Geography Overview

Maps are among the most powerful of human inventions, showing us where we are, where we have been, and where we might go in the future. They are essential tools in nearly every aspect of social life, enabling politicians to govern their people, soldiers to defend against invasions, and merchants to conduct trade and commerce. As noted in the *Introducing World History* essay, maps also create mental images of the world and, hence, help shape the way people look at the world and their place in it.

Maps are especially useful for the historian or student of history. Historical maps show us where different peoples lived and interacted, at one point in time or over long periods. Typically, they use lines, symbols, shading, and text to present a combination of physical and political information. The physical part pertains to the natural world—the shape of landmasses and bodies of water—and serves as a kind of background or screen onto which political information is projected. Categories of political information commonly featured on historical maps include the location and names of important cities and states, the changing borders of nations and empires, and the routes people traveled as they explored, migrated, traded, or fought with one another. In order to read a historical map, one must first understand its legend. The legend provides a key for interpreting the map's graphical symbols.

The first map in this overview, Map 1.3: The Indo-European Migrations and Eurasian Pastoralism, uses colored shading to show that around 4000 B.C.E. a people called the Indo-Europeans lived by the Caucasus Mountains in western Asia, and blue arrows to show that over the next three thousand years various Indo-European tribes migrated into western and northern Europe, Central and southwestern Asia, and northern India. Black capital letters are used to name important regions of human settlement, such as Anatolia and Mesopotamia, and black italic capitals for topographical features, such as mountains and desert. Red italic capitals indicate how people in different parts of Eurasia and Africa sustained themselves at this time—whether by raising livestock, farming, hunting and gathering, or some combination of these.

Every map is designed to convey only selected categories of information and, therefore, may leave certain questions about the geographical area and its inhabitants at either the same or different points in history unanswered. Thus, Map 1.3 tells us very little about the other human populations that lived in Eurasia between 4000 and 1000 B.C.E. The names *Sumer* and *Akkad* appear, but their status as regions where the world's first urban societies arose is something the student will only discover by reading the beginning of Chapter 2 and looking at Map 2.1 Ancient Mesopotamia. Arrows show the probable routes taken by different Indo-European tribes as they migrated from their homeland, but these tribes are not named, and the student must read the rest of Chapter 2 and all of Chapter 3 before learning that they included the Greeks in Europe and the Aryans in northern India.

To introduce you to the maps in this text, and the world history they help to illuminate, seven maps have been reproduced in this section, each provided with an analytical introduction and set of questions. Every part of the world is covered, and every historical period is represented by one map—except for the Early Modern Era, which is represented by two maps. The introductions help explain the content of each map by placing it in its broader historical context. That context includes the other maps in this text, and these are referenced whenever possible. For almost any subject about which the student would like to learn more, there are several maps that should be consulted. A list of all the maps in this text follows the table of contents.

The Indo-European Migrations and Eurasian Pastoralism

After the first human communities learned to domesticate native plants and animals, between 11,500 and 7,000 years ago, two types of cultures arose: farming societies in fertile river basins and pastoral societies in areas dominated by grassland, mountainous terrain, or desert (see Map 1.2). Important early farming societies include the city-states of Sumer and Akkad in Mesopotamia (see Map 2.1), the Harappan cities of the Indus Valley in India (see Map 2.2), the Egyptian and Nubian states along the Nile River in Africa (see Map 3.1), and the Shang state by the Yellow River in China (see Map 4.1). Bordering these peoples were pastoral societies who raised livestock as their main source of food and raw material and lived in smaller, dispersed groups over large areas of Eurasia, Africa, and Arabia. One such society, or collection of tribes, were the Indo-Europeans, who lived near the Caucasus Mountains around 4000 B.C.E. Over the next three thousand years, various Indo-European peoples migrated from their homeland: the Greeks settled in the eastern Mediterranean, the Hittites in central Anatolia, and the Aryans in northern India. Most European languages and many languages of southwestern Asia, Central Asia, and India are direct descendants of the prehistoric language spoken by the Indo-Europeans.

Maps referenced

MAP 1.2 **The Origins of Agriculture** (p. 19)

MAP 2.1 **Ancient Mesopotamia** (p. 32)

MAP 2.2 **Harappan Culture and Aryan Migrations** (p. 40)

MAP 3.1 **Ancient Egypt and Nubia** (p. 53)

MAP 4.1 **Shang and Zhou China** (p. 78)

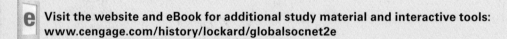 Visit the website and eBook for additional study material and interactive tools: www.cengage.com/history/lockard/globalsocnet2e

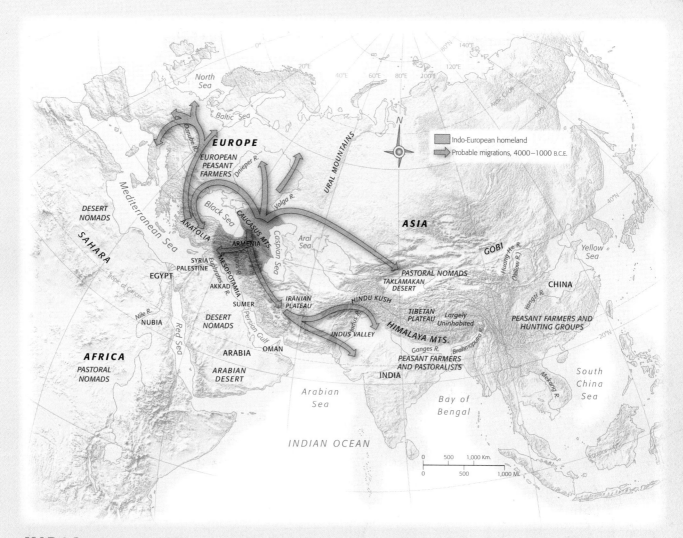

MAP 1.3
The Indo-European Migrations and Eurasian Pastoralism
Some societies, especially in parts of Africa and Asia, adapted to environmental contexts by developing a pastoral, or animal herding, economy. One large pastoral group, the Indo-Europeans, eventually expanded from their home area into Europe, southwestern Asia, Central Asia, and India.

Questions

1. The Indo-Europeans were pastoral nomads, most of whom later became farmers. Which regions on this map are suited to pastoralism and which to farming economies?

_____

_____

_____

2. The blue arrows on this map show the probable migration routes taken by various Indo-European tribes from 4000 to 1000 B.C.E. Identify the main geographical features (rivers, seas, mountain ranges, etc.) of the Indo-European homeland and the regions settled by Indo-Europeans during their migrations.

_____

_____

_____

THE ROMAN EMPIRE, CA. 120 C.E.

Rome was founded in the eighth century B.C.E. by the Latin people, a tribe of Indo-European pastoralists. In 509 B.C.E., influenced by the cultures of the neighboring Greek and Etruscan city-states (see Map 8.1), the Romans established a republic—a form of government in which political power is exercised by elected representatives of the people. The Roman Republic became a great military power, defeating the trading empire of the Carthaginians, and, by 58 B.C.E., under Julius Caesar, the Celtic tribes in Gaul (modern France). With the rise to power of Octavian, who defeated Mark Antony and Queen Cleopatra of Egypt at the naval Battle of Actium in Greece in 31 B.C.E., the Republic became a military dictatorship. At the time of Emperor Hadrian's death in 138 C.E., the Roman Empire dominated the whole of the Mediterranean basin, bounded in the west by the Atlantic Ocean, in the south by the Sahara Desert, to the north by Germanic and Celtic tribes, and to the east by the Parthian empire and the Arabian Desert. The Roman Empire was unified by a network of over 150,000 miles of roads and linked to the peoples of Africa and Asia by numerous land and sea trade routes (see map on page 233, "Great Empires and Trade Routes").

Maps referenced

MAP 8.1   **Italy and the Western Mediterranean, 600–200** B.C.E. (p. 182)

SNT 2   **Great Empires and Trade Routes** (p. 233)

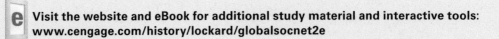 **Visit the website and eBook for additional study material and interactive tools:** www.cengage.com/history/lockard/globalsocnet2e

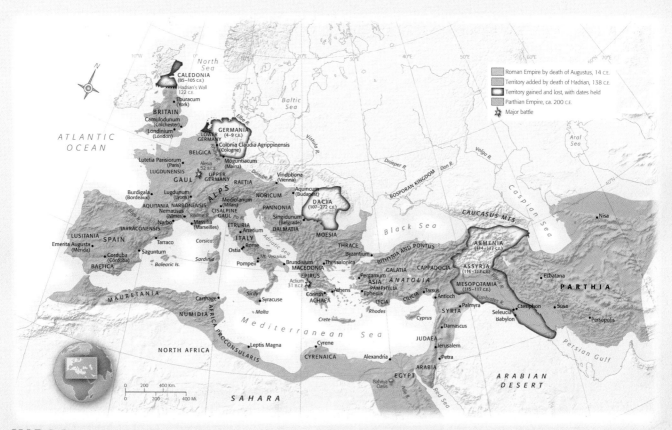

MAP 8.2
The Roman Empire, ca. 120 C.E.

The Romans gradually expanded until, by 120 C.E., they controlled a huge empire stretching from Britain and Spain in the west through southern and central Europe and North Africa to Egypt, Anatolia, and the lands along the eastern Mediterranean coast.

Questions

1. Which three rivers helped define the borders of the Roman Empire by the death of Augustus (Octavian) in 14 C.E.?

2. Which Roman emperor had a 73-mile wall built to secure the province of Britain from Celtic tribes to the north?

DAR AL-ISLAM AND TRADE ROUTES, CA. 1500 C.E.

The rise and spread of Islam in the Intermediate Era is paralleled by that of Christianity in Europe and Buddhism in Asia (see the map on page 378, "World Religions and Trade Routes, 600–1500"). By 750 C.E. the Umayyad Caliphate had conquered Spain and North Africa in the west (see Map 10.1), and a year later Arab armies defended their conquest of Central Asia by defeating Chinese forces from the Tang Empire at the Battle of Talas (see Map 11.1). From its capital in Baghdad, the Abbasid Caliphate ruled an empire stretching from Egypt to the Indus River (see Map 10.2). Like Latin culture in Europe, Arabic literature and science flourished during this period; new long-distance trade routes enriched Arab merchants and rulers and stimulated interest in the wider world. The confidence and curiosity of Islamic culture at this time are shown by the life and writings of the fourteenth-century Moroccan jurist and explorer Ibn Battuta. Logging more than 60,000 miles in thirty years, Ibn Battuta traveled to the far reaches of the Islamic world, from Timbuktu in the West African empire of Mali (see Map 12.1) to the Delhi Sultanate in India (see Map 13.1) and the cities of Pasai and Melaka in Southeast Asia (see Map 13.3).

 Visit the website and eBook for additional study material and interactive tools: www.cengage.com/history/lockard/globalsocnet2e

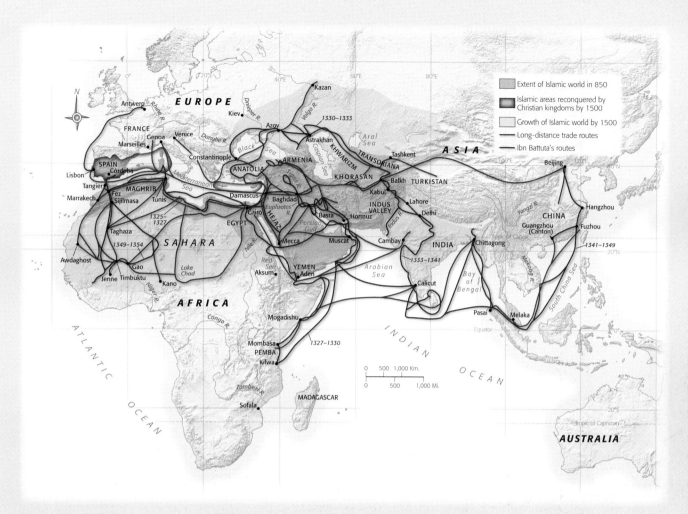

MAP 10.3
Dar al-Islam and Trade Routes, ca. 1500 C.E.

By 1500 the Islamic world stretched into West Africa, East Africa, and Southeast Asia. Trade routes connected the Islamic lands and allowed Muslim traders to extend their networks to China, Russia, and Europe.

Questions

1. Which European cities conducted maritime trade with Islamic societies in the Intermediate Era?

2. Islam spread to which western European land during the early Intermediate Era? (See also Map 10.1.)

THE ATLANTIC ECONOMY

The rise of European political and economic power in the Early Modern Era was made possible by maritime exploration (see Map 15.1) and missions of conquest in the Americas (see Map 17.1). In four voyages between 1492 and 1504, Christopher Columbus crossed the Atlantic Ocean and surveyed much of the Caribbean Basin, claiming it for Spain. Hernán Cortés sailed from Cuba to eastern Mexico and conquered the Aztec Empire in 1521, and in 1535 the Inca Empire in South America was conquered by Francisco Pizarro. By 1700, Portugal controlled Brazil, while England, France, and Spain claimed most of North America (see Map 17.2). European colonization was devastating to indigenous peoples. The introduction of infectious diseases like smallpox, to which Native Americans had no immunity, reduced their population by 90 percent from 1500 to 1700. Millions of West Africans were enslaved and transported to the Americas, where they mined gold and silver and produced sugarcane and tobacco on plantations (see Map 16.2). European states prospered from the development of capitalist economies, and the revenue from colonial slave labor and increased global trade put them in a position to dominate the world.

Maps referenced

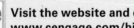 **Visit the website and eBook for additional study material and interactive tools: www.cengage.com/history/lockard/globalsocnet2e**

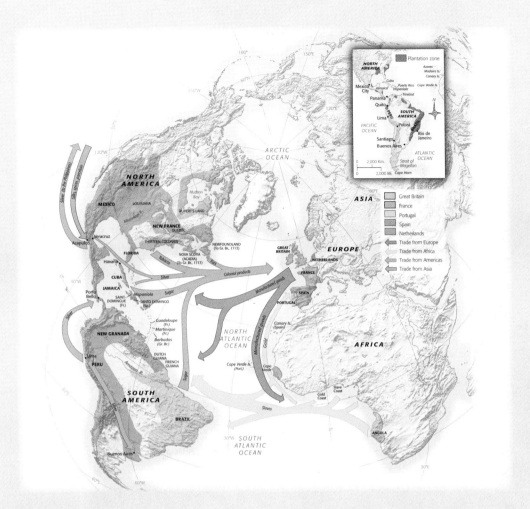

MAP 17.3
The Atlantic Economy

The Atlantic economy was based on a triangular trade in which African slaves were shipped to the Americas to produce raw materials that were chiefly exported to Europe, where they were turned into manufactured goods and exported to Africa and the Americas.

Questions

1. Which Caribbean islands were colonized by Spain, France, and Great Britain?

_____

_____

2. Which Spanish American port imported silks, spices, and porcelain from Asia?

_____

_____

3. Settlers from which American colony exported furs to Europe?

_____

_____

_____

U.S. Expansion Through 1867

The successful revolution in 1776 of Great Britain's thirteen North American colonies inaugurated a series of revolutions throughout the Western Hemisphere. Apart from Cuba and Puerto Rico, all of Spain's Latin American colonies achieved independence by 1840 (see Map 19.2). In 1783 the United States extended as far west as the Mississippi River; in 1803 its territory was doubled by the Louisiana Purchase; by 1848, after a war with Mexico, the territories of Texas, New Mexico, and California were annexed. Beginning in England in the 1770s, the Industrial Revolution had—and continues to have—far-reaching effects on the social and political history of the world. Europe's population soared, and industrial capitalism enriched nations and wealthy investors, but also impoverished and dislocated millions of people. From 1821 to 1920 more than 30 million Europeans emigrated to the United States (see Map 20.1). In 1865, after a bloody Civil War, slavery was abolished in the southern states. Only four years later, a large and diverse workforce, including African Americans and Chinese immigrants, completed the first transcontinental railroad. Immigrants from Britain also settled Oceania during the Modern Era (see Map 20.3), seizing the lands of Aborigines in Australia and Maori in New Zealand, just as European colonists had seized the lands of Native Americans two centuries before.

Maps referenced

MAP 19.2 **Latin American Independence, 1840** (p. 526)

MAP 20.1 **European Emigration, 1820–1910** (p. 548)

MAP 20.3 **Australia and New Zealand** (p. 570)

 Visit the website and eBook for additional study material and interactive tools: www.cengage.com/history/lockard/globalsocnet2e

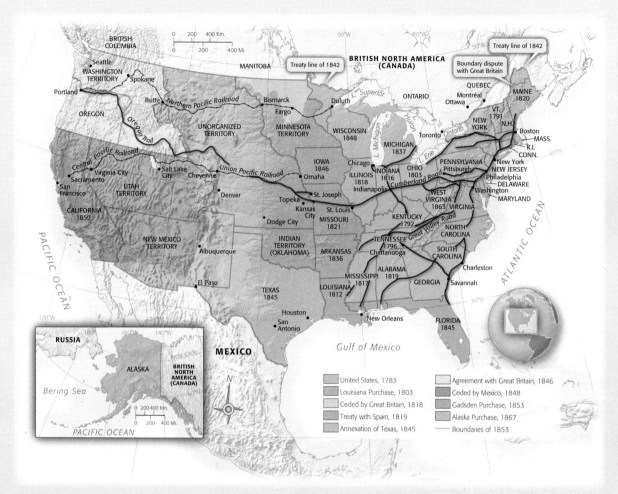

MAP 20.2
U.S. Expansion Through 1867
The United States expanded in stages after independence, gaining land from Spain,
France, Britain, and Mexico until the nation stretched from the Atlantic to the Gulf
and Pacific coasts by 1867. During the same period Canadians expanded westward
from Quebec to British Columbia.

Questions

1. First mapped in 1811, the Oregon Trail became the primary overland route
   for settlers migrating to the Pacific Northwest. Which future states did it pass
   through?

2. Which cities in the western United States benefited from the California Gold
   Rush of 1849?

3. The first transcontinental railroad was a joint effort of the Union Pacific and
   Central Pacific Railroads. What two cities did it join by 1869?

AFRICA IN 1914

After losing their American colonies, European nations projected their power to the south and east, and by 1914 they had colonized most of Africa, India, and Southeast Asia (see Map 19.4). Numerous Africans resisted European colonization, such as the Mandinka king Samory Toure, who fought the French in West Africa, and the confederation of Shona and Ndebele peoples, who fought the British in Southern Rhodesia. Ultimately, however, a combination of deceitful diplomacy and superior firearms made the Europeans unstoppable. Belgium seized the Congo River Basin, France took control of most of West Africa, and Great Britain conquered lands in a north-south band stretching from Cairo to Cape Town. The remaining African territories, with the exception of independent Ethiopia and Liberia, were colonized by Germany, Italy, and Portugal. The spread of Muslim culture beyond the Middle East and Central Asia, begun in the Intermediate Era, was unaffected by European colonialists and Christian missionaries: today Islam is the majority religion in northern Africa and Southeast Asia (see Map 26.3 and Map 30.2).

Maps referenced

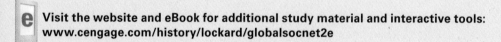 **Visit the website and eBook for additional study material and interactive tools: www.cengage.com/history/lockard/globalsocnet2e**

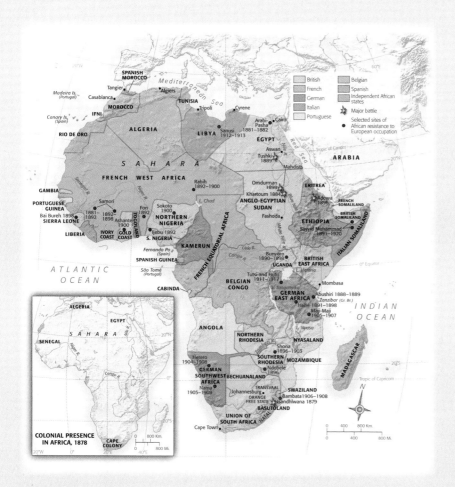

MAP 21.1
Africa in 1914
Before 1878 the European powers held only a few coastal territories in Africa, but in that year they turned to expanding their power through colonization. By 1914 the British, French, Belgians, Germans, Italians, Portuguese, and Spanish controlled all of the continent except for Ethiopia and Liberia.

Questions

1. Which European state had a single African colony?

2. What world religions are predominant in northern and southern Africa, respectively (see also Map 26.3)?

3. Around which two African river basins did the British and French base their colonies?

WORLD POPULATION GROWTH

World population increased more rapidly in the contemporary era than at any time in history: from 2.5 billion to more than 6.5 billion. This map shows the relative size of nations as measured by their populations in 2002. It also shows their projected average annual growth rates between 2002 and 2015. Currently, population growth is moderate in the world's five largest nations, and higher in developing nations like Pakistan, Nigeria, and Mexico. For a number of reasons, including women's desire to work outside the home and to prevent pregnancy by using birth control, Japan and many European nations have declining birthrates and aging populations. Since 1900 there has been a massive increase in global industrial output, consumption of resources, and all forms of pollution. Although the developing nations of Asia have the largest populations, most of the world's wealth is concentrated in North America, western Europe, and Japan (see the map on page 938, "Global Distribution of Wealth"). In 2000, over 1 billion people were desperately poor. People living in wealthier nations consume a much greater share of the earth's raw materials and cause more damage to the environment than those in developing nations. The average American consumes some twenty times the resources of the average Pakistani.

Map referenced

SNT 6   **Global Distribution of Wealth** (p. 938)

 Visit the website and eBook for additional study material and interactive tools:
www.cengage.com/history/lockard/globalsocnet2e

MAP 26.2
World Population Growth
This map shows dramatically which nations have the largest populations: China, India, the United States, Indonesia, and Brazil. It also shows which regions experience the most rapid population growth: Africa, South Asia, and Central America.

Questions

1. In 2002, the population of India was how many times greater than that of the United States? How many times greater was the population of China?

2. What challenges confront developing nations with large and growing populations?

3. What are some things developing nations can do to meet these challenges?

SOCIETIES, NETWORKS, AND TRANSITIONS

A GLOBAL HISTORY

Second Edition

Volume I: To 1500

Craig A. Lockard

University of Wisconsin—Green Bay

WADSWORTH
CENGAGE Learning

Australia • Brazil • Japan • Korea • Mexico • Singapore • Spain • United Kingdom • United States

WADSWORTH
CENGAGE Learning™

Societies, Networks, and Transitions, 2e, Volume I
Craig A. Lockard

Senior Publisher: Suzanne Jeans

Senior Acquisitions Editor: Nancy Blaine

Development Manager: Jeff Greene

Senior Development Editor: Tonya Lobato

Assistant Editor: Lauren Floyd

Editorial Assistant: Emma Goehring

Senior Media Editor: Lisa Ciccolo

Senior Marketing Manager: Katherine Bates

Marketing Coordinator: Lorreen Pelletier

Marketing Communications Manager: Christine Dobberpuhl

Senior Content Project Manager: Carol Newman

Senior Art Director: Cate Rickard Barr

Print Buyer: Becky Cross

Senior Rights Acquisition Account Manager: Katie Huha

Text Permissions Editor: Tracy Metivier

Senior Photo Editor: Jennifer Meyer Dare

Photo Researcher: Carole Frohlich

Production Service: Lachina Publishing Services

Text Designer: Henry Rachlin

Cover Designer: Dutton & Sherman Design

Cover Image: Church of St. George, Lalibela, Ethiopia: Robert Harding Picture Library/ SuperStock

Compositor: Lachina Publishing Services

For product information and technology assistance, contact us at
Cengage Learning Customer & Sales Support, 1-800-354-9706
For permission to use material from this text or product,
submit all requests online at **www.cengage.com/permissions**
Further permissions questions can be emailed to
permissionrequest@cengage.com

Library of Congress Control Number: 2009935606

Student Edition:

ISBN-13: 978-1-4390-8535-6

ISBN-10: 1-4390-8535-8

Wadsworth
20 Channel Center Street
Boston, MA 02210
USA

Cengage Learning is a leading provider of customized learning solutions with office locations around the globe, including Singapore, the United Kingdom, Australia, Mexico, Brazil, and Japan. Locate your local office at: **international.cengage.com/region**

Cengage Learning products are represented in Canada by Nelson Education, Ltd.

For your course and learning solutions, visit **academic.cengage.com**

Purchase any of our products at your local college store or at our preferred online store **www.ichapters.com**

Printed in the United States of America
1 2 3 4 5 6 7 13 12 11 10 09

BRIEF CONTENTS

Contents

PART I

FOUNDATIONS: ANCIENT SOCIETIES, TO CA. 600 B.C.E. 1

HISTORICAL CONTROVERSY

SOCIETIES • NETWORKS • TRANSITIONS

MAPS

FEATURES

PREFACE

Awareness of the need for a universal view of history—for a history which transcends national and regional boundaries and comprehends the entire globe—is one of the marks of the present. Our past [is] the past of the world, our history is the first to be world history.[1]

—GEOFFREY BARRACLOUGH

British historian Geoffrey Barraclough wrote these words over two decades ago, yet historians are still grappling with what it means to write world history, and why it is crucial to do so, especially to better inform today's students about their changing world and how it came to be. The intended audience for this text is students taking introductory world history courses and the faculty who teach them. Most of these students will be taking world history in colleges, universities, and community colleges, often with the goal of satisfying general education requirements or building a foundation for majoring in history or a related field. Like the contemporary world, the marketplace for texts is also changing. Both students, many of whom have outside jobs, and instructors, often facing expanded workloads, have increasing demands on their time. New technologies are promoting new pedagogies and a multiplicity of classroom approaches. Hence, any textbook must provide a sound knowledge base while also enhancing teaching and learning whatever the pedagogy employed.

To make this second edition even more accessible than the first edition, we have changed from a two-column to a more reader-friendly one-column format, streamlined and shortened the narrative, and added a brand-new map program. We believe that these changes will make the text more visually dynamic, easier to follow, and even more user friendly. Furthermore, students and many faculty are more interested in technology than ever before, and this second edition places more emphasis on the many website resources that are available through icons that tell students where to find online primary sources and interactive maps related to the text, as well as through a suggested list of online resources at the end of each chapter. I believe that these changes and additions enhance the book's presentation and clarity and enable it to convey the richness and importance of world history for today's students and tomorrow's leaders while also making the teaching of the material easier for both high school and college instructors using this text.

Twenty-first-century students, more than any generation before them, live in multicultural countries and an interconnected world. The world's interdependence calls for teaching a wider vision, which is the goal of this text. My intention is to create a meaningful, coherent, and stimulating presentation that conveys to students the incredible diversity of societies from earliest times to the present, as well as the ways they have been increasingly connected to other societies and shaped by these relationships. History may happen "as one darn thing after another," but the job of historians is to make it something more than facts, names, and dates. A text should provide a readable narrative, supplying a content base while also posing larger questions. The writing is as clear and thorough in its explanation of events and concepts as I can make it. No text can or should teach the course, but I hope that this text provides enough of a baseline of regional and global coverage to allow each instructor to bring her or his own talents, understandings, and particular interests to the process.

I became involved in teaching, debating, and writing world history as a result of my personal and academic experiences. My interest in other cultures was first awakened in the multicultural southern California city where I grew up. Many of my classmates or their parents had come from Asia, Latin America, or the Middle East. There was also a substantial African American community. A curious person did not have to search far to hear music, sample foods, or encounter ideas from many different cultures. I remember being enchanted by the Chinese landscape paintings at a local museum devoted to Asian art, and vowing to one day see some of those misty mountains for myself. Today many young people may be as interested as I was in learning about the world, since, thanks to immigration, many cities and towns all over North America have taken on a cosmopolitan flavor similar to my hometown.

While experiences growing up sparked my interest in other cultures, it was my schooling that pointed the way to a career in teaching world history. When I entered college, all undergraduate students were required to take a two-semester course in Western Civilization as part of the general education requirement. Many colleges and universities in North America had similar classes that introduced students to Egyptian pyramids, Greek philosophy, medieval pageantry, Renaissance art, and the French Revolution, enriching our lives. Fortunately, my university expanded student horizons further by adding course components (albeit brief) on China, Japan, India, and Islam while also developing a study abroad program. I participated in both the study abroad in Salzburg, Austria, and the student exchange with a university in Hong Kong, which meant living with, rather than just sampling, different customs, outlooks, and histories.

Some teachers and academic historians had begun to realize that the emphasis in U.S. education on the histories of the United States and western Europe, to the near exclusion of the rest of the world, was not sufficient for understanding the realities of the mid-twentieth century. Young Americans were being sent thousands of miles away to fight wars in countries, such as Vietnam, that few Americans had ever heard of. Newspapers and television reported developments in places such as Japan and Indonesia, Egypt and Congo, Cuba and Brazil, which had increasing relevance for Americans. Graduate programs and scholarship directed toward Asian, African, Middle Eastern, Latin American, and eastern European and Russian history also grew out of the awareness of a widening world, broadening conceptions of history. I attended one of the new programs in Asian Studies for my MA degree, and then the first PhD program in world history. Thanks to that program, I encountered the stimulating work of pioneering world historians from North America such as Philip Curtin, Marshall Hodgson, William McNeill, and Leften S. Stavrianos. My own approach, developed as I taught undergraduate world history courses beginning in 1969, owes much to the global vision they offered.

To bring some coherence to the emerging world history field as well as to promote a global approach at all levels of education, several dozen of us teaching at the university, college, community college, and secondary school levels in the United States and Canada came together in the early 1980s to form the World History Association (WHA), for which I served as founding secretary and, more recently, as a member of the Executive Council. The organization grew rapidly, encouraging the teaching, studying, and writing of world history not only in the United States but all over the world. The approaches to world history found among active WHA members vary widely, and my engagement in the ongoing discussions at conferences and in essays, often about the merits of varied textbooks, provided an excellent background for writing this text.

THE AIMS AND APPROACH OF THE TEXT

Societies, Networks, and Transitions: A Global History provides an accessible, thought-provoking guide to students in their exploration of the landscape of the past, helping them to think about it in all its social diversity and interconnectedness and to see their lives with fresh understanding. It does this by combining clear writing, special learning features, current scholarship, and a comprehensive, global approach that does not omit the role and richness of particular regions.

There is a method behind these aims. For forty years I have written about and taught Asian, African, and world history at universities in the United States and Malaysia. A cumulative seven years of study, research, or teaching in Southeast Asia, East Asia, East Africa, and Europe gave me insights into a wide variety of cultures and historical perspectives. Finally, the WHA, its publications and conferences, and the more recent electronic listserv, H-WORLD, have provided active forums for vigorously discussing how best to think about and teach world history.

The most effective approach to presenting world history in a text for undergraduate and advanced high school students, I have concluded, is one that combines the themes of connections and cultures. World history is very much about connections that transcend countries, cultures, and regions, and a text should discuss, for example, major long-distance trade networks such as the Silk Road, the spread of religions, maritime exploration, world wars, and transregional empires such as the Persian, Mongol, and British Empires. These connections are part of the broader global picture. Students need to understand that cultures, however unique, did not emerge and operate in a vacuum but faced similar challenges, shared many common experiences, and influenced each other.

The broader picture is drawn by means of several features in the text. To strengthen the presentation of the global overview, the text uses an innovative essay feature entitled "Societies, Networks, and Transitions." Appearing at the end of each of the six chronological parts, this feature analyzes and synthesizes the wider trends of the era, such as the role of long-distance trade, the spread of technologies and religions, and global climate change. The objective is to amplify the wider transregional messages already developed in the part chapters and help students to think further about the global context in which societies are enmeshed. Each "Societies, Networks, and Transitions" essay also makes comparisons, for example, between the Han Chinese, Mauryan Indian, and Roman Empires, and between Chinese, Indian, and European emigration in the nineteenth century. These comparisons help to throw further light on diverse cultures and the differences and similarities between them during the era covered. Finally, each essay is meant to show how the transitions that characterize the era lead up to the era discussed in the following part. In addition, the prologues that introduce each of the six eras treated in the text also set out the broader context, including some of the major themes and patterns of wide influence as well as those for each region. Furthermore, several chapters concentrate on global rather than regional developments.

However, while a broad global overview is a strongly developed feature of this text, most chapters, while acknowledging and explaining relevant linkages, focus on a particular region or several regions. Most students learn easiest by focusing on one region or culture at a time. Students also benefit from recognizing the cultural richness and intellectual creativity of specific societies. From this text students learn, for instance, about Chinese poetry, Indonesian music, Arab science, Greek philosophy, West African arts, Indian cinema, Latin American economies, and Anglo-American political thought. As a component of this cultural richness, this text also devotes considerable attention to the enduring religious traditions, such as Buddhism, Christianity, and Islam, and to issues of gender. The cultural richness of a region and its distinctive social patterns can get lost in an approach that minimizes regional coverage. Today most people are still mostly concerned with events in their own countries, even as their lives are reshaped by transnational economies and global cultural movements.

Also a strong part of the presentation of world history in this text is its attempt to be comprehensive and inclusive. To enhance comprehensiveness, the text balances social, economic, political, and cultural and religious history, and it also devotes some attention to geographical and environmental contexts as well as to the history of ideas and technologies. At the same time, the text highlights features within societies, such as economic production, technological innovations, and portable ideas that had widespread or enduring influence. To ensure inclusiveness, the text recognizes the contributions of many societies, including some often neglected, such as sub-Saharan Africa, pre-Columbian America, Southeast Asia, and Oceania. In particular, this text offers strong coverage of the diverse Asian societies. Throughout history, as today, the great majority of the world's population has lived in Asia.

ORGANIZING THE TEXT

All textbook authors struggle with how to organize the material. To keep the number of chapters corresponding to the twenty-eight or thirty weeks of most academic calendars in North America, and roughly equal in length, I have often had to combine several regions into a single chapter to be comprehensive, sometimes making decisions for conveniences sake. For example, unlike texts that may have only one chapter on sub-Saharan Africa covering the centuries from ancient times to 1500 C.E., this text discusses sub-Saharan Africa in each of the six chronological eras, devoting three chapters to the centuries prior to 1500 C.E. and three to the years since 1450 C.E. But this sometimes necessitated grouping Africa, depending on the era, with Europe, the Middle East, or the Americas. Unlike texts that may, for example, have material on Tang dynasty China scattered through several chapters, making it harder for students to gain a cohesive view of that society, I want to convey a comprehensive perspective of major societies such as Tang China. The material is divided into parts defined as distinct eras (such as the Classical and the Early Modern) so that students can understand how all regions were part of world history from earliest times. I believe that a chronological structure aids students in grasping the changes over time while helping to organize the material.

For the second edition I have reorganized Part II. The chapter on southern and Central Asia now leads off this part as Chapter 5, introducing the development and beliefs of Buddhism as well as examining Central Asian societies such as the Sogdians and Huns. This makes the discussion of Buddhism and of the Silk Road in Chapter 6 on East Asia more understandable. The coverage of the Greeks and Persians in the Eastern Mediterranean (Chapter 7) is now followed immediately by the chapter on the Western Mediterranean and Roman Empire (Chapter 8).

DISTINGUISHING FEATURES

Several features of *Societies, Networks, Transitions: A Global History* will help students better understand, assimilate, and appreciate the material they are about to encounter. Those unique to this text include the following.

Introducing World History World History may be the first and possibly the only history course many undergraduates will take in college. The text opens with a short essay that introduces students to the nature of history, the special challenges posed by studying world history, and why we need to study it.

Balancing Themes Three broad themes—uniqueness, interdependence, and change—have shaped the text. They are discussed throughout in terms of three related concepts—societies, networks, and transitions. These concepts, discussed in more detail in "Introducing World History," can be summarized as follows:

- **Societies** Influenced by environmental and geographical factors, people have formed and maintained societies defined by distinctive but often changing cultures, beliefs, social forms, institutions, and material traits.
- **Networks** Over the centuries societies have generally been connected to other societies by growing networks forged by phenomena such as migration, long-distance trade, exploration, military expansion, colonization, the spread of ideas and technologies, and webs of communication. These growing networks modified individual societies, created regional systems, and eventually led to a global system.
- **Transitions** Each major historical era has been marked by one or more great transitions sparked by events or innovations, such as settled agriculture, Mongol imperialism, industrial revolution, or world war, that have had profound and enduring influences on many societies, gradually reshaping the world. At the same time, societies and regions have experienced transitions of regional rather than global scope that have generated new ways of thinking or doing things, such as the expansion of Islam into India or the European colonization of East Africa and Mexico.

Through exposure to these three ideas integrated throughout the text, students learn of the rich cultural mosaic of the world. They are also introduced to its patterns of connections and unity as well as of continuity and change.

"Societies, Networks, and Transitions" Minichapters A short feature at the end of each part assists the student in backing up from the stories of societies and regions to see the larger historical patterns of change and the wider links among distant peoples. This comparative analysis allows students to identify experiences and transitions common to several regions or the entire world and to reflect further on the text themes. These features can also help students review key developments from the preceding chapters.

Historical Controversies Since one of the common misconceptions about history is that it is about the "dead" past, included with each "Societies, Networks, and Transitions" feature is a brief account of a debate among historians over how an issue in the past should be interpreted and what it means to us today. For example, why are the major societies dominated by males, and has this always been true? Why and when did Europe begin its "great divergence" from China and other Asian societies? How do historians evaluate contemporary globalization? Reappraisal is at the heart of history, and many historical questions are never completely answered. Yet most textbooks ignore this dimension of historical study; this text is innovative in including it. The Historical Controversy essays will help show students that historical facts are anything but dead; they live and change their meaning as new questions are asked by each new generation.

Profiles It is impossible to recount the human story without using broad generalizations, but it is also difficult to understand that story without seeing historical events reflected in the lives of men and women, prominent but also ordinary people. Each chapter contains a Profile that focuses on the experiences or accomplishments of a woman or man, to convey the flavor of life of the period, to embellish the chapter narrative with interesting personalities, and to integrate gender into the historical account. The Profiles try to show how gender affected the individual, shaping her or his opportunities and involvement in society. Several focus questions ask the student to reflect on the Profile. For instance, students will examine a historian in early China, look at the spread of Christianity as seen through the life of a pagan female philosopher in Egypt, relive the experience of a female slave in colonial Brazil, and envision modern Indian life through a sketch of a film star.

Special Coverage This text also treats often-neglected areas and subjects. For example:

- It focuses on several regions with considerable historical importance but often marginalized or even omitted in many texts, including sub-Saharan Africa, Southeast Asia, Korea, Central Asia, pre-Columbian North America, ancient South America, the Caribbean, Polynesia, Australia, Canada, and the United States.
- It includes discussions of significant groups that transcend regional boundaries, such as the caravan travelers and traders of the Silk Road, Mongol empire builders, the Indian Ocean maritime traders, and contemporary humanitarian organizations such as Amnesty International and Doctors Without Borders.
- It features extensive coverage of the roots, rise, reshaping, and enduring influence of the great religious and philosophical traditions.
- It blends coverage of gender, particularly the experiences of women, and of social history generally, into the larger narrative.
- It devotes the first chapter of the text to the roots of human history. After a brief introduction to the shaping of our planet, human evolution, and the spread of people around the world, the chapter examines the birth of agriculture, cities, and states, which set the stage for everything to come.
- It includes strong coverage of the world since 1945, a focus of great interest to many students.

Witness to the Past Many texts incorporate excerpts from primary sources, but this text also keeps student needs in mind by using up-to-date translations and addressing a wide range of topics. Included are excerpts from important Buddhist, Hindu, Confucian, Zoroastrian, and Islamic works that helped shape great traditions. Readings such as a collection of Roman graffiti, a thirteenth-century tourist description of a Chinese city, a report on an Aztec market, and a manifesto for modern Egyptian women reveal something of people's lives and concerns. Also offered are materials that shed light on the politics of the time, such as an African king's plea to end the slave trade, Karl Marx's *Communist Manifesto,* and the recent *Arab Human Development Report.* The wide selection of document excerpts is also designed to illustrate how historians work with original documents. Unlike most texts, chapters are also enlivened by brief but numerous excerpts of statements, writings, or songs from people of the era that are effectively interspersed in the chapter narrative so that students can better see the vantage points and opinions of the people of that era.

LEARNING AIDS

The carefully designed learning aids are meant to help faculty teach world history and students actively learn and appreciate it. A number of aids have been created, including some that distinguish this text from others in use.

Geography Overview Located at the front of the text-book, the Geography Overview pairs key maps found in the text with critical-thinking questions that help students interpret the variety of geographic and historical information that a map can convey.

Part Prologue and Map Each part opens with a prologue that previews the major themes and topics—global and regional—covered in the part chapters. An accompanying world map shows some of the key societies discussed in the part.

Chapter Outline, Primary Source Quotation, and Vignette A chapter outline shows the chapter contents at a glance. Chapter text then opens with a quotation from a primary source pertinent to chapter topics. An interest-grabbing vignette or sketch then funnels students' attention toward the chapter themes they are about to explore.

Focus Questions To prepare students for thinking about the main themes and topics of the chapter, a short list of thoughtfully prepared questions begins each chapter narrative. These questions are then repeated before each major section. The points they deal with are revisited in the Chapter Summary.

Special Boxed Features Each chapter contains a Witness to the Past drawn from a primary source, and a Profile highlighting a man or woman from that era. The Historical Controversy boxes, which focus on issues of interpretation, appear at the end of each part and before each "Societies, Networks, and Transitions" essay. Questions are also placed at the end of the primary source readings, historical controversies, and profiles to help students comprehend the material.

Maps and Other Visuals Maps, photos, chronologies, and tables are amply interspersed throughout the chapters, illustrating and unifying coverage and themes.

Section Summaries At the end of each major section within a chapter, a bulleted summary helps students to review the key topics.

Chapter Summary At the end of each chapter, a concise summary invites students to sum up the chapter content and review its major points.

Annotated Suggested Readings and Endnotes Short lists of annotated suggested readings, mostly recent, and websites providing additional information are also found at the end of each chapter. These lists acknowledge some of the more important works used in writing as well as sources of particular value for undergraduate students. Direct quotes in the text are attributed to their sources in endnotes, which are located at the end of the book.

Key Terms and Pronunciation Guides Important terms likely to be new to the student are boldfaced in the text and immediately defined. These key terms are also listed at the end of the chapter and then listed with their definitions at the end of the text. The pronunciation of foreign and other difficult terms is shown parenthetically where the terms are introduced to help students with the terminology.

NEW TO THIS EDITION

In developing this new edition, I have also benefited from the responses to the first edition, including correspondence and conversations with instructors and students who used the text. Incorporating many of their suggestions, this second edition is somewhat shorter than the first. The chapter structure is now streamlined by combining some materials and hence eliminating superfluous heads. Yet the new one-column format also allows for short call-outs of paragraph topics to be placed in the margins, along with key terms and definitions, helping students to organize the material and study for exams. New "eBook and Website Resources" sections at the end of every chapter indicate important corresponding online assets, including Primary Sources and Interactive Maps. I have also eliminated redundancies, corrected factual errors, and revised the suggested readings lists.

In addition to all these changes, I have updated the narrative to incorporate new scholarly knowledge and historical developments since the first edition was completed in 2006. Hence, many chapters include new information. Paleontology, archaeology, and ancient history are lively fields of study that constantly produce new knowledge, and the chapters in Part I include updates on subjects such as human evolution, the spread of modern humans, the rise of agriculture, the emergence of states, and early human settlement in the Americas. Later chapters incorporate new material on such subjects as politics in Muslim Spain, the invention of the Cherokee alphabet, and the contributions of the abolitionist Frederick Douglass. As most readers know, many important developments have occurred in the last few years, and hence the chapters in Part VI have required the most revision. As a result, Chapter 26 on the Global System includes, among other topics, new material on the 2008–2009 global recession, increasing global warming, the spread of Christianity (especially Pentacostalism), political protests and instant messaging (especially in China and Iran), and the world response to the death of Michael Jackson. Chapter 27 on East Asia examines economic challenges, human rights protests in China, violence in Tibet and Xinjiang, Japanese politics, and North Korean developments and regional tensions. The discussion of Europe and Russia in Chapter 28 ponders recent economic challenges, immigration issues, Russian-Georgian tensions, Vladimir Putin's government, and changing attitudes toward the European Union. In Chapter 29 on the Americas, I have added

material on such topics as the Reagan and Bush legacies, the 2008–2009 economic meltdown, the election of Barack Obama, the wars in Iraq and Afghanistan, politics in various Latin American nations, the drug wars in Mexico and Colombia, and Chinese investment. New material in Chapter 30 on the Middle East and Africa includes Turkish politics, continuing Israel-Arab conflicts, the 2009 Iran elections, Iraq and Afghanistan updates, conflicts in Somalia, politics in varied African nations, the spread of Christianity, and the growing Chinese economic presence. Finally, Chapter 31 addresses the 2009 Indian elections, India's challenges, Pakistani politics, the Sri Lankan defeat of Tamil rebels, the Southeast Asian economic crisis, and politics and violence in various Southeast Asian nations. These chapters should give students a good introduction to the world in which they live.

ANCILLARIES

A wide array of supplements accompany this text to help students better master the material and to help instructors teach from the book.

Instructor Resources

PowerLecture CD-ROM with ExamView® and JoinIn® This dual-platform, all-in-one multimedia resource includes the Instructor's Resource Manual; a Test Bank (developed by Candace Gregory-Abbott of California State University, Sacramento; includes key term identification and multiple-choice, short answer/essay, and map questions); Microsoft® PowerPoint® slides of lecture outlines and of images and maps from the text, which can be used as offered or customized by importing personal lecture slides or other material; and JoinIn® PowerPoint® slides with clicker content. Also included is ExamView®, an easy-to-use assessment and tutorial system that allows instructors to create, deliver, and customize tests in minutes. Instructors can build tests with as many as 250 questions using up to 12 question types; using ExamView®'s complete word-processing capabilities, they can enter an unlimited number of new questions or edit existing ones.

HistoryFinder This searchable online database allows instructors to quickly and easily download thousands of assets, including art, photographs, maps, primary sources, and audio/video clips. Each asset downloads directly into a Microsoft® PowerPoint® slide, allowing instructors to easily create exciting PowerPoint presentations for their classrooms.

eInstructor's Resource Manual Prepared by Rick Gianni of Purdue University Calumet, this manual has many features, including instructional objectives, annotated chapter outlines, chapter summaries, lecture suggestions, suggested debate and discussion topics, and writing and research assignments. It is available on the instructor's companion website.

WebTutor™ on Blackboard®, WebTutor™ on WebCT®, and WebTutor™ on Angel® With WebTutor™'s text-specific, preformatted content and total flexibility, instructors can easily create and manage their own custom course website. Its course management tool gives instructors the ability to provide virtual office hours, post syllabi, set up threaded discussions, track student progress with the quizzing material, and much more. For students, WebTutor™ offers real-time access to a full array of study tools, including animations and videos that bring the book's topics to life, plus chapter outlines, summaries, learning objectives, glossary flashcards (with audio), practice quizzes, and weblinks.

Student Resources

Book Companion Site This website features a wide assortment of resources to help students master the subject matter. Prepared by Jason Ripper of Everett Community College, it includes a glossary, flashcards, crossword puzzles, learning objectives, preclass quizzes, tutorial quizzes, critical thinking exercises, and matching exercises. Throughout the text, icons direct students to relevant exercises and self-testing material located on the student companion website, which can be accessed at: *www.cengage.com/history/lockard/globalsocnet2e.*

CL eBook This interactive multimedia ebook links out to rich media assets such as Internet field trips and MP3 chapter summaries. Through this ebook, students can also access self-test quizzes, chapter outlines, focus questions, fill-in-the-blank exercises, chronology puzzles, essay questions (for which the answers can be emailed to their instructors), primary source documents with critical thinking questions, and interactive (zoomable) maps. Available on iChapters.

iChapters The website *www.iChapters.com* saves students time and money by giving them a choice in formats and savings and a better chance to succeed in class. iChapters.com, Cengage Learning's online store, is a single destination for more than 10,000 new textbooks, eTextbooks, eChapters, study tools, and audio supplements. Students have the freedom to purchase a-la-carte exactly what they need when they need it. They can save 50 percent on the electronic textbook and can pay as little as $1.99 for an individual eChapter.

Wadsworth World History Resource Center Wadsworth's World History Resource Center gives students access to a "virtual reader" with hundreds of primary sources, including speeches, letters, legal documents and transcripts, poems, maps, simulations, timelines, and additional images that bring history to life, along with interactive assignable exercises. A map feature including Google Earth™ coordinates and exercises will aid in student comprehension of geography and use of maps. Students can compare the traditional textbook map with an aerial view of the location today. It's an ideal resource for study, review, and research. In addition to this map feature, the resource center also provides blank maps for student review and testing.

Writing for College History, 1e Prepared by Robert M. Frakes, Clarion University, this brief handbook for survey courses in American history, Western Civilization/European history, and world civilization guides students through the various types of writing assignments they encounter in a history class. Providing examples of student writing and candid assessments of student work, this text focuses on the rules and conventions of writing for the college history course.

The History Handbook, 1e Prepared by Carol Berkin of Baruch College, City University of New York, and Betty Anderson of Boston University, this book teaches students both basic and history-specific study skills, such as how to read primary sources, research historical topics, and correctly cite sources. Substantially less expensive than comparable skill-building texts, *The History Handbook* also offers tips for Internet research and evaluating online sources.

Doing History: Research and Writing in the Digital Age, 1e This text was prepared by Michael J. Galgano, J. Chris Arndt, and Raymond M. Hyser of James Madison University. Whether they are starting down the path as a history major or simply looking for a straightforward and systematic guide to writing a successful paper, students will find it an indispensable handbook to historical research. This text's "soup to nuts" approach to researching and writing about history addresses every step of the process, from locating sources and gathering information to writing clearly and making proper use of various citation styles to avoid plagiarism. It enables students to learn how to make the most of every tool available—especially the technology that helps them conduct the process efficiently and effectively.

The Modern Researcher, 6e Prepared by Jacques Barzun and Henry F. Graff of Columbia University, this classic introduction to the techniques of research and the art of expression is used widely in history courses but is also appropriate for writing and research methods courses in other departments. Barzun and Graff thoroughly cover every aspect of research, from the selection of a topic through the gathering, analysis, writing, revision, and publication of findings. The research process is presented not as a set of rules but through actual cases that put the subtleties of research in a useful context. Part One covers the principles and methods of research; Part Two covers writing, speaking, and getting one's work published.

Reader Program Cengage Learning publishes a number of readers, some containing exclusively primary sources, others a combination of primary and secondary sources, and some designed to guide students through the process of historical inquiry. A complete list of readers can be found at *www.cengage.com.*

CUSTOM OPTIONS

Cengage Learning offers custom solutions for this course that can tailor-fit students' learning needs—whether it's making a small modification to *Societies, Networks, and Transitions* to match the syllabus or combining multiple sources to create something truly unique. Instructors can pick and choose chapters, include their own material, and add additional map exercises along with the *Rand McNally Historical Atlas of the World* to create a text that fits the way they teach. They can ensure that students get the most out of their textbook dollar by giving them exactly what they need. A Cengage Learning representative can help instructors explore custom solutions.

Rand McNally Historical Atlas of the World, 2e This valuable resource features over seventy maps that portray the rich panoply of the world's history from preliterate times to the present, illustrating how cultures and civilizations were linked and interacted. The maps make it clear that history is not static; rather, it is about change and movement across time, a process of expansion, cooperation, and conflict. This atlas includes maps that display the world from the beginning of civilization; the political development of all major areas of the world; Africa, Latin America, and the Middle East in increased detail; the current Islamic World; and the world population change in 1900 and 2000.

Document Exercise Workbook Prepared by Donna Van Raaphorst, Cuyahoga Community College, this is a two-volume collection of exercises based around primary sources.

FORMATS

The text is available in a one-volume hardcover edition, a two-volume paperback edition, a three-volume paperback edition, and as an interactive ebook. *Volume I: To 1500* includes Chapters 1–14; *Volume II: Since 1450* includes Chapters 15–31; *Volume A: To 600* includes Chapters 1–9; *Volume B: From 600 to 1750* includes Chapters 10–18; and *Volume C: Since 1750* includes Chapters 19–31.

ACKNOWLEDGMENTS

The author would like to thank the following community of instructors who, by sharing their teaching experiences and insightful feedback, helped shape the final textbook and ancillary program:

Susan Autry, Central Piedmont Community College
Brett Berliner, Morgan State University
Edward Bond, Alabama A & M University
Gayle K. Brunelle, California State University, Fullerton
Clea Bunch, University of Arkansas at Little Rock
Steve Corso, Elwood-John Glenn High School
Gregory Crider, Winthrop University
Jodi Eastberg, Alverno College
Eve Fisher, South Dakota State University
Rick Gianni, Purdue University Calumet
Candace Gregory-Abbott, California State University, Sacramento
Gregory M. Havrilcsak, University of Michigan–Flint
Linda Wilke Heil, Central Community College
Mark Hoffman, Wayne County Community College District
Bram Hubbell, Friends Seminary
Frances Kelleher, Grand Valley State University
Kim Klein, Shippensburg University
Rachel Layman, Lawrence North High School
Christine Lovasz-Kaiser, University of Southern Indiana

John Lyons, Joliet Junior College
Mary Ann Mahony, Central Connecticut State University
Laurence Marvin, Berry College
Patrick McDevitt, University at Buffalo SUNY
David K. McQuilkin, Bridgewater College
Bill Mihalopoulos, Northern Michigan University
W. Jack Miller, Pennsylvania State University–Abington
Edwin Moise, Clemson University
Aarti Nakra, Salt Lake Community College
Peter Ngwafu, Albany State University
Melvin Page, East Tennessee State University
Craig Patton, Alabama A & M University
William Pelz, Elgin Community College
Paul Philp, John Paul II HS/Eastfield Community College
Jason Ripper, Everett Community College
Rose Mary Sheldon, Virginia Military Institute
Anthony Steinhoff, University of Tennessee–Chattanooga
Bill Strickland, East Grand Rapids High School
Kurt Waters, Centreville High School

The author would also like to acknowledge the following instructors who lent their insight and guidance to the previous edition: Siamak Adhami, Saddleback Community College; Sanjam Ahluwalia, Northern Arizona University; David G. Atwill, Pennsylvania State University; Ewa K. Bacon, Lewis University; Bradford C. Brown, Bradley University; Gayle K. Brunelle, California State University–Fullerton; Rainer Buschmann, California State University, Channel Islands; Jorge Canizares-Esguerra, State University of New York–Buffalo; Bruce A. Castleman, San Diego State University; Harold B. Cline, Jr., Middle Georgia College; Simon Cordery, Monmouth College; Dale Crandall-Bear, Solano Community College; Cole Dawson, Warner Pacific College; Hilde De Weerdt, University of Tennessee, Knoxville; Anna Dronzek, University of Minnesota, Morris; James R. Evans, Southeastern Community College; Robert Fish, Japan Society of New York; Robert J. Flynn, Portland Community College; Gladys Frantz-Murphy, Regis University; Timothy Furnish, Georgia Perimeter College; James E. Genova, The Ohio State University; Deborah Gerish, Emporia State University; Kurt A. Gingrich, Radford University; Candace Gregory-Abbott, California State University, Sacramento; Paul L. Hanson, California Lutheran University; A. Katie Harris, Georgia State University; Gregory M. Havrilcsak, University of Michigan–Flint; Timothy Hawkins, Indiana State University; Don Holsinger, Seattle Pacific University; Mary N. Hovanec, Cuyahoga Community College; Jonathan Judaken, University of Memphis; Thomas E. Kaiser, University of Arkansas at Little Rock; Carol Keller, San Antonio College; Patricia A. Kennedy, Leeward Community College–University of Hawaii; Jonathan Lee, San Antonio College; Thomas Lide, San Diego State University; Derek S. Linton, Hobart and William Smith Colleges; David L. Longfellow, Baylor University; Erik C. Maiershofer, Point Loma Nazarene University; Afshin Marashi, California State University, Sacramento; Robert B. McCormick, University of South Carolina Upstate; Doug T. McGetchin, Florida Atlantic University; Kerry Muhlestein, Brigham Young University–Hawaii; Peter Ngwafu, Albany State University; Monique O'Connell, Wake Forest University; Annette Palmer, Morgan State University; Nicholas C. J. Pappas, Sam Houston State University; Patricia M. Pelley, Texas Tech University; John

Pesda, Camden County College; Pamela Roseman, Georgia Perimeter College; Paul Salstrom, St. Mary-of-the-Woods; Sharlene Sayegh, California State University, Long Beach; Michael Seth, James Madison University; David Simonelli, Youngstown State University; Peter Von Sivers, University of Utah; Anthony J. Steinhoff, University of Tennessee-Chattanooga; Nancy L. Stockdale, University of Central Florida; Robert Shannon Sumner, University of West Georgia; Kate Transchel, California State University, Chico; Sally N. Vaughn, University of Houston; Thomas G. Velek, Mississippi University for Women; and Kenneth Wilburn, East Carolina University.

The author has incurred many intellectual debts in developing his expertise in world history, as well as in preparing this text. To begin with, I cannot find words to express my gratitude to the wonderful editors and staff at Wadsworth, Cengage Learning— Nancy Blaine, Tonya Lobato, Carol Newman, and Jean Woy—who had enough faith in this project to tolerate my missed deadlines and sometimes grumpy responses to editorial decisions or some other crisis. I also owe an incalculable debt to my development editor on the first edition, Phil Herbst, who prodded and pampered and helped me write for a student, rather than scholarly, audience. Tonya Lobato adroitly supervised the second edition. Carole Frohlich ably handled photos; Charlotte Miller, maps; Susan Zorn, copyediting; Jake Kawatski, indexing; and Katherine Wetzel, general project management. Katherine Bates provided great help with marketing. I also owe a great debt to Pam Gordon, whose interest and encouragement got this project started. Ken Wolf of Murray State University prepared the initial drafts of several of the early chapters and in other ways gave me useful criticism and advice. I am grateful to Edwin Moise, Michelle Pinto, Rick Gianni, and Ibrahim Shafie for pointing out factual errors in the first edition. I would also like to acknowledge the inspiring mentors who helped me at various stages of my academic preparation: Bill Goldmann, who introduced me to world history at Pasadena High School in California; Charles Hobart and David Poston, University of Redlands professors who sparked my interest in Asia; George Wong, Bart Stoodley, and especially Andrew and Margaret Roy, my mentors at Chung Chi College in Hong Kong; Walter Vella, Robert Van Niel, and Daniel Kwok, who taught me Asian studies at Hawaii; and John Smail and Philip Curtin, under whom I studied comparative world history in the immensely exciting PhD program at Wisconsin. My various sojourns in East Asia, Southeast Asia, and East Africa allowed me to meet and learn from many inspiring and knowledgeable scholars. I have also been greatly stimulated and influenced in my approach by the writings of many fine global historians, but I would single out Philip Curtin, Marshall Hodgson, L. S. Stavrianos, William McNeill, Fernand Braudel, Eric Hobsbawm, Immanuel Wallerstein, and Peter Stearns. Curtin, Hobsbawm, and McNeill also gave me personal encouragement concerning my writing in the field, for which I am very grateful.

Colleagues at the various universities where I taught have been supportive of my explorations in world and comparative history. Most especially I acknowledge the friendship, support, and intellectual collaboration over three and a half decades of my colleagues in the interdisciplinary Social Change and Development Department at the University of Wisconsin-Green Bay (UWGB), especially Harvey Kaye, Lynn Walter, Larry Smith, Andy Kersten, Kim Nielsen, Andrew Austin, and the late Tony Galt, as well as members of the History faculty. I have also benefited immeasurably as a world historian from the visiting lecture series sponsored by UWGB's Center for History and Social Change, directed by Harvey Kaye, which over the years has brought in dozens of outstanding scholars. My students at UWGB and elsewhere have also taught me much.

I also thank my colleagues in the World History Association (WHA), who have generously shared their knowledge, encouraged my work, and otherwise provided an exceptional opportunity for learning and an exchange of ideas. I am proud to have helped establish this organization, which incorporates world history teachers at all levels of education and in many nations. Among many others, I want to express a special thank-you to longtime friends and colleagues in the WHA from whom I have learned so much and with whom I have shared many wonderful meals and conversations.

Finally, I need to acknowledge the loving support of my wife Kathy and our two sons, Chris and Colin, who patiently, although not always without complaint, for the many years of the project put up with my hectic work schedule and the ever-growing piles of research materials, books, and chapter drafts scattered around our cluttered den and sometimes colonizing other space around the house. Kathy also spent many hours selflessly helping me to complete chapter revisions to meet deadlines for the second edition.

ABOUT THE AUTHOR

Craig A. Lockard is Ben and Joyce Rosenberg Professor of History in the Social Change and Development Department at the University of Wisconsin–Green Bay, where since 1975 he has taught courses on Asian, African, comparative, and world history. He has also taught at SUNY-Buffalo, SUNY-Stony Brook, and the University of Bridgeport, and twice served as a Fulbright-Hays professor at the University of Malaya in Malaysia. After undergraduate studies at the University of Redlands, during which he was able to spend a semester in Austria and a year as an exchange student at a college in Hong Kong, the author earned an MA in Asian Studies at the University of Hawaii and a PhD in Comparative World and Southeast Asian History at the University of Wisconsin–Madison. His published books, articles, essays, and reviews range over a wide spectrum of topics: world history; Southeast Asian history, politics, and society; Malaysian studies; Asian emigration and diasporas; the Vietnam War; and folk, popular, rock, and world music. Among his major books are *Southeast Asia in World History* (2009); *WORLD* (2009); *Dance of Life: Popular Music and Politics in Modern Southeast Asia* (1998); and *From Kampung to City: A Social History of Kuching, Malaysia, 1820–1970* (1987). He was also part of the task force that prepared revisions to the U.S. National Standards in World History (1996). Professor Lockard has served on various editorial advisory boards, including the *Journal of World History* and *The History Teacher,* and as book review editor for the *Journal of Asian Studies* and the *World History Bulletin.* He was one of the founders of the World History Association, served as the organization's first secretary, and is currently a member of the Executive Council. He has lived and traveled widely in Asia, Africa, and Europe.

Note on Spelling and Usage

Transforming foreign words and names, especially those from non-European languages, into spellings usable for English-speaking readers presents a challenge. Sometimes, as with Chinese, Thai, and Malay/Indonesian, several romanized spelling systems have developed. Generally I have chosen user-friendly spellings that are widely used in other Western writings (such as *Aksum* for the classical Ethiopian state and *Ashoka* for the classical Indian king). For Chinese, I generally use the *pinyin* system developed in the People's Republic over the past few decades (such as *Qin* and *Qing* rather than the older *Chin* and *Ching* for these dynasties, and *Beijing* instead of *Peking*), but for a few terms and names (such as the twentieth-century political leaders *Sun Yat-sen* and *Chiang Kai-shek*) I have retained an older spelling more familiar to Western readers and easier to pronounce. The same strategy is used for some other terms or names from Afro-Asian societies, such as *Cairo* instead of *al-Cahira* (the Arabic name) for the Egyptian city, *Bombay* instead of *Mumbai* (the current Indian usage) for India's largest city, and *Burma* instead of *Myanmar*. In some cases I have favored a newer spelling widely used in a region and modern scholarship but not perhaps well known in the West. For example, in discussing Southeast Asia I follow contemporary scholarship and use *Melaka* instead of *Malacca* for the Malayan city and *Maluku* rather than *Moluccas* for the Indonesian islands. Similarly, like Africa specialists I have opted to use some newer spellings, such as *Gikuyu* rather than *Kikuyu* for the Kenyan ethnic group. To simplify things for the reader I have tried to avoid using diacritical marks within words. Sometimes their use is unavoidable, such as for the premodern Chinese city of *Chang'an;* the two syllables here are pronounced separately. I also follow the East Asian custom of rendering Chinese, Japanese, and Korean names with the surname (family name) first (e.g., *Mao Zedong, Tokugawa Ieyasu*). The reader is also referred to the opening essay, "Introducing World History," for explanations of the dating system used (such as the Common Era and the Intermediate Era) and geographical concepts (such as Eurasia for Europe and Asia, and Oceania for Australia, New Zealand, and the Pacific islands).

Introducing World History

This introduction helps you take the important "first step" toward understanding the scope and challenge of studying world history. By presenting the main concepts and themes of world history, it serves as your guide in exploring the story of the world presented in the rest of the book while providing a foretaste of the lively debates among historians as they try to make sense of the past, especially how societies change and how their contacts with one another have created the interconnected world we know today. By examining world history, you can better understand not only how this connection happened, but also why.

What Do Historians Do?

History is the study of the past that looks at all of human life, thought, and behavior and includes both a record and an interpretation of events, people, and the societies they developed. Therefore, the job of the historian is to both describe *and* interpret the past. Although beginning students generally see history as the story of "what happened," most professional historians want to make sense of historical events. Two general concepts help historians in these efforts. When they look at humans in all their historical complexity, historians see both changes and continuity. The legal system in the United States, for example, is unlike any other in the world, and yet it has been shaped in part by both English and ancient Roman legal practices.

Historians face their greatest challenges in their role as interpreters of the past. Although historians agree on the need for extensive evidence to support their generalizations, they often disagree on how an event should be interpreted. Often the disagreements reflect political differences. In 1992 a widely publicized disagreement took place on the occasion of the 500-year anniversary of the first cross-Atlantic voyage of Christopher Columbus to the Western Hemisphere in 1492. Some historians pictured Columbus as a farsighted pioneer who made possible communication between the hemispheres, while others saw him as an immoral villain who mistreated the local peoples, beginning a pattern of exploitation by Europeans. Similar debates have raged about whether it was necessary for the United States to drop atomic bombs on Japan in 1945, killing thousands of Japanese civilians but also ending World War II.

While the events of the past do not change, our understanding of them does, as historians both acquire new information and use the old information to answer new questions. Only within the past fifty years, for example, have historians studied the diaries and journals that reveal the important role of women on the home front during the American Civil War. Recently historians have used long-neglected sources to conclude that, a millennium ago, China had the world's most dynamic economy and sophisticated technology. Similarly, historians have recently discovered, in the West African city of Timbuktu, thousands of old books written in African languages, forcing a rethinking of literacy and scholarship in West African societies hundreds of years ago.

What history "tells us" is constantly evolving. New evidence, changing interests, and the asking of new questions all add up to seeing things in a new light. As you read the text, remember that no text contains the whole or final truth. Historical revision, or changing understanding of the past, is at the heart of historical scholarship. This revision and the difficulties of interpretation also make history controversial. In recent years heated debates about what schools should teach about history have erupted in many countries, including Japan, India, France, and the United States.

Historians bridge the gap between the humanities and the social sciences. As humanists, historians study the philosophies, religions, literatures, and arts that people have generated over the ages. As social scientists, historians examine political, social, and economic patterns, though frequently asking questions different from those asked by anthropologists, economists, political scientists, and sociologists, who are generally more concerned with the present and in theoretical questions. Historians also study people in their many roles and stations in life—the accomplishments of the rich and famous as well as the struggles and dreams of common women and men—and must be familiar with the findings of other relevant academic disciplines.

Why Study World History?

World or global history is the broadest field of history. It studies the human record as a whole and the experiences of people in all the world's inhabited regions—Africa, the Americas, Asia, Europe, and the Pacific Basin—and also helps us better understand individual societies by making it easier to look at them comparatively. Studying history on a global scale also brings out patterns of life, cultural traditions, and connections between societies that go beyond a particular region, such as the spread of Buddhism, which followed the trade routes throughout southern and eastern Asia nearly two thousand years ago. World history takes us through the forest of history in which the individual societies represent the individual trees. World history helps us comprehend both the trees and the forest, allowing us to situate ourselves in a broader context.

This helps us understand our increasingly connected world. Decisions made in Washington, D.C., Paris, or Tokyo influence citizens in Argentina, Senegal, and Malaysia, just as events elsewhere often affect the lives of people in Europe and North America. World historians use the widest angle of vision to comprehend how diverse local traditions and international trends intermingle. International trends spread from many directions. Western phenomena such as McDonald's, Hard Rock Cafes, French wines, Hollywood films, churches, the Internet, cell phones, and text messaging have spread around the world but so have non-Western products and ideas, among them Mexican soap operas, Chinese food, Japanese cars, Indonesian arts, African rhythms, and the Islamic religion. When we study individual nations, we must remember that, for all their idiosyncrasies, each nation develops in a wider world.

Along with the growing interconnectedness of the world, a global perspective highlights the past achievements of all peoples. The history of science, for example, shows that key inventions—printing, sternpost rudders, the compass, the wheelbarrow, gunpowder—originated in China and that the modern system of numbering came from India, reaching Europe from the Middle East as "Arabic" numerals. Indeed, various peoples—Mesopotamians, Egyptians, Greeks, Chinese, Indians, Arabs—built the early foundation for modern science and technology, and their discoveries moved along the trade routes. The importers of technology and ideas often modified or improved on them. For example, Europeans made good use of Chinese, Indian, and Arab technologies, as well as their own inventions, in their quest to explore the world in the fifteenth and sixteenth centuries. The interdependence among and exchanges between peoples is a historical as well as a present reality.

THE WORLD HISTORY CHALLENGE

When we study world history, we see other countries and peoples, past and present. We do not, however, always see them accurately. Nevertheless, by studying the unfamiliar, world history helps us to recognize how some of the attitudes we absorb from the particular society and era we live in shape, and may distort, our understanding of the world and of history. Coming to terms with this mental baggage means examining such things as maps and geographical concepts and acquiring intellectual tools for comprehending other cultures.

Broadening the Scope of Our Histories

During much of the twentieth century, high school and college students in North America were often taught some version of a course, usually called Western Civilization, that emphasized the rise of western Europe and the European contributions to modern North American societies. This course recognized the undeniably influential role of Western nations, technologies, and ideas in the modern world, but also reflected historians' extensive acquisition of data on Europe and North America compared with the rest of the world. This approach often exaggerated the role that Europe played in world history before modern times, pushing Asian, African, and Native American peoples and their accomplishments into the background while underplaying the contributions these peoples made to Europe. Students usually learned little about China, India, or Islam, and even less about Africa, Southeast Asia, or Latin America.

In the 1960s the teaching of history began to change in North America. The political independence of most Asian, African, and Caribbean nations from Western nations fostered a more sophisticated understanding of African, Asian, Latin American, Native American, and Pacific island history in North America and Europe. The increased knowledge has made it easier to write a history of the entire globe. As a result, world history courses, rare before the 1960s, became increasingly common in U.S. universities, colleges, and high schools by the late twentieth century and have been proliferating in several other countries, such as Australia, Canada, South Africa, China, and the Netherlands.

Revising Maps and Geography

Maps not only tell us where places are; they also create a mental image of the world, revealing how peoples perceive themselves and others. For example, Chinese maps once portrayed China as the "Middle Kingdom," the center of the world surrounded by "barbarians." This image reflected and deepened the Chinese sense of superiority over neighboring peoples. Similarly, 2,500 years ago, Greek maps showed Greece at the center of the inhabited world known to them.

Even modern maps can be misleading. For example, the Mercator projection (or spatial presentation) still used in many school maps in North America and elsewhere and standard in most atlases, is based on a sixteenth-century European model that distorts the relative size of landmasses, greatly exaggerating Europe, North America, and Greenland while diminishing the lands nearer the equator and in the Southern Hemisphere. Hence, Africa, India, Southeast Asia, China, and South America look much smaller than they actually are. In the United States, maps using a Mercator projection have often tellingly placed the Americas in the middle of the map, cutting Asia in half, suggesting that the United States, appearing larger than it actually is, plays the central role in the world. Some alternative maps give a more accurate view of relative size. For example, the oval-shaped Eckert projection uses an ellipse that shows a better balance of size and shape while minimizing distortion of continental areas. A comparison between the Mercator and Eckert world maps is shown on the following spread.

The same shaping of mental images of geography found in maps is also seen in concepts of geographical features and divisions, such as continents, the large landmasses on which most people live. The classical Greeks were probably the first to use the terms *Europe, Africa,* and *Asia* in defining their world 2,500 years ago, and later Europeans transformed these terms into the names for continents. For centuries Western peoples have taken for granted that Europe is a continent although Europe is not a separate landmass, and the physical barriers between it and Asia are not that significant. If mountains and other geographical barriers define a continent, one can make a better case for India (blocked off by truly formidable mountains) or Southeast Asia than for Europe. At the same time, seeing Asia as a single continent is also a problem, given its spectacular size and geographical diversity. Today world geographers and historians usually consider Europe and Asia to constitute one huge continent, Eurasia, containing several subcontinental regions, such as Europe, South Asia, and East Asia.

Popular terms such as *Near East, Middle East,* or *Far East* are also misleading. They were originally formulated by Europeans to describe regions in relationship to Europe. Much

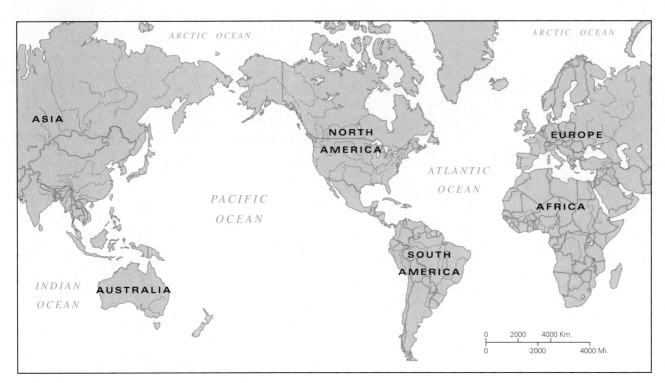

Mercator Projection

depends on the viewer's position; Australians, for example, often label nearby Southeast and East Asia as the "Near North." Few Western scholars of China or Japan today refer to the "Far East," preferring the more neutral term *East Asia*. This text considers the term *Near East*, long used for western Asia, as outdated, but it refers to Southwest Asia and North Africa, closely linked historically (especially after the rise of Islam 1,400 years ago), as the Middle East, since that term is more convenient than the alternatives. The text also uses the term *Oceania* to refer to Australia, New Zealand, and the Pacific islands.

Rethinking the Dating System

A critical feature of historical study is the dating of events. World history challenges us by making us aware that all dating systems are based on the assumptions of a particular culture. Many Asian peoples saw history as moving in great cycles of birth, maturation, and decay (sometimes involving millions of years), while Westerners saw history as moving in a straight line from past to future (as can be seen in the chronologies within each chapter). Calendars were often tied to myths about the world's creation or about a people's or country's origins. Hence, the classical Roman calendar was based on the founding of the city of Rome around 2,700 years ago, reflecting the Romans' claim to the territory in which they had recently settled.

The dating system used throughout the Western world today is based on the Gregorian Christian calendar, created by a sixteenth-century Roman Catholic pope, Gregory XIII. It uses the birth of Christianity's founder, Jesus of Nazareth, around 2,000 years ago as the turning point. Dates for events prior to the Christian era were identified as B.C. (before Christ); years in the Christian era were labeled A.D. (for the Latin *anno domini,* "in the year of the Lord"). Many history books published in

Europe and North America still employ this system, which has spread around the world in recent centuries.

The notion of Christian and pre-Christian eras has no longer been satisfactory for studies of world history because it is rooted in the viewpoint of only one religious tradition, whereas there are many in the world, usually with different calendars. Hence, the Christian calendar has little relevance for the non-Christian majority of the world's people. Muslims, for example, who consider the revelations of the prophet Muhammad to be the central event in history, begin their dating system with Muhammad's journey, within Arabia, from the city of Mecca to Medina in 622 A.D. Many Buddhists use a calendar beginning with the death of Buddha around 2,500 years ago. The Chinese chronological system divides history into cycles stretching over 24 million years. The Chinese are now in the fifth millennium of the current cycle, and their system corresponds more accurately than does the Gregorian calendar to the beginning of the world's oldest cities and states, between 5,000 and 6,000 years ago. Many other alternative dating systems exist. Selecting one over the others constitutes favoritism for a particular society or cultural tradition.

Therefore, most world historians and many specialists in Asian, African, and European history have moved toward a more secular, or nonreligious, concept, the Common Era. This system still accepts as familiar, at least to Western readers, the dates used in the Western calendar, but it calls the period after the transition, identified by Christians with the birth of Jesus, a "common" era, since many influential, dynamic societies existed two millennia ago throughout the world, not only in the Judeo-Christian Holy Land. Two millennia ago, the beginning of the Common Era, the Roman Empire was at its height, Chinese and Indian empires ruled large chunks of Asia, and many peoples in the Eastern Hemisphere were linked by trade and religion to a greater extent than ever before. Several African societies also flourished, and states and cities had long before

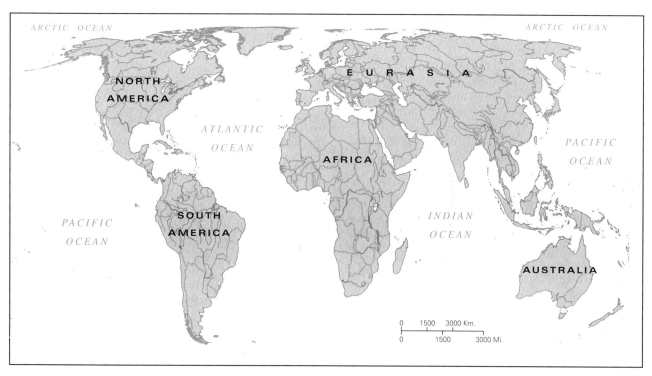

Eckert Projection

developed in the Americas. Hence this period makes a useful and familiar benchmark. In the new system, events are dated as B.C.E. (before the Common Era) and as C.E. (Common Era, which begins in year 1 of the Gregorian Christian calendar). This change is an attempt at including all the world's people and avoiding preference for any particular religious tradition.

Rethinking the Division of History into Periods

To make world history more comprehensible, historians divide long periods of time into smaller segments, such as "the ancient world" or "modern history," each marked by certain key events or turning points, a process known as **periodization**. For example, scholars of European, Islamic, Chinese, Indonesian, or United States history generally agree among themselves on the major eras and turning points for the region they study, but world historians need a system that can encompass all parts of the world, no easy task since most historic events did not affect all regions of the world. For instance, developments that were key to eastern Eurasia, such as the spread of Buddhism, or to western Eurasia and North Africa, such as the spread of Christianity, did not always affect southern Africa, and both the the Americas and some Pacific peoples remained isolated from the Eastern Hemisphere for centuries.

Given the need for an inclusive chronological pattern, this book divides history into periods, each of which is notable for significant changes around the world:

1. **Ancient (100,000–600 B.C.E.)** The Ancient Era, during which the foundations for world history were built, can be divided into two distinct periods. During the long centuries known as Prehistory (ca. 100,000–4000 B.C.E.), Stone Age peoples, living in small groups, survived by hunting and gathering food. Eventually some of them began simple farming and living in villages, launching the second period, the era of agrarian societies. Between 4000 and 600 B.C.E., agriculture became more productive, the first cities and states were established in both hemispheres, and some societies invented writing, allowing historians to study their experiences and ideas.

2. **Classical (600 B.C.E.–600 C.E.)** The Classical Era is marked by the creation of more states and complex agrarian societies, the birth of major religions and philosophies, the formation of the first large empires, and the expansion of long-distance trade, which linked distant peoples.

3. **Intermediate (600–1500 C.E.)** The Intermediate Era comprises a long middle period or "middle ages" of expanding horizons that modified or displaced the classical societies. It was marked by increasing trade connections between distant peoples within the same hemisphere, the growth and spread of several older religions and of a new faith, Islam, and oceanic exploration by Asians and Europeans.

4. **Early Modern (1450–1750 C.E.)** During the Early Modern Era, the whole globe became intertwined as European exploration and conquests in the Americas, Africa, and southern Asia fostered the rise of a global economy, capitalism, and a trans-Atlantic slave trade while undermining American and African societies.

5. **Modern (1750–1945 C.E.)** The Modern Era was characterized by rapid technological and economic change in Europe and North America, Western colonization of many Asian and African societies, political revolutions and ideologies, world wars, and a widening gap between rich and poor societies.

6. **Contemporary (1945–present)** The Contemporary Era has been marked by a more closely interlinked world, including the global spread of commercial markets, cultures, and communications, the collapse of Western colonial empires, international organizations, new technologies, struggles by poor nations to develop economically, environmental destruction, and conflict between powerful nations.

Understanding Cultural and Historical Differences

The study of world history challenges us to understand peoples and ideas very different from our own. The past is, as one writer has put it, "a foreign country; they do things differently there."[1] As human behavior changes with the times, sometimes dramatically, so do people's beliefs, including moral and ethical standards. For example, in Asia centuries ago, Assyrians and Mongols sometimes killed everyone in cities that resisted their conquest. Some European Christians seven hundred years ago burned suspected heretics and witches at the stake and enjoyed watching blind beggars fight. Across the Atlantic, American peoples such as the Aztecs and Incas engaged in human sacrifice. None of these behaviors would be morally acceptable today in most societies.

Differences in customs complicate efforts to understand people of earlier centuries. We need not approve of empire builders, plunderers, human sacrifice, and witch burning, but we should be careful about applying our current standards of behavior and thought to people who lived in different times and places. We should avoid **ethnocentrism**, viewing others narrowly through the lens of one's own society and its values. Historians are careful in using value-loaded words such as *primitive, barbarian, civilized,* or *progress* that carry negative or positive meanings and are often matters of judgment rather than fact. For instance, soldiers facing each other on the battlefield may consider themselves civilized and their opponents barbarians. And progress, such as industrialization, often brings negative developments, such as pollution, along with the positive.

Today anthropologists use the term **cultural relativism** to remind us that, while all people have much in common, societies are diverse and unique, embodying different standards of proper behavior and thought. For instance, cultures may have very different ideas about children's obligations to their parents, what happens to people's souls when they die, or what constitutes music pleasing to the ear. Cultural relativism still allows us to say that the Mongol empire builders in Eurasia some eight hundred years ago were brutal, or that the mid-twentieth-century Nazi German dictator, Adolph Hitler, was a murderous tyrant, or that laws in some societies today that blame and penalize women who are raped are wrong and should be protested. But cultural relativism discourages us from criticizing other cultures or ancient peoples just because they are or were different from us. Studying world history can make us more aware of our ethnocentric biases.

THE MAJOR THEMES

Determining major themes is yet another challenge in presenting world history. This text uses certain themes to take maximum advantage of world history's power to illuminate both change and continuity as we move from the past to the present. Specifically, in preparing the text, the author asked himself: What do educated students today need to know about world history to understand the globalizing era in which they live?

Three broad themes help you comprehend how today's world emerged. These themes are shaped around three concepts: societies, networks, and transitions.

1. **Societies** are broad groups of people that have common traditions, institutions, and organized patterns of relationships with each other. The societies that people have organized and maintained, influenced by environmental factors, were defined by distinctive but often changing cultures, beliefs, social forms, governments, economies, and ways of life.

2. **Networks** are arrangements or collections of links between different societies, such as the routes over which traders, goods, diplomats, armies, ideas, and information travel. Over the centuries societies were increasingly connected to other societies by growing networks forged by phenomena such as population movement, long-distance trade, exploration, military expansion, colonization, the diffusion of ideas and technologies, and communication links. These growing networks modified individual societies, connected societies within the same and nearby regions, and eventually led to a global system in which distant peoples came into frequent contact.

3. **Transitions** are passages, changes, events, or movements that reshape societies and regions. Each major historical era was marked by one or more great transitions that were sparked by events or innovations that had profound, enduring influences on many societies and that fostered a gradual reshaping of the world.

The first theme, based on societies, recognizes the importance in world history of the distinctiveness of societies. Cultural traditions and social patterns differed greatly. For example, societies in Eurasia fostered several influential philosophical and religious traditions, from Confucianism in eastern Asia to Christianity, born in the Middle East and later nourished both there and in Europe. Historians often identify unique traditions in a society that go back hundreds or even thousands of years.

The second theme, based on networks, acknowledges the way societies have contacted and engaged with each other to create the interdependent world we know today. The spread of technologies and ideas, exploration and colonization, and the growth of global trade across Eurasia and Africa and then into the Western Hemisphere are largely responsible for spurring this interlinking process. Today networks such as the World Wide Web, airline routes, multinational corporations, and terrorist organizations operate on a global scale. As this list shows, many networks are welcome, but some are dangerous.

The third theme, transitions, helps to emphasize major developments that shaped world history. The most important include, roughly in chronological order, the beginning of agriculture, the rise of cities and states, the birth and spread of philosophical and religious traditions, the forming of great empires, the linking of Eurasia by the Mongols, the European seafaring explorations and conquests, the Industrial Revolution, the forging and dismantling of Western colonial empires, world wars, and the invention of electronic technologies that allow for instantaneous communication around the world.

With these themes in mind, the text constructs the rich story of world history. The intellectual experience of studying world history is exciting and will give you a clearer understanding of how the world as you know it came to be.

KEY TERMS

history	ethnocentrism	societies	transitions
periodization	cultural relativism	networks	

SUGGESTED READING

After each chapter and essay, you will find a short list of valuable books and useful websites to help you explore history beyond the text. The books listed below will be of particular help to beginning students of world history because they examine the field of world history, offer an overview of history, or place key themes in a broad context for the general reader. The websites listed are megasites containing links to many essays, primary readings, and other sources.

Books

Bender, Thomas. *A Nation Among Nations: America's Place in World History*. New York: Hill and Wang, 2006. Looks at the history of the United States as part of modern world history.

Bentley, Jerry H. *Shapes of World History in 20th Century Scholarship*. Washington, DC: American Historical Association, 1996. A brief presentation of the scholarly study of world history.

Buschmann, Rainer F. *Oceans in World History*. Boston: McGraw-Hill, 2008. An innovative overview of how oceans connected distant societies.

Chanda, Nayan. *Bound Together: How Traders, Preachers, Adventurers, and Warriors Shaped Globalization*. New Haven: Yale University Press, 2007. A lively examination by an Indian journalist.

Christian, David. *Maps of Time: An Introduction to Big History*. Berkeley: University of California Press, 2004. A detailed but pathbreaking study by an Australian scholar that mixes scientific understandings into the study of world history.

Crossley, Pamela Kyle. *What Is Global History?* Malden, MA: Polity Press, 2008. Briefly examines approaches to understanding world history.

Dunn, Ross, ed. *The New World History: A Teacher's Companion*. Boston: Bedford/St. Martin's, 2000. A valuable collection of essays on various aspects of world history and how it can be studied. Useful for students as well as teachers.

Fernandez-Armesto, Felipe. *Pathfinders: A Global History*. New York: W.W. Norton, 2006. Readable survey of exploration.

Headrick, Daniel R. *Technology in World History*. New York: Oxford University Press, 2009. Good summary of this important topic.

Hodgson, Marshall G. S. *Rethinking World History: Essays on Europe, Islam, and World History*. Edmund Burke III, ed. New York: Cambridge University Press, 1993. Written by one of the most influential world historians for teachers and scholars but also offering many insights for students.

Manning, Patrick. *Migration in World History*. New York: Routledge, 2005. Explores population movements from prehistory to today.

McNeill, J. R., and William H. McNeill. *The Human Web: A Bird's-Eye View of World History*. New York: W.W. Norton, 2003. A stimulating overview of world history using the concept of human webs to examine interactions between peoples.

McNeill, William H., et al., eds. *Berkshire Encyclopedia of World History*, 5 vols. Great Barrington, MA: Berkshire, 2005. One of the best of several fine encyclopedias, with many essays on varied aspects of world history.

Nieberg, Michael S. *Warfare in World History*. New York: Routledge, 2001. Focuses on wars as agents of long-term change.

Ponting, Clive. *A New Green History of the World: The Environment and the Collapse of Great Civilizations*. New York: Penguin, 2007. Provocative study by a British scholar for a general audience.

Stavrianos, Leften S. *Lifelines from Our Past: A New World History*. rev. ed. Armonk, NY: M. E. Sharpe, 1997. A brief but stimulating reflection on world history by a leading scholar.

Stearns, Peter N. *Western Civilization in World History*. New York: Routledge, 2003. A brief examination of how Western civilization fits into the study of world history.

Wiesner-Hanks, Merry E. *Gender in World History*. Malden, MA: Blackwell, 2001. A pioneering thematic survey of a long-neglected subject.

WEBSITES

Bridging World History (*http://www.learner.org/courses/world history/*). Rich site with essays and multimedia presentations.

The Encyclopedia of World History (*http://www.bartleby.com/67/*). A valuable collection of thousands of entries spanning the centuries from prehistory to 2000.

Internet Global History Sourcebook (*http://www.fordham.edu/halsall/global/globalsbook.html*). An excellent set of links on world history from ancient to modern times.

Internet History Sourcebooks Project (*http://www.fordham.edu/halsall/*). Huge invaluable collection of public domain historical readings on many topics and regions.

Women in World History (*http://chnm.gmu.edu/wwh/*). Invaluable collection of links covering many societies and all eras.

World Civilizations (*http://www.wsu.edu/~dee*). An Internet anthology maintained at Washington State University.

World History Connected (*http://worldhistoryconnected.press/illinois.edu)/*). This e-journal contains essays of use to both students and teachers.

World History for Us All (*http://worldhistoryforusall.sdsu.edu*). A growing site with useful essays and other materials, sponsored by San Diego State University.

World History Sources (*http://worldhistorymatters.org*). Valuable annotated links on different subjects, based at George Mason University.

FOUNDATIONS: ANCIENT SOCIETIES, TO 600 B.C.E.

Most of us carry pictures in our minds of the world's ancient peoples and their ways of life: prehistoric cave dwellers huddling around a fire, wandering desert tribes, towering pyramids, and spectacular ruins of cities and temples. In fact, the centuries between 100,000 and 600 B.C.E. saw the evolution of these and many other social and cultural phenomena, more complex and often more significant to us today than these mental pictures convey. These centuries also saw humans take the first steps in establishing regular contacts and exchanges, often those of trade, with one another, creating the networks that linked many societies over wide areas.

Human societies have emerged only recently in earth's long history. Simple life began on earth over 3 billion years ago. Several million years ago in Africa the earliest near ancestors of humans began to walk upright and use simple tools. Gradually they evolved into modern humans who commanded language, controlled fire, and eventually populated the entire world. For thousands of years, small bands of people, carrying their stone and wood tools as they moved from campsite to campsite, lived by hunting and gathering. With the first great transition in human history, the introduction of agriculture some 10,000 years ago, people began to deliberately cultivate plants and raise draft animals. Although some societies remained hunters and gatherers or herders, most people around the world shifted eventually to farming. Congregating in villages and towns and farming the neighboring fields with their simple hoes and plows, they experienced profound changes in their ways of life. For some societies, the production of an agricultural surplus—more food than was needed by the farmers—and growing commercial activity provided the economic and labor support that enabled the development of formal governments and religious institutions. Farming, town life, trade, and more advanced technology set the stage for the second great transition, the building of cities and the forming of states.

The world's first societies emerged in various parts of the world, and each society gradually created its own distinctive traditions. The first cities and states arose between 5,500 and 4,000 years ago in the lands stretching from southern Europe and northern Africa eastward through western and southern Asia to China. For most of history the vast majority of the world's people lived in these regions of Africa and Eurasia. Between 5,000 and 3,000 years ago cities and states also developed in the Americas. The most densely populated ancient societies emerged where agriculture, aided by irrigation, flourished: in large river valleys, particularly the floodplains of the Nile in Egypt, the Tigris-Euphrates in Mesopotamia, the Indus in India, and the Yellow in China. The ancient world also benefited from great advances in metalworking, especially of copper, bronze, and iron, which spread widely. Growing networks of trade and transportation

Cuneiform Tablet This letter, impressed on a clay tablet in Mesopotamia around 1900 B.C.E., records a merchant's complaint that a shipment of copper that he had paid for contained too little metal. Mesopotamian letters, written chiefly by merchants and officials, were enclosed in envelopes made of clay and marked with the sender's private seal.

Courtesy of the Trustees of the British Museum

increasingly connected many societies to each other by land and sea. Although societies exchanged ideas, products, and technologies with others, each ancient society created unique religions, cultural values, social structures, and systems for recording information. These traditions sometimes continued over several thousand years, even though modified with time. A few traditions, such as the ancient Hebrew and Indian religions, have survived into the present.

Contacts between peoples in different regions had already begun to increase greatly with the appearance of farming. Societies traded agricultural and hunting tools, as well as minerals, wood, clothing, and food. Between 2500 and 600 B.C.E. the Eastern Hemisphere experienced much more active trading networks. Improved transportation, including seaworthy sailing vessels, horse-drawn chariots, and camel caravans, fostered trade by shrinking distances. Long-distance trade served to spread ideas and expand horizons. Some peoples migrated far from their ancestral homes, with major movements into the Pacific islands (Oceania) and the southern half of Africa. Like trade, other encounters between societies, friendly or hostile, often became major forces for change.

Most ancient societies, such as Egypt and Mesopotamia, have long since disappeared, leaving only crumbling ruins or long-buried artifacts to remind us of their achievements. In their ancient forms, these societies never survived through the centuries, although their religions and values often influenced the societies that displaced them, and many of their descendants still live in the region. On the other hand, the Chinese and Indian societies persisted in some recognizable form and are familiar to us today. The Ancient Era built the framework for much that came later.

NORTH AND CENTRAL AMERICA
The ancestors of Native Americans migrated into North America from Asia thousands of years ago. They gradually occupied the Americas, working out ways of life compatible with the environments they lived in. While many remained hunters and gatherers, the first American farming began in Mexico and spread to various North American regions. The Olmecs of Mexico built cities atop huge artificial mounds and created an alphabet and religious traditions that influenced nearby peoples. Other North Americans also built settlements around large mounds.

SOUTH AMERICA
Some Native Americans reached South America thousands of years ago. Farming developed early along the Pacific coast and in the Andes Mountains region. The first cities, such as Caral in coastal Peru, arose around the same time as early cities in Egypt and India. Cities were later established in the Andes Mountains. The major Andean states influenced the art and religion of many other South American societies.

© Cengage Learning

WESTERN ASIA

The world's first farmers probably lived in western Asia, east of the Mediterranean Sea, where the oldest known cities and states also arose. The diverse societies that formed in the Tigris-Euphrates River Valley in Mesopotamia developed bronzeworking, writing, science, and mathematics, and they also traded with India and Egypt. Western Asians perfected iron technology, which eventually spread around Eurasia. The Phoenicians were the greatest traders of the Mediterranean region and also invented an alphabet later adopted by the Greeks. Another notable people, the Hebrews, introduced a monotheistic religion, Judaism.

EUROPE

Ancient cities and states formed on the Mediterranean island of Crete and in Greece. Minoans, the residents of Crete, were successful maritime traders. After their collapse, the Mycenaeans of mainland Greece traded widely and exercised regional power until they declined. Migrants into Greece mixed with the Mycenaeans to form the foundation for later Greek society. These southern European societies worked bronze and participated in trade networks linking them to North Africa, eastern Europe, and western Asia.

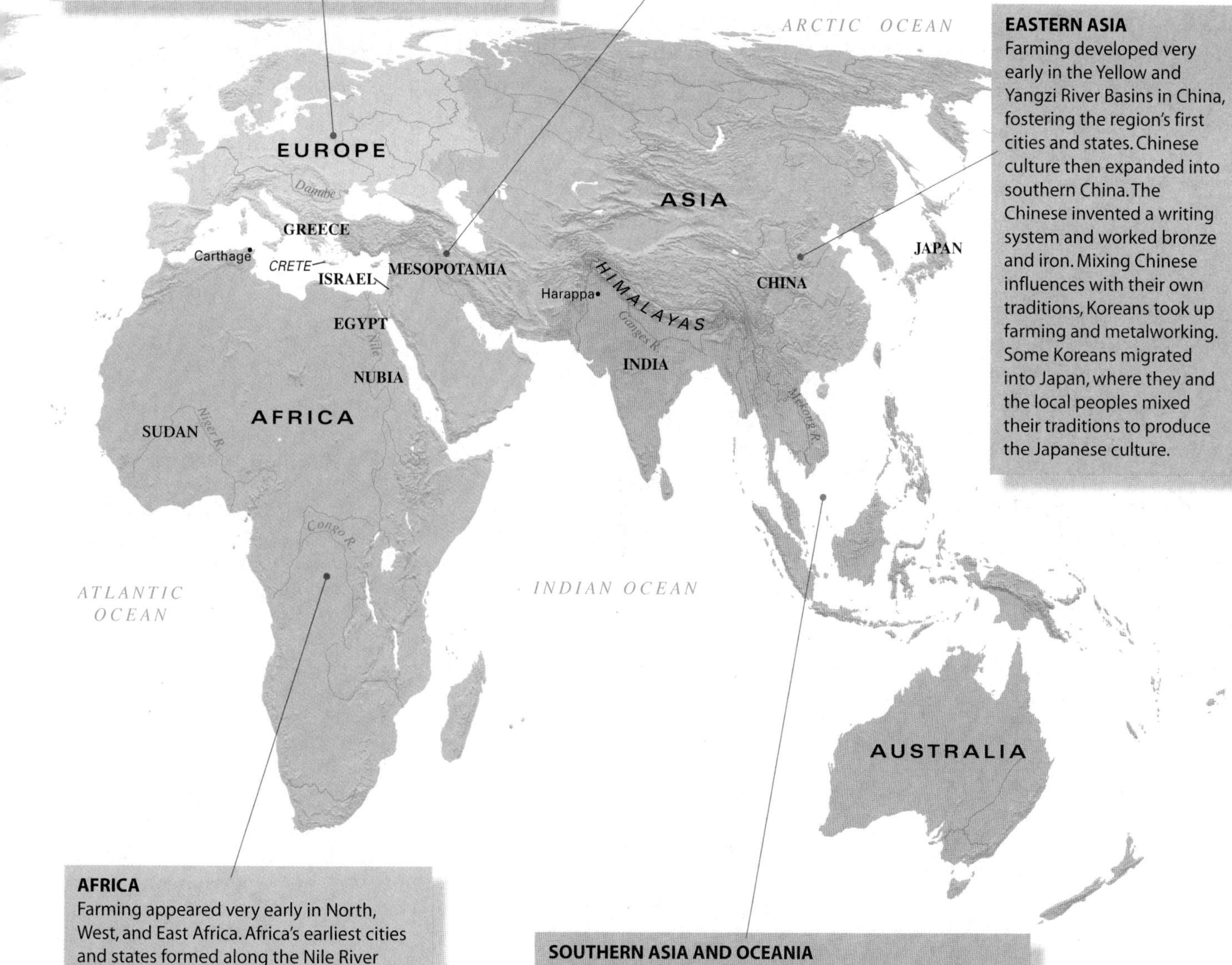

EASTERN ASIA

Farming developed very early in the Yellow and Yangzi River Basins in China, fostering the region's first cities and states. Chinese culture then expanded into southern China. The Chinese invented a writing system and worked bronze and iron. Mixing Chinese influences with their own traditions, Koreans took up farming and metalworking. Some Koreans migrated into Japan, where they and the local peoples mixed their traditions to produce the Japanese culture.

ARCTIC OCEAN

EUROPE

Danube

GREECE

Carthage

CRETE ISRAEL MESOPOTAMIA

EGYPT

NUBIA

AFRICA

SUDAN *Niger R.*

ASIA

Harappa *HIMALAYAS*

Ganges R.

INDIA

JAPAN

CHINA

Mekong R.

Nile

Congo R.

ATLANTIC OCEAN

INDIAN OCEAN

AUSTRALIA

AFRICA

Farming appeared very early in North, West, and East Africa. Africa's earliest cities and states formed along the Nile River Valley in Egypt. The Egyptians invented a writing system and flourished from productive agriculture and trade with other African societies and Eurasia. Cities and states also arose in Nubia, just south of Egypt. Africans south of the Sahara Desert developed ironworking technology very early, and iron tools and weapons helped the Bantu-speaking peoples gradually expand from West Africa into Central and East Africa.

SOUTHERN ASIA AND OCEANIA

Farming and metalworking developed early in South and Southeast Asia. The people of the Harappan cities in the Indus River Basin grew cotton, made textiles, and traded with western and Central Asia. After the Harappan society collapsed, Aryan peoples from western Asia moved into India, and the mixing of Aryan and local traditions formed the basis for the Hindu religion. Meanwhile, Austronesian peoples migrated from Taiwan into the Southeast Asian and Pacific islands. Southeast Asians pioneered in maritime trade and formed their first states. Hunters and gatherers flourished in Australia.

THE ORIGINS OF HUMAN SOCIETIES, TO CA. 2000 B.C.E.

Kazuyoshi Nomachi/Pacific Press Photo

Tassili Archers
Thousands of ancient paintings on rock surfaces and cave walls record the activities of African hunters, gatherers, and pastoralists. This painting of archers on a hunt was made in a rock shelter on the Tassili plateau of what is today Algeria, probably long before the Sahara region had dried up and become a harsh desert.

*W*e are long past the time when we could deal with the human story apart from the life story, or the earth story, or the universe story.

—Cosmologist Brian Swimme and Historian Thomas Berry[1]

The human story was already old and the life story far older when, at Abu Hureyra (AH-boo hoo-RAY-rah) in the Euphrates (you-FRAY-teez) River Valley of what is now Syria, a group of villagers became some of the first farmers, thus taking a large step in shaping world history. People who hunted game and gathered vegetables and nuts occupied Abu Hureyra 13,000 years ago, when the area was wetter and blessed with many edible wild plants and herds of Persian gazelles. But a long cold spell brought a drought, challenging their good life; to survive, the Abu Hureyra villagers began to cultivate the most easily grown grains and later also raised domesticated sheep and goats. By 7600 B.C.E. they had shifted completely to farming and animal herding.

FOCUS QUESTIONS

1. According to most scientists, what were the various stages of human evolution?
2. How did hunting and gathering shape life during the long Stone Age?
3. What environmental factors explain the transition to agriculture?
4. How did farming and metallurgy establish the foundations for the rise of cities, states, and trade networks?

The Abu Hureyra farmers pursued a life familiar to rural folk for millennia afterwards. Several hundred people crowded into a village of narrow lanes and courtyards. Families dwelled in one-story, multiroom mud houses with polished plaster floors, some decorated with red designs. At night family members studied the sky and pondered the mysteries of the universe. Men did much of the farm work while women carried heavy loads on their heads, prepared meals, and ground grain in a kneeling position, an activity that was hard on arms, knees, and toes. Work for both women and men involved repetitive tasks and called for muscle power. Many villagers suffered from arthritis and lower back injuries. Abu Hureyra was abandoned in 5000 B.C.E.

Prehistory includes a vast span of time, from the earliest humans to the beginnings of agriculture and the emergence of complex societies with cities and states. Much of what we know about these millennia comes from archaeologists, who study the material remains of past cultures, and anthropologists, who study human biology and culture in relation to the physical and social environment. During the long saga of our planet, all living creatures appeared and developed, including eventually humans. Over many millennia humans evolved physically, mentally, and culturally, learning to make simple tools and then spreading throughout the world. Later most societies, like the Abu Hureyra villagers, made the first great historical transition from hunting and gathering to farming and animal herding. This transition profoundly changed the relationship between people and the environment and prompted the working of metals for better tools. The rise of agriculture all over the world made possible another important transition, the emergence of larger societies with cities and states. In turn this stimulated long-distance trade and the rise of social, cultural, and economic networks linking distant societies.

e Visit the website and eBook for additional study materials and interactive tools: www.cengage.com/history/lockard/globalsocnet2e

PREHISTORY: THE COSMOS, EARTH, AND THE ROOTS OF HUMANITY

According to most scientists, what were the various stages of human evolution?

Some scholars have promoted a "big history" that places the development of human societies and networks in a much longer and more comprehensive framework, the "universe story." They argue that we cannot comprehend the rise of complex societies without a knowledge of prefarming peoples, the ancestors of humans, and, before that, the beginning of life on earth and the formation of our planet within the larger cosmic order. Recurring patterns of balance and imbalance and of order and disorder in the natural world, such as global warming and cooling, have always played a role in human history. Inspired by such large forces around them, people have speculated about the origins of the cosmos, earth, life, and humanity for countless generations. Over the years their views have been integrated into religions.

Perceptions of Cosmic Mysteries

Human development on earth constitutes only a tiny fraction of the long history of the universe, which most astronomers think began in a cosmic Big Bang explosion some 14 billion years ago. As the universe expanded, matter coalesced into stars, and stars formed into billions of galaxies spread over vast distances. Our solar system emerged about 4.5 billion years ago out of clouds of gas. On our planet, earth, the developing atmosphere kept the surface warm enough for organic compounds to coalesce into life forms. This is the story presented by modern science.

Over the centuries most human societies, to explain their existence, have crafted creation stories and cosmologies, systematic expressions of their views on the natural and supernatural worlds. These explanations have varied greatly, but usually they have involved myths or legends of some divine creator or creators. The earliest known creation story, from Mesopotamia, claimed that heaven and earth were formed as one in a primeval sea and then were separated by the gods, humanlike beings unperceivable to mortals and far more powerful. Mesopotamian beliefs influenced the seven-day creation story in the Hebrew book of Genesis.

Many cosmological traditions, however, were very different. Ancient Hindu holy books, for example, describe the creation of a universe out of nothingness: "There was neither non-existence or existence then; there was neither the realm of space nor the sky which is beyond. Darkness was hidden by darkness in the beginning, emptiness."[2] Then a great heat formed the cosmos and generated life. The ancient Chinese believed that the universe was created out of chaos and darkness and that the creator Pan Ku fashioned the sun, moon, and stars to put everything in proper order. The result was a unifying force in the universe, known as the "way," or *dao* (DOW). A related Chinese theory, *feng shui* (fung-SHWAY), suggests that the earth itself contains natural forces that people must comprehend in order to properly situate buildings and graves. Some ideas from the feng shui tradition have recently gained a following in Western countries.

Early Life and Evolutionary Change

"Life," meaning organisms that are able to consume food, grow, and reproduce with a genetic code, has a long history. Simple, single-celled life emerged by perhaps 3.5 to 3.8 billion years ago and remained dominant until about a half billion years ago, when life forms became increasingly complex and proliferated in incredible variety. Animal life colonized the land between 400 and 500 million years ago and evolved into many species. Throughout its long history, life has been influenced by natural forces such as geology and climate. Volcanic and earthquake activity caused by plate movements has influenced human history, and sometimes intense volcanic eruptions have dramatically altered regional climates. As we will see, warmer or cooler climates helped shape human societies and also sometimes undermined them.

Most natural scientists agree that living things change over many generations through evolution, the process by which they modify their genetic composition to adapt to their environment. In the nineteenth century the British biologist Charles Darwin explained the process with his theory of natural selection. He believed individuals developed variations that helped them to compete for food and domination within their own species and to triumph over rival species. Scientists still debate evolution's precise mechanisms, but modern biology has mostly confirmed Darwin's

 Primary Source: The *Rig Veda* Read how Indra, "the thunder-wielder," slew Vritra, "firstborn of dragons," and how Purusha created the universe through an act of ritual sacrifice.

Life on Earth

CHRONOLOGY

	Cosmos	Human Evolution	Prehistory Transitions
14 billion years ago	**14 billion years ago** Big Bang **4.5 billion years ago** Solar system and earth	**5–6 million years ago** Earliest proto-humans	
400,000 B.C.E.		**400,000–200,000 B.C.E.** *Homo sapiens* **135,000–100,000 B.C.E.** Modern humans in Africa	
100,000 B.C.E.		**100,000 B.C.E.** Modern humans in Eurasia	**100,000–9500 B.C.E.** Old and Middle Stone Ages **9500–8000 B.C.E.** New Stone Age; beginning of agriculture **3500–3200 B.C.E.** First cities in western Asia **3000 B.C.E.** Introduction of bronze **1500 B.C.E.** Introduction of iron

basic insights that species, including humans, are shaped by their changing biological and physical environment.

A half dozen massive species extinctions have occurred in the past 400 million years. For example, 250 million years ago gigantic volcanic eruptions produced enough climate-changing gases to almost wipe out all life. The best-known extinction involved the dinosaurs, which flourished for 150 million years before dying out about 65 million years ago, probably from environmental changes: the cooling of the planet from increasing volcanic activity, the cataclysmic impact of one or several large asteroids or comets smashing into the earth, or both. The resulting toxic acid rain and long winter destroyed food sources, thus killing off about 70 percent of all species. The demise of the dinosaurs opened the door for mammals to rise and flourish. One group of these mammals eventually evolved into humans. So far humans have been lucky. Scientists estimate that 99 percent of all species eventually became extinct when conditions changed dramatically, as they did for the dinosaurs. In our own time, species have been dying rapidly over the past two hundred years, most likely because of environmental changes such as pollution, habitat removal, and global warming generated by human activity.

Eventually, after several billion years, evolutionary changes among one branch of mammals led to the immediate ancestors of humans. Humans are part of the primate order, the mammal category that includes the apes. Our closeness to the apes is shown by the fact that over 98 percent of human DNA is the same as that of chimpanzees. Human–chimp lines diverged sometime before 5 or 6 million years ago.

Humans ultimately became dominant among large animal species by using their superior brain to gain an evolutionary edge. One key to their success was the ability to form *complex* social organizations that emphasized cooperation for mutual benefit. Humans also developed tools, mastered fire, and learned how to use speech, all of which gave them great advantages. Ultimately they began using a more complex technology that enabled them to manipulate the physical environment in many ways to meet their needs.

Hominids (HOM-uh-nids), a family including humans and their immediate ancestors, first evolved 5 to 6 million years ago from more primitive primates. The first chapters of the human story began in Africa, where the span of human prehistory is much longer than anywhere else. The most extensive fossil evidence comes from the southern African plateau and the Great Rift Valley of East Africa, a wide, deep chasm stretching from Ethiopia south to Tanzania. There are heated disagreements among scientists over fossil and artifact remains and whether teeth, skulls, and bones belong to ancestors of humans or of apes. Fossil discoveries point to several stages and branches in early human evolution (see Chronology: Hominid Evolution). A common ancestral, apelike group lived in the woodlands and savannahs of East Africa. One division (the ancestors of most apes) began

Species Extinctions

Human Ancestors

hominids A family including humans and their immediate ancestors.

CHRONOLOGY
Hominid Evolution

20 Million B.C.E. Common ancestor to humans and apes (Africa)

5–6 Million B.C.E. Earliest proto-humans

4–5 Million B.C.E. Australopithecines

2.5 Million B.C.E. *Homo habilis*

2.2–1.8 Million B.C.E. *Homo erectus*

400,000–200,000 B.C.E. *Homo sapiens* (archaic humans)

135,000–100,000 B.C.E. *Homo sapiens sapiens* (modern humans)

australopithecines Early hominids living in eastern and southern Africa 4 to 5 million years ago.

Homo habilis ("handy human") A direct ancestor of humans, so named because of its increased brain size and ability to make and use simple stone tools for hunting and gathering.

Homo erectus ("erect human") A hominid that emerged in East Africa probably between 1.8 and 2.2 million years ago.

Pioneers in Eurasia

specializing in forest dwelling and climbing with all four limbs. Another division developed occasional and then permanent bipedalism, walking upright on two feet. This made more activity possible because it left the hands free for holding food or babies, manipulating objects, and carrying food back to camp. Bipeds, being higher off the ground, could also scan the horizon for predators or prey.

Several hominid groups apparently coexisted at the same time, but only one led to modern humans. Several branches of early hominids known as **australopithecines** (aw-strah-lo-PITH-uh-seens) lived in eastern and southern Africa 4 or 5 million years ago. The brains of these proto-humans were about one-third the size of our brains. One example was found in Ethiopia, where archaeologists unearthed the bones of a small female, named Lucy by anthropologists, who lived some 20 years and probably walked mostly on her feet. Scholars disagree as to whether these hominids might be the ancestors to modern humans.

Some 2.5 million years ago one branch of australopithecines evolved into our direct ancestor, a transition probably due to environmental change. The earth cooled, fostering the first of a series of Ice Ages, which covered large areas of northern Eurasia and North America with deep ice sheets and glaciers. This cooling pattern also affected Africa and its hominid inhabitants, bringing a drier climate and more open habitats. Increased intelligence was needed to deal with the challenges posed by this climate change. **Homo habilis** (HOH-moh HAB-uh-luhs) ("handy human") was so named because of this species' larger brain size and its ability to make and use simple stone tools for hunting and gathering. Stone choppers and later hand axes made possible a more varied diet, more successful hunting, and larger groups that could cooperate to share food. The other branches of australopithecines died out, losing the competition to *Homo habilis.*

As hominid societies developed, males increasingly became the hunters or scavengers for meat and females the gatherers of nuts and vegetables. The receding of the forests and their food sources may have made meat a more crucial protein source. Nonetheless, gathering still probably brought more food than hunting or scavenging. Indeed, these early humans were probably mainly vegetarians, like many primates today. In any case, cooperation between the sexes and group members was the key to survival and probably involved communication through gestures and vocal cries.

Homo Erectus and Migrations Out of Africa

Probably between 1.8 and 2.2 million years ago, some more advanced hominids evolved from *Homo habilis* in East Africa. Most scholars have termed these hominids **Homo erectus** ("erect human"). Their achievements were remarkable. They had a brain about two-thirds the size of ours and eventually developed a more complex and widespread tool culture that included hand axes, cleavers, and scrapers. They spread to other parts of Africa, preferring the open savannah.

Between 1 and 2 million years ago, as southern Eurasia developed a warmer climate, some *Homo erectus* bands began migrating out of Africa, carrying with them refined tools, more effective hunting skills, and an ability to adapt to new environments. Perhaps the first migrants were following game herds. This was the first great migration in human history, and it corresponded to the ebb and flow of the Ice Ages as well as the periodic drying out of the Sahara region. Over thousands of years these hominids came to occupy northern Africa, the Middle East, South and Southeast Asia, China, Europe, and perhaps Australia. Some of the earliest non-African sites, perhaps 1.8 million years old, have been found in the Caucasus (KAW-kuh-suhs) Mountains of western Asia. Farther east, bones and tools discovered in Chinese caves and skulls from the island of Java in Indonesia, then connected to mainland Asia, have been dated at 1.6 to 1.9 million years ago. These finds suggest that *Homo erectus* may have been widespread in East and Southeast Asia by 1.5 million years ago. Fossils from eastern Siberia date back 300,000 years, indicating how adaptable and resourceful the species had become if it could survive in that brutal climate. Europe has proved a bigger puzzle. These hominids lived in Spain by 800,000 B.C.E. However, their tool cultures differed somewhat from those of Chinese *Homo erectus*, indicating cultural diversity and perhaps, some scholars believe, major variation from the Asian species.

By 500,000 years ago *Homo erectus* in China lived in closely knit groups, engaged in cooperative hunting, and probably used both wood and bamboo for containers and weapons. Most lived in caves, but some built simple wooden huts for shelter. Their hand axes were the Swiss army knives of their time, with a tip for piercing, thin edges for cutting, and thick edges for scraping and chipping. Scientists debate whether *Homo erectus* could use speech.

One of the key discoveries, how to start and control fire, was perhaps the most significant human invention ever. But we do not yet know precisely where or when people first used fire or how many millennia it took for knowledge of fire to spread widely. Fire opened up many possibilities, providing warmth and light after sunset, frightening away predators, and making possible a more varied diet of cooked food, which tasted better and fostered group living and cooperation as people gathered together around campfires and hearths. Fire also enabled ancestral humans to spread to cooler regions, such as Europe and eastern Asia.

The Evolution and Diversity of *Homo Sapiens*

The transition from *Homo erectus* to archaic forms of **Homo sapiens** ("thinking human"), a species that was physically close to modern humans, began around 400,000 years ago in Africa. By 200,000 years ago a more complex tool culture was widespread, evidence for *Homo sapiens* occupation. With this development humanity became a single species, despite some superficial differences. Eventually members of *Homo sapiens* were the only surviving hominids.

Members of *Homo sapiens* had many advantages over *Homo erectus*. With a larger brain, they were more adaptive and intelligent, able to think conceptually. Archaic *Homo sapiens* may have used language, lived in fairly large organized groups, built temporary shelters, created crude lunar calendars, and killed whole herds of animals. They also raised more children to adulthood. Possession of symbolic language gave *Homo sapiens* an advantage over earlier hominids and all other creatures, allowing them to share information over the generations. Language enabled people to adjust to their environment and overcome challenges not just individually but also collectively.

Scientists debate precisely how and where *Homo erectus* evolved into *Homo sapiens,* and several competing theories explain the transition. Some scholars argue that the evolution into *Homo sapiens* occurred in different parts of the Afro-Eurasian zone. The most widely supported scenario, known as the African Origins theory, suggests that *Homo sapiens* evolved only in East Africa and then spread throughout Afro-Eurasia, displacing and ultimately dooming the remaining *Homo erectus* groups. The evidence for this theory includes the fact that (so far, anyway) the earliest *Homo sapiens* remains have been found in East Africa. One of the most useful tools in tracing human evolution is the study of genetic codes, which mostly support the African Origins theory.

Whether the evolution into *Homo sapiens* occurred only in Africa or on several continents, all humans came to constitute one species that could interbreed and communicate with each other. There were a few differences in physical features, such as skin and hair color and eye and face shape, but it remains unclear whether these developed earlier or later in *Homo sapiens* evolution. The diverse groupings that evolved from *Homo sapiens* were once labeled "races," meaning large groups that shared distinctive genetic traits and physical characteristics. But the race concept is for good reasons often dismissed by experts for its inability to classify human populations. Observable physical attributes such as skin color and eye shape reflect a tiny portion of one's genetic makeup

John Reader/Photo Researchers, Inc.

The Laetoli Footprints   Some 4 million years ago in Tanzania, three australopithecines walked across a muddy field covered in ash from a nearby volcanic eruption. When the mud dried, their tracks were permanently preserved, providing evidence of some of the earliest upright hominids.

Homo sapiens ("thinking human") A hominid who evolved around 400,000 years ago and from whom anatomically modern humans (*Homo sapiens sapiens*) evolved around 100,000 years ago.

Debating Race

and thus cannot always predict whether two groups are genetically similar or different. There has been much genetic intermixing between human populations, and many people are difficult to classify. Humans are much more similar than different.

Sometime between 150,000 and 100,000 years ago in Africa, anatomically modern humans with slightly larger brains, known as *Homo sapiens sapiens*, developed out of *Homo sapiens*. With this biological change, language and culture expanded in new directions and developed many variations. Scholars debate whether creativity, intelligence, and even language abilities were innate to *Homo ssapiens sapiens,* as suggested by engraved pigments in South African caves from 75,000 to 100,00 years ago, or arose only some 50,000 years ago, possibly as a result of a genetic mutation. With this great transition humanity reached its present level of intellectual and physical development, and humans established the foundation for the constant expansion of information networks to a global level.

Modern humans eventually developed their languages in ways that made possible complex cultures with shared learning. Spoken language was the main method of communication for much of history. Perhaps there was one original language used by all humans. But eventually, some 5,000 or 6,000 languages emerged around the globe. Some languages, such as English and German, have a clear common ancestry, but scholars debate the relationships and origins of most of the world's languages. Human intellectual development also included abstract, symbolic thought, which was revealed early in decoration and art. Ocher (O-ker), for example, a natural red iron oxide, was mined in various African locations and probably used for body decoration. The gorgeous cave and rock art of southwestern Europe, Africa, western Asia, and Australia has been traced back at least 30,000 to 40,000 years. These creations probably had magical, religious, or ritual purposes, such as the celebration of spirits or valued animals.

The Globalization of Human Settlement

Between 50,000 and 12,000 years ago much of the world was settled by restless modern humans. As people spread, genetic differences grew and *Homo sapiens sapiens* proved able to adapt to many environments all over the world. By 100,000 years ago some had already left Africa to settle in Palestine. *Homo sapiens sapiens* settlement might not have expanded much beyond Africa and southwestern Asia until 50,000 years ago. But rising sea levels at the end of the last Ice Age may also have covered evidence that might allow us to trace migration routes along the southern Asian coasts. Eventually modern humans reached central and eastern Eurasia, from where some moved on to Australia, the Americas, and Europe (see Chronology: The Spread of Modern Humans).

Modern humans crossed to the eastern fringe of Asia before they populated Europe (see Map 1.1). They arrived in India and Southeast Asia between 40,000 and 50,000 years ago, in China between 35,000 and 50,000 years ago, and in Europe between 35,000 and 45,000 years ago. To reach Australia from Southeast Asia across a very shallow sea required rafts or boats, but modern humans may have settled there between 60,000 and 45,000 B.C.E. While New Guinea had human settlers between 50,000 to 60,000 years ago, the peopling of the Pacific islands to the east began much later, around 2000 B.C.E.

Beginning around 200,000 years ago, a vibrant new tool culture developed in Europe that has been identified with the **Neanderthals** (nee-AN-der-thals), hominids who were probably related to *Homo erectus* populations. The Neanderthals gradually spread to inhabit a wide region stretching from Spain and Germany to western and Central Asia; fossils have also been found in North Africa. Skillful hunters, the Neanderthals maintained social values, buried their dead, and cared for the sick. Their cranial capacity equaled or even exceeded that of *Homo sapiens,* and they had larger bodies. Although they probably lacked spoken language, they were capable of communication. They also used tools, made bone flutes, and wore jewelry. The relationship of the Neanderthals to *Homo sapiens sapiens* is debated. By 70,000 years ago both Neanderthals and modern humans lived in Palestine. When the modern, tool-using humans known as **Cro-Magnons** (krow-MAG-nuns) arrived in Europe from Asia, they also coexisted with Neanderthals for several millennia. DNA studies suggest that Neanderthals were a rather different species from Cro-Magnons. There is little convincing evidence of significant interbreeding. Around 28,000 years ago, the last Neanderthals died out. Whether they were ultimately annihilated, outnumbered, outcom-

Neanderthals Hominids who were probably descended from *Homo erectus* populations in Europe and who later spread into western and Central Asia.

Cro-Magnons The first modern, tool-using humans in Europe.

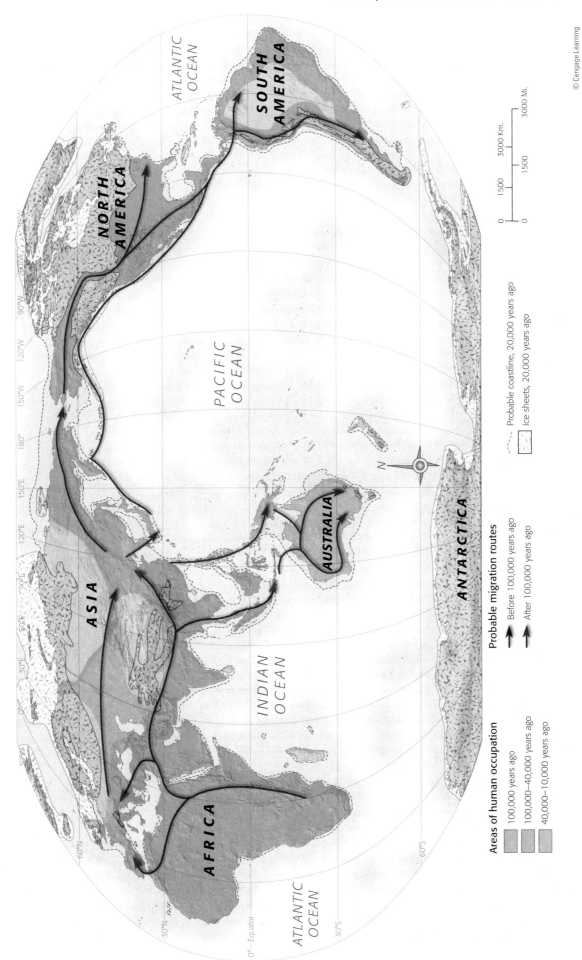

Areas of human occupation

- 100,000 years ago
- 100,000–40,000 years ago
- 40,000–10,000 years ago

Probable migration routes

- Before 100,000 years ago
- After 100,000 years ago

- - - - Probable coastline, 20,000 years ago

Ice sheets, 20,000 years ago

 **Interactive Map**

Map 1.1
Spread of Modern Humans Around the Globe

Most scholars believe that modern humans originated in Africa and that some of them began leaving Africa around 100,000 years ago. Gradually they spread out through Eurasia. From Eastern Asia some crossed to the Americas.

peted, or assimilated by the more resourceful and adaptable *Homo sapiens sapiens,* who had better technology and warmer clothing, remains unknown.

Peopling the Americas

Archaeologists long thought that the peopling of the Americas came very late and that the earliest migration into North America occurred only 12,000 to 15,000 years ago. But recent discoveries have led some scholars to speculate that the pioneer arrivals may have crossed from Northeast Asia, probably in very small numbers, as early as 20,000 or possibly even 30,000 or 40,000 years ago (see Chapter 4). At various times a wide Ice Age land bridge connected Alaska and Siberia across today's Bering Strait, and the evidence for a migration chiefly from Asia over thousands of years is strong. The first settlers moved by land or by boat along the coast. Gradually people of Asian ancestry settled throughout the Western Hemisphere, becoming the ancestors of today's Native Americans.

SECTION SUMMARY

- To fully understand human history, it is helpful to first examine the origins of our planet, the beginning of life on earth, and our prehuman ancestors.

- Throughout the millennia, various peoples have developed stories of creation and universal order.

- In order to survive, species must adapt to their changing environments.

- Humans are closely related to chimpanzees and other great apes; they eventually became dominant because of their use of intelligence.

- Early hominids first evolved in Africa (most likely East Africa) 4 to 6 million years ago.

- Of the early hominids, our direct ancestor, *Homo habilis,* was most successful because it used simple stone tools.

- *Homo erectus* developed more refined tools and migrated to Eurasia and throughout Africa.

- *Homo sapiens* had larger brains and evolved into modern humans, who developed language and spread throughout the world.

- Though humans from different parts of the world may have different appearances, their genetic differences are insignificant.

THE ODYSSEY OF EARLY HUMAN SOCIETIES

> How did hunting and gathering shape life during the long Stone Age?

Paleolithic The Old Stone Age, which began 100,000 years ago with the first modern humans and lasted for many millennia.

Mesolithic The Middle Stone Age, which began around 15,000 years ago as the glaciers from the final Ice Age began to recede.

Neolithic The New Stone Age, which began between 10,000 and 11,500 years ago with the transition to simple farming.

For thousands of years humans lived at a very basic level during what is often called the Stone Age, although they also used other materials, such as wood and bone, to help them sustain life. The Stone Age included three distinct periods. The long **Paleolithic** (pay-lee-oh-LITH-ik) period (or Old Stone Age) began about 100,000 years ago. The **Mesolithic** (mez-oh-LITH-ik) period (Middle Stone Age) began around 15,000 years ago, when the glaciers from the final Ice Age receded. Major meat sources in Eurasia and North America that were adapted to Ice Age climates, such as the vast herds of woolly mammoths and mastodons, died out from warming climates, catastrophic disease, or zealous hunting by humans. During the Paleolithic and Mesolithic eras peoples organized themselves into small, usually mobile, family-based societies. The **Neolithic** (nee-oh-LITH-ik) period (New Stone Age) began between 9500 and 8000 B.C.E. in Eurasia, with the transition from hunting and gathering to simple farming.

Hunting, Gathering, and Cooperation

Small groups of twenty to sixty members were the earliest and simplest forms of society. Their subsistence life depended on fishing, hunting live animals, scavenging for dead or dying animals, and gathering edible plants, a way of life that depended on naturally occurring resources. Members cooperated in gathering or hunting to obtain food. Improved tools made possible both more food options and better weapons against predators or rivals. Hunting became more important when the bow and arrow were invented in Africa, Europe, and southwestern Asia at least 15,000 years ago. Now hunters could kill large animals at a safer distance. Although men gained prestige from being the main hunters, meat was usually a small part of the diet.

Survival Strategies

The gathering by women of edible vegetation such as fruits and nuts was probably more essential for group survival than obtaining meat, and it gave women status and influence. Ethnographic studies indicate that this is still true among many of the remaining hunting and gathering peoples today. Furthermore, women probably helped develop new technologies such as grinding stones, bone needles, nets (possibly used to catch small animals like rabbits and foxes), baskets, and primitive cloth. The oldest known woven cloth clothing was made in eastern Europe some 28,000 years ago. Pottery was made at least 12,500 years ago in Japan.

The hunting and gathering way of life may not have been as impoverished and unfulfilling as we sometimes imagine it was, with people continually searching for food in harsh environments. Many societies were creative, inventing fishhooks, harpoons, fuel lamps, dugout boats, and canoes. Studies over the past fifty years of groups who still hunt and gather, such as the Mbuti (em-BOO-tee) of the Congo rain forest and the !Kung of the Kalahari Desert, have found that they enjoy varied, healthy diets, surprisingly long life expectancies, considerable economic security, and a rich communal life. Many spend only ten to twenty hours a week in collecting food and establishing camps. Generally these people have plenty of time for activities such as music, dance, and socializing. On the other hand, hunters and gatherers have always faced serious challenges. Early humans had to make their own weapons and clothing and construct temporary huts. For some groups, life remained precarious and many died young, since not all enjoyed access to adequate food resources.

Hunting and gathering generally encouraged cooperation, which led to closely knit communities based on kinship. Members were able to communicate with one another, and they also passed information from one generation to another, conveying a sense of the past and traditions. Gradually humans increased in numbers, and societies became more complex. In societies founded on family ties, personal relationships were paramount, while little value was given to obtaining material wealth. The mostly nomadic way of life made individual accumulation of material possessions impractical. These small groups shared food resources among the immediate family and friends, thus helping to ensure survival. Cooperative work and food sharing also promoted an intense social life.

Cooperation and Conflict

But living close to others did not always result in harmony and mutual affection. Those who violated group customs could be killed or banished, temporarily or permanently, and sometimes groups split apart because of conflicts. Most hunters and gatherers lived in small bands that had no system of government or leader; everyone played a needed role, and social responsibilities linked people together. In these egalitarian social structures, all members in good standing often had equal access to resources. At the same time, groups often tended to reward the most resourceful members.

Women and men probably enjoyed a comparable status, as they do in many hunting and gathering societies today. As key providers of food, women may have participated alongside men in group decision making. They also likely held a special place in religious practice as bearers of life. Midwives were highly respected. **Matrilineal** (mat-ruh-LIN-ee-uhl) **kinship** patterns, which trace descent and inheritance through the female line, were probably common, as they are today in these societies. But these societies mostly maintain a clear sexual division of labor and give men some advantages over women. Although childbearing influenced women's roles, women were not constantly pregnant. Since it was necessary to limit group size to avoid depleting resources from the environment, most hunting and gathering societies practiced birth control and abortion. In addition, the practice of breastfeeding an infant for several years suppressed ovulation and created longer intervals between pregnancies. Paleolithic populations grew slowly, perhaps by only 10 percent a century.

matrilineal kinship A pattern of kinship that traces descent and inheritance through the female line.

Cultural Life and Violence

Some aspects of culture that we might recognize today were taking shape, such as religious belief. As people sought to understand dreams, death, and natural phenomena, they developed a perspective known as **animism** (ANN-uh-miz-um), the belief that all creatures, as well as inanimate objects and natural phenomena, have souls and can influence human well-being. Many early peoples also practiced **polytheism** (PAUL-e-thee-ism), the belief in many spirits or deities. Since spirits were thought capable of helping or harming a person, **shamans** (SHAW-mans), specialists in communicating with or manipulating the supernatural realm, became important members of the group. Many shamans were women.

Some activities with a social function that we might consider essential for enjoyment developed early, including music, dance, making and drinking beer or wine, and painting on rocks and cave walls. Primitive flutes can be traced back 45,000 years. Dancing and singing may have promoted feelings of togetherness and lessened personal rivalries.

animism The belief that all creatures as well as inanimate objects and natural phenomena have souls and can influence human well-being.

polytheism A belief in many spirits or deities.

shamans Specialists in communicating with or manipulating the supernatural realm.

Egalitarian, self-sufficient societies enriched by spirituality and leisure activities may sound appealing to many modern people, but this was not the complete story. Violence between and within different societies has been a part of human culture throughout history, and the seeds were planted in the Paleolithic period. People were hunters, but they were also hunted by predators such as bears, wolves, and lions. This reality may have instilled in early societies not only a terror of dangerous animals, apparent in myths and folklore, but also a tendency to justify violence. Men were often expected to prove their bravery to attract females.

War and Peace

Anthropologists disagree about whether humans are inherently aggressive and warlike or peaceful and cooperative. The experiences of societies still based on hunting and gathering or simple agriculture suggest that both patterns are common. Some peoples, such as the Hopi and Zuni Indians of the American Southwest, the Penan of Borneo, and many Australian Aborigines, have generally avoided armed conflict. But most societies have engaged in at least occasional violence, such as when their survival or food supply was threatened. Some societies have admired military prowess and male bravado. For example, the Dani of New Guinea, who engaged in frequent conflict with their neighbors, lost a third of their men to war-related death.

Humans may not be genetically programmed for either violence or cooperation. They have a capacity but not a compulsion for aggressive behavior. On the other hand, humans may naturally seek self-preservation; social and cultural patterns that have promoted certain behaviors, such as violence against neighboring groups, have often arisen in response to environmental conditions that have threatened existence.

Cave Paintings in Europe This Ice Age painting of bison is from a cave at Altamira, Spain. Many paintings on cave walls have been found in France and Iberia. Paleolithic peoples all over the world painted pictures of the animals they hunted or feared as well as of each other, suggesting an increasing self-awareness.

The Heritage of Hunting and Gathering

Hunting and gathering never completely disappeared. Throughout history some peoples have found this way of life the most realistic strategy for survival. Although not environmentalists in the modern sense, most recent hunting and gathering societies have made only a marginal impact on the surrounding environment because of their small numbers and limited technology. Since they have learned to live within environmental constraints, these peoples could be seen as highly successful adapters. Although it has generated little material wealth, hunting and gathering has remained viable for many societies, such as Australian Aborigines, until

modern times. Indeed, Australia was the only inhabitable continent where agriculture never developed before modern times, largely because populations remained small, much of the continent was harsh desert, and the Aborigines were such skillful hunters and gatherers. But trade routes spanned the continent, and many Aborigines developed detailed notions of land management as well as rich mythologies about their origins and their relationship to the fragile environment.

Although we must be cautious in comparing modern hunters and gatherers to peoples who lived several millennia ago, today's few remaining hunting and gathering peoples, to the extent that they have not yet been significantly changed by the outside world, can probably reveal much about ancient societies (see Profile: The !Kung Hunters and Gatherers). But this way of life, which has survived for many millennia, may disappear during the twenty-first century. In recent decades many hunters and gatherers have seen their lives disrupted or destroyed by logging, commercial fishing, plantation development, dam building, tourism, and other activities that exploit their environments. For example, in the Amazon Basin, the burning of rain forests and opening of new land for farming or mining overwhelms many Native American groups. In the end these peoples, defenseless against modern technology, may have to make the same transition to new survival strategies as other peoples did millennia ago.

SECTION SUMMARY

- During the Paleolithic and Mesolithic eras, people lived in small groups of hunters and gatherers.

- In general, women gathered fruits and nuts, which provided the majority of the food, while men hunted game.

- Hunting and gathering groups were usually close-knit and egalitarian, though violence was not unknown.

- Anthropologists are undecided as to whether humans have a natural tendency toward violence or peace.

- Some hunting and gathering groups still exist, but they are threatened by modernity.

THE AGRICULTURAL TRANSFORMATION, 10,000–4000 B.C.E.

What environmental factors explain the transition to agriculture?

Between 10,000 and 11,500 years ago, people who had survived largely by hunting and gathering during the Mesolithic period began to develop simple agriculture. This momentous change marked the beginning of the Neolithic period, a time when humans began to master the environment and change natural biological relationships in unprecedented ways. People now deliberately altered the ecological system by cultivating the soil, selecting seeds, and breeding animals that could help them survive. The often-used term *Agricultural Revolution* is misleading, because the development did not involve rapid, electrifying discoveries but occurred over hundreds of years. Nonetheless, the shift from hunting and gathering to farming was one of the greatest transitions in history, and it changed human life all over the world. The production of a food surplus set the stage for everything that came later, including cities, states, social classes, and long-distance trade.

Environmental Change and the Roots of Agriculture

Probably the first farmers did not even see themselves as pioneers forging a new way of life. Even before farming began, some people were preparing themselves for permanent village life. Some, like the villagers at Abu Hureyra in Syria, were settling alongside lakes or in valleys rich in wild grains that were easy to collect. Around the world, archaeologists have discovered clay-walled houses from the Neolithic period, as well as baskets, pottery, pits for storing grain, and equipment for hunting, fishing, and grain preparation. However, documenting the steps taken in the transition to agriculture and settled life is not easy. For the earliest periods we have no written sources, since writing appeared only around 3500 B.C.E. Many material artifacts still lie buried, while others have long since turned to dust or were covered by rising sea levels.

Climate change was probably one key factor in triggering the shift to agriculture. After the last great Ice Age, the earth entered a long period of unusual warmth, which still persists. The melting glaciers caused rising sea levels, covering about a fifth of previously available land. Some scholars contend that the spread of the Persian Gulf, the Black Sea, and the Mediterranean onto once occupied lowlands may have led to legends in the Middle East of a great flood and human expulsion from a "garden of Eden." Rising sea levels also covered over many land links, including those connecting the British Isles to continental Europe and Japan to Asia. Another factor was probably population growth. Around 10,000 B.C.E., the world population had grown to perhaps 5 or 10 million, and in

Climate Change and Population Growth

THE !KUNG HUNTERS AND GATHERERS

Although we need to remember that all societies change over time, often in response to environmental conditions, the remaining hunting and gathering peoples today may give us a glimpse of how some prehistoric peoples lived. The !Kung, a subgroup of the San people (once known as Bushmen), live in the inhospitable Kalahari Desert in southwestern Africa, chiefly in what is today Botswana and Namibia. Several thousand years ago they were widespread in the southern half of Africa, and some probably adapted to desert life a long time ago.

The !Kung became skilled hunters and gatherers. Women obtain between 60 and 80 percent of the food, collecting nuts, berries, bulbs, beans, leafy greens, roots, and bird eggs, as well as catching tortoises, small mammals, snakes, insects, termites, and caterpillars. While the women gather, the men hunt animals, snare birds, and extract honey from beehives. These hunters are skilled trackers who can follow animal tracks and other clues for many miles without rest. The !Kung utilize some fifty species of plants and animals for food, medicine, cosmetics, and poisons. Although Western peoples may disregard many of the food sources because of cultural biases, these sources are in fact highly nutritious. Termites, for example, are about half protein.

The !Kung have adapted well to a harsh environment. Even during periodic drought conditions that devastate the more vulnerable farmers, the diversity of !Kung food sources ensures a steady supply. Furthermore, their diet is low in salt, carbohydrates, and saturated fats, and high in vitamins and roughage. Their diet, combined with a relatively unstressful life, helps them avoid modern health problems like high blood pressure, ulcers, obesity, and heart disease. But because they live far from clinics, they die more easily from accidents and malaria, and some scholars doubt that their diet is nutritionally sound. Nonetheless, !Kung life expectancy is similar to that in many industrialized countries.

Since they spend only about fifteen to twenty hours a week in maintaining their livelihood, the !Kung have ample free time for resting, conversing, visiting friends, and playing games. Children have few responsibilities because their labor is not needed for the !Kungs' survival. The !Kung value interdependence between the genders and are willing to do the work normally associated with the opposite sex. For example, fathers take an active role in child rearing. The intense social life is symbolized by a large communal space in the midst of the camp surrounded by family sleeping huts; they prefer companionship to privacy. The !Kung strongly discourage aggressiveness. Their folk stories praise the animal tricksters who evade the use of force.

Throughout history farming peoples have affected hunters and collectors. The !Kung have faced many challenges in recent decades that have altered the lives of many bands. Most are no longer completely self-sufficient. They trade desert products to nearby farming villages for tools and food. Others have been drafted into the military, have taken up wage labor, or have been displaced because their territory has been claimed by governments or business interests. Today, forced or induced to abandon their traditional ways of life, some disoriented !Kung have moved to dilapidated, impoverished villages on the edges of towns. The future for their ancestral lifestyle is unpromising.

THINKING ABOUT THE PROFILE

1. What role does the gathering by women play in the !Kung economy?

2. How does the traditional !Kung way of life promote leisure activity?

3. What problems do the !Kung face today?

!Kung Women Returning to Camp These !Kung women in the Kalahari Desert of southwestern Africa are returning to camp after gathering wild berries and vegetables, sometimes by using digging sticks. Many Stone Age societies were sustained by such activity.

M. Shostak/Anthro-Photo

some regions hunting and gathering could no longer meet the basic needs of everyone, especially as good land was submerged. Soon food gatherers gravitated to areas rich in wild grains and grazing animals, some of them abandoning their nomadic ways to live permanently near these rich food sources.

The Great Transition to Settled Agriculture

Crop Domestication

The environment continued to change, posing new challenges. The earth cooled again briefly about 9000 B.C.E., reducing food supplies, and a drought in the Middle East presented a crisis for some food-gathering societies because they had no real concept of saving or storing for the future. Responding to the challenges, hunters and gatherers began to store food and learn how to cultivate their own fields. Some people experimented with new foods, especially cereal grains collected in a wild state. Former hunters and gatherers began to pioneer **horticulture** (HORE-tee-kuhl-chur), the growing of crops with simple methods and tools, such as the hoe or digging stick. These efforts eventually resulted in a profound reorganization of human society. Women may well have taken the lead in domesticating plants and some animals and in molding clay for storage and cooking pots. As the chief gatherers, women knew how plants grew in certain types of soil and sprouted from seeds, and they also knew the amount of water and sunshine needed to sustain plants. Women are generally the main food producers in horticultural societies today.

horticulture The growing of crops with simple methods and tools.

One major food-producing strategy was shifting cultivation, a method still practiced today by millions of people, especially in Southeast Asia, Africa, and Latin America. Shifting cultivation was especially adaptable in wooded areas, where people could clear trees and underbrush by chopping and burning (hence the common term *slash and burn*). Once the area was cleared, people loosened the soil with digging sticks and finally scattered seeds around the area. Natural moisture such as rain helped the crops mature. But since the soil became eroded after a few years, shifting cultivators moved periodically to fresh land, returning to the original area only after the soil had recovered its fertility.

Ruins of Abu Hureyra The site of this ancient village overlooks the floodplain of the Euphrates River in northeastern Syria. The earliest settlement included intersecting pits that were turned into huts by roofs of reeds, branches, and poles.

Farming promoted many radical changes in the way people lived and connected with their environments. Whether agriculture made life more secure, predictable, and healthy than hunting and gathering remains subject to debate. But the domestication of plants and animals increased the production of food in a given amount of land. Agriculture could produce a much higher yield per acre and thus could support much denser populations in the same area. Permanent settlements also made possible the storage of food for future use, since the pots and buildings did not have to be moved periodically. Most people apparently believed farming was necessary for survival.

However, since farmers depended on fewer plant foods than food gatherers, they were in some ways more vulnerable to disaster from drought or other natural catastrophes. Food shortages may have become more rather than less common. The earliest farmers could probably grow enough to feed themselves and their families with three or four hours of work a day. But as they required more food to feed growing populations, they were forced to exploit local resources more intensively and to work harder in their fields. Some people complained. The Hebrew writer who recorded the biblical garden of Eden story blamed women for the hard work of farming: "Cursed is the ground for your sake; in toil you shall eat of it all the days of your life. In the sweat of your face you shall eat bread til you return to the ground."[3] Agriculture eventually depended on peasants, mostly poor farmers who worked small plots of land that were often owned by others. Hard-working peasants were the backbone of most societies before the Industrial Revolution.

© Oxford University Press. Photo: Andrew M.T. Moore

The Globalization and Diversity of Agriculture

The agricultural transformation eventually reached across the globe. Agriculture came first to Eurasia, where geography favored the movement of people to the east or west along the same general latitude, without abrupt climatic changes. By contrast, the Americas are constructed along a north-south axis, and northern and southern temperate regions are linked only through a huge tropical zone stretching from southern Mexico to northern and eastern South America. Some peoples, such as those in Australia and the Arctic, did not or could not make the transition from food gathering because of environmental and geographical constraints. Nonetheless, the different regions all contributed significantly to the discovery and production of the food resources we use today.

Where did agriculture begin? Most archaeologists believe the earliest transition to farming occurred in the area of southwestern Asia known as the "Fertile Crescent." This includes what is today Iraq, Syria, central and eastern Turkey, and the Jordan River Valley. This region had many fast-growing plants with high nutritional value, such as wheat, barley, chickpeas, and peas. The breakthrough came between 9500 and 8000 B.C.E. Food growing also began independently in several other parts of the world, although we still do not know precisely when (see Map 1.2). Hot, humid climates such as those in Southeast Asia, tropical Africa, and Central America are poor for preserving plant, animal, and human remains. But clearly several Asian peoples were among the earliest farmers. Crop cultivation began around 7000 B.C.E. in China and New Guinea, 7000 or 6000 B.C.E. in India, 5000 or 4000 B.C.E. in Thailand, and 3000 B.C.E. in Island Southeast Asia.

The dates for the beginning of agriculture vary considerably (see Chronology: The Transition to Agriculture, 10,000–500 B.C.E.). In the Mediterranean region, farming began in the Nile Valley by at least 6000 B.C.E., if not earlier, and in Greece by 6500 B.C.E. Agriculture reached northward to Britain and Scandinavia between 4000 and 3000 B.C.E. Farming may have spread into Europe with migrants from western Asia who intermarried with local people. While some historians suspect that farming in the southeast Sahara dates to between 8000 and 6000 B.C.E., others doubt it began that early. People in Ethiopia were farming by 4500 B.C.E. In the Americas cultivation apparently began in central Mexico between 7000 and 5500 B.C.E. and in the Andes (ANN-deez) highlands by 6000 B.C.E., if not earlier. Farming reached the Amazon Basin by 1500 B.C.E., Colorado by 1000 B.C.E., and the southeastern part of North America by 500 B.C.E.

The earliest crops that were grown varied according to local environments and needs. Millet dominated in cold North China, rice in tropical Southeast Asia, wheat and barley in the dry Middle East, yams and sorghum in West Africa, corn in upland Mesoamerica, and potatoes in the high Andes. Some crops such as flax were grown for fiber to make clothing. Other plants had medicinal properties. Southwest Asians began making wine from grapes and beer from barley between 6000 and 3000 B.C.E. Over time farming became deeply ingrained in the psychology, social life, and traditions of many societies (see Witness to the Past: Food and Farming in Ancient Cultural Traditions). Farming technology gradually improved. People living in highlands where slopes are steep, such as in Peru, Indonesia, China, or Greece, made their fields on terraces, which were laborious to construct and maintain. Then, as more people moved from highlands into valleys, they used water from nearby marshes or wells or built large-scale water projects such as irrigation canals.

Animal Domestication

The domestication of animals for human use developed in close association with crop raising. As they were bred in captivity, animals were gradually modified from their wild ancestors. Men may have tamed and looked after the larger animals such as oxen and cattle, while women may have taken charge of smaller species such as sheep and pigs. Wild boars were domesticated into pigs in several different regions. Animals were raised to supply meat and leather, to aid in farming, to produce fertilizer, or to supply transportation. For example, horses and camels made long-distance travel and communication easier. Plows became more efficient tools when pulled by oxen or cattle. One disadvantage was that domesticated animals passed on diseases to humans, although this eventually led to immunities among peoples in Eurasia.

Humans and Animals

CHRONOLOGY

The Transition to Agriculture, 10,000–500 B.C.E.

9500–8000 B.C.E. Southwestern Asia (Fertile Crescent)

7000 B.C.E. Nubia (date disputed), China, Mexico, New Guinea

6500 B.C.E. Greece

6000 B.C.E. Northwestern India, Egypt, Andes, West Africa (disputed)

5000 B.C.E. Thailand

4900 B.C.E. Panama

4500 B.C.E. Ethiopia

4000 B.C.E. Britain, Scandinavia

3000 B.C.E. Island Southeast Asia, tropical West Africa

1500 B.C.E. Amazon Basin

1000 B.C.E. Colorado

500 B.C.E. Southeast North America

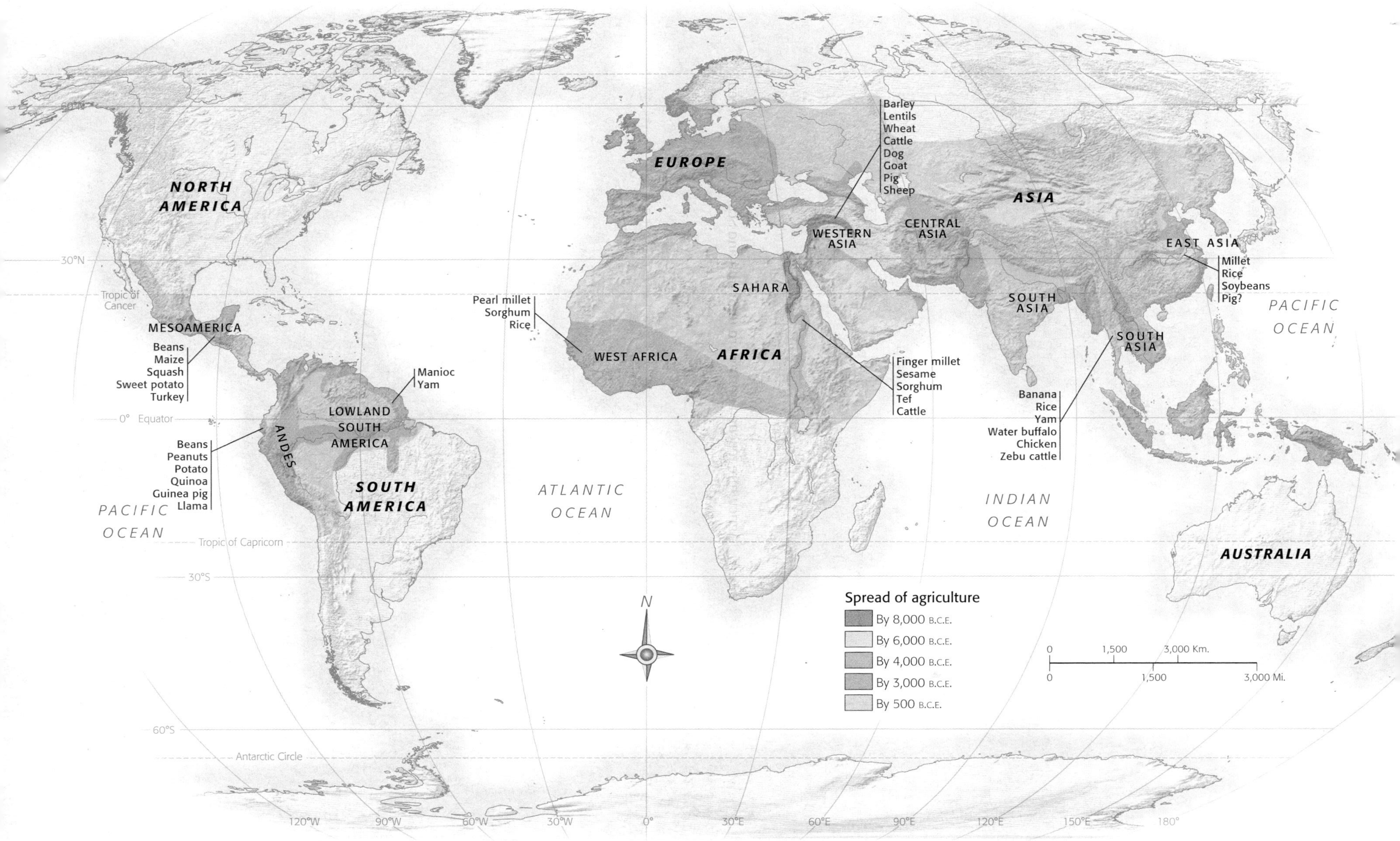

Map 1.2
The Origins of Agriculture

Between 11,500 and 7,000 years ago, people in western Asia, North and sub-Saharan Africa, southern Asia, East Asia, New Guinea, Mesoamerica, and South America developed agriculture independently and domesticated available animals. Later most of these crops and some of the animals spread into other regions.

NORTH AMERICA

MESOAMERICA
Beans
Maize
Squash
Sweet potato
Turkey

LOWLAND SOUTH AMERICA
Beans
Peanuts
Potato
Quinoa
Guinea pig   Llama

Manioc
Yam

SOUTH AMERICA

ANDES

PACIFIC OCEAN

ATLANTIC OCEAN

Tropic of Cancer

Equator

Tropic of Capricorn

Antarctic Circle

30°N

0°

30°S

60°S

120°W

90°W

60°W

30°W

EUROPE

WEST AFRICA

AFRICA

SAHARA

Pearl millet
Sorghum
Rice

Finger millet
Sesame
Sorghum
Tef
Cattle

WESTERN ASIA
Barley
Lentils
Wheat
Cattle
Dog
Goat
Pig
Sheep

CENTRAL ASIA

ASIA

SOUTH ASIA

SOUTH ASIA

Banana
Rice
Yam
Water buffalo
Chicken
Zebu cattle

INDIAN OCEAN

EAST ASIA
Millet
Rice
Soybeans
Pig?

PACIFIC OCEAN

AUSTRALIA

N

0°   30°E   60°E   90°E   120°E   150°E   180°

© Cengage Learning

Spread of agriculture

By 8,000 B.C.E.

By 6,000 B.C.E.

By 4,000 B.C.E.

By 3,000 B.C.E.

By 500 B.C.E.

0   1,500   3,000 Km.

0   1,500   3,000 Mi.

3,000 Mi.

e Interactive Map

Food and Farming in Ancient Cultural Traditions

As agriculture became an essential foundation for survival, it became increasingly important in the traditions and mindsets of societies around the world. The following excerpts show three examples of how food and farming were reflected in the cultural traditions of ancient societies. The first, an Andean ritual chant many centuries old, is a prayer for successful harvests addressed to an ancient deity. The second is from a farmer's almanac from eighteenth-century B.C.E. Mesopotamia that offers guidance on cultivating a successful grain crop; this excerpt deals with preparing the field and seeding. The third reading, a song collected in China around 3,000 years ago, celebrates a successful harvest and explains how some of the bounty will be used.

Andean Chant

Oh Viracocha, ancient Viracocha, skilled creator, who makes and establishes
"on the earth below may they eat, may they drink" you say; for those you have established, those you have made
may food be plentiful.
"Potatoes, maize, all kinds of food may there be"

Excerpt from Farmer's Almanac

Keep a sharp eye on the openings of the dikes, ditches and mounds [so that] when you flood the field the water will not rise too high in it. . . . Let shod oxen trample it for you; after having its weeds ripped out [by them and] the field made level ground, dress it evenly with narrow axes weighing [no more than] two thirds of a pound each. . . . Keep your eye on the man who puts in the barley seed. Let him drop the grain uniformly two fingers deep. . . . If the barley seed does not sink in properly, change your share. . . . Harvest it at the moment [of its full strength].

Chinese Harvest Song

Abundant is the year, with much millet, much rice;
But we have tall granaries,
To hold . . . many myriads and millions of grain.
We make wine, make sweet liquor,
We offer it to ancestor, to ancestress,
We use it to fulfill all the [religious] rites,
To bring down blessings upon each and all.

THINKING ABOUT THE READING

1. Who did the Andeans believe determined the success of their harvest?
2. How did Mesopotamian farming depend on draft animals and cooperation?
3. How did ancient Chinese farmers use surplus grain and rice to fulfill obligations?

Sources: Brian M. Fagan, *Kingdoms of Gold, Kingdoms of Jade* (London: Thames and Hudson, 1991), p. 88; *The Book of Songs*, translated by Arthur Waley (London: George Allen and Unwin, 1954), ©1954 by permission of The Arthur Waley Estate.

Much remains unclear about the chronology and location of animal domestication. For example, dogs may have been domesticated from gray wolves by at least 12,000 or perhaps 15,000 years ago in East Asia or the Middle East. Dogs were welcome for companionship, guarding, assistance in hunting, and sometimes food. Migrants took Asian dogs to the Americas. Sheep, goats, pigs, chickens, and cattle were all domesticated in the Middle East and South Asia between 9000 and 7000 B.C.E. Some contested evidence also suggests early cattle domestication in East Africa and in the Sahara region . The first domesticated horses and donkeys, which date back to around 4000 B.C.E., enabled the improved transportation that stimulated long-distance trade networks.

Zoological Differences

Zoological differences among the continents were crucial to the evolution of advanced agriculture. Eurasia contained many species of large, plant-eating, herding mammals whose habits and mild dispositions made their domestication into draft animals possible. But outside Eurasia, the lack of draft animals hindered the development of agriculture. Africa (except for cattle) and Australia lacked such animals, and most of the candidates in the Americas, such as the horse and camel, were extinct by 10,000 B.C.E. The only American possibilities were the gentle llamas and alpacas of the South American highlands. Though Andean people used them as pack animals by 3500 B.C.E., they were not well suited for farming.

Agriculture and Its Environmental Consequences

At the same time that the environment influenced farming, the resulting population growth also contributed to environmental changes, some with negative consequences such as cutting trees.

Human activities have had an impact on environments since the time of *Homo habilis*. Indeed, Stone Age hunters in both hemispheres may have contributed to the extinction of many animal species. But intensive agriculture more radically altered the ecology, especially as technology improved. Technological innovation solved some problems for a while, but it did not always prove advantageous in the long run. For example, the invention of the plowshare made it easier to loosen dirt and eliminate weeds so that seeds could be planted deeper in nutrient-rich soil. But it also exposed topsoils to water and wind erosion. Similarly, vast irrigation networks provided the economic foundations for flourishing agriculture and denser settlement. But irrigation requires more labor than dry farming, and it also tends to foster centralized governments that can allocate the water resources among the people, with the result that more controls are placed on people's behavior. In addition, adding water to poor soils can produce waterlogged land and also produce a thick salt surface that ruins farming. In Mesopotamia and the Americas, where irrigation ultimately created deserts, it helped account for the rise and fall of entire societies.

Various activities contributed to environmental destruction. Farming and animal raising placed new demands on the land. Goats, for example, caused considerable damage as they browsed on shrubs, tree branches, and seedlings, thus preventing forest regeneration. Cattle required much pasture. People exploited nearby forests for lumber to build wagons, tools, houses, furniture, and boats. Contemporary observers were aware of the deforestation. For example, twenty-four centuries ago the philosopher Plato bemoaned the deforestation of the Greek mountains, which he called "a mere relic of the original country. What remains is like the skeleton of a body emaciated by disease. All the rich soil has melted away, leaving a country of skin and bone."[4] Overgrazing and deforestation in the mountains feeding the main rivers produced silt that contained harmful salt and gypsum, which moved downstream to the sea, clogging canals and dams.

The changing relationship of humans to their environment with farming generated new religious ideas. Early sacred and philosophical texts often justified human domination over nature. For example, the authors of the Hebrew book of Genesis believed God told humans to "be fruitful and multiply; fill the earth and subdue it; have dominion over the fish of the sea, over the birds of the air, and over every living thing that moves upon the earth."[5] Many ancient thinkers saw an ordered world in which every part had a role and purpose in a divine plan, with humans the ultimate beneficiaries.

Environmental Destruction

Seated Goddess from Western Asia
This baked-clay figure from one of the oldest towns in western Asia, Çatal Hüyük in Anatolia, shows an enthroned female, probably a goddess giving birth, guarded on both sides by catlike animals—perhaps leopards.

C. M. Dixon/Ancient Art & Architecture Collection

SECTION SUMMARY

- The shift from hunting and gathering to farming had tremendous consequences, but it occurred gradually, over hundreds of years.

- The end of the last great Ice Age and increased population density led people to shift from hunting and gathering to farming.

- Settled farming could support much denser populations and allowed for food storage, but it also led to some new health problems.

- Farming probably began in the area of southwestern Asia known as the "Fertile Crescent."

- Irrigation and other technological advances led to larger crops but also caused great environmental damage.

THE EMERGENCE OF CITIES AND STATES

How did farming and metallurgy establish the foundations for the rise of cities, states, and trade networks?

Farming generated more complex societies. Given the prospects for ample food, some western Asian people moved to fertile areas to farm. They unloaded their stone tools, clay pots, and plant seeds and built flimsy huts of mud and reeds. Families formed small villages, which had more children to help in the fields. They built houses with a sleeping platform, bread oven, grain silo, and a corral for their domesticated animals. Older women served as religious specialists, acting as midwives, reciting myths, and composing verses. Over time people began to see themselves as part of larger communities. To honor a special deity the villagers built a temple. Eventually these villages with their temples grew into the first cities. In turn, cities established a foundation for the rise of states, trade networks, and writing.

The Rise of New Technologies

Metallurgy

Agriculture also fostered new technologies. Many times in history people came up against a serious resource problem, such as lack of food and water, and had to overcome the problem or perish. Often their solution was to develop some new technology, and many of these inventions had long-lasting value. One innovation, metalworking, made possible a new level of human control over resources supplied by the environment. The first metalworking was done with copper, used in Europe for making weapons and tools as early as 7000 B.C.E. and in the Middle East by 4500 B.C.E. In fact, copper mining may have been the first real industry of the ancient world. Traded over considerable distances, copper also became perhaps the first major commodity to enjoy a world market. Gold was also used and valued very early. These two soft metals could be fairly easily cut and shaped with stones.

Soon specialist craftsmen emerged to mine and work metals. By 3000 B.C.E. some of these specialists in western Asia had developed heating processes by which they could blend copper together with either tin or arsenic to create bronze. The bronze trade became a major spur to commerce in early Mesopotamia. By 1500 B.C.E. the technology for making usable iron had also been invented, although it took many centuries for people to perfect the new alloy for practical use. Bronze and iron made better, more helpful, and more durable tools (such as plows), but they also made more deadly weapons, and their use shaped many societies of the ancient and classical worlds (see "Societies, Networks, Transitions," page 96).

Urbanization and the First Cities

Urban Life

Agriculture also fostered population growth. By using cow's milk and grain meal for infant's food, women could now breastfeed for a shorter period and consequently bear children more frequently. In the Middle East the population is believed to have grown from less than 100,000 in 8000 B.C.E. to over 3 million by 4000 B.C.E. Some farming villages grew into substantial, often prosperous towns. In one of the oldest towns, Çatal Hüyük (cha-TAHL hoo-YOOK) in central Turkey, roughly 10,000 residents lived in cramped mud-brick buildings. The residents decorated the white plaster walls of their houses with paintings. Çatal Hüyük and similar towns became centers of long-distance trade. By around 3700 B.C.E. Tell Hamoukar (Tell HAM-oo-kar) in northeastern Syria had grown from a village into a town enclosed by a defensive wall. It contained both a bakery and a brewery, evidence of some residents organizing people and resources, and seems to have had a growing bureaucracy, perhaps even a king. By 3500 B.C.E. Tell Hamoukar had grown into a city that later traded with the cities of southern Mesopotamia. Road networks linked the various cities of the Tigris-Euphrates Basin.

As people grouped together, they pioneered new ways of living. Permanent settlements became larger, dominating nearby villages and farms. A city is a permanent settlement with a greater size,

Çatal Hüyük A view of rooms and walls in one of the first known towns, Çatal Hüyük in eastern Turkey. The ruins contained many art objects, murals, wall sculpture, and woven cloth.

James Mellaart/Catalhoyuk Research Projects

population, and importance than a town, and it usually contains many shops, public markets, government buildings, and religious centers. Cities emerged where farmers produced more food than they needed for themselves and so could be taxed or coerced to share their excess crops. This surplus was critical to sustain people with no time or land for farming, and priests, scribes, carpenters, and merchants increasingly congregated in the growing settlements.

What some call the urban revolution constituted a major achievement in different parts of the world, perhaps as significant as the agricultural transformation. In Southwest Asia the first small cities were formed between 3500 and 3200 B.C.E.; they were administered by governments and dominated by new social hierarchies. Soon cities appeared elsewhere, many surrounded by walls (see Chronology: The Rise of Cities). City people enjoyed new amenities. Many streets were lined by small shops and crowded with makeshift stalls selling foodstuffs, household items, or folk medicines. Hawkers peddled their wares from door to door. Craftsmen in workshops fashioned the items used in daily life, such as pottery, tools, and jewelry. Some of the goods made, mined, or grown locally were traded by land or sea to distant cities. Thus the rise of cities reshaped societies and fostered networks of communication and exchange.

Urban Revolution

The Rise of States, Economies, and Recordkeeping

Food production and urbanization eventually led to the formation of states: formal political organizations or governments that controlled a recognized territory and exercised power over both people and things. The people within them, often from diverse ethnic and cultural backgrounds, did not necessarily share all the same values or allegiances. Furthermore, they exchanged influences with neighboring peoples. Complex urban societies organized into states developed at least 3,000 years ago on all the inhabited continents except Australia.

These urban societies relied on diversified economies that generated enough wealth to support a division of labor and social, cultural, and religious hierarchies. Farmers, laborers, craftsmen, merchants, priests, soldiers, bureaucrats, and scholars served specialized functions. The priests served the religious institutions that emerged as societies organized and standardized their beliefs. Some states constructed monumental architecture, such as large temples, palaces, and city walls. While men dominated most of the hierarchies and heavy labor, women also played key economic roles. Women made the cloth: preparing the raw materials, spinning the yarn, weaving the yarn into fabrics, and fashioning and sewing the clothing, blankets, and other useful items, while passing along their knowledge from mother to daughter. Most urban societies were connected to elaborate trade networks extending well beyond the immediate region. By 4000 B.C.E. a network of merchant contacts linked India and Mesopotamia, 1,250 miles apart. Clay counting tokens used for trade had appeared by 3100 B.C.E., if not earlier. By 5000 B.C.E. the first seafaring vessels had been built around the Persian Gulf

The early urban societies also introduced cultural innovations such as recordkeeping and literature. A system of recordkeeping could involve a written language, such as those developed by the Egyptians, Greeks, Chinese, and Maya, among others. Or records could be kept by a class of memory experts, such as the professional "rememberers" among many African and South American peoples. In most literate societies writing was usually reserved for the privileged few until recent centuries, so knowledge of literature was not widespread unless it was passed on orally. Most societies created rich oral traditions of stories, legends, historical accounts, and poems that could be shared with all the people.

Some historians apply the term *civilization* to larger, more complex societies such as ancient Egypt and China, but this is a controversial concept with a long history of abuse. Since ancient times some peoples have seen themselves as "civilized" and criticized their neighbors, or any people unfamiliar to them, as "barbarians." Modern historians may focus too much on societies, such as Egypt, that left more of an archaeological and written record, giving lesser attention to those societies that did not. The term *civilization* could also refer to a large grouping of people with a common history and traditions, such as the Chinese, Maya, Arabs, or western Europeans. Or it could be restricted to those large, complex urban societies that developed or borrowed certain useful patterns such as bureaucratic governments, monumental architecture, and writing. Thus the term is too subjective to have much value in understanding world history. It is not used in this text.

CHRONOLOGY
The Rise of Cities

3500–3200 B.C.E. Western Asia

3500–3000 B.C.E. Northwestern India

3100–3000 B.C.E. Egypt

3100–2500 B.C.E. Peru

2000 B.C.E. Northern China

1800 B.C.E. Nubia

1600 B.C.E. Crete

1200 B.C.E. Mesoamerica (Mexico)

100 C.E. West Africa

The Rise of Pastoral Nomadism

pastoral nomadism
An economy based on breeding, rearing, and harvesting livestock.

Some societies adopted an alternative to agriculture and cities known as **pastoral nomadism**, an economy based on breeding, rearing, and harvesting livestock. The interaction between pastoral nomads and settled farmers was a major theme in history for many centuries. On the marginal land unsuitable for farming, some people began specializing in herding, moving their camps and animals seasonally in search of pasture. They traded meat, hides, or livestock to nearby farmers for grain. Both trade and conflict between the two contrasting groups, farmers and herders, became common. Pastoral nomadism involved dispersed rather than concentrated populations. Yet some pastoral nomads exercised a strong influence on societies with much greater populations.

Pastoral nomads mostly concentrated in grasslands and deserts, which could sustain only small populations. Grasslands covered much of central and western Asia from Mongolia to southern Russia, as well as large parts of eastern and southern Africa. An even more inhospitable area was the Sahara region of northern Africa, which by 2000 B.C.E. was part of a great arid zone stretching from the western tip of Africa eastward through Arabia into western Asia and then to the frontiers of China.

Pastoral Life

Living along or beyond the frontiers of settled farming, the pastoralists lived very differently than farmers, but they were not culturally unsophisticated. For example, they domesticated horses in Central Asia around 4300 B.C.E. and camels in Arabia around 3000 or 2500 B.C.E. Although they had few material possessions, like other societies, pastoralists often had humane values and a rich cultural life. The nomadic pastoral life had many similarities regardless of the region. Since a large area was needed to support each animal, herds had to be kept small to prevent overgrazing. As a result, the herders lived in small, dispersed groups, generally organized by extended families that were often part of **tribes**, associations of clans that traced descent from a common ancestor.

tribes Associations of clans that traced descent from a common ancestor.

There were also many differences among pastoralists. While some societies maintained egalitarian social structures, others were headed by chiefs. In some of the pastoral societies of Central Asia, women seem to have held a high status and to even have served as warriors. Burial mounds in Turkestan contain the remains of what may be female warriors from 2,500 years ago. These women, unusually tall, were buried with daggers, swords, and bronze-tipped arrows. Some pastoralists became tough, martial peoples who were greatly feared by the farmers. Central Asian pastoralists like the Huns and Mongols played a central role in world history before modern times.

Indo-European Expansion

Among the pastoral nomads who had a great historical influence were the various tribes known collectively as the **Indo-Europeans**. Historians derive this term from the original common tongue that spawned the many related languages spoken today by these peoples' descendants. Scholars have long debated where the original Indo-European homeland was located, but it was probably in the Caucasus Mountains, the adjacent southern Russian plains to the north, or in eastern Anatolia (modern Turkey). Eventually, because of the spread of these seminomadic and strongly patriarchal tribes and their languages, most people in Europe, Iran, and northern India came to speak Indo-European languages.

Indo-Europeans Various tribes who all spoke related languages deriving from some original common tongue and who eventually settled Europe, Iran, and northern India.

Indo-European expansion apparently occurred in several waves. Some Indo-Europeans may have moved into Europe and Central Asia as early as 6500 or 7000 B.C.E., perhaps carrying with them not only their language but also farming technology. The culturally mixed people who resulted may have been the ancestors of the Celts and Greeks. Sometime between 3000 and 2000 B.C.E. many of the Indo-European pastoralists were driven from their western Asian homeland by some disaster. The various tribes dispersed in every direction, splitting up into smaller units and driving their herds of cattle, sheep, goats, and horses with them. As they encountered farming peoples, they turned to conquest in order to occupy the land (see Map 1.3).

This dispersal set the stage for profound changes across Eurasia. The Hittites gained dominance in Anatolia and then, around 2000 B.C.E., expanded their empire into Mesopotamia. Other tribes pushed on between 2500 and 1500 B.C.E., some to the west into Greece, some east as far as the western fringe of China, some south into Persia (Iran). From Persia some tribes moved southeast through the mountain passes into northwestern India. Everywhere they went the Indo-Europeans spread their languages and imposed their military power, eventually absorbing or subduing the peoples they encountered. Most eventually abandoned pastoral nomadism for farming, but their spread opened a new chapter in the history of Europe, the Middle East, and India.

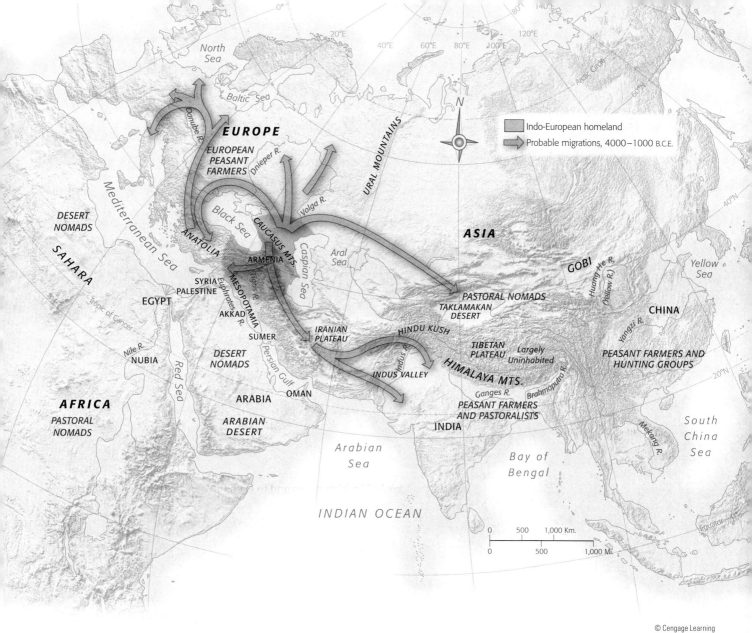

Map 1.3

The Indo-European Migrations and Eurasian Pastoralism

Some societies, especially in parts of Africa and Asia, adapted to environmental contexts by developing a pastoral, or animal herding, economy. One large pastoral group, the Indo-Europeans, eventually expanded from their home area into Europe, southwestern Asia, Central Asia, and India.

© Cengage Learning

 **Interactive Map**

SECTION SUMMARY

- Metals such as bronze and iron helped improve farming tools and weaponry.

- Highly productive farming allowed for the formation of the first cities, which became centers of trade.

- People in cities developed forms of recordkeeping and writing.

- Pastoral nomads, or herders, kept their animals in areas that were unsuitable for farming.

- Herders played an important role in spreading culture across Eurasia, though most eventually took up farming.

CHAPTER SUMMARY

The story of humans and their societies constitutes only a tiny part of the broader 4.5-billion-year history of the earth. Some 4 million years ago our hominid ancestors emerged in Africa, learning to walk upright, to make and use tools, and to control fire. Eventually, evolution produced modern humans, who developed language and more complex social structures. During the long Paleolithic age, all humans, using simple technologies and living in small groups, hunted wild animals and gathered wild plants, surviving by maintaining a balance with their environment. While many such societies survived over the millennia, eventually environmental changes and other factors encouraged most peoples to adopt farming.

Beginning between 10,000 and 11,500 years ago, the climate warmed and populations increased. Some people began to grow their own food. The great transition from hunting and gathering to a farming-based economy also involved the domestication of wild animals. Farming probably emerged first in southwestern Asia. By 2000 B.C.E. various peoples in Eurasia, Africa, and the Americas were farming. Agriculture led to larger populations and changed people's relationship to the environment. It also set the stage for another transition, the emergence of the first societies with cities, states, social classes, and recordkeeping. In the Afro-Eurasian zone, where many peoples were in contact with others, these societies first developed between 3000 and 3500 B.C.E. The first cities and states formed in sub-Saharan Africa and the Americas between 3000 and 1000 B.C.E. Some people living in the grasslands and deserts became nomadic pastoralists and interacted with settled farmers. The formation of distinctive societies and increased contact between peoples inaugurated a new era of human history.

KEY TERMS

hominids	Neanderthals	matrilineal kinship	pastoral nomadism
australopithecines	Cro-Magnons	animism	tribes
Homo habilis	Paleolithic	polytheism	Indo-Europeans
Homo erectus	Mesolithic	shamans	
Homo sapiens	Neolithic	horticulture	

EBOOK AND WEBSITE RESOURCES

 PRIMARY SOURCE
The *Rig Veda*

 INTERACTIVE MAPS
Map 1.1 Spread of Modern Humans Around the Globe
Map 1.2 The Origins of Agriculture
Map 1.3 The Indo-European Migrations and Eurasian Pastoralism

LINKS

About Archaeology (http://archaeology.about.com/science/archaeology). Contains much material on archaeology and ancient societies.

ArchNet Home Page (http://archnet.asu.edu/). This Arizona State University site contains links to information on human origins, prehistory, and archaeology.

Becoming Human (http://www.becominghuman.org/). Material on hominds compiled at Arizona State University.

Evolution of Modern Humans (http://anthro.palomar.edu/homo2/default.htm). Valuable site maintained by Palomar College.

Human Origins Program (http://anthropology.si.edu/humanorigins/). Smithsonian Institution site covers a range of topics.

Internet Ancient History Sourcebook (http://www.fordham.edu/halsall/ancient/asbook.html). Good collection of essays and links on prehistory.

The Internet Public Library: Archaeology (http://www.ipl.org/div/subject/browse/soc06.00.00/). Extensive collection of links on the ancient world and prehistory.

World Civilizations (http://www.wsu.edu/~dee/). A useful collection of materials on prehistory and ancient history, operated by Washington State University.

**Plus flashcards, practice quizzes, and more. Go to:
www.cengage.com/history/lockard/globalsocnet2e.**

SUGGESTED READING

Barfield, Thomas J. *The Nomadic Alternative*. Englewood Cliffs: Prentice Hall, 1993. Examines current and past nomadic societies in Asia ad Africa.

Bellwood, Peter. *First Farmers: The Origins of Agricultural Societies*. Malden, MA: Blackwell, 2005. A detailed scholarly account summarizing recent knowledge.

Bogucki, Peter. *The Origins of Human Society*. Malden, MA: Blackwell, 1999. A detailed and up-to-date scholarly study of human prehistory.

Christian, David. *Maps of Time: An Introduction to "Big History."* Berkeley: University of California Press, 2004. The most extensive presentation of the "big history" approach.

Clark, Robert B. *The Global Imperative: An Interpretive History of the Spread of Humankind*. Boulder, CO: Westview, 1997. A well-written, brief overview of human expansion and the development of agriculture.

Diamond, Jared. *Guns, Germs and Steel: The Fates of Human Societies*. New York: W.W. Norton, 1997. A fascinating interpretation of early human societies, with emphasis on environmental influences.

Fagan, Brian. *The Long Summer: How Climate Changed Civilization*. New York: Basic Books, 2004. An up-to-date assessment of the connection between history and climate over the past 5,000 years.

Fagan, Brian. *People of the Earth: An Introduction to World Prehistory*, 12th ed. Upper Saddle River, NJ: Prentice-Hall, 2006. A standard overview of human evolution and prehistory, from early hominids through the Neolithic.

Goudsbloom, Johan. *Fire and Civilization*. London: Penguin, 1992. Examines the impact of fire use on prehistorical and early farming peoples.

Lee, Richard B. and Richard Daly. *The Cambridge Encyclopedia of Hunters and Gatherers*. New York: Cambridge University Press, 2004. A major source on these societies today.

Manning, Patrick. *Migration in World History*. New York: Routledge, 2005. A provocative study of human migrations, with much on prehistory and ancient history.

Megarry, Tim. *Society in Prehistory: The Origins of Human Culture*. New York: New York University Press, 1995. A sociological study of human evolution and Stone Age societies.

Mithen, Steven. *After the Ice: A Global Human History, 20,000–5000 BC*. Cambridge: Harvard University Press, 2004. An unorthodox but fascinating portrayal, based on the latest research, of 15,000 years of prehistory.

Panter-Brick, Catherine. *Hunter-Gatherers: An Interdisciplinary Perspective*. New York: Cambridge University Press, 2001. Scholarly study of past and present peoples.

Ristvet, Lauren. *In the Beginning: World History from Human Evolution to the First States*. New York: McGraw-Hill, 2007. Readable overview of prehistoric patterns.

Tattersall, Ian. *The World from Beginnings to 4000 BCE*. New York: Oxford University Press, 2008. A brief, up-to-date survey of human prehistory and the Neolithic period.

ANCIENT SOCIETIES IN MESOPOTAMIA, INDIA, AND CENTRAL ASIA, 5000–600 B.C.E.

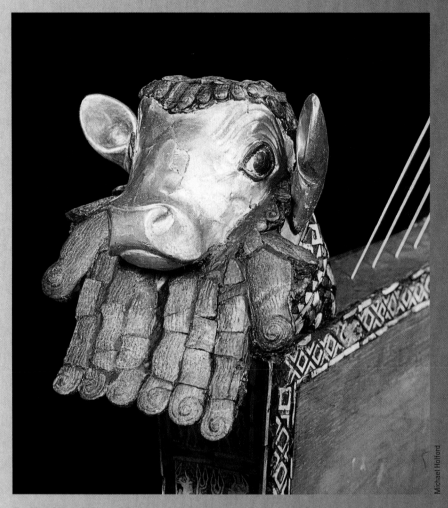

Michael Holford

Bull's Head from Sumerian Lyre
This bull's head is part of the soundbox of a wooden harp. The harp, made in Sumeria around 2600 B.C.E., is covered with gold and lapis lazuli and reflects the popularity of music in Mesopotamian society.

I nanna filled Agade [a Mesopotamian city], her home, with gold. She filled the storerooms with barley, bronze, and lumps of lapis lazuli [a stone used in jewelry]. The ships at the wharves were an awesome sight. All the lands around rested in security.

—POEM PRAISING THE GODDESS OF LOVE AND GENEROSITY, WRITTEN IN 2250 B.C.E.[1]

S ome 5,000 years ago in the Mesopotamian (MESS-uh-puh-TAIM-ee-an) city of Uruk (OO-rook), an unknown artist carved a beautiful narrative relief on a large stone-pedestaled vase, the first such sculpture known in history, and donated it to the city's temple for the goddess of love, Inanna (ih-NON-a), the first known goddess in recorded history. The scenes of domestic and religious life celebrate a festival honoring the goddess. The artist divided the vase into three bands, each illustrating different aspects of Uruk life and traditions. The lowest band presents an agricultural scene, with sheep, barley, and water, the staples of the area's economy. The central band portrays a procession of men carrying foodstuffs that they will present as gifts of gratitude to Inanna. Finally, the uppermost band features a female figure wearing a tall horned headdress, perhaps Inanna or her priestess. The vase reflects artistic skill and also pictures for us the social order and rituals of one of the world's earliest cities.

Sometime after the people in southwest Asia and India had become comfortable with the farming technology necessary for successful living, they began to make the next great transition by founding the first cities like Uruk and states. Various urban societies eventually formed in the Indus Valley in northwestern India and all along the **Fertile Crescent**, a large semicircle of fertile land that included the valleys of the Tigris (TIE-gris) and Euphrates (you-FRAY-teez) Rivers stretching northwest from the Persian Gulf to the eastern shores of the Mediterranean Sea. The Mesopotamians divided their specialized workers into full-time farmers, professional soldiers, government officials, artisans, traders, and priests. Ancient Indians also established social classes and the foundations for several religions of enduring appeal.

The Mesopotamians and Indians were among various Afro-Eurasian peoples who built the foundations to sustain large populations. For at least three millennia a large majority of the world's population has lived in an arc stretching from Egypt and Mesopotamia eastward through India to China and Japan. The people of western Asia created the first systematic use of writing for both business transactions and literature, the first working of bronze, the first large states, and the first institutionalized religions to worship deities like Inanna. These societies also constructed networks to exchange products and information over long distances by land and sea. The city Agade (uh-GAH-duh) was visited by traders from near and far. Over time southwest Asia became a crossroads or bridge between Europe, Africa, and southern Asia and a great hub for trade and communication networks extending to distant lands.

FOCUS QUESTIONS

1. Why did farming, cities, and states develop first in the Fertile Crescent?
2. What were some of the main features of Mesopotamian societies?
3. What were some of the distinctive features of the Harappan cities?
4. How did Indian society and the Hindu religion emerge from the mixing of Aryan and local cultures?

Fertile Crescent A large semicircular fertile region that included the valleys of the Tigris and Euphrates Rivers stretching northwest from the Persian Gulf to the eastern shores of the Mediterranean Sea.

e Visit the website and eBook for additional study materials and interactive tools: www.cengage.com/history/lockard/globalsocnet2e

Early Mesopotamian Urbanized Societies, to 2000 b.c.e.

Why did farming, cities, and states develop first in the Fertile Crescent?

Small city-states emerged in Mesopotamia around 5,000 years ago, especially in the southern part of the Tigris-Euphrates Valley. Geography played a key role in this region's transition to farming, urbanization, and state building. The connections between diverse peoples helped cultures change and grow. Over the centuries various peoples moved into the area, each adopting and building on the achievements of their predecessors. Their cities were dominated by religious temples and had elaborate social class structures. As conquerors combined various city-states into a series of ever larger states, empires were formed, and Mesopotamian societies were soon linked by trade to the Mediterranean and North Africa.

Western Asian Environments

Geographical Foundations

Life in these early societies owed much to the geographic features that brought people together. Most early urban societies began first in wide river valleys such as the Tigris-Euphrates, Indus, and Nile Valleys because such places provided life-giving irrigation for the crops that supported larger populations. In Mesopotamia (the Greek word for the "land between the rivers"), the flooding of the Tigris and Euphrates Rivers made possible a flourishing society. The Tigris-Euphrates Basin stretches from the western edge of the Persian Gulf through today's Iraq into Syria and southeastern Turkey. The long river valley promoted interaction, both friendly and hostile, between peoples. For example, it invited frequent invasions through mountain passes by people living to the north and east. To the northwest is the mountainous Anatolia **(ANN-uh-TOE-lee-uh)** Peninsula (modern Turkey). East of Mesopotamia lay Iran (known through most of history as Persia), a land of mountains and deserts and the pathway to India and Central Asia. To the south the Arabian peninsula, largely desert, was characterized by oasis agriculture and nomadic pastoralism.

Although water was plentiful, other characteristics of this region and its climate were not so generous. Ancient Mesopotamia had a climate similar to southern California today. Most rain fell in the winter, and summer temperatures in some places reached 120 degrees Fahrenheit. During the long, scorching summer, the land baked stone-hard and searing winds blew up a choking dust. Vegetation withered. In the winter, winds, clouds, and the occasional rains made for stormy days. In spring the rains and melting snows in the nearby mountains swelled the rivers to flood level, sometimes submerging the plains. Still, the annual but unpredictable floods created natural levees that could be drained and planted, and the nearby swamps contained abundant fish and wildlife.

Diverse peoples and languages contributed to the history of western Asia. Many different peoples settled the region, some of them speaking Semitic languages, including Arabic and Hebrew, which are related to some African tongues. Speakers of Turkic and of Indo-European languages such as Persian, Armenian, and Kurdish arrived later. Europeans later referred to southwestern Asia as the Orient, Asia Minor, or the Near East (since it was part of the "East" nearest to them), and to the region along the eastern Mediterranean coast as the Levant **(luh-VANT)** ("rising of the sun"). Geographers today use the label "southwest Asia" and often lump the region together with Islamic North Africa under the broader concept of the "Middle East," since Europeans saw it as midway between East Asia (the "Far East") and themselves ("the West").

The Tigris and Euphrates Rivers, which flow southeast from eastern Anatolia, fostered several Mesopotamian societies. The modern city of Baghdad is midway up the Tigris, and the ancient city of Babylon was only a few miles away on the Euphrates. Such cities arose when the population of farmers and herders in the fertile hills on either side of these rivers increased and needed more food. Possibly pushed by a cooler climate, they left the hill country and created the first towns in the marshy areas near the head of the Persian Gulf. After moving

CHRONOLOGY
Mesopotamia, 5500–330 b.c.e.

5500 b.c.e. First Sumerian settlements

3200 b.c.e. First cuneiform writing

3000–2300 b.c.e. Sumerian city-states

2750 b.c.e. Model for legendary Gilgamesh rules Uruk

ca. 2500–2100 b.c.e. Jiroft

ca. 2350–2160 b.c.e. Akkadian Empire unifies Mesopotamia

ca. 2100–2000 b.c.e. Neo-Sumerian Empire led by city of Ur

ca. 2000 b.c.e. *Epic of Gilgamesh* written in cuneiform

ca. 1800–1595 b.c.e. Old Babylonian Empire

ca. 1790–1780 b.c.e. Hammurabi's Law Code

ca. 1600–1200 b.c.e. Hittite Empire

ca. 1115–612 b.c.e. Assyrian Empire

745–626 b.c.e. Height of Assyrian Empire

ca. 626–539 b.c.e. Chaldean (Neo-Babylonian) Empire

ca. 539–330 b.c.e. Persian Empire

CHRONOLOGY

	Mesopotamia	India and Central Asia
3000 B.C.E.	**3000–2300** B.C.E. Sumerian city-states	
2500 B.C.E.	**2350–2160** B.C.E. Akkadian Empire	**2600–1750** B.C.E. Harappan city-states
		2200–1800 B.C.E. Oxus cities
2000 B.C.E.	**1800–1595** B.C.E. Old Babylonian Empire	**1600–1400** B.C.E. Aryan migrations
		1500–1000 B.C.E. Aryan age
1000 B.C.E.	**1115–605** B.C.E. Assyrian Empire	

to the river valleys, they worked together to build elaborate irrigation canals so they could grow food after the annual floods. This irrigation had significant consequences, for it necessitated the cooperation that laid the foundations for organized societies and then cities. Yet irrigation also slowly degraded the soil, the salts it added eventually creating infertile desert.

The Pioneering Sumerians and Their Neighbors

People built the first Mesopotamian cities and states in Sumer (soo-MUHR), the lower part of the Tigris-Euphrates Valley in southern Iraq (see Map 2.1). The Sumerians originally came from the north or the east and settled in southern Mesopotamia about 5500 B.C.E. By 3500 B.C.E. Uruk had grown into a city, eventually reaching a population of 50,000. Some scholars suspect that other Mesopotamian peoples, such as those in the north at Tell Hamoukar (see Chapter 1), may have been as important as the Sumerians in forging the first states. But our knowledge of the Sumerians is much more extensive.

By 3000 B.C.E. Sumerians had created a network of city-states, urban centers surrounded by agricultural land controlled by the city and used to support its citizens (see Chronology: Mesopotamia, 5500–330 B.C.E.). These earliest territorial political units allowed Sumerian societies to grow to several million people by 2500 B.C.E. Uruk was surrounded by 5 miles of fortified walls and had extended its influence through trade as far north as modern Turkey by 3500 B.C.E. An attack by Uruk on Tell Hamoukar is the world's oldest known example of large-scale organized warfare.

Sumerians were clearly proud of their cities. A Sumerian myth begins with the lines "Behold the bond of Heaven and Earth, the city. Behold the kindly wall . . . its pure river, its quay where the boats stand. Behold its well of good water. Behold its pure canal."[2] The Sumerians felt that city life made them superior to others. The city-dwellers lived in mud-baked brick houses constructed around courtyards. The largest building in any Sumerian city was the temple, or **ziggurat** (ZIG-uh-rat), a stepped, pyramidal-shaped building (almost an artificial mountain) that was seen as the home of that city's chief god. One of these temples may have inspired the later Hebrew story of the tower of Babel (BAY-buhl/BAH-buhl).

ziggurat A stepped, pyramidal-shaped temple building in Sumerian cities, seen as the home of the chief god of the city.

Sumerian Society and Economy

In Sumerian society some people had higher ranks than others. At first decision-making assemblies of leading citizens governed the cities. Scholars have long debated whether these assemblies, which included elders and other free citizens, amounted to a kind of democratic government. The assemblies seem to have appointed a city leader, sometimes a woman, with both secular and religious authority. However, with the waging of wars, rulers, priests, and nobles came to dominate large numbers of lower-class people, workers, and slaves. Women lost the right to be elected leader and serve in the assemblies. War leaders became kings, or hereditary monarchs, and weakened the power of the assemblies and priests. The nobility and priests controlled most of the land in and around the city, which was tilled by tenant farmers or slaves. Thus many common people became dependent on the nobles or priests for their survival. A Sumerian proverb claimed that "the poor man is better dead than alive; if he has bread, he has no salt; if he has salt, he has no bread."[3] The many slaves, who included captives taken in battles and criminals, were treated as personal property but allowed to marry. Eventually royal officials, nobility, and priests controlled most of the economic life of the cities.

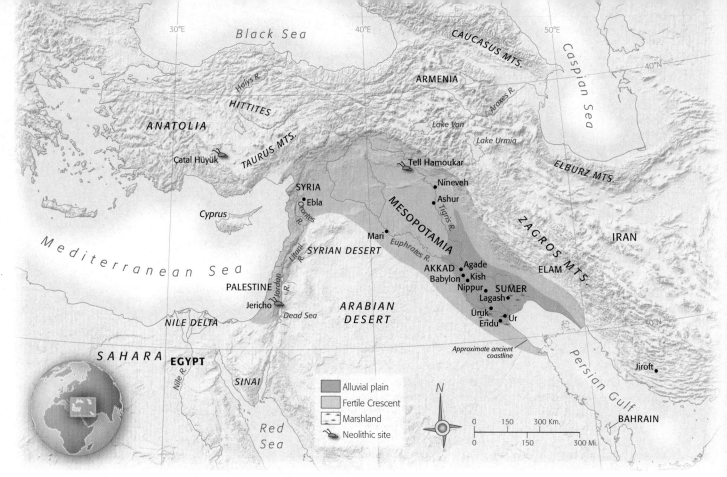

Map 2.1
Ancient Mesopotamia

The people of Mesopotamia and the adjacent regions of the Fertile Crescent pioneered farming. The Mesopotamians also built the first cities and formed the first states. The Sumerian cities dominated southern Mesopotamia for over a millennium, only to lose power to societies from northern Mesopotamia.

e Interactive Map

patriarchy A system in which men largely control women and children and shape ideas about appropriate gender behavior.

As the first of many male-governed societies, Sumeria introduced **patriarchy**, a system in which men largely control women and children and also shape ideas about appropriate gender behavior. Sumerian women were generally subservient to men and excluded from government, but they could inherit property, run their own businesses, and serve as witnesses in court. A queen enjoyed much respect as the wife of the king. Sumerian religion also allowed a woman to be the high priestess if the city divinity was female. Sumerians treasured the family; a proverb suggested the importance of women in the family but also the stereotypes they faced: "The wife is a man's future; the son is a man's refuge; the daughter is a man's salvation; the daughter-in-law is a man's devil."[4]

The trade networks involving Sumeria may have been some of the first in world history with significant consequences. Because of their location and lack of natural resources, the Sumerian cities engaged in extensive trade, which helped form networks with neighboring societies.

Trade and Trade Networks

Sumerians imported copper from Armenia in the Caucasus Mountains and then discovered how to mix it with tin to make bronze. This alloy made for stronger weapons, which they often used against each other. Thus the Bronze Age originated in western Asia, and later the use of bronze helped shape other societies in Eurasia and North Africa. The Sumerians also imported gold, ivory, obsidian, and other necessities from Anatolia, the Nile Valley, Ethiopia, India, the Caspian Sea, and the eastern shore of the Mediterranean.

The Persian Gulf became a major waterway, with many trading ports. Bahrain (bah-RAIN) Island served as a transshipment point for goods flowing in from all directions and as a hub where various traders and travelers met. Mesopotamian merchants traveled to this port carrying textiles, leather objects, wool, and olive oil and returned with copper bars, ivory, precious objects, and rare woods from various western Asian societies and India. Mesopotamian traders traveled widely. Trade helped people learn and profit from each other's skills and surplus goods.

The Sumerians also seem to have had some trade and other connections with another urban-based farming society, Jiroft (JEER-oft) in southeastern Iran. Jiroft emerged sometime between 3000 and 2500 B.C.E., which had an economy based on cultivating date palms. Jiroft, which had emerged by 2500 B.C.E., had an economy based on gaily decorated capital city had lofty red brick towers, and the rulers supplied craftsmen to Uruk. The ruins of Jiroft city include a two-story citadel, a Sumerian-like ziggurat, the world's oldest known board games, and staggering numbers of decorated vases, goblets, cups, and boxes. The people adorned their products with precious stones from India and Afghanistan.

Jiroft

Sumerian Writing and Technology

The Sumerians were innovators in many areas. Although a few scholars think the Egyptians, Indians, or Chinese might have developed a simple writing system at least as early, most still credit the Sumerians with producing the first written records. Trade and the need to keep accurate records of agricultural production and public and private business dealings led around 3200 B.C.E. to the **cuneiform** (kyoo-NEE-uh-form) (Latin for "wedge-shaped") writing system, by which temple recordkeepers, or scribes, began to keep records of financial transactions by making rough pictures (say, of an animal or fish) on soft clay with a stylus that made wedges in the clay. They then baked the bricks on which these pictograms were scratched. Sumerian scribes soon let a stylized version of the pictogram stand for an idea, and later they converted an even more abstract version into a phonetic sign describing a speech sound.

Writing

cuneiform ("wedge-shaped") Latin term used to describe the writing system invented by the Sumerians.

Writing provided a way of communicating with people over long distances and allowed rulers to administer larger states. Those who controlled the written word, like those who master electronic communication in our day, had power, prestige, and a monopoly over a society's official history. Writing also gave temple scribes and other religious leaders the power to determine how written texts attributed to the gods or political authorities should be interpreted. Since writing required mastery of at least three hundred symbols, few people learned to write, and those who did largely came from the upper class. In part to produce scribes, the Sumerians created the world's first schools, where strict instructors beat students for misbehavior or sloppy work. A clay tablet from the eighteenth century B.C.E. describes the life of a pupil who spent twenty-four days a month in school and was frequently beaten: "My teacher said: 'Your hand [writing] is unsatisfactory.' [He] caned me. I [begin to hate] the scribal art."[5] However, because cuneiform eventually transformed pictures into phonetic sounds, it made the written word more accessible, even for people whose only goal was a good recipe for a meal of red broth and meat.

Writing became crucial in history for a number of reasons. First, written language made it easier to express abstract ideas and create an intellectual life based on a body of literature. The

Hirmer Verlag München

Overview of Early City of Uruk   This photo shows the ruins of one of the earliest Mesopotamian cities, a rich source of art objects and fine architecture. The best-known king of Uruk was the legendary Gilgamesh.

oldest known signed poetry was composed by Enheduanna (en-who-DWAHN-ah), a Sumerian priestess and princess living around 2300 B.C.E. Royal women were often authors. In addition, a written language based on clearly understood symbols allowed communication among people who spoke different languages but understood the same written symbols. For example, the number 5 is understood today the same way by Spanish speakers, who pronounce it "cinco," and German speakers, who say "funf." Finally, writing was one key to the interaction among societies. It not only gave a strong sense of identity to all who shared the language but also eventually encouraged the spread of trade and culture, including religion, to those outside a particular homeland.

Sumerian Inventions

Sumerians were innovative in many areas. They pioneered the first use of the wheel, glass, and fertilizer, inventions that we still live with today. Sumerians also created some of the earliest calendars, which were based on their observations of the movements of various celestial bodies, and one of the first mathematical systems, based on the number 60. Remnants of this system can be seen today in our 60-minute hours and 60-second minutes. Many other peoples eventually adopted all of these inventions. Humanity also owes to the Sumerians the decision to divide night and day into twelve hours each. Like us, the Sumerians enjoyed alcoholic beverages. Although they were not the first to convert barley into beer, they designated a special goddess to supervise its production, called Ninkasi or "the lady who fills the mouth." The many taverns fostered early drinking songs: "I will summon brewers and cupbearers to serve us floods of beer and keep it passing round! Our hearts enchanted and our souls radiant."[6]

The Akkadian Empire and Its Rivals

Sargon's Empire

Eventually the political structure of the region changed. For centuries each city had its own king who ruled the people in the name of the city's god. This independence ended about 2350 B.C.E. when Sargon (SAHR-gone), the ruler of Akkad (AH-kahd), a region just north of Sumer whose capital was Agade, conquered Uruk as a prelude to uniting the other Sumerian cities under the rule of his family. Sargon formed the world's first known empire, a large state controlling other societies through conquest or domination. The Akkadians enslaved many other people in addition to the Sumerians; in fact, slaves constituted perhaps a third of the empire's population. Under Sargon trade between Mesopotamia and India reached a peak. Indeed, Akkad became the major center for regional trade, and merchant ships from as far as Oman (O-mahn) in eastern Arabia and, even further away, India, docked at the wharves, carrying copper and various exotic products.

Sargon's empire soon came into conflict with one created by another imperial city, Ebla (EBB-luh), in northern Mesopotamia. Ebla had created a large empire based on trade that stretched from eastern Turkey to the ancient city of Mari (MAH-ree), several hundred miles north of Akkad. The Akkadian Empire was destroyed by the twenty-first century B.C.E., probably from a combination of internal conflicts, external attacks, and less rainfall. A disastrous drought between 2200 and 1900 B.C.E. affected much of Eurasia. Mesopotamian societies such as Sumer and Akkad were powerless against abrupt climate change. Sumerian legends expressed dread of the periodic droughts: "The famine was severe, nothing was produced. The fields are not watered. In all the lands there was no vegetation [and] only weeds grew."[7] Irrigation canals silted up and settlements became ghost towns as people migrated.

As the Akkadian Empire collapsed, a new Sumerian dynasty led by Ur took over much of the lower valley between 2100 and 2000 B.C.E., forming the Neo-Sumerian Empire. Some Ur kings boasted of their commitment to art and intellectual life, one ordering that the places of learning

The Royal Standard of Ur This mosaic from around 2500 B.C.E., made of inlaid shells and limestone, was found in a royal tomb. It depicts various aspects of life in the Mesopotamian city-state of Ur. The bottom panel shows a four-wheeled battle wagon drawn by a horselike animal. The middle panel features soldiers wearing armor and helmets. The top panel shows war prisoners being brought before the king.

British Museum/Michael Holford

should never be closed. But Ur was devastated by a coalition of enemies and sacked and burned along with other Sumerian cities. Its temples were destroyed, its populations killed or enslaved, and its treasures plundered. A surviving lamentation describes the destruction of Ur: "Ur is destroyed, bitter is its lament. The country's blood now fills its holes like hot bronze in a mould. Our temple is destroyed, the gods have abandoned us, like migrating birds. Smoke lies on our city like a shroud."[8]

The Akkadians, Eblaites, and the later Sumerians established the first empires in history, even though their creations were short-lived and were not the large bureaucratic organizations we see in later empires. They were largely collections of city-states that acknowledged one city as overlord. It soon became clear that whoever had the best army would dominate Mesopotamia.

SECTION SUMMARY

- The first urban societies of Mesopotamia developed in the Tigris-Euphrates Basin.

- Sumerian society was hierarchical and patriarchal.

- The earliest writing system was probably the cuneiform system, developed by the Sumerians.

- The world's first empire, the Akkadian Empire, was founded by Sargon in an area just north of the Sumerians.

LATER MESOPOTAMIAN SOCIETIES AND THEIR LEGACIES, 2000–600 B.C.E.

What were some of the main features of Mesopotamian societies?

The Sumerians and Akkadians established a pattern of city living, state building, and imperial expansion. From 2000 B.C.E. and continuing for the next 1,500 years, a series of peoples coming mainly from the north—the Babylonians, Hittites, and Assyrians—successively dominated Mesopotamia and created new empires. Each made important contributions to the politics, laws, culture, and thought of the region. This pattern changed only when the entire area was incorporated into the Persian Empire in 539 B.C.E.

The Babylonians and Hittites

Several states dominated Mesopotamia during the second millennium B.C.E., beginning with Babylon. In 1800 B.C.E. the Amorites (AM-uh-rites), a Semitic people, conquered Babylon, a city about 300 miles north of the Persian Gulf, and gradually extended their control in the region. Babylon's most famous king, Hammurabi (HAM-uh-rah-bee), who ruled from 1792 to 1750 B.C.E., reunified Mesopotamia. Hammurabi had nearly three hundred laws collected and posted on a black basalt pillar. These laws were designed, he said, "to make justice appear in the land, to destroy the evil and the wicked [so] that the strong might not oppress the weak."[9] It remains famous today because some of its principles appeared later in the laws of the Hebrews and also because of its most noted principle, the law of retaliation: an eye for an eye and a tooth for a tooth.

The Babylonians

By 1595 B.C.E. the Babylonian Empire had disintegrated in the face of attacks by the Hittites (HIT-ites), an Indo-European people who moved into Mesopotamia from their base in central Anatolia. The Hittites were most famous for their later use of iron weapons, which were superior to those made of bronze, but these had not yet been invented when the Hittites invaded Mesopotamia. The Hittites expanded their power until they met the equally strong Egyptians in Syria and Palestine. The Hittites may also have used the first known biological weapons, since one of their tactics was to send plague victims into enemy lands. The Hittite Empire dominated various parts of western Asia from 1600 to 1200 B.C.E. but treated their subjects less harshly than the Babylonians. They followed a tolerant attitude toward other religions and adopted many Mesopotamian gods, establishing a tradition of tolerance in the region.

The Hittites

The Assyrian Empire and Regional Supremacy

In 1115 B.C.E. the Assyrians (uh-SEER-e-uhns) began conquering an empire in western Asia that was eventually larger than any before, the first that was more than a collection of city-states. They did this by creating a large, well-organized military; systematically using terror against enemies; and devising methods of bureaucratic organization that later empires imitated. One of the greatest kings, Tiglath-pileser (TIG-lath-pih-LEE-zuhr) III (745–727 B.C.E.), conquered the entire eastern shore of the Mediterranean. Later Assyrian rulers added Egypt to the empire. One

Assyrian king described himself with some accuracy as "obedient to his gods and receiving the tribute of the four corners of the world."[10] Using iron weapons while their enemies still relied on softer bronze ones, the Assyrians launched armies of over 50,000 men that were carefully divided into a core of infantrymen aided by cavalry and horse-drawn chariots. They conducted sieges in which they used battering rams and tunnels against the city walls of their enemies. They also employed guerrilla, or irregular hit-and-run, tactics when fighting in the forests or mountains.

Assyrian Government

Assyrian kings created a systematic bureaucracy to rule over several million people in the Tigris-Euphrates heartland alone. To improve their administrative control, the rulers used horsemen to create an early version of the "pony express," which allowed them to send messages hundreds of miles within a week. Some kings were both brutal and learned. Ashurbanipal (ah-shur-BAH-nugh-pahl) (680–627 B.C.E.) founded a great library to collect tablets from all over the country. He boasted of his learning, noting that, in school, he learned to solve complex mathematical problems and discovered the "hidden treasure" of writing.

Violence and the Fall of the Assyrians

The Assyrians were most remembered, and deplored, for their brutality, which ultimately contributed to their downfall. King Ashurbanipal bragged about mutilating and burning prisoners. After destroying the state of Elam in Iran, he boasted that "like the onset of a terrible hurricane I overwhelmed Elam. I cut off the head of . . . their braggart king. In countless numbers I killed his warriors." As to the capital city, "I destroyed it, I devastated it, I burned it with fire."[11] Soldiers routinely looted cities, destroyed crops, and both flailed and impaled their enemies. To prevent revolts, the Assyrians often simply moved people to another part of the vast empire. For example, according to legends, inhabitants of one of the two Hebrew kingdoms were sent to Mesopotamia, where they disappeared from history (see Chapter 3). Yet the Assyrians also tolerated other religions, a policy that allowed the Hebrew faith to survive the conquest of their state.

The terror tactics undermined Assyrian popularity. In 612 B.C.E., a coalition including the Chaldeans (kal-DEE-uhns) (also known as neo-Babylonians) captured the Assyrian capital at Nineveh (NIN-uh-vuh). The Chaldeans, who formed the last Mesopotamian empire, adopted the Assyrian administrative system and flourished from 626 B.C.E. until they were conquered by the much larger Persian Empire in 539 B.C.E. Their most memorable ruler, Nebuchadnezzar (NAB-oo-kuhd-nez-uhr) II (r. 605–562 B.C.E.), a brutal strongman, rebuilt Babylon and adorned it with magnificent palaces and the elaborate terraced "hanging gardens," which were built to please one of his wives and which became famous throughout the ancient world. Nebuchadnezzar led the conquest of the remaining Hebrew kingdom in 586 B.C.E.

Mesopotamian Law

Several very different documents tell us much about Mesopotamian life and beliefs. The eighteenth-century B.C.E. Law Code of Hammurabi gives us a good look at the social structures of this early urban society (see Profile: Hammurabi the Lawgiver). Hammurabi's Code makes clear both what people valued and how people themselves were valued; it is also one of the earliest systematic records we have of how ancient peoples viewed laws, government, and social norms. The Code probably reflected a high crime rate in the cities, no doubt because of the tremendous gap between rich and poor. Families were responsible for the crimes of any of their members. To keep lines of inheritance clear, Hammurabi prescribed harsh punishments for sexual infidelity and incest, as did many societies. Women who violated social norms generally suffered harsher punishments than men, just as the eyes and teeth of poor men or slaves were worth less than the same body parts among the upper classes. Each slave was branded with the owner's symbol, and some endured harsh lives of forced labor. Yet, while it may seem contradictory to their status as property, some slaves also owned their own assets, carried on business, and even acquired their own slaves.

Hammurabi's Code

The Code also addressed economic issues. In this class-conscious society, a surgeon could lose his hand if his patient was a free man who failed to survive the operation, certainly a disincentive to take up medicine. If the patient was a slave, however, the surgeon had only to replace him with another. If a builder's house collapsed and killed its inhabitants, the builder could be executed. The existence of a thriving commercial class is confirmed by the existence of high interest rates on loans. In general, the punishments in Hammurabi's Law Code tell us how precarious life must have been in this society, where even a single small break in an irrigation canal wall could spell disaster.

Hammurabi the Lawgiver

No person personifies Mesopotamian society better than Hammurabi, a Babylonian king (r. 1792–1750 B.C.E.) who was also at times a diplomat, warrior, builder of temples, digger of canals, and, most famously, lawgiver. Many surviving tablets, inscriptions, and letters, some from Hammurabi himself, made the king and his era the best documented in Mesopotamian history. He seems to have been a good administrator and able general who governed fairly and efficiently. Like other Mesopotamian kings, Hammurabi probably had a chief queen and various concubines, as well as several sons and daughters.

When Hammurabi became king, Babylon (which meant "gateway of the gods" in Akkadian) was an insignificant city-state. To expand its power, Hammurabi shrewdly allied with the powerful king of Ashur, probably by becoming a vassal, and allowed him to conquer some nearby cities. For some years Hammurabi's small domain remained one of many rival states, as noted by one of his officials: "There is no king who by himself is strongest. Ten or fifteen kings follow Hammurabi." Like other kings, Hammurabi had intelligence agents in other cities keeping him abreast of important developments such as pending alliances and troop movements. A spy for another king became close to him, writing that "whenever Hammurabi is perturbed by some matter, he always sends for me. He tells me whatever is troubling him, and all of the important information I continually report to my lord." After his army repulsed an invasion by a coalition of rivals, a confident Hammurabi engaged in a long series of wars that added all of southern Mesopotamia and then much of the north to his kingdom. Finally he conquered the strongest power, his former ally Ashur.

Kingship brought responsibilities. Hammurabi's letters reveal him sitting in an office at his palace, dictating to a secretary who recorded his orders or thoughts with a reed stylus on a clay tablet. Most letters conveyed commands to governors. Messengers brought letters from officials, which the secretary read aloud. In his replies, Hammurabi tried to resolve problems, for example, suggesting ways to clear a flooded shipping channel, warning delinquent tax collectors of their

Hammurabi Receiving the Law Code The top of this stela, which is 8 feet high, shows the powerful sun-god, Shamash, on his throne bestowing the famous Law Code to King Hammurabi.

obligations, punishing corrupt officials, improving agricultural productivity, or protecting frontiers. He also held daily audiences for petitioners seeking justice. Many decisions concerned temple property and administration, indicating the link between church and state.

Hammurabi realized the need to have uniform laws in his diverse country. He compiled older laws, recent legal decisions, and social customs, arranged them systematically, and placed them on an 8-foot block of basalt stone in the temple of Babylon's patron god, Marduk. At the top, an artist pictured Hammurabi receiving the symbols of kingship from Shamash, the sun-god and lawgiver. The Code of 282 laws informed citizens of their rights and demonstrated to both gods and people that the king was doing his job to uphold justice in a moral universe.

For close to four millennia, the principles of this ancient Mesopotamian law code have intrigued us. The Code reflected the harsh views of the era. It mandated two kinds of punishments, a monetary penalty and a retribution in kind, and the harshness of the punishment depended on the class of the people involved. The Code recognized three social classes: nobles and landowners, commoners, and slaves. Many of Hammurabi's laws discouraged burglary by prescribing instant death for those caught. This emphasis may have reflected the fact that mudbrick homes were not very secure. On the other hand, prostitution was legal. Some laws protected women and children from abuse and arbitrary treatment. For example, a husband who divorced his wife because she bore no sons had to return the dowry she brought into the marriage and forfeit the money he had given her parents for a bridal price. Since the Hebrews borrowed some of these laws, often in modified form, and passed them into Christian and Islamic traditions, Hammurabi's legacy remains influential today.

THINKING ABOUT THE PROFILE

1. How did Hammurabi increase the power of Babylon?
2. What were the purposes of his great Law Code?

Note: Quotations from William H. Stiebing, Jr., *Ancient Near Eastern History and Culture* (New York: Longman, 2003), 88–89.

Mesopotamian Religion and Literature

Gods and Godesses

Like most early people, the Mesopotamians believed in a host of gods and goddesses, such as Inanna, later called Ishtar (ISH-tar), the beautiful goddess of love who created desire. But this polytheistic religion imposed no moral demands. These divinities came with human weaknesses, yet they were powerful enough to punish humans, who were created to serve them. People saw themselves as subject to the gods' whims. The gods were housed in massive and opulent temples, where ritual ceremonies were held. The Babylonians and later the Assyrians changed the names of some of the earlier Sumerian gods but maintained the basic Sumerian view of the universe.

Epic of Gilgamesh

The *Epic of Gilgamesh* (GILL-guh-mesh), first written down about 2000 B.C.E. but revised and retold by Mesopotamians for 1,500 years, reveals some of their religious values and attitudes. Perhaps humanity's first epic adventure story, *Gilgamesh* echoes Hammurabi's view of the world as a dangerous place in which happiness is hard to find. Although only one part of a very rich legacy of literature and mythology, *Gilgamesh* had the most enduring and widespread influence, enriching the traditions of varied Eurasian societies.

Primary Source: The *Epic of Gilgamesh* Find out how Gilgamesh's friend Enkidu propels him on a quest for immortality, and whether or not that quest is successful.

In one version of the Gilgamesh story, the hero, modeled after a real king in Uruk about 2750 B.C.E. and created to be two-thirds god and one-third man, engages in a series of adventures involving both the gods and men. With his friend Enkidu, Gilgamesh challenges and defeats the evil but divine giant who guards a mysterious cedar forest. Following this adventure, Gilgamesh rejects a proposal from Ishtar, the goddess of love, telling her that she is fickle and recounting the disagreeable things she has done to her previous lovers, such as turning one of them into a wolf. In revenge at being snubbed, Ishtar causes the death of Enkidu. Reflecting on the death of his friend, Gilgamesh decides to search for the key to eternal life, an ultimately futile quest involving many setbacks that reflects the general pessimism of Mesopotamian culture. A Uruk master scribe lamented around 1300 B.C.E.: "Gilgamesh, what you seek you will never find. For when the Gods created Man they let death be his lot, eternal life they withheld. Let your every day be full of joy, love the child that holds your hand, let your wife delight in your embrace, for these alone are concerns of humanity."[12]

Legacy of *Gilgamesh*

Scholars have noted the similarities between this story and stories found in the later Hebrew book of Genesis. In both there is a paradise: the garden of Eden for the Hebrews, Dilmun for the Mesopotamians. In both a great flood destroys humankind. In both a man challenges the god(s). And in both a serpent comes between a man and immortality. However, although the writer or writers of Genesis may been influenced by *Gilgamesh,* there are some differences in tone and attitude between the Babylonian and Hebrew versions. In the Hebrew story, God sends a flood to punish humans for evil living. In more urban Mesopotamia, where floods were frequent and destructive, the gods "decide to exterminate mankind" because "the uproar of mankind is intolerable and sleep is no longer possible by reason of the babel."[13] But a dissenting god causes his favorite mortal to survive by building a boat and loading it with his family and "the seed of all living creatures, the game of the field, and all the craftsmen."

The parallels between the Gilgamesh legend and Genesis remind us that the Gilgamesh story became widely known far beyond Mesopotamia. Some motifs can be found in the literature of the Greeks, such as the Homeric epics. They also reappear in the much later Islamic period, such as the stories of Aladdin and Sinbad, and they are still found in the folk cultures of some villages. The Gilgamesh epic became one of the many unique traditions that shaped the societies of southwestern Asia and made them different from other early societies such as India and Egypt.

SECTION SUMMARY

- The Babylonians, Hittites, Assyrians, and Chaldeans created empires in Mesopotamia.

- The Babylonian king Hammurabi created a legal framework that included harsh punishments and reflected strict class divisions.

- The Assyrian Empire, known for its brutality, dominated a large region but was finally defeated by a coalition of enemies.

- The *Epic of Gilgamesh,* which shows parallels with the book of Genesis, reflects Mesopotamian values and perspectives, including a pessimistic view of life.

THE EARLIEST INDIAN AND CENTRAL ASIAN SOCIETIES, 6000–1500 B.C.E.

What were some of the distinctive features of the Harappan cities?

India developed a society with cultural features vastly different from those of the Middle East, Europe, or China. Aided by environmental factors, some Indians made the transition to farming very early, and the first cities and states east of Mesopotamia were founded around 2600

B.C.E. (see Chronology: Ancient India and Central Asia, 7000–600 B.C.E.). Most scholars trace the foundations of Indian urban society to the city-states and the widespread Bronze Age culture they shared, often called **Harappan** (huh-RAP-un), that were centered in the Indus (IN-duhs) River Valley and nearby rivers in what is now Pakistan and northwest India. Harappan culture eventually covered some 300,000 square miles, the largest in geographical extent of the ancient societies. Although the Harappans built no pyramids like the Egyptians or ziggurats like the Sumerians, they developed a remarkable society. To the north, an urban society also developed in Central Asia.

Harappan Name given to the city-states and the widespread Bronze Age culture they shared that were centered in the Indus River Valley and nearby rivers in northwest India.

South Asian Environments and the Rise of Farming

River valley environments strongly shaped the early societies of India, just as they did Mesopotamia, Egypt, and China. The Indian subcontinent, about half the size of Europe, is rimmed by the Indian Ocean and the Himalayan Mountains, which boast the half dozen highest peaks in the world, including Mt. Everest at nearly 30,000 feet. The Himalayas, which stretch some 1,500 miles from east to west, inhibited regular communication between China and India. Just north of the Himalayas, the Tibetan Plateau is the source of great rivers, including the Indus and Ganges in India, the Yellow and Yangzi in China, and the Irrawaddy and Mekong in Southeast Asia, which eventually reach great plains and deltas. The land proved highly fertile in these river basins, allowing for productive farming and dense settlement. Rice and wheat became the staple crops for most peoples in both South and East Asia, and scavenging animals like chickens and pigs were more important food sources than beef cattle, which requires extensive pasture.

Geographical Foundations

As with all societies, India's distinctive features resulted in part from its physical environment and climate. The fertile north Indian plains, watered by the Indus and Ganges Rivers, are relatively flat and so encouraged cultural unity and the formation of cities and kingdoms. By contrast, mountainous south India developed more cultural diversity. The southern peoples and languages differ greatly from those of north India. Other regions with highly distinctive local cultures include Bengal, framed by the delta of the Ganges River, and the fertile island of Sri Lanka (once known as Ceylon), just a few miles off India's southern tip.

South Asian Regions

The tropical climate affected Indian life. Some areas enjoy high rainfall, especially in the south and northeast, but much of the northwest is today desert. Although the annual rains sustain life, seasonal flooding can be a chronic problem. Water has been an especially sacred commodity in Indian life and thought, and a frequent subject of literature. Because they had many domesticated cattle, most Indians learned to consume dairy products, including yogurt, a local invention. Thanks to surpluses of wheat and barley, by 3000 B.C.E. the population of the Indus Valley may have reached 1 million, and regional trading networks emerged, setting the stage for the emergence of cities.

Harappan Cities

Around 2600 B.C.E., the first Indian urban society emerged from regional cultures in the Indus River Valley, a semiarid region similar ecologically to the Nile and Tigris-Euphrates Valleys (see Map 2.2). Along the banks of the Indus, which later inspired the English term *India,* and nearby rivers such as the Saraswati, a vibrant urban-based culture thrived for hundreds of years and planted some seeds for the rich Indian culture that endures to the present. Silt spread by regular river floods served as a natural fertilizer, while nearby forests provided enough wood for baking the bricks used in building cities. Like the Nile in Egypt, the flat, easily navigable Indus and its tributary rivers gave Harappan society considerable uniformity. Most of the Harappan cities were in the Punjab (PUHN-jab) and Sind provinces of modern Pakistan, a crossroads of major trading routes, but some were hundreds of miles to the west or east. Indeed, the Indus culture covered an area far larger than the Mesopotamian and Egyptian cultures combined. The two major Indus cities, called by archaeologists Harappa and Mohenjo-Daro (moe-hen-joe-DAHR-oh), stood 400 miles apart. The 1,500 Harappan cities and towns contained a total population of perhaps 5 million people at their zenith.

CHRONOLOGY

Ancient India and Central Asia, 7000–600 B.C.E.

7000–6000 B.C.E. Agriculture begins in Indus River Basin

2600–2500 B.C.E. Harappan cities established

2300–1900 B.C.E. Harappan cities at height

2200–1800 B.C.E. Oxus cities in Central Asia

1900–1750 B.C.E. Harappan society collapses in Indus Basin

1600–1400 B.C.E. Beginning of Aryan migrations into India

1500–1000 B.C.E. Aryan age of conquest and settlement

1000–700 B.C.E. Compilation of *Brahmanas*

1000–450 B.C.E. Height of Indo-Aryan synthesis

800–600 B.C.E. Compilation of *Upanishads*

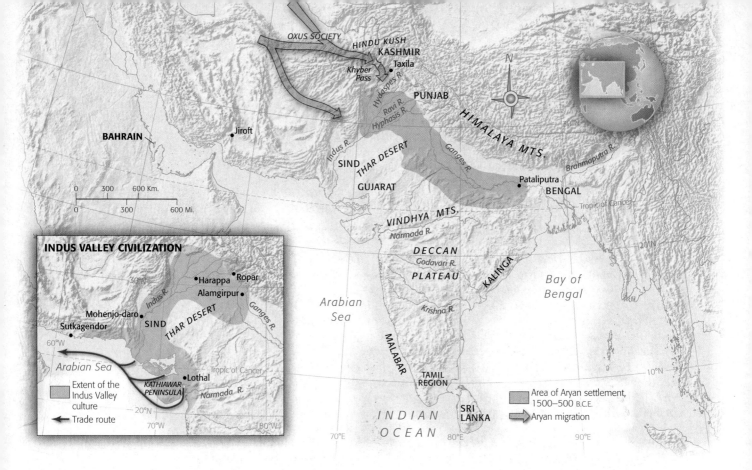

Map 2.2
Harappan Culture and Aryan Migrations

The Harappan culture emerged in the city-states of the Indus River Basin. They had collapsed by around 1500 B.C.E., when the Aryan peoples from Iran began migrating into India and setting up states.

e **Interactive Map**

City Life

All the cities had many common features, in construction as well as in society, government, religion, and culture. The uniformity among Harappan cities reveals a society that valued order, organization, and cleanliness. Administrators used the same pattern, carefully laying out the cities using a north-south grid pattern with wide streets and large rectangular city blocks. They built most buildings of sturdy baked brick molded to a standardized size. Residential and commercial districts were separated from a smaller area for public affairs. Shops probably lined the main streets. The largest city, Harappa, some 3 $1/3$ miles in circumference, contained perhaps 80,000 people at its height. Massive brick ramparts 40 feet thick at their base partially protected it from the river waters and any potential human attackers. Large granaries provide evidence of wealth and stored voluminous supplies, perhaps of wheat for the local population, or export goods. The Harappan people had exceptional housing for ancient times. More affluent residents lived in spacious homes constructed on strong brick foundations with interior courtyards that provided considerable privacy. But even the common people enjoyed well-built accommodations.

The urban Harappans enjoyed the most advanced sanitation system in the ancient world. Most houses had a bathroom and drains to carry away the wastewater. The covered drains along the city streets were a technological masterpiece and more sanitary than those found in many modern cities. Indeed, not until modern times did urban sanitation anywhere duplicate and then exceed Harappan models. The close attention to providing and carrying away water and the huge public baths suggest an emphasis on washing and personal cleanliness for ritual purity, which later became important in Indian religion.

Dravidian A language family whose speakers are the great majority of the population in southern India.

Scholars debate the identity of the Harappan people. Most believe that they spoke a **Dravidian** (druh-VID-ee-uhn) language, although speakers of other languages may also have lived there. The term *Dravidian* refers to a specific language family and the people who speak these languages. Most modern Dravidian speakers live in southern India, where they are the great majority of the population.

Ruins of Mohenjo-Daro The photo shows the great bath at Mohenjo-Daro. Like modern Indians, the Harappans valued bathing for hygienic and possibly religious reasons.

Josephine Powell, photographer. Courtesy of Special Collections, Fine Arts Library, Harvard College

Harappan Society and Its Beliefs

The Harappan governments, social system, and religious beliefs remain a puzzle. The available evidence for an organized monarchy is thin, and there were no elaborate palaces, temples, or monuments glorifying leaders. Each city was probably independent, perhaps governed by some powerful guild of merchants or a council of commercial, landowning, and religious leaders. The ruins contain few weapons, suggesting that, in contrast to Mesopotamia, war was uncommon. But some people owned beautiful objects of personal adornment, such as necklaces and beads, while others apparently lacked such valuable possessions. The ruins also contain many toys made from clay or wood, indicating a prosperous society that valued leisure for children.

Harappan society had unusual gender relations for that era, different from the rigid patriarchies that characterized Mesopotamia or China as governments grew more powerful. Apparently Harappan husbands moved into their wives' households after marriage, a practice that suggests a matrilineal system. Yet some customs harmed women. At least some Harappans may have practiced *sati* (suh-TEE), the custom of a widow killing herself by jumping onto the funeral pyre as her dead husband is being cremated.

Harappan city-dwellers developed an artistic appreciation, mixing art with religion and even commerce. They made small, square, clay seals, possibly used by merchants for branding their wares. Some of the seals contain brilliant portraits of indigenous animals, including bulls and water buffaloes as well as the tigers, elephants, and rhinoceros that inhabited the nearby forests. Small bronze statues of dancers suggest the Harappans enjoyed dance. Most scholars argue that the Harappans created a written language by at least 2600 B.C.E., although other historians question whether the Harappans had a true writing system comparable to the Mesopotamians and Chinese. By Harappan times the seals, pottery, and various clay tablets contained some four hundred different signs that were completely unrelated to the scripts of Mesopotamia and Egypt. Unfortunately, modern scholars have not been able to decipher the Indus language. Most likely many of the signs represent the names of merchants, businesses, or the commodities being sold.

Government and Gender Relations

Arts and Writing

Harappan Religion

Shiva The Hindu god of destruction and of fertility and the harvest.

Some Harappan religious notions contributed to Hinduism, a religion that developed after Harappan times. For example, one of the seals features a human figure sitting in a yogalike position, surrounded by various animals. The figure appears to have multiple faces, a regular feature of later Hindu icons, and may depict what later became the great Hindu god **Shiva** (SHEEV-uh) in one of his major roles as "Lord of the Beasts." Harappans apparently already worshiped Shiva in his dual role as god of destruction and of fertility and the harvest. Possibly the later Hindu notions of reincarnation and the endless wheel of life derived from Harappan beliefs. Mother-goddess worship seems also to have been prominent in Harappan religious life, as it was in the Fertile Crescent and ancient Europe. Many small clay figurines featuring exaggerated breasts and hips may have represented the mother goddess. Such artistic representations of voluptuous female deities remain common today in India. The goddesses symbolized earth and the life-bearing nature of women. Whereas a female orientation largely disappeared in the religions of many other societies, it remained prominent in Hinduism.

The Harappan Economy and the Wider World

Agriculture

The Harappan cities were hubs tied to surrounding regions, especially southwestern and Central Asia, through trade and transportation networks that fostered extensive contact. This foreign trade grew out of a diverse local economy based on cultivating barley and wheat and producing cotton and metal products. These innovations helped Harappan society to remain stable and prosperous for hundreds of years. A highly sophisticated irrigation system and animal husbandry aided farming. Harappans or their ancestors domesticated the camel, zebu (oxen), elephant, chicken, and water buffalo. The raising of fowl enriched the diet, and water buffalo and zebu greatly aided farming as draft animals. Possibly the Harappans worshiped these two animals, becoming the basis for the later respect accorded cows in Hinduism.

Harappans also made other long-lasting contributions. They invented cotton cloth and made cotton textiles for clothing, one of ancient India's major gifts to the world. For many centuries, cotton spinning and weaving remained the most significant Indian industry, producing materials for eager markets both at home and abroad. Cotton was a chief item in the interregional trading system, shipped in bulk to Mesopotamia. Since there were few metals in the Indus Basin, the Harappans obtained metals in exchange for cotton and other products.

Harappan Seal The seal from Mohenjo-Daro features a humped bull. The writing at the top has yet to be deciphered.

The desirable Harappan agricultural and manufactured products led to extensive foreign trade that linked India with the wider world of western and Central Asia. A huge dock, massive granaries, and specialized factories at the coastal port of Lothal reflected a high-volume maritime trade. Many Harappan seals found at the Mesopotamian city of Ur suggest a steady trade between 2300 and 2000 B.C.E. Bahrain Island in the Persian Gulf functioned as a major crossroads for the Harappan-Sumerian trade. The Harappans exported surplus food, cotton, timber products, copper, and gold, as well as luxury items such as pearls, precious stone products, ivory combs, beads, spices, peacock feathers, and inlay goods made from shell or bone. The Harappans imported precious stones from southern India and silver, turquoise, and tin from Persia and Afghanistan.

J. M. Kenoyer/Courtesy, Department of Archaeology and Museums, Government of Pakistan

The Decline and Collapse of Harappan Society

Eventually, Harappan society declined, for reasons not altogether clear. Sometime between 1900 and 1750 B.C.E. a combination of factors disrupted the urban environment of this once wealthy and highly efficient society. By 1700 B.C.E. most of the Harappan cities had been destroyed or abandoned, although a considerable rural population remained. The decay is obvious in the archaeological excavations. Seals and writing began to disappear. The careful grid pattern for city streets was abandoned, the drainage systems deteriorated, and even home sizes were reduced. Some evidence points to plundering and banditry.

Harappan decline may have resulted from several factors. Perhaps the Harappans exhausted the land. Some evidence points to ecological catastrophes resulting from climate change, deforestation, increased flooding, excessive irrigation of marginal lands, and soil deterioration. Apparently rainfall decreased significantly, one major river, the Sarawati, drying up entirely. These catastrophes probably led to economic breakdown. The crop surpluses that had long sustained the cities disappeared, and people abandoned farms. Perhaps disease epidemics weakened the population.

The end of some of the Indus Valley cities may have been sudden, the result perhaps of a disastrous flood. A mud slide after an earthquake may have temporarily dammed the Indus River or one of its tributaries, unleashing an awesome flood that quickly overwhelmed low-lying cities. The hoards of jewelry, skeletons buried in debris, and cooking pots found strewn across kitchens indicate hastily abandoned homes. The rising floodwaters may have been accompanied by more earthquakes. The chaos of the last days spread rapidly along the river. Harappa, located on higher ground, and some other cities survived a while longer, although with much reduced populations.

The fate of the Harappan people and their cultures is unclear. Some cities east of the Indus Valley remained populated for several more centuries, practicing modified forms of Harappan culture until around 1300 B.C.E. Many Harappans may have migrated into central and southern India, mixing with local Dravidian populations. They carried with them a culture, technology, and agriculture that contributed to the Indian society to come. The calamities left the remaining Indus peoples weak and unable to resist later migrations of peoples from outside.

Central Asian Environments and Oxus Cities

Central Asia is the vast area of plains (**steppes**), deserts, and mountains that stretches from the Ural Mountains and Caspian Sea eastward to Tibet, western China, and Mongolia. Before modern times Central Asians played a role in history far greater than their relatively small populations would suggest, not only as invaders and sometimes conquerors but also as middlemen in the long-distance trade that developed on the land routes between China, India, the Middle East, and Europe.

steppes The plains of Central Asia.

Much of Central Asia offered a harsh living environment suitable mainly for pastoralists. It was inhabited largely by people speaking Ural-Altaic languages, including various Turkik and Mongol tongues. Many different peoples lived in the region known today as Turkestan, from east of the Caspian Sea to Xinjiang (SIN-john) on China's western frontier. Large-scale population movements and frequent warfare between competing tribal confederations became common. Most of the steppe societies had skilled horsemen and were led by warrior chieftains. Some Central Asian peoples attacked and occasionally conquered northern China, and over the centuries various Central Asian peoples also migrated through the mountain ranges into northwest India.

Central Asian Societies

Although much of Central Asia was steppe lands, some areas supported city life. Archaeologists regularly find previously unknown sites, such as Jiroft in southern Iran, to expand our knowledge. In recent years these discoveries have revealed an early urban society in Central Asia, which some call the Oxus (OX-uhs), after the river that runs through the area. The Oxus society apparently thrived between 2200 and 1800 B.C.E., when the Harappan culture was also at its height, building walled cities with mud-brick buildings around desert oases in what is now Uzbekistan and Turkmenistan. Enjoying a wetter climate than now, the people grew wheat and barley. They also forged bronze axes, carved figurines of women from stone and ivory, and decorated pottery. A tiny stamp seal with letter-like symbols dated to 2300 B.C.E. is evidence for writing, and so far the writing has not been linked to any other society. The Oxus cities, perhaps independent city-states, were situated along the "Silk Road" trade routes between India and China, suggesting that this trade may be older than is often thought. They were closely linked to the Harappans and probably traded with China, Jiroft, and Mesopotamia. Eventually the cities were abandoned and, over the centuries, buried by sand.

SECTION SUMMARY

- The earliest Indian urban society, the Harappan, emerged in the Indus River Valley around 2600 B.C.E.

- The peaceful Harappans had well-planned cities with advanced sanitation, a culture that gave women high status, and a written language.

- The Harappans invented cotton cloth, and Harappan cities enjoyed extensive foreign trade with western and Central Asia.

- Harappan cities declined for unknown reasons, possibly due to environmental catastrophe.

- The steppes of Central Asia were home to mostly horsemen, but evidence of an urban society has been discovered on the Oxus River.

THE ARYANS AND A NEW INDIAN SOCIETY, 1500–600 B.C.E.

How did Indian society and the Hindu religion emerge from the mixing of Aryan and local cultures?

Aryans Indo-European-speaking nomadic pastoralists who migrated from Iran into northwest India.

Throughout India's long history, many people migrated from elsewhere into the subcontinent, some of them conquering parts of India, and the assimilation of these various newcomers resulted in an increasingly diverse Indian society. One such group of invaders were the **Aryans** (AIR-ee-unzs), Indo-European-speaking nomadic pastoralists who migrated into northwest India, expanded across northern India, and introduced new traditions to the area. The Aryan expansion between 1500 and 1000 B.C.E. built the foundation for a new society that mixed Aryan culture with the traditions of the indigenous peoples, including the Dravidians. Over many centuries a fusion of Aryan and Dravidian cultures occurred that historians label the **Indo-Aryan synthesis**, forging a new social system and Hinduism, a religion of diverse beliefs. But the Aryans had a greater impact in the north than in the mostly Dravidian south, which retained its own languages and writing systems. Despite regular contact with western, Central, and Southeast Asia, the patterns that developed were so distinctive and enduring that India even today is unlike any other society.

Indo-Aryan synthesis The fusion of Aryan and Dravidian cultures in India over many centuries.

The Aryan Peoples and the Vedas

Aryan Migrations

Most scholars agree that the Aryans began migrating by horse-drawn chariot from Iran (the Persian word for "Aryan") or Turkestan into northwestern India between 1600 and 1400 B.C.E., after the collapse of the Harappan cities. The migration to India came when rainfall in the Indus region was increasing again, improving economic conditions. Some historians and Indian nationalists argue that Aryan settlement in India was far older and that the Harappans may have been Aryans. However, in the mainstream view, the Aryans arrived in small groups over several centuries, bringing with them a rich oral literature and unusual ideas about government, society, and religion. For the next 500 years, the Aryans expanded throughout northern India as more arrived. But archaeologists have found little material evidence, such as pots or weapons, that might tell us more about Aryan migration and settlement. Furthermore, unlike the Chinese and Greeks, ancient Indians never developed a tradition of historiography, the study and writing of history, perhaps because their conceptions of time emphasized the temporary nature of existence.

Vedas The Aryans' "books of knowledge," the principal source of religious belief for Hindus: a vast collection of sacred hymns to the gods and thoughts about religion, philosophy, and magic.

Much of what we know about the ancient Aryans comes from their literature, the **Vedas** (VAY-duhs) ("books of knowledge"). A vast collection of sacred hymns to the gods and thoughts about religion, philosophy, and magic, the Vedas were based on oral accounts carefully preserved by bards, the memory experts of each Indo-European tribe, through a vibrant oral tradition. The Vedas reflected the world-view of the priestly class and were already old when written down. They are the principal early source of Hindu religious belief. From the Vedas we can infer that the Aryans were organized into tribes that frequently moved their settlements. Their class system consisted of warriors, priests, and commoners. They were a cattle-raising people, as is reflected in one of the hymns: "A bard am I, my father a leech, And my mother a grinder of corn. Diverse in means, but all wishing wealth, Alike for cattle we strive."[14]

Conflict and Conquest

They were also a militaristic people who harnessed horses to chariots and skillfully wielded bows and arrows and bronze axes. They had fought their way through blistering deserts and snowy mountains to reach India. Some Vedas celebrate Aryan victories against fortified settlements inhabited by peoples, probably including Dravidians, who had darker skins than the Aryans: "For fear of thee fled the dark-hued races, scattered abroad, deserting their possessions."[15] The various Aryan tribes could unite against a common enemy, but most of the time they fought against each other.

Sanskrit The classical language of north India, originally both written and spoken but now reserved for religious and literary writing.

In India the Aryans mixed their language with those of local people, creating **Sanskrit** (SAN-skrit), the classical written and spoken language of north India, through which the Vedas were preserved. By the fourth century B.C.E., however, vernacular (everyday) Indo-European spoken languages like Hindi and Bengali had become dominant in north India, and Sanskrit gradually became mostly a written language for religious and literary works. Since few Indians today learn to write or speak Sanskrit, some fear the language may eventually become extinct.

Early Aryan Government, Society, and Religion

The early Aryan political and social structure was tribal and marked by persistent military conflict. Each tribe was governed by an autocratic male, known as a *raja,* who sought as much power for himself and his group as possible. The most powerful tribe seems to have been the Bharata (BAA-ray-tuh). Later the **Mahabharata** (MA-huh-BAA-ray-tuh) ("Great Bharata"), an Aryan epic and the world's longest poem, spun a complex and entertaining tale of many cousins and their titanic battles for supremacy. Reflecting life around 1000 B.C.E., the *Mahabharata* is, like Homer's *Iliad*, drenched in the blood of endless struggles over succession and supremacy. The *Ramayana* (ruh-MA-yawn-uh) ("The Story of Rama"), another Aryan epic written down sometime after 500 B.C.E., may be based on the extension of Aryan power into southern India.

> **Mahabharata** ("Great Bharata") An Aryan epic and the world's longest poem.

Aryan family structure was patriarchal, with the father dominating his wives and children. In the centuries to follow, both male supremacy and a hierarchy based on age became the standard Indian family pattern. The Aryans developed a living pattern known as the joint family, also common in China, in which the wives of all the sons moved into the larger patriarchal household, which included members from three or even four generations. The status of Aryan women changed with time. The early Aryans educated both daughters and sons in the Vedas. One Vedic hymn encouraged women to speak publicly, and women may have composed some of the hymns. Later women became more restricted and daughters less valued. They needed to obtain dowries (gifts for the prospective in-laws) in order to marry, could not participate in the sacrifices to gods, and did not inherit property.

> **Aryan Families**

The Vedas also reveal something of Aryan recreational interests. The leading sports seem to have been horse-drawn chariot racing and gambling. Both dice and chess were invented in India. Gambling features prominently in the *Mahabharata;* one raja loses his kingdom through his fondness for games of chance. The Aryans were fond of wine and music, using such instruments as lutes, flutes, and drums. Song and dance remain an integral component of Indian religious worship and ritual.

As sacred texts, the Vedas contained considerable information about Aryan religion, the significance of various gods, and the role of priests. Each Aryan tribe boasted its own bards, poets who were also priests. Because they alone had memorized the Vedic hymns, these bards presided over sacrifices and rituals. The oldest and most important Veda, the *Rig Veda* ("Verses of Knowledge"), probably composed between 1500 and 1000 B.C.E., contains over 1,000 poems written in Sanskrit, most of them soliciting the favor of Aryan gods.

> **Aryan Religion**

The Aryans worshiped a pantheon of nature gods, to whom they offered sacrifices. The *Rig Veda* describes some thirty-three deities, several of which are prominent. They are led by the thunderbolt-wielding war-god Indra (INN-druh), who is ever youthful, heroic, and victorious. Many poems celebrate the awesome power of the deities, as in the following tribute to the storm-gods: "You are terrible and powerful, O storm gods. You bring everlasting rain in the desert. Dark rain clouds shroud the sky, Turning day into night, drenching the earth."[16] Aryan religion also included speculations on the deepest mysteries of existence. One poem, the "Hymn of Creation," is one of the most ancient expressions of questions about the creation of the universe: "Who really knows? Who will here proclaim it? Whence was this creation? The gods came afterwards, with the creation of the universe. Who then really knows whence it has arisen?"[17] This hymn also suggests a time before time when there was no space or sky, night or day, life or death. Then, in a kind of Big Bang, the cosmos was created by the power of heat (see Chapter 1).

Aryan Expansion and State Building in North India

Many Aryans eventually moved eastward into the Ganges (GAN-geez) Valley between 1000 and 450 B.C.E., building kingdoms and mixing with local peoples. During this time they changed through conflict, cooperation, and assimilation with the peoples they encountered. They eventually adopted Dravidian systems of farming, village structure, and some religious concepts, but they also contributed their language, social system, and many religious beliefs to the mix.

Throughout north India, city development and economic growth encouraged political consolidation into kingdoms. By the sixth century B.C.E. sixteen major Aryan kingdoms stretched from Bengal westward to the fringes of Afghanistan, most of them in the central Ganges region. However, kings did not have unlimited power; they were still advised by councils of warriors. Thus no kingdom was yet strong enough to conquer all the others and create a unified government for all north India until the establishment of the Mauryan Empire in 321 B.C.E. (see Chapter 7).

> **Political Development**

The Roots of the Caste System

The Indo-Aryan synthesis modified the social structure, which became increasingly complex as the expanding Aryans integrated diverse people. Perhaps incorporating some Harappan traditions, a four-tiered class division emerged that comprised the **brahmans** (BRAH-munz),

> **brahmans** The priests, the highest-ranking caste in Hindu society.

[17]Burton Stein, *A History of India.* Copyright ©1988 by Wiley-Blackwell Publishing Ltd. Reprinted with permission.

Aryan Warfare Vedic stories remain popular in modern India. This scene from an old temple wall of Aryan warfare depicts embattled gods and demons from the *Mahabharata*.

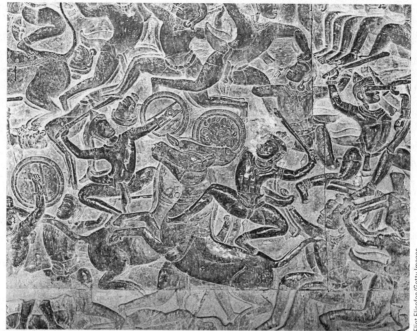

Eliot Elisofon/Getty Images

kshatriyas Warriors and landowners headed by the rajas in the Hindu caste system.

vaisyas The merchants and artisans in the Hindu caste system.

sudras The poorer farmers, farm workers, and menial laborers in the Hindu caste system.

or priests; the **kshatriyas** (kuh-SHOT-ree-uhs), the warriors and landowners; the **vaisyas** (VIGH-shuhs), or merchants and artisans; and the **sudras** (SOO-druhs), mostly poorer farmers, farm workers, and menial laborers. The Aryans allocated the three highest categories to themselves. The priests enjoyed many special privileges as guardians and interpreters of sacred knowledge. Over time the sudras, mostly of non-Aryan origins, were locked into a permanent low status and were prohibited from studying the magically potent Vedic hymns.

The Sanskrit term for a class division, or ritual status, was *varna* (VARN-uh), which meant "[skin] color." The term suggests that the lighter-skinned Aryans wanted to maintain their domination over, and purity from "pollution" by, the darker-skinned indigenous people. Many centuries later, Portuguese visitors referred to the system as *castas* ("pure"); hence the origin of the Western term *caste*. Aryans used religion to justify this class system. One of the hymns in the *Rig Veda* attributed the classes to the Lord of Beings, the originator of the universe: "When they divided the Man, into how many parts did they divide him? What was his mouth, what were his arms, what were his thighs and his feet called? The brahman was his mouth, of his arms was made the kshatriya. His thighs became the vaisya, of his feet were born the sudra."[18]

The Caste System

caste system The four-tiered Hindu social system comprising hereditary social classes that restrict the occupation of members and their relations with members of other castes.

pariahs The large group of outcasts or untouchables below the official Hindu castes.

Gradually, over many centuries, this four-tiered class hierarchy evolved into the immensely complex **caste system**. Each hereditary social class was restricted to certain occupations, and its members were restricted in their relations with members of other castes. For example, only members of closely allied groups could intermarry. Below the caste system were a large group of outcasts (**pariahs**) or untouchables, labeled such because the higher castes considered their touch defiling. The pariahs performed tasks considered "unclean," such as tanning animal hides and removing manure. This system, firmly in place by 500 B.C.E., differed in many respects from the modern caste system. Although the system was never rigid and changed over time, it provided the basic structure of Hindu society for several millennia.

Indo-Aryan Society and Economy

Bhagavad Gita

Bhagavad Gita ("Lord's Song") A poem in the *Mahabharata* that is the most treasured piece of ancient Hindu literature.

The Vedas reveal some of the expectations and attitudes of ancient Indian society. For example, contained within the *Mahabharata* is a philosophical poem called the ***Bhagavad Gita*** (BAA-guh-vad GEE-tuh) ("Lord's Song"), the most treasured piece of ancient Hindu literature (see Witness to the Past: Hindu Values in the *Bhagavad Gita*). It encourages people to do their duty to their superiors and kinsmen resolutely and unselfishly. It also explains that death is not a time of grief because the soul is indestructible. The other great ancient epic, the *Ramayana*, resembles the *Odyssey* of the Greek Homer in that it tells of endless court intrigues and a hero's wanderings while his wife remains chaste and loyal.

We know something of Indo-Aryan gender relations. The *Ramayana* illustrates the early Hindu notion of perfect manhood and womanhood through the main characters: Rama, the husband, and Sita (SEE-tuh), his wife, who demonstrate mutual loyalty, devotion, and self-sacrifice. But Sita

Hindu Values in the *Bhagavad Gita*

The *Bhagavad Gita*, a philosophical poem in the *Mahabharata*, helped shape the ethical traditions of India while providing Hindus with a practical guide to everyday life. The following excerpt is part of a dialogue between the god Krishna (Vishnu) and the poem's conflicted hero, the warrior Arjuna (are-JUNE-ah), on the eve of a great battle in which Arjuna will slaughter his uncles, cousins, teachers, and friends. The reading summarizes some of Krishna's advice in justifying the battle. Krishna suggests that Arjuna must follow his destiny, for while the physical body is impermanent, the soul is eternal. The slain will be reborn. Furthermore, humans are responsible for their own destiny through their behavior and mental discipline. They also, like Arjuna, need to fulfill their obligations to society.

The wise grieve neither for the living nor for the dead. There has never been a time when you and I and the kings gathered here have not existed, nor will there ever be a time when we will cease to exist. As the same person inhabits the body through childhood, youth, and old age, so too at the time of death he attains another body. The wise are not deluded by these changes.

When the senses contact sense objects, a person experiences cold or heat, pleasure or pain. These experiences are fleeting; they come and go. Bear them patiently. . . . Those who are not affected by these changes, who are the same in pleasure and pain, are truly wise and fit for immortality. Assert your strength and realize this!

The impermanent has no reality; reality lies in the eternal. Those who have seen the boundary between these two have attained the end of all knowledge. Realize that which pervades the universe and is indestructible; no power can affect this unchanging, imperishable reality. The body is mortal but he who dwells in the body is immortal and immeasurable. . . . As a man abandons worn-out clothes and acquires new ones, so when the body is worn out a new one is acquired by the Self, who lives within. . . . Death is inevitable for the living; birth is inevitable for the dead. Since these are unavoidable, you should not sorrow. . . .

Now listen to the principles of yoga [mental and physical discipline to free the soul]. By practicing these you can break through the bonds of karma. On this path effort never goes to waste, and there is no failure. . . . When you keep thinking about sense objects, attachment comes. Attachment breeds desire, the lust of possession that burns to anger. . . .

They are forever free who renounce all selfish desires and break free from the ego-cage of "I," "me," and "mine" to be united with the Lord. This is the supreme state. Attain to this, and pass from death to immortality. . . . Strive constantly to serve the welfare of the world; by devotion to selfless work one attains the supreme goal of life. Do your work with the welfare of others always in mind.

THINKING ABOUT THE READING

1. What key aspects of Hindu thought are revealed in the poem?
2. How do the attitudes toward life, death, and desire influence the behavior of individuals?
3. What are some of the viewpoints in this ancient poem that might be considered universal in their appeal?

Source: From *The Bhagavad Gita,* trans. by Eknath Easwaran, founder of the Blue Mountain Center of Meditation, copyright 1985. Reprinted by permission of the Nilgiri Press, P.O. Box 256, Tomales, CA 94971, www.easwaran.org.

is also patient and faithful in supporting her husband and family. The Sita ideal strongly influenced cultural expectations of womanhood, especially in north India. Women enjoyed a higher status in south India, where both matriarchal and matrilineal traditions persisted for centuries, and goddesses remained especially central to religious life. But even in the north some women mastered the Vedas and mixed freely with men.

Indo-Aryan technology derived from both foreign and local developments. The Aryans used iron, especially once they reached iron-rich districts in the Ganges region around 1000 B.C.E. Soon after they arrived in India they made the transition from a pastoral economy to a combination of pastoral and agricultural pursuits that emphasized grains like barley and wheat. One Veda prays: "Successfully let the good ploughshares' thrust part the earth, successfully let the ploughman follow the beasts of draft."[19] The use of plows and the expansion of irrigated agriculture greatly increased the available food supply and thus fostered population growth. India's population in 500 B.C.E. has been estimated at 25 million, including 15 million in the Ganges Valley.

Hinduism: A New Religion of Diverse Roots

Although Indian religion has changed much since the Harappans, it has remained unique. Nothing in the Middle East or Europe remotely resembles basic bedrock Indian beliefs such as reincarnation. What modern Indians would clearly recognize as Hinduism had probably not fully formed until the beginning of the Common Era. The term Hinduism was not applied to these traditions until recent centuries. But the foundations were clearly established in ancient times. Hinduism

47

can be seen historically as a synthesis of Aryan beliefs with Harappan and other Dravidian traditions that developed over many centuries. As the religion became more complex, it probed ever more deeply into cosmic mysteries, resulting in ferment and questioning.

Hindu Beliefs

The Hindu religious system became one of the richest and most complex in the world, with gods, devotions, and celebrations drawn from various regional cultures. The Aryans gradually turned from their old tribal gods to deities of Harappan origin such as Shiva. Hence the rise of the great gods of Hinduism: *Brahma* (BRA-ma) (the Creator of life); *Vishnu* (VISH-noo) (the Preserver of life); and *Shiva* (among other functions, the Destroyer of life). Vishnu is a benevolent deity who works continually for the welfare of the world. Shiva personifies the life force and embodies both constructive and destructive power. Hinduism never developed a rigid core of beliefs uniting all followers; instead, it loosely linked together diverse practices and cults that shared a reverence for the Vedas. The Vedic thinkers were influenced by pre-Aryan meditation techniques and mystical practices of possible Harappan origin, such as those that were later known as *yoga*. In the eternal quest for divine favor, the Hindus came to believe that everyone must behave properly so that the universe can function in an orderly manner. They came to see human existence as temporary and fleeting and only the realm of the gods as eternal.

Religious Development

The Vedas underwent three major stages of development to become accepted as revealed literature. The earliest stage included the poems and hymns in the *Rig Veda* and several other collections. From around 1000 to 700 B.C.E. a series of prose commentaries on the earlier Vedas appeared, elaborating on the meaning of the Vedic literature and also prescribing proper procedures for worshiping the gods. These commentaries are called the **Brahmanas** (BRA-ma-nus), since they emphasize the central role of the priests, or brahmans. At this time, the prevailing religion can be termed Brahmanism. Later still, between 800 and 600 B.C.E., a third group of more philosophical writings appeared, mostly in the form of 108 poetic dialogues known as the **Upanishads** (oo-PAHN-ih-shahds) ("sitting around a teacher"). These writings, which speculated on the ultimate truth about the creation of life, offered a striking contrast to the emphasis on ritual, devotion, and ethics in the older works because they came from an atmosphere of questioning and rebellion against priestly power. They also gave women more importance; for example, the dialogues include the story of an exceptionally learned female. The religious atmosphere of ancient India was dynamic, with growing tensions between competing ideas about the nature of existence and appropriate human behavior. For example, the *Ramayana* contrasts the luxury-filled decadence of the royal courts with the austere existence of hermit-sages dwelling in the forest and practicing forms of meditation and mysticism. The movements that developed out of this ferment in the first millennium B.C.E. transformed the framework of Indian religion, fostering both Buddhism and the modified form of Brahmanism known today as Hinduism, as we shall see in Chapter 5.

Brahmanas Commentaries on the Vedas that emphasize the role of priests (brahmans).

Upanishads Ancient Indian philosophical writings that speculated on the ultimate truth about the creation of life.

SECTION SUMMARY

- The Indo-European Aryans, a cattle-raising tribal people, migrated into north India 3,500 years ago.

- The Vedas, written in Sanskrit, are religious writings that reveal information on the Aryan religion and their patriarchal culture.

- Aryan priests supervised the worship of the religion's many nature gods.

- Eventually Aryans built kingdoms in the Ganges River Basin.

- Aryan and local cultures mixed together over the centuries and eventually produced a unique four-tiered caste system.

- The *Bhagavad Gita,* which emphasizes one's earthly duty and the soul's immortality, became the most treasured piece of Indian literature.

- Hinduism developed over many centuries but never became a rigid belief structure.

- The philosophical *Upanishads* represented a departure from the emphasis on priestly ritual.

CHAPTER SUMMARY

Mesopotamian society and early Indian society were two of humankind's first experiments with farming, cities, and states, both using technologies that were unheard of in Neolithic times. These ancient societies also developed different religious notions, social systems, and political structures. They were shaped by the challenges and opportunities of flood-prone river valleys: Mesopotamian society arose between the Tigris and Euphrates Rivers, and Harappan society arose in the Indus River Valley. Mesopotamians introduced the first cities and states, the cuneiform system of writing, bronze metalworking, mathematics, and science. Their many kingdoms were united under several different empires. Mesopotamia was also part of the early trade networks linking the Mediterranean Basin with India. Such connections among societies were a crucial and continuing part of history.

In northwest India the Harappans built peaceful, bustling, and well-planned cities. They produced cotton products and developed sophisticated sanitation systems. The Harappans also participated in a trading network that reached into the Fertile Crescent and Central Asia. After the Harappan collapse, Aryan migrants established political control. The mixing of Harappan and Aryan cultures shaped a new Indian society, establishing the foundation for a caste system and the religion of Hinduism.

KEY TERMS

Fertile Crescent	Shiva	*Mahabharata*	pariahs
ziggurat	steppes	brahmans	*Bhagavad Gita*
patriarchy	Aryans	kshatriyas	*Brahmanas*
cuneiform	Indo-Aryan synthesis	vaisyas	*Upanishads*
Harappan	Vedas	sudras	
Dravidian	Sanskrit	caste system	

EBOOK AND WEBSITE RESOURCES

e PRIMARY SOURCE
The *Epic of Gilgamesh*

e INTERACTIVE MAPS
Map 2.1 Ancient Mesopotamia
Map 2.2 Harappan Culture and Aryan Migrations

LINKS

Exploring Ancient World Cultures (http://eawc.evansville.edu/). Excellent site run by Evansville University, with essays and links on the ancient Near East and Europe.

Harappa: The Ancient Indus Valley and the British Raj in India and Pakistan (www.harappa.com). Essays and photos on the Indus societies and excavations.

Indus Valley Civilization (http://ancienthistory.about.com/od/indusvalleyciv/Indian_Subcontinent.htm). Gives access to many sites and links on ancient India, run by About.com.

Internet Ancient History Sourcebook (http://www.fordham.edu/halsall/ancient/asbook.html). Exceptionally rich collection of links and primary source readings.

Internet Indian History Sourcebook (http://www.fordham.edu/halsall/india/indiasbook.html). An invaluable collection of sources and links on ancient India.

Plus flashcards, practice quizzes, and more. Go to: www.cengage.com/history/lockard/globalsocnet2e.

SUGGESTED READING

Allchin, F. R. *The Archaeology of Early Historic South Asia: The Emergence of Cities and States.* Cambridge: Cambridge University Press, 1995. A scholarly overview.

Avari, Burjor. *India: The Ancient Past. A History of the Indian Sub-Continent from 7000 BC to AD 1200.* New York: Routledge, 2007. A balanced, up-to-date overview.

Basham, A. L. *The Wonder That Was India,* 3rd ed. London: Macmillan, 1968 (reprinted 1999 by Rupa and Company, New Delhi). An older study but still the best survey of premodern India.

Bottero, Jean. *Everyday Life in Ancient Mesopotamia.* Baltimore: Johns Hopkins University Press, 2001. Summarizes recent discoveries about Mesopotamian social and cultural life.

Crawfurd, Harriet. *Sumer and the Sumerians,* 2nd ed. Cambridge: Cambridge University Press, 2004. An up-to-date and interdisciplinary summary of the achievements of the Sumerians.

Dunstan, William E. *The Ancient Near East.* New York: Harcourt Brace, 1998. Designed for the general reader, this work makes sense of the confusing array of states and empires in western Asia.

Kenoyer, Jonathan Mark. *Ancient Cities of the Indus Valley Civilization.* New York: Oxford University Press, 1998. A valuable, well-illustrated summary of the most recent discoveries.

McIntosh, Jane. *A Peaceful Realm: The Rise and Fall of the Indus River Civilization.* Boulder, CO: Westview, 2001. A comprehensive, well-illustrated survey of the Harappans, based on recent archaeological research.

Noble, D. Brendan. *The Ancient World: A Social and Cultural History,* 7th ed. Upper Saddle Back, N.J.: Prentice Hall, 2009. Survey text with much on Mesopotamia.

Sandars, N. K., trans. *The Epic of Gilgamesh.* New York: Penguin Books, 1972. An easy introduction to the ancient Mesopotamian world-view.

Stiebing, William H. *Ancient Near Eastern History and Culture.* New York: Longman, 2003. An up-to-date survey of ancient western Asia, Egypt, and the eastern Mediterranean.

Thapar, Romila. *Early India from the Origins to AD 1300.* Berkeley: University of California Press, 2002. A valuable revision of the standard history of early India, detailed and comprehensive.

Wolpert, Stanley. *A New History of India,* 8th ed. New York: Oxford University Press, 2009. One of the most readable survey texts.

ANCIENT SOCIETIES IN AFRICA AND THE MEDITERRANEAN, 5000–600 B.C.E.

George Holton/Photo Researchers, Inc.

Abu Simbel
The great temple with its colossal statues at Abu Simbel overlooking the Nile River in Egypt was built as a monument to honor the powerful thirteenth-century B.C.E. pharaoh Rameses the Great, who presided over empire building and economic prosperity.

> Behold, the heart of his majesty was satisfied with making a very great monument; never has happened the like since the beginning. He made it as an everlasting fortress. It is wrought with gold and many costly stones.
>
> —Temple inscription at Thebes, Egypt, fourteenth century B.C.E.[1]

Around 1460 B.C.E. Queen Hatshepsut (hat-SHEP-soot), the powerful ruler of Egypt, issued a decree to build a temple on the banks of the Nile River for the glory of the highest god, Amon-Re (AH-muhn-RAY). The temple would have terraced gardens planted with fragrant myrrh. To obtain the myrrh, the queen ordered an expedition to be sent down the Red Sea to Punt (poont) on the coast of northeast Africa, probably modern Somalia (so-MAH-lee-uh). Egyptian ships had previously visited Punt at various times. Now Hatshepsut, for reasons of commerce, religion, and personal ambition, ordered that contact with Punt to be renewed. The new expedition was extremely successful, returning with myrrh trees, jewels, incense, and other treasures. Like other rulers before and after her, Queen Hatshepsut commemorated her achievements with inscriptions and pictures, in this case by summarizing the results of the trading expedition on the walls of her magnificent new temple: "The loading of the cargo-boats with great marvels of Punt, with all the good woods, ebony, pure ivory, gold, monkeys, [and] skins of leopard. Never were brought such things to any king, since the world was."[2] To obtain such luxury products, Egyptians became ship-builders and sailors, becoming connected to a much wider world. Foreign trade made Egypt the ancient world's wealthiest society.

Among the Egyptians and some other African and eastern Mediterranean societies—including the Hebrews, Minoans (mih-NO-uhns), Mycenaeans (my-suh-NEE-uhns), Phoenicians (fo-NEE-shuhns), and early Greeks—we see the same kind of dramatic changes resulting from contact among different peoples that fostered urban life in Mesopotamia and India. Egypt greatly influenced neighboring peoples and was also influenced by them. This interaction among neighbors promoted cultural development in the Nile Valley and the Mediterranean. Like the Tigris-Euphrates and Indus Valleys, the Nile Valley made possible population growth, social organization, large state structures, and elaborate religious systems.

Ancient peoples also created unique and complex societies elsewhere in Africa and the eastern Mediterranean. Diverse sub-Saharan African societies developed or borrowed farming and metal technologies, and some built cities. However, unlike Egypt's spectacular pyramids, over the centuries many of the sub-Saharan people's monuments and buildings were covered by rain forest, blowing sand, or wayward rivers. Meanwhile, on the islands and shores of the eastern Mediterranean, various peoples traded widely, built cities whose ruins still interest visitors, and developed religious concepts that endure to this day.

FOCUS QUESTIONS

1. How did the environment shape ancient Egypt?
2. What were some unique features of Egyptian society?
3. What were some achievements of the ancient Nubian, Sudanic, and Bantu peoples?
4. What were the contributions of the Hebrews, Minoans, Mycenaeans, Phoenicians, and Dorian Greeks to later societies in the region?

e Visit the website and eBook for additional study materials and interactive tools: www.cengage.com/history/lockard/globalsocnet2e

THE RISE OF EGYPTIAN SOCIETY

How did the environment shape ancient Egypt?

The formation of Egyptian society involved interactions among many different peoples, producing a mixed society so successful that it survived in more or less its basic form for nearly 2,000 years. The classical Greek historian Herodotus (heh-ROD-uh-tuhs) called Egypt the "gift of the Nile" because it owed its existence to the Nile River. The river valley's African location allowed the Egyptians to develop many traditions and ideas completely different from those in nearby Mesopotamia, Palestine, and Crete.

North African Environments

North Africa, a region stretching from Morocco to the Red Sea, has been shaped by several environmental features. In ancient times maritime routes in the Mediterranean Sea linked societies along its shores and islands and enabled the spread of products, ideas, technologies, and peoples. The Red Sea connected Egypt to northeast Africa, Arabia, and India. Agriculture, then and now, is mainly possible only in a narrow fertile valley in Egypt nourished by the Nile River. To the west of the Nile lies the vast Sahara Desert, which stretches all the way to the western coast of Africa. In northwestern Africa (today's Tunisia, Algeria, and Morocco) mountain ranges separate the desert from the Mediterranean and Atlantic coastal plains, where farming is also possible.

The Nile River is the key to understanding the formation of Egyptian society (see Map 3.1). The settlers in the northern Nile Valley enjoyed many centuries of uninterrupted development thanks to the inhospitable deserts on both sides of the valley. This environment allowed Egypt to thrive for a thousand years without significant outside challenge. Since the Nile was navigable and slow moving, boats drifted northward with the current and used southerly winds to move south; thus the river was a great highway that promoted political stability and uniformity. By the fourth millennium B.C.E. the grasslands and forests of earlier times had turned to desert and the valley was fertile only because of the silt deposited by the fall flooding of the Nile.

Foundations of Egyptian Society

The same process that transformed farming societies into urban societies in Mesopotamia took place a few centuries later, around 3100 or 3000 B.C.E., in the Nile Valley. Here too, with little rainfall, irrigation works were necessary to take advantage of the rich silt. But unlike the 100-mile-wide Tigris-Euphrates Valley, the river valley here was only 10 miles wide, with the result that the population was more protected from the outside and more concentrated.

The Nile Valley continued to be shaped by the arrival of new peoples. Many of the earliest settlers were migrants from a Sahara region that had been fertile but began drying out some 6,000 to 7,000 years ago. This environmental change forced the peoples to move to the grasslands of western Africa, the northern coast, or into the Nile Valley. Other early migrants came from western Asia and from the Horn of Africa, southeast of Egypt. The Egyptian population eventually included peoples of Semitic, Berber (BUHR-bur), Ethiopian, Somali, black African, and, later, Greek origins. Egypt also enjoyed close relationships with the Nubians, black African peoples living along the Nile in what is today southern Egypt and northern Sudan. The ancient Egyptian language belonged to the Afro-Asiatic family, which included Semitic and Berber languages and many African tongues. Most of the people in northwest Africa were Berbers.

Unlike the floods in Mesopotamia, the Nile floods came on an exact schedule. Egyptians formed a central government to organize large numbers of people to prepare the cropland to take best advantage of the flooding, such as by building dikes to contain the floodwater used in irrigation. The backbreaking work required to maintain the irrigation canals reminds us that, for peasants at least, a complex society was a mixed blessing. If the floodwaters were not carefully channeled, little would grow. In periods of political disorder, when weak central governments left the dikes untended, the desert spread and famine struck the land. When order prevailed and the dikes were maintained, the valley could support a high population. By 1000 B.C.E., the population had reached 3 or 4 million. Given their general good fortune, it is not surprising that Egyptians saw themselves as the center of the world. As far as they knew for many centuries, they were.

In earliest times, the 100-mile-long area from the modern city of Cairo down the Nile to the sea was considered Lower Egypt or the northern kingdom, at the end of which was the fertile Nile

CHRONOLOGY

	Egypt	Sub-Saharan Africa	Eastern Mediterrnean
3000 B.C.E.	**2686–2181** B.C.E. Old Kingdom		
2000 B.C.E.	**2040–1786** B.C.E. Middle Kingdom **1550–1064** B.C.E. New Kingdom	**2000** B.C.E.**–1000** C.E. Bantu migrations **1800–1500** B.C.E. Nubian kingdom of Kerma	**2000–1400** B.C.E. Minoan Crete **1600–1200** B.C.E. Mycenaea **1500–650** B.C.E. Phoenicia
1000 B.C.E.		**900** B.C.E. Rise of Kush	**1000–722** B.C.E. Hebrew kingdoms

Delta (see Map 3.1). The area from Cairo to Aswan (AS-wahn), some 650 miles south, was Upper Egypt or the southern kingdom. These two states were united by the legendary Upper Egyptian King Menes (MEH-neez) in about 3000 B.C.E. The rest of Egyptian history is usually divided into three successive eras: the Old Kingdom (2686–2181 B.C.E.), the Middle Kingdom (2040–1786 B.C.E.), and the New Kingdom (1550–1064 B.C.E.). During each period various dynasties ruled Egypt, and the intermediate periods were marked by disorder or foreign conquest. After 1075 B.C.E. Egypt increasingly fell victim to the empire building of western Asian, Mediterranean, and other African peoples.

pharaohs Rulers of ancient Egypt.

The Old Kingdom: Egypt's Golden Age

When we think of ancient Egypt, most of us picture the Old Kingdom because of the pyramids built in this splendid era. The pyramids, which have awed visitors for thousands of years, illustrate the Egyptian self-confidence of this period. Perhaps the greatest and most enduring of the ancient world's construction projects, they reflected a powerful government, unsurpassed organizing talent, a prosperous society, and unique values and beliefs (see Chronology: Ancient Egypt, 3100–525 B.C.E.). The largest pyramid, that of the twenty-fifth-century pharaoh Cheops at Giza, is nearly 500 feet high, covers an area of nearly 200 square yards, and remained the tallest building in the world until the twentieth century. All the nearly 6 million tons of limestone used in the building was moved into place on ramps and wooden rollers by tens of thousands of workers without the benefit of winches, pulleys, or scaffolds. Most of the workers were not slaves, and many were highly skilled artisans. Workers and their families lived in villages where the government supplied them with ample food and good housing. This did not prevent complaints, however. One disgruntled draftsman wrote to his superior: "If there is some beer, you do not look for me, but if there is work, you do look for me. I am a man who has no beer in his house."[3]

The rulers of Egypt, known as **pharaohs** (FAIR-os) (from *per-o* or "great house"), had immense power to order such projects because their subjects believed them to be the divine

Map 3.1
Ancient Egypt and Nubia

The Egyptian and Nubian societies developed along the Nile River. Egypt traded with, and sometimes controlled, the peoples of the Levant on the eastern Mediterranean coast.

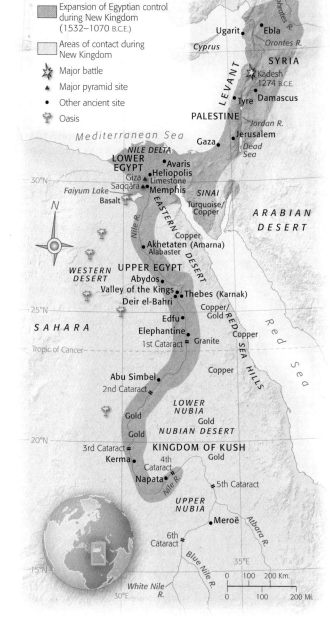

Old Kingdom (2575–2134 B.C.E.) and Middle Kingdom (2040–1640 B.C.E.)

Expansion of Egyptian control during New Kingdom (1532–1070 B.C.E.)

Areas of contact during New Kingdom

✸ Major battle

▲ Major pyramid site

• Other ancient site

Oasis

e Interactive Map

CHRONOLOGY
Ancient Egypt, 3100–525 B.C.E.

3100–3000 B.C.E. Upper and Lower Egypt unified

2686–2181 B.C.E. Old Kingdom and age of pyramids

2181–2041 B.C.E. First Intermediate Period

2040–1786 B.C.E. Middle Kingdom

1786–1550 B.C.E. Second Intermediate Period

1550–1064 B.C.E. New Kingdom

1064–525 B.C.E. Third Intermediate Period

hieroglyphics The Egyptian writing system, which evolved from pictograms into stylized pictures expressing ideas.

offspring of the sun-god Re, the creator of heaven, earth, and humans. Pharaohs also had soldiers as well as the authority of priests and religion to support their rule. Writing, invented by 3000 B.C.E., enabled the administration to function smoothly. The Egyptian writing system of **hieroglyphics** (hi-ruh-GLIF-iks), like Sumerian cuneiform, evolved from pictograms into stylized pictures expressing ideas. The pharaohs, who were considered the owners of all the land and people in Egypt, governed a highly centralized state from the city of Memphis, strategically located where the Nile Valley met the delta. A chief minister supervised the administrative structure and ensured that taxes were collected, grain properly stored in government warehouses, and salaries paid to government officials. Most ministers came from noble families, but occasionally pharaohs recruited for talent. One advised his son: "Do not distinguish the son of a noble man from a poor man, but take to thyself a man because of the work of his hands."[4]

The royal government also expanded trade through regional networks. The pharaohs dispatched expeditions east to Arabia, south to Nubia (NOO-bee-ah), and northeast to Lebanon, Syria, and Anatolia. Although the Egyptians may not have invented international maritime trade, the records from the Pharaoh Snefru (SNEF-roo) around 2600 B.C.E. provide the first known written accounts of this activity. They describe the arrival of forty ships filled with cedar logs, probably from today's Lebanon, to make the cedar wood doors of the royal palace.

Some historians believe that the expense of the great royal tombs eventually impoverished the country during the final decades of the twenty-second century B.C.E. The royal governors became more independent of the ruler at Memphis, whose authority was thereby weakened. Egyptian beliefs led people to accept this development. Many peasants reasoned that if the power of the ruler was weakened, it must mean that the gods were displeased. But environmental change may also have undermined the government. A dramatic and sudden drop in rainfall led to many years of poor harvests and starvation in Upper Egypt. The demise of the Old Kingdom led to a century of social disorder during which thieves ransacked some royal tombs. One scribe lamented the consequences of this upheaval: "The son of the high-born is no longer to be recognized. Men do not sail to Byblos (BIB-loss) [Phoenicia] today. Gold is diminished. To what purpose is a treasure without its revenues? Laughter hath perished. It is grief that walketh through the land."[5]

The Middle Kingdom and Foreign Conquest

The pharaohs of a new dynasty restored strong government, moving the capital to Thebes in the south and establishing stronger control over the governors. This Middle Kingdom lasted for 400 years and saw Egyptian influence extend to Palestine and, briefly, to Nubia. Amon-Re, a fusion of two great gods, now became Egypt's chief god and was proclaimed the ancestor of the divine pharaoh.

However, foreign conquest and domestic disorder brought an end to the Middle Kingdom. The Hyksos (HICK-soes), an iron-using Semitic people from Syria and Palestine, conquered a portion of the Nile Delta region. Hyksos rule led to further divisions: an Egyptian dynasty began to rule Upper Egypt from Thebes, and the Nubians established yet a third state. The Hyksos adopted Egyptian customs and brought several improvements to Egypt that would later pay dividends, including increased trade with the peoples of the eastern Mediterranean and Mesopotamia, and military innovations, such as iron and the practice of using smaller shields, body armor, powerful bows, and, especially, horse-drawn chariots.

The New Kingdom and Egyptian Expansion

Empire Building

In the mid-1500s B.C.E. a dynamic new set of rulers reestablished Egypt's regional power and fostered social and religious changes. Using the new military technology, the pharaohs began the most expansionist period of ancient Egyptian history. During the New Kingdom, Egypt became more active in the western Asian and Mediterranean worlds. By 1500 B.C.E. its rulers were leading armies on repeated campaigns into Palestine, Syria, and the Euphrates River, as well as south into Nubia. Foreigners from Libya in the west and from as far away as Babylon in the east came to serve in the Egyptian court. Egypt's power derived partly from its position as the major regional supplier of gold, which it obtained mostly from Nubia and Punt.

For a few years Egypt was ruled by the female pharaoh introduced at the beginning of this chapter. Hatshepsut (r. ca. 1479–1458), the daughter and wife of pharaohs, ruled in her own name

Great Pyramid at Giza Three Egyptian pharaohs from the twenty-sixth century B.C.E. were buried in these magnificent pyramids, which symbolized the power of Old Kingdom Egypt. The rearmost pyramid, built for Pharaoh Cheops, remains the largest all-stone building ever constructed anywhere.

between 1473 and 1458. The Egyptians had no word for a female ruler and described a queen only as the "king's wife." To ensure that she looked like a proper pharaoh, Hatshepsut apparently wore male clothing and the headdress and false beard that were symbols of royalty. Hatshepsut supervised military campaigns in both the north and south and also sponsored the marine expedition to Punt to collect luxury goods.

Another New Kingdom pharaoh, Amenophis **(AH-men-o-fis)** IV (r. 1353–1333), rebelled against the priests of Amon-Re and promoted the worship of a new sun-god, Aten, who he claimed was the only god (other than the pharaoh himself). Amenophis changed his name to Akhenaten **(AH-ke-NAH-tin)** ("servant of Aten") and wrote a famous hymn to Aten: "Beginner of Life. How manifold are thy works? They are hidden from the sight of men, O Sole God. Thou didst fashion the earth according to thy desire."[6] His experiment with **monotheism**, the belief in a single, all-powerful god, has long intrigued historians because it occurred at roughly the same time that the Hebrews were developing their belief in a single god. Some scholars see cross-cultural influences at work, since Hebrews were within the Egyptian sphere of influence, and some may have lived in Egypt. Some Hebrew psalms and proverbs are clearly derived from Egyptian writings, including Akhenaten's hymn to Aten. At Akhenaten's death, however, the priests successfully pressured his successor to return to Amon-Re worship.

The New Kingdom continued its military successes for a while before faltering. The high point of Egyptian empire building was reached when Rameses **(ram-ih-SEEZ)** II (r. 1290–1224) signed a treaty with the Hittites dividing Syria and Palestine between them. In 1208 B.C.E. Libyan tribes invaded the Nile Delta. Although they were pushed out, Egypt began its long decline as a power in the eastern Mediterranean. From about 750 to 650 B.C.E., a dynasty of pharaohs from the kingdom of Kush in Nubia ruled Egypt. They adopted Egyptian customs and wrote their language in hieroglyphics. Finally, Egypt was conquered by the Assyrians in the seventh century and by the Persians in the late sixth century B.C.E.

Religious Diversity

monotheism The belief in a single, all-powerful god.

SECTION SUMMARY

- The regular flooding of the Nile River provided the ancient Egyptians with a highly fertile valley and a dependable growing season.

- A strong central government allowed the Egyptians to make the most of their agricultural system.

- The pyramids were built by the Egyptian pharaohs of the Old Kingdom, thought to be descendants of the sun-god.

- During the Middle Kingdom, the Egyptian capital moved from Memphis to Thebes.

- The New Kingdom was a time of Egyptian expansion into western Asia and the Mediterranean, but it ended with the decline of Egyptian dominance.

EGYPTIAN SOCIETY, ECONOMY, AND CULTURE

What were some unique features of Egyptian society?

Like other ancient societies, the Egyptians had many distinctive customs, technologies, and beliefs. Egypt was a generally tolerable place to live. Perhaps because of the Nile inundation each fall, Egyptians of all social classes, blessed with many centuries of good crops, seemed to view themselves as favored. One writer celebrated the Nile Delta as "full of everything good— its ponds with fish and its lakes with birds. Its meadows are verdant, its melons abundant. Its granaries are so full of barley that they come near to the sky."[7] Although many peasants and workers worked hard and had fewer comforts than the upper classes, they at least had a life that was secure and a routine that was predictable. Women enjoyed considerable freedom. Finally, Egyptian cities could grow rich by trading with many distant suppliers and markets.

Society

Like other urban societies, Egypt was divided into social classes with different responsibilities and roles. The pharaoh theoretically owned everything in the kingdom and had particular estates reserved for him. The priests and nobles owned 80 to 90 percent of all the usable land (see Profile: Hekanakhte, an Egyptian Priest). The scribe, or "writing man," held an honored upper-class occupation. "Be a scribe," a young man was advised in one source. "Your limbs will be sleek. Your hands will grow soft. You will go forth in white clothes with courtiers saluting you."[8] Not all enjoyed such amenities. Peasants maintained the irrigation works and paid high taxes. At the bottom of society were slaves, perhaps 10 or 15 percent of the population. They were mostly prisoners of war and foreigners, including Nubians and people from Palestine, among them some Hebrews. Most worked in the homes of the wealthy, in the palaces, or on temple estates. Some helped build pyramids and monuments.

Social Classes

Egyptians valued security and regularity more than social equality. Since it was relatively easy to plant in the soft soil left after the floods, they did not need heavy plows. Despite occasional grueling labor on construction projects, peasants showed little discontent except during the troubled intermediate periods. Although the rich ate meat and the poor had beer, bread, and beans ("beer and bread" was an ancient Egyptian greeting, much like "have a good day"), most people thought themselves lucky. Their massive tombs and mummies may seem gloomy to us today, but their temples were once bright with paint and gold. Egyptians told bawdy stories (often about their gods), played musical instruments such as flutes, pipes, and harps, and got drunk. Both men and women used cosmetics to enhance their physical attractions, including scented oils and colorful eyeliners. In seeking beauty aids, Egyptians became the world's first chemists. Young people wrote sentimental poems to sweethearts. One love poem by a girl reported on a swim with her lover:

> Diving and swimming with you here,
> Gives me the chance I've been waiting for,
> To show my looks,
> Before an appreciative eye.
> My bathing suit of the best material.
> Nothing can keep me from my love,
> Standing on the other shore.[9]

Gender roles were flexible, and women had more independence and rights, especially in law, than women in any other ancient society. Hatshepsut was the most famous of at least four women pharaohs. The status of New Kingdom Egyptian women was higher than that of women in Mesopotamia or later in classical Greek and Roman society, and legal distinctions seemed to be based more on class than on gender. A woman could inherit, bequeath, and administer property, conclude legal settlements, take cases to court, initiate divorce, and testify. Some women could probably read and write, and many were involved in well-paying economic activities. Women weavers produced some of the finest cloth in world history. Wives also enjoyed rough equality with husbands and assumed the public and family responsibilities of their deceased spouses. Women served as doctors and priestesses, and a few women even held administrative positions. Despite all these exceptions, public duties were normally reserved for men. An Old Kingdom sage advised men to "love your wife at home, as is proper. Fill her belly and clothe her back. Make her heart glad as long as you live. You should not judge her, or let her gain control."[10]

Gender Relations

Cities, Trade, and Technology

Mesopotamian cities had been trading centers almost from their beginnings. Egyptian cities, by contrast, were largely administrative centers to house tax collectors, artisans in government workshops, shopkeepers, and the priests who cared for the local temple. Most trade involved the

HEKANAKHTE, AN EGYPTIAN PRIEST

Hekanakhte (heh-KHAN-akt) who lived about 2000 B.C.E., was the *ka*-priest of a chief government minister who had died a generation earlier. As a *ka*-priest, it was his duty to tend the tomb of his patron, near the city of Thebes, in order to protect the deceased individual's guardian spirit or soul (*ka*). Wealthy individuals, like the great minister Ipi whom Hekanakhte served, left money or other resources to support a priest who would perform these duties. If the *ka* were not honored with these ceremonial offerings, Egyptians feared that it would die a "second death" or be annihilated.

In this case, the minister Ipi had left a large estate to support Hekanakhte and his family. Hekanakhte also supervised other properties left to his care, and he had to be gone visiting them much of the year. We know much about him because during his absences he wrote many letters to his eldest son, Mersu. Mersu read and eventually discarded them in a local tomb, where they were forgotten but where the dry desert climate preserved them until they were discovered by an archaeologist in 1922. These letters give us an interesting picture of family life in the Middle Kingdom. We discover that Hekanakhte had a large family that included five sons, two of them married, and all of them living at home. He also supported his mother, a poor female relative, and a widowed daughter.

Perhaps because he had such a large household, Hekanakhte's letters to Mersu give advice on cultivating and tending the grain crops. Some of the letters were written during a bad year, when harvests were slim because of inadequate Nile flooding. The priest tells his son that he is sending some food, but he carefully lists what each family member is to receive. He tells Mersu to remind family members not to complain, since "half life is better than dying together." Hekanakhte orders that only those who work should get food and urges Mersu to "make the most of my land, strive to the uttermost, dig the ground deep with your noses." He also tells his son

exactly what seeds to plant and where to plant them. And he warns his son not to overpay the help, saying that if he does, his own personal funds will be reduced. Trust between father and son seems to have been in short supply.

Family disputes in Hekanakhte's household were a frequent topic in these letters. Apparently Hekanakhte had spoiled Mersu's younger brother, Snerfu, because he constantly reminds Mersu to give this youngest son things he wants. In addition, Hekanakhte apparently decided late in life, after his wife died, to take a young concubine, Iutenhab (YOU-ten-hob), who disrupted the household with her many requests. In one letter, the priest tells his son to fire a maid who had offended Iutenhab. Given the nagging tone of many of Hekanakhte's letters to his long-suffering son, it may not surprise us that one of the letters found in the debris of the tomb had been left unopened.

THINKING ABOUT THE PROFILE

1. What were the duties of a *ka*-priest?
2. What do these letters tell us about family relationships in this social class?

Note: Quotations from Barbara Mertz, *Red Land, Black Land: Daily Life in Ancient Egypt* (New York: Dodd, Mead, 1978), 127.

Measuring and Recording the Egyptian Harvest This wall painting from a tomb in the city of Thebes shows officials and peasants figuring the size of the annual harvest.

Michael Holford

Economic Life

import of luxury goods by the wealthy. Also, Egyptian city-dwellers, unlike their Mesopotamian counterparts, did not think of themselves as attached to the city. They were, like all Egyptians, subjects of the pharaoh. Most Egyptians lived in villages, and market towns were scattered up and down the river. The Egyptians' long-distance trade systems were more wide-ranging than those of the Mesopotamians. Egyptians traded with sub-Saharan Africans as far south as the Congo River Basin, with the Berber peoples of Libya and Algeria to the west, with the societies along the Red Sea to the east, with Palestine, Phoenicia, and Mesopotamia to the northeast, and with southeastern Europe. Gold, semiprecious stones, and such exotic things as frankincense, myrrh, ivory, ostrich feathers, and monkeys came from sub-Saharan Africa through Nubia or via the Red Sea and were exchanged for furniture, silver, tools, paper, and linen. Egyptians mined copper in the nearby Sinai (SIGH-nigh) Peninsula and along the Red Sea coast, and the Nile Delta provided papyrus and waterfowl.

Mathematics and Science

The Egyptians understood enough mathematics and physics to make the pyramids perfectly level and to match the corners of each pyramid with the four points of the compass. The Egyptians also used a solar calendar that divided the year into 365 days and twelve months, more accurate than the Sumerian lunar calendar. Egyptian arithmetic, however, was less sophisticated. The Egyptians understood fractions, but they had no concept of zero. In medicine, Egyptians used both surgery and herbal remedies to treat illnesses. They recognized that the heart was a pump, were able to cure some eye diseases, and did some dental work. Modern observers still admire Egyptian technical skill in treating the dead, reflected in the mummies held in museums worldwide. Using a form of salt found abundantly in Egypt, and taking advantage of the extremely dry climate, Egyptian morticians were able to preserve human tissue well enough that the distinct features of individuals can be seen 4,000 years later.

Religion

Gods and Myths

Egyptian religious and moral beliefs included many myths, unique views of death, and some 2,000 gods and goddesses, most of them benevolent. Like their Mesopotamian counterparts, the Egyptian gods were created to explain nature, but they were also made in the image of humans and shared human weaknesses. The emphasis on preserving bodies indicates a chief feature of Egyptian religion, the belief that a person's soul could be united with his or her body after death, but only if the body was properly preserved. In the Old Kingdom, only pharaohs could expect this afterlife, which mirrored life on earth. By the Middle Kingdom, however, all who could afford some form of mummification and whose souls passed a final moral judgment after death were candidates for immortality. As a result, people devoted vast resources to this quest.

Primary Source: Egyptian *Book of the Dead* Read the number of potential sins that would likely tarnish a journeying spirit and prevent entrance into the realm of the blessed.

The most dramatic and long-lived of the Egyptian myths is the story of Osiris (oh-SIGH-ris), a god-king, and his wife Isis (EYE-sis). Murdered by his brother, Osiris descended to the underworld, where he established justice there as he had done on earth. A famous Egyptian drawing from the *Book of the Dead,* which depicts the afterlife, shows Osiris weighing the heart of a dead princess against the symbol of justice and truth. The *Book of the Dead* describes a confession that the dead person is to repeat as part of this judgment by Osiris. This confession includes statements by the deceased indicating that he or she has not murdered or cheated anyone.

Because of the *Book of the Dead,* the durability of the pyramids, other Egyptian tombs, and mummified remains, some scholars have viewed the ancient Egyptians as people preoccupied with death and the afterlife. However, the tombs are the only artifacts that remain because they were made of stone. The Egyptians were probably not as preoccupied with death as the physical remains suggest. They no doubt enjoyed life as much or more than other people. Many wall paintings suggest that even the lower classes accepted their lot as part of the natural order of things and found ways to cope. They show farmers and herders telling jokes, women bringing them their lunches, children squabbling, and shepherds asleep under a tree, a dog or flask of beer beside them. They could find solace in religion and awe of the pharaoh who sat, as the gods ordained, at the apex of the social pyramid.

SECTION SUMMARY

- Though Egyptian society was divided into classes, with the rich enjoying lavish lifestyles, even the poor were relatively comfortable.

- Women had greater independence and rights in Egypt than in any other ancient society, but their roles were still quite limited.

- Ancient Egyptians had great technical skill in architecture, medicine, and preserving the dead.

- Ancient Egyptians believed they could obtain immortality if their bodies were mummified and if they passed a moral judgment after death.

- Ancient Egyptians traded widely with societies in sub-Saharan Africa and western Asia.

ANCIENT SUB-SAHARAN AFRICAN SOCIETIES

What were some achievements of the ancient Nubian, Sudanic, and Bantu peoples?

Africa is the original homeland for all of humanity, and Egypt was only the best-known of the early farming societies and states that emerged on the continent. Africans fostered varied societies that became linked to each other and the wider world by growing networks. Just as the annual Nile floods fostered Egypt's distinctive development, so the environment also influenced sub-Saharan Africans and helped or hindered their early development of farming and technology. While historians tend to emphasize state building and monarchs, many Africans rejected political centralization, choosing public participation rather than kings and bureaucracies. However, strong states emerged in Nubia and the Sudan. Meanwhile, migrating **Bantu (BAN-too)** spread farming, iron metallurgy, and their languages widely in the southern half of the continent.

Sub-Saharan African Environments

Both geography and climate have shaped African history. Africa, with one-fifth of the earth's landmass, is the second largest continent after Eurasia and occupies more space than the United States, Europe (excluding Russia), China, and India combined. The equator bisects Africa, giving most of the continent a tropical climate. Lush rain forests have flourished along West Africa's Guinea coast and in the vast Congo River Basin in the heart of the continent. These equatorial regions are home to many insects, parasites, and bacteria that cause debilitating diseases like malaria, yellow fever, and sleeping sickness. Since the last is deadly to cattle and horses, it was impractical to use a plow or wheel. Most of the continent, however, is parched desert or savannah grasslands. African weather can be erratic, with fluctuating and often unpredictable rains. Rain quickly diminishes north and south of the equator, producing a huge dry zone that receives less than 10 inches of rain a year. The deserts have largely been occupied by pastoral societies and herds of large wild animals. In some regions the poor-quality soil has been easily eroded by overuse, fostering low agricultural productivity. Nonetheless, early farmers cultivated the grassland-covered region known as the **Sudan (soo-DAN)**, which stretches along the southern fringe of the Sahara Desert from the western tip of Africa to the Nile Basin.

Geography has often hindered communication. The eastern third of Africa includes extensive plateau and mountain regions, where in some plateau districts great lakes and volcanic soils have permitted denser populations. The eastern highlands also produced great river systems, including the Nile, the Congo, and, in the south, the Zambezi **(zam-BEE-zee)**, but all these rivers have numerous rapids and waterfalls that have limited boat travel. Only the Niger **(NIGH-jer)** River, which flows through the West African plains, is navigable over large distances. Prevailing winds also made it difficult to sail along the West African coast, and much of the African coast has sandbars that create great swells, making it difficult to land a boat. Furthermore, there are few bays, gulfs, inland seas, or natural harbors to serve as maritime hubs. Only along the eastern, Red Sea, and Mediterranean coasts did a few protected bays and prevailing winds favor seagoing trade.

The catastrophic climatic change that created and expanded the Sahara Desert strongly shaped early African societies. In 3500 B.C.E. the Sahara region was relatively wet, a rich grazing land with lakes and rivers and occupied by societies that flourished from hunting, gathering, fishing, and some farming. Ancient rock art portrays people dancing, worshiping, riding chariots, and tending horses and cattle. The paintings endow women with dignity as they raise children, gather plants, and make baskets, pottery, and jewelry. Then, as rain patterns shifted southward, **desertification**, the process by which productive land is transformed into mostly useless desert, began. By 2000 B.C.E. the Sahara region was harsh desert. People contributed to this process by overgrazing marginal lands and burning forests to create grasslands. The same desertification processes continue today on the Sahara's southern fringe. The Sahara was left largely to nomadic herders of cattle, goats, and camels, and most other inhabitants migrated to the north and south or into the lower Nile Valley. Eventually the Sahara marked a general boundary between the Berber and Semitic peoples along the southern Mediterranean coast and the darker-skinned peoples in the rest of Africa. But the desert barrier did not prevent considerable social, cultural, and genetic intermixing and exchange.

Bantu Sub-Saharan peoples who developed a cultural tradition based on farming and iron metallurgy, which they spread widely through great migrations.

Geographical Foundations

Sudan A grassland region stretching along the southern fringe of the Sahara Desert from the western tip of Africa to the Nile Valley.

The Expanding Sahara

desertification The process by which productive land is transformed into mostly useless desert.

The Origins of African Agriculture

Africa's geographical disadvantages did not prevent agriculture from developing early as the result of both local and imported discoveries. Some 12,000 or 13,000 years ago, people in the eastern Sahara were perhaps the first in the world to make pottery, probably for storing food and water, two centuries earlier than Middle Eastern people. Between 8000 and 5000 B.C.E., people in Nubia and the Sahara region had become farmers, followed by Ethiopians (see Chronology: Ancient Sub-Saharan Africa, 8000 B.C.E.–350 C.E.). By 2500 B.C.E. farming was widespread in West, Central, and East Africa. In West Africa almost all food crops developed from local wild African plants like sorghum, millet, yams, and African rice. Rice gradually spread south to become a major crop in the rain forest zone. People in the eastern Sahara domesticated cotton and worked it into fabrics using spindles of baked clay, perhaps by 5000 B.C.E. Other crops came later from outside Africa, including wheat, barley, and chickpeas from the Middle East and bananas from Southeast Asia. But the movement went in both directions. Crops domesticated in West Africa such as sorghum and sesame reached India and China well before 2000 B.C.E.

Animal domestication presented a great challenge to sub-Saharan Africans. Cattle were probably domesticated very early from local sources in the southern Sahara and East Africa. But no other African animals were suitable for domestication, and some were dangerous predators. Rock art reveals possible failed attempts to domesticate giraffes, antelopes, and elephants. Most draft animals had to come from North Africa and Eurasia. Goats and sheep were brought in from the Middle East.

African peoples overcame geographical challenges in many ways. The major response to difficult climate and soils was to create a subsistence economy, rather than the high-productivity agriculture possible in Egypt, China, India, Southeast Asia, or southern Europe. One such subsistence strategy, pastoral nomadism, became the specialty of some groups in dry regions. Others chose farming by shifting cultivation, a creative adaptation to prevailing conditions. Shifting cultivators moved their fields around every few years, letting recently used land lie fallow for a while to regain its nutrients. If not abused, this system worked well for centuries. Only in a few fertile areas was intensive sedentary agriculture possible.

Ancient African Metallurgy

Most sub-Saharan peoples learned to make metal tools and weapons. Copper may have been mined in the Sahara by 1500 B.C.E. There was no pronounced bronze age, and generally the use of bronze came around the same time as or later than iron. Sub-Saharan Africans were among the world's earliest ironworkers, probably making iron by at least 1000 B.C.E. on the northern fringe of the Congo Basin. Iron smelters were built around 900 B.C.E. in **Iron Technology** the Great Lakes region, slightly earlier than the first Egyptian works. Between 600 and 300 B.C.E., iron was being mined, smelted, and forged widely in West and East Africa, with West Africans possibly being influenced by iron and bronze metallurgy established on the North African coast after 700 B.C.E. Since major iron ore deposits were rare, ore and iron artifacts had to be transported over long distances. Mining and working iron were both difficult operations, and those who did them probably occupied a special position in the community. Among the Haya (HI-uh) people in Tanzania (TAN-zeh-NEE-uh), when a new king was installed on the throne, he made a ritual visit to the blacksmith's hut, symbolizing the special relationship between the king and the ironworkers.

Iron technology gradually improved and the number of products increased. In many places miners had to dig open pits or even put down vertical shafts to reach ore deposits deep underground. Furnaces for smelting ranged from simple open holes in the ground to elaborate clay structures 6 or 8 feet high with blower systems. The craftsmen made spear blades and arrowheads for warriors and hunters; hoes, axes, machetes, and knives for farmers and traders; bangles and rings for jewelry; gongs to produce music; hammers, hinges, and nails for household use; and iron bells for ceremonies and rituals.

Agriculture and metallurgy came to various African regions at different times, depending on circumstances, and they spread to the southern half of the continent last. Originally much of this region was inhabited by expert hunters and gatherers such as the !Kung (see Chapter 1), success-

CHRONOLOGY
Ancient Sub-Saharan Africa, 8000 B.C.E.–350 C.E.

8000–5000 B.C.E. Earliest agriculture in the Sahara and Nubia

5000–4000 B.C.E. Earliest agriculture in Ethiopia

3100–2800 B.C.E. First Nubian kingdom (disputed)

2500 B.C.E. Widespread agriculture in West, Central, and East Africa

2000 B.C.E. Beginning of Bantu migrations

1800–1500 B.C.E. Kerma kingdom in Nubia

1200 B.C.E. Early urbanization in western Sudan

1000–500 B.C.E. Bantu settlement of Great Lakes region

1000–500 B.C.E. Beginning of trans-Saharan trade

1000–500 B.C.E. Early ironworking technology

900–800 Mande towns

900 B.C.E.–350 C.E. Early Kush

ful adapters to their environment who had little incentive to develop agriculture or ironworking. Gradually most of these groups were pushed farther south by iron-using farmers.

Early Urban Societies in Nubia

The first known urban African state after Egypt emerged in the region known in ancient times as Nubia (see Map 3.1), occupying what is today the northern half of the country of Sudan and far southern Egypt. Like Egyptians, Nubians turned to the Nile for survival. The region is mostly desert, but a thin area along the Nile was fertile, and copper and gold could be mined nearby. The first Nubian kingdom may have formed as early as 3100 B.C.E. Egypt dominated the region for many centuries, occasionally through military occupations. Egypt and Nubia also established a two-way trade, with Egypt exporting materials such as pottery and copper items to Nubia and importing ivory, ebony, ostrich feathers, and slaves from the Nubians. An independent Nubian kingdom, Kerma (CARE-ma), appeared between 1800 and 1600 B.C.E. Extensive ruins of stone and mud-brick buildings, massive cemeteries, and large towers testify to a prosperous and well-organized society. Kerma was also distinguished for painted pottery and copper vessels and weapons. Around 1500 B.C.E. Egyptian forces once again occupied Nubia and destroyed the Kerma state.

When Egyptian power declined around 900 B.C.E., after the end of the New Kingdom, a larger Nubian state known as Kush (koosh) emerged, laying the foundations for a golden age of trade, culture, and metallurgy. The Kushites conquered Egypt in the eighth century B.C.E. but were pushed out by the Assyrians after nearly a century of occupation. Kush became a major regional trading hub. Overland caravan routes linked Kush with the Niger Basin, the Congo Basin, and the Ethiopian highlands. This enterprising society provided goods from central and southern Africa to the Mediterranean and Red Sea regions, as well as to markets as distant as India and China. From these places Kush imported Roman goblets and Chinese copper vessels.

Kush clearly benefited from its contacts with other societies, adding imported ideas to Nubian traditions. For example, irrigation technology imported from Egypt and western Asia made farming possible in this barren area. In religion, Kushites worshiped both Egyptian and local gods and buried their kings in Egyptian-style pyramids. A sixth-century B.C.E. inscription tells us that King Aspelta (as-PELL-ta), as the son of the Egyptian sun-god, Ra, built for his son a pyramid of white stone. However, while Kushite art reflected Egyptian and even sometimes Greek influence, the overall effect remained distinctively Nubian. The unique Kushite society may have also been matrilineal, and some women held key political positions, including that of queen. Kings sometimes traced their descent back through female ancestors.

Eventually Kush linked the peoples of Africa and the Mediterranean. By 600 B.C.E. Kush had become the major African producer of iron, a position that gave it an even more crucial economic influence on the ancient world. The ancient Greek poet Homer described Kushites as "the most just of men; the favorites of the gods. The lofty inhabitants of Olympus (oh-LIM-pus) (home of Greek gods) journey to them, and take part in their feasts."[11]

The Sudanic Societies and Trade Networks

In ancient times peoples in the Sudan grasslands of West Africa also developed towns and long-distance trade routes, and perhaps a few small kingdoms. Trade extended to Nubia and Egypt. By 1200 B.C.E. farmers in Mauritania (MORE-ee-TAIN-ee-uh) had built over two hundred stone villages and towns in what is now mostly uninhabited desert. They may have been the ancestors of the Mande (MAN-da) peoples, who now occupy a large area of the western Sudan. By 900 or 800 B.C.E. population increase had changed walled villages into large, well-constructed towns. Eventually this flourishing society was swallowed by the expanding Sahara and the people probably moved south.

Nubia and the Nile

Coronation Stela of Kushite King Aspelta (ca. 600 B.C.E.) The stela and inscription celebrate the coronation of King Aspelta. Related to the royal line through his mother, he was chosen from among many candidates by high priests acting in the name of the gods.

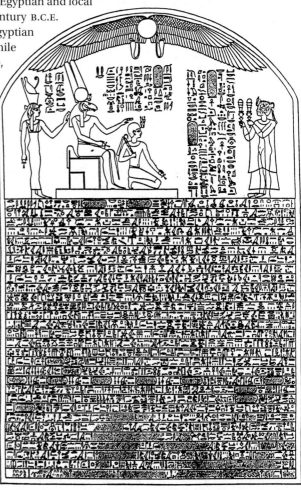

British Museum Press. Reproduced with permission.

Nok Terracotta Sculpture of Head Elaborate, life-size, technically complex sculptures reveal something of Nok material life in ancient Nigeria. Some figures sit on stools, carry an axe, or wear beads.

Werner Forman/Art Resource, NY

Long-distance trade, especially the caravan routes crossing the Sahara Desert, greatly aided the growth of Sudanic societies by forging enduring communication networks. The earliest caravan activity dates back to 1000 or 500 B.C.E. Gradually some groups took up commerce as their primary activity. The trans-Saharan trade depended on pack animals introduced by Berbers from North Africa, initially mules and horses and later camels. First domesticated in parched Arabia, camels stimulated trans-Saharan trade because they could endure many days of caravan travel without water. Eventually a large trade system linked the Sudanic towns with the southern Mediterranean coast and the forest zone to the south.

African societies gradually shaped their beliefs into complex artistic and religious traditions. On the southern fringe of the Sudan, in what is now central Nigeria, the Nok people, mostly farmers and herders, were working iron by 500 B.C.E., and they created enduring artistic traditions. Nok artists fashioned exquisite terracotta pottery and sculpture, including life-size and realistic human heads. The later art of several Nigerian societies shows Nok influence. While each society developed some distinctive notions of the cosmic order and their place within it, there were common patterns (see Witness to the Past: The World-view of an African Society). Many peoples, like the Mande and the Igbo (EE-boh), believed in one divine force or supreme being, either male or female, who created the cosmos, earth, and life and then remained remote from human affairs. Africans needing immediate spiritual help appealed to secondary gods and spirits. Thus sub-Saharan African religion became a mix of monotheism, polytheism, and animism.

The Bantu-Speaking Peoples and Their Migrations

Today people who speak closely related Bantu languages occupy most of Africa south of a line stretching from today's Kenya in the east to Cameroon in West-Central Africa. All of these societies can trace their distant ancestry back to the same location in West-Central Africa originally occupied by the Bantu (see Map 3.2). In their migrations, the Bantu incorporated many of the peoples they encountered and modified their own cultures to suit local conditions. The Bantu occupation of central, eastern, and southern Africa is the result of one of the great population movements in world history, a saga similar to that of the sea voyages that resulted in the settlement of the Pacific islands and the Indo-European migration into western and southern Eurasia. As the Bantu spread out over a wider area, they gradually divided into over four hundred different ethnic groups.

Bantu Migrations

The Bantu originated along the Benue (BAIN-way) River in eastern Nigeria and western Cameroon (KAM-uh-roon). But agricultural progress fostered overcrowding by 2000 B.C.E., spurring some to migrate eastward into the lands just north of the Congo River Basin. Bantu settled the Great Lakes region of East Africa between 1000 B.C.E. and 500 B.C.E. Some land-short Bantu from the Benue also began moving south into the Congo River Basin. Bantu mixed with the local peoples, exchanging technologies and cultural patterns.

Bantu Technologies

The Bantu benefited from metallurgy and agricultural technologies. They had learned to smelt iron, a knowledge that they spread along the Bantu communication network. Metallurgy allowed the Bantu to use iron tools and weapons to open new land and subdue the small existing populations. Although skilled farmers, some also adopted cattle and goat raising. By 2,000 years ago some Bantu living in northeast Africa had also learned to grow domesticated bananas and plantains (large bananas) imported from Southeast Asia, as well as sorghum (SOAR-gum) from the Nile Valley. These high-yielding crops replaced yams as their primary staple food and provided a spur to population growth, encouraging new migration into southern Africa.

The World-view of an African Society

Few primary sources survive for the ancient period in sub-Saharan Africa. Although it is difficult to extrapolate the distant past from contemporary oral traditions, we can get some insight into ancient understandings of the natural and spiritual realms from such accounts. This excerpt on the world-view of the Igbo people in southeastern Nigeria was compiled by an Igbo anthropologist, who summarized Igbo thought. Many Igbo perspectives may well derive from the Nok and Bantu cultures, whose ancestral homelands are near the region where the Igbo live today.

There is the world of man peopled by all created beings and things, both animate and inanimate. The spirit world is the abode of the creator, the deities, the disembodied and malignant spirits, and the ancestral spirits. It is the future abode of the living after their death. . . . Existence for the Igbo is a dual but interrelated phenomenon involving the interaction between the material and the spiritual, the visible and the invisible, the good and the bad, the living and the dead. . . . The world of the "dead" is a world full of activities. . . . The principle of seniority makes the ancestors [in the world of the "dead"] the head of the [extended kinship system in the world of man]. . . .

The world as a natural order which inexorably goes on its ordained way according to a "master plan" is foreign to Igbo conceptions. Rather, their world is a dynamic one—a world of moving equilibrium. It is an equilibrium that is constantly threatened, and sometimes actually disturbed by natural and social calamities. . . . But the Igbo believe that these social calamities and cosmic forces which disturb their world are controllable and should be "manipulated" by them for their own purpose. The maintenance of social and cosmological balance in the world becomes . . . a dominant and pervasive theme in Igbo life. They achieve this balance . . . through divination, sacrifice, and appeal to the countervailing forces of their ancestors . . . against the powers of the malignant spirits. . . . The Igbo world is not only a world in which people strive for equality; it is one in which change is constantly expected. . . . Life on earth is a link in the chain of status hierarchy which culminates in the achievement of ancestral honor in the world of the dead. . . .

The idea of a creator of all things is focal to Igbo theology. They believe in a supreme god, a high god, who is all good. . . . The Igbo high god is a withdrawn god. He is a god who has finished all active works of creation and keeps watch over his creatures from a distance. . . . Although the Igbo feel psychologically separated from their high god, he is not too far away, he can be reached, but not as quickly as can other deities who must render their services to man to justify their demand for sacrifices. . . . Minor gods [can] be controlled, manipulated, and used to further human interests. . . . Given effective protection, the Igbo are very faithful to their gods.

THINKING ABOUT THE READING

1. How do the Igbo understand the relationship between the human and spiritual worlds?

2. What is the role of the supreme god in their polytheistic theology?

3. How might their beliefs about the relationship of the human and spiritual realms shape Igbo society?

Source: From Uchendu, THE IGBO OF SOUTHEAST NIGERIA, 1E © 1965 Wadsworth, a part of Cengage Learning, Inc. Reproduced by permission.

SECTION SUMMARY

- African geography is extremely varied, ranging from jungles with abundant rainfall to deserts with practically no rainfall.

- The area now covered by the Sahara Desert was once lush and fertile, but it gradually dried out as rain patterns shifted southward.

- Small-scale agriculture flourished in Africa, though widespread disease made it difficult to domesticate animals.

- Sub-Saharan Africans worked with iron at the same time or before they worked with bronze.

- Early sub-Saharan societies were linked by trade.

- Nubia had a close relationship with Egypt, which eventually destroyed the Nubian kingdom of Kerma.

- The Nubian kingdom of Kush increased in power as Egypt declined and became a major trading hub linking the peoples of Africa to the Mediterranean.

- Caravan routes through the Sahara allowed for trade and for links among widely separated African peoples.

- The Bantu spread widely throughout Africa, mixing their culture and traditions with those of local peoples.

Map 3.2
Bantu Migrations and Early Africa

The Bantu-speaking peoples spread over several millennia throughout the southern half of Africa. Various societies, cities, and states emerged in West and North Africa.

 **Interactive Map**

EARLY SOCIETIES AND NETWORKS OF THE EASTERN MEDITERRANEAN

What were the contributions of the Hebrews, Minoans, Mycenaeans, Phoenicians, and Dorian Greeks to later societies in the region?

During the second millennium B.C.E., when the Egyptian and Mesopotamian societies were rising and falling, smaller bronze- and then iron-using societies in the eastern half of the

Mediterranean Basin were developing influential ideas or establishing cities and states. Among these, the Hebrews created the foundation for three major religions. The Minoans became a flourishing economic bridge between western Asia and southeastern Europe, and the warlike Mycenaeans built the first cities in Greece. The Phoenicians created an important new alphabet, established colonies in the western Mediterranean, and forged trade links with people as far away as England, fostering networks connecting many ancient societies. Greek migrants also began building an influential society.

Eastern Mediterranean Environments

The history and diet of peoples living around the eastern Mediterranean were influenced by the regional climate, with its cool, rainy winters and hot, dry summers, and by the Mediterranean Sea. On the plains of the northern shores, people grew grain and made bread. The many hills also encouraged the planting of olive trees and grape vines, and both olive oil and wine became export crops. Pastoralism was common in the drier lands of Lebanon and Palestine. Finally, the eastern Mediterranean Sea, a mostly placid body of water, fostered boat building, maritime trade, and other contacts between diverse societies (see Map 3.3).

Geographical Foundations

One of the densest populations emerged in Greece, located across the Aegean (ah-JEE-uhn) Sea from Anatolia. The Greeks were destined to live in relatively small, independent city-states and to be a seafaring, trading people. Unlike Mesopotamia and Egypt, where river valleys invited the creation of large political units, Greece consists of small valleys separated by numerous mountains. Physical separation encouraged political fragmentation and intellectual diversity. Greece also has an extensive coastline with many good harbors. Greeks could travel by sea east to Ionia (today western Turkey), south to Crete, or west to southern Italy more easily than they could establish connections with nearby inland towns. Thus the Mediterranean linked the societies of the Greek peninsula to other peoples such as the Minoans, Egyptians, and Phoenicians.

The Hebrews and Religious Innovation

The Hebrews, a Semitic people, were one of many groups of pastoral nomads led by powerful men known as patriarchs (from the Greek word for "rule by the father"). Their population was small, their economic and technological developments unimpressive, and their political achievements short-lived. The united Hebrew monarchy lasted less than a century. Yet the Hebrew contribution to religious history, especially to Christian and Islamic traditions, exceeds that of either the Mesopotamians or Egyptians.

The various books of the Hebrew Bible contain their basic laws and are the main source for their early history. The Hebrews trace their ancestry back to Abraham, a patriarch who supposedly lived in Mesopotamia sometime between 2000 and 1500 B.C.E. (see Chronology: The Eastern Mediterranean, 2000–539 B.C.E.). Whether Abraham was a real person or mythical may never be resolved by archaeological research. The patriarch and his two sons, Isaac and Ishmael, are considered the spiritual ancestors of three monotheistic religions—Judaism, Christianity, and Islam—which are often called the Abrahamic faiths and collectively have some 3 billion followers today. Historians and archaeologists have heatedly debated the historical reliability and antiquity of the Hebrew Bible, which was probably based in part on oral traditions. Little of it can be confirmed by archaeology. Some scholars think the biblical books are quite old, while others argue that most or all of the books were composed after 700 B.C.E. to support the claims of Hebrew political and religious factions. Some Bible stories seem based on Mesopotamian and Egyptian traditions, such as the great flood in the *Epic of Gilgamesh,* suggesting the spread of ideas. For example, some of the advice in the Hebrew Book of Proverbs, such as helping neighbors rather than acquiring wealth, closely echoes ideas in more ancient Egyptian writings. These ongoing controversies in biblical scholarship underline the importance of Hebrew religion to later history.

In the biblical account, Abraham led a few followers on a migration from southern Mesopotamia to Palestine, on the Mediterranean coast. Although born into a polytheistic world, Abraham recognized one supreme god. Peoples from Palestine had migrated, either voluntarily or as slaves, to Egypt since at least 2000

CHRONOLOGY
The Eastern Mediterranean, 2000–539 B.C.E.

2000–1500 B.C.E. Possible time frame for Abraham (biblical account)

2000–1400 B.C.E. Minoan society

1630 B.C.E. Volcanic eruption destroys Thera (Santorini)

1600–1200 B.C.E. Mycenaean society

1500–650 B.C.E. Phoenician society

1300–1200 B.C.E. Hebrew Exodus from Egypt led by Moses (biblical account)

1200–800 B.C.E. Greek "Dark Age"

1250 B.C.E. Destruction of Troy, possibly by Mycenaeans

1000 B.C.E. First Hebrew kingdom (biblical account)

922–722 B.C.E. Hebrew kingdoms of Israel and Judah

750 B.C.E. Carthage colony established by Phoenicians

722 B.C.E. Assyrian conquest of Israel

586 B.C.E. Neo-Babylonian (Chaldean) conquest of Judah

539 B.C.E. End of Babylonian captivity

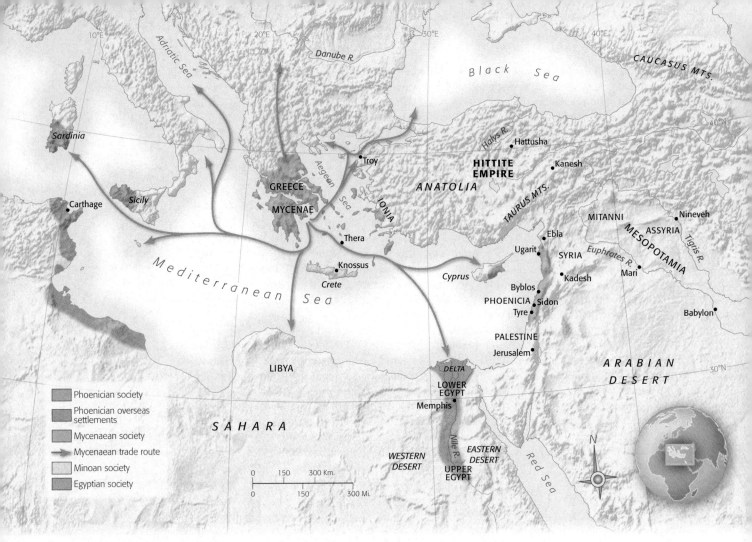

Map 3.3
The Ancient Eastern Mediterranean

The Hebrew, Minoan, Mycenaean, Phoenician, and Greek societies developed along the eastern shores of the Mediterranean Sea. They exchanged goods and ideas with each other and with other western Asians and the Egyptians.

e Interactive Map

B.C.E. A group of Hebrews who had gone to Egypt to escape drought and been enslaved were freed and left Egypt, probably in the thirteenth century. This "Exodus" from Egypt and eventual return to Palestine was led by Moses, whom the later Hebrews believed to be the founder of their religion. Moses gave his name to a code of laws, including the Ten Commandments.

Around 1000 B.C.E. the Hebrews had enough unity to establish a monarchy centered in the small city of Jerusalem. But Hebrew unity proved short-lived. After the death of King Solomon in 922 B.C.E., the monarchy split into a northern kingdom of Israel and a southern kingdom of Judah. In 722 the Assyrians conquered Israel and resettled its inhabitants elsewhere in their empire. When Assyria fell, the Hebrew prophet Nahum (NAY-hum) expressed the joy of many: "Nineveh [the Assyrian capital] is laid waste; who will bemoan her? All who hear the news of you will clap their hands over you."[12] In 586 the Chaldeans conquered Judah and moved its leaders to Babylon. The bitterness of the "Babylonian Captivity" was reflected in a Hebrew psalm: "By the rivers of Babylon, there we sat down, yea, we wept when we remembered Zion."[13] This exile ended in 539 when the Persians conquered the Chaldeans and allowed the Hebrews to return to Palestine. Later Palestine became part of the Roman Empire. The Jews were again dispersed after a revolt against Roman rule in 70 C.E., and from that time until the establishment of modern Israel in 1948 C.E., there was no Jewish state.

Despite their lack of political power, the religious history of the Hebrews, especially their ethical code, makes them memorable in world history. Over their long history the Hebrews developed four religious concepts that made them stand out among ancient peoples and that later influenced the Western and Islamic traditions: monotheism, morality, messianism, and meaning in history. Many Hebrews worshiped a single god, *Yahweh* (YA-way). They believed Yahweh had made an agreement, or covenant, with their earliest patriarchs and reinforced it when Moses received the Ten Command-

Hebrew Political History

Religious Concepts

66

ments. If they would obey him, he would protect them. Some neighboring peoples may also have adopted monotheistic views around the same time. Gradually the Hebrews reshaped monotheism, asserting that there is only one God, Yahweh, for all peoples, as the prophet Isaiah proclaimed: "There is no other God besides Me, a just God. Look to Me, and be saved, all you ends of the earth!"[14]

Hebrew holy men known as prophets refined two other Hebrew religious concepts, morality and messianism. These men emphasized that it was not enough to obey the Bible's social and ritual commandments. Following Yahweh also meant leading a moral life, refraining from lying, stealing, adultery, and persecution of the poor and oppressed. One of the differences between the code of Hammurabi and the law of Moses was that the latter also emphasized compassion for the poor. Also, unlike the Mesopotamian law, Hebrew law required that only the wrongdoer be punished, and not members of his or her family. Hebrew ethics emphasized mercy as well as justice. Another major concept, **messianism**, was the belief that God had given the Hebrew people a special mission in the world. As the Hebrews faced their time of troubles after the division of Solomon's kingdom, and especially after the fall of Judah to the Chaldeans, messianism acquired a broad spiritual meaning of bringing proper ethical behavior to all peoples. The book of Isaiah refers to Israelites as models from whom other people can learn moral truth: "I will give you as a covenant to the people, as a light to the [nations]. To open blind eyes, to bring out prisoners from the prison, those who sit in darkness."[15] This idea later inspired Christian missionary work.

messianism The Hebrew belief that their God, Yahweh, had given them a special mission in the world.

The final contribution is the idea that history itself has meaning and that it moves forward in a progressive, linear fashion and not in great repetitive cycles. Sanctifying a linear view of time meant that this earthly world was where human beings worked out their salvation by choosing good over evil. This belief also helped give birth later to the idea of progress, the notion that the future will be better than the past. It stood in contrast to ideas enshrined in the Indian religions of Hinduism and Buddhism that the material world is illusory and that time is cyclical.

Minoan Crete and Regional Trade

An influential urban society and network hub, now called Minoan (mi-NO-an), thrived on the island of Crete (kreet) between about 2000 and 1400 B.C.E. Crete lies just south of the Aegean Sea and the Greek peninsula, a strategic location that made it a logical center for sea trade between Egypt, western Asia, and southeastern Europe. Historians have remained intrigued by the achievements of Minoan society. Some of the cities had indoor plumbing and streets with drains and sewers, like the cities in ancient India. Paintings and sculptures show some Mesopotamian and Egyptian influences, but they are also different in style. Minoans apparently worshiped a large number of female deities, including an important mother goddess. The Minoans built no fortresses or defensive walls, apparently relying on their fleet to protect them. Around 1630 B.C.E. many cities on the island were destroyed, perhaps from earthquakes that followed a massive volcanic explosion that blew apart the nearby island of Thera (THER-uh) (today's Santorini). The

Minoan Cities

The Captivity of Israeli Women at Nineveh This relief comes from the palace of the Chaldean king Sennacherib in Nineveh. It was probably carved at the beginning of the seventh century B.C.E.

Erich Lessing/Art Resource, NY

Julie M. Fair

sinking of most of Thera and the dispersal of the survivors may have given rise to the legend of the lost continent of Atlantis.

The first great Mediterranean sea power, the Minoans were innovators and played a key role in regional trade. They pioneered a mixed agriculture that was well suited to the region's sunny, dry climate. Minoans traded extensively with Sicily, Greece, and the Aegean islands and sent wine, olives, and wool to Egypt and southwest Asia. Ancient Crete also served as a hub or meeting place connecting, through trade, western Asians and North Africans with various European societies. The Cretan ports were counterparts to the Persian Gulf ports that linked western and southern Asia. Though the Minoans' writing has not been deciphered, tablets found in the palace appear to be written in two scripts, one perhaps of Mesopotamian origin and the other related to early forms of Greek.

The Mycenaeans and Regional Power

The Mycenaeans, Indo-Europeans named after the city of Mycenae (my-SEE-nee) in southern Greece, also became an important power between 1600 and 1200 B.C.E. after migrating into the Greek peninsula. A warrior society, their graves contain bronze swords and armor. Their state-controlled economy was tightly organized by the king and his scribes. Eventually the Mycenaeans conquered Crete (whose Minoan society had already collapsed), all of southern Greece, and the Aegean islands, forming an empire from which they collected taxes and tribute. They continued the Minoan trading networks, dispatching ships to Sicily, Italy, and Spain and into the Black Sea, and also engaged in war with rivals, operating out of strong fortresses. According to legends, around 1250 the Mycenaeans conquered Troy, a prosperous Hittite trading port along the northwestern coast of Anatolia. This event inspired Homer's epic story, the *Iliad,* some 500 years later. Scholars differ as to whether an actual Trojan War ever took place, and some suspect that the Homeric stories combine oral accounts of various conflicts. Whatever their accuracy, they strongly influenced the later Greeks and Romans.

By 1200, however, the Mycenaeans themselves faced collapse, although the reasons remain unclear. A prolonged drought resulting from climate change or a possible series of earthquakes may have been factors. Many historians blame civil wars and attacks by warlike Indo-Europeans known as the Dorian Greeks, who were migrating into the peninsula. In the several centuries after 1200 various groups known as "Sea Peoples" pillaged and disrupted trade throughout the Aegean and eastern Mediterranean. But eventually a creative society emerged in Greece that incorporated many influences from the Dorian Greeks, Mycenaeans, Phoenicians, and Egyptians.

The Phoenicians and Their Networks

The Phoenicians linked Mediterranean and southwest Asian peoples by trade networks and by their invention of a phonetic alphabet. Between 1500 and 1000 B.C.E. this Semitic people, known

68

to the Hebrews as the Canaanites (KAY-nan-ites), established themselves along the narrow coastal strip west of the Lebanon mountains, where they built the great trading cities of Tyre (tire), Sidon (SIDE-en), and Byblos (BIB-los). Tyre was a major hub, the place where luxury goods from many societies were collected and the finest artists and craftsmen worked. The Hebrew prophet Ezekial denounced the rich, vibrant city and the extraordinary network of mercantile connections: "Your borders are in the midst of the seas. All the ships of the sea were in you to market your merchandise."[16] Although sometimes dominated by Egypt, these cities were fiercely competitive and independent states headed by kings. While the Phoenicians spoke a common language and worshiped the same gods, they never united. The Phoenicians' relatively rich land was the home of the now long-gone "cedars of Lebanon" prized by the tree-starved Sumerians, Egyptians, and Hebrews. The most famous cultural achievement of the Phoenicians, their simplification of Mesopotamian cuneiform writing into an alphabet of twenty-two characters, became the basis of later European alphabets.

Trading Cities

Only a few tablets containing information on Phoenician government, society, and religion survive. Most of what we know comes from Egyptian, Greek, and Hebrew sources; these peoples generally admired the Phoenicians' skills as scribes, seafarers, engineers, and artisans but also denounced them as immoral profiteers and cheaters. The Phoenician image as schemers, deserved or not, survives into modern times. Our term for a shameless woman, Jezebel, is derived from a princess of Tyre. Yet the Phoenician creation of an alphabet helped spread Phoenician influence in the Mediterranean.

Between 1000 and 800 B.C.E., the seafaring Phoenicians began to replace the declining Mycenaeans as the leaders in Mediterranean trade with western Asia. In addition, the Phoenicians became experts in new methods of dyeing cloth, and they may have traveled as far as England to get supplies of tin. They established colonies or trading posts beyond the Strait of Gibraltar on the southern coast of Spain and in Morocco, Sicily, and southern Italy. Some historians think the Phoenicians may have reached the Canary Islands and Madeira, off the coast of Morocco. Thus the Phoenicians became the greatest mariners of the ancient Mediterranean.

Trade and Colonization

Between 1000 and 500 B.C.E., the Mediterranean Sea became a major source of goods and wealth, partly because of Phoenician efforts. Solid bars of precious metals served as currency. Using their colonies as ports for resupply and repair, the Phoenicians traveled long distances to secure iron, silver, timber, copper, gold, and tin, all valuable commodities in western Asia and Egypt during the second and first millennia B.C.E. Legends suggest that around 600 B.C.E., under the sponsorship of the Egyptian king, a Phoenician fleet may even have sailed around Africa in an expedition lasting three years, but these journeys cannot be substantiated. In 650 B.C.E. the Assyrians conquered the Phoenician home cities and brought an end to their dynamic power, but some Phoenician colonies lived on. The most famous colony was Carthage in North Africa near what is today Tunis. Carthage became the capital of a major trading empire and the chief competitor to the Romans in the western Mediterranean by the third century B.C.E. As great sailors the Carthaginians later explored far down the coast of West Africa.

The Eclectic Roots of Greek Society

The fall of the Phoenicians and the Mycenaeans set the stage for another seafaring people, the Greeks, to found an influential urban society. During the centuries from the destruction of Mycenae around 1200 B.C.E. down to around 800 B.C.E., called the Greek "Dark Age," organized states and writing disappeared, the economic and social environment changed considerably, and there was great population movement. Dorian Greeks settled much of the Greek peninsula, and many Mycenaeans dispersed, some settling the offshore islands and others crossing the Aegean Sea to Ionia, where they established cities. The Greek world, scattered, as the philosopher Plato later put it, like frogs around a pond, became a mix of Mycenaean and Dorian peoples and traditions. Various tribes struggled for power.

Although the Greeks were famous as maritime traders, they were also warriors. Their respect for military strength is reflected in the works of Homer, oral epics written down between the eleventh and the eighth centuries B.C.E. that became an integral part of the Greek tradition. Historians disagree as to whether Homer was an actual person or the collective name for several authors who compiled these epic poems, perhaps a composite of various stories, into a narrative. Many themes in the epics may reflect influences from Mesopotamian literature such as the *Epic of Gilgamesh*, indicating the spread of ideas around the eastern Mediterranean world.

Homeric Epics

The first Homeric epic, the *Iliad*, is set during an attack by some Greek cities, led by their king Agamemnon (ag-uh-MEM-non), on Troy. The poem emphasizes the value of valor in war but also warns its readers against excessive pride. Arrogance leads the Greeks to make some nearly fatal mistakes. For example, the Greek hero Achilles (uh-KIL-eez) refuses to fight after a quarrel with Agamemnon. When Achilles' friend Patroclus (puh-TROW-klus) takes Achilles' place in the battle and is killed by Hector, the Trojan leader, a remorseful Achilles then kills Hector, warning that there can be no truce until one of them has fallen. The poem ends when Hector's father, Priam, comes to ask Achilles for his son's body. Achilles is moved by Priam's courage, and both men share their grief. This poem and Homer's second epic, the *Odyssey*, a story of the adventures of Odysseus (oh-DIS-ee-us), or Ulysses, who is returning home after the Trojan War, portrayed the Greek gods as superheroes who intervened frequently to help their human friends and hinder their enemies. The Homeric world measured virtue by success in combat rather than justice or mercy. Yet these great epics continue to be read, not only because of their dramatic and often brutal war scenes, but also because they tell us something about the tragedy of human life. This emphasis on both human power and suffering remained a part of Greek literature throughout the following centuries.

The Homeric epics and belief in the gods that they introduced greatly influenced the emerging Greek society. The Greeks also borrowed ideas from neighboring peoples, including the Egyptians and western Asians, although the degree of outside influence on early Greek culture is debated (see the Historical Controversy feature in "Societies, Networks, Transitions," page 94). Certainly the Mediterranean was a zone of interaction for peoples living around its rim. Phoenician ships, which had avoided a turbulent Greece for several hundred years, began to show up again, restoring Greek contact with the eastern Mediterranean and its regional trade networks. Soon the Greeks adopted and modified the Phoenician alphabet. These centuries built a foundation for a dynamic Greek society in the Classical Era.

SECTION SUMMARY

- Mountainous Greece favored the development of many small, independent communities, rather than one homogenous community.

- The Hebrews were politically fragmented, but their religious writings, with their emphasis on monotheism, morality, messianism, and meaning in history, have had a tremendous impact on religious history.

- Minoan Crete was the first great Mediterranean sea power and had a well-developed urban infrastructure.

- Around 1250 B.C.E., the Mycenaeans possibly conquered Troy; this event later inspired Homer's epic, the *Iliad*.

- The Phoenicians, the region's greatest maritime traders, simplified the Mesopotamian cuneiform writing into an alphabet, which served as the basis for later European alphabets.

- The Homeric epics, the *Iliad* and the *Odyessy*, greatly influenced the emerging Greek society, which was a synthesis of Mycenaean and Dorian Greek peoples.

CHAPTER SUMMARY

Egypt is often called "the gift of the Nile" because it arose in the flood-prone Nile River Valley. The Egyptian system lasted for several thousand years in its basic form. The Egyptians developed a state led by kings and invented the hieroglyphics writing system. In their stable and predictable environment, they developed a more optimistic world-view and culture than the Mesopotamians. Egyptians also participated in trade networks linking western Asia and the Mediterranean Basin with sub-Saharan Africa and India.

Many sub-Saharan African peoples also invented or adopted agriculture and metallurgy, both of which built the framework for cities and states. An environment of grasslands, forests, and the expanding Sahara Desert shaped their history, and the gradual drying out of the Sahara region forced many people to migrate. Cities arose early in Nubia (along the central Nile), probably stimulated by long-distance trade and contacts with Egypt. The Sudan fostered distinctive cultures. The Bantu peoples, in one of the greatest migrations in history, spread their farming and iron-based culture and languages widely in the southern half of Africa.

The Mediterranean societies also benefited from regional connections. The trade routes of the seafaring Minoans, Mycenaeans, and Phoenicians enriched the peoples of western Asia and the Mediterranean Basin by bringing them material goods, markets, cultural contacts, and a practical new alphabet. The Hebrews' evolving understanding of their mission, and of Yahweh, was influenced by their contact with Egyptians and Mesopotamians. Some of these contributions, such as the Phoenician alphabet and Hebrew religious and ethical concepts, have influenced many peoples down to the present day. Greece arose from interaction among several Mediterranean societies in a turbulent period during which Homer wrote his great epics.

KEY TERMS

pharaohs	**monotheism**	**Sudan**	**messianism**
hieroglyphics	**Bantu**	**desertification**	

EBOOK AND WEBSITE RESOURCES

e **PRIMARY SOURCE**
Egyptian *Book of the Dead*

e **INTERACTIVE MAPS**
Map 3.1 Ancient Egypt and Nubia
Map 3.2 Bantu Migrations and Early Africa
Map 3.3 The Ancient Eastern Mediterranean

LINKS

African Timelines (http://web.cocc.edu/cagatucci/ classes/hum211/timelines/htimelinetoc.htm). Offers many links to essays and other sources on Africa; maintained by Central Oregon Community College.

Ancient Jewish History (http://www.us-israel.org/ jsources/Judaism/jewhist.html). Offers much useful information.

Exploring Ancient World Cultures (http://eawc.evansville .edu/). Excellent site run by Evansville University, with essays and links on the ancient Near East and Europe.

Internet African History Sourcebook (http://www .fordham.edu/halsall/africa/africasbook.html). This site contains much useful information and documentary material on ancient Africa.

Internet Ancient History Sourcebook (http://www .fordham.edu/halsall/ancient/asbook.html). Exceptionally rich collection of links and primary source readings.

Plus flashcards, practice quizzes, and more. Go to: www.cengage.com/history/lockard/globalsocnet2e.

SUGGESTED READING

Armstrong, Karen. *The Great Transformation: The Beginning of Our Religious Traditions*. New York: Alfred Knopf, 2006. Good discussion of ancient religions.

Castledon, Rodney. *Minoans: Life in Bronze Age Crete*. New York: Routledge, 1993. A valuable recent survey.

Connah, Graham. *African Civilization: An Archaeological Perspective*, 2nd ed. Cambridge: Cambridge University Press, 2004. A good overview of early African societies; emphasizes the rise of cities and states.

Dunstan, William E. *The Ancient Near East*. New York: Harcourt Brace, 1998. Designed for the general reader, this work makes sense of the confusing array of states and empires in western Asia and Egypt.

Ehret, Christopher. *The Civilizations of Africa: A History to 1800*. Charlottesville: University of Virginia Press, 2002. A pathbreaking introduction to African history, with nearly half devoted to the ancient period.

Grimal, Nicolas. *A History of Ancient Egypt*. Oxford: Blackwell, 1992. A clear account of this society for beginning students.

Harris, Nathaniel. *History of Ancient Egypt: The Culture and Lifestyle of the Ancient Egyptians*. New York: Barnes and Noble, 1997. A richly illustrated overview of Egyptian life.

Markoe, Glenn E. *The Phoenicians*. Berkeley: University of California Press, 2000. A fine account of the history, cities, economy, and literature of this maritime society.

McNutt, Paula M. *Restructuring the Society of Ancient Israel*. Louisville: Westminster John Knox Press, 1998. Survey of knowledge and scholarly debates.

Mertz, Barbara. *Red Land, Black Land: Daily Life in Ancient Egypt*, rev. ed. New York: Peter Bedrick, 1990. A lively and readable recreation of the lives and values of ancient Egyptians.

Newman, James L. *The Peopling of Africa: A Geographic Interpretation*. New Haven: Yale University Press, 1995. An excellent summary of what we know about the early history and migrations of Africa's people.

Niditch, Susan. *Ancient Israelite Religion*. New York: Oxford University Press, 1997. An account of the Hebrew religion that shows its debt to the Canaanites as well as those features that made it unique.

Shaw, Ian, ed. *The Oxford History of Ancient Egypt*. New York: Oxford University Press, 2004. A well-rounded, up-to-date survey.

Stiebing, William H. *Ancient Near Eastern History and Culture*, 2nd ed. New York: Longman, 2008. An up-to-date survey of ancient western Asia, Egypt, and the eastern Mediterranean.

Tyldesley, Joyce. *Hatshepsut: The Female Pharaoh*. New York: Viking, 1996. A readable biography of this remarkable leader.

Welsby, Derek A. *The Kingdom of Kush: Napatan and Meroitic Empires*. Princeton: Markus Wiener, 1996. A well-illustrated and up-to-date survey of Kushite society.

AROUND THE PACIFIC RIM: EASTERN EURASIA AND THE AMERICAS, 5000–600 B.C.E.

Bildarchiv Preussischer Kulturbesitz/Art Resource, NY

Shang Axe Head
The Shang Chinese made some of the ancient world's finest bronze tools. This axe head, decorated with a human face, may have been used to behead rivals of the Shang rulers.

He encouraged the people and settled them. He called his superintendent of works [and] minister of instruction, and charged them with the building of the houses. Crowds brought the earth in baskets. The roll of the great drum did not overpower [the noise of the builders].

—CHINESE POEM FROM THE SECOND MILLENNIUM B.C.E.[1]

According to Chinese tradition, around 1400 B.C.E. a ruler named Pan Keng supervised the building of a new capital city, Anyang (ahn-yahng), on a flat plain alongside the Huan River. The king and his officials supervised the citizens in the hard construction labor, which was done to the beat of a drum. The king had high expectations for his new capital. Thanks to the rich soil, productive farms would stretch out into the distance. The river could supply water and aid in defense. People could find timber, hunt, or seek relief from the summer heat in mountains a short chariot ride away. Anyang was likely China's first planned city. Surrounded by four walls facing the points of the compass, it reflected the ancient adage that without harmony nothing lasts. Three and a half millennia later archaeologists digging at Anyang found exquisite ritual bronzes and "dragon bones," animal bones carved with some of the earliest Chinese writing. For hundreds of years, local chemists, not knowing their priceless historical value, had been grinding up these bones to make folk medicine. But they showed that ancient China, like Mesopotamia and Egypt, had both cities and a writing system. Although Anyang's buildings crumbled with time and ruling families came and went, the legacy of early China did live on for centuries.

Cities, states, agriculture, and trade networks developed in various societies on both sides of the Pacific Ocean. People in China and Korea were among the earliest people in the world to develop farming and metalworking, and Southeast Asians pioneered in maritime technology. The ancient Chinese established a foundation for a society that has retained many of its original ideas and customs down to the present day. Despite formidable geographical barriers, China and Southeast Asia also became connected very early to other parts of Eurasia by trade networks. On the American side of the Pacific, too, many peoples underwent the great transitions to farming, cities, and complex social structures. Although mountains, deserts, and forest barriers tended to isolate North, Central, and South American societies from each other, regional networks of exchange still formed during the ancient period.

FOCUS QUESTIONS

1. How did an expanding Chinese society arise from diverse local traditions?

2. What were some key differences between the Shang and Zhou periods in China?

3. How did the traditions developing in Southeast and Northeast Asia differ from those in India and China?

4. How do scholars explain the settlement and rise of agriculture in the Americas?

Visit the website and eBook for additional study materials and interactive tools:
www.cengage.com/history/lockard/globalsocnet2e

THE FORMATION OF CHINESE SOCIETY, 6000–1750 B.C.E.

How did an expanding Chinese society arise from diverse local traditions?

China was one of the first societies with cities and states, joining Harappa, Mesopotamia, Egypt, and Minoan Crete in pioneering new ways of life. Societies change in part through contact with each other, but forbidding desert and mountain barriers, including the high Tibetan (tuh-BET-en) Plateau on China's western borders, complicated contact with China, although they did not prevent some influences from crossing borders. But productive farming, creative cultures, and the rise of states laid the framework for a distinctive society, now at least 4,000 years old.

China and Its Regional Environments

The Chinese faced many challenges in communicating both with each other and with distant peoples. China's vast size, combined with a difficult topography, made transportation difficult and also encouraged regional cultural and political loyalties. The early Chinese were sometimes divided into competing states, and governments struggled to enforce centralizing policies. The Himalayas (him-uh-LAY-uhs), the Tibetan Plateau, and great deserts inhibited contact with South and West Asia. However, the Chinese did have regular exchanges, including both trade and conflict, with the peoples in Central Asia, North Asia, Southeast Asia, and Tibet, whose cultures, languages, and ways of life were very different from the Chinese. The Chinese sometimes extended political control over these peoples and sometimes were invaded and even conquered by them.

Geographical Foundations

China's large land area was one major factor that fostered regionalism. Modern China covers as much land as western and eastern Europe combined. But most people lived in the eastern third of the modern country. Most Chinese also lived in inland river valleys rather than along the coast. As a result, maritime commerce was not very significant until 1000 C.E. China's three major river systems helped shape Chinese regionalism. The Yellow, or Huang He (hwang ho), River; the Yangzi (yahng-zeh), or Yangtze, River; and the West, or Xijiang (SHEE JYAHNG), River all flow from west to east and hence do not link the northern, central, and southern parts of China. The Yellow River, sometimes termed "China's sorrow" because of its many destructive floods, flows some 3,000 miles through north China to the Yellow Sea, but it is easily navigable only in some sections. The more navigable but also flood-prone Yangzi, the world's fourth-longest river, flows through central China, a region of moderate climate that has long had the densest population. The shorter West River system helps define mountainous and subtropical south China.

China's neighboring regions had diverse environments and distinctive cultures. The deserts and grasslands of Central Asia, with their blazing hot summers and long, bitterly cold winters, were mostly unpromising for intensive agriculture. The rugged, pastoralist Central Asian societies that lived there traded with, warred against, and sometimes conquered the settled farmers of China, Korea, and India. The Central Asians who most affected Chinese history included diverse Turkik-speaking peoples, some of whom lived in the dry Xinjiang (SHIN-jee-yahng) region of far western China. The Tibetans were subsistence farmers and herders. The ancient Chinese also forged occasional relations with people in mainland Southeast Asia, Manchuria, and Korea.

Early Chinese Agriculture

Agriculture in China began around 7000 B.C.E., perhaps 1,000 years later than in Mesopotamia (see Chronology: Ancient China, 7000–600 B.C.E.). The remains of Neolithic settlements have been discovered all over China, suggesting the diverse roots of Chinese society. The Yellow and Wei River Valleys in north China were major centers of early farming. The modest annual rainfall and frequent flooding made the region somewhat similar to the Nile, Tigris-Euphrates, and Indus Basins. In addition, winds blowing in from the Gobi Desert of Mongolia to the northwest deposited massive amounts of dust, which enriched the soils of north China. The people planted the wheatlike, highly drought-resistant millet. Later, wheat, likely imported from India or

CHRONOLOGY

Ancient China, 7000–600 B.C.E.

7000 Agriculture begins in Yellow River Basin

5000 Agriculture begins in Yangzi River Basin

5000–3000 Yangshao culture in northern China

3000–2200 Longshan culture in northern China

2600 Copper mining

2183–1752 Xia dynasty in northern China (disputed)

1752–1122 Shang dynasty in northern China

1400 Beginning of bronze-casting industry

1122–221 Zhou dynasty

CHRONOLOGY

	China	Japan and Southeast Asia	The Americas
10,000 B.C.E.		**10,000–300 B.C.E.** Jomon culture	
5000 B.C.E.	**5000–3000 B.C.E.** Yangshao culture	**4000–2000 B.C.E.** Austronesian migrations	
3000 B.C.E.	**3000–2200 B.C.E.** Longshan culture		**3000–1600 B.C.E.** Peruvian cities
2000 B.C.E.	**1752–1122 B.C.E.** Shang dynasty **1122–221 B.C.E.** Zhou dynasty		**1200–300 B.C.E.** Olmec **1200–200 B.C.E.** Chavín
1000 B.C.E.		**1000–800 B.C.E.** First Southeast Asian states	

Mesopotamia, became northern China's main cereal grain. Ancient songs tell us something about the farming routine:

> They clear away the grass, the trees; Their ploughs open up the ground. In a thousand pairs they tug at weeds and roots, Along the low grounds, along the ridges. They sow the many sorts of grain, The seeds that hold moist life. How that blade shoots up, How sleek, the grown plant.[2]

Farther south, the Chinese in the Yangzi River Basin began cultivating rice by 5000 B.C.E. Thus very early two distinct agricultural traditions emerged. In the cooler, drier north drought-tolerant crops like wheat, millet, pears, and apricots were mainstays. In the wetter, warmer southern half of China, irrigated rice predominated. But rice became so important that for several thousand years Chinese have greeted each other by asking, Have you eaten rice yet?, and have described losing a job as breaking one's rice bowl.

Highly productive agriculture was always a key to China's success. Making wise use of the land, the Chinese sustained reasonably adequate diets over many millennia. Despite sporadic famine, the Chinese people were basically well fed and well housed throughout much of history, beginning in ancient times. Productive farming also promoted population growth: China contained between 2 and 4 million people by 3000 B.C.E. The Chinese ate well enough that they came to perceive food as more than simple fuel. Cooking became an art form and an essential component of social life, and a God of the Kitchen became an important deity of folk religion. Many regional cooking variations developed, as any traveler will see by exploring the Cantonese, Hunanese (hoon-ahn-eez), Mandarin, and Sichuanese (SUH-chwahn-eez) restaurants in large cities around the world. The use of chopsticks for eating meals probably goes back 4,000 years.

Neolithic China included several societies with distinctive regional traditions that established a foundation for Chinese cultural development. The Yangshao (YANG-shao) ("painted pottery") culture, which began in the middle Yellow River region around 5000 B.C.E., covered an area of north China larger than Mesopotamia or Egypt. Yangshao people made fine painted pottery, used kilns, bred pigs and dogs, weaved thread, and buried their dead in cemeteries, suggesting belief in an afterlife. They also raised silkworms and fashioned the silk into clothes. In the centuries to follow, silk making become a unique Chinese activity, and Chinese silk was exported all over Eurasia. Music was popular; a 7,000-year-old seven-holed flute is the oldest still playable musical instrument ever found anywhere in the world. Evidence for jade carving, for which the Chinese later became famous, has been found in several regions. Finally, since floods and earthquakes were common, the early Chinese sought various ways to avert disaster. This search led to religious speculation and experimentation with techniques to predict the future.

The Growth and Spread of Chinese Culture

About 3000 B.C.E., when the Sumerians were building their cities, the exchange of ideas and technologies over the developing trade networks began to produce an expansive Chinese culture out

[2]*The Book of Songs*, translated by Arthur Waley (London: George Allen and Unwin, 1954), © copyright by permission of The Arthur Waley Estate.

Peasant Life in Zhou China The decorations on bronze vessels from Zhou China offer information on peasant life. This decoration, from the Warring States Period, shows people in varied activities: fighting, hunting, making music, performing rituals, and preparing food.

of various regional traditions. As late as 2000 B.C.E. many societies with different cultures and languages remained in China, but gradually the societies in northern and central China merged their traditions into a common social and cultural zone. The Yellow River Basin remained a major core of creativity. The Longshan (LUNG-shahn) ("black pottery") culture flourished between 3000 and 2200 B.C.E. Occupations were now more specialized, fostering a division of labor and social classes. The Longshan people built strong houses, lived in walled villages and towns, and had weapons. They also made pottery almost as hard as metal, carved high-quality jade, and created a simple pictographic writing system. Millennia before any other society, the Chinese of this era also used industrial diamonds to polish ceremonial ruby and sapphire axes, giving them a fine sheen. Chinese in other regions also made contributions. For example, the people in the Yangzi Basin produced distinctive traditions of agriculture, animal domestication, town building, and bronze metallurgy that were at least as old, if not older, than those of north China.

E. Consten, Das alte China

During the first millennium B.C.E., Chinese identity and customs gradually expanded from the Yellow and Yangzi Basins into south China. The Chinese displaced or absorbed most of the indigenous (in-DIJ-uh-nuhs) peoples (the original inhabitants) in the south, although many ethnic minorities still live there. This mixing of different peoples produced a Chinese culture that encompassed many regional traditions and, at times, different states, all held together by many common customs as well as a standardized written language. Political unity helped but was not essential to this sense of a shared cultural identity.

Population growth and shared culture made possible the first state. Chinese historians labeled this state the Xia (shya) (Hsia) dynasty (2183–1752 B.C.E.), but its existence is still debated. A possible Xia capital city, one square mile in size, was built around 2000 B.C.E. near the Yellow River. The Xia may have presided over an occupationally diverse society including scribes, metallurgists, artisans, and bureaucrats. Some influences also filtered in from Central Asia, including the horse and chariot, ironworking, and certain philosophies, but in general, the Chinese themselves developed the ideas and institutions that gave their society the ability to expand, grow, adapt, and coordinate large populations. Many of the ancient traditions remain influential even today.

SECTION SUMMARY

- Early Chinese society was concentrated inland from the sea and was frequently fragmented into various states.

- In the cold, dry Chinese north, crops such as wheat and millet were grown, while in the wetter, warmer south, rice was dominant.

- Members of the Yangshao ("painted pottery") society were skilled craftspeople who excelled at carving, weaving, and village design.

- As time passed, the widely diverse Chinese peoples began to knit themselves together in one broad society with traditions that persist to this day.

- The first Chinese state may have appeared late in the third century B.C.E.

THE RESHAPING OF ANCIENT CHINESE SOCIETY, 1750–600 B.C.E.

What were some key differences between the Shang and Zhou periods in China?

China had clearly made the great transition to cities and states when the Shang (shahng) dynasty established a powerful state and an expanding culture based on bronze technology. The Shang were followed by a more decentralized, iron-using Zhou (joe) dynasty, when the Chinese improved writing and developed literature. Some religious notions of enduring influence in China also appeared in these centuries. Isolation from other Eurasian states fostered a feeling of cultural superiority. The Chinese perceived themselves surrounded by less developed neighbors who either adopted Chinese customs or invaded China to enjoy its riches. Strong governments, technological developments, and writing helped make China the most influential East Asian society.

The Shang Dynasty Reshapes Northern China

The Shang (1752–1122 B.C.E.), the first Chinese dynasty that can be well documented, began around the same time that Hammurabi ruled in Babylon and the Harappan society was collapsing in India. A people from the western fringe of China, the Shang, like the Aryan migrants into India, had adopted horse-drawn chariots for warfare and owed their success partly to contacts with Central Asian pastoralists. They conquered the eastern Yellow River Basin, imposing a hierarchy dominated by landowning aristocrats (see Map 4.1), presiding over a growing economy and the building of more cities. However, many Chinese outside Shang control maintained their own states and unique customs.

The Shang established an authoritarian state, perhaps in part to coordinate irrigation and dam building. Shang kingship was passed on to a monarch's brother or son. Kings presented themselves as father figures who headed the country as a father did a family, claiming both political and spiritual leadership. Like the Aryans who were then moving into India, they devoted much of their energy to military matters, using a lethal combination of archers, spearmen, and charioteers. One of their concerns was defending their northern borders, a recurring theme in Chinese history. The relative prosperity of China in comparison to the marginal existence possible in the grasslands and deserts beyond the frontiers often prompted pastoral nomads to invade the Yellow River Valley.

Economically and technologically the Shang was a flourishing period. Many cities were built as administrative and commercial centers. Anyang, the ruler Pan Keng's new capital city discussed in the chapter opening, was surrounded by a wall 30 feet high and 60 feet wide that enclosed 4 square miles; altogether, the city and its suburbs spread out over some 10 square miles. It apparently took some 10,000 workers eighteen years to build Anyang, reflecting considerable political and social organization. Technology improved, especially with the introduction of bronze in 1400 B.C.E. and the earliest porcelain. This was the great age of bronze, and the Shang are often considered the most skilled bronze casters in the Afro-Eurasian world. They produced flawless bronze arrows, spears, sculpture, pots, and especially ritual vessels for drinking wine. The Shang also produced glazed pottery that was the forerunner of the porcelain ("china") for which the Chinese would later become so famous.

The Shang social hierarchy was dominated by landowning aristocrats, many of them government officials. They enjoyed luxurious surroundings, and their residences were built on cement-like foundations. Aristocratic women also enjoyed a high status. For example, Fuhao (foo-HOW), a wife of a Shang king, led military campaigns and owned large estates. Shang leaders and their families were buried in elaborate royal tombs with great quantities of valuable objects.

Shang Bronze Pots These bronze ritual vessels, some featuring animal designs, were made during the Shang or early Zhou period. They were used for ceremonies.

Courtesy of the Trustees of the British Museum

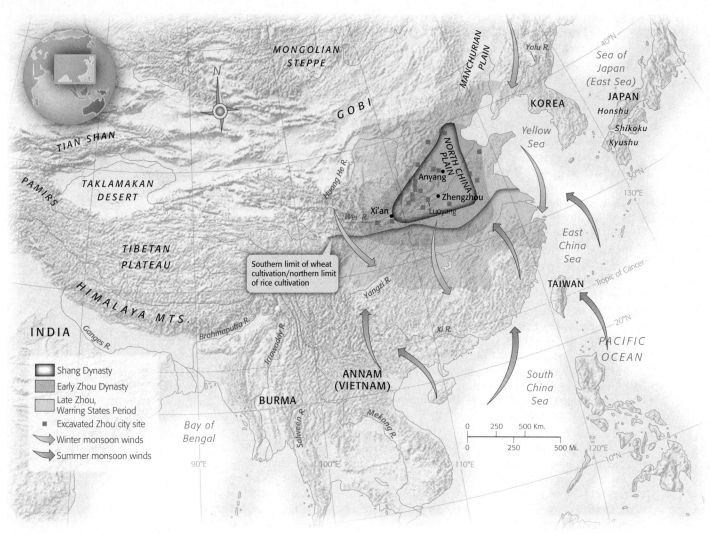

Map 4.1
Shang and Zhou China

The earliest Chinese states arose in north China along the Yellow River and its tributaries. The bronze-using Shang dynasty presided over the first documented state and were succeeded by the iron-using Zhou, who governed much of north and central China.

Interactive Map

However, many people were commoners, included skilled artisans, scribes, and merchants. The scribes may have formulated the world's earliest simple decimal system. Farmers and laborers, including many slaves, occupied the bottom of the social hierarchy, and they were often mobilized by the powerful state for major building projects. The Shang were harsh masters. They practiced human and animal sacrifice as part of their religious observances, often using slaves as victims.

The Shang's momentous contribution was an elaborate writing system. In an attempt to predict the future, influential people wrote questions addressed to the gods on bones of animals and *Shang Writing* tortoise shells. The variety of subjects included the abundance of the next harvest, the outcome of a battle, the weather, or the birth of an heir. For example, one inquired whether "if the king hunted, whether the chase would be without mishap."[3] Some prestigious officials were experts in interpreting the future with these bones. The writing found on oracle bones was clearly the forerunner of today's Chinese writing.

The Early Zhou and Their Government

Political Change As Shang power faded, the Zhou, a state on the western fringe of China, invaded and overthrew the Shang, forming a new dynasty, the Zhou (1122–221 B.C.E.), and a new type of government. The Duke of Zhou supposedly urged that "we must go on, abjuring all idleness, until our reign is universal and there shall not be one who is disobedient to our rule."[4] But the decentralized Zhou system differed considerably from the Shang approach. A relatively weak central government ruled over small states that had considerable autonomy but owed service obligations to the king.

This decentralization reflected the Zhou realization that, despite their impressive military technology, Chinese culture had spread too far for them to administer the entire society effectively. The royal family directly ruled the area around their capital but parceled out the rest to followers and relatives. The regional leaders became local lords with much local power. Hence the Zhou kings presided, however symbolically, over a much larger land area than that of the Shang, from southern Manchuria to the Yangzi Basin (see Map 4.1).

To solidify their position, the Zhou justified their triumph over the Shang with a new concept: the **Mandate of Heaven**. According to this belief, rulers had the support of the gods ("heaven") so long as conditions were good. However, when there was war, famine, or other hardships, heaven withdrew its sanction and rebellion was permissible. The decadent and cruel Shang, the Duke of Zhou argued, lost their right to rule because their last kings mocked the gods by their behavior. But over time this radical new concept was used against the Zhou and all later dynasties. Monarchs lost their legitimacy if their misrule led to a crisis. Ever since the Chinese have invoked the Mandate of Heaven to justify the demise of a discredited government.

Furthermore, Chinese scholars began to view their political history in terms of the **dynastic cycle**. Instead of seeing a straight line of progress in history, as the Hebrews did, the Chinese focused on dynasties of ruling families, all of which more or less followed the same pattern as their predecessors. The cycle always began with a new dynasty, which brought peace and prosperity for a few decades. Then overexpansion and corruption led to increasingly costly government, bankruptcy, social decay, and rebellions, eventually resulting in a new dynasty. This concept shaped Chinese thinking for the next 2,500 years.

The Zhou system was unstable, plagued by chronic warfare between the various substates, with larger substates conquering smaller ones. As a result, the 1,700 substates of the early Zhou years were reduced to 7 by 400 B.C.E. These larger substates now had considerable power in counteracting the weakening Zhou kings. Furthermore, Central Asians were obtaining faster ponies, forcing the Chinese to erect better defenses against their relentless pressure.

Mandate of Heaven A Chinese belief that rulers had the support of the supernatural realm as long as conditions were good, but rebellion was justified when they were not.

dynastic cycle The Chinese view of their political history, which focuses on dynasties of ruling families.

Early Zhou Society and Economy

Zhou government not only brought political fragmentation and a figurehead monarchy, but it also fostered a rigid society clearly divided into aristocrats, commoners, and slaves. The nobility, who owed allegiance to the king as vassals but governed their own realms as they liked, owned large estates defended by private armies and worked by slaves. As influential commoners, the merchants had more freedom of action and often became rich. The majority of slaves were soldiers from rival ministates captured in the frequent wars. Criminals and sometimes their relatives were enslaved for their misdeeds. Peasants were mostly bound to the soil on aristocracy-owned land (see the Witness to the Past: The Poetry of Peasant Life in Zhou China), assigned work and punished if it was not done. Their songs reflected resignation: "We rise at sunrise, We rest at sunset. Dig wells and drink, Till our field and eat—What is the strength of the emperor to us?"[5] Yet, there were some checks on landowner power. The more repressive and exploitive lords lost many of their workers and slaves, who migrated or absconded, depopulating the land and ruining the landlord.

Gender roles were rigid in this patriarchal society. All marriages were arranged by parents. A song from the times states: "How does one take a wife? Without a matchmaker she cannot be got." Before or after marriage most women worked hard, and their assigned place was in the home, preparing food, doing housekeeping, and making clothes. Women at all levels were expected to be submissive, and they enjoyed no official role in public affairs. While many elite women were literate, few peasant women or men enjoyed opportunities to learn to read and write. Both genders valued friendship and kinship, as another song illustrates: "Of men that are now, None equals a brother. When death and mourning affright us, Brothers are very dear."[6]

Zhou China nurtured many significant technological and economic developments. Ironworking reached China from Central Asia by around 700 B.C.E. Iron made much better plows and tools than bronze but also improved weaponry for the increasing warfare. Newly introduced soybeans provided a rich protein source and also enriched the soil. Chinese agriculture became so productive, and surpluses so common, that the population by 600 B.C.E. was around 20 million. Trade grew, merchants became more prominent, and China developed a cash economy with copper coins.

Zhou social life often revolved around food. The Chief Cook of the ruler was a high state official, and lavish feasts cemented social ties. Indeed, the banquet was a chief tool of diplomacy at

Social Patterns

Iron and Agricultural Technology

The Poetry of Peasant Life in Zhou China

We can learn something of the lives of ancient Chinese common folk, especially the peasants who worked the land, from *The Book of Songs*, a collection of 305 poems, hymns, and folk songs compiled between 1000 and 600 B.C.E.

Some songs address ordinary people at their labor. Men weed the fields, plant, plow, and harvest. Women and girls gather mulberry leaves for silkworms, carry hampers of food to the men in the fields for lunch, and make thread:

The girls take their deep baskets, And follow the path under the wall, to gather the soft mulberry-leaves.

Some of the songs deal with courtship and love, sometimes revealing strong emotion, as in this song by a girl about a prospective sweetheart:

That the mere glimpse of a plain cap, Could harry me with such longing, Cause me pain so dire. . . . Enough! Take me with you to your house. . . . Let us two be one.

Within the family, the father had nearly absolute authority over his wife and children. When the family patriarch died, his wife became the family head. Children were expected to obey their parents, but some songs reveal that mutual affection and gratitude were common:

My father begot me. My mother fed me, Led me, bred me, Brought me up, reared me, Kept her eye on me, tended me, At every turn aided me. Their good deeds I would requite.

Peasant lives were filled with toil and hardship, but they could find some relief from drudgery in friendship and kinship. Entertaining relatives and friends was a major leisure activity:

And shall a man not seek to have his friends? He shall have harmony and peace. I have strained off my liquor in abundance, the dishes stand in rows, and none of my brethren are absent. Whenever we have leisure, let us drink the sparkling liquor.

Peasants faced many demands on their time and labor. Songs complain and even protest about an uncaring government and its rapacious tax collectors:

Big rat, big rat, Do not gobble our millet! Three years we have slaved for you. Yet you took no notice of us. At last we are going to leave you, And go to the happy land . . . where no sad songs are sung.

Some songs record abject poverty and misery:

Deep is my grief. I am utterly poverty-stricken and destitute. Yet no one heeds my misfortunes. Well, all is over now. No doubt it was Heaven's [the supernatural realm's] doing. So what's the good of talking about it!

Zhou peasants needed all the help they could get, and some songs seem to be prayers to Heaven to bless their lives:

Good people, gentle folk—Their ways are righteous. . . . Their thoughts constrained. . . . Good people, gentle folk—Shape the people of this land. . . . And may they do so for ten thousand years!

THINKING ABOUT THE READING

1. What do the songs tell us about the importance of families and friends to the Zhou Chinese?

2. What did peasants think about those who ruled them? Can you say why?

Source: The Book of Songs, translated by Arthur Waley (London: George Allen and Unwin, 1954) © copyright by permission of The Arthur Waley Estate.

all levels of society, often lubricated by wine: "When we have got wine, we strain it; When we have got none, we buy it!"[7] However, the costly and complicated ceremonies enjoyed by the rich did not extend down to peasants, who had little money for anything more than basic hospitality.

The Evolution of Chinese Writing and Religion

A distinctive Chinese writing system arose to solve the special problems posed by the many, often mutually unintelligible spoken languages. Some six hundred dialects of Chinese are still spoken today, a heritage of many local cultures. Most of the Chinese north of the Yangzi River speak closely related Northern Mandarin dialects, but other Chinese, especially in the southern half of China, have vastly different dialects. Chinese from Guangzhou (GWAHN-cho) and Beijing (bay-JING) would not understand each other if they only spoke their local dialects. Another difficulty is that the monosyllabic Chinese languages are tonal: that is, the stress placed on a sound changes its meaning. For example, depending on the tone employed by the speaker, in

Mandarin the sound *ma* can mean "mother," "hemp," "horse," or the verb "to curse." It can also indicate a question. To overcome these problems, the Chinese gradually developed one written language based not on sound but on characters. The pictographs of early Shang times resemble crude pictures of an object, such as a man or bird. Later they evolved into complex ideographs, in which characters stand for ideas and concepts. Some 50,000 new characters have been created since the Shang (see Figure 4.1). The practicality of this system became apparent in modern times when Chinese linguists faced great difficulty converting tonal words into a Western-type alphabet.

As in Mesopotamia and Egypt, writing had vast social and cultural implications, promoting political and cultural unity by making possible communication between people speaking different dialects. Otherwise the Chinese might have split into many small countries, as occurred in India and Europe for much of history. Thus writing helped to create the largest society on earth, unifying rather than dividing peoples of diverse ancestries, regions, and languages. The written language also gave prestige to those who mastered it. As the writing brush became the main writing instrument, writing became an art form, and every literate Chinese became something of an art-

大	大	Large *(frontal view of "large" man)*
日	日	Sun
甘	曰	To speak *(mouth with protruding tongue?)*
廿	口	Mouth
䇠	言	Speech *(vapor or tongue leaving mouth)*
尸	户	Door, house *(left leaf of double door)*
㞢	心忄	Heart, mind *(picture of physical heart)*
夕	夕	Evening, dusk *(crescent moon)*
朩	木	Tree, wood *(tree with roots and branches)*
魚	魚	Fish
屮屮	艸	Grass *(growing plants)*
𣪊	鼓	Drum *(drum on stand; hand with stick)*

Figure 4.1 Evolution of Chinese Writing This chart shows early and modern forms of Chinese characters, revealing how pictographs, often recognizable, matured into increasingly abstract ideographs.

ist. Yet the demands of memorizing thousands of characters mostly limited literacy to the upper classes with the time and money to study writing. Education, scholarship, and literature became valued commodities.

Chinese ideas on the mysteries of life and the cosmic order also developed in ancient times. Shang religion emphasized ancestor worship, magic, mythology, agricultural deities, and local spirits. These ideas evolved by later Zhou times into distinctive ideas, including the notion of a generalized supernatural force the Chinese called *tian* (tee-an), which was believed to govern the universe. The **Yijing** (yee-CHING) (Book of Changes), a collection of sixty-four mystic hexagrams and commentaries that was used to predict future events, later became influential throughout East Asia. The *Yijing*'s main theme was that heaven and earth are in a state of continual change.

The *Yijing* was closely related to Chinese cosmological thinking as expressed in the theory of *yin* and *yang*, which had appeared in simple form as early as the Shang period. To the Chinese, yin and yang are the two primary cosmic forces that power the universe through their interaction. Neither one permanently triumphs; rather they are balanced, in conflict and yet complementary in a kind of cosmic symphony. Many things were correlated with these principles:

Yang: bright, hot, dry, hard, active, masculine, heaven, sun

Yin: dark, cold, wet, soft, quiescent, feminine, earth, moon

Given the Chinese preference for hierarchy, yang was superior to yin, and male superior to female. Thus the philosophy justified inequalities in society. The yin-yang dualism remains important throughout East Asia. The Chinese strongly influenced their neighbors in Korea, Vietnam, and Japan, and over the centuries many Chinese ideas and institutions diffused to the peoples on their fringe.

***Yijing* (Book of Changes)** An ancient Chinese collection of sixty-four mystic hexagrams and commentaries upon them that was used to predict future events.

SECTION SUMMARY

- The western Shang established an authoritarian state, with the king playing the role of father to the entire country.

- Under the Shang, society became increasingly stratified, divided up into a dominant aristocracy, a middle class, farmers and laborers, and slaves.

- After a slave rebellion overthrew the Shang, the Zhou established a more widespread, less centralized empire.

- The Zhou introduced the concepts of rule by the "Mandate of Heaven" and of the dynastic cycle, which have endured to this day.

- A common written language provided a unifying link for the Chinese, who spoke hundreds of different dialects (many of which are still spoken today).

- One of the first Chinese books was the *Yijing*, which was related to the idea of the universal opposing forces, *yin* and *yang*.

ANCIENT SOUTHEAST AND NORTHEAST ASIANS

How did the traditions developing in Southeast and Northeast Asia differ from those in India and China?

China's neighbors in Southeast and Northeast Asia also made important early contributions in farming and technology in an environment somewhat different from China and India. These cultures, although influenced by China or India, demonstrated many unique characteristics. Chinese influence was especially strong in Korean and Japan, beginning in the Shang period. But the Koreans and Japanese had already established the foundations for complex societies. Over the following centuries they integrated Chinese influences with their own ideas and customs, maintaining separate ethnic identities.

CHRONOLOGY
Northeast and Southeast Asia, 10,000–600 B.C.E.

10,000–300 B.C.E. Jomon culture in Japan

8000–6000 B.C.E. Agriculture begins in Southeast Asia

7000–4000 B.C.E. Agriculture begins in New Guinea

5000–2000 B.C.E. Agriculture begins in Korea

4000–2000 B.C.E. Austronesian migrations into Southeast Asia islands

2000–1500 B.C.E. Bronze Age begins in Southeast Asia

1600–1000 B.C.E. Melanesian and Austronesian migrations into South Pacific

1000–800 B.C.E. First Southeast Asian states

1000 B.C.E. Austronesian settlement of Fiji and Samoa

Southeast Asian Environments and Early Agriculture

While historically linked to both China and India, Southeast Asian peoples developed in distinctive ways that were shaped in part by geography and climate. Southeast Asia, which stretches from modern Burma (or Myanmar) eastward to Vietnam and the Philippines and southward through the Indonesian archipelago, is separated from the Eurasian landmass by mountain and water barriers. The region has a tropical climate, with long rainy seasons. Rain forests once covered much of the land. But the great rivers that flow through mainland Southeast Asia, such as the Mekong (MAY-kawng), Red, and Irrawaddy (ir-uh-WAHD-ee) Rivers, also carved out broad, fertile plains and deltas that could support dense human settlement.

The topography both helped and hindered communication. Southeast Asians say that the water unites and the land divides. The shallow seas fostered maritime trade, seafaring, and fishing and linked the large islands such as Sumatra (soo-MAH-truh), Java (JA-veh), and Borneo (Kalimantan) to their neighbors. In contrast, the heavily forested highlands inhibited overland travel and encouraged diverse religions, languages, and states. An Indonesian proverb well describes the mosaic of cultures that resulted: different fields, different grasshoppers; different pools, different fish.

Agriculture and technology arose early. Some scholars think that, as in the Fertile Crescent, the transition to food growing began in Thailand and Vietnam by 8000 or 9000 B.C.E., but most doubt that it began earlier than 6000 B.C.E. (see Chronology: Northeast and Southeast Asia, 10,000–600 B.C.E.). Horticulture may have began in the island of New Guinea even earlier. Rice was probably first domesticated in south or central China first and then spread into Southeast Asia, where it became a major crop. Southeast Asians may have been the first to cultivate bananas, yams, and taro and domesticated chickens, pigs, and perhaps even cattle. Southeast

Asians also developed or improved technologies originally from India, Mesopotamia, and China. By 1500 B.C.E. fine bronze was being produced in northeast Thailand in villages like Ban Chiang (ban chang), whose people lived in houses perched on poles above the ground, still a common pattern in Southeast Asia. Ban Chiang women made beautiful hand-painted and durable pottery. Village artists fashioned jewelry and many household items of bronze and ivory. Elsewhere in Eurasia the Bronze Age was synonymous with cities, kings, armies, huge temples, and defensive walls, but in Southeast Asia bronze metallurgy derived from peaceful villages. Evidence for trade networks can be found in Dong Son village, Vietnam, where people made huge bronze drums that have been found all over Southeast Asia. Tin mined in Southeast Asia may have been traded to the Indus cities. Southeast Asians worked iron by 500 B.C.E., several centuries later than northern China.

Migration and New Societies in Southeast Asia and the Pacific

Gradually new societies formed from local and migrant roots. The early Southeast Asians probably included the Vietnamese, Papuans (PAH-poo-enz), Melanesians (mel-uh-NEE-zhuhns), and Negritos (ne-GREE-tos). Migrants came into Southeast Asia from China sometime before the Common Era, assimilating local peoples or prompting them to migrate eastward through the islands. Today Papuans and Melanesians are found mostly in New Guinea and the western Pacific islands, while the few thousand remaining small-statured, dark-skinned Negritos mostly live in remote mountains and islands. The newcomers probably mixed their cultures and languages with those of the remaining indigenous inhabitants, producing new peoples such as the Khmers (kuh-MARE) (Cambodians), who later established states in the Mekong River Basin.

Over the course of several millennia peoples speaking Austronesian (AW-stroh-NEE-zhuhn) languages and possessing advanced agriculture entered island Southeast Asia from the large island of Taiwan, just east of China. Beginning around 4000 B.C.E., Austronesians began moving south into the Philippine Islands, and by 2000 B.C.E. some moved into the Indonesian archipelago (see Map 4.2), settling Java, Borneo, and Sumatra. Austronesian languages became dominant in the Philippines, Indonesia, the Malay Peninsula, and the central Vietnam coast. Indonesian islanders were the major seafaring traders of eastern Eurasia before the Common Era.

The Austronesian migrations affected other regions as well. Melanesians had migrated eastward into the western Pacific islands beginning around 1500 or 1600 B.C.E., carrying Southeast Asian crops, animals, and house styles as far east as Fiji. Traveling in outrigger canoes and, later, in large double-hulled canoes, some Austronesians also sailed east into the Pacific, mixing their cultures, languages, and genes with those of the Melanesians. By around 1000 B.C.E. Austronesian settlers had reached Samoa and Tonga. These voyages were intentional efforts at discovery and colonization by fearless mariners who developed remarkable navigation skills, reading the stars with their eyes and the swells with their backs as they lay down in their canoes.

The ancient western Pacific culture known as **Lapita**, stretching some 2,500 miles from just northeast of New Guinea to Samoa, was marked by distinctive pottery and a trading network over vast distances. In Samoa and Tonga, Polynesian culture emerged from Austronesian roots. Some Polynesians eventually reached as far east as Tahiti and Hawaii, both 2,500 miles from Tonga.

The Austronesians, Khmer, Vietnamese, and others established societies based on intensive agriculture, fishing, and interregional commerce. By 1000 B.C.E. Austronesian trade networks stretched over 5,000 miles, from western Indonesia to the central Pacific. Austronesians built advanced boats and carried out maritime trade with India by 500 B.C.E. Indonesian cinnamon even reached Egypt. The Vietnamese created the first known Southeast Asian states between 1000 and 800 B.C.E. and believed in a god that "creates the elephants [and] the grass, is omnipresent, and has [all-seeing] eyes."[8]

The Foundations of Korea and Japan

Korea and Japan are neighbors, but they were shaped by different environments (see Map 4.1). The 110 miles of stormy seas that separate them at their closest point did not prevent contact between the two societies but did make it sporadic. Korea occupies a mountainous peninsula some 600 miles long and 150 miles in width. Japan is a group of 3,400 islands stretching across

Erich Lessing/Art Resource, NY

Dong Son Bronze Drum These huge Dong Son bronze drums, named for a village site in Vietnam, were produced widely in ancient Southeast Asia and confirm the extensive long-distance trade networks.

Pacific Cultures

Lapita The ancient western Pacific culture that stretched some 2,500 miles from just northeast of New Guinea to Samoa.

Geographical Foundations

Map 4.2
The Austronesian Diaspora

Austronesians migrated from Taiwan into Southeast Asia, settling the islands. Later some of these skilled mariners moved east into the western Pacific, settling Melanesia. Eventually some of their ancestors settled Polynesia and Micronesia.

e Interactive Map

several climatic zones. Over 90 percent of the land is on three islands: densely populated Honshu (hahn-shoo), frigid Hokkaido (haw-KAI-dow) in the north, and subtropical Kyushu (KYOO-shoo) in the south. Because mountains occupy much of Japan, only a sixth of the land is suitable for intensive agriculture. The archipelago is also weak in all metals except silver.

Koreans

Koreans began farming between 5000 and 2000 B.C.E.. Later they creatively adapted rice growing, which originated in warm southern lands, to their cool climate. As Korean agriculture became more productive, the population grew rapidly, generating a persistent migration of Koreans across the straits to Japan. Growing occupational specialization led to small states based on clans. In a pattern still common today, female shamans led the animistic religion. Despite centuries of contact, the Koreans were never assimilated by the neighboring Chinese, in part because the nontonal Korean and tonal Chinese spoken languages were very different. Korean belongs to the Ural-Altaic language family and is related (although not closely) to Mongol, Turkish, and the Eastern Siberian tongues.

The ancient Koreans imported some useful ideas, adopting bronze and then ironworking, probably from China and Central Asia. Shang refugees brought more Chinese culture and technology, but Koreans also created their own useful products and technology, including some of the era's finest pottery. To contend with the frigid winters, the early Koreans invented an ingenious method of radiant floor heating, still widely used today, that circulates heat through chambers in a stone floor. Much later both the Chinese and Romans devised similar schemes.

The ancient Japanese were more isolated than the Koreans from China and no less creative. Human settlement began perhaps 40,000 years ago, before rising sea levels isolated Japan from the mainland. Pottery, for example, was produced earlier than in China and is among the world's oldest. The identity of these early settlers is unknown, but they were probably the ancestors of the Ainu (I-noo), who are genetically close to other East Asians despite their unusually light skin and extensive body hair. The ancestral Ainu built seaworthy boats, for they settled the Kurile (KOO-reel) Islands north of Japan and traded with eastern Siberia. Ainu relics have also been found in the Aleutian (ah-LOO-shan) Islands off Alaska, suggesting some connection there in ancient times. Ancestral Ainu also were perhaps among the northeast Asians who settled the Americas. Today the remaining few thousand Ainu, who mostly live on Hokkaido and Sakhalin Island, face cultural extinction.

Little is known about when the non-Ainu ancestors of today's Japanese arrived in the islands. Some may have come from Korea beginning 3,000 or 4,000 years ago. Ainu and newcomers mixed over the millennia. Genetic studies link modern Japanese to the Ainu, Siberians, and especially Koreans.

Jomon Society

The best documented Japanese early society is called **Jomon** (JOE-mon) ("rope pattern"), because of the ropelike designs on their pottery. The Jomon period began around 10,000 B.C.E. and endured until 300 B.C.E. The Jomon were probably an Ainu culture that was divided by various languages and regional customs, a diversity that may have reflected the arrival of migrants from Korea. However, the major migrations that brought waves of iron-using settlers from Korea came later, between 500 and 700 B.C.E. The Jomon traded with Korea and Siberia.

The Jomon lived primarily from hunting, gathering, and fishing, but by 5000 B.C.E. they lived in permanent wooden houses containing elaborate hearths, probably the centers for family gatherings. A wide range of foods made up their well-balanced, highly nutritious diet, including shellfish, fish, seals, deer, wild boar, and yams. The Jomon may have been better fed than the Chinese and Korean farmers. There is no evidence for complex agriculture until around 500 B.C.E.

A very different spoken language helped preserve cultural distinctiveness despite much Chinese cultural influence over the centuries. Whether the Japanese language was spoken by the Jomon or brought by later immigrants remains uncertain. Japanese is distantly related to modern Korean and not at all to the surviving Ainu languages. Probably between 500 B.C.E. and 500 C.E., most of the Ainu languages were overwhelmed by a Japanese language possibly based on a now lost Korean dialect. The environment also helped shape the language. Perhaps in response to increasingly crowded conditions, the language promoted tact and vagueness, and the Japanese became adept at nonverbal understanding. These tendencies, which are useful in discouraging social conflict, remain part of Japan's unique heritage.

Dogu Figurine Jomon fired-clay figures, like this one, typically portray women and may have been used in fertility rites. Many have a heart-shaped face and elaborate hairstyle.

Jomon The earliest documented culture in Japan, known for the ropelike design on its pottery.

Tokyo National Museum/The Art Archive

SECTION SUMMARY

- The peoples of Southeast Asia established early maritime trading networks, while inland geographical boundaries led to the development of extremely diverse cultures.

- Extensive migration occurred among China, Southeast Asia, and the Pacific islands.

- Korea and Japan, while being strongly influenced by the Chinese, were shaped by different environments and created unique cultures and societies.

- Partly because of its distinct language, Korea was never assimilated into China and developed special technologies, such as radiant floor heating, to meet its needs.

- The ancestors of modern Japanese probably included, among others, the Ainu, the Jomon, and later the Koreans.

- Japan's language promoted tact and vagueness, probably to prevent social conflict in an increasingly populated area.

ANCIENT AMERICANS

How do scholars explain the settlement and rise of agriculture in the Americas?

After the migrations of humans from Eurasia to the Americas thousands of years ago, American societies developed in isolation from those in the Eastern Hemisphere. Early Americans created diverse cultures that often flourished from hunting and gathering, and later Americans, in some regions, pioneered agriculture and, in Mexico and the Andes, created urban societies and states. Population movement and adaptations to differing environments shaped these varied people's most ancient history, but Americans also shared some common ideas.

Diverse American Environments

Most of the land area of the Western Hemisphere is found on two continents, North and South America, which are linked by the long, thin strand of Central America. A string of fertile islands, both large and small, also rings the Caribbean Sea from Florida to Venezuela. Unlike the east-west axis of Eurasia, the Americas lie on a north-south axis, with a large forest-covered tropical zone separating more temperate regions. This meant that migrating peoples or long-distance travelers encountered very different environmental and climatic zones.

Geographical Foundations

Although the total land area is smaller, the Western Hemisphere contains as much diversity of landforms and climate as the Eastern. Extensive tropical rain forests originally covered much of Central America, the Caribbean islands, and the vast Amazon and Orinoco (or-uh-NO-ko) River Basins of South America, making intensive farming difficult, although some people developed simple farming. Rain-drenched forests also once covered the northern Pacific coast and southern Chile, while the southeastern part of North America had more temperate woodlands. The long winters in much of North America made hunting and gathering the most practical subsistence option. Great mountain ranges discouraged communication. Like the Himalayas in Asia, the high Andes, which stretch nearly 5,000 miles down the western side of South America, limited travel. In North America, the Rocky Mountains also provided an east-west barrier. Mountains also run along the Pacific coast of North America, trapping rain clouds and creating huge deserts in western North and South America, as well as extensive grasslands in the interior of the continents. Some of the great river systems, such as the Mississippi, fostered long-distance trade.

The Antiquity and Migration of Native Americans

The ancestry and antiquity of Native Americans generate scholarly debate. Most anthropologists agree that modern Native Americans are descended from stone tool–using Asians who crossed the Bering Strait from Siberia to Alaska, probably when Ice Age conditions lowered ocean levels and created a wide land bridge. Some may have crossed by boat even when no land bridge existed. Seeking game like bison, caribou, and mammoths, migrants could have moved south through ice-free corridors or by boat along the Pacific coast and gradually dispersed throughout the hemisphere. Waves of migrants, probably in small numbers, from different cultural backgrounds in East and North Asia might account for the over two thousand languages among Native Americans. The last wave some 5,000 years ago brought the Inuit (IN-oo-it) and Aleuts (AH-loots).

Debates on Origins

The traditions of many Native American peoples place their origins in the areas where they lived 500 years ago, but some may have lived in these places for many centuries before that. While their origin stories, rich in spiritual meaning, deserve respect, much evidence supports the notion of ancient migration from Asia. No remains of any hominids earlier than modern humans have been found in the Americas. Furthermore, the common ancestry of modern Native Americans is clear from the remarkable uniformity of DNA, blood, virus, and teeth types, which all connect them to peoples in northeast Asia. Some evidence hints that the ancestors of the Ainu, skilled boat-builders in Japan, might have been early migrants. A few recent tool and skeletal finds in North America and Brazil resemble those in Southeast Asia. Several scholars have also suggested that some tool cultures in eastern North America are similar to those of Stone Age peoples who lived in Spain and France several millennia earlier. But the evidence for possible European or Southeast Asian ancestry is sparse. If such migrants did once settle in the Americas, they likely died out or were absorbed by the peoples of Northeast Asian ancestry.

American Origins

Clovis A Native American culture dating back some 11,500 to 13,500 years.

The question of when the first migrants arrived in the Americas perplexes archaeologists. Most trace the migration back to the **Clovis** culture some 11,500 to 13,500 years ago, named after spear points discovered at Clovis, New Mexico, but widespread in North and Central America (see Chronology: The Ancient Americas, 40,000–600 B.C.E.). However, skeletons and artifacts have lately been discovered in North and South America that are much older. Monte Verde (MAWN-tee VAIR-dee), a campsite in southern Chile that is over 10,000 miles from the Bering Strait, may be at least 12,500 years old. Some think it is much more ancient. Monte Verde people lived in rectangular houses with log foundations and exploited a wide variety of vegetable and animal foods. Various other sites in North America, Mexico, and Brazil challenge the Clovis-first theory, but none offers conclusive evidence that convinces skeptics. Various sites in Pennsylvania, South Carolina, and

Virginia may place people in eastern North America between 17,000 and 19,000 years ago. These scattered discoveries hint at but do not yet prove an ancient migration somewhere between 20,000 and 40,000 years ago. The debate will rage for years to come as more sites are excavated.

The earliest Americans, known to scholars as Paleo-Indians, survived by hunting, fishing, and gathering while adapting to varied environments. Being skilled hunters and armed with spears, they may have helped bring about the extinction of large herbivore animals such as horses, mammoths, and camels, which disappeared from the Western Hemisphere between 9000 and 7000 B.C.E. A similar die-off of animals also occurred in Eurasia at the end of the Ice Age, suggesting that climate change was a factor. Most likely, the extinctions of the animals in both hemispheres was caused by some combination of overhunting, environmental change, and perhaps an apocalyptic disease that affected the large mammals. Hunters mostly shifted to smaller game. But on the North American Great Plains, many peoples hunted bison, without benefit of horses. Only in the nineteenth century C.E. did this hunting way of life become impossible, as newly arrived white Americans slaughtered the bison herds on which these Native Americans depended.

Some people in favored locations flourished from hunting, fishing, and gathering for many millennia. In the Pacific Northwest, coastal peoples built oceangoing boats and sturdy wood houses. Along the Peruvian coast deep-sea fishermen exploited the rich marine environment. The Monte Verde villagers used more than fifty food plants and twenty medicinal plants. In southern California the Chumash (CHOO-mash) society, like the Jomon culture of Japan, lived well from a varied vegetation and meat diet that included large marine mammals such as seals. The Chumash built large, permanent villages headed by powerful chiefs. Yet Pacific coast peoples such as the Chumash were also subject to climate change, which periodically brought drought by altering plant and animal environments.

The eastern third of what is now the United States also provided an abundant environment for hunting and gathering, augmented by trade. By 4000 B.C.E. extensive long-distance trade networks linked people over several thousand miles from the Atlantic coast to the Great Plains. Dugout canoes moved copper and red ocher from Lake Superior, jasper (quartz) from Pennsylvania, obsidian from the Rocky Mountains, and seashells from both the Gulf and East Coasts. Great Lakes copper was traded as far away as Mexico, New England, and Florida.

Early Societies and Their Cultures

Over many millennia Americans organized larger societies and developed some distinctive social and cultural patterns that emphasized cooperation within families, animistic religion, and, for some, building huge mounds. Most people lived in egalitarian bands linked by kinship and marriage. Hunting was often a communal activity. Americans shared a belief in supernatural forces, spirits, or gods. For example, men often sought a personal guardian spirit through a visionary experience induced by fasting, enduring physical pain, or taking hallucinogenic drugs. Shamans claiming command over spirits or animal souls were vehicles to connect the human and spirit worlds. The ceremonies for such events as initiations into adult life and courtship probably included ritual dancing. Since the land furnished food, most Americans revered the earth as sacred. Some of them also adopted creation stories that were widely shared with other peoples.

Some Americans organized communities around **mound building**, the construction of huge earthen mounds, often with temples on top. The oldest mound so far discovered, in Louisiana, dates to 2500 B.C.E. Beginning around 1600 B.C.E., some peoples in North America's eastern woodlands and Gulf Coast also developed distinctive mound-building cultures. One major site, Poverty Point in northeastern Louisiana, was occupied between 1000 and 500 B.C.E. (see Profile: The Poverty Point Mound Builders). Occupying about 3 square miles and home to perhaps 5,000 people at its height, Poverty Point had the most massive earthworks in all the Americas at that time. The largest mound, an effigy of a bird that can only be seen from the air, was 70 feet high, comparable to an eight-story apartment building, and 700 feet long. Poverty Point served as the hub of a trading system, importing goods from as far away as the Ohio and upper Mississippi River Valleys and exporting stone and clay products such as pendants and bowls to Florida, Missouri, Oklahoma, and Tennessee.

CHRONOLOGY
The Ancient Americas, 40,000–600 B.C.E.

40,000–20,000 B.C.E. Possible earliest migrations to Americas (disputed)

11,500–9,500 B.C.E. Beginning of Clovis culture

8000 B.C.E. Beginning of agriculture in Mesoamerica and Andes

6000 B.C.E. Potato farming in Andes

4000 B.C.E. Early trade routes in North America

2500 B.C.E. Earliest mound-building cultures

3000–2500 B.C.E. Farming along Peruvian coast

3100–1600 B.C.E. Peruvian city of Caral

2500 B.C.E. Agriculture in lower Mississippi Valley

2000 B.C.E. Earliest agriculture in southwestern North America

1500 B.C.E. Agriculture in Amazon Basin

1200–300 B.C.E. Olmec

1200–200 B.C.E. Chavín

1000–500 B.C.E. Poverty Point culture

650 B.C.E. Olmec writing

---

mound building The construction of huge earthen mounds, often with temples on top, by some ancient peoples in the Americas.

THE POVERTY POINT MOUND BUILDERS

While the spectacular mounds at Poverty Point are the site's most striking legacy, the archaeological research has also revealed a remarkable community. The inhabitants did not need farming because their location, in a fertile valley nourished by annual Mississippi River floods, offered a benign hunting and gathering environment and a gentle climate. The people enjoyed a rich and varied diet that many modern people might envy. Men used simple weapons—for example, spears, spear throwers, darts, and knives—to hunt. The woods provided turkey, duck, deer, and rabbit, while the rivers offered bass, catfish, alligator, and clams. Women collected acorns, hickory nuts, walnuts, wild grapes, persimmons, sunflower seeds, squash, and gourds.

Life seems to have been agreeable. The people lived in wood houses around a central plaza and six mounds, probably governed by chiefs. In their houses men and women crafted many tools and art objects, some of which they traded hundreds of miles away. Small decorated baked-clay balls, found by the thousands in the ruins, were heated for use in cooking or boiling water. Since cooking was women's work, women probably made these clay balls, perhaps helped by their children. Each woman had her own preference for design and shape. Stoneworkers also ground and polished hard stones into ornaments and useful artifacts, and they chipped various stones into points, blades, and cutting tools. Those with an artistic bent made solid-clay female figurines, sometimes pregnant, possibly as fertility symbols. Using red jasper, they fashioned beautiful bead necklaces, bird-head pendants, and human effigies.

Located at the intersection of important waterways, Poverty Point was the central hub for a large region and was linked to trade networks that supplied the townsmen with Appalachian metal for bowls and platters, stone from the Ozarks and Oklahoma, and flint from as far away as Illinois and Ohio. The finely crafted red jasper items, often shaped like animals such as owls, have been found in distant settlements. Some of the Poverty Point men may have ventured out on trading expeditions or to bring home valuable stones from as far away as Missouri. Men and perhaps women undoubtedly arrived regularly in canoes full of trade goods to exchange.

At times the people were mobilized to build new mounds or rebuild old ones that were eroding with time. The complete earthworks contain an immense 1 million cubic yards of soil;

to make them, the people probably had to transport 35 to 40 million 50-pound basket loads to the site. Several thousand people may have participated in the construction, and the project had to be carefully planned and directed so that it followed a geometric design. The mounds perhaps aided astronomical observations as a solar calendar, or perhaps served as a regional ceremonial center for social, political, or religious purposes. Some priestly or ruling class may have lived atop the mounds, as was common in some mound-building societies around the hemisphere. At least 150 smaller satellite sites, scattered along the Mississippi for several hundred miles, all contain similar artifacts, suggesting that Poverty Point was the center of both an economic and a political network.

The culture disappeared by 500 B.C.E., the people having dispersed to smaller settlements. There are no signs of war or major environmental change. Perhaps some political or religious crisis disrupted society. Whatever the case, the Poverty Point people and their culture were lost to history, leaving only the badly eroded but still impressive ruins of today.

THINKING ABOUT THE PROFILE

1. What sort of life did the Poverty Point people experience?
2. What role did Poverty Point play in the region?

Gilcrease Museum, Tulsa, Oklahoma

Poverty Point Jasper Bead Trade goods, such as this red jasper bead shaped like a locust, were produced at Poverty Point in Louisiana and traded over many hundreds of miles in eastern and central North America.

The Rise of American Agriculture

Americans were some of the earliest farmers, but they developed very different crops than the peoples of Afro-Eurasia. Population growth, long-distance trade, and the ebb and flow of weather conditions helped spark this great transition. Hunting and gathering peoples were vulnerable to devastating droughts in years when the periodic weather change known today as *El Niño* (EL

NEE-nyo) warmed the Pacific Ocean, shifting both rainfall patterns and the marine environment, perhaps prompting them to experiment with growing food sources. Some of the chief crops, such as maize (corn), were much more difficult to master than the big-seeded grains of the Fertile Crescent. Furthermore, since there were no potential draft animals, farmers needed to be creative in growing and transporting food.

Some Americans made the transition not long after Southwest Asians had. In Mesoamerica (the region from central Mexico through northern Central America), bottle gourds and pumpkins may have been raised by 8500 or 8000 B.C.E. and maize, sweet potatoes, and beans by 3500 B.C.E. Andes people cultivated chili peppers and kidney beans by about 8000 B.C.E. Later potatoes and maize flourished there. Some Andeans, like early farmers in Eurasia, built elaborate irrigation canals that created artificial garden plots. By 3000 or 2500 B.C.E. societies along the Peruvian coast raised cotton, squash, and maize. By 1500 B.C.E. farming had spread to the Amazon Basin. Farming later spread to North American societies, probably influenced by a wetter climate. The southwestern peoples were particularly ingenious in adapting farming to their poor soils and desert conditions, growing maize, squash, beans, and corn. By 2500 B.C.E. people in the lower Mississippi Valley grew sunflowers and gourds. Eventually maize, beans, and squash became mainstays from the Southwest to the northeastern woodlands, providing a nutritionally balanced diet. **Early Farming**

Three basic farming patterns eventually shaped American societies. People in the highland and valley regions of Mesoamerica relied on maize, beans, and squash. Another pattern emphasizing potatoes and other frost-resistant tubers was developed in the high altitudes of the Andes. Tropical forest societies in South America grew manioc, sweet potatoes, and root crops. The differing farming patterns proved significant for later world history because the great diversity later enriched modern food supplies. Americans domesticated more different plants than had all the Eastern Hemisphere peoples combined, including three thousand varieties of potatoes, as well as chocolate, quinine, and tobacco.

The Americans practiced less intensive agriculture than people in the Eastern Hemisphere because of the lack of draft animals. The only large herd animals available for domestication, the llama and alpaca of the Andes, were tamed by 3500 B.C.E., mostly for use as pack animals and wool sources. Americans domesticated turkeys and guinea pigs for eating. But there were no surviving counterparts to horses, cattle, and oxen. With no animals to aid in pulling, people could not use a plow or wheel. In any case, wheeled vehicles were useless in the steep Andes and the tropical rain forests. People made other innovations, including various ingenious irrigation schemes such as terracing of hillsides and the floating gardens in Central Mexico, which turned swamps into productive fields. But the intensive farming that supported huge populations in China or India was not possible in the Americas.

The lack of draft animals also meant that Americans were exposed to fewer infectious diseases and epidemics. In the Eastern Hemisphere, domesticated animals passed diseases such as measles and smallpox to humans through germs and parasites, precipitating outbreaks that could kill many people. Historians disagree over whether Americans may have been healthier than people across the oceans. Many of them enjoyed long lives, but many people also suffered from various ailments. Furthermore, isolation from the Eastern Hemisphere left Native Americans vulnerable to the diseases brought by Europeans and Africans beginning in 1492 C.E., for which they had no immunity. These diseases eventually killed the great majority of Native Americans. **Health**

Farming Societies, Cities, and States

Archaeologists are learning more about the social and cultural patterns that led to cities and states among early farming peoples. Communal activity was essential in early villages as people cooperated for survival. In the northern Andes, people fashioned the oldest known ceramics in the hemisphere between 3000 and 2500 B.C.E. Institutionalized religions took shape, led by a priestly caste. Some Mesoamericans practiced human sacrifice by 7000 B.C.E., and human sacrifice became common in both Mesoamerica and the Andes to honor the gods and keep the cosmos in balance. Far earlier than the more famous Egyptian mummies, some South American and North American societies developed processes for mummifying the bodies of the deceased through drying, perhaps because of religious beliefs about death and the afterlife. Like the North American mound builders, some Andean and Mesoamerican societies also began building permanent structures for religious, governmental, or recreational purposes. Pacific coast and Andean cultures in South America constructed some of the oldest monumental architecture, including stepped pyramids, by the third millennium B.C.E., about the same time as Egypt, India, and China. A site in southern Mexico from 5000 B.C.E. contained a dance ground or ball **Ancient Religions** **Architecture** court, and ceremonial ballgames involving small teams of players attempting to knock a rubber ball through a high stone hoop became a fixture of Mesoamerican life for millennia.

The First Cities

Agriculture, monumental construction, population growth, and long-distance trade provided a foundation for the first cities and states in the Andes and Mesoamerica between 3000 and 1000 B.C.E. (see Map 4.3). People worked metals like copper, gold, and silver to create tools, weapons, and jewelry. Growing towns with public buildings became centers of political, economic, and religious activities. Massive ceremonial centers hundreds of feet long were constructed along the Peruvian coast, and elsewhere huge mounds laid the foundation for great pyramids. Between 4000 and 1 B.C.E. the population of the Americas grew from 1 or 2 million to around 15 million; over two-thirds of this number were concentrated in Mesoamerica and western South America. Long-distance trade routes also became more common, moving commodities such as obsidian, mirrors, seashells, and ceramics.

South American Societies: Caral and Chavín

Chavín The first major urban civilization in South America (900–250 B.C.E.).

Olmec The earliest urban society in Mesoamerica.

Olmec Head This massive head from San Lorenzo is nearly 10 feet high. The significance of such heads (and the helmets they wear) remains unclear, but they might represent chiefs, warriors, or gods.

The first large settlements built around massive stone structures emerged around 3100 B.C.E. in the Norte Chico region between the Andes and the Pacific coast in north-central Peru. The largest of these settlements and America's first known city, Caral, was built perhaps as early as 2500 or 3000 B.C.E., about the same time as the Harappan cities and the Egyptian pyramids. Caral had some 3,000 residents and was a 150-acre complex of plazas, pyramids, and residential buildings that probably required many thousands of laborers to build. The major pyramid, 60 feet tall and covering the equivalent of four football fields, contained an amphitheater capable of seating hundreds of spectators for civic or religious events. The local economy was clearly able to support an elite group of priests and planners who lived in large, well-kept rooms atop the pyramids. Eventually some twenty pyramid complexes occupied land for many miles around.

We know only a little of Norte Chico life. The economy was based on marine resources such as fish and growing squash, sweet potatoes, fruits, beans, and cotton. The Norte Chico people do not seem to have made ceramics or enjoyed many arts and crafts. However, Caral was a major hub for trade routes extending from the Pacific coast through the Andes to the Amazonian rain forest. There is evidence for human sacrifice. The people evidently enjoyed music, and many animal bone flutes have been found. But Caral collapsed for unknown reasons around 1600 B.C.E., several hundred years before the rise of the better-known American societies of Chavín and the Olmec.

Nathaniel Tarn/Photo Researchers, Inc.

Chavín (cha-VEEN), situated 10,000 feet above sea level in northwestern Peru, emerged the same time as the Olmec, around 1200 or 1000 B.C.E., and collapsed by 200 B.C.E. The Chavín people created flamboyant sculpture and monumental architecture. They also developed a highly original art focusing on real or mythical animals, and they worked gold and silver. Chavín exercised considerable influence in surrounding regions. At its height, the main city probably had some 3,000 inhabitants. Elaborate burial sites reveal class divisions. Chavín became a major regional power, trading widely with the coast and spreading its religious cult to distant peoples. The people worshiped two main deities, and their ceremonial center became a site of pilgrimage for the faithful from a wide area. Chavín perpetuated some of the architectural and religious patterns that became common in the Andes. Its capital, Chavín de Huántar, was located high in the Andes Mountains of Peru. Chavín became politically and economically dominant in a densely populated region that included two distinct ecological zones, the Peruvian coastal plain and the Andean foothills.

Mesoamerican Societies: The Olmec

The **Olmec** (OHL-meck), a people who lived along the Gulf coast of Mexico, formed the earliest known urban society in Mesoamerica by 1200 or 1000 B.C.E., flourishing until 300 B.C.E. (see Map 4.3). Each Olmec city was probably ruled by a powerful chieftain. Olmec cities reflected engineering genius. The earliest city, known today as San Lorenzo, was built on an artificial dirt platform three-quarters of a mile long, half a mile wide,

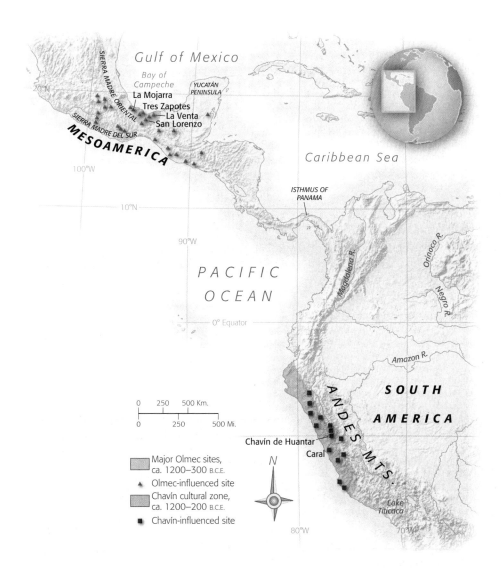

and 150 feet high. Home to some 2,500 people, San Lorenzo was situated above fertile but frequently flooded plains. Another Olmec city, La Venta, included huge earth mounds that required massive labor to build. The stones for Olmec sculptures and temples had to be brought from 60 miles away, and some of the blocks weigh more than 40 tons. The Olmec studied astronomy to correctly orient their cities and monuments with the stars.

The Olmec created remarkable architecture, art, and a writing system. The purpose of the huge sculptured stone heads they erected is unknown, but they might represent rulers. The Olmec built temples and pyramids in ceremonial centers and palace complexes. Their artists carved human and animal figures as well as supernatural beings in sculpture and relief. By around 650 B.C.E. the Olmec had also developed perhaps the first simple hieroglyphic writing in the Americas, which influenced other Mesoamerican peoples, especially the Maya. Mesoamerican writing kept records of kings, rituals, and the calendar, much as writing did in Egypt.

Olmec Arts and Writing

Commerce and the networks it created were a key to Olmec influence. The Olmec traded with Mexico's west coast and Central America, importing basalt, obsidian, and iron ore. One of the major trade goods was jade, which the Olmec fashioned into ceremonial objects, masks, and jewelry. The Olmec may also have exploited cocoa trees for chocolate. Extensive communication between the Olmec and neighboring peoples contributed to some cultural homogeneity in Mesoamerica, especially in religion. Olmec religious symbols and myths emphasized fearsome half-human, half-animal supernatural beings, the prototypes of later Mesoamerican deities. Religious ceremonies required precise measurement of calendar years and time cycles, which fostered mathematics and writing. Although Olmec society eventually disappeared, the Olmec established enduring patterns of life, thought, and kingship in Mesoamerica that influenced later peoples like the Maya (see Chapter 9).

Olmec Economy

SECTION SUMMARY

- The lands of the Western Hemisphere are smaller in area than those of the Eastern and are constructed on a north-south axis rather than an east-west one, but they are just as varied in terms of landforms and climate.

- Scientific evidence suggests that Native American peoples migrated from Eurasia to North America at least 12,000 years ago, and possibly between 20,000 and 40,000 years ago.

- Early American peoples survived by hunting, gathering, and fishing, as well as trading over large distances, but some societies clustered around huge mounds that served religious purposes.

- Mutual cooperation, earth worship, personal connections with guardian spirits, and shamanism were prominent features in early American cultural and spiritual life.

- In response to the challenges posed by different climates, American peoples domesticated more different plants than all the peoples of the Eastern Hemisphere.

- Lacking draft animals, Americans came up with ingenious approaches to farming, but they could not grow the amount of food necessary to support the population levels of India or China.

- The absence of draft animals also meant that Native Americans were not exposed to many diseases before the arrival of Europeans and Africans after 1492 C.E.

- Various technological breakthroughs led to the development of urban societies in Mesoamerica and the Andes, including Caral, America's first known city.

- Chavín of South America and the Olmec in Mesoamerica were early urban societies that served as patterns for later American urban societies.

CHAPTER SUMMARY

Chinese society emerged in river valleys, where the Chinese made the transition to agriculture, cities, and states. The Himalayan Mountains, the Tibetan Plateau, and vast deserts allowed only sporadic contact between China and most other societies. Gradually an expanding Chinese society incorporated many local traditions. The Shang built a powerful state while developing bronze technology and a unique writing system. The Zhou replaced the Shang and presided over a more decentralized system that saw further technological and cultural development, including more advanced writing and literature. China's neighbors in Southeast Asia, Korea, and Japan were also creative in farming and technology, forming unique cultural identities and traditions. Austronesians migrating into Southeast Asia were skilled mariners, and some of them settled the western Pacific islands.

Scholars still debate the origin and antiquity of settlement in the Americas, but most conclude that migrants moved from eastern Eurasia by land or boat many millennia ago. For centuries, hunting, fishing, and gathering supported a viable way of life. The Americas did not have the rich farmland and draft animals common in Eurasia. Nonetheless, farming appeared nearly as early as in the Eastern Hemisphere, a result of population growth, climate change, and technological development. Americans domesticated a wide variety of crops and also forged long-distance trade networks, religious institutions, cities, and states.

KEY TERMS

Mandate of Heaven	**Lapita**	**mound building**
dynastic cycle	**Jomon**	**Chavín**
Yijing	**Clovis**	**Olmec**

EBOOK AND WEBSITE RESOURCES

e **INTERACTIVE MAPS**
Map 4.1 Shang and Zhou China
Map 4.2 The Austronesian Diaspora
Map 4.3 Olmec and Chavín Societies

LINKS

Ancient and Lost Civilizations (http://www.crystalinks .com/ancient.html). Offers some useful essays on various world regions and ancient cultures.

Ancient Mesoamerican Civilizations (http://angelfire .com/ca/humanorigins/index.html). Links and information about the Olmec and other premodern societies.

Internet East Asian History Sourcebook (http://www .fordham.edu/halsall/eastasia/eastasiasbook.html). An invaluable collection of sources and links.

Internet Guide for China Studies (http://www.sino .uni-heidelberg.de/igcs/). A good collection of links on premodern and modern China.

The Ancient East Asia Website (http://www.ancient eastasia.org/). Offers useful essays and other materials on China, Japan, and Korea.

Plus flashcards, practice quizzes, and more. Go to: www.cengage.com/history/lockard/globalsocnet2e.

SUGGESTED READING

Barnes, Gina L. *China, Korea and Japan*, rev. ed. New York: Thames and Hudson, 2000. A well-illustrated summary of the archaeology.

Chang, Kwang-Chih. *The Archeology of Ancient China*, 4th ed. New Haven: Yale University Press, 1986. The major study of ancient China and lavishly illustrated.

Coe, Michael D. *Mexico: From the Olmecs to the Aztecs*, 7th ed. London: Thames and Hudson, 2005. A readable overview of pre-Columbian Mexico, with much on the Olmec.

Creel, Herlee G. *The Birth of China: A Survey of the Formative Period of Chinese Civilization*. New York: Frederick Ungar, 1961. This study remains one of the best introductions to the society of early China.

Ebrey, Patricia, et al. *East Asia: A Cultural, Social, and Political History*, 2nd ed. Boston: Houghton Mifflin, 2009. An excellent survey text on the region.

Ebrey, Patricia Buckley. *The Cambridge Illustrated History of China*. New York: Cambridge University Press, 1999. A readable survey incorporating recent findings.

Fagan, Brian M. *Kingdoms of Gold, Kingdoms of Jade: The Americas Before Columbus*. London and New York: Thames and Hudson, 1991. A nicely illustrated and readable introduction.

Fairbank, John K., Edwin O. Reischauer, and Albert M. Craig. *East Asia: Tradition and Transformation*, rev. ed. Boston: Houghton Mifflin, 1989. A major text with good coverage of ancient China, Korea, and Japan.

Fiedel, Stuart J. *Prehistory of the Americas*, 2nd ed. Cambridge: Cambridge University Press, 2008. A readable introduction.

Habu, Junko. *Ancient Jomon of Japan*. New York: Cambridge University Press, 2004. Excellent study of Jomon society.

Higham, Charles. *The Archaeology of Mainland Southeast Asia*. Cambridge: Cambridge University Press, 1989. A useful and scholarly study of early Southeast Asia.

Higham, Charles. *The Bronze Age of Southeast Asia*. New York: Cambridge University Press, 1996. Scholarly study of ancient Southeast Asia and China.

Imamura, Keiji. *An Introduction to Prehistoric Japan: New Perspectives on Insular East Asia*. Honolulu: University of Hawaii Press, 1996. An up-to-date introduction to what is known about early Japan.

Keightly, David N., ed. *The Origins of Chinese Civilization*. Berkeley: University of California Press, 1983. Scholarly essays on various aspects of ancient China.

Kirch, Patrick V. *The Lapita Peoples: Ancestors of the Oceanic World*. London: Blackwell, 1997. A recent overview of the ancient Pacific peoples.

Totman, Conrad. *A History of Japan*. Malden, MA: Blackwell, 2000. A recent survey with much on this era.

Patriarchy and Matriarchy in the Ancient World

Today, as in the past, men generally hold political, economic, and religious power in most societies. This dominance is due to patriarchy, a system whereby men largely control women and children, shape ideas about appropriate gender behavior, and generally dominate society. Many people assume that patriarchal social organization springs from some innate characteristic of the human species, symbolized by the common expression that this is a "man's world." But the situation is more complex historically.

THE PROBLEM

The prevalence of patriarchy raises three important questions. First, was there ever a time when women held equal power and status to men? Second, was matriarchy, in which women enjoy social and political dominance, ever common? And third, assuming women once enjoyed a higher status in society, can we identify a particular period when patriarchy triumphed? These questions spark heated scholarly debates.

THE DEBATE

The first question is the easiest to answer. Historians are reasonably sure that, among many peoples, women had greater equality with men during the Stone Age. The small, closely knit societies, like the !Kung of southern Africa, were often egalitarian, had weak leaders, and had little private property to fight over. But, despite a rough equality due to women's ability, essential for a society's survival, to gather food and medicinal herbs, there is little evidence that many prefarming societies allowed women more publicly recognized authority than men. Some peoples who practiced simple farming, such as the Iroquois, Cherokee, Hopi, and Zuni in North America, gave women considerable influence within a matrilineal culture, even if men usually had ultimate decision-making power.

In response to the second question, some scholars have argued that a "golden age of matriarchy" existed before the rise of urban societies and states in Europe and the Middle East, and perhaps also in India, Japan, Southeast Asia, and the Americas. Supporters of the ancient matriarchy thesis point to the many figurines of females, many perhaps of goddesses, unearthed at archaeological sites worldwide. They believe that goddess worship correlated with high female status and that women were cherished for giving birth and nurturing the young, which gave them a connection to the earth and spirits. Patricia Monaghan identifies more than 1,500 different goddesses worldwide, representing everything from mother to warrior.

Perhaps the most debated recent studies are by Lithuanian archaeologist Marija Gimbutas, whose writings, based on discoveries at sites such as Çatal Hüyük in Turkey, the Minoan palace at Knossos, and Stonehenge, portray ancient people in Europe and Anatolia as egalitarian and peaceful farmers led by influential women. These female-oriented societies, she says, were destroyed around 3500 B.C.E. by more violent Indo-European nomads from Central Asia, who brought patriarchy with them. From then on, patriarchy spread across Europe. Similarly, Riane Eisler and Judith Lorber describe ancient, goddess-worshiping farming cultures in eastern and southern Europe, where men and women ruled equally, with no war or inequalities of wealth. And like Gimbutas, they contend that Indo-European newcomers imposed male governments on these earlier societies.

Most scholars dispute the views of Gimbutas, Eisler, and Lorber about ancient matriarchies and equal status for each gender. For example, Lotte Motz, Lucy Godison, and Christine Morris argue that goddess worship theories are unproven. Motz claims that female images are no more common in early Europe than those of men and animals. Furthermore, the figurines may have been used in fertility rites rather than revered as spiritual forces. Motz and Cynthia Eller also suggest that mother goddess theories reflect not ancient realities but modern political and cultural attitudes, including a feminism that challenges patriarchy and biases about women's roles. Nor can we assume, such critics say, that worshiping female deities, if it happened, actually gave real power to women. After all, the patriarchal ancient Mesopotamians and Greeks worshiped various female deities, including a goddess of love, and many modern patriarchal cultures, including the Chinese, Japanese, Hindu Indian, and Yoruba, have female deities in their pantheons. Many Europeans have revered the Virgin Mary over the past two millennia, but men have still dominated European society.

If the notion of ancient matriarchies transformed by force into patriarchies cannot be proven, we are still left with the third question, how and when did patriarchy emerge? Anthropologist Sherry Ortner argues for a slow but inevitable transition from the egalitarianism of food collecting to male domination in the early cities and states. To Ortner, patriarchy was a product of technological and social upheavals rather than a will to power by aggressive men. Childbearing played a role because, while women stayed home having and raising children, men could travel and engage in more paid work and governmental, leisure, and religious activities, as well as warfare. That led to the gender stereotypes of women in unpaid work at home and men at paid work elsewhere. Also arguing for a gradual change, anthropologist Elizabeth Barber contends that farming people needed products, such as metal ores, that had to be gained through long-distance trade. This gave power to the more mobile and physically stronger men, who could travel to distant places and transport the heavy cargoes home. To be sure, knowledge of cloth making and the fiber arts gave women importance in ancient societies, since men also used products such as clothing and blankets; nevertheless, patriarchy emerged gradually as society slowly changed and began to reward strength and mobility.

There is considerable evidence that men increased their power over women in many early urban societies. Historian Gerda Lerner analyzed male power in the Mesopotamian city-states, where kings or male assemblies ruled. Law codes

Erich Lessing/Art Resource, NY

Goddess Figure This female figure, probably a mother-goddess, found in France was probably used in fertility rights. Such figures have been found in many ancient societies studied by archaeologists.

such as Hammurabi's favored men, and only women could be divorced or sold into slavery for adultery. Laws also restricted women's freedom of movement and treated them as private property. By this time, Lerner argues, gods had become more important than goddesses, and male power was legally recognized and sanctioned by religion.

EVALUATING THE DEBATE

What, then, was the status of women in ancient societies? The weight of scholarship favors those who doubt that full-blown matriarchal societies were once widespread. But few societies have ever been entirely controlled by the activities or wishes

of men. Until recently historians and archaeologists have neglected the role of women. When we study ancient societies, we may unknowingly be influenced by modern patriarchal attitudes, since these are prominent in today's culture. We are more likely to study kings and wars than the beginnings of herbal medicine, cloth production, and the role of women as negotiators in community disputes. We have not heard the last word from scholars on the question of ancient matriarchies and patriarchies, but their disputes have made us more aware of the role of women in history.

THINKING ABOUT THE CONTROVERSY

1. Why can worship of a mother-goddess be understood in different ways?

2. Why do we need to understand patriarchy to comprehend world history?

EXPLORING THE CONTROVERSY

Some major works supporting the ancient goddess and matriarchy thesis include Marija Gimbutas, *Goddesses and Gods in Old Europe, 6500–500 B.C.: Myths and Cult Images* (Berkeley: University of California Press, 1982); Gimbutas, *The Language of the Goddess: Unearthing the Hidden Symbols of Western Civilization* (New York: Harper and Row, 1989); Gimbutas, *The Living Goddesses* (Berkeley: University of California Press, 1999); and Riane Eisler, *The Chalice and the Blade: Our History, Our Future* (San Francisco: Harper and Row, 1995). Judith Lorber challenges basic assumptions about gender in *Paradoxes of Gender* (New Haven: Yale University Press, 1994). Patricia Monaghan, *The New Book of Goddesses and Heroines* (New York: Llewellyn Publications, 1997), provides a useful reference on mythological and legendary female deities from many lands and eras.

Strong criticism of the ancient matriarchy thesis can be found in Lucy Godison and Christine Morris, eds., *Ancient Goddesses: The Myths and the Evidence* (Madison: University of Wisconsin Press, 1999); Lotte Motz, *The Faces of the Goddess* (New York: Oxford University Press, 1997); and Cynthia Eller, *The Myth of Matriarchal Prehistory: Why an Invented Past Won't Give Women a Future* (Boston: Beacon Press, 2001). Among major books on the making of patriarchy and gender roles are Elizabeth Barber, *Woman's Work: The First 20,000 Years: Women, Cloth, and Society in Early Times* (New York: W.W. Norton, 1994); Gerda Lerner, *The Creation of Patriarchy* (New York: Oxford University Press, 1986); and Sherry Ortner, *Making Gender: The Politics and Erotics of Culture* (Boston: Beacon Press, 1997).

Ancient Foundations of World History, 4000–600 B.C.E.

People today live in the shadow of the ancient peoples who began farming and later founded the Bronze Age cities in western Asia, Africa, South Asia, East Asia, and southern Europe. These ancient centuries, and the transitions that marked them, constructed the foundations for much that came later, including organized societies and the growing networks that connected them.

After thousands of years of prehistory, some peoples congregated in villages and began to practice agriculture. This was perhaps one of the two greatest transitions in human history, the other being the Industrial Revolution of the eighteenth and nineteenth centuries C.E. We can thank early farmers for giving us, between 10,000 and 5000 B.C.E., valuable inventions such as pottery, cloth, and the plow. Agriculture was the essential building block that stimulated other major developments, in particular the founding of cities and states and the invention of metalworking. New developments then fostered other changes. For example, better means of transportation allowed people, goods, ideas, and even diseases to travel longer distances in a shorter time. This transportation also became the basis for networks of trade and cultural exchange linking distant societies. In turn, this wider sharing of ideas helped bring about further transformations in social and cultural patterns. Today, like the ancients, we still get our food mostly from intensive agriculture and livestock raising, work metals into useful products like tools, ride in wheeled vehicles and boats that allow us to travel over long distances, worship in religious buildings, and often live in cities, where people representing several classes and many occupations work and trade. These cities are located in powerful states that are administered by bureaucratic governments and protected by military forces.

Ancient transitions happened as the result of many influences, among them environmental factors such as disease, climate change, the availability of fertile land, and the annual flooding of rivers. Local conditions helped shape such distinctive societies as Sumeria, Egypt, Nubia, Minoan Crete, Phoenicia, the Harappan cities, Shang China, and the Olmec. At the same time, there was much contact and communication among Eurasian and northern African societies as well as long-distance migrations by peoples like the Austronesians, Bantu, and Indo-Europeans. Such movement ensured that even largely distinctive societies shared certain common features.

Technological Foundations

We can thank the ancient peoples for inventing useful technologies such as metallurgy and for vastly improving transportation. Today we take these technologies for granted; indeed, they are basic to modern industrial life. In ancient times, however, people developed these technologies to help them solve particular problems. Once developed, they had many consequences. For example, metallurgy became a key to economic growth. Bronze and, a few centuries later, iron aided agricul-

ture, transportation, and communication. Improvements in land and sea transportation helped move people and products over long distances, fostering trade networks. Expanded trade encouraged cities, and metal weapons and improved transportation allowed city rulers to build or expand states.

The Copper and Bronze Ages

The first metal to be worked was copper. Stoneworkers discovered that heating copper reduced it to liquid form and allowed it to be shaped in a mold. As it cooled, it could be given a good cutting edge. Many peoples in both hemispheres made copper tools and weapons, and they traded copper widely. Excavations of sunken trading ships from this era in the Mediterranean often discover large cargoes of copper. The Sumerian city-states were the first great metal-using society, followed soon after by the Egyptians, who used copper instruments to build the great pyramids. But metallurgy also led to deforestation, as forests were cut to make charcoal to fire the kilns. For example, it took 140 pounds of wood to produce 1 pound of copper.

Beginning around 3000 B.C.E. in western Asia, metalworkers figured out how to mix copper with tin or arsenic to create bronze. This discovery launched the Bronze Age in Afro-Eurasia. The Sumerians were the first society known to use bronze in commerce. Between 2600 and 2000 B.C.E. bronze technology was adopted or invented in Egypt, eastern Europe, Nubia, India, China, and Southeast Asia. The Chinese were the greatest users and mass producers of bronze. In South America, some peoples made use of another copper-arsenic alloy, as well as silver and gold.

Bronze technology affected life. Easier to make and more durable than copper, bronze was well suited for tools, drinking vessels, and weapons. In Hebrew tradition, the formidable biblical Philistine warrior Goliath had a bronze helmet, bronze armor on his legs, and a bronze javelin. Bronze making probably spurred both trade networks and warfare. Since tin deposits are less common than copper, tin was traded over great distances, and industries arose to obtain copper and tin and to manufacture bronze products. Armies were formed in part to protect mines, markets, and trade routes. Metalsmiths were so valuable that invading armies often carried them home in captivity. Finally, copper and bronze, as well as gold and silver, were used for the first coins, which gradually became the major medium of exchange.

The Iron Age

The making of iron provided the next technological breakthrough (see map). Western Asia had little tin but large quantities of iron ore. Iron was much harder to work than copper: artisans needed to produce higher temperatures, and heating produced a spongy mass rather than a liquid. Eventually inventive workers, possibly in the Hittite kingdom along the Black Sea or in Palestine, discovered a completely new but laborious technology that involved repeatedly heating and hammering the iron and plunging the result into cold water.

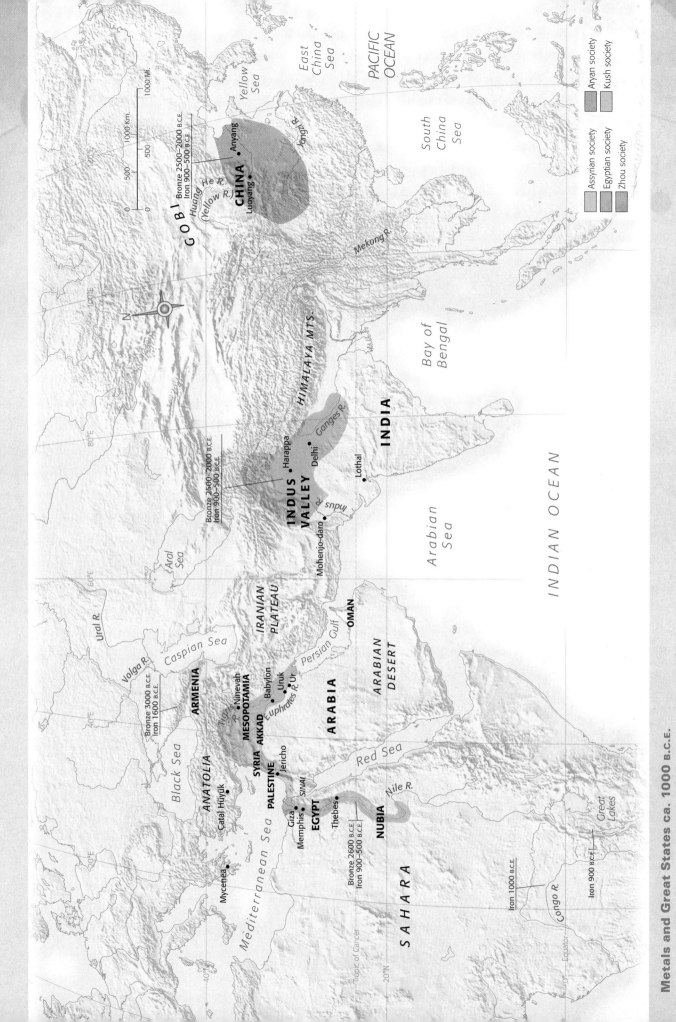

Metals and Great States ca. 1000 B.C.E.

The earliest states arose in river valleys—the Nile, Tigris-Euphrates, Indus, and Yellow—and these early states also worked metals, first bronze and then iron, to produce tools and weapons.

e | **Interactive Map**

Legend:
- Assyrian society
- Egyptian society
- Zhou society
- Aryan society
- Kush society

Map labels:

PACIFIC OCEAN

East China Sea
Yellow Sea
South China Sea

GOBI
CHINA
Anyang
Luoyang
Huang He R. (Yellow R.)
Yangzi R.
Bronze 2500–2000 B.C.E.
Iron 900–500 B.C.E.

Mekong R.

HIMALAYA MTS.

INDUS VALLEY
Harappa
Delhi
Mohenjo-daro
Lothal
Indus R.
Ganges R.
INDIA
Bronze 2500–2000 B.C.E.
Iron 900–500 B.C.E.

Bay of Bengal

Aral Sea

IRANIAN PLATEAU

Caspian Sea
Volga R.
Ural R.

ARMENIA
Bronze 3000 B.C.E.
Iron 1600 B.C.E.

ANATOLIA
Çatal Hüyük

Black Sea
Mycenae
Mediterranean Sea

Tigris R.
Ninevah
Babylon
Uruk
Ur
Euphrates R.
MESOPOTAMIA
AKKAD
SYRIA
PALESTINE
Jericho
SINAI

OMAN
Persian Gulf
ARABIA
ARABIAN DESERT

EGYPT
Giza
Memphis
Thebes
Nile R.
NUBIA
Bronze 2600 B.C.E.
Iron 900–500 B.C.E.

Red Sea

SAHARA

Tropic of Cancer
20°N

Iron 1000 B.C.E.
Iron 900 B.C.E.
Congo R.
Great Lakes
Equator

INDIAN OCEAN
Arabian Sea

N

1000 Mi.
1000 Km.
500
0

40°E   60°E   80°E   100°E

The Iron Age began in western Asia and Egypt by around 1600 B.C.E. Between 900 and 500 B.C.E. iron technology was also adopted or invented in Greece, India, western and central Europe, Central Asia, China, Southeast Asia, and West and East Africa. Some peoples acquired iron through trade, and others through contact with ironworking peoples like the Bantu. Since ironworking never developed in the Americas or Australia, these societies had no iron weapons or tools. Eurasians and Africans may have benefited from having societies close enough to each other to regularly exchange ideas. In contrast, many thousands of miles, much of it rain forest or desert, separated the societies of Mesoamerica from those in the Andes region, limiting contact.

Ironworking brought many advantages. The metal was both more adaptable and cheaper to make than bronze. With it people could produce better axes for cutting wood, plows for farming, wagon wheels for transport, and swords for warfare. For example, in Hebrew tradition, the Israelites could not drive the Canaanites out of the Palestinian lowland because they had iron chariots. Centuries later metalworkers learned how to add carbon to iron to make steel. But like many technologies, iron proved a mixed blessing. While it improved farming, it also made for deadlier weapons. Armies equipped with iron-tipped weapons enjoyed a strategic advantage over their neighbors. Although iron shields afforded some protection, more men may have died as warfare became more frequent.

Transportation Breakthroughs and Human Mobility

Metalworking was only one of several valuable technologies invented in ancient times. Land transport was dramatically transformed by the anonymous inventor of the wheel, to whom we owe much. Wheels were first used in pottery making, an activity that involved both men and women. But sometime between 3500 and 3200 B.C.E., probably in Mesopotamia, artisans found that fitting an axle to a cart allowed two wheels (often made of iron) to turn freely, and the wheeled cart was invented. Wagons followed rapidly, and then horse-drawn chariots. These wheeled vehicles made possible longer journeys and enabled people to carry more cargo, increasing long-distance trade. This increased travel inspired the first maps, drawn in Mesopotamia around 2300 B.C.E.

These maps, drawn onto small tablets and then baked, recognized distant relationships in portraying agricultural land, town plans, and the world as known to Babylonians. Such a map from the sixth or seventh century B.C.E. reveals how trade and communication had expanded their horizons. The map shows the Babylonian world, including rivers, canals, cities, and neighboring states, in the center of a flat earth, with the remote lands on the fringe inhabited by legendary beasts. The mapmaker noted that his sketch showed the "four corners" of the earth.

The inventors of the first boats are unknown. The ancestors of Australian Aborigines and some of the first migrants to the Americas may have used boats, perhaps canoes or rafts, to reach their destinations many thousands of years ago. Archaeologists have discovered the remnants of 10,000-year-old boats in northwest Europe. By 5000 B.C.E. people living in Mesopo-tamia and along the Nile had invented square sails, and wind could then be harnessed to drive boats through the water. The use of sails spread quickly. Reed and tar boats began sailing between Kuwait, on the Persian Gulf, and India. The Greek writer Homer reported how the Mycenaeans prepared ships for voyages: "they dragged the vessel into deeper water, put the mast and sails on board, fixed the oars in leather hoops, all ship-shape, and hauled up the white sail."[1] Austronesians were probably the first to construct boats capable of sailing the deep oceans. As with land transport, better ships made it easier for distant peoples to come into contact with one another and share their ways of life. Maritime trade networks, such as those linking Pacific islands with Southeast Asia and the eastern Mediterranean with northwest Europe, stretched over vast distances.

The invention and spread of wheeled vehicles and boats also made it easier for people to migrate over longer distances. The ancient era saw several great migrations involving large numbers of people. Using seagoing boats, especially large outrigger canoes, Austronesians sailed to and settled most of the widely scattered Pacific islands. Using carts and chariots, Indo-European peoples occupied large areas of Eurasia. Traveling by foot or in canoes, and also possessing iron technology, Bantu-speaking peoples settled the forests and grasslands of the southern half of Africa.

Urban and Economic Foundations

The first cities, some of them with populations over 100,000, became the cultural focal points and organizing centers for surrounding regions. The first states formed around cities, which also fostered the first writing. The urban revolution also encouraged expanded economic activities, so that merchants became prominent members of society. In turn, merchants established the first long-distance trade networks that connected people over long distances and helped spread the influence of urban societies.

The Functions and Social Organization of Cities

From the very beginning, ancient cities served a variety of functions. Some, like several Mesopotamian cities and South American cities such as Caral and Chavín, developed as centers for religious ceremonies. An Akkadian text boasted that, in Uruk, "people are resplendent in festive attire, where each day is made a holiday."[2] Cities in Egypt and China, by contrast, seem to have been founded chiefly as administrative centers to govern the surrounding territories. Many others, including the Harappan, Nubian, and Olmec cities, formed around marketplaces. Perhaps the first large city, Tell Hamoukar in Mesopotamia, sat alongside a major trade route. Many cities served all these functions.

Cities produced more organized societies by fostering more elaborate class structures than could be found in the countryside. Political elites staffed the government bureaucracies such as the law courts, while religious leaders directed the

Terracotta Figures from Harappan Cities These terracotta figures found in the ruins of Harappa show the diverse hairstyles and ornaments popular in the city. Archaeologists believe that these indicate the diversity of social classes and ethnic groups that inhabited Harappa.

Georg Helms/Harappa Archaeological Research Project, Courtesy Dept. of Archaeology and Museums, Govt. of Pakistan

temples. In Mesopotamian, Egyptian, Chinese, Harappan, and American cities, these upper-class groups generally lived in the center, around the temples and public buildings. Just outside this central zone, the middle-class merchants and skilled craftsmen lived with their families above their workshops and stores. This was true in both Sumerian Ur and Chinese Anyang. In Mesopotamia, craftsmen accounted for 20 percent of the city population. Different neighborhoods were often defined by occupation. For example, at Anyang potters apparently concentrated in one district, metalworkers in another. On the city outskirts lived the laborers, including household servants, small farmers, and slaves. Cities also attracted people from neighboring societies, and ethnically diverse populations were common. Some merchants migrated from elsewhere but probably maintained ties to their hometowns through the extensive commercial networks.

Most urban women led busy lives. As households began to stir each morning, women prepared a quick meal for husbands and sons heading out to their work, perhaps as artisans, peddlers, soldiers, or laborers. Many used pots and pans made of copper or bronze to cook and serve the food. After cleaning up the meal, many women walked through dusty streets to market stalls to buy food grown on nearby farms. As they returned home, they may have passed children playing in the narrow alleys, perhaps watched by grandparents. In some societies, the wealthier women were increasingly restricted inside walled courtyards. The poorest women and men begged, searched through trash, or offered their services to those who were better off.

Cities, Trade, and Networks of Exchange

Because trade was a major city activity, merchants became prominent members of urban society. In their shops and mar-

ket stalls, they made available products from near and far. One of the most popular products was salt, which was used to preserve and add taste to food. Another was obsidian, a volcanic glass that made sharp tools and was found naturally only where volcanic activity had occurred. Diverse peoples, among them Greeks, Pacific islanders, and Mesoamericans, actively sought obsidian. By 1500 B.C.E. long-distance traders supplied various Mediterranean and Middle Eastern societies with opium and other drugs, which were mostly used to ease the pain of disease, surgery, and childbirth. As it does today, trade could also foster disagreements. An Ur merchant, complaining about the poor quality of copper shipped from Bahrain, wrote to the sender: "Who am I that you treat me in this manner and offend me?"[3]

Growing trade required the creation of currencies, without which our modern economic life would be impossible. Simple forms of money, mostly varied weights of precious metals like silver, were invented between 3000 and 2500 B.C.E. in Mesopotamian cities. Legal codes were then written that specified fines, interest rates, and even the ideal price of some common goods. By 600 B.C.E. the first gold coins were being struck in Anatolia. Money made exchange easier, especially in cities, and it may have stimulated the development of mathematics as a tool for calculating wealth. Various ancient societies in both hemispheres developed some system of mathematics.

Trade networks moving objects of value, from raw materials to luxury goods, linked major cities and even distant societies. Between 4000 and 3000 B.C.E. traders began shipping minerals, precious stones, and other valued commodities over long distances, and Mesopotamia became a commercial hub linking southern Asia with Egypt. Beginning around 1200 B.C.E., heavily urbanized Phoenicia, which established many trading ports around the Mediterranean, became the first known society to flourish mostly through interregional commerce rather than farming. Gradually trade routes expanded over long distances, increasing contacts between societies with different cultures and institutions. Goods traveled initially by riverboat and by donkey or horse caravans. By 2000 B.C.E., however, sea trading in the Mediterranean Sea, Persian Gulf, and Indian Ocean had become more important.

Some areas became trade centers. Mesopotamia was the center of a vast trade network, with links eastward to India and Central Asia and westward to Egypt and Italy. Its location as the hub of this network allowed it to draw ideas, produce, and people from a huge hinterland. Similarly, Egypt connected Africa and Eurasia. By 2000 B.C.E. cities like Dilmun on Bahrain Island in the Persian Gulf flourished as trade hubs located between major societies. The Persian Gulf itself has served as a contact zone for over five millennia.

Trade fostered other transitions. The need to guide ships or caravans to distant destinations, as well as the belief that the changing skies could influence human activity (astrology), sparked the study of the stars. Babylonian astrological beliefs and the zodiac may have been spread by trade to western Asia and southern Europe, where they became popular.

Victor Boswell/NGS

Fragments of Egyptian-Hittite Treaty This carved stone fragment contains a treaty, signed around 1250 B.C.E., between Egypt and the Hittite kingdom in Anatolia that ended a war between the two states. The treaty is inscribed in the widely used cuneiform script of the Akkadian language. It eloquently demonstrates the reality of ancient warfare but also expresses the age-old quest for peace.

Political Foundations

Closely related to urbanization was the emergence of the first states, with their bureaucratic structures and powerful ruling elites. States marked a transition to more complex and organized societies. The first known states formed in Mesopotamia around 3500 B.C.E. and in Egypt by 3000 B.C.E. Between 3000 and 1000 B.C.E. states were also established in India, China, Vietnam, Nubia, and southeastern Europe, as well as in Mesoamerica and South America. Today we take for granted the notion of large political units to whom people owe allegiance, but in the ancient world they were major innovations. Among the consequences of states was the rise of conflict between them as well as with nearby pastoral peoples, which resulted in increased warfare. Although warfare long predates state building, now it was waged on a larger scale, becoming a common pattern in world history.

Kings and Political Hierarchies

States were hierarchically organized political structures. The rulers—mostly kings and emperors, but sometimes queens, such as the Egyptian Hatshepsut—ruled over many rural peasants and city-dwellers living within the territories they controlled. These people paid taxes, in money or in agricultural products, in acknowledgment of the king's ability to keep order, promote justice, and protect his subjects from harm. The great

Law Code associated with the Babylonian ruler Hammurabi is one illustration of this basis of ancient governments. Many kings sought the kind of support accorded the Aryan kings in the Hindu sacred writings: "Him do ye proclaim, O men as kings and father of kings, the lordly power, the suzerain of all creation, the eater of the folk, the slayer of foes, the guardian of the law."[4] Bureaucracies were formed to administer the states, including the first empires. As royal power increased, the institutions that allowed merchants and other leading citizens to participate in government, such as the assemblies in Sumerian cities, lost their importance.

The rulers of large states had to possess legal and military power to reward their supporters and punish their enemies. This required sufficient income from either taxes or the spoils of war. Some of this money was also used to build great monumental architecture, such as the Egyptian pyramids and Olmec mounds whose ruins still astonish tourists. Rulers also had to convince their subjects that they ruled, either as gods themselves (such as the pharaoh of Egypt) or with the permission of divine forces (such as the Zhou dynasty rulers in China, who claimed to rule by the "Mandate of Heaven"). We often imagine ancient pharaohs and emperors as all-powerful despots, and in many respects they were. But kingship was not always an easy job. Officials might ignore their policies, rivals could challenge them, and disenchanted groups might rebel.

After states came empires, which were generally formed by conquest. The Akkadian Sargon in Mesopotamia established the earliest known imperial state around 2350 B.C.E. Sargon's use of a standing army (with over five thousand soldiers) set the pattern that prevailed in the Fertile Crescent for the next several millennia as various states gained influence or control over their neighbors, often to secure scarce resources like silver, copper, or timber. Various ancient societies established empires, among them Assyrians, Egyptians, Mycenaeans, and Hittites. This expansion prompted states to set up forts on their frontiers to control the local population and the flow of traffic. An Egyptian inscription ordered a garrison along the Nile "to prevent any Nubian from passing northward, whether on foot or by boat," except for traders or messengers.[5]

States and Warfare

With the rise of competing states and improved military technology, warfare became more common. One of the chief tasks of the ruler was to protect and perhaps expand his state, and often rulers waged war to acquire land and capture people. More land and population meant more resources and tax revenues. As part of the rise of warfare as an institution, rulers were expected to be or honor heroic warriors. Even today people remember the legends of great ancient warriors (real or mythical) like Hercules at Troy or Arjuna in the *Bhagavad Gita*. Ancient soldiers were armed with "shock" weapons such as clubs or swords and "missiles" such as arrows or spears. Warfare by settled peoples required a powerful state. To wage war, kings had to marshal resources such as food and metals as well as recruit soldiers. They also had to discourage dissent and instill among the population a sense that warfare was worthwhile. Opposition to the ruler and his policies was viewed as treason and could mean death or imprisonment.

In Afro-Eurasia many wars matched states against pastoral nomads, who were attracted by the wealth of the farming societies and their cities. These mobile nomads, often viewed by the farming peoples as "barbarians," pioneered the development of chariot and cavalry warfare and possessed many horses or camels. Between 2000 and 1000 B.C.E. nomadic peoples occasionally conquered cities and states. Eventually many of these pastoralists, such as the Hittites in western Asia and the Aryans in India, adopted some of the ways of the conquered farmers, while the urban peoples acquired the pastoralists' military technologies. Incursions into farming societies by nomadic pastoralists remained an important pattern in world history until the seventeenth century C.E.

Ancient armies, like modern ones, depended on their weapons and on soldiers who were not always enthusiastic about their job. One Egyptian text said of a soldier: "He is awakened when an hour has passed and he is driven like an ass. He works till the sun sets. He is hungry, his body is exhausted, he is dead while still alive. His body is broken with dysentery."[6] Some conscripts in Zhou China shared the disenchantment: "What plant is not wilting? What man is not taken from his wife? Alas for us soldiers!"[7] Then as now, soldiering was a dangerous activity that required bravery and self-discipline.

Warfare became increasingly lethal as weaponry and strategy improved. When the Assyrians swept through Mesopotamia in the ninth century B.C.E., their advanced cavalry and siege weaponry enabled them to level and burn the great city of Babylon. Later the Assyrians themselves experienced defeat, as their capital, Ninevah, fell to "the noise of the whip and of rattling wheels, galloping horses, clattering chariots!"[8] Even though many ancient cities were surrounded by defensive walls, they were still vulnerable to well-armed foes. But the costs of war, in treasure and people, also prompted rulers to make peace treaties with rival powers and prompted prophets to call for beating "their swords into ploughshares, their spears into pruning hooks; nation shall not lift up sword against nation."[9] The quest for peace was as old as the urge to wage war.

Social and Cultural Foundations

Beginning around 3500 B.C.E. the social forms common to hunters and gatherers began to change as more and more people settled down to farming and developed more organized societies. Metallurgy, cities, and states fostered new structures, systems, and attitudes, along with social inequality and more varied activities. Perhaps the two most significant cultural innovations were writing, which allowed for record-keeping and improved communication, and institutionalized religion, which shaped the values and behavior of societies. The social and cultural patterns that emerged in antiquity endured because they fulfilled basic human needs for group survival and personal satisfaction.

Inequality, Conflict, and Leisure

The shift from the relatively egalitarian ethos of hunting and gathering to a more hierarchical social organization changed people's lives. Increasingly people were divided into social classes, with the wealthier groups controlling the distribution and consumption of economic resources. Ancient graves reveal the differences in social status. Some graves were elaborate, filled with offerings of material goods such as jewelry, and others were very simple. Legal codes, such as that of Hammurabi, usually favored the wealthy.

At the same time, with productive agriculture, populations grew. Between 8000 and 500 B.C.E. the world's population jumped from 5 or 10 million up to an estimated 100 million. The great majority of these people lived in Mesopotamia (the most densely populated area), Egypt, India, China, and southeastern Europe. People were also living longer than during the Stone Age, when a third died before age twenty and only a tenth lived past forty. Bronze Age peoples lived into their early forties, and probably 5 to 10 percent lived past sixty.

With less equality but more people, the potential for social conflict increased. Most communities included haves and have-nots, landlords and landless, free citizens and slaves. The gap between rich and poor made crime a serious problem that was addressed through harsh codes like that of Hammurabi. Theft was common in major Mesopotamian and Egyptian cities. Large enslaved populations, which included debtors and prisoners of war, might revolt. Slavery was more pervasive in Mesopotamia than in China, Egypt, and India, but slave-holding was common in all ancient agricultural societies.

Patriarchy was another source of inequality and remains a feature of life today (see Historical Controversy: Patriarchy and Matriarchy in the Ancient World). Men increasingly believed that women were unsuited to run governments, and few of them were allowed to do so. Social changes that required heavy physical labor in farming, warfare, and long-distance trade influenced gender and family relations. Women now became known as the "weaker sex" and were often assigned chiefly domestic tasks. An ancient Chinese saying asserted that "men plow and women weave."[10] Although women continued to produce some of the pottery and most of the cloth, they were no longer equal contributors to food needs because they now spent more time at home. In farming families, women were also encouraged to bear a larger number of children to help in the fields. In many places, men, especially rulers and the rich, had multiple wives or took concubines. In some societies, among them Sumeria, Egypt, and Shang China, the remnants of older matrilineal family systems were only fading memories, but middle-class urban women fought hard to retain their property and other rights. Sexual options became more limited for women because men wanted to ensure that their personal wealth would be passed on to their children of known paternity. Increasingly dependent on men for support, women became more preoccupied with physical appearance, hoping to attract male favor. Women used eye makeup and perfume, both invented in ancient Egypt and still popular today.

Despite the social inequality and long hours of toil, leisure activities developed that are familiar to us today. For example, the Sumerian city-dwellers enjoyed dancing and music and invented beautiful, elaborate harps and lyres for their pleasure. Zhou Chinese music lovers preferred flutes and drums, and Egyptians preferred metal horns. Music was used for worship, festivals, and work, but the oldest known love songs had also appeared by 2300 B.C.E. in Egypt. Wrestling became a popular sport in many cultures. Alcoholic drinks like beer and wine were also common, often consumed in public taverns. Drinking became an integral part of leisure and social relationships in many societies. Homer summed up the pleasures favored in early Greece: "The things in which we take a perennial delight are the feast, the lyre [a musical instrument], the dance, clean linen in plenty, a hot bath and our beds."[11] These are pleasures that most modern people share, indicating that some things have not changed much in 3,000 years.

Writing and Its Consequences

Imagine how different our modern worlds of education and work would be without reading and writing. Although limited to a relatively small group of people for much of history, writing was a critical invention of several early societies. A Sumerian legend recalled a key discovery: "The High Priest of Kulaba formed some clay and wrote words on it as if on a tablet; with the sun's rising [to dry the clay], so it was!"[12] Writing fostered increasing occupational specialization, including the emergence of clerks, scribes, bureaucrats, and eventually teachers, scholars, and historians.

Initially developed chiefly to keep commercial accounts, codify legends and rituals, or record political proclamations, writing later gave birth to literature, historiography, sacred texts, and other forms of learning and culture that could now be transmitted and expanded. For example, writing helped spread the Sumerian epic of Gilgamesh so widely that it influenced the Hebrew book of Genesis and the *Iliad* and the *Odyssey* of the Greek Homer many centuries later. Similarly, Indian stories such as the *Ramayana* became popular in Southeast Asia. Writing also allowed rulers to communicate over long distances with district governors and foreign leaders, and it allowed merchants to make arrangements with merchants in other cities, enhancing the role of communication networks.

Writing, however, had contradictory consequences. On the one hand, it clearly stimulated creativity and intellectual growth while allowing for a spread of knowledge. But writing also often became a tool for preserving the social and politi-

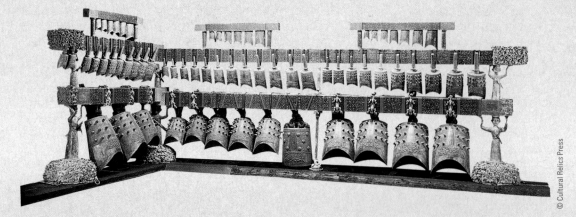

Bell of Marquies   Music had a key function in the court life of Zhou China. This sixty-four-piece bell set was found in the tomb of a regional ruler, which also contained many flutes, drums, zithers, pan pipes, and chimes. Five men using mallets and poles were needed to play this set of bells.

cal order, especially when literacy was restricted to a privileged elite such as bureaucrats, lawyers, or priests. For example, a soldier in Zhou China complained that he and his colleagues wanted to return home, but they "were in awe of the [official] orders in the tablets."[13] Sacred literature was also frequently closed to debate, since it supposedly came from the gods.

Institutionalized Religions

The rise of agriculture and then cities gradually transformed the belief that nature was alive with spiritual forces (animism) to more systematic theologies and organized religious observances. These beliefs and practices gave order and meaning to people's lives and may have promoted cooperation and a sense of community. Ideas about the fate of individual humans after death as well as notions of right and wrong differed widely as societies developed unique traditions and beliefs. While most ancient peoples were polytheists or animists, believing in many gods or spirits, a few, such as the Hebrews and some African societies, were monotheists, believing in one high god who presided over the universe.

Full-time religious specialists also evolved, often replacing the shamans, the part-time spiritual leaders associated with earlier times. With the rise of agriculture and larger communities, a priestly class arose who were seen as able to communicate with the gods and interpret their will. Because they provided essential services such as writing or calculating the time of the annual floods, priests were the first social group to be freed from direct subsistence labor. They also staffed the temples, which in some cities were massive monumental buildings serving thousands of believers.

The supernatural and natural worlds were usually explained through myths, stories about the past or about the interaction of gods with the human world. Mythology explained the birth of the universe, the progression of seasons, the uncertainties of agriculture, the flooding of rivers, and human dramas such as battlefield losses and victories. Myths and legends were included in sacred books. Several thousand years later some of these ancient books, such as the Hindu Vedas and the Hebrew Bible, are still revered by many millions of people.

Institutionalized religions influenced societies. Because religious ceremonies and ideas provided supernatural sanction for the social and political order, they became a powerful force for social control. Challenging the political or social system, which was seen as divinely inspired, now constituted blasphemy and condemned one to eternal punishment after death. Many of the ancient religions, led by men and worshiping chiefly male gods, supported patriarchal attitudes. Religious views also spread from one society to another. For example, Egyptian ideas of the afterlife and a final Day of Judgment were influential around the larger Mediterranean basin. Hebrews may have acquired their notions of a weekly Sabbath and a Garden of Eden from Mesopotamians. Many centuries later all these ideas were reflected in Christianity and Islam.

Suggested Reading

Books

Adas, Michael, ed. *Agricultural and Pastoral Societies in Ancient and Classical History*. Philadelphia: Temple University Press, 2001. A useful collection of essays on various aspects of premodern world history.

Armstrong, Karen. *The Great Transformation: The Beginning of Our Religious Traditions*. New York: Knopf, 2006. Good discussion of ancient religions and beliefs.

Bogucki, Peter. *The Origins of Human Society*. Malden, MA: Blackwell, 1999. A detailed and up-to-date scholarly study of prehistory and the rise of ancient societies.

Casson, Lionel. *The Ancient Mariners: Seafarers and Sea Fighters of the Mediterranean in Ancient Times*, 2nd ed. Princeton, NJ: Princeton University Press, 1991. A fascinating study of ancient maritime trade and connections.

Christian, David. *Maps of Time: An Introduction to "Big History."* Berkeley: University of California Press, 2004. The most extensive presentation of the "big history" approach, with much on the ancient era.

Curtin, Philip D. *Cross-Cultural Trade in World History*. Cambridge: Cambridge University Press, 1984. A pioneering comparative study.

Diamond, Jared. *Guns, Germs and Steel: The Fates of Human Societies*. New York: W.W. Norton, 1997. A fascinating interpretation of prehistoric and ancient human societies, with emphasis on environmental influences.

Fagan, Brian. *The Long Summer: How Climate Changed Civilization*. New York: Basic Books, 2004. An up-to-date assessment of the connection between history and climate over the past 5,000 years.

Fagan, Brian M. *People of the Earth: An Introduction to World Prehistory*, 12th ed. New York: Longman, 2003. Contains much up-to-date material on the ancient societies and prehistory.

Headrick, Daniel R. *Technology: A World History*. New York: Oxford University Press, 2009. Valuable discussion of ancient agriculture and metallurgy.

Manning, Patrick. *Migration in World History*. New York: Routledge, 2005. A provocative study, with much on prehistory and ancient history.

Matossian, Mary Kilbourne. *Shaping World History: Breakthroughs in Ecology, Technology, Science, and Politics*. Armonk, NY: M.E. Sharpe, 1997. A general examination of science, technology, and ecology, with much material on early farmers and the ancient societies.

Ristvet, Lauren. *In the Beginning: World History from Evolution to the First States*. New York: McGraw-Hill, 2007. Good overview of topics on ancient global history.

Snooks, Graeme D. *The Dynamic Society: Exploring the Sources of Global Change*. London: Routledge, 1996. A challenging view of world history by an economist, with much on the ancient world.

Trigger, Bruce D. *Understanding Early Civilizations.* New York: Cambridge University Press, 2003. A detailed scholarly examination of ancient societies, including Egypt, Mesopotamia, and Shang China.

Wood, Michael. *Legacy: The Search for Ancient Cultures.* New York: Sterling, 1994. A well-written survey of ancient societies for the general reader.

WEBSITES

Ancient and Lost Civilizations (*http://www.crystalinks.com/ancient.html*). Offers some useful essays on various world regions and ancient cultures.

Exploring Ancient World Cultures (*http://eawc.evansville.edu/*). Excellent site run by Evansville University, with essays and links on the ancient Near East, Egypt, India, China, and Europe.

Geology Project (*http://www.unr.edu/sb204/geology*). Provides brief but useful information on the history of copper, bronze, and iron technology.

Internet Ancient History Sourcebook (*http://www.fordham.edu/halsall/ancient/asbook.html*). An exceptionally rich collection of links and primary source readings.

Internet Global History Sourcebook (*http://www.fordham.edu/halsall/global/globalsbook.html*). An excellent set of links on world history from ancient to modern times.

World Civilizations (*http://www.wsu.edu/~dee/TITLE.HTM*). A useful collection of materials on prehistory and ancient history, operated by Washington State University.

BLOSSOMING: THE CLASSICAL SOCIETIES AND THEIR LEGACIES, CA. 600 B.C.E.–CA. 600 C.E.

The Classical Era, roughly the centuries between 600 B.C.E. and 600 C.E., was a formative period that saw a flourishing of societies and networks in nearly every inhabited part of the globe. The foundations for this era had been laid with the agricultural transition and the rise of the first cities and states in both the Eastern and Western Hemispheres. The classical societies typically became more complex and often larger than their ancient predecessors, and their art, literature, politics, and religion have had a lasting significance. Today's popular images of the Classical Era—Greek philosophers debating the meaning of existence, Roman gladiators battling in the Colosseum, and the Buddha meditating under a leafy tree—while limited, testify to the ongoing prominence this era has held in our thought.

These centuries saw innovations in thought, government, writing, and metalworking and an increase in long-distance trade aided by new transportation technologies. Improved communications between societies spread ideas and products, helping foster change. Trading zones expanded, and societies as distant from each other as Persia and China established diplomatic communication. People began to envision a larger world than their own village or kingdom, and that larger world changed them. In the increasingly cosmopolitan milieu of the Eastern Hemisphere, for example, Chinese influence began to reshape Korea and Japan, Indian religions and political ideas sparked state building in Southeast Asia, and Greek culture reached into Europe, Asia, and Africa. In the ferment sparked in the Eastern Hemisphere by local growth and contact with other societies, many of the laws, political traditions, literatures, philosophies, and religions associated with the major cultures emerged. Similarly, in both sub-Saharan Africa and the Americas, societies exchanged religious ideas, trade goods, and notions of government. Population movement into the Pacific islands (Oceania) and southern Africa continued.

The early classical centuries in Greece, Israel, Persia, India, and China were marked by philosophical speculation. This creative evolution in human thought between 600 and 250 B.C.E., often called the Axial Age, laid the groundwork for the core beliefs of some classical societies. Many of the greatest thinkers in history, such as Buddha, Confucius, and Socrates, lived at the same time or were near-contemporaries. Several billion people in Asia continue to revere the teachings of Confucius and the Buddha, Hebrew thinkers influenced later religions, and schools in North America and western Europe still introduce students to the ideas of the classical Greek philosophers.

Between 350 B.C.E. and 250 C.E. large parts of the Afro-Eurasian zone were transformed by large regional empires.

Courtesy of the Trustees of the British Museum

Persian Rhyton This gilded silver drinking cup, made in Persia in the fourth or fifth century B.C.E., has the figure of the ibex, a local animal, at the base. The cup is an example of the artistic treasures produced by classical peoples.

During the imperial age great states dominated the Mediterranean Basin, western Asia, India, and China. Diverse peoples, including Persians, Hellenistic Greeks, Romans, Mauryan Indians, and Han Chinese, presided over regional empires greater in scale than any that had come before. Some of the empire builders, such as the Macedonian Alexander the Great and the Roman Julius Caesar, are still famous today. Eventually, however, the empires overextended themselves territorially and collapsed. In contrast, most American and sub-Saharan African states were small and often decentralized.

The great Afro-Eurasian empires were in regular contact with each other by way of extensive trade networks. Distances narrowed. The best-known network was the overland Silk Road, named after the main commodity shipped, which linked China across Central Asia with India, the Middle East, and Europe. Caravans also linked North and West Africa across the harsh Sahara Desert, while trade routes around the Indian Ocean connected Southeast Asia and India with East Africa and Western Asia. Thanks to conquest or trade, Greek and Roman ideas and institutions permeated the Mediterranean region, and Indian cultural influences spread into Central, East, and Southeast Asia. Deadly diseases, such as plague, also moved along the trade routes, killing millions. Thus societies all over the world were increasingly altered, at times dramatically, by contact with others through various kinds of networks of trade, migration, disease, and conquest. Nonetheless, despite this contact, major societies largely remained distinct from each other.

As the Afro-Eurasian empires declined, divided, or collapsed, three religions rose in influence and enjoyed a wide appeal: Buddhism, Hinduism, and a new faith, Christianity. As these religions crossed cultural boundaries, attracting people of diverse backgrounds, they became universal religions, promoting social stability while also fostering cultural exchange. Since the Classical Era, regions have often been identified with their dominant religion, such as Hindu India or Christian Europe. These religious heritages were formed in the Classical Era.

NORTH AND CENTRAL AMERICA
The Maya established a long-lasting series of rival city-states in Mexico and Central America that flourished from creative farming, science, trade, and writing. Great cities based on trade also appeared elsewhere in Mexico. North of Mexico, town-dwelling farming societies emerged. Especially influential, the Mound Builders in eastern North America fostered long-distance trade networks stretching from the Atlantic Ocean and Gulf of Mexico to the Great Lakes.

SOUTH AMERICA
New states that used innovative agriculture emerged along the Peruvian coast and in the Andes highlands. The Moche, while warring with their neighbors, also created sophisticated pottery and art. In the Andes, Tiwanaku produced art and thought that influenced neighboring societies. Long-distance trade networks also connected various societies in South America.

EUROPE

Greek city-states, notably Athens, experimented with democracy and fostered philosophy and science. By conquering a large empire, Alexander the Great spread Greek culture into western Asia and Egypt. The Romans built an empire that encompassed the Mediterranean Basin and much of Europe, spreading Roman influence. By late Roman times Christianity was becoming the dominant religion in the Mediterranean, and Germanic tribes migrated into southern Europe, contributing to the collapse of Roman power. To the east, Byzantium conquered a large empire while mixing Roman, Greek, and Christian traditions.

WESTERN ASIA

The Persians established a large empire over much of western Asia and Egypt, promoting Persian thought. After their collapse the Hellenistic Greeks dominated the region and spread Greek culture. The Hellenistic Greeks were then displaced by the Romans. In Roman-ruled Palestine the teachings of a Hebrew, Jesus, sparked a new religion, Christianity, which during the later Classical Era spread around the Mediterranean Basin. With Roman decline the Persians regained power over much of western Asia.

EASTERN ASIA

Chinese philosophies emerged during a time of rapid change, and Confucianism, Daoism, and Legalism became enduring influences. The Qin dynasty reunified China, and then the Han dynasty established a huge empire and overland trade with western Asia and Rome. When the Han collapsed, Buddhism filtered in from India. Chinese science and technology during this era were innovative. Koreans and Japanese formed states and imported Confucianism, Buddhism, and political models from China.

ARCTIC OCEAN

GERMANS

EUROPE

Danube

ROMAN EMPIRE

BYZANTIUM

GREECE

Carthage

ASIA

PERSIA

EGYPT

PALESTINE

Nile R.

HIMALAYAS

Ganges R.

CHINA

JAPAN

KUSH

GHANA

Niger R.

AFRICA

AKSUM

INDIA

Congo R.

CAMBODIA

Mekong R.

ATLANTIC OCEAN

INDIAN OCEAN

INDONESIA

AUSTRALIA

AFRICA

Egypt fell successively under Persian, Hellenistic Greek, and finally Roman rule. Carthage was another major North African power and trade center until the Romans conquered the region. In northeast Africa, Kush was a trade center and major iron producer, and another trading state, Aksum, adopted Christianity. Trading cities and then empires, notably Ghana, emerged in the Sudan region. Elsewhere the Bantu peoples continued their expansion, settling much of central, eastern, and southern Africa. Long-distance trade networks connected West Africans with North Africa and East Africans with India and western Asia.

SOUTHERN ASIA AND OCEANIA

Buddhism arose in India, where it was later adopted by the kings of the region's first empire, the Mauryas. However, Hinduism remained India's majority faith, and Buddhism later split into rival schools. Indians traded with western Asia, Africa, Rome, and Southeast Asia. Various groups migrated into India from Central Asia. The Gupta kingdom made India a world leader in science, and Indian influence, including Buddhism and Hinduism, spread into Southeast Asia, helping foster states. Maritime trade linked Southeast Asia with China, India, western Asia, and East Africa. During this same time Austronesians continued settling the Pacific islands and traded with each other over vast distances.

CLASSICAL SOCIETIES IN SOUTHERN AND CENTRAL ASIA, 600 B.C.E.–600 C.E.

C.M. Dixon/Ancient Art & Architecture Collection

Gold Coin
This gold coin, showing a horseman, was made in India during the reign of King Chandragupta II, who presided over a great and prosperous Indian empire, with a dynamic economy, between 380 and 415 C.E.

T he merchants used to move about in the rivers as they wished, in the forests as if in gardens and on mountains as if in their own houses. As [the King] used to protect the earth so it too gave him gems out of mines, corns from the fields, and elephants from forests.

—INDIAN WRITER KALIDASA (KAHL-I-DAHSS-uh), FIFTH CENTURY C.E.[1]

S ometime around 80 C.E. an unknown Greek boarded a trading ship that left the Egyptian port of Berenike (BER-eh-nick-y) headed for India. The ship sailed down the Red Sea and then along the coast of Arabia, braving the dangers from pirates. At the Indus River the merchants exchanged clothing, silverware, and glassware for semiprecious stones from Afghanistan, Chinese silks, and Indian textiles. Proceeding down India's west coast, they stopped near present-day Bombay, trading silverware and Italian wine for pepper. The travelers then reached the great port of Muziris (MOO-zir-us) in southwest India, where the sailors probably haunted the waterfront dives. A second-century Indian poet recorded the arrival of such ships at Muziris: "The beautiful vessels stir white foam on the river, arriving with gold and departing with pepper."[2] The ship then sailed around the southern tip of India and up the east coast, stopping to collect pearls, textiles, spices, and gems. Finally the ship returned to Egypt, the merchants aboard hoping to make a fortune from their cargo.

From Egypt, western Asia, and East Africa ships arrived annually at Indian seaports to trade, collecting fabulous trade goods, such as pepper, cinnamon, cotton, and gems, for sale in distant markets. India also attracted sojourners and permanent settlers arriving by sea or overland. For those who arrived over the mountains from windswept Central Asia, the Indian sun was a blazing fury and the drenching summer rains a shock. To all the newcomers, the Indian culture and religion were more unusual than the climate. But Indian society was adaptable and accommodating. Most immigrants found themselves gradually enfolded into Indian religions, which allowed for many paths to understanding. Hinduism was resilient, bending to meet the varying needs of dissimilar people. This adaptability also helped Indian culture to spread into Southeast Asia.

The Classical Era was a time of flowering in South and Southeast Asia, particularly in state building, the development of new trade networks, and religious thought. Many of the patterns forged in this era endured into modern times. Several great empires brought unusual political unity to South Asia and made India a leading world power. India also remained closely connected to land and sea networks of exchange that helped reshape the society. Hinduism developed new schools of thought, while Buddhism (BOO-diz-uhm) arose to become a major faith in many parts of Asia. Meanwhile, various Central and Southeast Asian societies established states and social systems that differed greatly from those in India and China while becoming major participants in international maritime trade.

FOCUS QUESTIONS

1. How did Buddhism and the Mauryas shape Indian society?

2. What were some of the ways in which classical India connected with and influenced the world beyond South Asia?

3. What were the main achievements of the Gupta era?

4. How did Southeast Asians blend indigenous and foreign influences to create unique societies?

e Visit the website and eBook for additional study materials and interactive tools:
www.cengage.com/history/lockard/globalsocnet2e

THE TRANSFORMATION OF INDIAN SOCIETY, RELIGION, AND POLITICS

How did Buddhism and the Mauryas shape Indian society?

The forging of a new society from the synthesis of Aryan and local traditions continued for centuries, affecting many aspects of life and thought. The distinctive caste system became a key foundation of Indian society, and Hinduism grew even more diverse and complex. In addition, Jainism and Buddhism were born out of the religious ferment of the Axial Age, that great philosophical awakening across Eurasia during the early Classical Age that spawned many new ways of thinking from Greece to China. India's first large centralized state, the Mauryan (MORE-yuhn) Empire, emerged in part as a response to contact with peoples to the west. Like the Hellenistic Greeks and Romans, the Mauryans were linked to trade and communication networks.

Caste and Indian Society

Village Scene, Second Century C.E.
In classical times most Indians lived in villages. This drawing of a village scene is based on a relief made at Amaravati, a Buddhist temple complex built in the second century C.E. It shows members of different caste groups carrying out various village activities.

The social configuration we know today as the caste system began to take shape early in the Classical Era. Members of a caste generally practiced a common occupation: some were priests, others warriors, merchants, artisans, or farmers, while still others performed the more menial tasks. Caste membership was also supported by Hindu values, including beliefs in reincarnation. Although the social and religious characteristics became similar throughout India over the centuries, the caste system was never uniform and unchanging. Still, it produced a social stability that allowed it to persist for several thousand years.

Over time the caste system became more fully developed. A political and legal document with advice for a Hindu king, usually known as the Code of Manu (MAN-oo), formalized many rules regarding caste relations. Gradually, during the first millennium of the Common Era, the four main castes (*varna*) subdivided into thousands of subcastes known as *jati* ("birth groups"), each with its own rules and, frequently, occupational specialization. Eventually the caste system became hereditary. Each person was born into a certain caste that maintained a moral code stipulating such duties as family maintenance and specifying which jatis could supply marriage partners. Strong food regulations prescribed the types of food that could be consumed by each caste, who could cook and serve the food, and who could accompany the diner. Gradually vegetarianism became more common among the higher castes, and cows were protected against being killed. Beef eating was probably common in ancient times, but by 500 C.E. pious Hindus avoided eating beef because the cow had come to be considered sacred, the symbol of life and motherhood. Cows wandered at will, eating whatever grain they found. Foreign observers have often argued that the cows spread disease and consume scarce food resources. However, some anthropologists argue that cow tolerance makes economic sense, ensuring an ample supply of cow dung for fuel and fertilizer as well as milk.

Hindu ideas sanctioned the caste system. The doctrine of *karma* held that one's status in the present life was determined by deeds in past lives. Every action had repercussions, and the sum of one's karma in past lives determined one's fate in this life. The three top caste groupings were considered further along the path of reincarnation. Low-caste Indians were held responsible for their status because of their presumed past sins. Their only hope lay in dutifully performing their present duties

From A. L. Balsham, *The Wonder That Was India* [London: Sidgwick and Jackson, 1954]

CHRONOLOGY

	India	Southeast Asia
600 B.C.E.	**563–483** B.C.E. Life of the Buddha	
400 B.C.E.	**322–185** B.C.E. Mauryan Empire	
200 B.C.E.		**111** B.C.E.**–939** C.E. Chinese colonization of Vietnam
1 C.E.	**50–250** C.E. Kushan era	**ca. 75–550** C.E. Funan **ca. 192–1471** C.E. Champa
200 C.E.	**320–550** C.E. Gupta era	

and obligations. Below the formal caste system were the untouchables, or *pariahs* (puh-RYE-uhz). Some 10 percent of the population, untouchables were generally condemned to trades and crafts regarded as undesirable (such as carrying water to village houses) or unclean because their function involved being polluted by filth or the taking of animal life. They worked as sweepers of village streets, fishermen, butchers, gravediggers, tanners, leatherworkers, and scavengers, and they lived largely in their own neighborhoods.

The caste system has functioned in some form for the past 2,500 years, providing stability and security. It promoted mutual aid within each caste and regulated village life, as subcastes exchanged goods or services with other subcastes in the village. Regional variations also developed: no single hierarchy or ranking was recognized throughout India. In south India, Bengal, and northwestern India, the caste system remained less complex. This system contributed greatly to the long-term continuity of Indian society, providing meaning and direction to the lives of Indians. Caste, along with village and family, became the pillar of Indian society, contributing to a group orientation and an acceptance of authority. It still remains strong in many villages. However, today the system has been rapidly breaking down in the larger cities. It is difficult to avoid close contact with members of other castes while eating in a restaurant, being confined in a hospital, or working in an office or factory.

Caste in Indian Life

The Shaping of Hinduism

The religion known today as Hinduism faced increasing dissent during the Classical Era, fostering new thinking. Power had been concentrated in the priestly class, the *brahmans*. They alone had mastered the scriptures and hymns for worship and presided over rituals. Enriched by gifts from the devout, many priests became wealthy landowners. Eventually, however, some Indians resented priestly wealth and corruption, and new movements emphasized new approaches to worship and spirituality, especially meditation, over ritual. The critics proposed other paths to spiritual fulfillment. Some of their writings were collected in the *Upanishads*, the final portion of the vast Hindu scriptures.

New Spiritual Movements

As a result of this new spirituality, Hinduism's highest ideal came to be the escape from sensual pleasures and the material world (seen as an "illusion") and the joining of one's individual soul with **Brahman**, the Universal Soul, or Absolute Reality, that fills all space and time. To achieve this goal, some seekers rejected society and sought mystical unity with the divine. *Yoga* (YOH-guh) ("yoke" or "union") was a system of physical and mental exercises that emphasized control of breathing to promote mental concentration, calmness, and a trancelike state that produced a mystical awareness of a universal soul. Holy men who abandoned worldly pleasures through such practices as yoga were greatly admired. Union with the universal soul meant ending the cycle of reincarnation through devotion to God, selfless action, and knowledge achieved through intense meditation. Only by escaping from one's ego could a person end the round of reincarnation and finally achieve the ultimate bliss of merging with Brahman, described in the *Upanishads* as a deep, dreamless sleep. But achieving this state necessitated abandoning the desires and actions that prevent release from earthly lives. "In thinking 'This is I' and 'That is mine,'" warns the *Upanishads*, "one binds himself to himself, as does a bird with a snare!"[3]

Brahman The Universal Soul, or Absolute Reality, that Hindus believe fills all space and time.

Spiritual Practices

New forms of worship stressed devotion or prayer focused on specific gods such as Vishnu or Shiva. Every home had a shrine to worship such deities. Frequent religious festivals had mass appeal, and great throngs made annual pilgrimages to sacred places such as the Ganges River. Eventually the spiritual quest led to new schools of Hindu thought such as **Vedanta** (vay-DAHNT-uh), meaning the "completion" of the Vedas. Vedanta offered mystical experience, a belief in the underlying unity of all reality, and sophisticated interpretations of the countless gods found in popular Hinduism, a diversity often summed up by the phrase "33,000 gods." Vedanta thinkers rejected polytheism and viewed these gods and spirits as only manifestations of the single Absolute Reality that pervades everything. The *Upanishads* states that Brahman is

Vedanta ("Completion of the Vedas") A school of classical Indian thought that offered Hindus mystical experience and a belief in the underlying unity of all reality.

> *God, all gods, the five elements—earth, air, fire, water, ether; all beings, great or small, born of eggs, born from the womb, born from heat, born from soil; horses, cows, men, elephants, birds; everything that breathes, the beings that walk and the beings that walk not.*[4]

Hinduism developed a broad and tolerant approach to religious differences. Many invaders swept into India, but most of them found a place in Hinduism, which incorporated a wide variety of beliefs, even integrating some non-Hindu figures into devotional cults. Indians worshiped God in many forms. As an old Indian folk song puts it: "Into the bosom of the great sea, flow streams that come from hills on every side. Their names are various as their springs. And thus in every land do men bow down, To one great God, though known by many names."[5] Hinduism developed not as a cohesive, rigidly defined theology with a centralized church but as a broad collection of loosely connected sects with many variations of belief and practice. Toleration and accommodation allowed Hinduism to retain its popularity among both the better educated and the villagers, despite the clearly inequitable divisions of caste and the burdens of karma.

Hindu Tolerance

Jainism and Buddhism

Two dissident ascetics eventually gave up on reforming Hinduism and founded new movements that became separate religions, Jainism (JINE-iz-uhm) and Buddhism. Jain ideas were organized by a famed teacher, Mahavira (MA-ha-VEER-a) ("Great Hero"), the pampered son of a tribal chief who abandoned his affluent life to wander naked as an ascetic around 500 B.C.E. Mahavira practiced self-torture as the route to salvation, eventually starving himself to death. The basic tenet of **Jainism** is that life in all forms must be protected because everything, including animals, insects, plants, and even sticks and stones, has a separate soul and is alive. While walking, a devout Jain sweeps the ground to avoid stepping on insects and wears a cloth over the nose to prevent inhaling insects. In Mahavira's words, "All things living, all beings whatever, should not be slain, or treated with violence."[6] Jains are vegetarians, but the most devout will not even eat vegetables such as carrots or potatoes because uprooting them damages the microorganisms living in the soil. Most Jains became merchants and bankers and are prominent today in India's economic elite. Given the emphasis on austere behavior and a spartan diet, the Jain sect never became very large; there are perhaps 1 million Jains in the world today. But Jainism had a major intellectual influence on Hindu ideas of nonviolence. Twenty-five centuries after Mahavira, Mohandas Gandhi, a devout Hindu, utilized Jain ideas in developing his philosophy of nonviolence and passive resistance to generate political change.

Mahavira and Jainism

Jainism An Indian religion that believes that life in all forms must be protected because everything, including animals, insects, plants, sticks, and stones, has a separate soul and is alive.

More important in the long run than Jainism was **Buddhism**, based on the teachings of a major Axial Age thinker, which eventually spread out of India to become a major faith in Central, East, and Southeast Asia and Sri Lanka. The religion's founder, Siddartha Gautama (si-DAHR-tuh GAUT-uh-muh) (563–483 B.C.E.), was a prince of a small kingdom in what is now southern Nepal and a contemporary of Confucius, Mahavira, and several other Axial Age thinkers. As with Jesus of Nazareth and Confucius, his life and thought are known largely through the accounts written by his followers. Siddartha led a privileged, carefree, and self-indulgent life, and then was shocked when he ventured from the palace and encountered the miseries experienced by common people. He abandoned his royal life, wife, and family to search for truth as a wandering holy man, living in the forest, practicing yoga, meditating, begging for his food, and nearly dying from fasting. He met skeptics who argued that there is no afterlife or god. Eventually, Siddartha believed he understood cosmic truths and began traveling to teach his new religion, attracting many disciples, who called him the Buddha ("The Enlightened One"). He also rejected the Hindu caste system as immoral.

Buddhism A major world religion based on the teachings of the Buddha that emphasized putting an end to desire and being compassionate to all creatures.

Buddha emphasized the Four Noble Truths (see Witness to the Past: Basic Doctrines in the Buddha's First Sermon): that this life is one of suffering and ignorance; that suffering stems from desiring what one does not have and clinging to what one already has for fear of losing it; that one must stop all desire; and that one does this by following the Noble Eightfold Path of correct

The Four Noble Truths

Worship of Buddhist Relics In the first century c.e. Buddhists erected a pillar containing this frieze of a stupa housing relics of the Buddha. The stupa is surrounded by throngs of worshipers and pilgrims making music and bringing offerings to honor the Buddha.

views, intent, speech, actions, trade (or profession), effort, mindfulness, and concentration. Following this path means leading a good life that does no harm to others. To Buddhists, the world is in a constant state of flux; when mortals try in vain to stop the flow of events, they suffer. Buddhism is neither monotheistic nor polytheistic, and the Buddha was ambivalent as to whether a god or gods existed. Buddhists were encouraged to live morally, nonviolently, and moderately and consider the needs of others. For example, men were urged to treat their wives with respect. Asked to summarize his beliefs, the Buddha replied: "Avoid doing evil deeds, cultivate doing good deeds, and purify the mind."[7] The Buddha did not oppose acquiring wealth but believed that wealth alone did not bring happiness. He also condemned the irresponsible use of wealth, such as wasting it on drinking, gambling, and laziness rather than saving some for emergencies and donating some to worthy causes.

Although rejecting priestly power and the caste system, Buddha adopted many Hindu ideas and modified them. To be released from the chronic cycle of birth and rebirth, Buddhists were urged, as were Hindus, to abandon all sense of self. But the goal was not unity with Brahman but rather **nirvana** (neer-VAHN-uh) (literally, "the blowing out"), a kind of everlasting peace or end of suffering achieved through perfection of wisdom and compassion. Buddha also urged his followers to avoid taking animal life if possible. As a result, many Buddhists became vegetarians. Buddha also seems to have been the world's first religious leader to introduce the idea of **monasticism** (muh-NAS-tuh-siz-uhm), the pursuit of a life of penance, prayer, and meditation in a community of other seekers. He advocated that monks adopt chastity, poverty, and nonviolence and suspend family ties. Monks and nuns followed the rules of proper conduct and also used such techniques as yoga for concentration, meditation, and self-discipline. They begged for their food, thus affirming their humility and allowing believers to gain merit by giving them food and other necessities. Eventually Buddhism became a major influence on the first great Indian imperial state, the Mauryan Empire.

Foreign Encounters and the Rise of the Mauryas

For several centuries in this era, northwest India remained in close communication with Persia and then Hellenistic Greece. Under their great king, Darius, the Persians conquered much of the Indus River Valley in 518 b.c.e., bringing India to the attention of the Greek historian Herodotus, whose fabulous tales may have stimulated the imagination of the young Alexander the Great (see Chapter 7). By 326 b.c.e. Alexander's forces had reached the Indus River and soon subdued several small Aryan kingdoms east of the Indus (see Chronology: Classical India). Impressed with wealthy India, the Macedonian conqueror discussed religion and philosophy with Indian scholars and apparently dispatched his notes back to his own teacher, Aristotle, making some

Other Buddhist Beliefs

nirvana ("the blowing out") For Buddhists a kind of everlasting peace or end of suffering achieved through perfection of wisdom and compassion.

monasticism The pursuit of a life of penance, prayer, and meditation, either alone or in a community of other seekers.

Persian and Greek Invaders

Basic Doctrines in the Buddha's First Sermon

Buddhist tradition holds that, after achieving enlightenment, the Buddha preached his first sermon in a deer park in the outskirts of the Ganges city of Varanasi (Benares) around 527 B.C.E. The sermon became one of the most important sources of belief for all Buddhists. It laid out the framework of Buddha's moral message, including the Middle Way between asceticism and worldly life, the Noble Eightfold Path, and the Four Noble Truths. These are the most important concepts in all branches of Buddhism.

There are two ends not to be served by a wanderer. What are these two? The pursuit of desires and of pleasure which springs from desire, which is base, common, leading to rebirth, ignoble and unprofitable; and the pursuit of pain and hardship [asceticism], which is grievous, ignoble, and unprofitable. The Middle Way of the [Buddha] avoids both of these ends. It is enlightened, it brings clear vision, it makes for wisdom, and leads to peace, insight, enlightenment, and Nirvana. What is the Middle Way? It is the Noble Eightfold path—Right Views, Right Resolve, Right Speech, Right Conduct, Right Livelihood, Right Effort, Right Mindfulness, and Right Concentration. . . .

And this is the Noble Truth of Sorrow. Birth is sorrow, age is sorrow, disease is sorrow, death is sorrow; contact with the unpleasant is sorrow, separation from the pleasant is sorrow, every wish unfulfilled is sorrow—in short, all of the five components of individuality are sorrow.

And this is the Noble Truth of the Arising of Sorrow. It arises from craving, which leads to rebirth, which brings delight and passion, and seeks pleasure from here, now there—the craving for sensual pleasure, the craving for continued life, the craving for power.

And this is the Noble Truth of the Stopping of Sorrow. It is the complete stopping of the craving, so that no passion remains, leaving it, being emancipated from it, being released from it, giving no place to it.

And this is the Noble Truth of the Way which Leads to the Stopping of Sorrow. It is the Noble Eightfold Path. . . .

THINKING ABOUT THE READING

1. What does the Buddha mean by the Middle Way?
2. What causes suffering, and how can people stop it?
3. What conduct do these ideas promote?

Source: From *Sources of Indian Tradition, Vol. 1* by William Theodore de Bary et al., eds. Copyright © 1958 Columbia University Press. Reprinted with permission of the publisher.

CHRONOLOGY
Classical India

563–483 B.C.E. Life of the Buddha

326 B.C.E. Alexander the Great's army reaches western India

322–185 B.C.E. Mauryan Empire

269–232 B.C.E. Reign of Ashoka

200 B.C.E.–150 C.E. Division of Buddhism into Theravada and Mahayana schools

ca. 50–250 C.E. Kushan Empire in northwest India

ca. 320–550 C.E. Gupta era

Forming a Mauryan Empire

Greek thinkers aware of Buddhist and Hindu ideas. Faced with a rebellion by his soldiers, Alexander turned back before entering the Ganges Valley and returned to Persia. His legacy endured, however; Hellenistic cultural influence persisted in northwest India, and Greek artistic styles helped to shape Buddhist art. As an outpost of their Persian venture, the Greek imperialists set up a state in northern Afghanistan known as Bactria (BAK-tree-uh), which flourished as a regional power. Some Greeks also remained behind in northwest India, intermarrying with local women.

Alexander's invasion into western India created a political vacuum that was filled by the military forces of Chandragupta (CHUHN-druh-GOOP-tuh) Maurya, who established the first imperial Indian state, the Mauryan Empire (322–185 B.C.E.). Perhaps inspired by Alexander, Chandragupta transformed himself from the ruler of a Ganges state, Magadha (MAH-guh-duh), into the monarch of half the subcontinent (see Map 5.1). At its height the Mauryan Empire included parts of Afghanistan, most of north and central India, and large parts of south India. The Mauryas maintained diplomatic relations with many societies, including Greece, Syria, and Egypt. Chandragupta, skilled in manipulating power, was influenced by his chief adviser, Kautilya (cow-TILL-ya), who favored political centralization and compiled the initial draft of a manual for rulers on obtaining and holding power.

The empire was ruled by the most efficient government in the classical world. A large army and secret police maintained order, and spies kept government officials under constant surveillance. An ambassador from Greece particularly admired the conscientious justice system, in which the king presided personally over court sessions and settled disputes. To maintain the expensive government, the state heavily taxed agriculture, trade, mining, herding, and other economic activities. Village councils composed of older men from leading families enjoyed considerable local autonomy, a pattern that became entrenched over the centuries. The Mauryan monarch lived in great splendor, often in seclusion and surrounded by an entourage of women who cooked his food, served his wine, and in the evening carried him to his apartment, where they lulled him to sleep with music. To discourage opposition, since Vedic times Indian rulers had claimed to be blessed by the gods and endowed with supernatural and magical powers. Yet,

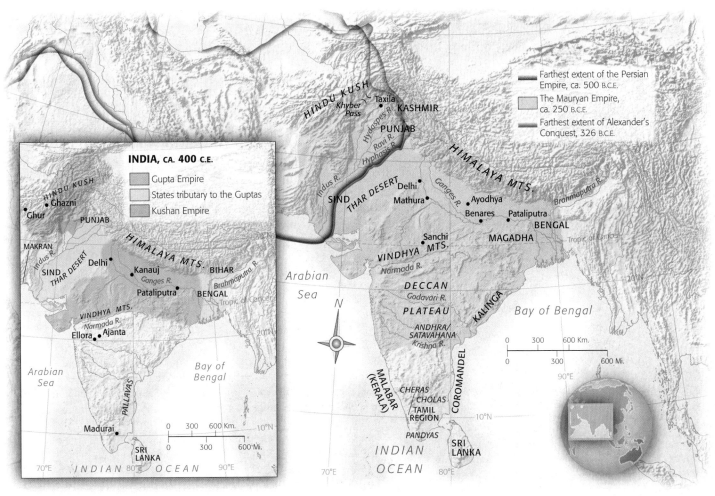

Map 5.1
The Mauryan Empire, 322–185 B.C.E.

During the Classical Era major states arose in north India, most notably the Mauryan, Kushan, and Gupta Empires. The brief encounter with the Greek forces led by Alexander the Great, which reached the Indus River Valley in 326 B.C.E., may have stimulated the Mauryas to build India's first empire.

e Interactive Map

the realization that excessive taxes and forced labor might drive the people into rebellion provided checks on autocratic power.

Mauryan Life, Institutions, and Networks

Many of the 50 to 100 million people in densely populated Mauryan India lived in cities, the centers for a prosperous economy. The Mauryan capital city, Patna (PUHT-nuh) (then called Pataliputra) on the Ganges River, was widely celebrated for its parks, public buildings, libraries, and a great university that attracted many foreign students. The accounts of Greek ambassadors suggest that Patna, with some 500,000 residents, was very likely the world's largest city. The fortified timber wall around the city, which had 570 towers, was roughly 21 miles long, suggesting that Patna was about twice as large as Rome several centuries later.

City Life

Mauryan prosperity depended on the world's most advanced trading system and craft industries. Many skilled woodworkers, ivory carvers, and stonecutters populated the cities, which also produced fine cotton fabrics. Products and merchants moved along the major east-west highway, which stretched from a seaport near present-day Calcutta (kal-KUHT-uh) through the Ganges and Indus Valleys to the borders of Afghanistan. Many foreign merchants resided in the empire, and an active exchange took place with China, Arabia, and the Middle East over trade networks. Artisan and merchant guilds, ruled by councils, supervised the private sector, while the government owned mines and forests and engaged in shipbuilding, arms manufacture, and textile production. Public granaries stored surplus food.

Mauryan Economy

Borromeo/Art Resource, NY

Ashoka Column
This 32-foot-tall sand-stone column, erected in northeast India around 240 B.C.E., weighs 50 tons. The inscriptions on the pillar outline Ashoka's achievements and offer advice on how citizens of the empire should behave.

Ashoka and Buddhist Monarchy

The Mauryas reached their height under Chandragupta's grandson, the enlightened king Ashoka (uh-SHOH-kuh) (whose name means "Sorrowless"), one of the major political and religious figures in world history. The ambitious Ashoka became a general and rose to power through a bloody campaign of eliminating rivals and expanding into frontier lands. We know much about Ashoka (r. 269–232 B.C.E.) from the many edicts he had carved in rocks and sandstone pillars. His early edicts boast of many enemies slain and captured. At some point, however, he experienced a spiritual conversion and became a devout Buddhist, proclaiming his remorse at past atrocities and his commitment to nonviolence. One edict noted that Ashoka "began to follow righteousness, to love righteousness. The greatest of all victories is the victory of righteousness."[8]

Ashoka spent his remaining years in power promoting the Buddha's pacifist teachings. He pledged to bear wrong without violent retribution, to look kindly on all his subjects, and to ensure the safety, happiness, and peace of mind of all living beings. To fulfill his pledge, he designed laws to encourage compassion, mutual tolerance, vegetarianism, and respect for all forms of life. He also sponsored many public works, including hospitals and medical care paid for by the state. Ashoka dispatched Buddhist missions to spread the religion into Sri Lanka, Southeast Asia, and Afghanistan. Despite his own strong beliefs, however, he neither made Buddhism the state religion nor persecuted other faiths. While Ashoka financed the building of Buddhist temples and *stupas* (STOOP-uhz) (domed shrines), government aid was distributed to all religious groups. The king argued that "all sects deserve reverence. By thus acting a man exalts his own sect and at the same time does service to the sects of other people."[9]

Ashoka styled himself "Beloved of the Gods," which meant he was considered at least a semideity. For both Hindus and Buddhists, the Mauryas created a political legacy of the universal emperor, a divinely sanctioned leader with a special role in the cosmic scheme of things.

Ashoka ruled with popular acclaim, but his successors were less able. Within a half century after his death, the Mauryan Empire had collapsed. Difficult communications in a large empire fostered local autonomy, and the mounting costs of a centralized bureaucracy drained the treasury. The end of the Mauryan Empire set a political pattern different from that of China, where long periods of unity were interspersed with short intervals of political fragmentation. In India, periods of unity were relatively brief, followed by prolonged fragmentation. But while Indians did not always possess political unity, they did possess a strong sense of cultural unity and loyalty to the social order, including the family and caste, rather than to the state.

SECTION SUMMARY

- The Indian caste system, which began to take form in the Classical Era, was based on the idea of karma and placed limits on one's occupation, diet, religious practice, and social interactions.

- New spiritual movements within Hinduism, such as yoga and Vedanta, challenged priestly control and emphasized the goal of escaping the ego.

- Jainism and Buddhism split off from Hinduism, but only Buddhism, which offered guidelines for achieving nirvana, gained wide appeal.

- Through the conquests by Darius and Alexander the Great, northwest India experienced significant influence from the West.

- After Alexander's retreat, Chandragupta established the first imperial Indian state, the centralized, autocratic Mauryan Empire, which included the Indus and Ganges Basins.

- The Mauryan capital city, Patna, was among the largest in the world, and the empire excelled in crafts and trade.

- King Ashoka, Chandragupta's grandson, became a pacifist convert to Buddhism, which he helped to spread to Sri Lanka, Southeast Asia, and Afghanistan.

- Unlike those of China, India's periods of unity were relatively brief; and, several decades after Ashoka died, the Mauryan Empire broke down.

SOUTH AND CENTRAL ASIA AFTER THE MAURYAS

| What were some of the ways in which classical India connected with and influenced the world beyond South Asia?

Although the end of the Mauryas in the early second century B.C.E. was followed by 500 years of political fragmentation before the rise of the next empire, that of the Guptas, these centuries saw increasing contact between India and the outside world. Indian cultural influence, especially Buddhism, spread into Central Asia. Various Central and West Asian peoples swept into northwestern India, conquering the Indus Valley and mixing with local peoples, who eventually absorbed the invaders and their ways. Substantial foreign trade and Buddhist missions to neighboring societies also occurred.

Indians and Central Asians

During this time India had constant relations with Central Asia, the area stretching from Russia eastward to the borders of China. The Turkestan region north of India, where many people spoke Turkik languages, was a key contact zone for networks stretching east to China, south to India, and west to Persia and Russia. As trade between China and western Asia developed, cities developed along the overland route (known as the "Silk Road") through Turkestan. The Sogdians (SAHG-dee-uhns), mostly Persian-speaking Zoroastrians or Buddhists who had a written language and literature, developed a flourishing mercantile society and dominated Turkestan's commerce. Over the centuries various pastoral Central Asian groups, unable to penetrate China's defenses or under pressure from Chinese expansion, moved westward, including the Huns, who developed the most effective weapon of the day, a reflex bow. Pressure from the horseback-riding Hun soldiers had long pushed various peoples into Europe. Some Huns followed into southern Russia and Hungary. In the fourth and fifth centuries C.E. Huns invaded the weakened Roman Empire (see Chapter 8).

The Silk Road and the Sogdians

Diverse peoples migrated through the mountain ranges into northwest India from Central Asia and western Asia, introducing new cultural influences. The Hellenistic kingdom of Bactria in Afghanistan was a crossroads between east and west where Greek, Persian, and Indian cultures met and mixed, and invaders from this city reintroduced Greek influence to the Indus Basin. Bactrian Greeks inspired a Greek- and Roman-influenced form of Buddhist painting and sculpture, but eventually they became absorbed into the broad fold of Indian society.

Migrations into India

In 50 C.E. the **Kushans** (KOO-shans) from Central Asia conquered much of northwest India while constructing an empire that also encompassed Afghanistan and many Silk Road cities. The Kushans promoted extensive trade between India and China, the Middle East, and the eastern Mediterranean. Some Kushan leaders embraced Buddhism and were instrumental in spreading the religion into Central Asia, from which it then diffused to China. The Kushans also encouraged the mix of Indian and Greco-Roman culture over a wide area. The much respected Kushan king Kanishka (ka-NISH-ka) (r. 78–144 C.E.) patronized artists, writers, poets, and musicians and tolerated all religions. Like invaders before them, the Kushans intermarried with local people, enhancing the hybrid character of the culture in northwestern India. When Kushan rule ended in 250, northern Indians replaced it with a patchwork of competing states.

Kushans An Indo-European people from Central Asia who conquered much of northwest India and western parts of the Ganges Basin, constructing an empire that also encompassed Afghanistan and parts of Central Asia.

South India and Sri Lanka

The political instability in northwestern India was duplicated elsewhere in the subcontinent, where there was frequent warfare between competing states. Some southern states had long flourished from maritime trade networks stretching from China to the Persian Gulf, and south India was renowned as far west as Greece and Rome for products such as gold. During this time both south India and the large island of Sri Lanka saw considerable political and cultural development. North Indian culture, partly rooted in Aryan traditions, spread southward, including Aryan myths, values, rituals, and ideas such as divine kingship, which appealed to south Indian rulers. South Indians also adopted the caste system, although in a less rigid form than in north India.

North Indian Influences

**Southern Regional
Traditions**

Despite their influence, however, Aryan ideas did not destroy regional traditions in south India. For example, the Tamils, who speak a Dravidian language and inhabit India's southeastern corner, developed a vigorous cultural tradition with poetry as the most esteemed art. The temple-filled mountain city of Madurai (made-uh-RYE) had several colleges and became a major center of Hinduism, literature, and education. A Tamil poem from the second century C.E. describes Madurai's function as a religious center filled with devout people:

> *The great and famous city of Madurai, Is like the lotus flower of God Vishnu. Its streets are
> the petals of the flower. God Shiva's temple is the center. The citizens are the plentiful pollen;
> The poor, the crowding beetles. And in Madurai, we wake to the chanting of the four Vedas,
> Sacred sculptures from the tongue of Brahma, born of the lotus flower.[10]*

Sri Lankan Society

Just south of India, on Sri Lanka (Ceylon), a very different south Asian society developed. Over the centuries, migrants from India intermarried with the local people, formed kingdoms, and eventually produced the Sinhalese (sin-huh-LEEZ) society. Sri Lanka became a trading hub between Southeast Asia and the Middle East. In the first century B.C.E. the Sinhalese, to improve their rice growing, began constructing one of the most intricate irrigation systems in world history, building canals dozens of miles long and artificial lakes covering thousands of acres, an engineering requiring complex hydraulic technology. Sri Lankan water control was comparable to that of ancient China and Mesopotamia. During Ashoka's reign Buddhist missionaries converted most Sri Lankans to Buddhism, and the Sinhalese came to view themselves as the protectors of Buddhism. Tamil-speaking Hindus also crossed the narrow straits and settled in the northern part of the island. For the next two millennia, Sinhalese Buddhist and Tamil Hindu societies coexisted, sometimes uneasily, in Sri Lanka.

Indian Encounters with the Afro-Eurasian World

Maritime Trade

The post-Maurya era stands out as a time of unprecedented Indian communication with other cultures and connection to networks of exchange. Even merchants from the Mediterranean visited India. India dispatched spices, cloth, silks, ivory, and works of art to the Roman Empire in exchange for gold coins, copper, tin, lead, and wine. Around 80 C.E. a Greek handbook for merchants interested in trade with India described sailing routes and India's products and culture. The author recommended a south Indian port offering a large quantity of cinnamon and pepper as well as multicolored textiles, tin, copper, gems, diamonds, sapphires, fine-quality pearls, ivory, and Chinese silk. Various Indian words were incorporated into the Greek language, especially words for spices, such as *ginger,* and for foods, like *rice.*

Indian Trade

Trade with China continued along the Silk Road, while many Indian traders traveled to Southeast Asia. Expanding foreign and domestic trade brought much wealth to the Indian commercial and artisan castes, fostering considerable economic growth. Gold coins led to the creation of banking and financial houses. But this commercial dynamism mostly occurred in the cities. Foreign products did not often reach the villages, where the bartering of services between farmers, craftsmen, and servants continued to define social and economic relations.

**Exporting Religious
Traditions**

Indian philosophy and religious ideas also gained a foreign audience. Some Indian philosophers seem to have visited western Asia, and their ideas may have influenced some of the religious movements percolating in the region. The Buddhist idea of monasticism also expanded from India to western Asia and may have influenced the rise of Christian monasticism. Buddhism and Buddhist art continued to spread into Central Asia, especially into the Silk Road cities. Indian cultural influence thus flowed out to the world, in a manner similar to the spread of Hellenistic Greek culture throughout the eastern Mediterranean and western Asia.

Religious Changes in South Asia

Buddhist Divisions

The post-Mauryan centuries saw considerable religious change, including the decline of Buddhism in India, the resurgence of Hinduism, and the arrival of both Christianity and Judaism. The division of Buddhism into two major schools with competing visions occurred in the two centuries just before the Common Era. Some followers criticized the religion as being remote from the real world, atheistic in its rejection of a god, excessively individualistic, requiring too much self-discipline, and denying any afterlife. In response, in the second century C.E., during the Kushan domination of northern India, the division into two schools, the mainstream Theravada (THERE-eh-VAH-duh) and the reformist Mahayana (MAH-HAH-YAH-nah), became complete.

Theravada, which means "Teachings of the Elders," remained closer to Buddha's original vision and clearly descended from Ashoka's Buddhism. To its followers the Buddha was not a god but rather a human teacher. Since the ever-changing universe had no supreme being or gods, people could only take refuge in the wise and compassionate Buddha, his teachings, and the community of monks who maintained them. Each believer was responsible for acquiring merit through devotion, meditation, and good works, such as feeding monks or supporting a temple. The only sure way to end rebirth and reach nirvana was to become a monk and abide by strict monastic rules, and many men did so for at least a few years.

The other school, **Mahayana** ("the Greater Vehicle" to salvation), was a more popularized and less demanding form of belief and practice. Mahayana developed many sects, most of which considered the Buddha a god. Mahayana followers found comfort in devotion to a loving deity (Buddha) and stressed charity and good works as paths toward salvation. A central concept is the **bodhisattva** (boe-dih-SUT-vuh) ("one who has the essence of Buddhahood"), a loving and compassionate "saint" who has died but postponed his or her own attainment of nirvana to help others find salvation. In China, Mahayanists converted nirvana into an appealing heaven, while the wicked were assigned to a terrifying hell. Some historians wonder whether Mahayana ideas about achieving salvation with the help of a saint contributed to Hebrew concepts of a messiah or the reverse. Perhaps the link, if any, was Persian Zoroastrianism, which may have influenced both Mahayana Buddhism and Christianity as it had earlier provided ideas to the Hebrews.

Although several Buddhist monastic orders and some believers remained, Indian Buddhism was gradually absorbed into Hinduism. Perhaps Buddhism was too pessimistic a faith, portraying life as suffering in contrast to the many life-affirming Hindu gods. But Buddhism flourished abroad by providing spiritual support in times of rapid political change or instability. It spread along the trade routes, accommodating itself to local traditions and faiths. The Mahayana school eventually became dominant in Central Asia, including Tibet and Mongolia, from where it filtered into China, Korea, Vietnam, and Japan. The Theravada school became entrenched in Sri Lanka and eventually expanded into mainland Southeast Asia, in the process replacing Mahayana Buddhism (see Map 5.2).

New religions also arrived in India. According to local legends, around 52 C.E. the Christian apostle St. Thomas established Christian churches and attracted followers along the Malabar (MAL-uh-bahr) coast of southwestern India. Such a trip along active maritime trade routes was certainly possible. Large Christian communities still flourish in the Malabar state of Kerala (KER-uh-luh), especially in the ancient coastal ports. Jewish settlers also came to India's west coast, where they established permanent communities in Kerala and to the north at Bombay. In the later twentieth century C.E., many Indian Jews emigrated to the new Jewish state of Israel.

Theravada ("Teachings of the Elders") One of the two main branches of Buddhism, the other being Mahayana, that arose just before the Common Era. Theravada remained closer to the Buddha's original vision.

Mahayana ("the Greater Vehicle" to salvation) One of the two main branches of Buddhism; a more popularized form of Buddhist belief and practice than Theravada. Mahayana Buddhism tended to make Buddha into a god and also developed the notion of the bodhisattva.

bodhisattva ("one who has the essence of Buddhahood") A loving and ever compassionate "saint" who has postponed his or her own attainment of nirvana to help others find salvation through liberation from birth and rebirth.

SECTION SUMMARY

- Various peoples, among them the Kushans from Central Asia, invaded northwest India and ended up adopting various aspects of Indian culture.

- Aspects of northern Indian culture spread to the south, and Buddhism was adopted in Sri Lanka.

- During the post-Mauryan era, there was great demand for Indian goods among traders from western Asia and the Mediterranean.

- Buddhism split into Theravada, a more traditional form, and Mahayana, a more accessible form.

- Buddhism declined in popularity in India as Hinduism adopted many of its ideas, but it spread to Central Asia, China, and Southeast Asia, where it flourished.

THE GUPTA AGE IN INDIA

What were the main achievements of the Gupta era?

In the fourth century C.E. the great Gupta (GOOP-tuh) Empire brought political unity to India once again. The Gupta era (320–550 C.E.) was a brilliant period that saw the assimilation of both immigrants and the foreign cultural influences that reshaped an ancient society. Today Indians consider the Gupta their golden age, with prosperity, tolerant government, and major contributions in science, medicine, mathematics, and literature. In comparison with the declining Roman Empire and turbulent post-Han China, Gupta India was perhaps the world's most dynamic society, visited by travelers and pilgrims from all over Asia.

Government and Economy

The Gupta family and their allies conquered most of north India. The Gupta Empire was somewhat like the Mauryan Empire in that the Gupta Empire was decentralized, with local rulers

Gupta Empire

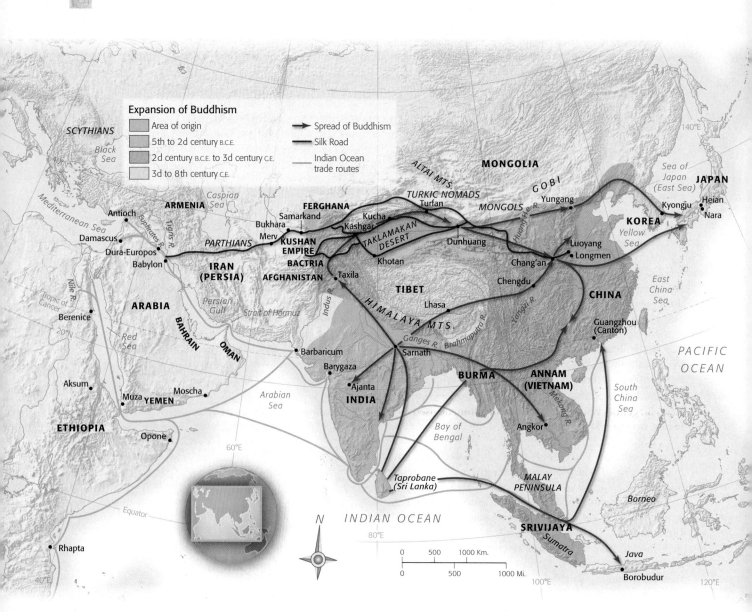

Map 5.2
The Spread of Buddhism in Asia, 100–800 C.E.

Buddhism originated in what is today Nepal and became a major religion in India during the Classical Era. From India it spread into Central Asia, China, Korea, Japan, and Southeast Asia as far east as Java.

Interactive Map

acknowledging Gupta overlordship. The Gupta zenith came under King Chandra Gupta II (r. 375–414), one of the most revered figures in Indian history, praised as enlightened, bold, and resourceful. Gupta India enjoyed a prosperity fostered by internal and external trade, the widespread use of gold and silver coins, and highly productive agriculture. India increasingly became the world's textile center, producing fabrics like linen, wool, and cotton; it also produced pepper and spices for export to the Middle East, Europe, China, and Indonesia. Although the Gupta government favored merchants and farmers, it continued the practice of using enforced labor for one day a month to assist in public projects. The Gupta rulers, like the Mauryas, operated all metal and salt mines as well as various industrial enterprises such as arms factories and textile mills.

Gupta Economy

Gupta Indians generally enjoyed domestic peace, personal freedom, and tolerance for minority views. One fifth-century Chinese Buddhist pilgrim, Faxian **(fah-shee-en)** (Fa-hsien), was impressed by the prosperity, state services, and humane justice system: "The people are very well off. The king governs without corporal punishment. Criminals are fined according to circumstances, lightly or heavily. Even in cases of repeated rebellion, they only cut off the right hand. The people kill no living thing."[11] While the rulers were Hindu, there was no official discrimination against Bud-

Gupta Tolerance

dhists or Jains. The Guptas even helped build a great Buddhist monastery and university at Nalanda (na-LAN-da), where students from all over Asia explored not only Buddhist subjects but also logic, medicine, and Hindu philosophy. However, as before the Gupta age, tolerance did not extend to the untouchables, who still occupied a degraded status.

The Gupta capital city, Patna, reflected prosperity, with hospitals that provided free care to the poor and handicapped. A great university attracted 10,000 students, many from other Asian societies. One observer reported that he saw in Patna "the workshops thriving along the royal road, the river furrowed by boats, and maidens flirting with youths in the parks on the outskirts of town."[12]

Gupta Society

Indian social patterns were never stagnant, and patriarchy became more dominant over time. As male authority grew, women's status gradually declined throughout northern India. By Mauryan times women enjoyed fewer opportunities to pursue intellectual or religious leadership. The *Mahabharata* warned men not to put "confidence in a woman or a coward, a lazybones, a violent man, a self-promoter, a thief, much less an atheist."[13] However, patriarchy remained weaker in south India. Some southern peoples were matrilineal, a kinship system still common in Kerala, and southern women often enjoyed more freedom and options than northern women. In contrast to the mostly male deities in the north, Hinduism in south India placed more emphasis on goddess worship, which may have given women higher status in society. An exception to the idea of the submissive female was also found in the *Kama Sutra*, a detailed sexual handbook written in the third century C.E. that offered ideas about gender that seem almost modern, including a liberal approach to sexual freedom and a somewhat understanding approach to homosexuality.

The Gupta age was not a golden age for women. Brahmans attempted to impose their rigid views on gender relations. The Code of Manu, devised by brahmans, tied women to the patriarchal family, urging that "in childhood a female must be subject to her father, in youth to her husband, and when her lord is dead, to her sons; a woman must never be independent."[14] The code restricted women's property rights and recommended early marriage to preserve chastity. It became common for girls to be married well before puberty, after negotiations were made between the senior men of the two families involved. In addition, widows could no longer remarry. The ancient custom of *sati* (suh-TEE), in which wives joined their late husbands on the funeral pyre, became more widespread. Many Indian writers denounced it, since families often forced an unwilling wife to agree.

Patriarchy and Gender Relations

Primary Source: The Code of Manu See how the principle of dharma justifies the traditional roles of men and women and of priests, warriors, merchants, and servants in Hindu society.

Gupta Science, Mathematics, and Culture

In the Gupta era intellectual and cultural pursuits flourished, and India became the world's leading producer of scientific knowledge, planting some of the roots of modern science. One of the world's major astronomers, mathematicians, and physicists, Aryabhata (AR-ya-BAH-ta) (ca. 476–550), taught that the earth was round, rotated on its own axis, and revolved around the sun as one of a family of planets. He also correctly analyzed lunar eclipses, accurately calculated the moon's diameter and the circumference of the earth, and precisely determined the length of a solar year at 365.36 days. In verse, Aryabhata discussed physics, including the earth's rotation and the nature of gravity. Many of these insights did not spread outside India until many centuries later.

Science and Aryabhata

In mathematics the Gupta Indians surpassed all other classical peoples. Aryabhata analyzed quadratic equations and the value of *pi*. The greatest Gupta achievement was the concept of zero and the consequent evolution of the decimal system. The base could have been any number; Indians probably chose 10 because it corresponded to the number of fingers. With this system, individual numbers were needed only for 0 through 9. By contrast, for the ancient Greeks each 8 in 888 was different. And for the Romans, 888 was written as DCCCLXXXVIII, rendering multiplication and division difficult. The simple and logical Indian numbering system eventually reached the Middle East and later was carried to Europe by Arabs, becoming known as Arabic numerals. Only in the fifteenth century, a thousand years after Gupta times, did European scientists and mathematicians adopt "Arabic" numerals, opening the door to modern science and mathematics. The Indian formulation of the zero and decimal system compares to the invention in western Asia of the wheel and alphabet: all pathbreaking and revolutionary in their consequences.

Decimals and Numerals

The Guptas were also remarkably creative in industrial chemistry and medicine. They made soap and cement, produced the world's finest tempered steel, and transformed sugar-cane juice into granulated crystals for easy storing or shipping. India's fine dyes and fabrics were later adopted

Chemistry and Medicine

Benoy K. Behl

Ajanta Cave Paintings   This painting, made on a cave wall in central India during or just after the Gupta era, depicts one of the Buddha's earlier lives as a king listening to his queen. This and other wall paintings made at Ajanta were part of a complex of Buddhist shrines.

by Europe; *cotton*, *calico*, and *cashmere* are all Indian words. The Guptas also built on a long tradition of medicine. Yoga practitioners required body control to promote mental and spiritual discipline, studying posture, breath control, and regulation of the pulse. Indian physicians also discovered the function of the spinal cord and sketched out the structure of the nervous system. The new knowledge of physiology and herbal medicines contributed to a better understanding of health. Gupta India had the world's best medical system, drugs, and therapeutic methods. Doctors sterilized wounds, did Caesarian deliveries, developed plastic surgery, and vaccinated patients against smallpox. By 1000 C.E. vaccination had traveled the trade routes to China, and by the 1700s to Europe.

The Gupta era was also a great period for literature and performing arts. Writing mostly in Sanskrit, Gupta writers produced religious works, poetry, and prose. The most popular writer, Kalidasa **(kahl-i-DACE-uh)** (ca. 400–455), rendered ancient legends and popular tales into drama and lyrics. Kalidasa's famous poem, "The Cloud Messengers," uses a passing cloud surveying the panoramic landscape to capture the heartache of lovers separated by a vast distance: "I see your body in the sinuous creeper, your gaze in the startled eyes of deer, your cheek in the moon, your hair in the plumage of peacocks, and in the tiny ripples of the river I see your sidelong glances."[15] Theater, music, and dance flourished, establishing the basis for the Indian performing arts of today. Instruments such as the lute, or *vina* **(VEE-nuh)**, and zither, or *sitar* **(si-TAHR)**, were adopted after being imported from western Asia. Improvisational instrumental pieces known as *ragas* **(RAHG-uhz)** were designed for religious and philosophical contemplation. Gupta artists also produced many religious sculptures and paintings, especially on cave or temple walls.

Decline of the Guptas

The arrival of Central Asian peoples brought an end to the Guptas. In the last half of the fifth century C.E. Huns conquered part of northwestern India. Although they were blocked by Gupta power, the cost of holding them off badly depleted the treasury. Soon the empire disintegrated, and other Central Asian invaders followed the Huns into north India. After the Gupta collapse, the varied Hindu states could not unite. India entered a period of fragmentation, political instability, and frequent warfare that persisted for several centuries and left Indians open to conquest by Muslim peoples.

Hun Invasion

Nevertheless, the many rival states that now constituted India remained part of the wider world. Seafarers from the southeastern coast made piratical raids deep into Southeast Asia, while the maritime trade linking southern India with Southeast Asia and China intensified dramatically. Cargo-laden Indian fleets sailed with the monsoon winds far to the east.

SECTION SUMMARY

- Under the decentralized Gupta Empire, based in northern India, the government attained prosperity while pursuing religious tolerance.

- Over time, the status of Indian women declined, particularly in the north.

- During the Gupta era, science, mathematics, literature, and the arts all thrived.

- The Guptas formulated the concept of zero, which made the decimal system possible and made mathematical computation infinitely more powerful.

- The Gupta Empire was greatly weakened by Hun invasion, and soon thereafter it collapsed and other Central Asian groups invaded India.

THE DEVELOPMENT OF SOUTHEAST ASIAN SOCIETIES

How did Southeast Asians blend indigenous and foreign influences to create unique societies?

In the tropical lands east of India and south of China, many societies borrowed political, religious, and cultural ideas from the two neighboring regions, although the impact of these ideas varied greatly. Southeast Asian states were products of indigenous as well as outside forces. Most of the early Southeast Asian societies were centered on coastal plains and in river valleys, where they flourished from both productive agriculture and extensive foreign trade and established enduring patterns in government, religion, and economics.

Austronesian Seafaring, Trade, and Migrations

Seafaring and maritime trade were major forces in the development of some Southeast Asian societies. One group of Austronesians (AW-stroh-NEE-zhuhns), the Malays (muh-LAYZ), enjoyed a strategic position for maritime commerce and intercultural exchange. The Straits of Melaka (muh-LAK-uh), between Sumatra (soo-MAH-tra) and Malaya (muh-LAY-a), had long been a crossroads through which peoples, cultures, and trade passed, some taking root in the area. The lands bordering the straits had also enjoyed fame as a source of gold, tin, spices, and forest products, some of which were traded as far west as Rome, and they became one of the world's most important contact zones. The prevailing climatic patterns in the South China Sea and Indian Ocean allowed ships sailing southwest and southeast to meet in the straits, where their goods could be exchanged.

Maritime Trade

Relief of Indonesian Ship   The Indonesians were skilled mariners. This rock carving, from a Buddhist temple in central Java, depicts a sailing vessel of the type commonly used by Indonesian traders in the Indian Ocean and South China Sea in this era. These ships also carried Indonesian colonists to East Africa and Madagascar.

Ancient Art & Architecture Collection

Malay States and Seafarers

Early in the Common Era small Malay trading states emerged in the Malay Peninsula and Sumatra, prospering from maritime commerce. Like the Phoenicians and Greeks, Malays specialized in maritime trade to distant shores, and they and other Melanesians became prominent in the expanding networks of exchange. In the third century B.C.E., Malay ships visited China using a sail that may have been the model for the revolutionary four-sided lateen (luh-TEEN) sail used later by Arabs and Polynesians, which allowed ships to sail directly into the wind. Malays opened the maritime trade between China and India by obtaining cinnamon grown on the China coast and carrying it across the Indian Ocean to India and Sri Lanka. Some Austronesian sailors returned from India with Indian ideas about government and religion. Other Austronesians from central Indonesia introduced Southeast Asian foods (especially bananas and rice), outrigger canoes, and musical instruments (including the xylophone) to East Africa.

Indian Ocean Connections

Between the fourth and sixth centuries C.E., instability in Central Asia disrupted the Silk Road, making the Indian Ocean connection more crucial. Some Southeast Asians benefited from the growing seagoing trade between China, India, and the Middle East. But the voyages held many dangers. For example, the Chinese Buddhist pilgrim Faxian, sailing from Sri Lanka to Sumatra in 414 C.E., reported that he "set sail on a large merchant ship which carried about two hundred passengers. A small boat trailed behind, for use in case the large vessel should be wrecked, as sailing on this sea was most hazardous. [We] were caught up in a typhoon [which] lasted for thirteen days. That sea is [also] infested with pirates."[16]

Austronesian Migrations

Austronesian seafaring also led to migration. Between 100 and 700 C.E. some Austronesians from southern Borneo (BOR-nee-oh) and Sulawesi (soo-luh-WAY-see) migrated across the Indian Ocean to the East African coast. Later most of them settled on the large island of Madagascar (mad-uh-GAS-kuhr), off the southeast coast of Africa. Today their descendants account for the majority of the island's population and speak Austronesian languages. Beginning in ancient times, other Austronesians moved from Southeast Asia into the western Pacific. Eventually their descendants, known today as the Polynesians (pahl-uh-NEE-zhuhns) and Micronesians (my-kruh-NEE-zhuhns), settled nearly all of the islands of the central and eastern Pacific (see Chapter 9). As a result of these movements, Austronesian-speaking societies stretched thousands of miles from Madagascar eastward through Indonesia and the Philippines to Hawaii and Easter Island in eastern Polynesia.

Indianization and Early Mainland States

First Cities and States

Various states developed on the Southeast Asian mainland by early in the Common Era, but their foundations had been established a few centuries earlier. The most populous societies emerged along the fertile coastal plains or in the valleys of great rivers like the Mekong and Red, where irrigated rice cultivation was possible, providing a highly productive and labor-intensive economic mainstay that could be sustained for many generations. Because it promoted social cooperation, this kind of economy led to centralized kingdoms. By 500 B.C.E. a few small states had emerged that used bronze and iron. The kings of Van Lang in northern Vietnam ruled through a landed aristocracy who controlled vast rice-growing estates worked by peasants. During the third century B.C.E. the earliest cities with monumental architecture appeared. At Co Loa, near modern Hanoi, King An Duong built a huge citadel surrounded by a wall 5 miles long and 10 yards wide. Urban societies also emerged among peoples such as the Khmers (kuh-MEERZ) (Cambodians).

Indianization The process by which Indian ideas spread into and influenced many Southeast Asian societies; a mixing of Indian with indigenous ideas.

Outside influences from China and India also generated change. In the second century B.C.E., Han China conquered northern Vietnam, imposing a colonial rule that endured for a millennium (111 B.C.E.–939 C.E.) and spreading many Chinese cultural patterns into Vietnam (see Chronology: Classical Southeast Asia). Chinese traders regularly visited many Southeast Asian states over the centuries. Elsewhere Indian influence was paramount in fostering a very different form of society. Around the beginning of the Common Era, Indian traders and brahman priests began regularly traveling the oceanic trade routes and settling in some of the states, where they married into or became advisors to influential families. They brought with them Indian concepts of religion, government, and the arts. Thus Gupta India provided a political model for Southeast Asians.

The process by which Indian ideas spread into and influenced many Southeast Asian societies is often termed **Indianization**, a mixing of Indian with indigenous ideas. This occurred about the same time as classical Greco-Roman culture was spreading around the Mediterranean. For a millennium, Southeast

CHRONOLOGY
Classical Southeast Asia

111 B.C.E.–939 C.E. Chinese colonization of Vietnam

39–41 C.E. Trung Sisters' rebellion in Vietnam

ca. 75–550 C.E. Funan

ca. 100–1200 C.E. Era of Indianization

ca. 192–1471 C.E. Champa

ca. 450–750 C.E. Zhenla states

Asian peoples such as the Khmers in the Mekong Basin, the Chams along the central coast of Vietnam, and the Javanese (JAH-vuh-NEEZ) on the fertile island of Java were closely connected to India, adapting Indian writing systems to local spoken languages. Mahayana Buddhism and Hinduism became popular in Southeast Asia, especially among the upper classes, fusing with indigenous animisms that focused on communicating with spiritual forces. Many Southeast Asians blended outside and local religions rather than following one exclusively. In politics, Southeast Asian rulers adopted the Indian concept of powerful kings who possessed supernatural powers and religious sanction, which made their positions difficult to challenge.

However, although centuries of borrowing helped shape Southeast Asians, they rarely became carbon copies of their mentors. Like the Japanese and western Europeans, they took ideas that they wanted from outsiders and adapted them to their own use, creating a distinctive synthesis. For example, the Hindu and Buddhist architecture and temples of Burma, Cambodia, or Java differed substantially from the South Asian models as well as from each other.

Funan, Zhenla, and Champa

Productive agriculture, maritime commerce, and Indianization fostered stronger mainland states. Between 75 and 550 C.E. Funan (FOO-nan) flourished in the fertile Mekong Delta of southern Vietnam. While the Khmer people made up most of the population, Austronesians did most of the maritime trade. Indianized Funan traded with China, valued literacy, and built complex irrigation systems to turn swamps into productive agricultural land. Funan apparently had some authority over Cambodia and southern Thailand (see Map 5.3). Trade goods from as far away as Rome, Arabia, Central Asia, and perhaps East Africa have been found in its ruins, and merchants from various countries (including India and China) lived in the major port city. Another Khmer state, Zhenla, in the middle Mekong basin, became prominent in the fifth century when Funan declined.

Meanwhile, the coastal, Austronesian-speaking Cham people of central Vietnam formed an Indianized state, or possibly several states, known as Champa (CHAM-pa), which tried to control the coastal commerce between China and Southeast Asia. The Chams, a strongly Hindu people, became renowned as sailors and merchants and sometimes resorted to piracy. They frequently fought the Vietnamese, who continually pushed southward. Champa existed from 192 to 1471 C.E., when the Vietnamese finally conquered Champa.

Map 5.3
Funan and Its Neighbors
The first large mainland Southeast Asian states emerged during the Classical Era. The major states included Vietnam, which became a Chinese colony in the second century B.C.E., Funan, Zhenla, and Champa.

 **Interactive Map**

Vietnam and Chinese Colonization

During Chinese colonial times, Vietnamese society was largely confined to what is today the northern third of Vietnam. China's final conquest and annexation of Vietnam in 111 B.C.E. ended the independence of a densely populated kingdom. The Chinese policy to assimilate the Vietnamese and implant Chinese values, customs, and institutions fostered some revolutionary changes. Chinese philosophies and religions like Confucianism, Daoism, and Mahayana Buddhism were adopted by most Vietnamese but also mixed with earlier ancestor and spirit worship. China's patriarchal family system, written language, and political ideas also sank deep roots.

Chinese Rule

Yet, while the Vietnamese adopted many Chinese patterns, they also sustained a hatred of Chinese rule and resisted cultural assimilation. The survival of the Vietnamese identity, language, and many customs during a millennium of colonialism constituted a display of national determination unparalleled in world history. Perhaps the Vietnamese were able to avoid cultural and national extinction because they already had several centuries of state building and cultural identity behind them when the Chinese colonized. A long history of resistance to the Chinese, a sense of nationhood, and a desire for independence also helped them resist assimilation. Chinese and later foreign conquerors such as the French in the modern era found that they had to conquer each village, one by one.

Vietnamese Resistance

Many revolts punctuated the Chinese colonial period, all of them well remembered today as symbols of patriotism. The rebellions were sometimes led by women, including the Trung Sisters

Anti-Chinese Revolts

(see Profile: The Trung Sisters, Vietnamese Rebels). Chinese officials recommended harsh retaliation to rebellion: "At every stream, cave, marketplace, everywhere there is stubbornness. Repression is necessary."[17] This history of resistance to foreign invaders meant frequent warfare. A Vietnamese Buddhist poet described the results: "War, no end to it, people scattered in all directions. How can a man keep his mind off it? The winds dark, the rains violent year after year, laying waste the land, over and over."[18] The Vietnamese eventually regained independence from China in the tenth century.

Economies, Societies, and Cultures

Regional Patterns

Despite the great differences between societies like Champa, Funan, and Vietnam, there were many commonalities throughout the region. Most of the larger Southeast Asian states were multiethnic in their population, including foreign merchants in temporary or permanent residence. Many Southeast Asians also lived well. Chinese envoys who visited Funan around 250 C.E. described walled cities, palaces, and houses occupied by people who ate with silver utensils and paid their taxes with gold, silver, perfumes, and pearls. The Chinese envoys were also impressed with the many books available and the well-kept archives, indicating that an Indian writing system was already in use. Commerce was prevalent in most places, but most Southeast Asians were farmers and fishermen living in self-sufficient villages held together by ties of kinship and a communal spirit of cooperation for mutual survival.

Family Systems and Gender Relations

Many Southeast Asian family systems contrasted with those in China or India. While the Vietnamese followed a patriarchal pattern like China, others developed flexible systems incorporating both paternal and maternal kin. The Chams were matrilineal, and their women enjoyed considerable political influence. Both Cham men and women could have more than one spouse. In Southeast Asia women generally enjoyed a higher status and played a more active public role than they did in China, India, the Middle East, and Europe; for example, they took charge of most village markets. The Southeast Asian pattern of inclusion and blending of religions and cultures, along with extensive trade, made Southeast Asian societies distinctive.

SECTION SUMMARY

- The lands bordering the Straits of Melaka were rich in natural resources, and their peoples engaged in wide-ranging maritime trade.

- Austronesians settled over a wide area, from Madagascar, off the coast of Africa, to the Pacific islands of Polynesia.

- Southeast Asians were influenced by both Chinese and Indian culture, but they retained distinct aspects of their native cultures.

- Some principal states in this era were Funan, Zhenla, and Champa on the Southeast Asian mainland.

- Vietnam showed great resistance in its long struggle against Chinese colonization.

- Though different from each other, Southeast Asian societies tended to be multiethnic and able to blend diverse elements into cultural unity.

CHAPTER SUMMARY

The Classical Era saw dramatic changes in India and Southeast Asia, some generated by outside influences such as migration and long-distance trade. India developed unique social systems and religious ideas. The caste system divided the population into categories based on descent and occupation. Hinduism flowered into various schools of speculative thought. Buddhism challenged Hinduism and the caste system in the first millennium B.C.E. Hinduism and Buddhism shared many beliefs, such as reincarnation and karma, but differed in their conception of gods and the path to ending reincarnation.

India's political, economic, and intellectual life also changed. The Mauryan Empire united India, and under Ashoka the empire reflected humane and peaceful Buddhist values. The Classical Era also saw the forging of deeper cultural and trade connections between India and other regions, and many peoples migrated into the country from Central Asia. Buddhism spread into

THE TRUNG SISTERS, VIETNAMESE REBELS

Some of the major anti-Chinese rebellions in Vietnamese history were led by women such as the Trung Sisters in 39 C.E. Even after 2,000 years, the Vietnamese honor the two sisters and their martyrdom with annual ceremonies at cult shrines dedicated to their memory. Our knowledge of the two sisters and their experiences is limited. Some historians consider them semimythical rather than flesh and blood. Their revolt was caused by Chinese attempts to raise taxes and consolidate their control over the indigenous landed aristocracy. The Trung Sisters became enshrined in images of brave but beautiful, sword-bearing women mounted on elephants, leading their troops against the Chinese.

The sisters are believed to have been daughters of a prominent family of landed aristocrats from near Hanoi. The older sister, Trung Trac, had married a member of another landed family. When her husband protested an increase in taxes by Chinese colonial authorities, he was apparently executed. The spirited sisters then sparked a rebellion that rapidly spread throughout the entire country and involved both the elite and the peasantry. With local Chinese officials in retreat, her followers declared Trung Trac queen of a newly independent country. Some sources suggest the sisters served as joint queens, ruling for two years. They abolished taxes, but, as traditionalists, they also sought to restore the pre-Chinese order dominated by landed aristocrats and protect local autonomy. Despite the sisters' aristocratic agenda, the common people joined the revolt because of their hostility to the authoritarian rule of the Chinese governors.

Han dynasty rulers, not about to allow this valuable part of their empire to secede, dispatched their most able general and his army to destroy the rebellion. As the fighting and repression intensified, most of the sisters' upper-class supporters abandoned their cause. Eventually their remaining forces were defeated in 41 C.E., and the sisters either committed suicide or were captured and executed. China now intensified its direct control of the colony and launched a more deliberate cultural assimilation policy to integrate Vietnam politically into China proper.

Although the revolt failed to dislodge the Chinese, the Trung Sisters established a model for later rebels, some of them also women. Another famous anticolonial leader, the nineteen-year-old Lady Trieu in the third century C.E., demonstrated a similar commitment. When advised to marry rather than fight, she replied: "I want to ride the storm, tread the dangerous waves, win back the fatherland and destroy the yoke of slavery. I don't want to bow down my head working as a simple housewife." The Lady Trieu seems an almost modern figure in her patriotic and social defiance.

Even in the nineteenth and twentieth centuries, Vietnamese women inspired by the Trung Sisters and Lady Trieu took up arms alongside men to fight oppressive governments and invading forces. Although men led the movements, women were prominent in the struggle against French colonialism and in the revolution by Communist forces to overthrow the U.S.-backed government in South Vietnam in the mid-twentieth century.

THINKING ABOUT THE PROFILE

1. What sparked the rebellion led by the Trung Sisters?

2. What does the experience of the Trung Sisters tell us about Vietnamese society under Chinese rule and the role of women in that society?

Note: Quotation is from Thomas Hodgkin, *Vietnam: The Revolutionary Path* (New York: St. Martin's, 1981), 22.

The Trung Sisters This painting by a Vietnamese artist shows the Trung Sisters riding into battle on war elephants against the Chinese.

both Central and Southeast Asia, becoming a major world religion. During the Gupta golden age, Indians achieved new knowledge in science and mathematics that later influenced the Middle East and Europe.

The states that emerged in Southeast Asia were based on maritime trade, rice agriculture, and the blending of local and foreign influences. The Austronesian sailors fostered trade networks over vast distances, and kingdoms arose in Cambodia and Vietnam. Indian religious, political, and cultural ideas had a great impact in many parts of the region, and China's conquest of Vietnam spread Chinese influence.

KEY TERMS

Brahman	Buddhism	Kushans	bodhisattva
Vedanta	nirvana	Theravada	Indianization
Jainism	monasticism	Mahayana	

EBOOK AND WEBSITE RESOURCES

 PRIMARY SOURCE
The Code of Manu

 INTERACTIVE MAPS
Map 5.1 The Mauryan Empire, 322–185 B.C.E.
Map 5.2 The Spread of Buddhism in Asia, 100–800 C.E.
Map 5.3 Funan and Its Neighbors

LINKS

Austronesian and Other Indo-Pacific Topics (http://w3 .rz-berlin.mpg.de/~wm/wm3.html). A useful collection to sources on Austronesian languages and cultures, operated by Germany-based scholars.

Internet Indian History Sourcebook (http://www .fordham.edu/halsall/india/indiasbook.html). An invaluable collection of sources and links on India from ancient to modern times.

Silk Road Narratives (http://depts.washington.edu/uwch/ silkroad/texts/texts.html). Explores cultural interaction in Eurasia through excerpts from Silk Road travelers.

Virtual Religion Index (http://virtualreligion.net/vri/). An outstanding site with many links on the history of Buddhism and Hinduism.

Plus flashcards, practice quizzes, and more. Go to: www.cengage.com/history/lockard/globalsocnet2e

SUGGESTED READING

Armstrong, Karen. *Buddha.* New York: Viking Penguin, 2001. A brief and readable introduction to the Buddha's life and thought.

Auboyer, Jeannine. *Daily Life in Ancient India: From 200 BC to 700 AD.* Translated by Simon Watson Taylor. London: Phoenix, 2002. A fascinating and readable examination of classical Indian society.

Avari, Burjor. *India: The Ancient Past. A History of the Indian Subcontinent from c. 7000 BC to AD 1200.* New York: Routledge, 2007. Good overview by an Indian scholar.

Basham, A. L. *The Wonder That Was India,* 3rd ed. London: Macmillan, 1968 (reprinted 1999 by Rupa and Company, New Delhi). Although dated, this is still the best general study of pre-Islamic India.

Foltz, Richard C. *Religions of the Silk Road: Overland Trade and Cultural Exchange from Antiquity to the Fifteenth Century.* New York: St. Martin's, 1999. An introduction to trade and the spread of religions, especially Buddhism, in Central Asia.

Frye, Richard N. *The Heritage of Central Asia: From Antiquity to the Turkish Expansion.* Princeton: Markus Wiener, 1996. One of the best surveys of Central Asia in this era.

Hall, Kenneth. *Maritime Trade and State Development in Early Southeast Asia.* Honolulu: University of Hawai'i Press, 1985. Useful study of trade, politics, and international connections.

Higham, Charles. *Early Cultures of Mainland Southeast Asia.* Chicago: Art Media Resources, 2002. Scholarly study with good coverage of this era.

Kulke, Hermann, and Dietmar Rothermund. *A History of India,* 2nd ed. London and New York: Routledge, 2010. A concise but stimulating general history that incorporates recent scholarship on the Classical Era.

Mabbett, Ian, and David Chandler. *The Khmers.* London: Blackwell, 1995. An authoritative study of early Cambodian history.

O'Reilly, Dougald J.W. *Early Civilizations of Southeast Asia.* Lanham, MD.: AltaMira Press, 2007. Excellent survey of classical Southeast Asia.

Oxtoby, Willard G. *World Religions: Eastern Traditions.* New York: Oxford University Press, 1996. Contains valuable essays on the Buddhist, Hindu, and Jain traditions.

Ray, Himanshu Prabha. *The Archaeology of Seafaring in Ancient South Asia.* New York: Cambridge University Press, 2003. A scholarly study of India's maritime trade and contacts in this era.

Shaffer, Lynda Norene. *Maritime Southeast Asia to 1500.* Armonk, NY: M.E. Sharpe, 1996. A very readable brief introduction to premodern Southeast Asia, including Funan and the Austronesian maritime trade.

Stein, Burton. *A History of India.* Malden, MA: Blackwell, 1998. A survey text especially strong on social and religious history.

Taylor, Keith Weller. *The Birth of Vietnam.* Berkeley: University of California Press, 1983. The major study on Vietnam before and during Chinese colonization.

Thapar, Romila. *A'soka and the Decline of the Mauryas.* Delhi: Oxford University Press, 1997. An update of an earlier study, with much information on the Mauryas.

Thapar, Romila. *Early India from the Origins to AD 1300.* Berkeley: University of California Press, 2002. A valuable revision of the standard history of early India, detailed and comprehensive.

EURASIAN CONNECTIONS AND NEW TRADITIONS IN EAST ASIA, 600 B.C.E.–600 C.E.

Courtesy, Dunhuang Academy/ Lois Conner, photographer

Fresco from Mogao Caves
The Mogao Caves, situated along the Silk Road in western China, contain many frescoes reflecting Silk Road life and the spread of Buddhism into the region. This fresco, painted in the third century C.E., shows a caravan resting at an oasis.

A fter the Han had sent its envoys to open up communications with the state of Da Xia [in today's Afghanistan], all the barbarians of the distant west craned their necks to the east and longed to catch a glimpse of China.

—CHINESE DIPLOMAT ZHANG QIAN, REPORTED BY HISTORIAN SIMA QIAN, CA. 100 B.C.E.[1]

In 138 B.C.E. the Chinese emperor, Wu Di (woo tee), sought to make contact with a Central Asian group, the Yuezhi (yueh-chih), in order to forge an alliance against their mutual enemy, another Central Asian group, the Xiongnu (SHE-OONG-noo), who were threatening China. An attendant at the imperial court, Zhang Qian (jahng chee-YEN), volunteered to undertake the dangerous diplomatic mission. A strong man known for his generosity who inspired trust and easily made friends with non-Chinese, Zhang set off on the overland journey west with only a small escort. After being captured by the Xiongnu and held prisoner for ten years, Zhang finally escaped. Hoping to complete his mission, he and his party made their way west, following a route that soon became known as one of the classical world's great networks of exchange: the Silk Road. They crossed the Pamir (pah-MEER) Mountains and visited lands in what is today Afghanistan and Turkestan, whose people already knew of China because they avidly imported Chinese silk (hence the name *Silk Road*). Although his diplomatic mission failed, after twelve years away Zhang brought back useful products, including the grape, and informed Wu Di about the lands to the west and their resources.

For over a millennium after Zhang's journey, China connected with the lands much farther west by way of overland trade and travel through Central Asia. Every year merchants gathered just outside the walls of the Chinese capital, Chang'an (CHAHNG-ahn) (today's Xian [SEE-ahn]), to form a caravan. The merchants loaded bundles of metals, ceramics, spices, scrolls of paintings, seeds, and above all piles of silk on their horses and donkeys. The veteran caravaners, Chinese and Central Asian, understood the dangers ahead, which could include blinding sandstorms and ruthless bandits, but also the fabulous profits that would be made from their venture. They traveled west for weeks, skirting the Great Wall of China. At the last outpost of Chinese society, marked by the Jade Gate, the horses and donkeys were exchanged for camels, better suited to the upcoming journey through harsh deserts. After weeks of travel across waterless wastes, the caravan crossed the snow-covered Pamir Mountains. Finally, several thousand miles from Chang'an, the travelers would arrive at the cities of Turkestan, where their precious commodities were traded or sold. Much of this cargo was then on its way to India, western Asia, and even southern Europe. In spite of great distances and immense geographical barriers, this vast network of trails tied China to the world beyond and made peoples as far west as Rome aware of China.

China and its neighbors, Korea and Japan, built their societies far away from the influence of the Middle East, India, and Europe, fostering unique technologies, governments, religions, and philosophies. But East Asians were also influenced by peoples, ideas, and commercial goods that traveled the trade networks from faraway places such as Central Asia and India. These were the centuries of the classical blossoming of East Asian cultures, which established frameworks for the development of these societies in the centuries to follow.

FOCUS QUESTIONS

1. **What were the distinctive features of the Chinese philosophies that emerged during the late Zhou period?**

2. **What developments during the Han dynasty linked China to the rest of Eurasia?**

3. **What outside influences helped shape China after the fall of the Han?**

4. **How did the Koreans and Japanese assimilate Chinese influences into their own distinctive societies?**

e Visit the website and eBook for additional study materials and interactive tools: www.cengage.com/history/lockard/globalsocnet2e

CHANGING CHINA AND AXIAL AGE THOUGHT, 600–221 B.C.E.

What were the distinctive features of the Chinese philosophies that emerged during the late Zhou period?

Chinese technology, science, and philosophy developed largely independently from outside influences. Yet Chinese originality also responded to many of the same challenges faced by other societies. The Chinese needed ideas to explain the workings of the universe and to bring order to their lives. Such ideas appeared during the late Zhou period, when changes in society and politics produced unsettled conditions. Chinese philosophers seeking to restore order spawned several schools of thought that endured for several millennia.

Late Zhou Conflicts

The Zhou dynasty endured for nearly 900 years (1122–221 B.C.E.), but after 500 B.C.E. it experienced rapid social and economic change as well as chronic warfare, worsened through advances in iron weapons (see Map 6.1). This era of particularly intense fighting is known as the "Warring States Period." Local lords did not challenge the Zhou king directly but increasingly ignored him, fighting instead among themselves for supremacy. This prolonged crisis fostered changes in many areas of Chinese life, not all of them detrimental. For example, despite the fighting, by 250 B.C.E. China had become the most populous society on earth, with 20 to 40 million people. Improving technol-

Warring States

Map 6.1
China in the Sixth Century B.C.E.

During the late Zhou era China was divided into competing, often warring, states, only loosely ruled by the Zhou kings. Some, such as Ch'u and Wu, were large. In the third century B.C.E. the westernmost state, Qin, conquered the others and formed a unified empire.

e Interactive Map

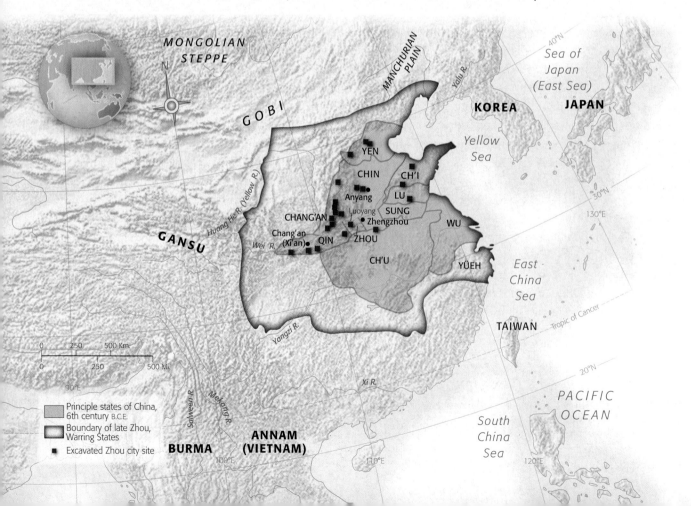

CHRONOLOGY

	China	Korea	Japan
1200 B.C.E.	**1122–221 B.C.E.** Zhou dynasty		
300 B.C.E.	**221–206 B.C.E.** Qin dynasty **206 B.C.E.–220 C.E.** Han dynasty	**108 B.C.E.–313 C.E.** Chinese colonization	**300 B.C.E.–552 C.E.** Yayoi culture
300 C.E.	**222–581 C.E.** Three Kingdoms and Six Dynasties	**350–668 C.E.** Koguryo Empire	
500 C.E.	**581–618 C.E.** Sui dynasty		**552–710 C.E.** Yamato state

ogy and communications also fostered commerce and cities. Political and economic power gradually shifted to the eastern part of the Yellow River Basin, while Chinese culture expanded south of the Yangzi River Basin, which became the major agricultural region because of its greater fertility and favorable climate. Social mobility also increased. Many peasants and slaves abandoned their homes and moved to open land or to the fast-growing cities. The growing merchant class also gained influence. A Chinese historian recorded the situation: "The law honors farmers, yet farmers have become poorer; the law degrades merchants, yet merchants have become richer."[2]

Late Zhou Technology and Science

China joined the Iron Age in the sixth century B.C.E., thus achieving equal technological footing with western Asia. Knowledge of ironworking, which probably filtered into China from Central Asia over trade networks, led to the use of iron-tipped ox-drawn plows, which improved agricultural productivity. The Zhou Chinese also became the first people to make the breakthrough to cast iron, which is much easier to shape into products; with this discovery they could make superior axes, hoes, ploughshares, picks, swords, and chariots. Indeed, Chinese iron plows were the world's most efficient farm tools before the second millennium C.E. The Chinese also made major advances in water control and conservation. In 250 B.C.E., for example, a vast complex of dikes, canals, and dams was constructed to control the fickle upper Yangzi River, a huge system that worked so well that it is still used today. Other advances included the growing of soybeans, which provided a rich protein source and enriched the soil. The late Zhou Chinese also invented the first compasses and became pioneers in mathematics, amending the Shang decimal system by adding a place for the zero in equations. While the Chinese had long produced silk from strands made by a caterpillar of a moth that fed on mulberry trees, in Zhou times they developed better methods of weaving the silk.

Iron Technology

One Hundred Philosophical Schools

The later Zhou was the most creative period in traditional Chinese thought, producing so many competing philosophies that it was called the era of the "hundred schools of thought." These diverse approaches were part of the widespread intellectual creativity in Eurasia during the Axial Age, so named because it fostered ways of thought that endured through the centuries. New philosophies and widening intellectual horizons also emerged in the Mediterranean world, western Asia, and India between 600 and 250 B.C.E. (see Chapters 5 and 7 and "Societies, Networks, Transitions," for Part II; see also Chronology: Classical China). To help explain the fighting and restore peace and harmony, philosophers across Eurasia emphasized ethical principles, criticized political conditions, and proposed new ideas about government and society. At the end of this period, powerful empires

CHRONOLOGY
Classical China

1122–221 B.C.E. Zhou dynasty

550–350 B.C.E. Height of Axial Age in China

481 B.C.E. Beginning of Warring States Period

551–479 B.C.E. Life of Confucius

221–206 B.C.E. Qin dynasty

206 B.C.E.–220 C.E. Han dynasty

141–87 B.C.E. Reign of Wu Di

105 C.E. Invention of paper

222–581 C.E. Three Kingdoms and Six Dynasties Era

581–618 C.E. Sui dynasty

Confucius Stone rubbing of a portrait of Confucius from an ancient temple. For 2,500 years Confucius was the most honored and influential Chinese thinker, remembered in countless paintings, woodblock cuts, and carvings on walls.

Confucianism A Chinese philosophy based on the ideas of Confucius emphasizing the relations among people.

The Analects The book of the sayings of Confucius collected by his disciples and published a century or two after his death.

filial piety The Confucian rule that children should respect and obey their parents.

emerged in China, India, and the Mediterranean that reflected a new order of technological and organizational planning. In China, the hundred schools resulted in part from the constant conflict during the Warring States Period and the increased knowledge of the outside world resulting from contact with Turkik pastoralists, who brought horses to China in exchange for grain, wine, and silks.

Chinese thought differed dramatically from that developed in other societies. From the late Zhou period onward, Chinese philosophy, unlike that in, for example, India, viewed people as social and political creatures within communities and placed less emphasis on an afterlife and powerful gods. While Chinese thinkers did not ignore the supernatural, and some practiced magic or mystical techniques, their main emphases were humanistic. This practical approach reflected the philosophers' position in society. Although literate and thoughtful, they were also pragmatic men who often served in government. Some wandered from one Zhou state to another offering their services, thus becoming teachers. Their disciples collected their sayings or thoughts into the classic texts venerated by later generations. The leading masters created with their followers the philosophies of Confucianism, Daoism, and Legalism, all of which ultimately stood the test of time and influenced China for the next two millennia. The divisions between and within the various schools were never rigid, but each had certain core ideas.

Confucius and His Legacy

The most influential new philosophy, **Confucianism** (kun-FYOO-shu-NIZ-um), was based on the ideas of Confucius and emphasized the relations among people. Kong Fuzi (kong foo-dzu) ("Master Kung"), better known in the West as Confucius, probably lived from 551 to 479 B.C.E. (see Chronology: Classical China). As with the Buddha in India or Jesus of Nazareth, we know of his life and ideas through the writings of followers. Confucius left no direct writings, but his sayings were collected by his disciples and published a century or two after his death in a book called ***The Analects*** (see Witness to the Past: *The Analects* and Correct Confucian Behavior). Born into a modest but aristocratic family, he attempted unsuccessfully to gain a government position in various states and then spent years as a teacher of dazzling ability. Over his career he taught some three thousand students from all social classes. The sage claimed that he had "never refused to teach anyone, even though he came to me on foot, with nothing more to offer as tuition than a package of dried meat."[3] Maintaining that education was the key to promoting morality, Confucius stressed the study of history, philosophy, literature, poetry, and music. Considering himself not a creator of new ideas but rather a transmitter of ancient wisdom, he revived traditional ideas and reorganized them into a coherent system of thought. Hence, he extolled the past as an example for the future.

Confucianism is not primarily a religion concerned with otherworldly issues, but a philosophy of social relations, a moral and ethical code designed to promote social stability. The Chinese never considered Confucius a god, but rather a wise sage to be honored by offerings. Confucius could best be described as an agnostic, arguing that, since people know little about life, they cannot know about death and the supernatural world. Like the Ionian Greeks a world away, Confucius was developing a rationalist view opposed to superstition. He asserted that wisdom was working to improve society and keeping one's distance from the gods and spirits while showing them reverence. The answer to the world's problems, Confucius argued, was virtue, ethics, and, above all, benevolence and moderation in behavior. Confucius also advised people to think about the future, contending that if they do not think about problems that are still distant, they will have to worry about them when they arrive.

Confucius advocated an autocratic but paternalistic form of government in which the ruler was responsible for the people's welfare. The family constituted the model for the state. Just as children should respect and obey their parents, a custom known as **filial piety** (FILL-eal PIE-uh-ty), so citizens should obey a fair government and play their assigned roles in a society defined by order and hierarchy: "Let the ruler be ruler, and the minister minister; let the father be father, and the son son."[4] Confucius talked about duty and obedience of inferiors to superiors: of wife to husband, son to father, younger to older, and citizen to king. But authority, he emphasized, must be wielded justly and wisely. Government was fundamentally a matter of ethics: if power was abused, it became illegitimate. When asked what thought should guide the conduct of both leaders and citizens throughout life, he replied: "Do not do to others what you yourself do not desire."[5]

The Analects and Correct Confucian Behavior

The Analects is the main record of Confucius and his thought that survived the Warring States Period and the book burnings of the next dynasty. Compiled by his disciples many years after his death, it is presented largely in the form of questions from his followers and answers, short aphorisms, or long discourses by the sage. Divided into twenty chapters, the book covers many topics, mostly peoples' conduct and aspirations. It became the most important book in China from the Han dynasty down to modern times. These fragments present a few of Confucius's thoughts about the correct behavior of gentlemen (the rulers and other leaders), sons and daughters, and people in general.

[About the gentleman], Confucius said, "The gentleman concerns himself with the Way [the natural order that is also a moral order]; he does not worry about his salary. Hunger may be found in plowing; wealth may be found in studying. The gentleman worries about the Way, not about poverty. . . . The gentleman reveres three things. He reveres the mandate of Heaven; he reveres great people; and he reveres the words of the sages. Petty people do not know the mandate of Heaven and so do not revere it. They are disrespectful of great people and they ridicule the words of the sage. The gentleman aspires to things lofty; the petty person aspires to things base. The gentleman looks to himself; the petty person looks to other people. The gentleman feels bad when his capabilities fall short of some task. He does not feel bad if people fail to recognize him. . . ."

[About filial piety or respect for parents], Confucius said, "Nowadays, filial piety is considered to be the ability to nourish one's parents. But this obligation to nourish even extends down to the dogs and horses. Unless we have reverence for our parents, what makes us any different? Do not offend your parents. . . . When your parents are alive, serve them according to the rules of ritual and decorum. When they are deceased, give them a funeral and offer sacrifices to them according to the rules of ritual and decorum. . . . It is unacceptable not to be aware of your parents' ages. Their advancing years are a cause for joy and at the same time a cause for sorrow. . . ."

[About humanity], Confucius said, "If an individual can practice five things anywhere in the world, he is a man of humanity. . . . [These are] Reverence, generosity, truthfulness, diligence, and kindness. If a person acts with reverence, he will not be insulted. If he is generous, he will win over the people. If he is truthful, he will be trusted by the people. If he is diligent, he will have great achievements. If he is kind, he will be able to influence others. . . . When you go out, treat everyone as if you were welcoming a great guest. Employ people as if you were conducting a great sacrifice."

THINKING ABOUT THE READING

1. What are some of the main qualities expected of a gentleman?
2. How might Confucian views on respect for parents have influenced the family system?
3. How did the advice reflect Confucius's humanistic emphasis?

Source: Reprinted with the permission of The Free Press, a Division of Simon & Schuster Inc. from CHINESE CIVILIZATION AND SOCIETY, A Sourcebook, Second Revised & Expanded Edition by Patricia Buckley Ebrey. Copyright © 1993 by Patricia Buckley Ebrey. All rights reserved.

Confucian teachings have had a more enduring influence on East Asia than those of any other thinker, becoming in some form or another the official doctrine in China, Korea, Vietnam, and Japan and helping set the common East Asian pattern of compromise. As a Chinese proverb advised, people should "bend like bamboo" to avoid conflict with other people. To promote harmony, Confucianism stressed adherence to rules of courtesy. For example, a book of etiquette from late Zhou times advised men on rules for visiting another man of equal status: if the host should "yawn, stretch himself, ask the time of day, order his dinner, or change his position, then [the guest] must ask permission to [leave]."[6] Confucian societies used ritual and etiquette to maintain stability and discipline. Confucian ideas were designed to promote social order and continuity across generations, and, in the centuries to follow, they generally did. China became one of the most stable societies in history.

Impact of Confucianism

The ideas of Confucius were revised to some extent by his followers and became increasingly rigid in application over the centuries, leading in some cases to a conservatism and inflexibility that Confucius might have condemned. Two of the main followers of Confucius represented opposing schools of interpretation. Both lived one and a half centuries later than their master. Mengzi (MUNG-dze) (Mencius) (372–289 B.C.E.) advocated a liberal, even permissive government in which the ruler embraced benevolence and righteousness as his main goals. Mengzi believed human nature was essentially good, and hence he was extremely optimistic about the prospects for society. Xunzi (SHOON-dze) (Hsun Tzu) (310–220 B.C.E.) disagreed; viewing human nature as essentially bad, he maintained that the state must enforce goodness and morality. Xunzi also contributed to the authoritarian tendencies of Confucianism by claiming that Confucian writings were the source of all wisdom.

Later Confucian Thinkers

Daoism and Chinese Mysticism

Daoism A Chinese philosophy that emphasized adaptation to nature.

The second major philosophy, **Daoism** (DOW-iz-um), taught that people should adapt to nature. Daoism's main ideas are attributed to Laozi (lou-zoe) (Lao Tzu or "Old Master"). According to legends, Laozi was an older contemporary of Confucius and a disillusioned bureaucrat who became a wandering teacher. If such a man ever lived, he probably did not write the two main Daoist texts, which were most likely composed during the third century B.C.E.

Daoist Beliefs

Daoism was a philosophy of withdrawal for people appalled by the warfare of the age. Daoist thinkers held that the goal of life was to follow the "way of the universe," or *dao*, described by Daoist teachers as "unfathomable, the ancestral progenitor of all things, everlasting. All pervading, dao lies hidden and cannot be named. It produces all things. He who acts in accordance with dao becomes one with dao."[7] Convinced that people could never dominate their environment, Daoists urged them to ally with it, becoming simple, without desire and striving, and content with what is. A Daoist text expressed disgust with everyday life: "To labor away one's whole lifetime but never see the result, and to be utterly worn out with toil but have no idea where it is leading, is this not lamentable?"[8] Daoists advised Chinese to conform to the great pattern of the natural world rather than, as was the emphasis of Confucians, to social expectations and governments. One of the main texts argued that the wise person prefers fishing on a remote stream to serving as emperor. To the Daoists, societies were obstacles and all governments corrupt and oppressive. Daoism was mystical and romantic, fostering an awareness of nature and its beauties. This attitude became pronounced in Chinese poetry and landscape painting, which often recorded towering mountains, roaring waterfalls, and placid lakes.

Diverse Traditions

Daoism later fragmented into several traditions. Popular Daoism became a religion of countless deities and magic. Some followers sought to find the elixir of immortality, often by experimenting with a wide variety of foods. By contrast, philosophical Daoism, which appealed to the better educated, suggested that the individual should turn inward and experience oneness with the universe. Daoist writers found it difficult to express their basic ideas in words, one claiming that "those who know do not speak; those who speak do not know."[9]

Some of the early Daoist writings contained stories such as this one, which is filled with mysticism, a sense of unity with nature, and a humbling relativism:

> One time, Chuang-tzu dreamed he was a butterfly, flitting around, enjoying what butterflies enjoy. The butterfly did not know that it was Chuang-tzu. Then Chuang-tzu started, and woke up, and he was Chuang-tzu again. And he began to wonder whether he was Chuang-tzu who had dreamed he was a butterfly dreaming that he was Chuang-tzu.[10]

Balancing Confucianism, Daoism tapped a different strand of Chinese experience, adding enjoyment, reflection, and a sense of freedom. Daoists advised Confucianists to flow with the heart rather than struggle with the intellect. The man in power was a Confucianist, but out of power he became a Daoist. The active bureaucrat of the morning became the dreamy poet or nature lover of the evening. Daoism complemented Confucianism by enabling the Chinese to balance the conflicting needs for social order and personal autonomy.

Legalism and the Chinese State

Legalism A Chinese philosophy that advocated harsh control of people by the state.

Among the dozens of other competing philosophies, **Legalism**, which advocated that the state maintain harsh control of people, also had an enduring influence. Borrowing ideas from the Confucian Xunzi, the Legalists emphasized that an authoritarian government must secure prosperity, order, and stability by controlling all economic resources and making people well disciplined through compulsory military duty and harsh laws. Taken to extremes, Legalism led to unrestrained state power. The ruler needed to be strong and to have no regard for the rights or will of the people. Legalists wrote that people can be controlled by means of punishments and rewards, commands and prohibitions, and they ridiculed Confucian humanism.

Although Legalism exercised a long-term influence on Chinese politics, the Chinese always balanced it with the more humane ideas of Confucius and Mengzi, who stressed moral persuasion rather than coercion. Hence, many Chinese did not follow one philosophy to the exclusion of others. Laws were sometimes severe, but local officials had flexibility in implementing them and took into account the social context.

SECTION SUMMARY

- Despite being marred by chronic civil warfare, China became the most populous society on earth, and its economy evolved rapidly.

- The belated development of iron technologies and other breakthroughs made China competitive with western Asia.

- Instability resulting from military conflict led intellectuals to question basic tenets of society and government, thus creating the era of the "hundred schools of thought."

- Three enduring Chinese philosophies from this period—Confucianism, Daoism, and Legalism—have influenced Chinese state and culture through two millennia.

- Chinese philosophies emphasized humanism rather than the supernatural or gods.

CHINESE IMPERIAL SYSTEMS AND THE WORLD

> What developments during the Han dynasty linked China to the rest of Eurasia?

Chinese society, more than Indian, Middle Eastern, or European societies, was characterized by cohesion and continuity, as well as by blending of diverse influences. For example, although China was often attacked and even occasionally conquered by Central Asians, the invaders maintained continuity with China's past by adopting Chinese culture, a process known as **Sinicization** (SIN-uh-sigh-ZAY-tion). But one major transition quickly changed the face of premodern China: the replacement of the multistate Zhou system by a centralized empire. Because of this development, China after 221 B.C.E. was different from the China before it and set the pattern for the centuries to follow. The new imperial China was forged by the harsh rulers of Qin (chin) and by the Han dynasty, which conquered a large empire, fostered foreign trade, and established enduring political patterns. During this time the Chinese family matured into its basic form, and the economy grew dramatically, affecting peasant life. Chinese examined their own history, looking for lessons from the past. The Han were also highly creative in technology and science, making advances in mathematics and health.

Sinicization The process by which Central Asian invaders maintained continuity with China's past by adopting Chinese culture.

The Qin Dynasty

Late Zhou political turmoil ended when the Qin dynasty (221–206 B.C.E.) conquered the other states and implemented repressive Legalist ideas, transforming the China of many states into an empire with a powerful authoritarian central government. Advised by Legalist thinkers, the state of Qin had gradually become the strongest state within the Zhou system, controlling the economy and establishing government monopolies over many trade goods. Like Sparta in Greece, the population was militarized, the men serving as citizen-warriors. Slowly Qin began conquering other Zhou states. The brutal prime minister, Li Si (lee SHE) (Li Ssu), a Legalist thinker and the chief deputy to the man who would eventually become the first emperor of all of China, argued that those who used the past to oppose the present, meaning the Confucians, had to be exterminated.

Qin Legalism

In 221 B.C.E. the Qin, after finally defeating and absorbing all the remaining Zhou states, established a new government that ruled most of the Chinese people. The first Qin ruler assumed the new and imposing title of Shi Huangdi (SHE hwang-dee) ("first emperor"). This extraordinary autocrat surrounded himself with mystery and pomp to enhance his prestige, but in so doing he also concealed himself from the consequences of his decrees. Shi Huangdi lived in carefully guarded privacy, moving secretly from one apartment to another in his vast palaces. To reveal his movements was a crime that was instantly punished with death. The new dynasty implemented dramatic policies. The Qin sent armies to incorporate much of southern China and, for a while, Vietnam into the empire. Many in the south were eventually assimilated into Chinese society. Mandating a total reordering of China along Legalist lines, the emperor constructed a monolithic and united state that sought to control all aspects of Chinese life. Given this unification, the name *Qin* is fittingly the origin of the Western name for China.

The First Emperor and His Empire

Qin Repression

Later Chinese historians viewed the Qin Empire as one of the most terrible periods in the country's long history. The common people hated the forced labor, strict laws, spies, general surveillance, and thought control that were paramount in the Qin police state. Intellectuals despised the Qin for launching attacks on non-Legalist thought, including Confucianism, as subversive doctrines. The Qin burned thousands of books and executed many scholars, often by burying them alive. In so doing they ended the intellectual creativity of the hundred schools.

Qin Achievements

Despite the repression, Shi Huangdi's policies led to many achievements, fostering public works projects, economic growth, and social change. The Qin standardized weights and measures, unified agricultural practices, and codified laws. To aid communication, they built roads, bridges, dams, and canals and ordered that all wheel axles be the same length so that wagons could use the ruts made by other wagons in the dusty roads. The Qin standardized the written language so that all literate Chinese anywhere in the empire could communicate easily. To foster economic growth, the Qin established state monopolies over essential commodities like salt, and ever since the Chinese have accepted a strong government role in economic matters. Taxes were high and involved forced labor on government projects. The harsh Qin laws also ended crime, as a later Chinese scholar conceded: "Nothing lost on the road was picked up and pocketed, the hills were free of bandits, men avoided quarrels at home."[11] Finally, Qin land reform undermined the power of the old aristocracy, a mighty blow to the Zhou social structure.

The Great Wall

The most famous public works project of the Qin era was the construction of an early and limited version of a Great Wall along China's northern borders as a barrier against the encroachment of Central Asian warriors. The Chinese traded with their Central Asian neighbors but also fought with and feared them. A few partial earthen walls had already been built in Zhou times, but the Qin consolidated these into a more formidable structure, later known as the Great Wall. As part of their tax obligation, vast numbers of laborers were drafted for building the Great Wall, one of the greatest architectural feats of the ancient world. Later dynasties periodically rebuilt and added to the wall. The present brick and stone wall that so astounds tourists derives mostly from reconstruction and expansion work six centuries ago, after which the wall stretched over 1,400 miles across north China. Properly manned, it could be an effective defense, but only the most affluent emperors could afford that expense. The wall was seldom successful in curbing invaders but was a symbolic affirmation of empire and territorial limits.

Qin Defeat

But the Qin dynasty itself was short-lived. Many hated Shi Huangdi, and his expansionist policies provoked conflict with neighboring peoples. His inner circle kept the first emperor's death in 210 B.C.E. secret for fear of general revolt. He was buried in a huge underground mausoleum together with seven thousand astonishingly realistic life-size terracotta horses and warriors brandishing real bronze weapons. When news finally spread of Shi Huangdi's death, peasant revolts broke out. In 206 B.C.E. the Qin forces were defeated by a rebel alliance. As the various rebel groups then vied for power, a former peasant led his forces to victory, establishing a new dynasty, the Han (HAHN).

The Great Wall This panorama from the region just north of Beijing shows a portion of the wall reconstructed in the fifteenth century C.E. The wall was an attempt to mark the northern boundary of China and keep out nomadic invaders.

Georg Gerster/Photo Researchers, Inc.

The Han Empire

The Han is the most respected Chinese dynasty because during these four centuries (206 B.C.E.– 220 C.E.) China became a major force in Eurasian trade, diplomacy, and imperialism. The Han built a huge empire stretching far into Central Asia (see Map 6.2), and trade across this area allowed greater contact with people to the west. Like the Qin, the Han built a strong state, but they also modified the Qin's harsh Legalist structure. The brilliance of Han rule and the expansion of Chinese society southward set the pattern for later dynasties and led the Chinese to call themselves the Sons of Han.

The middle Classical Era was the age of empires, when large segments of Eurasia and North Africa were dominated by large imperial structures like the Han. All the empires built on the ideas of the Axial Age sages, resolving the crises that had sparked their rise. But the classical empires eventually declined as their structures and finances weakened, the conquered populations revolted, and nomadic peoples invaded the imperial heartlands. The Han and Roman Empires reached their zenith around the same time and resembled each other in population, although Rome's empire was larger in territorial size. In 2 C.E. the Han Empire contained at least 60 million people, most of them in China proper, and the Roman Empire ruled some 55 million, most of them outside Italy.

Age of Empires

Map 6.2
The Han Empire

The Han Empire fluctuated in size but at its height controlled most of today's China, Korea, northern Vietnam, and a long corridor through Central Asia to Turkestan.

e **Interactive Map**

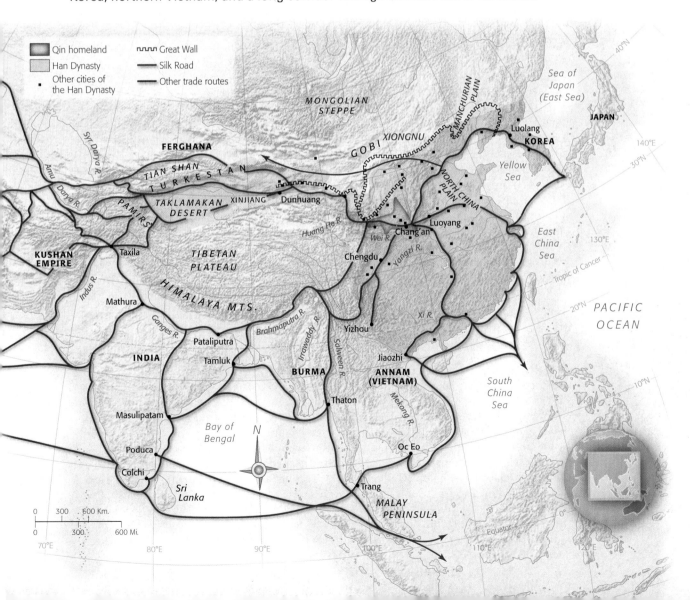

Emperor Wu Di

The pinnacle of Han imperial power came under the emperor mentioned in the chapter opening: Wu Di, who ruled for over half a century (141–87 B.C.E.). After he established firm control at home, Wu Di, a firm believer, like many Chinese emperors, that the best defense is a good offense, used bloody campaigns to counteract the encroaching pastoral nomads to the north and west. Some groups, such as the Huns, were deflected to the west, where they then disrupted the Roman Empire. The branch of Huns the Chinese called Xiongnu, a large tribal confederation, had constantly threatened China.

Han Expansion

Empire building and diplomacy soon linked China to western Eurasia as well as to Northeast and Southeast Asia. The Han sent ambassadors such as Zhang Qian to distant Central Asians seeking allies against common enemies. Wu Di also dispatched great armies, some numbering as many as 150,000 men, to conquer southwestern China, northern Korea, Vietnam, the Xinjiang (shinjee-yahng) region on China's western borders, Mongolia, and parts of Turkestan. Wu Di wrote a poem about a successful military campaign that brought many horses as tribute: "The heavenly horses are coming from the Far West. They crossed the Flowing Sands, for the barbarians are conquered."[12] The Chinese ruled Korea for four centuries and Vietnam for 1,000 years. Soon Chinese power extended even further, as states in today's Afghanistan acknowledged themselves vassals of China, sending tribute to Han emperors. But not all soldiers celebrated these achievements. One Han soldier wrote a protest song: "In the wilderness we dead lie unburied, fodder for crows. Tell the crows for us, 'We've always been brave men.'"[13] In later Han times a Chinese army of 90,000 men reached as far as the Caspian Sea in southeastern Russia, and a small force led by a General Gan Ying apparently traveled through Parthia to the Persian Gulf in 97 C.E., the first Chinese known to reach there. On his return General Gan reported on the customs and topography of these western states, as well as on the vast Roman Empire.

The Silk Road and Eurasian Trade

Silk Road A lively caravan route through Central Asia that linked China with India, the Middle East, and southern Europe.

The Han security presence in Central Asia fostered overland trade networks between China and western Asia. A lively caravan route, known as the **Silk Road** for its most valuable cargo, linked China with India, the Middle East, and southern Europe. Central Asian cities such as Kashgar (kahsh-gar) and Samarkand (SAM-mar-kahnd) grew up along the Silk Road to service the trade and the merchants. Indeed, the string of cities along the road was an important contact zone between East and West. Chinese silk, porcelain, and bamboo were carried west across the deserts and mountains to Baghdad and the eastern Mediterranean ports. Eventually some Chinese goods, especially silk, reached Rome. Since silk was lightweight and easily packed, large quantities were carried west by each caravan. Caravans then returned with horses and luxury goods such as Egyptian glass beads, Red Sea pearls, and Baltic amber.

The Silk Road trade networks greatly influenced the peoples who participated in the trade. To pay for Chinese luxuries, the Romans dispatched silver to China, causing a serious trade imbalance that contributed to the decline of the Western Roman Empire. Thus the Han Empire ultimately had a political and economic impact on distant Europe. Relations with Central and West Asians also brought new products to China, such as stringed musical instruments and new foods. Imperial power and foreign trade generated an economic boom and the rapid growth of commerce. The Silk Road network also fostered a Central Asian melting pot as peoples moved, met, and mixed.

Han Government and Politics

Han Politics

The Han government structure survived in its basic form until the early twentieth century. Whereas the Qin had sought to transform China in one brutal stroke, the Han were more pragmatic and cautious, relying on elements of Qin authoritarianism but using less repression. The Han softened Legalism with Confucian humanism, demonstrating that Confucian philosophy could maintain stability in the wake of momentous change. This Han pattern of mixing Legalism with Confucianism, power with ethics, characterized the Chinese political system for the next 2,000 years. During Han times the civil service developed to include some 130,000 officials, or 1 for every 400 to 500 people, a small number in relationship to the total population. The central government had a restricted role, mainly ensuring law, order, and border defense. Its bureaucrats collected taxes, administered the legal system, and officered military forces. Yet the many rebellions during Han times suggest that high taxes and demands that peasants provide military or labor service, such as rebuilding river dikes or repairing washed-out roads, generated occasional unrest.

The Han bureaucracy was staffed by educated men later called **mandarins**. Chinese proverbs claimed that the country might be won by the sword but could be ruled only by the writing brush—in other words, by an educated elite. The Han Chinese invented the civil service examination system to select officials based on merit. These exams tested knowledge of the Confucian writings, an indication that Confucianism was becoming the official state ideology, legitimizing the regime and promoting faithful service. The prestige of the scholars staffing the bureaucracy also moderated the tendency toward despotism, since they served as intermediaries between the emperor and the people. The development of the Han bureaucracy marked the rise of the **scholar-gentry**, a social class based on learning and officeholding but also on landowning, since many of the mandarins came from wealthy landowning families. Still, the social system was somewhat fluid. Scholars could not guarantee that their sons would be competent, and some poor men did rise by passing the civil service exams.

During the Han the concept of the Mandate of Heaven and of history in terms of the dynastic cycle became ingrained in Chinese thinking (see Chapter 4). Most premodern Chinese scholars believed that emperors ruled as deputies of the cosmic forces, but only so long as they possessed justice, benevolence, and sincerity. In each dynasty, able early rulers were succeeded by debauched weaklings, who indulged their pleasures, keeping harems of wives, concubines, and sometimes boys. When an emperor misruled, rebellion was justified. The rise and fall of dynasties also correlated with economic trends. A strong new dynasty initially generated security and prosperity, luring ambitious emperors into overextending imperial power and squandering human and financial resources, not only on expansion but also on court luxury. Such luxury included some extraordinary art produced for the Han elite; for example, the tomb of one princess contained a 2,000-piece jade suit that was sown with gold wire.

Wasteful expenditures created financial difficulties and military stagnation. Governments could no longer fund the large military commitment to protect the country, and some bureaucrats became corrupt. To meet the growing deficits the government raised taxes, forcing many poorer peasants to sell their land to large landlords, who could then evade taxes through their wealth and influence. This pattern was illustrated by Han emperor Wu Di. His glorious empire came at a huge cost, straining the imperial treasury. Some Han scholars opposed military expansion as a senseless waste of lives and tax revenues, and in 81 B.C.E. Wu Di's successor invited some of them to make their case before him. They did so, arguing that,

> at present, morality is discarded and reliance is placed on military force. Troops are raised for campaigns and garrisons are stationed for defense. It is the long-drawn-out campaigns and the ceaseless transportation of provisions that burden our people at home and cause our frontier soldiers to suffer from hunger and cold.[14]

But higher government officials responded that the spending was necessary to protect the country from the Xiongnu.

The Han dynasty finally collapsed in 220 C.E., not unlike the fall of Rome several centuries later. Critical factors for both empires included inadequate revenues, peasant revolts, powerful landed families contending for power, and raids by pastoralists from the borderlands. Across Eurasia the unusually warm conditions between 200 B.C.E. and 200 C.E. came to an end, and the colder weather affected agriculture. Both empires were also ravaged by epidemics in the second century C.E., which killed millions and thus reduced tax revenues.

Han Society and Economy

Han social life revolved around the family system, which endured for over 2,000 years because it offered many strengths. In part because of Confucian ideas, the family became the central focus of allegiance. Each person belonged to a large, continuing family that went backward and forward in time. The Chinese were expected to honor their ancestors while also considering the welfare of future generations. The family provided great psychological and economic security. The Chinese ideal was the joint family, that is, three or four generations living together under one roof. But only wealthy families could support the large houses and private courtyards that made the joint family way of life possible. The family was also an autocratic institution led by a patriarch, or senior male, who commanded respect. Chinese traced descent exclusively through the male line. Children were expected to respect both parents and to venerate their elders, and family interests always took precedence over individual ones. Laws held the family accountable for the actions of its members, discouraging disgraceful behavior by individuals.

mandarins Educated men who staffed the Chinese bureaucracy.

scholar-gentry A Chinese social class of learned officeholders and landowners that arose in the Han dynasty.

Han Ideology

Han Decline

Family System

Gender Relations and Women

This family system increasingly put most women at a disadvantage. Women were expected to be devoted to their parents, then to their husband and sons; care of the family and children was their central preoccupation. Parents arranged marriages with the goal of linking families, and a young wife joined her husband's family and was subject to the authority of his parents. Although many marriages seem to have been happy, the sorrows of unhappy women became a common literary theme. Many Chinese novels and plays concerned unrequited love or lovers forced to marry others. In one small part of central China, some women developed among themselves a special and secret form of writing, known as **nuxu** (nu-shu), to share their life experiences. Its origins remain obscure.

nuxu A secret form of writing developed by some Chinese women to share their experiences, possibly beginning in the Han period.

We know much about the experiences of Han women. Ban Zhao (ban chao), an accomplished historian, astronomer, and mathematician, wrote an influential book on women's place in society. Her advice to women stressed the Confucian obligations of selfless behavior, devotion, and obedience. Although gender roles became more rigid than they had been a few centuries earlier, many women engaged in some small-scale trade or worked long hours in the fields in addition to doing housework and caring for children. They also formed groups to spin or weave together. Women's experiences were never standardized, and the independence and influence they enjoyed depended on their age, social class, and local practices. There were always women like Ban Zhao who achieved wide acclaim. Some elite women received an education, and some were celebrated for their poetry writing. The mother of the Confucian thinker Mengzi was widely esteemed as a model of astuteness and assertiveness, yet she was reported by a male Han era biographer to have said that a "woman's duties are to cook the five grains, heat the wine, look after her parents-in-law, make clothes, and that is all!"[15] In contrast, some peasant women, who worked in the fields alongside their men, were strong-willed and exercised influence in their families and villages.

During the Han period and for over 2,000 years thereafter, China's economy was dominated by intensive farming, especially the growing of cereal crops by peasants. Landowning became the major goal of economic endeavor and investment, and peasants had to produce a food surplus for the 20 percent of the people living in towns and cities. Working fertile land, peasants achieved high yields, becoming some of the world's most efficient farmers through hard physical labor, especially in growing rice. Fields had to be flooded with irrigation water and drained, and the rice had to be sown, transplanted, and harvested, all by hand. Peasants did not lead easy lives. Most rarely went farther than the local market town to which they brought their produce. Family land and movable property were divided equally among sons. A Han scholar complained that poor peasants were left with too little land to live on and thus reduced to eating the food of pigs and dogs. As a result, many peasants were forced into tenancy to landlords. However, slavery, an important feature of Shang and Zhou society, became less common during the Han.

Population pressure and land shortage posed problems to peasants and also created political stability. By the second century B.C.E., practically all the good agricultural land in north and north-central China was being used. The labor-intensive nature of the economy was also apparent outside agriculture. Transportation meant porters with carrying poles, men pushing wheelbarrows, and men bearing the sedan chairs of the elite. Men also walked along narrow paths pulling boats upriver through the narrow gorges of the Yangzi River. While the famous sericulture (silk-making) industry produced silks and brocades of the finest weave, producing 150 pounds of silk required feeding and keeping clean the trays of 700,000 worms.

Han Farmer   Stone relief of Han farmer using an ox-drawn plow. These plows fostered the expansion of cultivated land during the Han.

From Patricia Buckley Ebrey, *The Cambridge Illustrated History of China*, 1996

Chinese Historiography

The Chinese developed one of the greatest traditions of studying and writing about history, known as historiography. The recording of history was probably inevitable among a people who looked to the past for guidance in the present. History writing in China goes back at least as far as the Zhou dynasty. Beginning with the Han, most dynasties employed a group of professional historians, such as the Han era's Sima Qian (Sl-mu tshen) (see Profile: Sima Qian, Chinese Historian). Later Chinese historians were influenced by Sima Qian's belief that past events, if not forgotten, also taught about the future. The Chinese historians tended to ignore social and economic history in favor of political history, concentrating on personalities, stories, wars, and the doings of emperors while neglecting long-term trends.

The greatest Chinese historians wrote monumental works and had much in common with each other. They aimed for objectivity, carefully separating their editorial comments from the narrative text. Like all historians, they still had to decide what to include and omit, focusing more on information about human beings and their foibles than on supernatural intervention. Historical literature also served as a manual for government, since it discussed the success and failure of past policies with the goal of achieving wisdom and promoting morality.

SECTION SUMMARY

- Through military conquest, the Qin dynasty unified the warring states into a new centralized, imperial China.

- Legalism, with its strict authoritarianism and negative view of human nature, was the dominant philosophy of the Qin rulers.

- Both the Han dynasty and the Roman Empire reached their peaks at about the same time, with roughly similar population sizes.

- The diplomatic and military expansion under the Han rulers set the stage for expanded trade, including the development of the Silk Road linking China to western Asia and Europe.

- The structure of government established during the Han, characterized by a blending of central and local authority and a softening of Legalism with Confucian humanism, endured until the early twentieth century.

- The family structure became the central social institution; its patriarchal hierarchy, codified in law, put the needs of the group above the needs of the individual.

- Despite subservience to all males in the family, some women of this period made many artistic and intellectual contributions.

- Peasant labor, as well as backbreaking labor in general, continued to be the foundation of the economy and characterized most people's existence.

CHINA AFTER THE HAN EMPIRE: CONTINUITY AND CHANGE

What outside influences helped shape China after the fall of the Han?

After the collapse of the Han in 221 C.E., China experienced three and a half centuries of disorder and political fragmentation known as the Three Kingdoms and Six Dynasties. China was divided into several states, once as many as sixteen, some ruled by Chinese and others by invaders. Just as the incursion of new peoples shaped Europe and India in the ashes of the Roman and Mauryan Empires, so this era in China was marked by frequent incursions by pastoral nomads. In the seventh century, the Chinese restored centralized government and reaffirmed the classical tradition.

Disunity, Invasion, and Cultural Mixing

The post-Han period was a troubled one as pastoral nomads crossed the Great Wall and attacked north China. They included the Huns, Mongols, and Turks, all of whom spoke Ural-Altaic languages. Although chiefly livestock herders, most used bronze and iron. Brutal winters and keen competition for good grazing land made them martial peoples scornful of but also attracted to the richer life available to the agricultural Chinese. Sometimes they succeeded in breaching the Great Wall thanks to their skills in horseback warfare, especially when they united in confederations under strong chiefs. These invasions produced what historians term the "Great Wall Complex": a natural Chinese paranoia about the security of borders and the perpetual fear of outsiders seeking to conquer. The Chinese believed that all non-Chinese were barbarians hoping to share in China's cultural glory and material wealth. This fear prompted them to rally to fight invaders. A much loved fifth-century ballad, perhaps based on an actual person, recalls the

Nomadic Invasions

SIMA QIAN, CHINESE HISTORIAN

Perhaps the greatest Han dynasty historian was Sima Qian (ca. 145–90 B.C.E.). His father, a high court official who also wrote about Chinese history, begged his son on his deathbed to continue compiling a history of China and its neighbors from earliest times. "I have failed to set forth a record of all the enlightened rulers and wise lords, the faithful ministers and gentlemen who were ready to die for duty," he conceded. His dutiful son replied, "I shall not dare to be remiss," and made the project his life's work. At the age of twenty, Sima Qian, who had grown up in the ancestral home in northwest China, began a grand tour of the empire. During the tour, he devoted time to examining historical sites, such as the tomb and family home of Confucius.

After receiving an official appointment in the Han government, the young scholar was sent on a mission to newly conquered territories in the southwest. Later he visited far northwestern outposts, including Mongolia, and also traveled extensively with the emperor Wu Di. Like his father, Sima Qian was appointed Grand Astrologer, a post dealing with time and the heavens, and helped to reform the calendar. But, being an honest man who spoke his mind, he alienated the emperor by defending a respected general whose brave attack against the Huns had failed for lack of support. As punishment Sima Qian was castrated.

Using his immense learning, combined with access to the vast imperial library containing the public records, Sima Qian produced his major book, *Records of the Grand Historian*. An invaluable source, *Records* covered some 2,000 years of history in 130 chapters, roughly 10,000 pages of text. Attempting to be universal, this monumental history ranges across a variety of topics, including astronomy, astrology, science, music, religious sacrifices, and economic patterns. It offers sketches of famous men from many walks of life, including political and military leaders, merchants, philosophers, scholars, comedians, assassins, rebels, bandits, and poets. *Records* also describes all foreign peoples and lands well known to the Chinese, from Korea to Afghanistan. Because it also covers rivers and canals, we know much of Wu Di's ambitious conservation and irrigation schemes. In addition, Sima Qian was the first historian to offer a comparative appraisal of China's various philosophical traditions, in which he showed particular sympathy to Daoism.

The book is strongest on the history of his times. Because Sima Qian's castration had embittered him toward Wu Di, some chapters are filled with covert satires on the emperor and warnings about his increasing power. His most original writing came in the chapters on people and contemporary affairs. Consider this criticism of those abusing their power:

We see that men whose deeds are immoral and who constantly violate the laws end their lives in luxury and wealth and their blessings pass down to their heirs without end. And there are others who expend anger on what is not upright and just, and yet, in numbers too great to be reckoned, they meet with misfortune and disaster. I find myself in much perplexity.

© British Library Board

Sima Qian   Painting of Sima Qian. This modern painting, by an unknown artist, imagines what Han China's great historian, Sima Qian, might have looked like.

Sima Qian's vital narrative and lively prose made his book popular reading among Chinese scholars for many centuries. Above all, the historian was concerned with both his literary and his moral legacy. As Sima Qian concluded, in words that still stir historians everywhere: "I have assembled and arranged the ancient traditions, and if they may be handed down and communicated surely I would have no regrets," and, "those who do not forget the past are masters of the future." Sima Qian set the standard to be followed by later historians in China.

THINKING ABOUT THE PROFILE

1. How did Sima Qian become a historian?

2. What does his life tell us about the pleasures and hazards of being a high official in Han China?

3. What made his historical writing so valuable to later readers?

Note: Quotations from Ben-Ami Scharfstein, *The Mind of China: The Culture, Customs, and Beliefs of Traditional China* (New York: Dell, 1974), 89–91; and Sima Qian, *Historical Records,* translated by Raymond Dawson (Oxford: Oxford University Press, 1994), 177.

deeds of a young woman warrior, Mulan, who disguises herself as a man in order to fight invading Central Asians. Only after she distinguishes herself in battle do her comrades discover her gender. The ballad makes a case for gender equality: "For the male hare has a lilting, lolloping gait, and the female hare has a wild and roving eye; But set them both scampering side by side, And who so wise could tell you 'This is he?'"[16] These invasions also prompted many Chinese to move south, solidifying the Chinese character of the Yangzi Basin.

The Chinese learned to endure both division and invasion by outsiders. In dealing with invaders, the Chinese developed a remarkable defense mechanism: assimilation. Most of the barbarian conquerors eventually ruled in a Chinese way, using the Confucian bureaucracy while also adapting many elements of Chinese culture. The Chinese believed that rule by foreigners could be tolerated as long as Chinese culture was respected and protected. Chinese culture, social institutions, and economic patterns thus proved able to survive the shock of conquest. But the Chinese also learned from the invaders. This merging of cultures provided a foundation for the later rejuvenation of a China that would be greater than the empires of Qin and Han. **Assimilation**

After the Han era, China became even more connected to the world outside, fostering a vital, cosmopolitan culture. One fifth-century emperor loved everything foreign: dress, art works, food, beds, chairs, harps, dances. Ideas and products traveled both directions along the Silk Road and by land and sea between China and Southeast Asia. Chinese objects from this era often showed Indian, Persian, Mesopotamian, Greek, or Roman influences. The graves of wealthy Chinese frequently contained Roman glass, Persian silver vessels, images of Greek gods, and cups made from Indonesian shells. China's openness to ideas from outside also led many Chinese to embrace an Indian religion, Buddhism. **China and the World**

Buddhism and China's Eclectic Religious Tradition

During the later Classical Era, universal religions—faiths that appealed to people from many cultures—became much more prominent in Eurasia and North Africa, marking another great transition. The decline and collapse of the great Afro-Eurasian empires, from China to Rome, produced political instability and social strife challenging established ways. In response, universal religions diffused along the trade networks: Christianity from western Asia to Europe, where it soon became the dominant religion; Hinduism throughout India and into Southeast Asia; and Mahayana (mah-HAH-YAH-nah) Buddhism into Central and East Asia. These universal religions incorporated existing local beliefs, creating hybrid artistic forms and value systems. The most pronounced synthesis took place in East Asia as Buddhism encountered earlier belief systems such as Confucianism. **Spread of Universal Religions**

Buddha Statue at Yungang This huge statue of the Buddha, created around 290 C.E., is 45 feet tall. It is one of thousands found along cliffs in western China and elsewhere along the Silk Road.

Werner Forman/Art Resource, NY

The Buddhist Age

The arrival of Buddhism was a momentous transition for East Asia, fostering the Buddhist Age in both Chinese and, more generally, Asian history between the fourth through the ninth centuries C.E. Buddhism in some form became dominant in much of East, Central, and Southeast Asia as well as in portions of South Asia (see Chapter 5). The basic Buddhist beliefs about overcoming suffering through good deeds and thoughts derived from the sixth-century B.C.E. teachings of the Indian sage known as the Buddha ("the Enlightened One"), but the religion later split into several rival schools. One of these, Mahayana Buddhism, was carried by merchants and missionaries along the Silk Road into Central Asia. From there it spread into western China during later Han times, serving to tie China to distant India. Later the religion spread from China to Korea, Vietnam, and Japan. Buddhism, a religion of compassion and gentleness, offered meaning and hope to people experiencing hardship, warfare, and instability. It also offered the Chinese a spiritual outlook largely missing in Confucianism, which appealed to reason and practical ethics but said little about gods or life after death, and it offered more than Daoist mysticism, which could not explain the fate of the individual in the cosmic order. Mahayana Buddhism thus promised salvation in an afterlife. But Buddhism also adapted to Chinese traditions. For example, the Buddhist notion of reincarnation clashed with Chinese beliefs in ancestor worship, so most Chinese never accepted this idea.

Buddhism in China

Because it had traveled from India through Central Asia, Chinese Buddhism acquired a cosmopolitan outlook. Buddhism's peaceful spread was accompanied by Indian artistic, literary, and cultural influences, such as the huge sculptures of the Buddha found along the Silk Road and in northwestern China. Many Buddhist missionaries entered China, and several hundred Chinese pilgrims went to India, either overland or along the sea route through Southeast Asia. For example, the monk Faxian (fah-shee-en) spent fifteen years in India and also visited Buddhist centers in Southeast Asia in the fifth century C.E. On their return to China the pilgrims spread knowledge of the societies they encountered.

The Three Ways

As a result of this mixing, by the middle of the first millennium C.E. an eclectic Chinese religious tradition embraced three very different viewpoints—Buddhism, Confucianism, and Daoism—known as "the three ways." The three schools interacted with each other, creating a rich synthesis, and many Chinese could no longer clearly differentiate between them. An old but still popular Chinese story has Confucius, Laozi, and Buddha walking and talking together, debating the merits of their respective positions; as they cross a bridge, they are obscured in mist. When spotted again only one somewhat larger figure can be seen in the distance. Yet some distinctions were maintained. Only Buddhism developed a fully organized church, with monks and nuns. Confucianism, a philosophy of social relations rather than a true religion, had no priests. Many Chinese, believing that people's needs could not be satisfied by any one set of doctrines and hence not identifying themselves exclusively with any of the three belief systems, saw the three traditions as different roads to the same destination, personal happiness.

Secular Worldviews and Popular Religion

Gradually a gap between the relatively secular worldview of the educated elite and the popular religion of the common people widened. The intellectuals favored Confucian humanism and Daoist naturalism, with moral perfection of humankind as the ultimate goal. Since Confucius and his followers had revealed a doctrine centered on humanity rather than on gods, many intellectuals viewed popular religion, with its gods, spirits, ghosts, and magic, as superstition. One Han scholar wrote that "the number of persons who have died since the world began must run into thousands of millions. If everyone of them has become a spirit, there must be at least one to every yard as we walk along the road."[17] Meanwhile, although more Chinese may have been indifferent to religion than was common elsewhere, many peasants, artisans, and merchants believed in thousands of gods and goddesses of Buddhist, Daoist, or animist origin, using shamans to communicate with the spirit realm. They also accepted notions of heaven and hell introduced by Mahayana Buddhism, and of **geomancy** (JEE-u-MAN-see), known in Chinese as *feng shui* (fung shway) ("wind and water"), a popular Daoist-influenced system for determining the auspicious settings of buildings and graves. Geomancy is still widely employed today in East Asia, and some architects even use it to assess the auspiciousness of modern houses and skyscrapers in North American and European cities.

geomancy Known in Chinese as *feng shui* ("wind and water"), a system for determining the auspicious settings of human dwellings and graves.

Science and Technology in the Classical Era

During this era China developed one of the world's oldest scientific and technological traditions, establishing along with the Indians, Mesopotamians, Egyptians, and Greeks the foundation for modern science. The Zhou and Han are credited with many important breakthroughs, including porcelain ("china"), rag paper, the water-powered mill, the shoulder harness for horses, the foot stirrup (possibly adapted from Central Asian models), the magnetic compass, the seismograph, the wheelbarrow, the stern-post rudder for boats, the spinning wheel, and linen. Most of these

Han Technology

inventions did not reach western Eurasia over the trade routes until a few centuries—in some cases a millennium—later. Paper may have been the most significant innovation. Before paper Chinese scribes wrote with a pointed stylus on strips of wood, bamboo, or woven cloth. Eventually an ingenious first-century C.E. artisan tried beating the cloth into fiber and forming thin sheets. In seeking ways to mass-produce Buddhist texts and images for believers and Confucian classics for students preparing for the examinations, Han craftsmen made ink rubbings on paper from stone carvings, often of entire Buddhist books. Elementary block printing was in limited use in China by the sixth century C.E. By the ninth century woodblock printing had become a major activity in East Asia.

The Han also made great strides in mathematics and science. Besides making the most accurate calculation of *pi* at the time, the Chinese were many centuries ahead of the rest of the world in the use of fractions, a simple decimal system, the concept of negative numbers, and in certain aspects of algebra and geometry. Around 190 C.E. they invented the *abacus,* a primitive computer still used widely in Asia today that proved an unparalleled tool for calculations. The abacus was constructed by fastening balls on wires attached to a board carved with divisions. Han astronomers compiled catalogues of stars, speculated on sunspots, and explained the causes of lunar eclipses. Astronomy was essential for an agricultural society, which needed accurate calendars to regulate planting and harvesting.

Han Mathematics and Science

Chinese science, especially medicine, owed much to the cosmological thinking exemplified in yin-yang dualism and also to Daoism, which inspired an interest in nature. To the Daoists the body was a microcosm of the universe. An enduring medical discovery, *acupuncture,* developed from the belief that good health was the result of proper yin-yang balance in the body. In this procedure, thin needles are inserted at predetermined points to alleviate pain or correct some condition. Chinese experts learned the parts of the body and how to read a pulse. Acupuncture is still practiced today and has spread around the world. The Chinese also stressed good hygiene and preventive medicine, including a well-balanced diet and regular exercise. In their quest for the elixir of immortality, Daoist alchemists discovered many edible foods, herbs, and potions that improved health, and they developed the greatest list of pharmaceuticals in the premodern world. By the Han period doctors could diagnose gout and cirrhosis of the liver. Many ancient Chinese folk remedies remain popular to this day in China.

Chinese Medicine

The Chinese also continued to develop innovative technologies. Although never a great seafaring people like the Austronesians and Greeks, the Chinese became some of the world leaders in shipbuilding, some taking up maritime trade. Even in Han times, Chinese ships carried trade goods back and forth to Korea, Japan, and Southeast Asia. By at least the fifth century C.E. the Chinese had constructed large oceangoing vessels with stern-post rudders for maneuvering, which permitted longer and farther journeys. Chinese ships and navigational skills were probably adequate to even cross the vast Pacific, although there is no compelling evidence that any did so.

Maritime Technologies

The Sui Reunification of China

To an observer in the fourth century it might have seemed that the Roman Empire, although visibly weakening, could endure, while the Chinese empire was overrun by "barbarian" invaders, broken apart, and turning to foreign, otherworldly religions. Yet China was eventually reunified under a powerful, centralized government, whereas Rome, facing the same kinds of challenges, fragmented and collapsed. Several factors contributed to China's reassembly. First, reestablishment of a centralized state was made easier by the large population of the Chinese core area, which was 50 million by 400 C.E., probably double the population of Europe. In addition, the Chinese shared more cultural unity than the varied peoples of western Asia, India, and Europe. The nomadic invaders, small in numbers, may have been easily absorbed in China. Culture and politics probably also played a role. Confucian ethical humanism, the merit-based civil service exams, and the Chinese writing encouraged cultural unity. In contrast, India contained many very different spoken languages but also diverse writing systems, and in Europe, the speakers of Romance languages based on phonetic alphabets splintered into many competing countries, never to be reunited.

Chinese Unity

The ruthless Sui (sway) dynasty (581–618 C.E.) played the same role in history as the Qin, reuniting China after several centuries of turmoil and division. The Sui emperors were tyrants but also patrons of arts and letters, and they created the largest library at that time in the world. Like the Qin, the Sui were builders, mobilizing 6 million forced workers to construct the Grand Canal linking the Yangzi and Yellow Rivers. At 1,200 miles long, the longest human-made channel ever constructed, the canal ensured the prosperity of later dynasties, since each year huge quantities

Sui Government and Society

Sui Decline

of grain could be shipped north. Tree-shaded parks and inns lined the route. However, like earlier dynasties, the Sui overreached and collapsed. Exhausting campaigns of conquest temporarily extended imperial frontiers into Korea and Central Asia, but the Sui drove the Chinese people too hard, resulting in overwork and food shortages. Soon rebellions broke out. The victor in the ensuing struggles established the Tang (tahng) dynasty (618–907 C.E.), which launched China into its great golden age, extending over many centuries, and linked it more closely to Korea and Japan, whose societies we turn to now.

SECTION SUMMARY

- Spurred by invasions of nomadic peoples from the north, the population shifted south, but the invaders were assimilated by existing Chinese government structures.

- Buddhism took root in China during this tumultuous period, spreading along the trade routes from India and melding with existing Confucian thought.

- The Chinese attitude toward religion was characterized by an easy interchange of beliefs, in which individuals drew from a variety of religious or philosophical perspectives depending on their need.

- Developments in science and medicine were influenced by Daoism, which promoted the idea of a yin-yang balance in the natural world.

- Fractured by invasions, Chinese reunification was nevertheless made easier by the population's shared written language, culture, and history.

- Like the Qin before them, the Sui rulers also reunited China using harsh measures but made lasting contributions, such as the Grand Canal.

KOREA, JAPAN, AND EAST ASIAN NETWORKS

How did the Koreans and Japanese assimilate Chinese influences into their own distinctive societies?

Large, densely populated China dominated East Asia for much of history. Consequently, eastern Asia did not develop the political diversity, with many rival states, that prevailed in India, western Asia, or Europe after classical times. Korea and Japan adopted intensive farming and thus became receptive to Chinese cultural influence. Although more developed than Japan for many centuries, Korea was often in the shadow of China. Separated by water, Japan was able to remain more independent. Yet both Korea and Japan creatively forged distinctive societies.

Korea and China

As a close neighbor, Korea experienced regular and extensive interaction with China, which brought many advantages but also political pressures. During the first millennium B.C.E. Chinese cultural and technological influences began permeating the Korean peninsula. Koreans adopted iron technology from the Chinese, including advanced weapons, which later fostered the rise of agriculture-based Korean states. However, these were soon overwhelmed by Chinese influence. In 108 B.C.E. Wu Di's Han armies, reportedly 60,000 troops strong, conquered northern Korea against fierce resistance. China ruled the territory as a colony for the next four centuries, providing models to the Koreans in government structure, architecture, and city planning (see Chronology: Classical Japan and Korea).

The end of Chinese colonization in 313 C.E. allowed Korean society to flower, and three native kingdoms emerged that dominated Korea between the fourth and seventh centuries, occasionally warring against each other. However, Chinese cultural influences, including the writing system and Confucianism, also spread more widely. Mahayana Buddhism, introduced from China in 372 C.E., strongly influenced Korean painting, sculpture, and architecture. But the Koreans never became carbon copies of the Chinese. For example, unlike in China, where family status rose or fell with dynastic change and civil service examination results, an aristocracy of inherited position thrived for most of Korean history. And although most Koreans adopted Buddhism, the animism that had long flourished never disappeared.

CHRONOLOGY
Classical Japan and Korea

300 B.C.E.–552 C.E. Yayoi culture in Japan

18 B.C.E. Rise of Koguryo in northern Korea

108 B.C.E.–313 C.E. Han Chinese colonization of Korea

250 C.E. Beginning of Yayoi tomb culture

350–668 C.E. Koguryo Empire

676–935 C.E. United Silla state

538 C.E. Introduction of Buddhism to Japan

552–710 C.E. Yamato state in Japan

604 C.E. First Japanese constitution

Eventually one Korean kingdom, Koguryo (ko-GUR-yo), became the most influential (see Map 6.3). In the fifth century, with China divided, Koguryo expanded far to the north, annexing much of Manchuria and southeastern Siberia and becoming one of the largest states in Eurasia between 350 and 668 C.E. At the same time, several smaller Korean states controlled the southern part of the peninsula. Koguryo's army repulsed seven major Chinese invasions by the Sui and Tang dynasties between 598 and 655 C.E., when a resurgent China was the most powerful state in eastern Eurasia. In 612 C.E. they routed an invading Sui army that, according to legend, numbered at least 1 million soldiers but was probably closer to a still formidable 300,000. The huge cost of the Chinese campaigns in Korea contributed to the collapse of the Sui dynasty. Finally, in 668 C.E., Chinese armies, allied with the southern Korean state of Silla (SILL-ah or SHILL-ah), overran Koguryo. Soon Silla drove out the Chinese armies and reunified much of Korea under the Silla state in 676.

Yayoi and Yamato Japan

Like Korea across the straits, Japan experienced dramatic change in this era. The pottery-making Jomon culture (see Chapter 4) persisted until around 300 B.C.E., when a new culture, Yayoi (ya-YOI), emerged, based on exceptionally productive wet rice farming and establishment of close links with Korea. During the Yayoi era (300 B.C.E.–552 C.E.), Korea remained a source of learning and population for Japan, with a continuous flow of Korean immigrants, including skilled craftsmen, scribes, and artists, as well as both Korean and

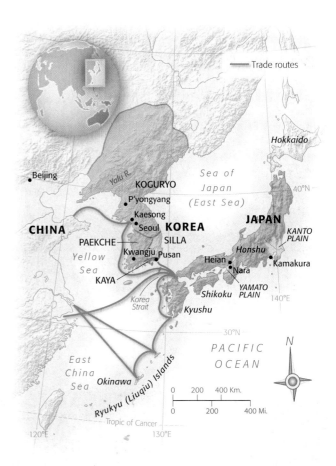

Map 6.3
Korea and Japan in the Fifth Century C.E. During the Classical Era Korea was often divided into several states. Koguryo in the north was the largest state, ruling part of Siberia. By the sixth century the Yamato state governed much of the main Japanese island, Honshu.

 **Interactive Map**

Chinese ideas and technology from the mainland into the islands. Korean migrants brought horses, and the armored warrior on horseback later became a vivid feature of Japanese life. Immigration from Korea continued until the ninth century. By 600 C.E. the Japanese people as we know them today had come together from the genetic and cultural mixing over many centuries of Korean immigrants with earlier settlers and the indigenous Ainu people.

The Yayoi also traded sporadically with China. A Chinese visitor in 297 C.E. left us much information about Yayoi society, reporting the preoccupation with taboos, class distinctions, and especially ritual cleanliness. Like modern Japanese, the Yayoi were fond of dancing, singing, drinking rice wine, and eating raw vegetables; experienced no theft and little other crime; and revered nature. The Yayoi used the potter's wheel, were expert weavers, and had mastered both bronze and iron technology, later fashioning iron into highly effective swords and armor. The Yayoi formed no centralized governments but were organized into many clans, each ruled by a hereditary priest-chieftain. During the second century C.E., when Japan was engulfed in conflict, a woman, Pimiko (pih-MEE-ko), became a powerful queen-priestess and brought peace by imposing strict laws. However, most clan elites were men who governed farmers, artisans, and a few slaves and who mobilized people to build hundreds of large earthen tombs, often surrounded by moats, all over south-central Honshu Island. The tombs housed the remains of prominent leaders, who were buried with jewels, swords, and clay figurines.

Japan entered the light of written history in the sixth century C.E. with the Yamato (YA-ma-toe) (552–710 C.E.), the first state ruling a majority of the Japanese people. The Yamato was centered in south-central Honshu, where the cities of Kyoto and Osaka now stand. Yamato was not a centralized state like Han China or Koguryo but rather a national government ruling over smaller groups based on territorial clans, each headed by a hereditary chief. Eventually Yamato extended its influence into southern Japan while expanding the northern frontier deep into Ainu territory.

Yamato was headed by emperors and occasionally empresses—all ancestors of the same imperial family that rules Japan today, fifteen centuries later. Political continuity under the same royal family gave the Japanese a strong sense of identity and cultural unity. The Japanese viewed their earlier history in mythological terms, believing the imperial family descended from the Sun Goddess. This beautiful spirit, *Amaterasu* (AH-mah-teh-RAH-soo), and her male consort experienced violent mood swings and periodic conflict that may have been modeled on the frequent storms,

Rise of Yamato

Yamato Government

Prince Shotoku This painting from the eighth century C.E. shows Prince Shotoku, one of the major Yamato leaders, and his sons in the Japanese clothing style of the times. Prince Shotoku launched a period of intensive borrowing from China.

Imperial Household Agency

volcanic eruptions, and earthquakes that rock the islands. Despite her tantrums, a female creator deity may also have reflected a high status for women in early Japan. Before the eighth century C.E. around half of the imperial sovereigns were women. However, patriarchy became the common pattern by 1000 C.E.

Japanese Isolation and Cultural Unity

The Japanese forged a particularly distinctive society through a mixing of the local and the foreign. The islands were over a hundred miles from the Eurasian mainland. Since communication with other societies was sporadic, mainly restricted to Korea and China, the Japanese had to become very creative. At the same time, the space and resources available to the steadily growing population on the mountainous islands were restricted, resulting in a tightly woven society with intense social pressures. Since personal privacy became rare in this crowded land, people learned how to erect psychological walls that allowed them to "tune out" the surrounding noise and activity.

Isolation also made the Japanese expert at borrowing selectively from the outside during periods of intensive contact. Japanese history featured an interplay between the indigenous (native) and the foreign, borrowing from Korea, China, and, much later, the West. While conscious of borrowing, the Japanese have always selected foreign ideas that suit their own needs, seldom leaving a borrowed idea in its original form. For example, they adopted the Chinese idea of an exalted emperor but not the concept of the Mandate of Heaven, which allowed for incompetent or tyrannical dynasties to be overthrown. The Japanese also created much of their own culture. Leading technological innovators for millennia, they developed the best tempered steel of the classical world. They also created artistic forms and styles of universal appeal, such as carefully planned gardens

Cultural Borrowing

and *bonsai* (bon-sigh) (miniature) trees, as well as ingenious solutions to chronic problems such as urban crowding and limited resources. Thus the Japanese house itself, containing thick straw floor mats, sliding paper panels rather than interior walls, a hot tub for communal bathing, and charcoal-burning braziers, conserved building materials and minimized fuel needs for heating and cooking.

Japanese Encounters with China

Japan was greatly influenced by the Chinese several times in history. The importation of Chinese ideas began on a large scale in the middle of the sixth century C.E. Mahayana Buddhism was introduced around 538 and became a major medium for cultural change, bringing, for example, new forms of art. Chinese teachers, artisans, and Buddhist monks crossed over to Japan, and Japanese journeyed to Korea and China, coming back as converts to Buddhism. Just as the Chinese maintained three distinct traditions of thought, in Japan Buddhism coexisted with the ancient animistic cult later known as **Shinto** (SHIN-toe) ("way of the gods"), which emphasized closeness to nature and enjoyed a rich mythology that included many deities.

A growing realization among Japanese leaders that China and Korea were much stronger than Japan in the political, economic, and cultural spheres led the Japanese to launch an era of deliberate borrowing from China to reshape Japanese society. The Yamato expanded relations with Sui China and began to reorganize government structures, integrating Chinese writing and Confucian notions of social organization and morality. The adoption of Chinese ideas accelerated under the auspices of Prince Shotoku (show-TOW-koo) (573–621 C.E.), an ardent Buddhist who sponsored the building of temples and also promoted Confucian values. His ideas also foreshadowed later Japanese values emphasizing group interests: "Harmony is to be cherished, and opposition for opposition's sake must be avoided as a matter of principle,"[18] he wrote into the first Japanese constitution, issued in 604. Shotoku became one of the most revered figures in Japanese history. His support for Buddhism has led some historians to compare Shotoku to the Indian king Ashoka, who also embraced Buddhism, and the Roman emperor Constantine, who promoted Christianity. Over the next two and a half centuries many official embassies were exchanged between China and Japan, further promoting the exchange of ideas.

Shinto ("way of the gods") The ancient animistic Japanese cult that emphasized closeness to nature and enjoyed a rich mythology that included many deities.

SECTION SUMMARY

- Like most of China, Korea and Japan were agricultural societies, a similarity that facilitated the easy transmission of Chinese culture.

- Korea's proximity to China led to the adoption of Chinese writing and other technologies in Korea.

- Both Buddhism and Confucianism from China permeated Korean culture and were blended with the native belief system of animism, keeping Korean culture distinctive.

- The flow of ideas and people from Korea and China to Japan introduced Buddhism, writing, and other influences into Japan, but the Japanese culture, arts, and religion remained distinctive.

- From the beginning, Japan's small land area prompted the Japanese to deal creatively with lack of space and the social problems of overcrowding.

- The Yamato were Japan's first centralized state and began actively importing cultural and political ideas from China in the sixth century.

CHAPTER SUMMARY

The classical societies that flowered in eastern Asia were distinctive in many ways. China was large, densely populated, and an innovator in government, culture, religion, science, and technology. During the warfare and political instability of the late Zhou period, Confucius promoted ethical values and suggested how people could live in harmony with each other through a well-defined and hierarchical social structure. In contrast, the Daoists advocated a life in accordance with the rhythms of the natural world. The Legalists argued that a powerful government must harshly regulate society to preserve order. These classical ideas persisted in Chinese thought into modern times. The Legalist leaders of the Qin dynasty used brutal policies to transform China into a centralized imperial state. Following the short-lived Qin, the great Han dynasty established a large Asian empire and traded with western Asia and Europe across the

Silk Road, becoming a major force in eastern Eurasia. The social structure became more patriarchal, and women were expected to be dutiful to their men.

After the Han collapsed, Central Asians frequently invaded and divided China politically. In this turbulent period, Mahayana Buddhism became popular in China, where it mixed with Confucianism, Daoism, and animism. Eventually the Sui dynasty reunified China, an achievement that contrasted with the Roman Empire in the West, which disintegrated into various fragments. China also became a model for neighboring societies. First the Koreans and then the Japanese adopted many Chinese ideas, including some technologies, writing, Confucianism, and Buddhism. But they also creatively blended them with their own unique traditions, resulting in a distinctive mix of the imported with the local.

KEY TERMS

Confucianism	Legalism	scholar-gentry
The Analects	Sinicization	nuxu
filial piety	Silk Road	geomancy
Daoism	mandarins	Shinto

EBOOK AND WEBSITE RESOURCES

e   INTERACTIVE MAPS
Map 6.1 China in the Sixth Century B.C.E.
Map 6.2 The Han Empire
Map 6.3 Korea and Japan in the Fifth Century C.E.

LINKS

History of China (http://www.chaos.umd.edu/history). Collection of essays and timelines on Chinese history maintained by the University of Maryland.

Internet East Asian History Sourcebook (http://www.fordham.edu/halsall/eastasia/eastasiasbook.html). An invaluable collection of sources and links on China, Japan, and Korea from ancient to modern times.

Internet Guide for China Studies (http://www.sino.uni-heidelberg.de/igcs/). Good collection of links on premodern and modern China, maintained at Heidelberg University.

Monks and Merchants (http://www.asiasociety.org/arts/monksandmerchants/index.html). Interesting essays, timelines, maps, and images for an Asia Society exhibition on the Silk Road as a zone of communication.

A Visual Sourcebook of Chinese Civilization (http://depts.washington.edu/chinaciv/). A wonderful collection of essays, illustrations, and other useful material on Chinese history.

Plus flashcards, practice quizzes, and more. Go to: www.cengage.com/history/lockard/globalsocnet2e

SUGGESTED READING

Adshead, S. A. M. *China in World History*, 3rd ed. New York: St. Martin's, 2000. A good introduction to Han China's interaction with Central Asia, western Asia, and Europe.

Clements, Jonathan. *Confucius: A Biography.* New York: Sutton, 2005. A brief study written for a popular audience.

Cotterell, Arthur. *The First Emperor of China.* New York: Penguin, 1981. A readable and fascinating study of the first emperor and his times.

Di Cosmo, Nicole. *Ancient China and Its Enemies: The Rise of Nomadic Power in East Asian History.* Cambridge: Cambridge University Press, 2002. An important study of China and the northern peoples from the Zhou through the Han dynasties.

Ebrey, Patricia Buckley. *The Cambridge Illustrated History of China.* New York: Cambridge University Press, 1996. A very readable survey with much on the classical period.

Ebrey, Patricia Buckley, et al. *Pre-Modern East Asia: to 1800: A Cultural, Social, and Political History,* 2nd. ed. Boston: Houghton Mifflin, 2009. An excellent survey of China, Japan, and Korea.

Hane, Mikiso. *Premodern Japan,* 2nd ed. Boulder, CO: Westview, 1991. A readable survey.

Hinsch, Bret. *Women in Early Imperial China.* Lanham, MD: Rowman and Littlefield, 2002. A stimulating study of the factors shaping women's experiences in Qin and Han China.

Holcombe, Charles. *The Genesis of East Asia, 221 B.C.–A.D. 907.* Honolulu: University of Hawai'i Press, 2001. A provocative examination of this era.

Hudson, Mark J. *Ruins of Identity: Ethnogenesis in the Japanese Islands.* Honolulu: University of Hawai'i Press, 1999. Scholarly study of forming Japanese identity and people.

Imamura, Kenji. *Prehistoric Japan: New Perspectives on Insular Japan*. Honolulu: University of Hawai'i Press, 1996. A scholarly study of the Yayoi and Yamato periods.

Lewis, Mark E. *The Early Chinese Empires: Qin and Han*. Cambridge: Belknap Press, 2007. Good study of these two dynasties.

Loewe, Michael. *Everyday Life in Early Imperial China: During the Han Period 202 B.C.–A.D. 220*. Indianapolis: Hackett, 2005. Reprint of a classic work on Han life and society.

Mote, Frederick W. *Intellectual Foundations of China*, 2nd ed. New York: Knopf, 1989. A brief, readable introduction to classical Chinese philosophy.

Seth, Michael J. *A Concise History of Korea from the Neolithic Period through the Nineteenth Century*. Latham, MD.: Rowman and Littlefield, 2006. One of the best general surveys of premodern Korea.

Shaughnessy, Edward L., ed. *China: Empire and Civilization*. New York: Oxford University Press, 2005. Contains many short essays on premodern Chinese society and culture.

Sima Qian. *Historical Records,* translated by Raymond Dawson. New York: Oxford University Press, 1994. A brief introduction to the writings of the Han era historian.

Wright, Arthur. *The Sui Dynasty: The Unification of China, A.D. 581–617*. New York: Alfred A. Knopf, 1978. A valuable study of government and society.

Western Asia, the Eastern Mediterranean, and Regional Systems, 600–200 B.C.E.

Ancient Art & Architecture Collection

Persepolis
During the height of their empire, Persian kings built a lavish capital at Persepolis, in today's Iran. This photo shows the audience hall, the part of the grand palace where the kings greeted their ministers and foreign diplomats.

> W onders are many on earth, and the greatest of these, is man, who rides the ocean. He is master of the ageless earth. The use of language, the wind-swift motion of brain he learned; found out the laws of living together in cities. There is nothing beyond his power.
>
> —CHORUS IN *ANTIGONE*, BY THE FIFTH-CENTURY GREEK PLAYWRIGHT SOPHOCLES (SAHF-uh-kleez)[1]

Thales (THAY-leez) and Anaximander (uh-NAK-suh-MAN-der), pioneering Greek philosophers and scientists, had the great fortune to grow up in prosperous Miletus (my-LEET-uhs), a commercial city on the southwestern coast of Anatolia (modern Turkey). Miletus had long served as a crossroads for the entire region, mingling Greek and foreign cultures. Young men like Thales and Anaximander haunted the bustling docks and seaside bars, listening to the reports of sailors returning from distant shores and of travelers from foreign lands. Milesian merchants sent ships to the far corners of the Mediterranean carrying the treasured wool developed by Miletus sheep breeders and the fine furniture produced by its cabinetmakers. Along the shores of the Black Sea, Milesian settlements supplied fish and wheat that enriched the city's traders. Some sailors brought scraps of learning from older societies such as Egypt and Mesopotamia. This intermingling led to new thinking about geography and cartography. Thales worked out a geometrical system to calculate the position of a ship at sea. Thales' student, Anaximander, made the first map of the Mediterranean world and the first Greek chart of the heavens. Later Hecataeus (HEK-a-TAU-us) of Miletus published a map of the world known to the Greeks, from India to Spain. Miletus matured into a great intellectual center and a meeting place for the Greek and Persian worlds.

The Greeks developed not only a penchant for maritime trade and an understanding of regional geography but also a unique society on the rocky shores of the Aegean Sea. In cities such as Miletus and Athens, they introduced many ideas and institutions that endured through the centuries. The view of humanity's greatness offered by Sophocles in the opening quotation reflects an obsession with individuality and freedom that made the Greeks role models for modern democracies. But the Greek achievements are only part of the story. Connected to a wider world through cities like Miletus, the Greeks flourished by participating in regional trade, colonizing other territories, and borrowing ideas from neighboring societies. Another creative society and even greater regional power, the Persian Empire, dominated the eastern Mediterranean and western Asia and also introduced many innovations that affected the lives of many peoples. Ultimately, the rival Greek and Persian societies were temporarily brought together in a political union that mixed Greek and Persian culture.

FOCUS QUESTIONS

1. How did the Persians acquire and maintain their empire?
2. What were some features of Greek government, philosophy, and science?
3. In what ways did Persians and Greeks encounter and influence each other?
4. What impact did Alexander the Great and his conquests have on world history?

Visit the website and eBook for additional study materials and interactive tools:
www.cengage.com/history/lockard/globalsocnet2e

THE PERSIANS AND THEIR EMPIRE

How did the Persians acquire and maintain their empire?

Although its period of greatest political influence lasted only two centuries, the Persian Empire played an important role in world history. The Persians established a larger, more multicultural empire than any people before them, encompassing Anatolian Greeks, Phoenicians, Hebrews, Egyptians, Mesopotamians, and Indians. Domination of the east-west trade routes made the empire the meeting ground of the early classical world. The Persians' wars with Greece and their empire building in western Asia paved the way for the later rule of the Greek Alexander the Great and his successors.

Building the Persian Empire

The Persian homeland was located on a plateau just north of the Persian Gulf (see Map 7.1). Overland routes connected Mesopotamia and Anatolia to India and Central Asia through Persia's mountains and deserts. The Caucasus Mountains between the Black and Caspian Seas were also linked to Persia historically. Two pastoral societies on the Persian plateau, the Indo-European Medes (MEEDZ) and the Persians, competed for power. By 600 B.C.E. the Persians were subjects of the Medes, who had joined with the Babylonians to overthrow the Assyrians (see Chronology: Persia, 1000–334 B.C.E.). But the Medes were soon displaced by the Persians.

Achaemenid The ruling family of the classical Persian Empire.

The Persian Empire, usually known as **Achaemenid** (a-KEY-muh-nid) Persia after the ruling family, was an extraordinary achievement. At its peak, it extended from the Indus Valley in the east to Libya in the west and from the Black, Caspian, and Aral (AR-uhl) Seas in the north to the Nile Valley in the south (see Map 7.1). This empire was created by a series of four kings. Cyrus II, better known as Cyrus the Great, began the expansion. Cyrus and his successors, Cambyses (kam-BY-seez) II, Darius (duh-RY-uhs) I, and Xerxes (ZUHRK-seez) I, conquered vast territories. Their autocratic but tolerant government established a model for later Middle Eastern empires and challenged the Greeks in the west.

Cyrus the Great (r. 550–530 B.C.E.) overthrew the Median king to become the "king of the Medes and Persians." By 539 he had conquered Mesopotamia, Syria, Palestine, Lydia (a kingdom in the western part of Anatolia), and all the prosperous Greek cities in Anatolia. As much diplomat as soldier, Cyrus followed moderate policies in the conquered territories, making only modest demands for tribute. After conquering Babylonia, Cyrus issued a proclamation on a cylinder, which some consider the world's first charter of human rights: "Protect this land from rancor, from foes, from falsehood, and from drought." Cyrus claimed that the main Babylonian god, Marduk (MAHR-dook), ordered him to help the Babylonians by becoming their ruler and bringing them "justice and righteousness."[2] Under his rule, the Jews taken to Babylon by the Assyrians were allowed to return to Palestine and rebuild their temple. When Cyrus was killed while campaigning against nomads east of the Aral Sea, he was replaced by his son Cambyses II (r. 530–522 B.C.E.), who subjugated Egypt and wisely presented himself as a new Egyptian ruler who would bring stability, good fortune, health, and gladness.

Cambyses' successor and distant cousin, Darius I (r. 521–486 B.C.E.), was a usurper who had seized power. Not a modest man, he boasted that "over and above my thinking power and understanding, I am a good warrior, horseman, bowman, spear-man."[3] Darius crushed a revolt in Egypt and spread Persian power east and west, even annexing Afghanistan and parts of the Indus River valley in northwestern India. Today many peoples in Afghanistan and Central Asia speak languages closely related to Persian. Darius claimed that within his territories he cherished good people, rooted out the bad, and prevented people from killing each other. To promote justice and ensure his posterity as a great lawgiver, he fashioned a law code for Babylon that basically reaffirmed Hammurabi's laws made almost 1,500 years earlier.

The Persians were among the classical world's greatest engineers and builders. For example, to forge closer links with Egypt, Darius completed the first Suez Canal, 125 miles long and 150 feet wide, that briefly connected the

CHRONOLOGY

Persia, 1000–334 B.C.E.

600 B.C.E. Persians become vassals of Medes

640 B.C.E. Kingship of Cyrus the Great

547–546 B.C.E. Conquest of Lydia

530–522 B.C.E. Kingship of Cambyses II

525–523 B.C.E. Conquest of Egypt

521–486 B.C.E. Kingship of Darius I

518 B.C.E. Persian conquest of Indus Valley

499 B.C.E. Rebellion by Ionian Greeks against Persian rule

499–479 B.C.E. Greco-Persian Wars

486–465 Kingship of Xerxes

404 B.C.E. Egyptian independence from Persia

330 B.C.E. Conquest of Persian Empire by Alexander the Great

CHRONOLOGY

	Greece	Persia	Hellenistic World
600 B.C.E.	**ca. 594 B.C.E.** Solon's reforms in Athens	**550–530 B.C.E.** Kingship of Cyrus the Great	
		525–523 B.C.E. Conquest of Egypt	
		521–486 B.C.E. Kingship of Darius I	
500 B.C.E.	**499–479 B.C.E.** Greco-Persian Wars		
	460–429 B.C.E. Periclean era in Athens		
	431–404 B.C.E. Peloponnesian War		
400 B.C.E.			**338 B.C.E.** Macedonian conquest of Greece
			336–323 B.C.E. Reign of Alexander the Great
			330 B.C.E. Occupation of Persia

Mediterranean and the Red Seas. Darius also began the building of a new capital at Persepolis (puhr-SEP-uh-luhs). The architecture of this spectacular city, centered on a massive stone terrace on which stood monumental royal buildings, was drawn from Egyptian, Mesopotamian, and Greek traditions, and its craftsmen and workers included Egyptians, Greeks, Hittites, and Mesopotamians.

Imperial Policies and Networks

Unlike their Assyrian and Babylonian predecessors, the Persian empire builders used laws, generous economic policies, and tolerance toward the conquered to rule successfully. Leading citizens came from many backgrounds. Generals might be Medes, Armenians, Greeks, Egyptians, or Kurds, a people living in the mountains just north of Persia and Mesopotamia. Some of the Persian techniques were imitated by their successors, including the Greeks and Romans, when they created even larger imperial structures several centuries later.

Persian Government

Although their power was in theory absolute, Persian kings were expected to consult with important nobles and judges. Each of the Persian provinces was governed by a **satrap** (SAY-trap) ("protector of the kingdom"), an official who ruled according to established laws and paid a fixed amount of taxes to the king each year. The Persians had several grand capitals, including Babylon and Susa (SOO-zuh) in Mesopotamia, before Persepolis was completed. Communications were aided by the "royal road" stretching 1,700 miles from east to west. A messenger of the

satrap ("protector of the kingdom") A Persian official who ruled according to established laws and procedures and paid a fixed amount of taxes to the emperor each year.

Bas Relief of Darius and Xerxes Holding Court This relief was carved in one of the palaces at the Persian capital of Persepolis.

Oriental Institute, University of Chicago, Photo #P57121

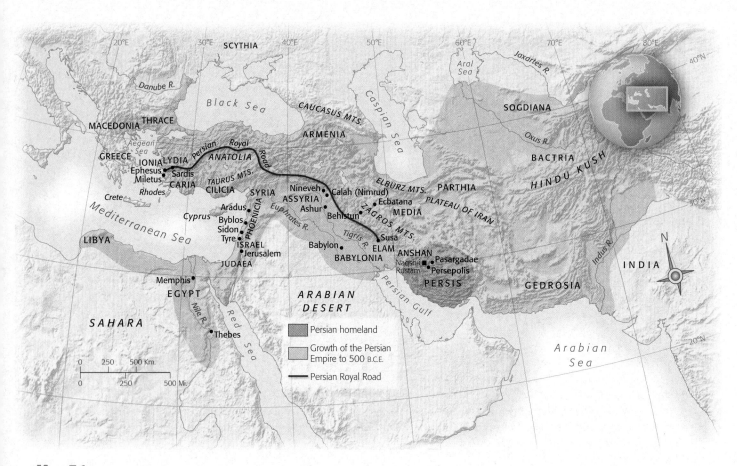

Map 7.1
The Persian Empire, ca. 500 B.C.E.

At its height around 500 B.C.E., the Persians controlled a huge empire that included northern Greece, Egypt, and most of western Asia from the Mediterranean coast to the Indus River in India.

 **Interactive Map**

king could travel the road by horse in nineteen days. The Persians became famous for building roads and then protecting those who traveled them. The Greek historian Herodotus marveled at the communication network, writing that "neither snow, nor rain, nor heat, nor darkness of night prevents these couriers from completing their designated stages with utmost speed."[4]

Persian Economy

The highways promoted economic growth and exchange, a second Achaemenid practice that strengthened their empire. The use of standard weights and measures, along with minted coins of recognized value, fostered trade throughout the empire. In addition, the Persian rulers did not steal the wealth of the conquered lands but allowed conquered peoples to continue to benefit from the same economic activities as before. Phoenicians, for example, continued their Mediterranean trade. To open new networks for exchanging goods and technologies, Darius sent an expedition to India that returned by sailing around Arabia to Suez. This expedition laid the foundation for the conquest of the Indus River Valley and also more maritime trade.

Cultural Mixing

Perhaps most crucial to their imperial success, the Persians generally treated the people they conquered with respect, allowing them to maintain their own social and religious institutions. In Egypt, for instance, Cambyses was a pharaoh, not a Persian ruler. The Persians prided themselves on their ability to unify vastly different peoples under the "king of kings," a title that respected other rulers with limited rights in their own territories. For this reason, many Greeks fought for Persia in the Greco-Persian Wars.

The Persians also utilized various official languages. Eventually, Aramaic (ar-uh-MAY-ik), spoken by many peoples of western Asia, became the official language. After a time Greek also was widely used. Herodotus reported of the Persians that "there is no nation which so readily adopts foreign customs. As soon as they hear of any luxury, they instantly make it their own."[5]

Persian Religion and Society

The Persians made another distinct contribution to later world history in their promotion of **Zoroastrianism** (zo-ro-ASS-tree-uh-niz-uhm), a religion founded by Zoroaster (whose name means "With Golden Camels") that later became the state religion of Persia. Some of the key ideas in Judaism, Christianity, and Islam are foreshadowed by, and perhaps even derived from, Zoroastrianism. Zoroaster was one of the first non-Hebrew religious leaders to challenge the prevailing polytheism. Scholars debate whether he lived between 630 and 550 B.C.E., as earlier studies concluded, or centuries earlier, perhaps around 1000 or 1200 B.C.E., as some recent studies suggest. He may have been a priest in the early Persian religion, which was closely related to the religion of the Aryans who migrated to India.

Zoroaster had a monotheistic vision of one supreme god, **Ahura Mazda** (ah-HOOR-uh MAZZ-duh) (the "Wise Lord"), who was opposed by an evil spirit, a Satan-like figure who was the source of lies, cowardice, and evil (see Witness to the Past: Good, Evil, and Monotheism in Zoroastrian Thought). Ahura Mazda allowed humans to freely choose between himself and evil, between heaven and hell. By serving Ahura Mazda, men and women were promoting ultimate goodness and truth. At the end of time, Zoroaster believed, Ahura Mazda would win a final victory over the spirit of evil and even hell would come to an end. Zoraster also banned use of intoxicants and animal sacrifice. However, some Persians worshipped other gods and several religions coexisted in Persia.

The Jews may have adopted some of their religious ideas about good and evil, God and the devil, heaven and hell, and a last judgment from Zoroastrians while the Jews were held captive in Babylon (586–539 B.C.E.). Such ideas were later incorporated into Christianity, and the Zoroastrian watchwords of "good thoughts, good words, good deeds" also became key ideas of other religions. Darius I did much to spread Zoroastrianism, publicly attributing his victories to Ahura Mazda and honoring him for creating earth, sky, and humankind. While Zoroastrianism was displaced in western Asia by Christianity and, later, Islam, the faith lives on today among small groups in Iran as well as in the wealthy Parsee (PAR-see) minority in India, descendants of Persian Zoroastrians.

The Persians did not develop as politically diversified a society as did the Greeks. At the top of the system were the nobles, many of them warriors who had been granted large estates by the king, followed by priests, merchants, and bankers. In Babylonian cities ruled by Persia these citizens met in formal assemblies to make important judicial decisions. Zoroastrian priests schooled the princes of the noble families to prepare for government careers. The middle class included brewers, butchers, bakers, carpenters, potters, and coppersmiths. Peasants and slaves constituted the bottom of the social structure. Many peasant farmers were impoverished, becoming poor renters or sharecroppers bound to the land. Slaves, mainly debtors, criminals, and prisoners of war, filled various functions. Some were apprenticed in trades while others operated small businesses.

Persian society was patriarchal and polygamous. Persian men believed that the greatest proof of masculinity was to father many sons, and many, especially at upper levels, had several wives. Persian women were usually kept secluded in harems and probably veiled themselves, an ancient practice in western Asia. But some queens and other noble women exercised strong influences on their husbands, and many even controlled large estates. A few women became independently wealthy. For instance, one entrepreneur of commoner origins, Irdabama, was a major landowner who not only controlled a large labor force of several hundred but also operated her own grain and wine business.

Warfare and Persian Decline

Darius and his successors eventually encountered some major problems. Darius campaigned unsuccessfully against the Scythians (SITH-ee-uhnz), warlike Indo-European pastoral nomads whose territory stretched from Ukraine to Mongolia. Skilled horsemen and master workers of gold and bronze, the Scythians had both fought and traded with the Greek cities. A more serious defeat came with the first Greco-Persian War, in which the tiny disunited Greek states turned back the world's most powerful empire. Persians and Greeks were rivals for regional power, but many Greeks lived in Persian territories. Inspired by Scythian resistance to Darius, some Greek cities on the Ionian (eye-OH-nee-uhn) coast of Anatolia rebelled against Persian control (see Map 7.1). In response Darius decided to attack the cities on the Greek peninsula that supported the Ionian Greek rebels. While the Persians failed to occupy most of Greece, they reclaimed the Ionian Greek cities, brutally punishing the most rebellious. Darius then turned to favoring democratic forces in Ionian cities, a tactical move he unrealistically hoped would inspire democrats in the peninsula to cooperate with Persian aims.

Xerxes (r. 486–465 B.C.E.), the son of Darius, tried again to conquer the Greeks in 480 B.C.E., attacking with a huge army and naval force; the result was a fierce two-year struggle. Perhaps

Zoroastrianism A monotheistic religion founded by the Persian Zoroaster, and later the state religion of Persia. Its notion of one god opposed by the devil may have influenced Judaism and later Christianity.

Ahura Mazda (the "Wise Lord") The one god of Zoroastrianism.

The Zoroastrian Legacy

Persian Class System

Families and Gender Relations

First Greco-Persian War

Second Greco-Persian War

Good, Evil, and Monotheism in Zoroastrian Thought

The Persian thinker Zarathustra, better known today as Zoroaster, the name given him by the Greeks, offered an ethical vision that, he believed, came from God. The early Persians apparently believed in three great gods and many lesser ones, but Zoroaster preached that only one of these, *Ahura Mazda* (the "Wise Lord"), was the supreme deity in the universe, responsible for creation and the source of all goodness. A rival entity, Angra Mainyu ("Hostile Spirit"), embodied evil and was the source of all misery and sin. Zoroaster asked people to join the cosmic battle for good and worship Ahura Mazda while opposing evil and Angra Mainyu, referred to as the Liar. This excerpt outlining Zoroaster's beliefs comes from one of the devotional hymns, the Gathas, contained within the Zoroastrian holy scriptures. It was written down in final form centuries after Zoroaster's life but was probably based on earlier writings by the prophet or his disciples.

Then shall I recognize you as strong and holy, Mazda, when by the hand in which you yourself hold the destinies that you will assign to the Liar [Angra Mainyu] and the Righteous [Ahura Mazda] . . . the might of Good Thought shall come to me.

As the holy one I recognized you, [Ahura Mazda], when I saw you in the beginning at the birth of Life, when you made actions and words to have their reward—evil for the evil, a good Destiny for the good—through your wisdom when creation shall reach its goal. At which goal you will come with your holy Spirit, O Mazda, with Dominion, at the same with Good Thought, by whose action the settlements [human societies] will prosper through Right. . . .

"I am Zarathustra, a true foe to the Liar, to the utmost of my power, but a powerful support would I be to the Righteous, that I may attain the future things of the infinite Dominion, so I praise and proclaim you, Mazda. . . ."

As the holy one I recognized you, [Ahura Mazda], when Good Thought [a good spirit created by Ahura Mazda] came to me, when the still mind taught me to declare what is best:

"Let not a man seek again and again to please the Liars, for they make all the righteous enemies."

And thus Zarathustra himself . . . chooses the spirit of thine that is holiest, Mazda. May Right be embodied, full of life and strength! May Piety abide in the Dominion where the sun shines! May Good Thought give destiny to men according to their works [good actions]!

This I ask you, tell me truly, Ahura. . . . Who determined the path of sun and stars? Who is it by whom the moon waxes and wanes again? . . . Who upheld the Earth beneath and the firmament from falling? Who the water and the plants? Who yoked swiftness to winds and clouds? . . .

This I ask you, tell me truly, Ahura—whether we shall drive the Lie away from us to those who being full of disobedience will not strive after fellowship with Right, nor trouble themselves with counsel of Good Thought. . . .

I will speak of that which [Ahura Mazda], the all-knowing, revealed to me first in this earthly life. Those of you that put not into practice this word as I think and utter it, to them shall be woe at the end of life. I will speak of that which the Holiest declared to me as the word that is best for mortals to obey: he, [Ahura Mazda] said, "They who at my bidding render [Zarathustra] obedience, shall all attain Welfare and Immortality by the actions of the Good Spirit." In immortality shall the soul of the righteous be joyful, in perpetuity shall be the torments of the Liars [the followers of evil]. All this does [Ahura Mazda] appoint by his Dominion.

THINKING ABOUT THE READING

1. What supreme powers did Zoroaster attribute to Ahura Mazda?
2. How did Zoroaster expect individuals to work for good and combat evil?
3. What fate awaited those who chose the path of evil?

Source: Yasnas 43–45, in James Hope Moulton, *Early Zoroastrianism* (London: Williams and Norgate, 1913), 364–370.

Xerxes' most effective ally was the Ionian Greek Queen Artemisia (AHRT-uh-MIZH-ee-uh), who was praised for her bravery and the wise counsel she gave the Persian king. But the Persian thrust failed. Although Xerxes still held a large chunk of the Greek world and regained control of Egypt, defeat in this second Greco-Persian War was a turning point in Persian history.

The Persian Empire was not finally conquered until the army of Alexander the Great defeated Persian forces in 330 B.C.E., but the seeds of decline were planted when Xerxes imposed heavy taxation on the satrapies, weakening support for Persian rule. By 424 B.C.E. the Persian Empire was suffering from civil unrest caused by fights within the Achaemenid family, currency inflation, and difficulty collecting taxes. Under Xerxes and his successors, the wise policies of Cyrus and Darius were gradually reversed. Many merchants and landlords were ruined by having to borrow money at very high interest rates, and fewer attempts were made to include other ethnic groups in governing. Some regions rebelled. For example, Egypt ended Persian control in 404 B.C.E. and restored pharaonic rule. Thus support for the increasingly remote kings weakened long before Alexander's superior armies ended Achaemenid Persia and its once-great empire.

Persian Collapse

- The Persian Empire, centered on a trade crossroads, was larger than any empire that preceded it.

- The Persians often won the support of peoples they had conquered through their respect for native cultures and their institution of the rule of law.

- The monotheistic Persian religion, Zoroastrianism, may have contributed some key ideas to Judaism, Christianity, and Islam.

- The Persian Empire suffered several setbacks, including an unsuccessful campaign against the Scythians and repeated failure to completely conquer Greece.

- Though the Persian Empire was conquered by Alexander the Great in 330 B.C.E., it had begun to decline over a century earlier.

THE RISE AND FLOWERING OF THE GREEKS

What were some features of Greek government, philosophy, and science?

When people today think of the classical Greeks, they envision the "golden age" of Athenian democracy, with philosophers debating the meaning of life and thinkers pondering the mysteries of science, but these were only part of a complex, often conflicted society. The Greeks had to struggle to forge democracy. How much of their culture the Greeks created and how much they adopted from others remains subject to debate. The Mediterranean was a zone of interaction for peoples living around its rim, and by 700 B.C.E. the Greeks became active participants in maritime trade. Soon this activity led to prosperity and new forms of government. Like people today, they debated how populations should be ruled, how leaders should be chosen, and how youngsters should be educated. But the Greek society modern people admire was also far from egalitarian and had many unattractive features.

The Greek City-States

The Greek world was shaped by varied influences. Mountainous terrain, coastal plains, and scattered islands encouraged the development of many city-states rather than one centralized state, as well as the maritime trade that fostered growth and prosperity between 800 and 500 B.C.E. (see Chronology: The Greeks, 750–338 B.C.E.). A growing population, a shortage of good farmland at home, and commercial interests led many Greeks to leave their home cities to establish new settlements along the Ionian coast, around the Black Sea, in Italy, and even the Mediterranean coasts of France and Spain (see Map 7.2). Trade and migration opened the Greeks to new ideas. Greeks even visited and lived in Egypt.

Prosperity led to a new conception of the city and the citizen's role in it. The result was the **polis (POE-lis)**, a city-state that became the major institution of classical Greek life and gave citizens a sense of community, loyalty, personal identity, and meaning. All business, from building a new temple to making war, was decided by the free male citizens meeting in an open assembly. The worst punishment a Greek could suffer was being asked to leave the polis. Some Greeks committed suicide rather than face ostracism. City-states competed fiercely with each other, including in sports events. The Olympic Games, begun in the eighth century B.C.E., were associated with a religious festival to honor the god Zeus. Each polis sent athletes who competed naked in track and field events or personal contests of strength, such as wrestling. The idea was to win, even if it meant cheating.

Not all inhabitants of the polis were equal. Many cities developed **oligarchy (AHL-uh-gar-kee)**, rule by a small group of wealthy leaders. As much as 80 percent of the population, including women, slaves, children, and resident foreigners, were not citizens and thus had no right to vote or hold office. Even among the citizens, members of old, aristocratic families were treated with greater respect than others. By the seventh century, however, aristocratic power weakened. Although aristocrats generally scorned trade in favor of the wealth to be gained from owning land, the growing trade created wealth for other citizens, allowing them to compete with the upper class. Furthermore, a new battle formation was developed that relied

polis A Greek city-state that embraced nearby rural areas, whose agricultural surplus then helped support the urban population.

oligarchy Rule by a small group of wealthy leaders.

CHRONOLOGY

The Greeks, 750–338 B.C.E.

ca. 750–550 B.C.E. Greek colonization in Mediterranean, Black Sea

ca. 594 B.C.E. Solon's reforms in Athens

561–527 B.C.E. Peisistratus tyrant in Athens

507 B.C.E. Athenian democracy under Cleisthenes

499–479 B.C.E. Greco-Persian Wars

477 B.C.E. Founding of Delian League

469–399 B.C.E. Life of Socrates

ca. 460–429 B.C.E. Era of Pericles in Athens

431–404 B.C.E. Peloponnesian War

428–347 B.C.E. Life of Plato

384–322 B.C.E. Life of Aristotle

338 B.C.E. Philip of Macedonia's conquest of Greece

Map 7.2
Classical Greece, ca. 450 B.C.E.

Greek settlements, divided into rival city-states, occupied not only the Greek peninsula but also Crete and western Anatolia. Two alliances headed by Athens and Sparta fought each other in the Peloponnesian War (431–404 B.C.E.).

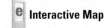 **Interactive Map**

on infantry more than the aristocracy-dominated cavalry. The city of Sparta perfected an infantry formation, the phalanx **(FAY-langks)**, that other cities quickly adopted. The phalanx consisted of a square of soldiers that moved in unison, each man protected with heavy armor and carrying a sword or spear. Greek armies became citizen-armies, not paid professional forces. As men other than aristocrats risked their lives for their polis, they wanted a greater role in governing it.

Roots of Democracy

The new military system, combined with population expansion and increased wealth from trade with the Greek cities in Ionia, contributed to the rise of democracy. Some Greeks tried to combine the contradictory ideas that people are politically free and that they also owe their loyalty to the community. Some Greeks also discovered how people could live with each other without being controlled by gods or kings, and many cities developed notions of political freedom and equality for adult male citizens. These were radical ideas for that era, or even for ours.

Athenian Political Change

Reform, Tyranny, and Democracy in Athens

The most dramatic political changes occurred in Athens, a polis on the eastern Greek peninsula of Attica. Athens became progressively more democratic, partly as a result of a crisis. The soil was wearing out, and farmers borrowed money and went deeply into debt. As the bad wheat harvests continued, farmers sold themselves and their families into slavery. The poor demanded reform. Around 594 B.C.E. the Athenians elected Solon (SOH-luhn), a general, poet, and merchant, to lead the city and rewrite the old constitution. To avoid civil war, he canceled the debts of the poor, forbade enslavement for default of debts, made wealth rather than birth the criterion for membership on the council that controlled the city, and established a Council of 400 to review issues before they came before an Assembly of Citizens, which now served as a court of appeals where people, rich or poor, could bring a case to court. However, he also reduced the freedom of women by, for example, allowing fathers to sell into slavery daughters who lost their virginity before marriage.

The Athenian path to a more democratic system came in several stages, from reform to tyranny to democracy. Solon's reforms failed to please either side in this social and economic struggle. The poor wanted him to give them land from the rich, while the aristocrats resented their loss of power. Tensions returned, allowing Peisistratus (pie-SIS-truht-uhs) (r. 561–527 B.C.E.) to seize power as a **tyrant**, not necessarily a brutal ruler but someone who ruled outside the law. Peisistratus gave the poor land he had confiscated from aristocratic estates and launched a building program, including an aqueduct to bring water directly to the city center.

Another aristocrat, Cleisthenes (KLICE-thuh-neez), established genuine democracy in Athens in 507 B.C.E. Instead of emphasizing noble birth or wealth as a criterion of citizenship, Cleisthenes created geographical units that chose people by lot to serve in a new Council of 500. The council submitted legislation to the Assembly, which consisted of 40,000 citizens who also selected by lot the city officials. In the mid-fifth century the power of the aristocrats was further reduced, and lower-income citizens were allowed to serve as officials. Euripides (you-RIP-uh-deez) described the system in his play, *The Suppliant Woman*: "The city is free, and ruled by no one man. The people reign, in annual succession. They do not yield power to the rich; the poor man has an equal share in it."[6] The Athenians believed that ordinary citizens could serve in any government positions except as military officers, and they chose representatives by lot rather than by more divisive elections. However, only a small aristocracy of adult males enjoyed these rights. Moreover, many Greeks did not think that democracy of any type was a good thing.

The Spartan System

In the Peloponnese (PELL-eh-puh-NEESE) peninsula in southern Greece, the landlocked city-state of Sparta followed a course much different from that of Athens (see Map 7.2). Spartans saw military power as essential to their prestige and influence. When the Spartans found themselves short of land, they conquered their neighbors rather than establish overseas colonies, then made the conquered peoples agricultural slaves with no political or human rights; slaves could be killed by a Spartan almost at will. Since slaves outnumbered Spartans ten to one, Sparta developed a rigid military state, led by two kings and a Council of Elders who were elected for life by an Assembly of all citizens over thirty. The Assembly could vote only yes or no to measures prepared for it by the Council of Elders and the king. Thus the Spartans discouraged independence of thought or behavior. Spartan boys who seemed physically unfit were generally taken to a remote rural area and allowed to die. The other boys were given a rigid military training and taught that self-discipline and courage were the highest virtues. One legend tells of a young boy who found a small fox and concealed it under his shirt while engaged in military drill. While standing quietly at attention, the boy suddenly fell over dead. The fox had eaten into his vital organs, but self-discipline had kept him from crying out in pain. From ages twenty to thirty, Spartan males served in the army, and they were allowed to live at home with their wives only after this time.

Although enjoying no political rights, Spartan women acquired a higher status than other Greek women, and their husbands' frequent absences from home allowed some of them to acquire wealth and land. Athenian men criticized Spartan women for their independence, portraying them as greedy, licentious, and needing male control. The playwright Euripides scolded the "Spartan maidens, allowed out of doors with the young men, running and wrestling in their company, with naked thighs."[7]

Religion, Rationalism, and Science

The Greeks may have been practical people, but they were also concerned with the supernatural realm. The multitude of gods and legends introduced by the Homeric epics profoundly shaped

Stages of Democracy

tyrant Someone who ruled a Greek polis outside the law, not necessarily a brutal ruler.

Military Power

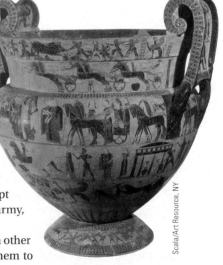

Scala/Art Resource, NY

Narrative Drawing on Pottery   The Francois vase, made around 570 B.C.E., is considered a masterpiece of narrative drawing on pottery, with fine detail and vivid coloring. It shows scenes of battle.

Greek thinking and values, although Greek religion also owed something to the Egyptians and Phoenicians. Chief gods and goddesses represented various natural and human activities. Zeus, a sky-god who guaranteed the natural and social order, was the leader. His wife, Hera (HEER-uh), represented marriage and the family. Poseidon (puh-SIDE-uhn), the brother of Zeus, was the lord of the sea. Athena, Zeus's favorite daughter, was the goddess of wisdom. Other notable deities were Apollo, patron of music, philosophy, and other finer things in life; Dionysus (DIE-uh-NYE-suhs), the god of wine; and Aphrodite (af-ruh-DITE-ee), goddess of sex and fertility. Although these gods and goddesses had human virtues and vices, they were also seen as immortal and more powerful than humans. To defy the gods was to invite disaster. Proper sacrifices to the gods, usually incorporated into festivals and official ceremonies, guaranteed harmony between humans and the heavens.

Rational Thought

Interest in the deeper meaning of life also led the Greeks to develop a rational approach to the search for truth. They produced some of history's greatest thinkers, joining the Mesopotamians, Egyptians, Indians, and Chinese in laying the foundation for modern science. Some Greek thinkers questioned supernatural explanations of natural events. The Ionian philosopher Xenophanes (zi-NAHF-uh-neez) was skeptical of the gods:

> *Mortals deem that the gods are begotten as they [humans] are, and have clothes like theirs and voice and form. . . . The Ethiopians make their gods black. The Thracians (THRAY-shuhns) say theirs have blue eyes and red hair.*[8]

Scientific Thought

Creative thought erupted throughout the Greek world. Thales of Miletus (ca. 636–546) was the first person we know of to perceive the universe as orderly and to seek a natural explanation of phenomena rather than attributing them to gods. Anaximander of Miletus (611–547) said the first creatures lived in water and came close to the idea, developed several millennia later, that human beings evolved from lower forms of life. Democritus (di-MAHK-ruht-uhs) announced his belief that all matter was composed of tiny seeds known as atoms and that these moved, creating different objects. Heracleitus (HER-uh-KLITE-uhs) of Ephasus (EF-uh-suhs) in Ionia declared that the universe is in a constant state of flux and that only change was permanent. The Ionian Pythagoras (puh-THAG-uh-ruhs) helped establish the foundations of modern mathematics by emphasizing the number 10 and developing the multiplication tables as well as major mathematical theorems.

These early thinkers laid the foundations of natural science and philosophy by emphasizing the explanatory power of human reason and evaluating evidence by human rather than divine standards. However, some Greek thinkers also opened the door to the more troubling idea that human standards are relative rather than absolute. The **Sophists** (SAHF-uhsts) emphasized skepticism and the belief that there is no ultimate truth. People have struggled with this twin legacy of Greek thinkers ever since.

Sophists Thinkers in classical Greece who emphasized skepticism and the belief that there is no ultimate truth.

Axial Age Philosophy and Thinkers

Axial Age Thinkers

Views of the Greek contribution to world thought often focus on the specific ideas of three major fifth- and fourth-century Athenian thinkers. The first two, Socrates and Plato, studied the nature of truth; the third, Aristotle (AR-uh-staht-uhl), examined the truth to be found in nature. These men were part of an outpouring of philosophical and religious genius across Eurasia between 600 and 200 B.C.E. that historians often term the Axial Age. The ideas of Buddha in India, Confucius in China, Hebrew prophets, Zoroaster, and various Greeks shaped classical societies and remained influential for many centuries.

Socrates

The earliest Greek philosophical giant, the Athenian Socrates (469–399 B.C.E.), believed that "the unexamined life" was not worth living. Shabbily dressed, eccentric, passionate, and indifferent to money and pleasure, he spent much time asking people leading questions that helped them examine the truth of their ideas, an approach called the **Socratic Method**. Unlike the Sophists, Socrates believed in absolute truths that would make people virtuous. But he also was suspicious of democracy, favoring government by the chosen few who had acquired superior knowledge. Although often credited as the founder of Western moral philosophy, some of his elitist views might be unpopular even today. For undermining the polis by asking so many, often embarrassing, questions and "corrupting the youth," Socrates was condemned to death for treason by the citizens of Athens in 399 B.C.E. The prosecutor said of him: "Socrates is an evil doer and a curious person, searching into things under the earth and above the heavens, and making the worse appear the better, and teaching all this to others."[9] Although he could have secured a lighter sentence or gone into exile, Socrates chose death, making him, in modern eyes at least, a

Socratic Method The method, introduced by Socrates, of asking people leading questions to help them examine the truth of their ideas.

martyr for truth and free expression, although most of his contemporaries may not have viewed him in this way.

Socrates' leading pupil, Plato (428–347 B.C.E.), became disillusioned with city politics after his mentor's execution. After a sojourn in Egypt, Plato founded a school in Athens that he called the Academy (the source of our word *academic*). Plato elaborated Socrates' belief in ultimate truth, beauty, and goodness, but he believed most people are ruled by emotions and cannot see reality. Only a special class, the Guardians, trained to use reason to control the emotions and will, can understand ultimate truth and goodness and therefore should govern. Later in his life, Plato retreated from this elitist conception and suggested that strong laws could control democratic excesses. Some charge that Plato's thinking sanctioned dictatorships in which a small group of men claimed special wisdom and virtue.

Aristotle (384–322 B.C.E.) was the Athenian philosopher whose ideas seem most similar to ours today. The son of a Greek physician working for the king of Macedonia, Aristotle came to Athens to study philosophy with Plato and eventually founded a school of his own. Like Socrates, he was charged with impiety, but he chose to go into exile. Aristotle offered many enduring insights. Although he distrusted democracy, he encouraged people to pursue their personal desires. Aristotle was pragmatic, emphasizing how human nature and physical nature worked rather than exploring the ultimate truths that lay behind our actions. His writings spanned the social sciences, humanities, and natural sciences. He was also one of the first psychologists, describing human emotions like affection, anger, bravery, fear, hate, joy, and pity. Aristotle was particularly interested in classifying and analyzing nature and dissecting animals, and he was the first to classify animals zoologically. His work was a key foundation for both Western and Islamic science. He also wrote works on logic and ethics and studied political systems. In philosophy, he speculated on **metaphysics**, the broad field that studies the most general concepts and categories underlying people and the world around them (such as "time" and "causation").

HIP/Art Resource, NY

Socrates This statue, made several centuries after his death, celebrates the Athenian philosopher Socrates, who had a strong influence on the thinking of Greek philosophers who came after him, including his student, Plato.

Literature

Greek cultural creativity, especially in Athens, reflected dynamism and freedom. Athens attracted many great writers and artists because prosperity generated spending money for entertainment. Perhaps the Athenians' most enduring contribution, drama, arose from annual religious festivals and was based on historical or mythological themes. Plays, which were mostly tragedies, were usually performed in outdoor amphitheaters and accompanied by music. The dramatists had different styles. Aeschylus (ESS-kuh-luhs) (525–456 B.C.E.) emphasized traditional values, the gods, and justice issues while portraying the disasters brought on by too much pride. Sophocles (SAUF-uh-klees) (ca. 497–406 B.C.E.) was a humanist, treating emotional issues with restraint. Aristophanes (AR-uh-STAHF-uh-neez) (448–380 B.C.E.) wrote comedies that ridiculed Athenians and their pretensions. For example, in *The Knights*, a general tries to convince an ignorant sausage seller to unseat the Athenian leader: "To be a leader of the people isn't for learned men, or honest men, but for the ignorant and vile."[10] Some of his criticism reflected Athenian losses during a terrible war. Some playwrights also offered vivid images of women who refused to be silenced or abused. In *Agamemnon* (ag-uh-MEM-non), a great tragic drama by Aeschylus, the wife of Agamemnon, the hero of the Trojan War, kills him upon his return for sacrificing their daughter to the gods to get a favorable wind to sail to Troy.

Greek lyric poets, especially in the Ionian cities, reflected an individualistic and openly intellectual way of thinking. For example, in contrast to Spartan heroism, Archilochus (ahr-KIL-uh-kuhs) mocked the Spartan order to their soldiers to "return with your shield—or on it," writing: "Some lucky Thracian has my shield, For, being somewhat flurried, I dropped it by a wayside bush, As from the field I hurried. To blazes with the shield. I'll get another just as good, When next I take the field."[11] Perhaps the most intensely personal poet was Sappho (SAFF-oh), from the Ionian island of Lesbos. A director of a girl's school, Sappho wrote passionate love lyrics to her students: "A host of horsemen, some say, is the loveliest sight upon the earth; some say a display of soldiery; some a fleet of ships, but I say it's whomever one loves."[12] Sappho was considered the equal of Homer as a poet, and her poems were read in the Mediterranean world long after her death.

metaphysics The broad field that studies the most general concepts and categories underlying people and the world around them (such as "time" and "causation").

e **Aristotle on Politics**
Discover the strengths and weaknesses, as Aristotle saw it, of kingdoms, aristocracies, and democracies.

Greek Society

The differences between social classes and genders were pronounced. Freedom was reserved primarily for males. Greek society consisted, from top to bottom, of free men (only some of whom

Social Classes

were citizens), many resident foreigners, free women, and slaves. Most free men, if not wealthy landowners or small farmers, worked as laborers, artisans, or shopkeepers. Resident foreigners, including Phoenicians, Lydians, and Syrians, were primarily merchants, bankers, and artisans. Many became wealthy, and they were required to serve in the military. Free women could not vote, hold office, or serve on juries. Socrates supposedly asked a colleague: "Is there anyone of your acquaintance with whom you have less conversation than your wife?" The reply: "Hardly anyone, I think."[13] Women from elite families generally stayed inside the home, in contrast to many less affluent women.

Slavery

About one-third of the population were slaves, mostly captives taken in battle or debtors. Slaves were often household servants or paid artisans, but many served as teachers, instructing generations of young people how to write and play music. Slaves also built some of the great buildings and worked on agricultural plantations or in mines owned by aristocrats. Life for many was harsh; slaves could be tortured and executed for mere suspicion of a crime.

Like the nuclear family system of the modern West but unlike the extended family pattern of many African and Asian societies, most Greek families consisted of a husband, a wife, and children. The principal tasks of women were to feed and clothe their families and to bear and raise children. While a woman did not have the same sexual freedom as men, she could own property and divorce her husband. Women's participation was also essential in religious festivals. For example, the oracle at the temple of Delphi (DELL-fye), which many leaders consulted to determine the will of Apollo, spoke through a woman's voice.

But women also experienced strong prejudice in a patriarchal society. Aristotle articulated the misogynist, or antiwoman, views of many men when he described women as deformed males. A popular saying expressed male views: "Respectable women should stay at home; the street is for worthless hussies." Some women expressed their discontent, as reflected in a tragic play by Euripides: "[Men] say we lead a safe life at home. What imbeciles! I'd rather stand to arms three times than bear one child."[14] In contrast to their role in politics, in Greek literature women are often powerful and capable of great anger, humor, faithfulness, and intelligence.

The last two are the chief qualities of Penelope, the wife of Ulysses in Homer's *Odyssey* who waits patiently for her husband, ruling the state wisely until his return while escaping the clutches of many men who want to marry her. In the bawdy comedy *Lysistrata* (lis-uh-STRAH-tuh) by Aristophanes, a group of women organize to end war by refusing to have sex with their husbands until the men stop fighting. Lysistrata tells her husband: "We women got together and decided we were going to save Greece. Listen to us and keep quiet, as we've had to do up to now, and we'll clear up the mess you've made."[15]

Some social customs might be considered controversial today. While their wives stayed at home, men attended parties, sometimes enlivened by the presence of courtesans celebrated for their wit and charm. Some courtesans had high status as free people and probably a good education, such as Aspasia (ass-PAY-zhee-uh), a vivacious, literate Milesian who operated a meetinghouse in Athens where educated men came for sex and conversation with intellectual women. An advocate of gender equality, Aspasia became the mistress of the Athenian leader Pericles (PER-eh-kleez), whose enemies accused her of writing his speeches, violating the tradition that politics was for men only. But most prostitutes were slaves whose lives were far different from Aspasia's.

Homosexuality has existed in all societies from earliest times, but Greek men were particularly open about their same-sex relationships. Artists fashioned many naturalistic statues of naked men and women. Diverse homosexual practices and relationships were tolerated. For example, homosexual behavior between older and younger upper-class men was accepted as part of a training or mentoring relationship for career preparation, and many famous Greeks had such relationships. In Sparta some top military units comprised homosexual couples. Boys and girls were often brought up separately, reducing heterosexual contact. But we must not assume that the concepts of same-sex or even opposite-sex relationships 2,500 years ago were precisely the same as those today.

Women Fetching Water The painting on this vase portrays everyday life in a Greek city. Women have congregated at a public fountain to fill jugs with water to be carried back home, where it will be used for drinking, cooking, and cleaning. The women's hair coverings and long robes reflect the fashion of the day.

Scala/Art Resource, NY

In general, men of superior status took for granted that, with or without consent, they could have intimate relations with anyone of inferior status, including servants, slaves, and foreigners. In contrast, nonelite Greeks often condemned homosexual relations between two adults.

SECTION SUMMARY

- The mountainous, maritime geography of Greece fostered the development of multiple city-states rather than one centralized state.

- The polis system of governance allowed extensive political rights for some but no political rights for many.

- Increased trade and the rise of the infantry reduced the power of Greek aristocrats.

- After a period of reform and tyranny, Athens emerged as a democracy for the minority who were citizens.

- Sparta had the strongest army in Greece and often attacked its neighbors and enslaved them.

- Though Greeks had a well-developed religion, they were also notable for their commitment to using reason to understand the world.

- Three of the greatest Greek philosophers were Socrates, who believed in absolute truths; Plato, who described an ideal society in the *Republic;* and Aristotle, who explored human nature and the workings of the physical world.

- Greek drama tended to focus on tragedy, as in the works of Euripides, Aeschylus, and Sophocles; writers like Aristophanes wrote comedies.

- Greek women were generally expected to stay at home and out of politics, but they were often featured as powerful characters in plays.

- Homosexual relations among men were considered acceptable and were common among the upper classes.

GREEKS, PERSIANS, AND THE REGIONAL SYSTEM

In what ways did Persians and Greeks encounter and influence each other?

The Greeks and Persians fought and connected with each other as well as with other societies. During the early fifth century B.C.E. Greek cities successfully fought a series of wars with the greatest power of western Asia, the Persian Empire. But the rival Greek states also fought ruinous wars with each other. Both Greeks and Persians borrowed many ideas from neighboring peoples, including the Egyptians and western Asians. The legacy of classical Greece and Persia for Europe and the Middle East is subject to debate.

The Greco-Persian Wars

The Greco-Persian conflict began in 499 B.C.E., when some Greek cities in Persian-held Anatolia, supported by Athens, rebelled against their Persian overlords; they were defeated in 494. To punish the peninsular Greeks, the Persian king Darius I dispatched a fleet to Greece in 492, but storms destroyed his ships. He then sent a larger Persian force into Greece, which was defeated at the Battle of Marathon in northern Greece in 490 B.C.E. Herodotus reported that the Greeks carried out a slaughter and the Persians fell in heaps, many of them drowning in the sea.

First Greek Victory

The Persians made another attempt to conquer the Greeks in 480 B.C.E., sparking the second war. Persia's King Xerxes sent a huge army, supported by the entire Persian navy, to engage an alliance led by Athens and Sparta. A Spartan force of three hundred fought to the death holding a strategic pass, but they were betrayed by some Greeks who showed the Persians a path around them. The Persians swept down into Athens and burned the city. Expecting final victory, they attacked the Athenian fleet trapped in the Bay of Salamis (SAL-uh-muhs). Surprisingly, the Greeks won the battle. The large Persian force was difficult to supply and control effectively, and the Athenians had also developed the world's most advanced fighting ship, the well-armored *trireme* (TRY-reem), which had three banks of oarsmen and deadly bronze rams. The following year (479) the Greeks defeated the remaining Persian infantry force at the battle of Plataea (pluh-TEE-uh). Some historians argue that the Greek victory over the Persians also led to a growing divide between "Europe" and "Asia," as the Greeks increasingly viewed themselves as different from, and superior to, the people to the east.

Second Greek Victory

Empire and Conflict in the Greek World

Michael Freeman Photography

Intra-Greek Warfare

Delian League A defensive league organized by Greek cities in the fifth century B.C.E. to defeat the Persians.

With the Persian threat ended, the old rivalries of the Greek cities reemerged. The period following the Greek victories was marked not only by great philosophers and playwrights but also by nearly constant warfare among Greek cities. To defeat the Persians the Greek cities had organized a defensive alliance, called the **Delian** (DEE-lee-uhn) **League**, led by the richest state and largest naval power, Athens, while other cities contributed funds or ships to the alliance. But in 467 the island of Naxos (NAK-suhs) tried to withdraw from the league and Athens refused, taking military action to stop Naxos. Some Athenians protested, worrying that a democracy, which allows varied opinions, could not manage an empire. But the Delian League had changed from a defensive alliance to an Athenian empire. In midcentury, Athens moved the league treasury to Athens and began to spend some of the money on Athenian civic improvements.

Periclean Athens

Peloponnesian War A long war between Athens and Sparta and their respective allies in 431–404 B.C.E. that resulted in the defeat of Athens.

The Acropolis The Acropolis dominated the surrounding city of Athens. The marble Parthenon at the center, dedicated to Athena, was built during the time of Pericles.

Athens reached its golden age under Pericles (ca. 495–429 B.C.E.), a visionary leader and spellbinding orator whose reforms brought more democracy to the legal system. Athenians had many reasons to be proud of their city, especially of the magnificent public buildings, such as the Parthenon (PAHR-thuh-nahn), a temple dedicated to the city's patron goddess, Athena, on the hilltop known as the Acropolis (uh-KRAHP-uh-luhs). But while Athenians embraced self-fulfillment and individualism, not all of them believed in unrestrained freedom, fearing that too much pride or self-expression spelled trouble. Playwrights, poets, and historians all taught how pride or arrogance could lead to punishment by the gods and personal disaster. Despite the warnings, the Athenians' arrogance and pride in their city eventually brought disaster, as increasing resentment of Athenian power by rival cities generated the long **Peloponnesian War** (431–404 B.C.E.) between Athens and Sparta and their respective allies. In a famous "funeral oration" delivered in memory of dead Athenian soldiers, the city's nationalistic leader, Pericles (r. 460–429 B.C.E.), reportedly contrasted Athenian democratic institutions and equality before the law with Spartan discipline and lack of freedom:

> . . . *We are called a democracy, for the administration is in the hands of the many and not of the few. . . . I have dwelt upon the greatness of Athens because I want to show you we are contending for a higher prize than those who enjoy none of these privileges. For in magnifying the city I have magnified the men whose virtues made her glorious.*[16]

In this speech Pericles introduced the novel ideas that war was not just to defend hearth and home but to spread better ideas and systems, and also that citizens who enjoyed freedom had a responsibility to their community. The assumption that because they had such high ideals Athenians were superior to their neighbors was one of the reasons other Greek cities despised Athens.

The war proved a disaster for Athens and a boon for Sparta. The Athenians' strategy was to use their navy to combat the superior land army of Sparta and its allies. But Athens was hit by a deadly plague in which a third of the population, including Pericles, died. The Athenians also blundered in an unwise attempt to capture Syracuse, a city founded by Greek settlers on Sicily. Later the Spartans, with Persian advice, destroyed the Athenian fleet. The victorious Spartans disbanded the Athenian navy, destroyed the city walls, and killed or exiled thousands of Athenians.

Although the war made Sparta the most powerful Greek state, decades of instability followed. The frequent conflicts between the Greek cities proved too destructive. Less than a century after the Peloponnesian War ended, Greece was conquered and became the base for a much greater empire led by the northern state of Macedonia.

Athenian Defeat

Historiography: Universal and Critical

The Greeks developed concepts of history that are still used today, but they did so in the context of their connections to other societies. Of course, peoples before them had some sense of history. The legends passed down through oral traditions, such as the stories in the Hebrew Bible and the Homeric epics, were narratives of history, although we cannot prove their accuracy. The Chinese also wrote historical accounts. But the Greeks were the first to pursue critical, analytical, and universal history. The two most famous Greek historians were Herodotus and Thucydides (thyou-SID-uh-deez).

Concepts of History

Herodotus (ca. 484–425 B.C.E.) wrote history on a scale never attempted before, providing most of what we know of the Greco-Persian Wars. Integrating information on geography and cultural traditions, Herodotus wrote vividly about neighboring societies such as Persia and Egypt. Born in a Persian-ruled Ionian city, he traveled around the Persian Empire and sojourned in Egypt, concluding that some Greek gods could be equated with Egyptian divinities. He visited Tyre, where he learned that Phoenicians had invented the alphabet. A sophisticated man with an inquiring mind, Herodotus lived for a time in Athens and portrayed the Athenians favorably, attributing the Greek victory over the Persians to the Greeks' free society, which gave them more incentive than the armies of the absolute Persian monarch. Because his interests and travels went well beyond the Greek world, Herodotus might be considered the first world historian. Although he too often reported unverified hearsay and failed to subject all of his material to critical scrutiny, he did not adopt Greek prejudices against other cultures, offering sympathetic views of the Persians and criticisms of the Greeks.

Herodotus

Much of what we know about Greek politics and wars during the fifth century B.C.E. comes from a single book, *The Peloponnesian War*, written by Thucydides (ca. 460–ca. 400 B.C.E.), an Athenian general who was exiled from Athens for losing an important battle. Despite his exile, Thucydides objectively evaluated the strengths and weaknesses of his home city, setting an example of careful observation. Unlike earlier writers, he added critical judgments to his narrative, for example, criticizing the Athenians for ignoring Pericles' warnings to attempt no new conquests. He also evaluated the strengths and weaknesses of democracy and asked fundamental questions about the nature of power. Thucydides looked for patterns and moral lessons in the past. Whenever historians seek to interpret the past, they are acknowledging a debt to Thucydides, a historian who was not just a teller of tales but also a teacher of wisdom.

Thucydides

Interregional Trade and Cultural Mixing

Throughout this time period the Mediterranean Basin remained a vast zone of exchange in which Greeks played the leading commercial role once dominated by Phoenicians, trading wine and olive oil through the eastern Mediterranean. They also established colonies and spread Greek culture. Like the Greeks, the Persians also welcomed foreign traders. Port cities like Persian-ruled Miletus in Ionia prospered as hubs of regional trade, and Persian gold coins were widely used in the Mediterranean Basin. Persian leaders patronized Greek traders living in their domains, and in 510 B.C.E. one of them, Scylax of Caryanda (SKY-lax of KAR-ee-AN-da), headed a Persian trade mission to India. Tribute flowed to the Persian capital, including camels from Arabia and Bactria, gold from India, horses from the Scythians, bulls from Egypt, leather goods from Anatolia, and silver from Ionia.

Trade Networks

Long-distance trade was crucial to the Mediterranean world in many ways. Merchants traveling elsewhere to trade eventually evolved into what historians call a **trade diaspora**, living

trade diaspora Merchants from the same city or country who live permanently in foreign cities or countries.

Athens as a Hub

permanently in foreign cities or countries. Most of the shipowners, traders, and moneylenders of Athens came from western Asia or from the Greek diaspora colonies such as Massalia (today's Marseilles) and the Crimea, and communities of expatriate Greek merchants were established in Egypt, western Asia, and around the Black Sea. Trade also contributed to the growth of a strong Athenian navy that helped the Greeks defeat the Persians. Athens became the leading Greek commercial and financial hub, controlling rich silver mines worked by over 20,000 slaves and importing huge amounts of wheat from Egypt, Sicily, and southern Russia. It developed a reputation as the most profitable and safest city to do business in, a place where even those of humble origins could achieve wealth.

Cultural Exchange

The Mediterranean Basin also provided a context for the intermingling of southern European, western Asian, and North African cultures. Though themselves highly creative, Persians and Greeks also learned much from other peoples. For example, Persians blended Ionian Greek, Mesopotamian, and Scythian art styles and motifs with their own traditions. Greeks were especially open to influences from the Phoenicians, Lydians, Egyptians, and Mesopotamians. Phoenician traders brought art forms and styles that inspired the Greeks to modify their columns, pottery, statues, and ceramic styles, and Greek music used many instruments and melodies from western Asia. The Greeks also adopted the Phoenician alphabet and several Phoenician, Egyptian, and Anatolian gods. In addition, many Greek colonists absorbed local influences. For example, Greeks in Massalia (modern Marseilles), on the southern coast of France, had to understand the local Celtic customs and language.

Greek Diaspora

Greeks visited, worked in, or settled in other societies, learning about other cultures. Many Ionian merchants lived in Egypt. The Athenian lawgiver Solon visited Egypt as a merchant, studied with priests, and wrote poems about living along the Nile. Some Egyptian medical ideas are found in his influential writings of the Athenian physician Hippocrates (hip-AHK-ruh-teez). Some Greeks even fought as mercenaries for Egyptian kings and worshiped Egyptian gods. Other Greeks served in Mesopotamian and Persian armies. The scientist Democritus visited Babylonia and Persia, and both Plato and Aristotle knew something about Zoroastrianism. Cosmopolitan Ionia, where Greek and Asian cultures mixed, produced pathbreaking thinking in philosophy and science, often under Persian patronage. In fact, rational thinking appeared there earlier than in Athens. Thales, a Lydian subject, studied in Egypt, where he learned geometry; he was the first Greek to inscribe a right-angled triangle and to determine the sun's course from solstice to solstice, something the Babylonians had long known how to do. The Ionian-born mathematician Pythagoras (ca. 580–ca. 500 B.C.E.) may have visited Egypt and Babylon.

The Persian and Greek Legacies

Persian Contributions

Both the Persians and Greeks influenced the peoples around them while leaving a rich legacy for later societies. Persians built the world's first large empire and multinational state, bringing together diverse societies under one flexible and tolerant canopy and fusing traditions from many cultures while spreading learning, such as Babylonian astronomy, to peoples such as the Greeks. Two thousand years later Persians still looked back to Cyrus the Great for inspiration. The Persians also made contributions to other cultures. Zoroastrian ideas influenced several religions, including Judaism, Christianity, and Islam, and many Persian words entered other languages. For example, the Persian word for "garden" became the English word *paradise*. Persian culture and language also strongly influenced Afghanistan and Central Asia. Under Persian rule, science and mathematics continued to develop in Ionia and Mesopotamia.

Many historians credit the Greeks with creating the Western tradition. They have admired the Greeks as the direct cultural, intellectual, and political ancestors of modern Europeans and North Americans, and they have perceived Greek society as culturally richer than any other before modern times. The Athenian era of Pericles, Plato, and Aeschylus is viewed as the "golden age" that launched Western literature, history, philosophy, science, and the democratic ideal. However, the view of Greece as the fountainhead of Western culture has problems. Some historians argue that the Romans founded the Western tradition. Perhaps, they suggest, the Greeks were an extension of the western Asian and North African societies that influenced them. From a modern perspective, the Greeks seem both very strange and quite familiar. Many Greek customs and social inequalities, especially their sometimes cruel

SECTION SUMMARY

- The Persians attacked the Greeks several times, but the Greeks, against great odds, fended them off.

- Following the Greek victory over the Persians, Athens's growing arrogance eventually led to the Peloponnesian War between Athens and Sparta, which ended with Spartan victory.

- Herodotus, who wrote of the Greco-Persian Wars, and Thucydides, who wrote of the Peloponnesian War, were the first historians to write critical and analytical history.

- The eastern Mediterranean and western Asia were zones of intense trade and cultural mixing.

- The long-held idea that the Greeks created the Western tradition is controversial, as are the merits of some Greek customs and ideas.

treatment of women and slaves, appall people today. To critics, Greek thinkers were not very liberal or secular, their democracy was elitist and flawed, and what ideas western Europe derived from the Greeks came in modified form through the Romans. Later, Europe rediscovered much of Greek thought through the Arabs. Moreover, modern science is based not only on Greek but also on Chinese, Indian, and Middle Eastern discoveries.

The debate suggests how fascinating the Greeks have been to various societies over the centuries, beginning with the Romans. Middle Eastern societies also treasured Greek thinkers and science, and Greek philosophy influenced some Islamic scholars. The debate also indicates that the Greeks, however imperfect their society, fostered ideas and institutions that were unusual for their time and that have endured for over two millennia.

THE HELLENISTIC AGE AND ITS AFRO-EURASIAN LEGACIES

What impact did Alexander the Great and his conquests have on world history?

Between 334 and 323 B.C.E., Alexander of Macedonia (MASS-uh-DUHN-ia), a student of classical Greek ideas, created a huge empire, spreading Greek culture over a wide area. Alexander's achievements established new networks of communication, and his legacy lived on for centuries in **Hellenism**, a widespread culture that combined western Asian (mainly Persian) and Greek (Hellenic) characteristics. During the Hellenistic Age, Greeks ruled over large parts of western Asia and North Africa, a domination that ended only with the rise of the Roman Empire and new Persia-based empires that continued to influence Middle Eastern history.

Hellenism A widespread culture flourishing between 359 and 100 B.C.E. that combined western Asian (mainly Persian) and Greek (Hellenic) characteristics.

Alexander the Great, World Empire, and Hellenism

The Greek disunity spawned by the Peloponnesian War opened the door to the armies of Macedonia to conquer a vast empire. The war had so weakened all the Greek cities that no one city could unite the peninsula. That task was left to the state of Macedonia, on the northern fringe of Greece. Led by King Philip II (382–336 B.C.E.), who developed a paid professional army and devised a more effective infantry phalanx, the Macedonian army conquered the Greek cities in 338 B.C.E. (see Chronology: Hellenistic Age, 359–100 B.C.E.). Two years later, on the eve of an expedition to Asia, Philip was assassinated. The hard-living, hard-drinking Philip had many enemies among Greeks, Persians, and Macedonian nobles.

Macedonian Conquest

Philip's twenty-year-old son, Alexander (r. 336–323 B.C.E.), a former student of Aristotle, became king. A fearless and resolute megalomaniac, his ambitions for conquest were evident as a child. Alexander reportedly lamented that, with such a multitude of other countries, it was a shame that he had not yet conquered even one of them. Later, he wrote to the Persian king that he was seeking vengeance on Persia for its invasions of Greece a century and half earlier. During his thirteen-year reign from 336 to his death in 323 B.C.E., Alexander, a brilliant military strategist and leader of men, used Macedonian, Greek, and mercenary troops to conquer the world from Greece east to western India, and from the Nile valley in the south to the Caucasus Mountains and the Black and Caspian Seas in the north. He employed ruthless tactics against enemies, sometimes destroying entire cities and slaughtering their inhabitants. The powerful Persian Empire was dismantled in three major battles between 334 and 331. The last Persian emperor, Darius III, was murdered by his own troops after Alexander had burned Persepolis and taken his place as Persian ruler. Alexander's forces then moved through Afghanistan, fighting difficult battles with the tough peoples of that mountainous region. The inhabitants destroyed their homes and farms rather than surrender. Many of Alexander's horses died and his grain ran out. Finally reaching the Indus Valley, the Macedonian wanted to move into the heart of India, but his exhausted and homesick troops refused to go farther. Alexander and his remaining troops made a difficult desert journey back to western Asia.

Rise of Alexander

Extraordinary for the times, Alexander saw himself as a new world ruler, a governor to all peoples. His empire incorporated most of the major ancient Afro-Eurasian societies, including Egypt, Crete, Mycenae, Phoenicia, Mesopotamia, and

CHRONOLOGY
Hellenistic Age, 359–100 B.C.E.

359–336 B.C.E. Reign of King Philip of Macedonia

338 B.C.E. Philip's conquest of Greek states

336–323 B.C.E. Reign of Alexander the Great

332 B.C.E. Invasion of Egypt

330 B.C.E. Occupation of Persia

327–325 B.C.E. Invasion of India

306–30 B.C.E. Ptolemaic Egypt

238 B.C.E. Parthian state in Persia

141 B.C.E. Parthians' conquest of Seleucids

Alexander Defeating Persians at Battle of Issus In this Roman copy of an earlier Greek painting, Alexander the Great is shown on his horse in the battle that brought defeat to Persian king Darius III in 333 B.C.E.

Scala/Art Resource, NY

the Indus Valley. The burning of Persepolis symbolized the end of one era of cultural exchange and the beginning of another.

Alexander initially organized his empire like the Persians. Although he was probably bisexual or homosexual and continued to have an intimate relationship with a male adviser, Alexander married a princess from Bactria (northern Afghanistan) and encouraged his soldiers to take Asian wives. He adopted the dress of a Persian ruler, wearing a purple and white cloak and a head ribbon previously worn by Persian royalty. After Alexander died in Babylon at age thirty-three, probably from a fever acquired after a night of heavy drinking, the conquered territories would retain a mixed Greek and Persian cultural flavor for centuries under the influence of Hellenism.

The Hellenistic Age and the Greek Heritage

The Hellenistic Age in the eastern Mediterranean and western Asia lasted several centuries. During this time, the Greek legacy was passed on in a form that fifth-century Greeks might have found hard to understand. Hellenistic culture placed less emphasis on individual freedom and the use of reason and more emphasis on the emotions. Some of Alexander's soldiers settled in Afghanistan and western India, and Greek ideas had an enduring influence on the local art. For centuries afterward people as far away as Ethiopia, Nubia, and western India studied the Greek language and borrowed Greek artistic styles.

Imperial Divisions

Alexander's empire soon fragmented. When asked to whom he left his empire, Alexander was alleged to have said: "to the strongest." Within twenty years, by the end of the fourth century B.C.E., Alexander's empire had been divided by his former generals, all Macedonians. A dynasty begun by Ptolemy (TAHL-uh-mee) controlled Egypt and the eastern Mediterranean coast; the family of Seleucus (suh-LOO-kuhs) controlled Persia, Mesopotamia, and Syria; and followers of Antigonus (an-TIG-uh-nuhs) controlled the Macedonian kingdom and northern Greece (see Map 7.3).

Parthian Empire

The dominance of the Hellenistic Seleucid kings, who governed Persia and Mesopotamia, was short-lived. They were challenged by the Parthians (PAHR-thee-uhnz), Indo-European pastoral nomads who migrated from Central Asia into eastern Persia in the third century B.C.E. In the second century B.C.E. the Parthians conquered large parts of Persia, Afghanistan, and Mesopotamia and seized the Seleucid capital on the Tigris River. Over the next few decades they expanded their empire into the Caucasus and then crushed an invading Roman army in 53 B.C.E. The Parthians adopted many Hellenistic traditions, making Greek the official state language. Gradually Persian influences grew stronger, and the Parthians became Zoroastrians. But frequent wars with the Romans, who replaced the other Hellenistic kingdoms, sapped their strength. In 224 C.E. the last Parthian ruler was defeated by a new Persian power, the Sassanians (suh-SAY-nee-uhnz), who ruled much of western Asia for the next four centuries, coming into frequent conflict with the Romans.

Hellenistic Cities and Economic Networks

City Life

Hellenistic cities differed from the polis in Golden Age Greece. Alexander had founded many cities named after him, the most famous of which was the still-surviving city of Alexandria on the Mediterranean coast of Egypt (see Map 7.3). Hellenistic cities were not politically independent

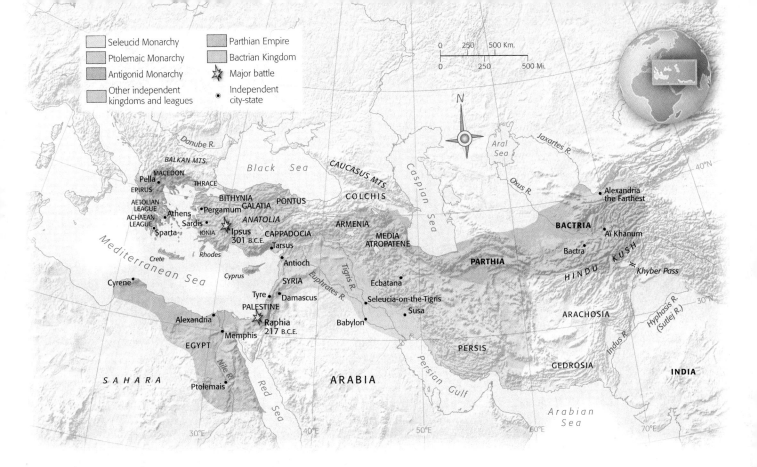

Map 7.3
The Hellenistic Kingdoms

The empire conquered by Alexander the Great was divided into rival Hellenistic kingdoms on his death in 323 B.C.E. By 140 B.C.E. the Parthians had conquered some of the eastern territories.

e Interactive Map

city-states but rather part of kingdoms, and their citizens did not enjoy much political participation. Wealthy aristocrats, professional soldiers, and bureaucrats ran the cities' governments. Although centers of Greek culture, the cities also existed in a predominantly non-Greek environment and so were influenced by local traditions. For example, the Ptolemaic dynasty in Egypt ruled with the pomp of the pharaohs. Hellenistic monarchs relied on Greeks, Persians, and others to govern, but they were vastly outnumbered by their Asian and African subjects.

The cities were no longer vibrant democratic communities, and the urban culture glorified hedonism. The upper classes enjoyed high living, and poets celebrated activities like horse racing, lovemaking, and drinking. A satirical Egyptian poem mocked a drunken and gluttonous harpist who showed up at weddings and festivals: "He disputes with the party-goers, shouting: 'I can't sing when I'm hungry, I can't hold my harp without my fill of wine!' And he drinks wine like two people and eats the meat of three."[17] Hellenistic cities were also more cosmopolitan and ethnically diverse than their earlier Greek counterparts. Alexandria, Egypt, for example, had large Egyptian, Greek, and Jewish populations and was a melting pot where many religions met and new ones sprouted up. It was here that the Zoroastrian holy books and the Hebrew Bible were translated into Greek. Many poets and scholars also moved to Alexandria. The Syrian Greek poet Meleager expressed the Hellenistic attitude: "Stranger, we live in the same motherland, the world."[18]

Alexander's conquests also linked the Mediterranean and western Asia in a vast trading network. Alexander used part of the great wealth he found in the Persian capital to build and repair roads and harbors. Greek colonists introduced or expanded money-based economies. Long-distance trade expanded rapidly as silk from China and sugar from India were traded for onions from Egypt, wood products from Macedonia, and olive oil from Athens. As caravans of vegetables and wine moved eastward, they crossed caravans of spices and other goods moving westward out of India, Arabia, and northeast Africa. This trans-Eurasian trading network remained strong long after the Hellenistic states had disappeared.

Trade Networks

Science, Religion, and Philosophy

<u>Scientific Thought</u>

Hellenistic thinkers maintained the classical Greek interest in scientific, religious, and philosophical questions. Scientists and mathematicians were rigorous in collecting and evaluating data, then offering hypotheses to explain mathematics problems, natural phenomena, and the workings of the universe. Alexandria in Egypt, with the largest library in the ancient world (700,000 papyrus scrolls), was the research center of the Hellenistic world, and Alexandrian thinkers and inventors anticipated the scientific, mathematical, and technological developments of the modern world. Here Euclid wrote his text on plane geometry, a book used for 2,000 years. Herophilus (hair-OFF-uh-lus) improved understanding of the brain and the nervous system. Aristarchus (AR-uh-STAHR-kuhs) proposed that the sun rather than the earth was the center of the universe, an idea most Europeans rejected for the next 1,000 years. The geographer Eratosthenes (ER-uh-TAHS-thuh-neez) calculated the circumference of the earth within about 200 miles. The inventor Hero devised a steam turbine, although it was treated only as an amazing toy. Other other major thinkers, such as the engineer and mathematician Archimedes, spent time in Alexandria (see Profile: Archimedes, a Hellenistic Mathematician and Engineer).

Greek philosophical and religious thought went in new directions. Some thinkers put less emphasis on reason to solve problems and more on resigning oneself to life in ways that often seemed fatalistic, taking life as it comes. The school of thought known as **Cynicism**, made famous by Ionia-born Diogenes (die-AHJ-uh-neez) (ca. 412–ca. 323 B.C.E.), emphasized living a simple life, shunning material things and all pretense. A famous legend of the meeting of Diogenes and a young Alexander conveys the flavor of Cynic philosophy. Diogenes asked Alexander about his greatest desire, and the Macedonian replied, "to subjugate Greece." Next he would subjugate Southwest Asia and then the world. And after that, Alexander said, "I will relax and enjoy myself," prompting Diogenes to reply: "Why not save yourself all the trouble by relaxing and enjoying yourself now?"[19]

Another Hellenistic philosophy, **Stoicism** (STOH-uh-siz-uhm), emphasized cooperating with and accepting nature, as well as the unity and equality of all people. Founded by Zeno (ZEE-noh) (ca. 334–ca. 265 B.C.E.) in Athens, Stoicism was a cosmopolitan and optimistic philosophy that accepted cultural diversity. Stoics also taught that the law of nature governing human affairs was common to all people and transcended the limited human laws created by kings. The Stoic emphasis on basic human equality survived over the centuries to influence modern lawmakers.

Hellenistic religion, like its major philosophies, offered people individual happiness and eternal life. The religion of Isis, originally an Egyptian fertility goddess, promised personal salvation. **Mithraism** (MITH-ruh-iz-uhm), a very popular cult that worshiped Mithra, a Persian deity associated with the sun, promised salvation, providing people were properly initiated into the community of the faith. Some historians believe that these Hellenistic religions, which shared features with Christianity, help explain the appeal of the teachings and life of Jesus several centuries later. Christianity borrowed from Mithraism the concept of purgatory as well as the winter solstice and birthday of Mithra (December 25). Hellenistic ideas also influenced the Romans (see Chapter 8) and remained important in western Asia and the eastern Mediterranean for many centuries.

Cynicism A Hellenistic philosophy, made famous by the philosopher Diogenes, that emphasized living a simple life, shunning material things and all pretense.

Stoicism A Hellenistic philosophy that emphasized the importance of cooperating with and accepting nature, as well as the unity and equality of all people.

Mithraism A Hellenistic cult that worshiped Mithra, a Persian deity associated with the sun; had some influence on Christianity.

SECTION SUMMARY

- After the Peloponnesian War, no Greek city was strong enough to unite the rest of the Greek peninsula.

- King Philip II of Macedonia conquered several Greek cities, and, after he died, his ambitious son Alexander the Great established an empire that ranged from Egypt to India.

- Alexander's legacy included a vast trading network that linked the Mediterranean, western Asia, and India, as well as the spread of Hellenism, a mix of Greek and Persian culture.

- Hellenism was marked by rigorous scientific inquiry, philosophies such as Cynicism and Stoicism that urged people to take life as it came, and mystical religions that had some influence on Christianity.

ARCHIMEDES, A HELLENISTIC MATHEMATICIAN AND ENGINEER

Archimedes was an outstanding mathematician, the greatest engineer of the Hellenistic world, and perhaps the most wide-ranging mind of his time. Some historians consider Archimedes and Aristotle the two greatest thinkers of Greek society. Archimedes was born around 287 B.C.E. to an influential family—his father was apparently an astronomer—in Syracuse, a Greek city on the island of Sicily. He studied in the intellectual capital of the Hellenistic world, Alexandria in Egypt, where inquisitive souls of financial means or, like Archimedes, political connections traveled widely and learned from varied cultures. In cosmopolitan Alexandria Archimedes became acquainted with famous scientists, including the astronomer Aristarchos. Eventually Archimedes returned to Syracuse, where he spent the rest of his days. We know little of his personal life and do not know whether he ever married.

In mathematics Archimedes introduced many new ideas, some of which added to Euclid's geometry. He offered a new system of numerals to handle large numbers; calculated the value of *pi*, the ratio of the circumference to the diameter of a circle, more accurately than anyone before him; and discovered the laws for finding the centers of gravity of plane figures. A book he wrote, lost for centuries but recently rediscovered, hints that 1,800 years before anyone else he was exploring calculus, the basis for much twenty-first-century technology. Archimedes also studied astronomy and built an instrument for measuring the movements of the sun, moon, and planets. This early clock may have inspired later timekeeping inventions.

Archimedes is equally well known for his engineering innovations. His later biographer, the Greek writer Plutarch, claimed that, like Plato, Archimedes disdained practical applications. Certainly he wrote much less about his applied than his theoretical studies. Nonetheless, his contributions were immense. He discovered "Archimedes' law," still tested in high school classrooms, which states that a body wholly or partly immersed in a fluid loses weight equal to the weight of the fluid displaced. This insight apparently came to him while in the public baths, as he watched water flow over the side as he entered the pool. According to Plutarch, he leaped from the pool and ran home naked, crying aloud: "Eureka!" ("I have found it!"). (The public nudity would not have astonished Greeks, who were used to seeing people in public without their clothes.) With such discoveries, Archimedes founded the science of hydrostatics, which involves balance and weights.

Archimedes also made other practical contributions. For instance, he supervised construction of the world's first three-masted ship, a huge combination of warship, yacht, and cargo ship that had horse stalls, fish tanks, cargo holds for wheat, and luxurious cabins. He also worked out the law of the lever and the theory of mechanical advantage, using his knowledge to launch his ship with the use of compound pulleys. He also solved a major problem of the time in irrigation and mining by discovering how to move great volumes of water up a steep incline by using a large pipe with a tightly fitted screw.

With Roman power on the rise, Archimedes was put in charge of Syracuse defenses. For a while Roman attackers were repulsed by his ingenious weapons, including missiles dropped from cranes that swung out over the fortified walls, and darts and balls delivered by catapults. Some legends, which many historians doubt, credit him with experimenting with mirrors to direct the sun's rays at enemy ships to set them on fire.

In 212 the Romans captured Syracuse and killed the aged Archimedes—according to one legend, as the famously absent-minded scientist was working on geometrical diagrams. This Roman triumph helped end the Hellenistic Age and begin the Roman Age in the central Mediterranean. The engineering and mathematical discoveries of Archimedes now became part of Roman and later world traditions.

THINKING ABOUT THE PROFILE

1. How did Archimedes' career reflect the Hellenistic Age?
2. Why was Archimedes considered one of the major classical engineers and mathematicians?

The Archimedes Palimpsest In 1889 scholars discovered a crumbling, long-lost parchment containing a copy of a major work by Archimedes, the treatise called "On Floating Bodies." This work, on buoyancy, suggests that he was centuries ahead of the rest of the world in his thinking on mathematics and physics, even suggesting ideas that did not reappear until the past several centuries.

CHAPTER SUMMARY

The Greeks and Persians dominated the Mediterranean and western Asia during the early Classical Era, influencing many other peoples in the region. The Persians built a huge multiethnic empire. Their emphasis on governing through mutual tolerance, a skillful bureaucracy, and good roads influenced the Macedonian Alexander the Great and his successors, as well as the Roman and the Muslim rulers of West Asia after them. Persian religious ideas, including Zoroastrianism, also spread to neighboring peoples such as the Hebrews. The Greeks reached their golden age during the fifth century. The Athenians practiced democracy, however imperfectly, in a society where there were many slaves and where women had few legal rights. Democracy developed as citizens demanded a voice in the decisions that ordered them to war. The classical Greeks were also pioneers in philosophy and science. Influenced by the increasing emphasis on reason, Greek thinkers like Socrates, Plato, and especially Aristotle established a foundation for critical thinking and natural science. Their legacy influenced people in both the Middle East and Europe.

The Greeks and Persians were also fierce rivals for regional power, fighting a series of destructive wars but also exchanging trade goods and ideas. The eastern Mediterranean zone fostered cultural mixing, maritime commerce, and the sharing of knowledge and products. Alexander the Great's conquests made Greek language and culture part of the eastern Mediterranean world for several centuries after his death. The Hellenistic world mixed Greek arts and philosophy with many Persian or western Asian ideas of government. The later Roman, Christian, and then Muslim rulers in these areas retained some of this Greco-Persian heritage.

KEY TERMS

Achaemenid	oligarchy	Delian League	Stoicism
satrap	tyrant	Peloponnesian War	Mithraism
Zoroastrianism	Sophists	trade diaspora	
Ahura Mazda	Socratic Method	Hellenism	
polis	metaphysics	Cynicism	

EBOOK AND WEBSITE RESOURCES

e PRIMARY SOURCE
Aristotle on Politics

e INTERACTIVE MAPS
Map 7.1 The Persian Empire, ca. 500 B.C.E.
Map 7.2 Classical Greece, ca. 450 B.C.E.
Map 7.3 The Hellenistic Kingdoms

LINKS

Ancient/Classical History (http://ancienthistory.about .com/library). Essays and timelines for many ancient civilizations and societies.

Diotima: Women and Gender in the Ancient World (http:// www.stoa.org/diotima/). Contains excellent materials on gender and women in the early Mediterranean world.

Exploring Ancient World Cultures (http://eawc.evansville.edu/). Excellent site run by Evansville University, with essays and links on the ancient Near East and Europe.

Internet Ancient History Sourcebook (http://www.fordham .edu/halsall/ancient/asbook.html). Exceptionally rich collection of links and primary source readings.

Livius: Articles on Ancient History (http://www.livius. org). Very useful site with many short essays on the Greeks, Persians, Parthians, Romans, and other ancient and classical societies.

Plus flashcards, practice quizzes, and more. Go to:
www.cengage.com/history/lockard/globalsocnet2e

SUGGESTED READING

Allen, Lindsay. *The Persian Empire.* Chicago: University of Chicago Press, 2005. A wonderfully illustrated recent survey of the classical Persians.

Armstrong, Karen. *The Great Transformation: The Beginning of Our Religious Traditions.* New York: Knopf, 2006. Good coverage of Greek and Persian religious development.

Briant, Pierre. *From Cyrus to Alexander: A History of the Persian Empire.* New York: Eisenbraun, 2001. An excellent and up-to-date survey.

Bridenthal, Renate, et al. *Becoming Visible: Women in European History,* 3rd ed. Boston: Houghton Mifflin, 1998. Contains excellent chapters on ancient and classical societies.

Brosius, Maria. *Women in Ancient Persia, 559–331 B.C.* New York: Oxford University Press, 1996. Examines women and their roles, providing a detailed picture of their lives.

Casson, Lionel. *The Ancient Mariners: Seafarers and Sea Fighters of the Mediterranean in Ancient Times,* 2nd ed. Princeton: Princeton University Press, 1991. A pathbreaking study of maritime trade, migration, and warfare.

Cook, J. M. *Persian Empire.* New York: Schocken, 1987. A useful scholarly survey, especially strong on political history.

Faceliere, Robert. *Daily Life in Greece at the Time of Pericles.* London: Phoenix, 2002. A detailed examination of various aspects of life in classical Athens.

Fox, Robin Lane. *Alexander the Great.* New York: Penguin, 2004. Updated edition of a readable introduction.

Levi, Peter. *The Greek World.* Oxford: Stonehenge, 1992. A comprehensive, well-illustrated, and readable survey.

Lloyd, G. E. R. *The Ambitions of Curiosity: Understanding the World in Ancient Greece and China.* New York: Cambridge University Press, 2002. An interesting scholarly study of the achievements and limitations of scientific inquiry in these two societies.

Martin, Thomas R. *Ancient Greece from Prehistoric to Hellenistic Times.* New Haven, CT: Yale University Press, 1996. A clear survey of Greek history, written for the general reader.

Pomeroy, Sarah B., et al. *Ancient Greece: A Political, Social, and Cultural History,* 2nd ed. New York: Oxford University Press, 2007. An excellent and readable overview.

Pomeroy, Sarah B. *Goddesses, Whores, Wives and Slaves: Women in Classical Antiquity.* New York: Schocken, 1995. An excellent study of women's lives in classical Greece and Rome.

Samons, Loren J., ed. *Athenian Democracy and Imperialism.* Boston: Houghton Mifflin, 1988. A valuable collection of writings on an important theme.

Vernant, Jean-Pierre, ed. *The Greeks,* translated by Charles Lambert and Teresa Lavender Fagan. Chicago: University of Chicago Press, 1995. A collection of essays interpreting Greek political, economic, social, and religious life.

Wood, Michael. *In the Footprints of Alexander the Great: A Journey from Greece to Asia.* Berkeley: University of California Press, 1997. A fascinating recreation of Alexander the Great's route to, and experiences reaching, India.

EMPIRES, NETWORKS, AND THE REMAKING OF EUROPE, NORTH AFRICA, AND WESTERN ASIA, 500 B.C.E.–600 C.E.

Erich Lessing/Art Resource, NY

Santa Sophia
The magnificent Santa Sophia Church in Constantinople, rebuilt during the reign of the emperor Justinian in the sixth century C.E., had interior walls covered in gold mosaics that glowed from reflected sunlight. This mosaic from the Zoe panel shows Jesus holding a Bible.

*R*emember, Roman, that it is for you to rule the nations. This shall be your task: to impose the ways of peace, to spare the vanquished and to tame the proud by war.

—Roman poet Virgil[1]

Around 320 B.C.E. Pytheas (PITH-ee-us), a scientist from the Greek colony of Massalia (ma-SAL-ya), today's city of Marseilles (mahr-SAY) on the Mediterranean coast of France, wrote a book about his remarkable travels in Europe. According to his account, the brave and curious Pytheas reached the western coast of France, from where he arranged to sail on a boat owned by local Celtic (KELL-tik) people to southwest England. He continued north through the Irish Sea and then ventured down the east coast of Britain before exploring the North Sea coast as far as Denmark. Some of his contemporaries called him a liar. Today many scholars credit Pytheas for providing Mediterranean societies with their first eyewitness account of the remote northern coast and its mysterious peoples, whom they considered dangerous barbarians.

The western Mediterranean where Pytheas lived was crisscrossed by trade networks: Greeks, Etruscans (ee-TRUHS-kuhns), Carthaginians (kar-thuh-JIN-ee-uhns), and the upstart Romans competed for economic resources and political power. These societies were all part of an interdependent world incorporating southern Europe, North Africa, and western Asia, where commodities flowed and ideas were exchanged. Three hundred years after Pytheas's voyage, Europe was much more closely linked, thanks largely to a people who in Pytheas's time were an ambitious but still minor power, the Romans.

The Roman success in creating a large empire and rich society, celebrated in the opening quote by the Roman poet Virgil, had a considerable impact on world history. Roman expansion reshaped much of Europe, marginalizing or incorporating the northern peoples while also transforming North African and western Asian politics. When the Roman Empire finally ended after half a millennium, it left several legacies for later European, western Asian, and North African societies. The Romans passed on to later Europeans legal and governmental concepts, some of which derived from the Greeks. Also during Roman times, Christianity emerged, forming the cultural underpinning of a post-Roman European society while also spreading in Asia and Africa.

A version of the Roman Empire in the eastern Mediterranean, Greek-speaking Byzantium (buh-ZANT-ee-uhm), served as a transcontinental trade center and a buffer between western Europe and West Asian states, including a revived Persian Empire. Byzantine-Persian struggles set the stage for the rise of another society, the Arabs.

FOCUS QUESTIONS

1. **What were the main political and social features of the Roman Republic?**
2. **How did the Romans maintain their large empire?**
3. **How did Christianity develop and expand?**
4. **How did the Byzantine and Sassanian Empires reinvigorate the eastern Mediterranean world?**

e Visit the website and eBook for additional study materials and interactive tools:
www.cengage.com/history/lockard/globalsocnet2e

ETRUSCANS, CARTHAGE, EGYPT, AND THE ROMAN REPUBLIC

▌What were the main political and social features of the Roman Republic?

By 300 B.C.E. the Mediterranean world was politically and culturally diverse, divided between Etruscans, Carthage, Greek city-states, various Hellenistic kingdoms including Egypt, and the rising Romans, who eventually dominated the entire region. The Romans learned much from the older Etruscan society that they eventually absorbed, and they were influenced by Greek ideas in building their republic. Eventually Rome conquered peoples in southern Europe and then beyond, establishing the framework of a huge empire.

European Geography, the Etruscans, and Early Rome

Geographical Foundations

Geography and climate were influential in shaping western Mediterranean society. The geological spine of Italy is the Apennine mountain range running down the eastern side of the narrow peninsula, to the west and north of which spread rich agricultural plains. This fertile land and mild climate fostered intensive agriculture. The Romans exported wine and olive oil while importing grain from the nearby islands of Sicily and Sardinia (sahr-DIN-ee-uh) and from northern Africa. In contrast to Greece, agricultural success and the ease of contact in the peninsula encouraged large states. Italy's inhabitants also were pressed to defend themselves against northern peoples attracted to the warmer lands of the south. These Indo-European Celtic and Germanic peoples living in the forested hills and plains of western and northern Europe made frequent invasions of Italy using passes through the Alps, a formidable complex of mountains.

As the Romans expanded beyond Italy, they drew upon the natural resources of the larger Mediterranean world (see Map 8.1) and beyond. Spain offered rich supplies of silver, copper, and tin. Egypt provided wheat. Beginning about 200 B.C.E., overland trade routes connected the Mediterranean with China along the famous Silk Road, named after the most important product acquired from East Asia, which was bartered in return for gold, silver, precious stones, and some textile products from the west.

The Etruscans

The Romans were greatly influenced by the Etruscans, who founded a dozen or so city-states in central and northern Italy by the eighth century B.C.E. The Etruscans were chariot warriors and also sailors who traded with the western Mediterranean islands and Spain. Eventually they dominated more of Italy and the nearby island of Corsica. They also had considerable contact and sometimes conflict with nearby Greek settlements. They adopted the Greek alphabet and myths, and Greek craftsmen worked in some Etruscan cities.

The Etruscan language is only partially understood, and none of their major literature survives. Their huge cemeteries with well-decorated tombs show that they were skilled artists and artisans, and their cities were well planned and linked together by a good road system. Each city apparently had its own king. The Etruscans were also known for working iron ore into excellent iron axes, sickles, and tools. Their rigid social system included slavery, although Etruscan women apparently had a high social status, conversing with men in public, driving their own chariots, owning real estate, and sometimes running businesses like pottery workshops.

Initially the relationship between the Romans and the Etruscans was peaceful. A small city-state in central Italy just south of Etruscan territory, Rome was established in the eighth century B.C.E. by Indo-European pastoralists known as the Latins (see Chronology: The Roman Republic, 753–58 B.C.E.). Built on seven hills along the Tiber River, Rome was originally founded as a base for trade with the Etruscans. However, the Etruscans soon dominated Rome. The Romans adopted the twenty-six-character alphabet that the Etruscans had themselves borrowed from the Greeks, as well as the Greek-inspired Etruscan phalanx infantry formation. Skilled Etruscan engineers taught the Romans to make the weight-bearing semicircular arch, which Romans used to construct city walls, aqueducts to carry water, and doorways. Although Etruscan kings won support by building new public buildings, at the end of the sixth century B.C.E. the last Etruscan king was driven out for his brutality, and Rome became independent. Later the Romans conquered and assimilated the Etruscans.

CHRONOLOGY The Roman Republic, 753–58 B.C.E.

753 B.C.E. Founding of Rome (traditional date)

ca. 616–509 B.C.E. Etruscan kings rule over Rome

509 B.C.E. Beginning of Roman Republic

265 B.C.E. Roman control of southern Italy

264–241 B.C.E. First Punic (Roman-Carthaginian) War

218–201 B.C.E. Second Punic War

149–146 B.C.E. Third Punic War

113–105 B.C.E. First German-Roman conflicts

60–58 B.C.E. Julius Caesar completes conquest from Rhine to Atlantic

CHRONOLOGY

	Roman Republic	Roman Empire	Byzantium and Western Asia
500 B.C.E.	**509** B.C.E. Roman Republic		
300 B.C.E.	**264–146** B.C.E. Punic Wars		
100 B.C.E.		**31** B.C.E.–**180** C.E. *Pax Romana* **7–6** B.C.E.–**30** C.E. Life of Jesus	
1 C.E.			**240–272** C.E. Founding of Sassanian Empire
300 C.E.		**395** C.E. Division of eastern and western empires	**330** C.E. Founding of Constantinople
500 C.E.		**476** C.E. Official end of western Roman Empire	**527–565** C.E. Reign of Justinian

The Roman Republic and Expansion

Using political ideas borrowed from the Greeks, the Romans built a system of self-government for their city-state. In 509 B.C.E. they established a republic, a state in which supreme power is held by the people or their elected representatives. Over the next three centuries, the Romans developed a system of representative government that introduced enduring political ideas. Many modern English words taken from Latin—such as *senate, citizenship, suffrage* (the right to vote), *dictator* (a man given full power), *plebiscite* (PLEB-i-site) (a special vote by citizens on a political issue), and even *republic*—suggest the influence of the Romans on modern political life.

Initially, power rested entirely with the aristocratic upper class, or **patricians** (puh-TRISH-uhnz). Patricians controlled the Senate, a body that had previously advised the kings and later dominated foreign affairs, the army, and the legislative body made up of soldiers, the **Centuriate Assembly**. The Senate, composed of three hundred former government officials, claimed the right to ratify resolutions of the Centuriate Assembly before they became law. As the Republic developed, the Centuriate Assembly elected two men each year to serve as **consuls**, who had executive power.

The patricians were heavily outnumbered by the commoners, or **plebeians** (pli-BEE-uhnz). As wealth flowed into Rome as a result of military expansion in the peninsula and then beyond, the plebeian soldiers wanted to share in this wealth. Long years of army service had taken them away from their farms and left them in debt, and they demanded a greater political voice and economic equality. A Roman historian reported the bitterness of a plebeian leader toward those who opposed reform: "[You] realize vividly the depth of the contempt in which you are held by the aristocracy. They would rob you of the very light you see by; they grudge you the air you breathe, the words you speak."[2] Political power, the plebeians believed, would allow them to pass laws that distributed the state's wealth more fairly.

Gradually social and political rights expanded. In 494 B.C.E. the plebeians selected two of their number, called **tribunes**, to represent their interests in the Centuriate Assembly, much as the consuls represented patrician interests. By 471 a separate Plebeian Assembly was established to elect tribunes and to conduct votes of the plebeian class, called plebiscites. Plebeians later gained the right to share with the patricians lands that the Roman state had won in war. Full equality for plebeians was won by 267 B.C.E., when their assembly became the principal lawmaking body of the state.

In the fourth century, the Roman Republic turned to imperialism, the control or domination by one state over another, as a way of resolving some of its problems. A major defeat at the hands of the Gauls (gawlz), a Celtic people who plundered Rome in 390 B.C.E., shocked Roman leaders, who decided to expand their territory to keep their frontiers safely distant from the city of Rome. Thus motivated, the Romans successfully fought wars with other Italian city-states. At the end of each conflict, they often granted either full or limited Roman citizenship to the inhabitants of the defeated cities. Being a Roman citizen thus became a great honor entitling a person to special legal treatment, an honor that fathers were proud to pass on to their sons. By wisely treating former enemies fairly, the Romans spread their power without encouraging revolts and ensured that more men would join their army.

patricians The aristocratic upper class who controlled the Roman Senate.

Centuriate Assembly A Roman legislative body made up of soldiers.

consuls Two patrician men, elected by the Centuriate Assembly each year, who had executive power in the Roman Republic.

plebeians The commoner class in Rome.

tribunes Roman men elected to represent plebeian interests in the Centuriate Assembly.

Imperialism

Map 8.1
Italy and the Western Mediterranean, 600–200 b.c.e.
During the early Classical Era the Etruscan cities in the north and the Greek city-states in the south held political power in Italy. Carthage held a similar status in northeast Africa. Eventually the Latins, from their base in Rome, became the dominant political force in the entire region.

 **Interactive Map**

Carthage, Egypt, and Regional Trade

The Carthaginians

After first conquering the Etruscan cities, weakened by conflicts with the Gauls, the Romans were then able to conquer the Greek cities in southern Italy and Sicily in 265 b.c.e. Across the sea from Sicily, however, the Romans encountered their greatest enemy, the Carthaginians. Both

The Roman Forum
The Forum, located amidst various religious and governmental buildings, was the center of Roman political life.

Carthage and Egypt played key roles in Mediterranean trade. The city-state of Carthage (KAHR-thij) was originally a Phoenician colony founded in 814 B.C.E. on the North African coast near where the city of Tunis is today. The other great power on the southern shores of the Mediterranean was Egypt, where the Hellenistic Greek Ptolemaic (taw-luh-MAY-ik) dynasty had fostered great prosperity for over a century.

With a fine harbor and a strategic position, Carthage grew into the wealthiest Phoenician outpost, described by a Greek from Sicily as having "gardens and orchards of all kinds, no end of country houses built luxuriously, land cultivated partly as vineyards and partly as olive groves, fruit trees, herds of cattle and flocks of sheep."[3] However, the autocratic city government experienced political instability as rival leaders vied for power, and differences between the prosperous Phoenician settlers and the native Berbers created tensions. The Carthaginians also fought frequent wars with their commercial rivals, the Greeks.

The Carthaginians used their maritime skills to develop trade networks. Around 425 B.C.E. an admiral, Hanno, led a naval expedition through the Strait of Gibraltar and down the coast of West Africa, seeking markets. He founded trading posts along Morocco's coast and sailed at least as far as the Senegal River. Other Carthaginian expeditions apparently reached the British Isles and perhaps several of the Atlantic islands off the northwest African coast. By the third century B.C.E. the Carthaginians had created an empire along the southern and western shores of the Mediterranean Sea, controlling a large part of Spain, much of the North African coast, and the islands of Corsica and Sardinia. In 264 B.C.E. they moved troops to Sicily to aid several Greek cities allied with them against Rome.

In Egypt, Ptolemaic power was becoming more tenuous by the second century B.C.E. The Ptolemies had increased agricultural and crafts production, in part by demanding more work from Egyptians. As in earlier times, Egypt remained a major supplier of wheat to other Mediterranean societies. It also exported papyrus, the preferred medium for scientific, philosophical, and literary texts throughout the region; textiles; pottery; and metal objects. Greeks and Phoenicians owned some of the ships that carried these goods to foreign ports. Despite the economic growth, many Egyptians tired of foreign occupation, hardship, and high taxes, and several rebellions threatened the government. In 180 B.C.E. Cleopatra I became sole ruler, the first in a long chain of assertive queens. During this time Egyptian rulers sought alliances with rising Rome to maintain their own independence. In 47 B.C.E., an ambitious eighteen-year-old became ruler as Queen Cleopatra VII, just as years of poor harvests and official corruption fostered more unrest. Her skills enabled the unstable country to maintain domestic peace and deflect Rome for nearly two decades.

Ptolemaic Egypt

The Punic Wars and Afro-Eurasian Empire

The result of Roman expansion southward was three Punic (PYOO-nik) Wars, which pitted the two major powers and bitter rivals, Rome and Carthage, against each other. The first Punic War

Carthage-Rome Conflict

(264–241 B.C.E.) resulted in several Roman naval expeditions against Carthage and finally ended with Roman occupation of Sicily, Corsica, and Sardinia. In the second conflict (218–201), the brilliant Carthaginian general Hannibal (247–182 B.C.E.) led his troops through Spain and France to invade Italy across the Alps, defeating every Roman army sent against them. Modern people may have images in their mind, probably accurate, of war elephants used by Hannibal's army lumbering through the rugged mountains. The Carthaginians had carefully trained these elephants to charge and possibly terrify the enemy on the battlefield. But the elephants and Hannibal's troops were not used to the snow and ice of the mountains, and they perished by the thousands.

Forming the Roman Empire

The arrival and early military success of Hannibal's force alarmed the Romans. With his supply lines overstretched, however, Hannibal could not conquer the Italian cities. Eventually the Romans drove him out and defeated Carthage, which had to surrender all its overseas possessions, including Spain. In the final Punic War (149–146), Romans laid siege to Carthage city and destroyed it, spreading salt on the fields around the city to make it difficult to plant crops there in the future. Northwest Africa became a Roman province, a source of copper, grain, and West African gold.

Roman victory encouraged additional Roman imperial expansion, aimed either at punishing Carthage's allies or at restoring stability. Rome ended Macedonian control of the Greek cities in 197 B.C.E. and in 146 B.C.E. made Greece and Macedonia into a Roman province. Few could resist the Roman infantrymen, armed with swords and rectangular shields, or the armor-clad Roman archers, who rode in carts carrying large crossbows, among the era's most feared weapons. By the middle of the first century B.C.E. the Romans had built an empire that commanded the entire Mediterranean and its vast resources, binding together Europe, western Asia, and North Africa. The empire included most of Anatolia, Syria, and Palestine, as well as much territory in northern and western Europe. The Ptolemies still controlled Egypt, but they were careful to not offend the Romans. The Romans absorbed much of the Hellenistic east, with its rich web of international commerce centered on several hubs, including Alexandria in Egypt, which distributed goods from as far away as India and East Africa.

The Decline of the Republic

But imperial success also led to major changes in Roman society. The Roman historian Tacitus (TASS-uh-tuhs) observed how the growth of empire increased the love of power: "It was easy to maintain equality when Rome was weak. World-wide conquest and the destruction of all rival[s] opened the way to the secure enjoyment of wealth and an overriding appetite for it."[4] Imperial expansion provoked various crises that reshaped Roman politics and undermined the Republic, turning the representative institutions into window-dressing. Warfare gave excessive power to military leaders, weakening the influence of the Senate, and growing Roman wealth increased the gap between the very rich and desperately poor. As the empire expanded, upper-class families bought farmland from peasants who had become impoverished by long service in the army. Many farmers then moved to the city of Rome, where the government supported hundreds of thousands of displaced people to maintain their loyalty. With fewer farmers willing to serve in the army, the tribune Tiberius Graccus (tie-BIR-ee-uhs GRAK-uhs) proposed turning over public land to farmers who agreed to serve in the Roman legions when needed. When the poor gathered in Rome to support this measure, some wealthy Romans panicked and spurred a mob to club Tiberius and many of his followers to death, demonstrating both the determination of the wealthy not to give up power and the mobilization of many poor people to support one leader or another. The Senate was unable to control the military leaders.

The changing nature of military power also undermined democracy. In 107 B.C.E., the victorious general Gaius Marius (GAY-uhs MER-ee-uhs) was elected consul for five straight years, violating a law that prohibited a person from holding the office more than one year. Marius brought his military veterans to pressure the senators to vote for a law that gave the veterans public land. Skillful military leaders thereafter used their armies to enhance their political power and outmaneuver civilian leaders and the Senate, resulting in civil and foreign wars. Between 78 and 31 B.C.E., ambitious military leaders expanded Roman territory in Europe and Asia, including Syria and Palestine, while finally destroying republican institutions within Rome itself.

Military Power and Politics

The young Julius Caesar proved the most ambitious. He completed the conquest of Europe from the Rhine River west to the Atlantic and sent the first Roman forces into Britain, after which he won a civil war against former allies. Caesar also weakened the Senate by enlarging it to nine hundred men, thus making it too large to be an effective governing body. Finally, in 44 B.C.E. he had himself declared "perpetual dictator" (see Chronology: The Roman Empire and Its Successors, 60 B.C.E.–526 C.E.). This act led to his assassination, made famous centuries later in the play *Julius Caesar* by the English author William Shakespeare.

Caesar's death led to civil war, the end of any pretence of democracy, and the conquest of Egypt. Caesar's adopted son, Octavian (ok-TAY-vee-uhn), fought Mark Antony, a general who had fallen in love with the Egyptian ruler Cleopatra. A remarkable personality who had borne a son by Julius Caesar, Cleopatra was described by a Greek historian as someone whose "presence was irresistible; the attraction of her person, the charm of her conversation, was something bewitching. She could pass from one language to another."[5] The turmoil and the Republic itself ended when Octavian defeated Antony and Cleopatra at the naval Battle of Actium (AK-tee-uhm), in Greece, in 31 B.C.E. Antony and Cleopatra committed suicide and their armies surrendered to Octavian, giving Rome control of Egypt. The Romans then placed Egypt under a tighter grip than most of their colonies, imposing heavy taxes and encouraging more wheat production to feed the city of Rome.

Civil War

SECTION SUMMARY

- The agricultural plenty of Italy allowed for the development of larger states than had been possible in Greece, and the Mediterranean Sea allowed for Roman expansion.

- The Etruscans, a non-Indo-European people most likely from western Asia, formed the first urban society in Italy; they influenced and were eventually conquered by the Romans.

- Rome formed a republic, in which citizens rule the state; initially upper-class patricians dominated, but over time the plebeians attained increasing amounts of power.

- After a major defeat by the Gauls, the Romans decided that the key to safety was to expand their territory so their frontiers would be safely distant from Rome.

- Rome defeated Carthage, its primary rival, in the Punic Wars and then conquered an empire.

- With the shift from Roman Republic to empire, military leaders gained power, farmers grew impoverished, and the people had less voice in government.

THE RISE AND DECLINE OF IMPERIAL ROME

How did the Romans maintain their large empire?

Athenians had pondered whether empire and democracy were compatible, and eventually they proved incompatible. Likewise, in Rome the rise of empire, with its clash of personal ambitions and greed created by the wealth gained through conquest, had important consequences. The expanding empire led to the replacement of the Republic with a more autocratic and arrogant imperial system. This period of imperial rule saw the full development of Roman culture and of those elements of the Roman heritage, such as law, that formed a significant legacy to European society. The Roman Empire lasted in the west for about five hundred years. Its decline began when a long period of internal and external disorder challenged the *Pax Romana*. Some of this decline resulted from various population movements that put pressure on the frontiers of the empire, leading to imperial division and then collapse.

Augustus and the *Pax Romana*

Rome and its empire were now ruled by emperors (*caesarsi*) who controlled the military and much of the government bureaucracy. This trend was begun by Octavian (63 B.C.E.–14 C.E.), who called himself Augustus, a Latin term meaning "majestic, inspiring awe." His long reign (r. 31 B.C.E.–14 C.E.) gave Augustus time to establish and consolidate a system in which the Senate appointed governors to the peaceful provinces while he governed provinces where troops were

Imperial Government

stationed. Augustus enacted or vetoed legislation and called the Senate into session. The writer Juvenal (JOO-vuhn-uhl) deplored the consequences of the lost popular voice and its replacement by entertainments to divert public attention: "The people that once bestowed commands now meddles no more and longs eagerly for just two things: bread and circuses."[6]

Pax Romana The period of peace and prosperity in Roman history from the reign of Augustus through that of Emperor Marcus Aurelius in 180 C.E.

The period in Roman history from Augustus through the reign of Emperor Marcus Aurelius (aw-REE-lee-uhs) in 180 C.E. is known as the **Pax Romana** ("Roman Peace"). For the first and last time, the entire Mediterranean world was controlled by one power and remained at peace for two centuries (see Map 8.2). Some historians refer to the Mediterranean Sea in those centuries as a "Roman lake." During this time Rome experienced few challenges from the Germanic peoples, who mostly remained east of the Rhine and north of the Danube Rivers. In western Asia the Romans faced only a weak Parthian kingdom in Persia and Mesopotamia. Whether in London or Paris, Vienna or Barcelona—all cities founded by the Romans—people lived under the same laws.

Peace and prosperity encouraged trade and population growth. Great fleets of ships moved mountains of goods around the Mediterranean Sea. Trade also flourished along the Silk Road between China and Rome through Central and western Asia. Rome governed a huge population, estimated at 54 million in the first century C.E., including 6 million in Italy. Rome may have been the world's largest city, with a half million to 1 million inhabitants. In this diverse empire the Roman ideal, like that of the Hellenistic Greeks, was cosmopolitan. Hence, Emperor Marcus Aurelius (r. 161–180 C.E.) wrote: "Rome is my city and country, but as a man, I am a citizen of the world."[7] Non-Romans were incorporated into the ruling class, and half of the Roman Senate were non-Italians. Men of wealth and military skill, whatever their ethnic background, could rise to the highest levels in the army and government. Many people migrated to Rome, bringing with them cultural forms such as musical instruments and dances. Thus the empire slowly changed into a multinational state that fostered diversity within unity. It was no accident that the phrase chosen as the slogan of the new United States in the eighteenth century C.E., *e pluribus unum* (EE PLUR-uh-buhs OO-nuhm), "one from many," is written in Latin.

Civic Virtue and Law

Roman society owed much to the Greeks' political, ethical, and philosophical ideas. But the Romans also made something distinctive from this Greek legacy, developing a practical way of looking at the world. In particular, the Romans extended the meaning of some of the classic Greek ideas, such as citizenship, and developed a concept of civic virtue, an idea close to what people today call public duty. Codified laws underpinned the Roman system and encouraged public responsibility. Several principles of Roman law have survived the centuries to become an accepted part of the laws of most modern nations and modern international law. For example, the Romans believed that all people, regardless of wealth or position, were equal before the law. They promoted individual responsibility; a family could not be held responsible for one member's misdeeds. Roman jurists also said that the burden of proof in a trial should rest with the person making the charge, not with the defendant.

The Roman concept of law was influenced by the Greek Stoic belief in eternal truths that transcended particular cultures. Leading Roman Stoics included the philosopher Seneca (4 B.C.E.–65 C.E.), the great Roman lawyer and essayist Cicero (106–43 B.C.E.), and the second-century emperor Marcus Aurelius (uh-REAL-yus), famous for his humanity and justice. These thinkers believed that all people were alike in their use of reason to determine that certain things were right and others wrong. Stoics promoted tolerance, moderation, and acceptance of life's travails. Because of such beliefs, the Romans generally allowed conquered peoples to govern themselves and keep their own customs and leaders so long as they paid their taxes and did not revolt.

Religion and Society

Roman religion and society, like government, changed over the centuries. Religion comprised a pantheon of gods and goddesses who were worshiped for practical reasons, such as to ensure good fortune. The Romans honored each god or goddess and expected favorable results. For example, specific gods or goddesses were associated with agricultural tasks, and there was even a goddess for thieves and one for door hinges. Roman religion was an integral part of civic life, there being no "separation of church and state" in Roman society. Priests were state officials who performed public sacrifices to please the gods and ceremonies promoting the welfare of the state. Reflecting these practical goals, Caesar Augustus commissioned the building in Rome of the *Ara Pacis,* or Altar of Peace, a sacrificial marble altar to celebrate the end of the wars of conquest in Gaul and Spain and, hopefully, launch a long era of peace. Not wishing to offend any divinity who might help them, the Romans also adopted the gods and goddesses of other

Gods and Godesses

Map 8.2
The Roman Empire, ca. 120 C.E.

The Romans gradually expanded until, by 120 C.E., they controlled a huge empire stretching from Britain and Spain in the west through southern and central Europe and North Africa to Egypt, Anatolia, and the lands along the eastern Mediterranean coast.

Legend:
- Roman Empire by death of Augustus, 14 C.E.
- Territory added by death of Hadrian, 138 C.E.
- Territory gained and lost, with dates held
- Parthian Empire, ca. 200 C.E.
- ★ Major battle

e Interactive Map

ATLANTIC OCEAN

North Sea

Baltic Sea

CALEDONIA (85–105 C.E.)

Hadrian's Wall 122 C.E.

Eburacum (York)

BRITAIN

Camulodunum (Colchester)
Londinium (London)

GERMANIA (4–9 C.E.)

LOWER GERMANY

Colonia Claudia Agrippinensis (Cologne)

Moguntiacum (Mainz)

UPPER GERMANY

BELGICA

Alesia 52 B.C.E.

Elbe R.

Rhine R.

RAETIA

ALPS

CISALPINE GAUL

Mediolanum (Milan)

Po R.

NORICUM

Vindobona (Vienna)

Aquincum (Budapest)

DACIA (107–272 C.E.)

Danube R.

PANNONIA

Singidunum (Belgrade)

DALMATIA

MOESIA

Vistula R.

Dnieper R.

Don R.

Volga R.

Aral Sea

Caspian Sea

BOSPORAN KINGDOM

GAUL

Lutetia Parisiorum (Paris)

Lugdunum (Lyons)

LUGDUNENSIS

AQUITANIA

NARBONENSIS

Nemausus (Nîmes)

Narbo

Massilia (Marseilles)

Rhône R.

Burdigala (Bordeaux)

TARRACONENSIS

Tarraco

Saguntum

Corduba (Córdoba)

BAETICA

LUSITANIA

Emerita Augusta (Mérida)

SPAIN

Ebro R.

Balearic Is.

Corsica

Sardinia

MAURETANIA

NORTH AFRICA

NUMIDIA

Carthage

AFRICA PROCONSULARIS

Leptis Magna

SAHARA

Mediterranean Sea

ITALY

ETRURIA

Arretium

Rome

Ostia

Pompeii

Mt. Vesuvius

Sicily

Syracuse

Malta

Adriatic Sea

Brundisium

Actium 31 B.C.E.

EPIRUS

MACEDONIA

Thessalonica

Corinth

Athens

ACHAEA

Crete

THRACE

Byzantium

Black Sea

BITHYNIA AND PONTUS

GALATIA

CAPPADOCIA

Pergamum

ASIA

ANATOLIA

PAMPHYLIA

Ephesus

LYCIA

CILICIA

Tarsus

Rhodes

Cyprus

Antioch

SYRIA

Damascus

Palmyra

Euphrates R.

Tigris R.

ARMENIA (114–117 C.E.)

ASSYRIA (116–117 C.E.)

MESOPOTAMIA (115–117 C.E.)

Seleucia

Babylon

Ctesiphon

CAUCASUS MTS.

PARTHIA

Nisa

Ecbatana

Susa

Persepolis

Persian Gulf

ARABIAN DESERT

JUDEA

Jerusalem

Petra

ARABIA

Red Sea

EGYPT

Alexandria

Nile R.

Bahriya Oasis

Cyrene

CYRENAICA

Scale: 0   200   400 Km.
0   200   400 Mi.

Ara Pacis The Altar of Peace, built in 9 B.C.E., resided in a large enclosure, whose walls contain relief sculptures. This scene depicts Mother Earth and her children, with the cow and sheep at her feet representing the prosperity resulting from peace.

Scala/Art Resource, NY

peoples. This was especially true of the Greek deities, which the Romans equated with their own gods. For example, the Greek leader of the gods, Zeus, became the Roman Jupiter, Zeus's wife Hera became the Roman Juno **(JOO-noh)**, and the Greek god of wine, Dionysus, became the Roman Bacchus **(BAK-uhs)**.

Social Classes

Although there was some mobility, Roman society remained stratified into sharply defined upper and lower classes, as well as sharply divided by wealth. Below the upper classes were middle-class merchants and artisans, who ranked above the urban workers. Many peasants became seriously impoverished. We know something of a wide range of the concerns and values of the middle and lower classes from the graffiti and tombstone memorials that they left (see Witness to the Past: The Voices of Common Romans).

As in Greece, slaves, one-third of the Italian population, occupied the bottom of the social ladder. Most slaves were war captives, but some people were enslaved as payment for debt or as the result of a crime. Some slaves lived very hard lives, working in mines, on vast plantations growing cash crops such as olives and grapes, or as oarsmen of Roman ships. A Roman historian described the lives of slaves working in a silver mine in Spain: "The slaves secure for their masters riches which are almost beyond belief. They, however, are physically destroyed, their bodies worn down. Many die because of the excessive mistreatment they suffer. They are given no break from their toil."[8] Most of the gladiators who fought in the arenas to entertain the public were highly skilled slaves who had studied at gladiator schools. In these deadly contests, few participants lived to old age. Slave rebellions were not uncommon and brutally crushed. The Romans were generous in freeing slaves after years of good service, but ex-slaves were still stigmatized socially.

Patriarchy and Gender Relations

Like most classical societies, the Romans were patriarchal. Only men had a political voice, and they enjoyed extensive power over women, children, and slaves. The oldest male in a family had the power of life and death over other family members and was even free to kill his children without fear of legal problems. Wives were advised to accept the extramarital sexual exploits of their husbands: "Let the matron be subject to her husband." Yet, some women stepped outside expected bounds. Seneca criticized those daring women who copied "male indulgences, they keep just as late hours, and drink as much liquor; they challenge men in carousing."[9]

Adult women also enjoyed some legal rights, including possession of their own property, even if married. Some women enjoyed considerable wealth, using it for such community ends as financing public monuments. Moreover, a wife could escape her husband's legal control by spending three days and nights away from his house, and she could sue her husband if he abandoned her. For example, a woman whose husband had moved to Alexandria and married another woman asked the court to make her husband return the dowry she brought to the marriage. Roman women also had more freedom to leave their homes and travel through the city than did their Greek sisters. Finally, abortion and contraception were common until they were outlawed around 200 C.E.

In the later years of the Republic, Romans became free to choose their own spouse. By 17 B.C.E., adultery and avoidance of marriage by both genders had become serious social problems. To attempt to halt a population decline among native Italians, a law was passed requiring men to marry or pay higher taxes. Views on human sexuality were diverse. For example, Romans were generally tolerant of homosexual activity and did not view it as immoral. Acknowledged homosexuals participated openly in Roman life.

Economy and Trade Networks

Roman society flourished from expanding trade and industry. Roman industries, such as mining and pottery making, depended mostly on slave labor. Those who acquired wealth beyond that needed for public display invested it in land rather than in business or industry. The Romans built over 150,000 miles of roads, most of them 4 feet thick. The phrase "all roads lead to Rome" reflects these accomplishments, as well as the fact that Rome became a communications center for a large area of Afro-Eurasia.

Maritime trade routes linked the Romans to peoples in Asia and Africa. The Egyptian port of Berenike (BER-eh-nick-y), on the Red Sea, was a transfer point for fabrics, spices, gems, and other exotic goods from India and Southeast Asia, frankincense and myrrh from Arabia, and ivory, drugs, tortoise shells, and slaves from Somalia and Ethiopia. During the *Pax Romana* over a hundred ships a year set off from Berenike and nearby ports for India. Merchant ships, the largest able to carry 1,200 tons of grain, plied the Mediterranean between Egypt and Rome. Roman coins have been found in India, China, and Vietnam.

Trade Routes

The Romans also traded widely over land. Roman-ruled North Africa obtained gold from West African societies across the Sahara Desert. The Silk Road across Central and western Asia allowed Chinese products to reach Rome. Romans shipped much gold and silver east in return for spices, jewelry, cut gems, glassware, and silk. Eventually, however, the Roman economy was harmed by the expanding Roman appetite for Chinese goods. The historian Pliny (PLIN-ee) the Elder bemoaned the wealth shipped east and blamed it on Roman women's fondness for silks, pearls, and perfumes: "India and China and [Arabia] together drain our empire. That is the price that our luxuries and our womankind cost us."[10] However, the criticism was misplaced, since both men and women coveted imported Asian goods.

Literature, Architecture, and Technology

As in the realm of public works and trade, the achievements of Roman literary culture during the late Republic and early empire were considerable, although they mostly reflected the views of the aristocratic elite. Virgil (70–19 B.C.E.) was Rome's greatest epic poet. To promote Roman greatness, his *Aeneid* (i-NEE-id) described the journey of the legendary Trojan hero Aeneas (i-NEE-uhs), who, according to the poem, left Troy and eventually founded the city of Rome. The love poems of Ovid (43 B.C.E.–17 C.E.) were irreverent and erotic, with his treatise on the art of love advising men to indulge their sexual cravings. In disgust, the moralistic emperor Augustus eventually sent Ovid into bitter exile along the Black Sea.

Poetry and History

Historians also made substantial contributions to Roman literature. Tacitus (56–117 C.E.) wrote a history of the early emperors in which he lamented the end of the Republic, which had a more open political atmosphere and sense of equality. He also authored a description of the Germanic tribes north of the Rhine and Danube, in which he contrasted the sexual purity and other virtues of the Germans with the vices of his fellow Romans. Of the corrupt emperor Domitian, Tacitus wrote that he "fancied that the voice of the Roman people [was] obliterated; he banished teachers of philosophy and exiled every noble pursuit, so that nothing honorable might anywhere be encountered."[11]

The Romans' quest to provide public services fostered notable architecture and engineering. The great dome of the Pantheon (PAN-thee-ahn), or temple to all the gods in Rome, has no interior-supporting pillars and forms a perfect sphere, as high as it is wide. The famous Colosseum in Rome was the world's largest outdoor arena until the twentieth century. Aqueducts carried water hundreds of miles from the mountains of Italy and Spain into the Roman cities. This abundance of water encouraged the development of public baths, which were social centers containing gardens, exercise and game rooms, and libraries. A Roman writer observed that baths, sex, and wine ruin bodies but make life worth living. The Romans are also remembered for some creature comforts. Some of the homes of the wealthier citizens were heated from furnaces under the floor that spread heat to the house through ductwork. The Koreans at the other end of Eurasia also developed similar heating systems. In addition, Romans invented glass windowpanes, scales with weights, chemical

Architecture and Engineering

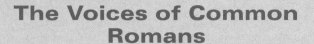

The Voices of Common Romans

As with most premodern societies, we know much more from the surviving records and literature about the prominent and wealthy Romans than about the common people who constituted most of the population. But we can learn something about the middle and lower classes from the graffiti preserved in the ruins of ancient cities like Pompeii and the epitaphs on tombstones. Romans used graffiti and epitaphs to voice frank opinions on many matters and to summarize their lives. Like modern graffiti, some of the remarks address sexual activities and bodily functions or insult rivals with profanity. The following are some examples of less profane but often humorous graffiti and epitaphs from various Roman cities.

Graffiti

I'm amazed, O wall, that you've not collapsed under the weight of so much written filth.

A bronze urn has disappeared from my tavern. Whoever returns it will get 65 sesterces reward. Whoever informs on the thief will get 20 sesterces, if we recover it.

Perarius, you're a thief.

No loiterers—scram!

Livia, to Alexander: "If you're well, I don't much care; if you're dead, I'm delighted."

Samius Cornelius, go hang yourself!

Stronnius is an ignoramus.

Crescens is a public whore.

Whoever doesn't invite me to dinner is a barbarian.

Whoever is in love, may he prosper. Whoever loves not, may he die. Whoever forbids love, may he die twice over!

Marcus loves Spendusa.

If you haven't seen the Venus that Apelles painted, take a look at my girl—she's just as beautiful.

Thraex makes the girls sigh.

All the goldsmiths support Gaius Cuspious Pansa for public works commissioner.

The mule-drivers support Gaius Julius Polybius for mayor. Genialis supports Bruttius Balbus for mayor. He'll balance the budget.

I ask you to support Marcus Cerrinus Vatia for public works commissioner. All the late-night drunks back him.

Epitaphs

If you wish to add your sorrow to ours, come here and shed your tears. A sad parent has laid to rest his only daughter, whom he treasured with sweet love as long as the Fates permitted. Now her dear face and form are mere shadow and her bones mere ash.

For my dearest wife, with whom I lived two years, six months, three days, and ten hours. On the day she died, I gave thanks before gods and men.

I was once famous, preeminent among thousands of strong Bavarian men. I swam across the Danube in full armor. I once shot an arrow in the air and split it with a second in midair. No Roman or barbarian ever beat me with a spear, no Parthian with the bow. This tombstone preserves the story of my deeds. But I am still unique, the first to do such things as these.

THINKING ABOUT THE READING

1. What do these graffiti tell us about political life?
2. What do the graffiti and epitaphs reveal about what common people valued?
3. In what ways do the sentiments seem familiar to modern readers?

Source: From *Lives and Times: A World History Reader, Volume I* 1st edition by HOLOKA/UPSHUR. © 1985 Wadsworth, a part of Cengage Learning, Inc. Reproduced with permission. www.cengage.com/permissions.

fertilizer, the theater curtain, the door key, the heavy plow, and a primitive dental drill. Finally, a calendar introduced by Julius Caesar created a year of 365 days and a few minutes. His calendar had to be reformed, but not until the sixteenth century.

The Decline of the Western Roman Empire

Political and Economic Problems

Political and economic problems eventually undermined the imperial system. Roman leaders had never found a good way to pass power on to a successor. The reliance on the army to decide who ruled resulted in twelve soldier-emperors between 235 and 260 c.e., none of whom died peacefully in old age. To control their possessions, the Romans spent more of their wealth to support a growing bureaucracy and the military, pushing the state toward bankruptcy. Paying the taxes was a particular problem in the western half of the empire, where serious inflation substantially decreased real wealth. The Roman economy was stronger in the east, where the older, larger cities provided a stronger tax base. Thus a serious "balance of payment" problem developed between the west and the east. The frontier lands west of Italy consumed more than they produced, and to pay for goods and food they had to constantly find more precious metals (such as gold and silver) or more wealth in the form of slaves, which they could sell or trade to the east for manufactured products.

No matter how advanced, with its aquaducts, central heating, and bureaucracy, the empire gradually decayed from within. Leaders became consumed by rivalries while corruption, ineptitude, and civil wars eroded government, making the state vulnerable to invaders. The early third century was a turning point. Roman rulers were forced by increasing costs and the difficulties of controlling a growing empire to end further conquests and merely defend the existing frontiers, cutting themselves off from the income that conquest provided and further impoverishing the government. Some gold and silver mines in the western lands became exhausted, as did some of the fertile soil in Italy, making goods more expensive. Alongside these troubles were a steadily widening gap between rich and poor, a serious trade deficit with China, declining levels of literacy, and growing corruption, apathy, and loss of public spirit. A cooler climate may have diminished crop yields. Because of contacts with distant lands, Rome was also increasingly vulnerable to the spread of diseases and epidemics that killed many thousands. A plague in the empire from 251 to 266 c.e., which reached Europe from North Africa, caused dramatic population decline and weakened Roman military forces. At the height of the epidemic, 5,000 people were said to have died each day just in the city of Rome.

Celtic and Germanic Societies and the Romans

The decline of Rome also corresponded with the rise of two northern European societies, Celts and Germans, both of Indo-European origin. The Celtic peoples, whose culture had developed by the twelfth century b.c.e. in the Danube River Basin north of the Alps, posed a challenge to the expanding Romans. Powerful chiefs ruled small Celtic states, and priests, known as *druids*, organized the worship of their many gods. Many Celts lived in large fortified towns, and some had coins and writing. Aided by bronze and then iron technologies, the Celts had occupied large sections of central and western Europe, from Germany and France to the British Isles and Spain. Fierce warriors and fine horsemen, by 400 b.c.e. Celtic tribes had raided into Italy, sacked Rome, and weakened the Etruscan states. A Roman writer describing the Celtic armies in Gaul said that the many trumpeters and horn blowers, as well as their war cries, terrified their opponents.

Celtic Societies

However, the well-drilled, disciplined Roman legions overwhelmed the Celtic fighters, which were divided by tribal rivalries. Most of the Celts were eventually colonized by the Romans or dislodged by the Germans. In 225 b.c.e. the Romans overran the Celts in northern Italy, and first the Carthaginians and then the Romans crushed Celtic power in Spain. Julius Caesar conquered the Celts of Gaul. In 60–61 c.e., however, the Romans faced a temporary setback when Celts led by a warrior-queen, Boudica (boo-DIK-uh) (d. 61 c.e.), destroyed several Roman settlements in England. Boudica had good reason to despise the Romans, who had pillaged her territory, flogged Boudica, and raped her daughters. A Roman historian lamented the defeat brought by a woman, which caused the Romans great shame. In retaliation, the Romans sent in a larger force, killing 80,000 of Boudica's subjects. The queen committed suicide rather than surrender to the Romans.

Roman Army Camp This carving shows a camp being built by Roman legionnaires during a military campaign. Soldiers' helmets, shields, and pikes are propped up at the right side. Some men build walls and dig ditches.

Celtic societies and culture remained strong mostly in Ireland and the rugged hills of Wales and Scotland, where the challenge of overcoming long lines of communication kept the Romans from extending their rule. Indeed, the Roman emperor Hadrian (HAY-dree-uhn) had a remarkable 73-mile-long rock wall built across northern England to keep Celtic tribes out of Roman territory. Celtic culture was eventually modified by Christianity, which reached Ireland in the fifth century. Today the Irish, Scottish, and Welsh people still honor their Celtic heritage, but few are fluent in their original Celtic languages. In most of mainland Europe and England, Celtic culture was gradually Latinized and Germanized, although even today pockets of Celtic identity can be found in Brittany (BRIT-uhn-ee) (western France) and in northwest Spain.

Gilles Mermet/Art Resource, NY

Life on a Late Roman Empire Estate The painting, of a fortified manor house and its surroundings, shows typical farming activity for each season.

The Germanic peoples put pressure on the empire's northern borders and eventually began migrating into the empire. German societies seem to have been organized in Scandinavia and the northern plains of Germany. No known German cities or states existed. The Roman historian Tacitus praised the Germans for their hospitality, noting that they considered it a crime to turn any visitor away from their door. Expanding to the south and west, the Germans inflicted several defeats on Roman legions in Gaul in 113 B.C.E. Although the Romans reorganized their legions and crushed the Germans, fear of Germanic invasions was a major reason the Romans expanded northward. As a result, some Germans were brought into the Roman fold, and some served in the Roman army. However, most Romans viewed the Germans as dangerous "barbarians."

For the next several centuries Romans and Germans watched each other warily on the fringes of the empire. German tribes joined to form confederations, whose combined strength made them a greater threat. Pushed by their own enemies such as the westward-moving Huns from Central Asia, some Germans began looking to the Roman lands for new homes, and German-Roman conflict intensified as Germanic peoples began moving into the empire. In 251 C.E. the Germans defeated a Roman army and plundered the Balkans. The declining Roman Empire was unable to field enough high-quality soldiers to defeat the invaders because its shrinking population meant that men needed to farm could not be spared for the army. In 381 the Romans began drafting men into service, but many draftees mutilated themselves to avoid service.

German expansion had a major impact on Roman society. High taxes needed to support the Roman armies alienated all classes, but they fell primarily on poor peasants, many of whom lost their land and became workers on large landed estates. Sometimes whole villages placed themselves under the protection of a wealthy landlord. This system, in which men and women worked the land of their patrons, eventually reshaped the peasant class as they gave up their freedom in exchange for protection. Meanwhile, the upper classes increasingly escaped the cities, which they had earlier supported with their money and public service, for their country estates. Thus Roman cities slowly but steadily shrank in size as fewer children were born and the upper classes moved away.

The Division of the Roman Empire

The mounting problems led to the division of the empire. Emperor Diocletian (DIE-uh-KLEE-shuhn) (r. 285–305) recognized the weakness of the western empire and divided the empire in half, making the Adriatic Sea an east-west dividing line. He ruled the east from Nicomedia (NIK-uh-MEED-ee-uh) in Anatolia and appointed another man, Maximian, as emperor in the west. A later emperor, Constantine (r. 306–337), temporarily reunited the empire under one ruler. He also established a new eastern capital on the Straits of Bosporus (BAHS-puhr-uhs), first named New Rome and then Constantinople (cahn-stan-tih-NO-pul)—today's Istanbul (IS-tahn-BUL). In 395 Constantinople became the capital of the eastern, or Byzantine Empire, which survived the western Roman Empire by nearly a thousand years.

Imperial Division and Roman Defeat

The worst military defeats suffered by Roman armies occurred in the fourth and fifth centuries C.E., forcing emperors to abandon claims to many territories, including Britain. In 410 the Germanic Ostrogoths (AH-truh-GAHTHS) (eastern Goths) plundered the city of Rome. Also around 410, a branch of the Huns, fierce horse-riding Central Asian pastoralists, conquered Hungary and later pushed various Germans west into Gaul, Italy, and Spain. Led by the able warrior Attila (uh-TIL-uh) (406–453), the Huns ravaged the Balkans and Greece before plundering northern Italy in 452. Hun power soon collapsed, but Rome was again sacked by another German group, the Vandals, in 455 C.E. The official end of the western empire came in 476, when Germans deposed the last Roman emperor.

The western Mediterranean world was now ruled by various Germanic kingdoms, including the Vandals in Northwest Africa, the Visigoths (VIZ-uh-gahths) in Spain, and the Ostrogoths in Italy. Another German group, the Franks, under their leader Clovis (KLO-vuhs), conquered what is now France and western Germany. Meanwhile, Germanic Angles and Saxons migrated into England. These Germanic peoples retained a considerable amount of Roman culture; moreover, some adopted local versions of Latin, which formed the basis for **Romance languages** such as French, Italian, and Spanish.

Romance languages
Languages that derive from Latin, such as French, Italian, and Spanish.

SECTION SUMMARY

- The *Pax Romana,* which began with Augustus, was a time of peace, prosperity, and cosmopolitan living, but also of imperial rule and a passive populace.

- The Romans set long-lasting legal standards and offered allegiance to a wide variety of gods, many of them borrowed from other peoples.

- Roman society was highly stratified; slaves performed much of the manual labor, and women, although accorded some significant legal rights, were generally subjugated.

- Rome served as a nexus for trade and communication, and it excelled in architecture and engineering.

- Beset by a range of problems, including uneasy succession, economic imbalance, overexpansion, climate change, and disease, the Roman Empire began to decline.

- The Celts, fierce warriors, posed a threat to the Romans, but they were eventually conquered and Latinized except for some in rugged areas of the British Isles.

- The Germans, whom the Romans considered barbarians, exerted a tremendous amount of pressure on the Roman Empire.

- The Roman Empire had trouble fielding enough soldiers or gathering enough money to fend off the German threat, since many of its poor had traded their rights for protection by the rich, and many of the rich had left the cities to live on their estates.

- The Roman Empire fell in 476 c.e., but an offshoot, the Byzantine Empire, lasted for another thousand years.

CHRISTIANITY: FROM WESTERN ASIAN SECT TO TRANSREGIONAL RELIGION

How did Christianity develop and expand?

The one institution that was a vigorous part of the life of the Roman cities even in the final decades of the western empire was the Christian church. Christianity arose in Palestine (in western Asia) in the first century c.e. as a Jewish sect (see Map 8.3). The religious and social institutions of Christianity accompanied Greco-Roman culture into the new Germanic kingdoms, and together they defined the culture of the new societies that dominated Europe in the centuries following the Classical Age. To understand the history of the Western societies, we need to analyze the rise and values of Christianity.

Roman Palestine and Jesus of Nazareth

Christianity was founded on the teachings of Jesus of Nazareth, a Jewish teacher in first-century c.e. Roman-ruled Palestine. Palestine and the surrounding region contained a mix of several traditions. For example, most people, including the Jews, spoke Aramaic (ar-uh-MAY-ik), the official language in the later Persian Empire, and most literate people wrote in Greek, a legacy of Hellenism. Various ideas from Egyptian, Mesopotamian, Phoenician, Persian, and Greek traditions undoubtedly influenced the Jewish and then Christian faiths. Palestine was one of the most restless Roman provinces and had a history of rebellion against Rome. Over the centuries the Hebrew prophets, such as Isaiah in the eighth century b.c.e. and Jeremiah, Ezekiel, and the "Second" Isaiah during the early Axial Age, explored the relations of the Hebrews to their God and other peoples. Jewish society was characterized by diverse beliefs and practices. Various mystical Jewish sects rejected both Hellenistic cosmopolitanism and the formal Jewish leadership. Jesus inherited these prophetic traditions and spoke of himself as the fulfillment of Jewish law.

Palestine and Hebrew Traditions

Much uncertainty surrounds the life of Jesus. Roman records confirm religious conflicts and instability in Palestine but make no mention of Jesus. According to Christian tradition, Jesus was a

Jesus and the Gospels

Jewish carpenter, teacher, and healer who probably lived from around 7 or 6 B.C.E. to 30 C.E. As with Buddha and Confucius, our knowledge of Jesus and his career comes from the writings of followers, primarily through the four gospel (literally "good news") accounts of the Christian New Testament. The earliest of these narratives, the Gospel of Mark, was written around 70 C.E., some forty years after the death of Jesus. Like the other three gospels in the official canon compiled in the middle of the second century C.E., Mark was written not as a historical account but as a faith statement, a "witness" to the power of God in the lives of the early followers of Jesus. As a result, modern theologians and historians vigorously debate the historical accuracy of gospel accounts. Several dozen other gospels or fragments of gospels were not included in the Christian Bible, and some of them differ considerably from the official gospels. Thus it is unclear whether the gospel accounts were based largely on eyewitness testimonies, oral traditions, or earlier writings that have since been lost.

The gospels describe Jesus as, among other things, a moral reformer who confronted the Jewish leaders, especially the *Pharisees* (FAR-uh-seez), a group that emphasized ritual purity, obeyed strict ceremonial laws, and awaited the coming of a messiah who would free them from the Romans. Jesus favored a simple life that included love of others, forgiveness of enemies, acceptance of the poor and other despised groups, and opposition to excessive legalism and ceremony. According to the Gospel of Matthew, Jesus summed up his teachings in two commandments: "Love God with all your heart, soul, and mind; and love your neighbor as yourself."[12] Matthew also reported that Jesus angered influential Jews and Romans by advising the wealthy to give their money to the poor since rich people were unwelcome in God's kingdom. Some modern theologians argue that Jesus made no claims to be divine or a "son of God," but described himself only as a healer and wisdom teacher. Other scholars emphasize that Jesus was seen as much more than a wisdom teacher by his followers.

Jesus's enemies, especially the Roman governor and a few Jewish religious leaders, accused him of treason against Rome, and Jesus was tried, convicted, and executed by crucifixion. Followers of Jesus claimed that he was revived or resurrected from death and that he "appeared to" his disciples. This belief in the continuing divine presence of Jesus probably motivated his followers to preach his message to others and honor his teachings by gathering for worship as a special sect within the first-century C.E. Jewish community.

Paul and the Shaping of Christianity

The evolution of the religion of Jesus into Christianity was greatly affected by the activities and writings of Paul of Tarsus (TAHR-suhs), a port city in southeast Anatolia. Paul was a first-century Romanized Jew from a Pharisee family who said that he was miraculously converted to belief in Jesus as a young man. He then spent the rest of his life spreading this faith to non-Jews, traveling extensively to western Asian and Greek cities before his death in a prison in Rome about 64 C.E. Paul's teaching emphasized that Jesus was a divine being, the "son of God" who earned forgiveness for the sins of humankind by his death on the cross. By accepting Jesus as the Christ (*Christus* meant "anointed one"), Paul taught, a person could be saved from damnation to an eternity in Hell. Paul also preached that a non-Jew who did not follow Jewish laws and ritual could become a follower of Jesus. By arguing that there was neither Jew nor Greek, slave nor free person but instead a spiritual equality, he was challenging fundamental Roman assumptions such as those behind slavery. These kinds of beliefs prompted many otherwise broad-minded Roman citizens to regard Christians as a threat. Paul's patriarchal views also strongly influenced Christian thinking. Paul valued celibacy above marriage and urged wives to be subject to their husbands and remain silent in church.

Paul and His Mission

Paul disagreed strongly with those in Jerusalem who believed that Christians had to follow Jewish laws. Paul's decision to exempt converts from undergoing the circumcision required by Jewish law was crucial for the success of Christianity, for, in those days before antibiotics and anesthesia, such operations would have discouraged many. Peter, the chief disciple of Jesus, agreed that God made no distinction between Jews and others, and in Roman Catholic tradition Peter became the first bishop of Rome (and hence the first pope). Peter was probably killed in Rome during the persecution of Christians in 64. Eventually, most Christians believed they were saved by faith in Jesus, not by following any Jewish tradition.

Jewish Revolt and Dispersal

The victory of Paul in convincing Peter to include non-Jews was crucial in establishing Christianity as a world religion (see Map 8.3). A Jewish revolt from 66 to 73 C.E. resulted in the Roman destruction of the Jewish temple in Jerusalem and the dispersion of many Jews to other lands. During the revolt the *Zealots*, a group of Jewish rebels, held out in a hilltop fort known as Masada (muh-SAHD-uh) overlooking the Dead Sea. Although the Romans eventually took the fort, Masada stood through history as a symbol of Jewish resistance to oppression. After the Roman victory, any Jew became discredited in Roman eyes, so it was fortunate for the early Christians that they had broken

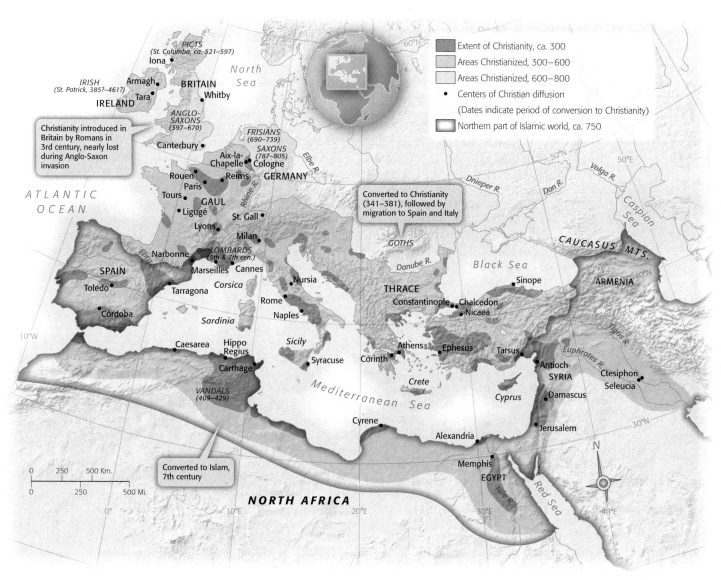

Map 8.3
Spread of Christianity

Christianity arose in Palestine in the first century C.E. and gradually gained footholds in parts of western Asia, North Africa, and southern Europe by 300 C.E. Over the next five centuries Christianity became the dominant religion in much of western and central Europe and expanded its influence in western Asia and North Africa.

 **Interactive Map**

with Judaism. Meanwhile, while Jews scattered across Eurasia and North Africa, the number of non-Jewish Christians continued to grow throughout the empire as the religion spread along the networks of trade and occupation throughout western Asia, North Africa, and southern Europe.

Christianity in the Mediterranean Zone

The Roman context shaped Christian growth and institutions. Christianity had similarities to "mystery religions," many from western Asia, that were becoming popular in the Roman world at the same time. Some had their roots in Persian and Hellenistic traditions. Like the followers of Mithra (MITH-ruh) or Isis (ICE-uhs), Christians believed in a life after death and had practices, such as a special initiation rite (baptism), that fostered a sense of religious community. But Christianity offered a greater emotional appeal than its competitors because of a belief in the spiritual equality of all people and a concern for the poor. Christians used the terms *heathen* and *pagan*, which had negative connotations, to describe those who followed polytheistic or animistic religions or were irreligious. These advantages helped Christianity gain greater acceptance. In 313 C.E. it became a legal religion by an edict of the Roman emperor Constantine, who believed

Christianity and
Eastern Religions

he had won a battle because of the help of the Christian God. After this the organized church, loosely headed by the bishop of Rome, became more significant. By 400 C.E. non-Christian faiths had been banned and Christianity had become the official Roman religion, thus uniting state and church in a troubled marriage for over a millennium.

But Christians also had to contend with theological divisions. For example, the sect of **Arianism** (AR-ee-uh-niz-uhm) taught that Jesus was not divine but rather an exceptional human being. To combat what most Christians saw as heresies and to establish core beliefs, the emperor Constantine called a church council at Nicaea (nye-SEE-uh), in Anatolia, in 325 C.E., where he ordered the bishops to resolve their doctrinal differences and determine which beliefs to follow. The **Nicene** (NYE-seen) **Creed** they produced became the official doctrine of the early church and is still recited in many denominations.

The early Christians borrowed much Greco-Roman culture. Their main difference with the state was to refuse to acknowledge the emperor's official divine status, for which they sometimes were persecuted. Nevertheless, as the Christian religion spread, most Christians were left alone to worship as they wished, and they, in turn, acquired a Roman education and even celebrated traditional Roman festivals along with the new Christian ones, such as the Christians' celebration of the birthday of Jesus on the date of the old Roman and Mithraist festival of the winter solstice. Early Christians also generally adopted the Greco-Roman tolerance toward homosexuality. There were also tensions between Christians and non-Christians, such as those that led to the murder of the philosopher Hypatia (hye-PAY-shuh) by Christian mobs in Alexandria around 416 C.E. (see Profile: Hypatia of Alexandria, a Pagan Philosopher). And some early church leaders already blamed the Jews for the death of Jesus. In general, however, Christians adapted successfully to Roman life.

By the early fifth century, the political and social leaders in most Roman cities were Christian, but some Christian leaders began to be troubled by their social and political success. Followers of Jesus were supposed to focus on spiritual instead of worldly success, on Heaven instead of earth. One result of this questioning was monasticism, the pursuit of a life of penance, prayer, and meditation, either alone or in a community of other seekers. For instance, Benedict of Nursia (ca. 480–ca. 543) became so disillusioned by the hedonistic life in Rome that he moved into a cave and later founded western Europe's first monastic order, the Benedictines (ben-uh-DIK-teenz). Benedict formulated monastic rules that explained how to live a spiritually fulfilling life. Many monks and nuns practiced **asceticism**, austere religious practices, such as intense prayer, that were used to strengthen spiritual life and seek a deeper understanding of God. As part of this increasing tendency to withdraw from society, some church leaders began to reemphasize the superiority of a life of virginity over that of marriage, a value earlier stressed in the writings of Paul.

Augustine and Roman Christianity

As Christianity expanded, it developed church institutions and produced thinkers who shaped the theology. In the declining decades of the empire, the North African bishop Augustine of Hippo (354–430 C.E.) redefined Christianity's relation to the Roman world and described Christian morality and history in a form that dominated western European culture for a thousand years. Augustine had tried several faiths before becoming a convinced Christian and eventually a priest, and then, in 395, bishop of Hippo, a city near Carthage. Like many Roman cities, Hippo had followers of many faiths, including various pagan and Persian traditions, all seen as heretical by the established church. After the sack of Rome by the Ostrogoths in 410, Augustine became troubled by the pagan accusation that it was the refusal of Christians to fight (many early Christians were pacifists) and the abandonment of the Roman gods that caused Roman society to wither. In his book, *City of God*, completed in 427, Augustine defended Christianity against its critics. He argued that the "city of God" comprised all who followed God's laws (i.e., Christians), while the "city of man" consisted of non-Christians, who ignored God's teachings and would be damned in a final judgment at the end of time. Augustine contended that all of history was in God's hands. He promoted a view of history as a straight line of progress from past to future, in which, at the end of history, Jesus would return to judge all humanity, living and dead.

In developing a moral thinking he viewed as superior to that of the tolerant Roman culture, Augustine also urged Christian men and women to remain celibate, viewing marriage as only for those with low self-control. He criticized sex outside of marriage, sanctioned sex within marriage only for procreation, and proclaimed men superior to women. Augustine's writings and theology strongly influenced the Roman Catholic tradition, as Christians increasingly separated themselves from hedonistic Roman traditions. For example, in 498 Christian leaders introduced an annual feast day in honor of St. Valentine to replace a holiday honoring Juno, the Roman goddess of love and marriage, and a popular, somewhat raunchy, Roman fertility festival.

Arianism A Christian sect that taught that Jesus was not divine but rather an exceptional human being.

Nicene Creed A set of beliefs, prepared by the council at Nicaea in 325 C.E., that became the official doctrine of the early Christian church.

asceticism Austere religious practices, such as intense prayer, that were used to strengthen spiritual life and seek a deeper understanding of God; began to be used in the Christian church in the fifth and sixth centuries C.E.

e Primary Source: Saint Augustine Denounces Paganism and Urges Romans to Enter the City of God In *City of God*, Augustine uses sarcasm to condemn the rituals of Rome's pre-Christian religion.

HYPATIA OF ALEXANDRIA, A PAGAN PHILOSOPHER

Hypatia was a female philosopher and mathematician in the old Hellenistic city of Alexandria in Egypt, then part of the Roman Empire. At a time when Christianity was becoming more influential, she followed a non-Christian polytheistic religion and thus in Christian eyes was a "pagan." Perhaps nothing better shows the complex relationship between Christians and pagans in the late Roman Empire, and the tension within the Christian community itself, than her murder at the hands of a Christian mob in 415 C.E. To critics of religious intolerance such as the eighteenth-century English historian Edward Gibbon, Hypatia was a beautiful woman torn to pieces by a fanatic mob because she believed in the Greek spirit of reason instead of, in his view, the irrational beliefs of Christianity. But it was not that simple.

Hypatia was born around 355 C.E., the daughter of a well-educated mathematician and astronomer. As a youth she studied the works of the mathematician Euclid and other great thinkers of the Hellenistic era and became known for making geometry intelligible to students. She was also attracted to the study of philosophy, but not of the purely rational sort Gibbon imagined. She became a neo-Platonist, a person who saw philosophy as almost a religion, a way to discover the hidden spirit of the divine within each person. She also stressed the feminine aspects of culture and argued that women benefited from honoring goddesses. Hypatia wrote commentaries on mathematical and astronomical subjects and lived quietly as a teacher, did not publicly participate in pagan worship, and, like many Christian women of her day, practiced celibacy, although she was married to another philosopher. Women philosophers were uncommon in those days, but Hypatia's wisdom and learning were celebrated. Admirers claimed she had "the spirit of Plato and the body of Aphrodite [the Greek goddess of love]." Her students were both pagan and Christian. One of them became a Christian bishop in Anatolia but remained Hypatia's lifelong friend.

Conditions in Alexandria began to change after 391 C.E., when the Roman emperor Theodosius forbade pagan worship in the empire. During the next twenty years, more and more Christians felt called to eradicate all non-Christian religions, and violent attacks on Jews and pagans became more frequent. By then Christians were a majority of the city population, though they were divided into feuding factions. Tensions grew worse in the city after the fanatic Cyril, who was generally intolerant of non-Christians, won election as bishop in 412. Since Hypatia was a close friend and supporter of Orestes, the city's Christian governor, his bitter rival Cyril spread the rumor that the widely respected Hypatia was a witch and practiced black magic. He also encouraged attacks on Jews.

In 415 a semimilitary gang of young Christians allied with Cyril dragged Hypatia from her carriage, stripped off her clothes, murdered her, and burned her body. Cyril had not ordered this, but he had created a social climate that made such a crime possible. After this event, Alexandria became a more thoroughly Christian city. The Jews, who had been a substantial community in Alexandria for over 600 years, were expelled, and Orestes returned to Rome. Cyril was never punished for his part in Hypatia's death.

Later critics were probably wrong to view Hypatia mostly as a martyr to her non-Christian beliefs. She was also, at least partly, a victim of a jealous bishop. However, Gibbon and others were correct to see her as one of the last representatives of a tolerant paganism rooted in the cosmopolitan ethos of Hellenistic and Roman culture, which was replaced by an intolerant form of Christianity. Her death also represented the displacement of philosophers from the public forum by religious men who claimed that the ideas they preached were superior because they came from God rather than from book learning.

THINKING ABOUT THE PROFILE

1. What does Hypatia's career tell us about Alexandrian society?

2. What does her experience reveal about conflicts between Christians and non-Christians in the late Roman Empire?

Note: Quotation from Maria Dzidzka, *Hypatia of Alexandria* (Cambridge: Harvard University Press, 1995), 5.

Statue of Hypatia This statue honors the great pagan philosopher and mathematician of fifth-century Alexandria who was murdered by Christian rivals.

Christianity filled the vacuum in the western Mediterranean as Roman government collapsed and many people left the cities in the fifth century. The population of the city of Rome fell from 800,000 in 300 to 60,000 in 530. The Christian clergy often provided the only semblance of order for those who remained. Church officials also achieved a huge boost when the Franks, a Germanic people, were converted to Latin Christianity under their ruler Clovis. Then, in the late sixth century, Europe was hit by many disasters, which were enumerated in 599 by an alarmed

Christian Society

Pope Gregory: "as the end of the world approaches, many things menace us which never existed before: inversions of the climate, horrors from the heavens and storms contrary to the season, wars, famine, plagues, earthquakes."[13] But the widespread mood of doom proved premature. A new age was dawning in western Europe. It was largely German and Christian in tone, with a Greco-Roman overlay of language and culture.

SECTION SUMMARY

- Christianity was born in Palestine, an area with a tradition of rebellion against Rome, and grew out of the Jewish prophetic tradition.

- Jesus opposed excessive legalism and ceremony, but scholars debate whether he saw himself as divine, or the "son of God."

- Paul was instrumental in spreading and shaping Christianity after Jesus's death, as well as in arguing that one did not have to be Jewish to become a Christian.

- Aided by the popularity of mystery religions similar to it and by the decline in quality of life, Christianity took hold and became the official Roman religion.

- In defending Christianity against its critics, Augustine distinguished between Christians, who would be saved, and non-Christians, who would be damned, and he also argued for strict standards of sexual morality that favored celibacy.

REVIVAL IN THE EAST: BYZANTINES, PERSIANS, AND ARABS

How did the Byzantine and Sassanian Empires reinvigorate the eastern Mediterranean world?

A century after Roman emperor Constantine dedicated his new capital city, later known as Constantinople, in 330 C.E., the western part of the empire fell to various German groups while the eastern empire fostered a new and distinctive society, Byzantium. Byzantium saw itself as a continuation of the Roman Empire but developed a different political structure as well as a culture and church that was more Greek than Latin. By taking the brunt of attacks by resurgent western Asian peoples such as the Sassanian Persians, Byzantium gave the struggling new states in western Europe time to develop into a separate Latin Christian culture. The Persian-Byzantine conflict also helped shape the rising Arab society.

Early Byzantium and the Era of Justinian

Byzantium's Empire

Byzantium emerged as the most powerful state in the eastern Mediterranean region, a status it maintained for many centuries. Its capital, Constantinople, straddled the narrow waterway linking the Aegean and Black Seas and separating Europe from western Asia, symbolically linking diverse peoples and traditions. The large eastern Roman Empire initially encompassed the Balkans, Greece, Anatolia, Syria, Palestine, and Egypt. Few emperors in Rome enjoyed the power that the Byzantine government had over its people, economy, and religious institutions.

The most important early ruler of the Byzantine Empire was the Emperor Justinian (juh-STIN-ee-uhn) (r. 527–565 C.E.) (see Chronology: Byzantium and Western Asia, 224–616 C.E.). Spurred on and advised by his powerful and ambitious wife, Theodora (THEE-uh-DOR-uh), Justinian was determined to defeat the German states in the west and reunite the old Roman Empire. His armies reconquered a large part of the western territories. They defeated the Ostrogothic kingdom in Italy in 563 after long years of fighting, but repeated battles for control of Rome left the city devastated, with only a few thousand impoverished, disease-ridden inhabitants. Moreover, Justinian's victories were accomplished only at the cost of high taxes, and he was barely able to defend his own domains from Huns, Persians, and various peoples migrating into Europe. During the first half of the seventh century, Justinian's successors had to fight the Sassanian Persians, and the western lands were once again lost (see Map 8.4).

Justinian's Government

Justinian also established a political pattern of despotism in which the Byzantine emperors were treated as near-gods by their subjects and thus gained absolute power over nearly every area of national life. They presided over a centralized and complex bureaucracy (hence our term *byzantine* for complicated and puzzling systems). Spies monitored the population. Justinian had many critics, among them the great Byzantine historian Procopius, who described the emperor as "at once villainous and amenable; as people say colloquially, a moron. He was never truthful with anyone. His nature was an unnatural mix of folly and wickedness."[14] But Justinian also collected all existing Roman laws into one legal code, preserving Roman legal principles for later generations.

In 540 the Byzantines encountered one of the most terrible epidemics in world history, often known as the plague of Justinian. The sickness, probably bubonic plague, began in Egypt and spread along the trade routes into western Asia before reaching Europe. At its height some 10,000 people a day perished. Ships were loaded with corpses, rowed out to sea, and abandoned. Agriculture largely halted and many communities were abandoned. A Christian bishop in Palestine wrote that "all the inhabitants, like beautiful grapes, were trampled and squeezed dry without mercy."[15] The plague returned several times until 590. When Justinian died at age eighty-three, his empire was much poorer, weaker, and less populated than it had been when he took power.

Byzantine Society, Economy, and Religion

Despite its many political misfortunes, the Byzantine Empire survived for centuries because of its social and economic strengths. The empire remained much more urban than western Europe. Constantinople grew to perhaps a million people and was described by a visitor as "a splendid city, how stately, how fair. It would be wearisome to tell of the abundance of all good things."[16] The rich in the cities lived in splendor, with luxury goods like silk clothes, carpets, and elegant tapestries provided by local industry. A huge gap separated rich and poor, but the Byzantine peasants faced unique restrictions. Laws required peasants who had lived many years in one place to remain there. They became bound to the soil, under the control of powerful landlords. Although Byzantine society was patriarchal, upper-class women in the large cities enjoyed influence, and some queens exercised considerable power. Women had the legal right to control their own property and to have their dowry returned if their husbands divorced them. However, men enjoyed greater legal safeguards, and wife-beating was common. In an era when maternal and infant mortality rates were high, pregnancy remained hazardous and childbirth dangerous.

The Byzantine economy flourished. Merchants and bankers were prominent members of the urban aristocracy and benefited from Constantinople's position astride the principal trade routes between Europe and Asia. Ships and caravans brought many products and resources to Constantinople: spices, cotton, and copper from India and Southeast Asia; jewels, silk, gold, and silver from China and Central Asia; gold, ivory, and slaves from Africa; cotton and grain from Egypt; grains, wool, and tin from northwestern Europe; olive oil and silver from Spain and Italy; timber, fur, copper, hides, and slaves from Russia and Scandinavia. The government placed a 10 percent tax on all goods that passed through the capital. Byzantine currency was internationally recognized, and Byzantine coins have been found as far away as China. But most trade with China and India had to go through Persian-controlled lands, and the Persian-Byzantine relationship alternated between uneasy peace and armed conflict.

The Byzantine society and culture, fundamentally Hellenistic Greek, inevitably diverged from the western Roman tradition in many ways, but especially in religion and culture. The Byzantines preserved and later passed on to the Latin west (often through the Muslims) the works of Plato, Aristotle, Homer, Sophocles, and other Greeks. The Christian church in the east also became separated from its Latin counterpart, over time evolving into the Greek Orthodox Church, which developed many customs and viewpoints quite foreign to the Roman church. Religion permeated all aspects of Byzantine life. The church, especially monasteries, gained control of considerable land and hence wealth. From the ruler, who controlled both temporal and religious affairs, to the ordinary citizen, religious questions were avidly discussed. Emperors proposed church reforms and called church councils to deal with what mainstream Christians considered heresies, including that of the **Monophysites** (muh-NAHF-uh-sites), who argued that Jesus had a single divine nature rather than both a divine and human form; and the **Nestorians**, who believed that the divine and human natures of Jesus were independent of each other. Christianity also affected gender relations. A goddess figure who represented urban prosperity was replaced by the much beloved Christian image of the Holy Virgin Mary, which gave women moral stature. But the church also viewed women as weak and inferior, both physically and morally, and easily tempted by sin.

Cities and Economic Life

CHRONOLOGY

Byzantium and Western Asia, 224–616 C.E.

224–226 B.C.E. Sassanians overthrow Parthians, begin building empire

306–337 B.C.E. Reign of Constantine

330 B.C.E. Founding of Constantinople

395 B.C.E. Final division of eastern and western empires

527–565 B.C.E. Reign of Justinian

540–590 B.C.E. Plague of Justinian

607–616 B.C.E. Sassanians conquer Syria, Palestine, and Egypt

Culture and Religion

Monophysites A heretical sect that argued that Jesus had a single divine nature rather than both a divine and a human form.

Nestorians A heretical Christian sect that believed that the divine and human natures of Jesus were independent of each other.

Interior of Santa Sophia Cathedral The great cathedral of Santa Sophia in Constantinople, rebuilt for Byzantine emperor Justinian, was famous for its spectacular interior.

Over time theological disputes between the eastern and western churches grew. In general, Greek Christians came to emphasize ritual and also refused to accept the notion that the bishop of Rome (later known as the pope) was superior in authority to the other bishops. Conflicts over authority and doctrine contributed to the final split between the Latin and Greek churches in the eleventh century. Meanwhile, the Monophysites formed the Armenian, Coptic, and Syrian Orthodox Churches. The Nestorians migrated to Persia, becoming the basis of the modern Chaldean and Assyrian Churches. From Persia they spread their faith along the Silk Road into India and China.

Byzantine art and architecture reflected the cultural diversity of this huge empire and was strongly influenced by western Asian traditions. The fusion of some Persian and Greco-Roman influences can be seen, for example, in the great dome in the Church of Santa Sophia (Holy Wisdom) in Constantinople, built under Justinian. The church was designed to symbolize inner Christian spirituality in contrast to human pride. Hence, the external appearance was modest but the interior was richly decorated with mosaics, marble columns, tinted glass, and gold leaf.

Sassanian Persians and Their Networks

Both the Roman Empire and the Byzantines had to deal with a revived Persia under the Sassanian dynasty, which generated frequent conflict during their four centuries of rule. Considering themselves the successors to the Achaemenids a half millennium earlier, the Sassanian court, based in modern Iraq, provided a focus for a brilliant culture mixing Hellenistic and Persian influences. Between 240 and 277 the Sassanians pursued empire. In the east they fought with the Kushans (KOO-shans), whose Afghanistan-based empire controlled parts of western India and Central Asia. The Sassanians overthrew the Parthians in 224 and spent the rest of the third century building their own empire. Eventually the Sassanians occupied much of Afghanistan and some of the Silk Road cities of Central Asia, but they lost these territories to the Huns in the fourth century C.E. To the west the Sassanians expanded into the Caucasus and Mesopotamia, creating chronic conflict with Rome in and around Syria. They also occupied parts of Arabia, including Yemen (YEM-uhn) in the south. In the sixth and early seventh centuries the Sassanians occupied the eastern Byzantine Empire, including Syria, Palestine, and Egypt (see Map 8.4). But years of war with Byzantium weakened both societies. In 651 the last Sassanian king was murdered and Arab Muslim armies gained control of all Sassanian territories.

Controlling much of the Persian Gulf, Sassanian Persia became a contact zone for international trade. Sassanian trade links stretched east as far as India, Central Asia, and China, and south into Africa. Byzantine and Sassanian coins were used as currency in the Silk Road cities. Persians produced some of the world's finest pottery, silver plates, pearls, brocades, carpets, and glassware, exchanging these for gems, incense, perfume, and ivory.

Sassanian Religion and Culture

In contrast to the religiously tolerant Achaemenids, the Sassanians mandated a state religion, Zoroastrianism. The government imposed orthodoxy, supporting the priesthood and sometimes persecuting other religions. However, state religions tend to decay, and Zoroastrianism was no exception. The Zoroastrian establishment became corrupt and rigid, and by the fifth century the faith was losing influence and followers. Yet Zoroastrianism spawned various religions that combined this faith with others. One of these new religions, Mithraism, became popular in the Roman Empire and spread as far west as England. Another new religion, **Manicheanism** (man-uh-KEE-uh-niz-uhm), founded by the Persian Mani (MAH-nee) (216–277 C.E.), was a blend of Zoroastrianism, Buddhism, and Christianity that emphasized a continuing struggle between the equally powerful forces of light and dark. Although Mani was executed for heresy, his faith suppressed by both the Sassanians and Christians, his religious dualism was later incorporated into Islam and some Christian sects.

Manicheanism A blend of Zoroastrianism, Buddhism, and Christianity, founded by Mani, that emphasized a continuing struggle between the equal forces of light and dark.

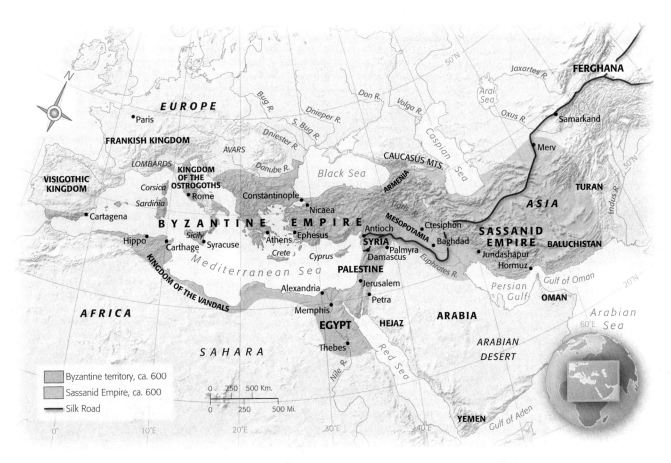

Map 8.4
The Byzantine and Sassanian Empires

By 600 C.E. the Byzantine Empire controlled much of southern Europe and the eastern end of the Mediterranean Basin, and the Sassanian Empire dominated most of
the rest of western Asia, part of Turkestan, and Egypt. Various Germanic kingdoms
held political sway in far western Europe, northern Europe, and northeast Africa.

e Interactive Map

As Zoroastrianism gradually lost influence, the state became more tolerant of diversity and
turned the capital city, Jundashapur, into a cosmopolitan intellectual center. Christian minorities
such as the Armenians of the Caucasus region were allowed freedom of religion, and the Sassanians also welcomed Nestorian Christians fleeing Byzantine repression. Foreign scholars migrated
to the newly tolerant state, as did Jews and others who feared persecution in Christian Europe. The
Sassanians also collected scientific and literary books from many neighboring peoples, translated
Greek writings, and established a renowned hospital and medical school. Sassanian Persia's mul-
ticulturalism provided a framework that enabled later Islamic governments to rule diverse peoples
and faiths. But Zoroastrianism, too closely connected to Sassanian domination, became only a
minor faith after Islam swept through the region.

Interregional Trade, Cities, and the Arabs

The ebb and flow of long-distance trade in western Asia, often influenced by the activities of the
Hellenistic Greeks, Romans, Byzantines, and Sassanians, helped foster Arab culture. Diverse
Semitic societies lived in the Arabian peninsula, a dusty region of mountains, dry plains, and
harsh deserts stretching from the Jordan River and Sinai southeast to the Indian Ocean. Most
of the Arabian peoples were pastoral nomads divided into tribes. Roman sources described
these mobile people: "All alike are warriors of equal rank, ranging widely with the help of swift
horses and slender camels."[17] Others lived from trade or farming. Eventually all of these groups
coalesced into the Arab society.

One of the peoples out of which Arab society arose were the Nabataeans (NAB-uh-TEE-uhnz),
who traded all over the Middle East and into Europe by land and sea. The Nabataean writing system
became the inspiration for the Arabic script. They also established a kingdom and built a major

Geographical Foundations

The Nabataeans

trading city, Petra (PE-truh), in today's Jordan, astride the overland caravan routes. Built in a narrow gorge, Petra had a population of 30,000 at its peak. The Petra residents developed an ingenious system for collecting and storing rainwater in this arid region. The ruins of Petra's spectacular tombs, with their elaborate facades carved into rock, still astonish visitors.

Beginning in the fourth century B.C.E., Petra flourished as a crossroads for goods moving between India, Arabia, Greece, and Egypt. But in 106 B.C.E. the Romans occupied Petra, and the city began a long decline as its trade shifted north to Palmyra (pal-MY-ruh), on the Euphrates River in today's Syria. Palmyra thrived until 273 C.E., when the Romans crushed a revolt led by the shrewd and ambitious Queen Septimia Zenobia (zuh-NO-bee-uh). After their conquest of the prosperous and ancient trading city in 114 B.C.E., the Romans had cultivated Palmyra to protect their eastern frontier. Taking advantage of Roman wars with the Goths, Zenobia sent her army into Egypt and then occupied much of Roman Asia. As ruler she invited Greek thinkers to Palmyra and encouraged religious tolerance. However, by controlling Egypt she controlled the Roman grain supply. After fierce battles the Romans reoccupied Palmyra and took Zenobia to Rome, where she died.

Yemenite Societies

The farming-based kingdoms that rose and fell in Yemen in southern Arabia since the days of the fabled Queen of Sheba around 1000 B.C.E. constituted another source for Arab culture. Yemen included an area of high, cool mountains and well-watered valleys. The Yemenite people were highly skilled, especially in civil engineering and architecture. They produced an abundant harvest with the aid of elaborate dams and terraces, and they constructed splendid cities in valleys and along mountainsides. City-states emerged, among them Saba, possibly the Sheba of the Hebrew Bible. The Yemenites traded by sea with India and East Africa, as well as across Arabia by land with the eastern Mediterranean and Mesopotamia. Frankincense from the region was prized as far away as Rome.

In the sixth century C.E. Arabian conditions began to change. Political disarray, an Ethiopian invasion, and commercial depression began to undermine Yemenite society and power. To the north, renewed conflict between the Sassanians and Byzantines led both of them to actively seek allies in central Arabia. As a result, Arabia became a political pawn caught between Orthodox Byzantium, Zoroastrian Persia, and Coptic Ethiopia. This situation also increased the traffic over land trade routes and fostered the settlement of many Christian and Jewish merchants in desert towns like Mecca (MEK-uh). Some Arabs adopted these religions. In the seventh century all these trends fostered the emergence of a new Arab faith, Islam, out of classical roots. Eventually Islamic armies overran most of the Byzantine Asian territories and the Sassanian Empire.

SECTION SUMMARY

- Justinian ruled the Byzantine Empire absolutely and tried to retake the Roman Empire, with mixed results.

- More urban and wealthy than western Europe, the Byzantine Empire served as a trading hub for goods from across Europe and Asia.

- Byzantine culture became more Greek and less Roman, and the Byzantine church denied the authority of the pope and came to emphasize ritual and doctrine to a greater degree than did the Roman church.

- The Sassanians revived the strength of Persia and adopted Zoroastrianism as a state religion.

- Arab culture began to rise out of tribes of pastoral nomads, the trading cities of Petra and Palmyra, and the farming-based kingdoms of Yemen.

CHAPTER SUMMARY

The middle and late Classical Era in the Mediterranean world and western Asia was shaped largely by the activities and cultures of the Romans, Germans, Greeks, and Persians. The Romans adopted and spread some of the values of the classical Greeks, while also making major contributions in government, law, and architecture. For several centuries they had a republic in which some of the people had a voice in government and elected Rome's leaders. To acquire more resources and preempt challengers, the Romans gradually expanded their territory until it encompassed much of Europe, North Africa, and western Asia. In the process they defeated and conquered rivals, including the Etruscans, Carthage, Egypt, and the Celts. Eventually the Republic was replaced by a more autocratic system led by powerful emperors. Controlling the far-flung territories was expensive, however, and the Roman forces became overextended. Soon the Romans were also defending their territories against the incursions of the Germanic peoples.

New forces also developed in the eastern end of the Mediterranean basin. Christianity arose out of Jewish society in Palestine and spread throughout the Mediterranean world, western Asia, and North Africa. The power of the Christian church rose as Roman political power declined. In the east Byzantium emerged out of the eastern Roman Empire, developing into a distinct society that incorporated Hellenistic Greek political and cultural traditions. It also fostered the Greek Orthodox Church. Meanwhile, the Sassanians reinvigorated Persian society and built a large empire, eventually putting pressure on Byzantium. These conflicts increased travel over the trade routes and generated new currents in Arab society.

KEY TERMS

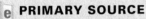

patricians	tribunes	Nicene Creed	Manicheanism
Centuriate Assembly	*Pax Romana*	asceticism	
consuls	Romance languages	Monophysites	
plebeians	Arianism	Nestorians	

EBOOK AND WEBSITE RESOURCES

e PRIMARY SOURCE
Saint Augustine Denounces Paganism and Urges Romans to Enter the City of God

e INTERACTIVE MAPS
Map 8.1 Italy and the Western Mediterranean, 600–200 B.C.E.
Map 8.2 The Roman Empire, ca. 120 C.E.
Map 8.3 Spread of Christianity
Map 8.4 The Byzantine and Sassanian Empires

LINKS

Diotima: Materials for the Study of Women and Gender in the Ancient World (http://www.stoa.org/diotima/). Contains excellent materials.

Exploring Ancient World Cultures (http://eawc .evansville.edu/). An excellent site with essays and links on the ancient Near East and Europe.

From Jesus to Christ: The First Christians (http://www .pbs.org/wgbh/pages/frontline/shows/religion). Valuable essays linked to a documentary series on U.S. Public Broadcasting.

Internet Ancient History Sourcebook (http://www .fordham.edu/halsall/ancient/asbook.html). An exceptionally rich collection of links and primary source readings.

Livius: Articles on Ancient History (http://www.livius .org). Very useful site with many short essays on the Romans.

The Roman Empire (http://www.roman-empire.net/). Offers extensive materials and essays on the Romans.

Plus flashcards, practice quizzes, and more. Go to: www.cengage.com/history/lockard/globalsocnet2e

SUGGESTED READING

Aldrete, Gregory S. *Daily Life in the Roman City: Rome, Pompeii, and Ostia.* Norman: University of Oklahoma Press, 2009. Readable and accessible.

Boren, Henry C. *Roman Society,* 2nd ed. Lexington, MA: D.C. Heath, 1992. An overview of how Roman society developed.

Chauveau, Michael. *Egypt in the Age of Cleopatra.* Ithaca: Cornell University Press, 2000. A wide-ranging, readable study by a French scholar.

Cunliffe, Barry. *Europe Between the Oceans: 9000 BC–AD 1000.* New Haven: Yale University, 2008. Innovative interdisciplinary study of European development.

Cunliffe, Barry. *The Ancient Celts.* New York: Penguin, 1997. A detailed but fascinating overview of Celtic history and culture.

Dupont, Florence. *Daily Life in Ancient Rome.* Oxford: Blackwell, 1992. Discusses material culture and social values.

Fox, Robin Lane. *Pagans and Christians.* New York: Alfred A. Knopf, 1987. Explores the early rise of Christianity.

Grant, Michael. *The Fall of the Roman Empire.* New York: Macmillan, 1990. A brief and readable account.

Lynch, Joseph H. *Early Christianity: A Brief History.* New York: Oxford University Press, 2009. Covers the foundations and first half millennium.

Pomeroy, Sarah B. *Goddesses, Whores, Wives and Slaves: Women in Classical Antiquity.* New York: Schocken, 1975. An excellent study of women's lives in classical Greece and Rome.

Taylor, Jane. *Petra and the Lost Kingdom of the Nebateans.* New York: I.B. Taurus, 2001. An overview of this pre-Arab society.

Treadgold, Warren. *A Concise History of Byzantium.* New York: Palgrave, 2001. A comprehensive recent survey.

Wiesehofer, Josef. *Ancient Persia.* London: I.B. Taurus, 2001. Scholarly essays on pre-Islamic Persia and the Sassanians.

Young, Gary K. *Rome's Eastern Trade: International Commerce and Imperial Policy, 31 BC–AD 305.* London: Routledge, 2001. A recent scholarly investigation of the Roman trading system.

CLASSICAL SOCIETIES AND REGIONAL NETWORKS IN AFRICA, THE AMERICAS, AND OCEANIA, 600 B.C.E.–600 C.E.

Werner Forman/Art Resource, NY

Aksum Stele
Early in the Common Era the kings of the African state of Aksum, in what is today Ethiopia, decorated their capital city with tall, flat-sided pillars known as steles, some nearly 70 feet high, possibly as monuments to the royal family.

*W*hen the day dawns the trader betakes himself to his trade; the spinner takes her spindle; the warrior takes his shield; the farmer awakes, he and his hoe handle; the hunter awakes with his quiver and bow.

—ANCIENT YORUBA PROVERB ABOUT DAYBREAK IN A WEST AFRICAN TOWN[1]

In the classical world, few settlements were as specialized as those serving the caravans that crossed the trackless sands of the vast Sahara Desert of Africa, a barren landscape where scorching sun and arid soil made it nearly impossible to plant crops or trees. The journeys were interrupted by rest stops at caravan way stations, isolated oasis towns with gardens, date palms, and flocks of sheep where weary travelers could find fresh water and restock before resuming their journeys. The round trip of many weeks between the cities of the North African coastal zone and those on the southern fringe of the desert held many dangers besides thirst and discomfort, including fierce raiders on horseback. Camels, the major beast of burden in the caravan trade, were not always cooperative animals and often waged battles of wills with their handlers, but they could travel many days without water. Thanks to these caravans and the brave men who led them, sub-Saharan African products reached a wider world, and goods and ideas from North Africa and Eurasia found their way along the trade networks to peoples living south of the Sahara.

The diverse societies that arose in sub-Saharan Africa, the Americas, and Oceania (the Pacific Basin) were all shaped by their environment, whether that was a desert like the Sahara, a highland, a flood-prone river valley, or a rain forest, savannah, seacoast, or small island. Societies were also influenced by their contacts—friendly, hostile, or both—with other societies. Various Africans established connections with the wider world through long-distance trade, such as that carried on by the camel caravans across the bleak Sahara or by boat around the Indian Ocean. These connections ensured that few societies were completely isolated. During the Classical Era diverse societies developed in sub-Saharan Africa, the Americas, and Australia, and intrepid mariners settled most of the Pacific islands. These various communities worshiped their own deities, created their own artistic styles, valued some products more than others, and evolved their own social and political structures, including some states. At the same time, they had much in common.

FOCUS QUESTIONS

1. What were some of the similarities and differences between Kush and Aksum?
2. How did the spread of the Bantus reshape sub-Saharan Africa?
3. How did the Mesoamerican, Andean, and North American societies compare with each other?
4. How were some of the notable features of Australian and Pacific societies shaped by their environments?

Visit the website and eBook for additional study materials and interactive tools: www.cengage.com/history/lockard/globalsocnet2e

CLASSICAL STATES AND CONNECTIONS IN NORTHEAST AFRICA

What were some of the similarities and differences between Kush and Aksum?

In classical times tropical Africa and Eurasia were connected largely through intermediaries, including the North Africans linked to the trans-Saharan caravan trade and the maritime traders of the Indian Ocean. Two African societies, Kush (koosh) in Nubia and Aksum (AHK-soom) in Ethiopia, became trading hubs and powerful states. Both enjoyed particularly close ties with Egypt and western Asia.

CHRONOLOGY
Classical Africa

2000 B.C.E.–1000 C.E. Bantu migrations into Central, East, and South Africa

800 B.C.E.–350 C.E. Meroë Kingdom of Kush

500 B.C.E.–600 C.E. Garamante confederation dominates trans-Saharan trade

400 B.C.E.–800 C.E. Aksum kingdom in Ethiopia

200 B.C.E. Founding of Jenne-Jenno

300 C.E. Introduction of Christianity to Kush and Aksum

ca. 500 C.E. Founding of kingdom of Ghana

Iron, Cities, and Society in Kush

The kingdom of Kush, along the Nile south of Egypt, existed from about 800 B.C.E. to 350 C.E. (see Chronology: Classical Africa), flourishing as the major African producer of iron and an important crossroads for trade between sub-Saharan Africa and the Mediterranean (see Map 9.1). Its capital city, Meroë (MER-uh-wee), became an industrial powerhouse of the classical world. Kush had many sources of iron ore, and heaps of iron slag litter the ruins of Meroë today. The Nubians in Kush imported pottery, fine ceramics, wine, olive oil, and honey from Egypt and western Asia, and they exported both iron and cotton cloth. Both the Greeks and Romans admired the Nubians. Some Nubians seem to have visited Greece, and others were members of the Persian armies that attacked Greece. Africans, possibly Nubians, went to Rome to trade or work as musicians, actors, gladiators, athletes, and day laborers in the city. At its height Meroë was a grand city of perhaps 25,000 inhabitants, containing massive temples, large brick-lined pools that may have been used for public baths, and rows of pyramids, similar to those in Egypt, where kings and queens were buried in splendor. The highly skilled builders used masonry, stonework, fired brick, and mud brick. As in the Indus cities, washing and sanitation facilities, with many latrines, serviced Meroë's population.

Kushite Society and Politics

Although influenced by Egypt, Kushite society and culture were distinctive. At the top of the social hierarchy were absolute monarchs, including some queens, who both governed the state and served as guardians of the state religion and the temples. Besides worshiping some Egyptian gods, Kushites considered their monarchs, like those in Egypt, to be divine. Inscriptions testify to the piety of rulers, and Roman sources report that kings were guided by laws and traditions:

> It is their custom that none of the subjects shall be executed, even if the person condemned to death appears to deserve punishment. Instead the king sends one of his servants bearing a symbol of death to the criminal. He upon seeing [it], immediately goes to his own house and kills himself.[2]

Queen mothers seem to have played an influential role in politics. Below the ruler were the military and bureaucratic elite. Kush's military officers led an army feared for both its weapons and the appearance of its soldiers. The Greek historian Herodotus described the soldiers of Kush:

> [They] were clothed in panthers' and lions' skins, and carried long bows made from branches of palm trees, and on them they laced short arrows made of cane tipped with stone. Besides this they had javelins, and at the tip was an antelope horn, made sharp like a lance; they also had knotted clubs. When they were going into battle they smeared one half of their body with chalk, and the other half with red ocher.[3]

Below the bureaucratic and military elite were free peasants and slaves. Women played a variety of economic roles, working in gold mines and engaging in farming and craft production. They also served as priestesses, perhaps specializing in the honoring of female deities.

Kushite Culture

Kushites enjoyed a rich culture. Some Greek-speaking teachers apparently lived at Meroë, and at least one Kushite king studied Greek philosophy. Meroë also had artists who produced highly polished, finely carved granite statues of their monarchs. Music played on trumpets, drums, harps, and flutes was a part of ceremonial and religious life, and some of the instruments may have been

CHRONOLOGY

	Africa	The Americas	Oceania
800 B.C.E.	**800 B.C.E.–350 C.E.** Kush		
400 B.C.E.	**400 B.C.E.–800 C.E.** Aksum		**300 B.C.E.–1200 C.E.** Polynesian settlement of Pacific
200 B.C.E.	**200 B.C.E.** Founding of Jenne-Jenno	**200 B.C.E.–600 C.E.** Hopewell mound builders **200 B.C.E.–700 C.E.** Moche **200 B.C.E.–750 C.E.** Teotihuacan **150 B.C.E.–800 C.E.** Flourishing of Maya society	
500 C.E.	**ca. 500 C.E.** Founding of Ghana		

imported from Egypt and Greece. People of all classes and both genders wore jewelry, and the ruins of at least one tavern have been found littered with thousands of goblet fragments, suggesting that wine was a popular drink. Finally, the presence of writing on numerous tombstones as well as graffiti suggests that literacy was widespread among all classes. Along with other distinctive achievements, Kushites developed their own alphabet, **Meroitic** (mer-uh-WIT-ik), a cursive script that can only be partly read today. Meroitic gradually replaced Egyptian hieroglyphics in monumental inscriptions. Indeed, over time Egyptian influence apparently faded while indigenous culture flourished.

Meroitic A cursive script developed in the Classical Era by the Kushites in Nubia that can only be partly read today.

The Legacy of Kush

After a millennium of power and prosperity, by 200 C.E. Kush was in decline, in part from environmental deterioration. Centuries of deforestation and overgrazing had helped produce a drier climate. Climate change was widespread in the world at that time, and it may have also hastened the decline of the Han Chinese and Roman Empires. Chronic warfare with the Ethiopian state of Aksum also contributed to Meroë's problems. In 350 C.E. an invasion by the Aksum army destroyed what remained of the Kush kingdom.

However, the culture of Kush was kept alive in some neighboring societies. Some of its people, including the rulers, may have migrated elsewhere in Africa, spreading their iron technology and culture. Some West African societies developed political traditions not unlike those in Kush, and some peoples now living a few hundred miles to the southwest of Meroë still show many signs of Kushite influence, including recreational activities (such as wrestling), fashion, body art, and material life.

Spread of Kushite Traditions

Several new kingdoms arose from the ashes of Kush, and contacts with the outside world eventually brought a new religion, Christianity, that became dominant in Nubia between the fourth and sixth centuries C.E. During this time many churches were built. Nubian Christianity was a branch of the **Coptic** (KAHP-tik) **Church**, which followed Monophysite thought (see Chapter 8) and had become influential in Egypt. Many Copts still live in Egypt. But the Christian kingdoms of Nubia, isolated from other Christians to the north by the Islamic conquest of Egypt in the seventh century C.E., gradually faded. Around 1400 C.E. Muslims conquered the last Christian Nubian state, and most people converted to Islam. Today only the ruins of Christian churches and monasteries of Nubia remain, along with the Meroite pyramids, the material legacy of Kush.

Coptic Church A branch of Christianity, based on Monophysite ideas, that had become influential in Egypt and became dominant in Nubia between the fourth and sixth centuries C.E.

The Aksum Empire and Society

Another literate urban African state, **Aksum**, emerged in the rocky but fertile Ethiopian highlands beginning around 400 B.C.E. Despite difficult geographical terrain and an unpredictable climate, its peoples traded with Egypt and also benefited from proximity to the Red Sea, the major maritime route between the Mediterranean Sea and the Indian Ocean. At the Red Sea's narrow-

Aksum A literate, urban state that appeared in northern Ethiopia before the Common Era and grew into an empire and a crossroads for trade.

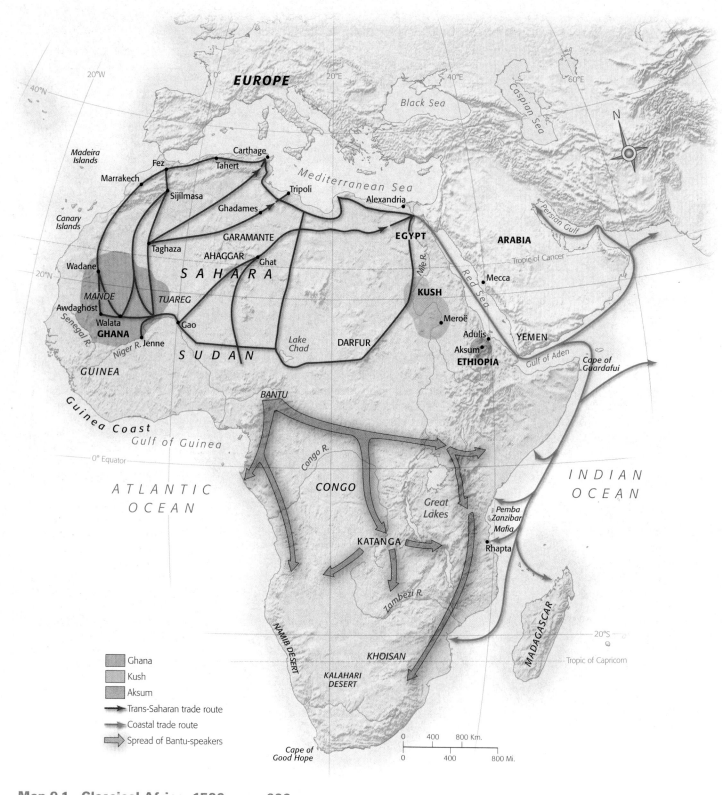

Key:
- Ghana
- Kush
- Aksum
- → Trans-Saharan trade route
- → Coastal trade route
- → Spread of Bantu-speakers

Map 9.1 Classical Africa, 1500 B.C.E.–600 C.E.
During this era, Kush, Aksum, and Jenne were major African centers of trade and government. Trade routes crossed the vast Sahara Desert, and the Bantu-speaking peoples expanded into central, southern, and eastern Africa.

e Interactive Map

est point, only 20 miles of water separates the southern tip of Arabia from Northeast Africa. Many Semitic people from Arabia crossed into Ethiopia and settled. Although many deep gorges inhibited communication across the plateau, accessibility to Arabia greatly benefited the northern Ethiopians and may have allowed them to establish links to the Hebrews. Ethiopian legends claim that the Queen of Sheba (Saba), who, according to biblical accounts, met the Hebrew King Solomon, was in fact an early Ethiopian monarch, Queen Makeda (ma-KAY-da), who went to Israel in search of knowledge. In the tale Makeda supposedly told her people:

> *Let my voice be heard by all of you, my people. I am going in quest of Wisdom and Learning. My spirit impels me to go and find them out where they are to be had, for I am smitten with the love of Wisdom and I feel myself drawn as tho by a leash toward Learning. Learning is better than treasures of gold, better than all that has been created upon earth.*[4]

Semitic immigrants from Yemen, the probable location of the ancient Sheba kingdom, may have brought the story with them to Ethiopia and adapted it for local needs. The son of Solomon and Makeda, Menelik (MEN-uh-lik), supposedly founded a new kingdom, called Aksum.

Located on the northern edge of the Ethiopian plateau near the Red Sea, Aksum was a center of agriculture and both bronze- and ironworking inhabited by the ancestors of the Amharic (am-HAR-ik) people who today dominate central Ethiopia. Between 400 B.C.E. and 100 C.E. Aksumites built their first temples and palaces of masonry, as well as a city, dams, and reservoirs. Irrigation and terracing supported productive farming. The Aksumites also developed an alphabet and enjoyed close economic and cultural exchange with both southwestern Asia and eastern Africa. In about 50 C.E. they built an empire that dominated a large section of Northeast Africa and flourished chiefly from trade. Soon Aksum had eclipsed Meroë and gained control of the trade between the Red Sea and the central Nile. It became so well known that the Persian prophet Mani included it with Persia, Rome, and China among the world's four great kingdoms.

The Aksumites traded all over the Middle East, eastern Mediterranean, and East Africa. The trade network also reached to Sri Lanka and India, and many Indian coins have been found at Aksum (see Witness to the Past: A Shopper's Guide to Aksum). The Aksumites exported ivory, gold, obsidian, emeralds, perfumes, and animals and imported metals, glass, fabrics, wine, and spices. They used the Greek language in foreign commerce and were the first sub-Saharan Africans to mint their own coins. Byzantium sent envoys to the court, seeking alliances against common enemies in Arabia. The Aksumites' extensive ties with the Semitic peoples of Yemen led to considerable genetic and cultural intermixing between these two peoples. The classical Amharic language, **Geez** (gee-EZ), is a mixture of African and Semitic influences. There was also much Hebrew influence on Ethiopian literature and religion. Indeed, the modern Amharic royal family, descendants of Aksumite kings, claimed ancestry from King Solomon and Queen Makeda. The Jewish communities known as *Falasha* (fuh-LAHSH-uh) have lived in northern Ethiopia for many centuries.

Aksum's social structure was dominated by kings who had a paternalistic attitude toward their people. A fourth-century C.E. king left an inscription in which he claimed: "I will rule the people with righteousness and justice, and will not oppress them."[5] Judging from their spectacular palaces, kings also enjoyed great wealth and power. A sixth-century Byzantine ambassador reported on the royal family's pomp and ceremony, writing that the king wore

From Graham Connah, *African Civilizations*, p. 44. Reproduced by permission of Cambridge University Press

Queen Amanitere
Queen Amanitere ruled Meroë along with her husband, King Natakamani, around 2,000 years ago. In this relief on the Lion Temple at Naqa, Kush, she holds vanquished foes by the hair while brandishing swords, thus demonstrating the power of the royal couple and the Kushite state.

Geez The classical Amharic language of Ethiopia, a mixture of African and Semitic influences.

a golden collar. He stood on a four-wheeled chariot drawn by four elephants; the body of the chariot was high and covered with gold plates. The king stood on top carrying a small gilded shield and holding in his hands two small gilded spears.[6]

Below the royal family was an aristocracy that supplied the top government officials, a substantial middle class including many merchants, and peasants and slaves, who could be conscripted for massive building projects.

The capital city of Aksum was a wealthy and cosmopolitan trading center widely known for its monumental architecture, including magnificent pillars, thin stylized representations of multistoried buildings (some over 100 feet high), many stone platforms, and huge palaces. The making and transporting of the huge monoliths and stone slabs required remarkable engineering skills.

The Aksum Legacy

Christianity became influential just as Aksum reached its height of economic and military power in the fourth century C.E. Christian missionaries traveled the trade routes from western Asia, with whom the Aksumites had long exchanged goods and ideas. The king adopted the faith, making Christianity the official religion of the kingdom. According to a Roman source, he "began to search out Roman merchants [at Aksum] who were Christian and to give them great influence and to urge them to establish [churches], supplying sites for buildings, and in every way promoting the growth of Christianity."[7] The king had political reasons for conversion, since he wanted to establish closer relations with Rome, Byzantium, and Egypt. But the Amharic population only slowly adopted the new faith. Ethiopian Christianity resembled the Coptic churches of Egypt and Nubia but also incorporated some of the long-entrenched spirit worship and various Hebrew practices, including the Jewish sabbath and kosher food.

Christianity in Aksum

Aksum eventually collapsed as a result of several forces. By 400 C.E., reduced rainfall and the resulting pressure on the land had produced an ecological crisis. Political problems added to imperial decline. In addition, the conquest of southern Arabia by Aksum's enemy, Sassanian Persia, in 575 diverted the Indian Ocean commerce from the port of Adulis. Then the rapid Islamic conquests of western Asia and North Africa beginning in the middle of the seventh century cut Aksum off from the Christian world. Aksum's trade withered, and it fell into economic stagnation, cultural decline, and political instability. By 800 C.E. the capital city was abandoned. Unlike Kush, Ethiopian society persisted in recognizable form. Over the centuries Christianity became a deeply ingrained local religion in the Ethiopian highlands, producing the unique Ethiopian Christianity of today. The Ethiopian church, closely connected to the monarchy, owned many landed estates. Ethiopians remained relatively isolated in their mountain fastness for the next ten centuries.

SECTION SUMMARY

- The kingdom of Kush in Nubia, with its capital city of Meroë, was a major African iron producer and crossroads of trade between sub-Saharan Africa and the Mediterranean.

- Kush was influenced by Egypt but was also remarkable for its rich culture and its fearsome warriors and absolute monarchs.

- Aksum, in the Ethiopian highlands, had contact with Egypt and Arabia, may have forged links with the Hebrews, and after a time eclipsed Meroë as the region's primary trade center.

- Aksum's king converted to Christianity as a means of establishing closer relationships with Rome, Byzantium, and Egypt.

- Like Kush, Aksum may have declined in part because of climate change, but it was also hurt by the Islamic conquest of its neighbors; unlike Kush, however, the society endured into modern times.

THE BLOSSOMING OF WEST AND BANTU AFRICA

| How did the spread of the Bantus reshape sub-Saharan Africa?

Complex urban societies also arose in West Africa, especially in the Sudanic region, on the Sahara's southern fringe, among peoples like the Mande (MAHN-day). These societies were linked to North Africa and beyond by trade networks. Meanwhile, Bantu-speaking Africans continued to spread their languages, cultures, and technologies widely, occupying the southern half of the continent. Some became connected to trade networks linked to east coast port cities.

A Shopper's Guide to Aksum

The following account of the trade of Aksum comes from the *Periplus of the Erythrean Sea*, written by an unknown Greek sometime in the second half of the first century C.E. The Periplus was a guide prepared for merchants and sailors that outlines the commercial prospects to be found in Arabia, the Indian Ocean, and the Persian Gulf. It also describes many of the bustling ports of this region. Hence, the *Periplus* is an excellent source for understanding Classical Era networks of exchange. In this excerpt, we learn about the port city of Adulis (A-doo-lis) on the Red Sea. Adulis, now called Massawa (muh-SAH-wuh), was the chief Aksumite trade distribution center, where goods from the Ethiopian interior and from faraway places such as India, Egypt, and the Mediterranean were brought for sale or transshipment.

Adulis [is] a port . . . lying at the inner end of a bay. . . . Before the harbor lies the so-called Mountain Isla, . . . with the shores of the mainland close to it on both sides. Ships bound for this port now anchor here because of attacks from the land [by bandits]. . . . Opposite Mountain Island, on the mainland, . . . lies Adulis, a fair-sized village, from which there is a three day's journey to Coloe, an inland town and the first market for ivory. From that place to the [capital] city of the people called Aksumites there is a five day's journey more; to that place all the ivory is brought from the country beyond the Nile. . . .

There are imported into these places [Adulis], undressed cloth made in Egypt for the Berbers; robes from . . . [modern Suez]; cloaks of poor quality dyed in colors; double-fringed linen mantles; many articles of flint glass, and others of . . . [agate] made in . . . [Thebes, Egypt]; and brass, which is used for ornament and in cut pieces instead of coin; sheets of soft copper, used for cooking utensils and cut up for bracelets and anklets for the women; iron, which is made into spears used against the elephants and other wild beasts, and in their wars. Besides these, small axes are imported, and adzes and swords; copper drinking cups, round and large; a little coin for those coming to the market; wine of Laodicea [on the Syrian coast] and Italy . . . ; olive oil . . . ; for the King, gold and silver plate made after the fashion of the country, and for clothing, military cloaks, and thin coats of skin. . . . Likewise from the district of Ariaca [on the northwest coast of India] across this sea, there are imported Indian cloth [fine-quality cotton]. . . . There are exported from these places ivory, and tortoise-shell and rhinoceros-horn. The most [cargo] from Egypt is brought to this market [Adulis] from the month of January to September.

THINKING ABOUT THE READING

1. What were some of the societies that were linked to the trade at Adulis?
2. What does this reading tell us about the networks of exchange that connected Aksum to a wider world?

Source: W. H. Schoff, trans. and ed., *The Periplus of the Erythraen Sea: Travel and Trade in the Indian Ocean by a Merchant of the First Century* (London, Bombay & Calcutta, 1912).

Sudanic Farming, Cities, and the Trans-Saharan Networks

In the vast but dry grassland region known as the Sudan (soo-DAN), lying in West and Central Africa between the Sahara and the tropical forests, societies adapted their economic life to the prevailing ecology. Most Sudanese became farmers living in small, largely self-sufficient villages, growing vegetables and cereal crops, especially millet and sorghum, that needed little water. West Africans also grew cotton and developed richly colored cotton clothing. The food grown in a large fertile delta region along one stretch of the Niger (NYE-juhr) River helped to feed the people of the trading cities.

Geographical Foundations

Some Sudanese along the Niger River congregated in large towns and cities that reached 30,000 or 40,000 in population. The major hub, Jenne-Jenno, located in what is now the nation of Mali, developed as early as 200 B.C.E. The residents built circular houses made of straw and coated with mud and also worked copper, gold, and iron, which they obtained from mines several hundred miles away. Gold dust and small copper ingots (ING-guhts) apparently served as currency throughout the Sudan. By 400 C.E. Jenne-Jenno had become a crucial transshipment point where goods arriving by camel or donkey caravan were exchanged for goods moved by boat along the Niger River. Jenne-Jenno continued to flourish as a commercial center for many centuries, closely tied, like other Sudanic cities, to hemispheric trade by the caravans across the Sahara. Eventually a wall over a mile in circumference surrounded the city to protect the residents. Built upon a

Ghana The first known major Sudanic state, formed by the Soninke people of the middle Niger Valley.

Mande Diverse Sudanic peoples who spoke closely related languages, shared many customs, and dominated the western Niger River Basin and adjacent areas of West Africa.

griots A respected class of oral historians and musicians in West Africa who memorized and recited the history of the group, emphasizing the deeds of leaders.

productive agriculture, Jenne-Jenno exported grain, fish, and animal products in exchange for metals. Historians suspect that Jenne-Jenno and other commercial centers in the Niger Valley were probably independent city-states for most of the first millennium C.E.

Large cities and states were less common in sub-Saharan Africa than in Eurasia and North Africa, in part because of smaller population densities. The African agricultural system, mostly based on shifting cultivation, suited the soils but could not generally support large settled populations. At the beginning of the Common Era the African continent may have contained between 15 and 25 million people, much less than half that of China. About half lived in Egypt, Kush, and along the Mediterranean coast. Small population densities meant that societies were held together by social and economic ties and did not require a powerful state to maintain order. The establishment of various caravan routes crossing the Sahara's barren sands, which greatly aided the growth of Sudanic societies by fostering interregional trade, began well before the Common Era. Eventually a large trade system spanned the Sahara, linking the Sudanic towns with the southern Mediterranean coastal societies such as Carthage. The gold used in coins minted in Carthage may have come from western Africa. Salt moving south to the Sudan and gold moving north to the Mediterranean drove the complex Saharan trade. Sudanic cities also shipped north cotton cloth, leather goods, pepper, and slaves, which the merchants in North Africa then sold to Europe.

Although Sudanic societies were largely self-sufficient, they needed salt mined in the central Sahara and along the West African coast. The salt trade was mostly controlled by the *Garamante* tribal confederation, which inhabited a large desert region north of the Sudan. These Berber (BUHR-buhr) people dominated the caravan trade routes as intermediaries from around 500 B.C.E. to 600 C.E., managing a vast commercial network. The Garamantes used camels as pack animals and horses to pull light chariots. To the Greeks and Romans, they were warlike barbarians, but in fact, these Saharans made the parched desert livable by combining pastoral stock raising with irrigated farming. They constructed several thousand miles of underground canals to cultivate their farms, lived in walled cities and villages, built stone citadels as military outposts, and were apparently governed by royal families. Their state collapsed around the same time as the Roman Empire, and the remnants were later overrun by Muslims.

West African States and Peoples

As in Kush and Aksum, commerce stimulated the growth of states in the Sudan and West Africa. Kingdoms apparently grew out of markets and taxed the trade in gold and other commodities. The Soninke (soh-NIN-kay) people of the middle Niger Valley formed the first known major Sudanic state, **Ghana** (GAH-nuh). Although Ghana existed by at least 700 C.E., it was probably formed several centuries earlier. Excavations of the probable capital city show a stone town that was built sometime between 500 and 600 C.E. Ghana reached its height as a trade-based empire in the ninth century and flourished until the thirteenth.

Diverse **Mande** (MON-day) peoples may have been typical of classical Sudanic societies. The Mande spoke closely related languages, shared many customs, and dominated the western Niger River Basin and adjacent areas. Mande speakers included such ethnic groups as the Soninke (who established Ghana), Mandinka (man-DING-goh), Malinke (muh-LING-kee), and Bambara (bam-BAHR-uh) peoples. By 900 or 800 B.C.E. Mande farmers lived in large walled villages, and they may have built Jenne-Jenno. Later, Mande speakers dominated much of the western Sudan.

The Mande groups shared many common social, political, and religious traditions. Their societies included aristocratic, warrior, and commoner classes and a special group of ritual and religious specialists. The Mande eventually developed theocracies in which chiefs and village heads combined religious and secular duties. A respected class of oral historians and musicians known widely as **griots** (GREE-oh) memorized and recited the history of the community, emphasizing the deeds of leaders. Many Mande of all classes enjoyed considerable prosperity, often from making their elaborate and

National Museum of African Art, Eliot Elisofon Photographic Archives, Smithsonian Institution. Photo by Frank Khory

A Jenne Warrior This statuette, about 2 feet tall and made of a baked clay known as terracotta, likely portrays a warrior in Jenne, probably of high status, although some experts believe it portrays a founding ancestor.

beautiful cotton clothing, which was traded widely. The Mande and other Sudanic peoples also developed some common ideas about religion, including animism. Although they believed in a distant creator god, spirits of nature and ancestors loomed large in daily life. The Mande drew no neat line between the living and the dead, and they also wanted to keep the favor of good spirits and avoid the hostility of bad ones.

Over time various peoples, including some from the Sudan, migrated into the Guinea (GIN-ee) coast, a migration made possible by new tools and agricultural techniques. The Guinea coast, which stretches some 2,000 miles from modern Senegal (sen-i-GAWL) to southeastern Nigeria (nie-JEER-ee-uh), was mainly covered by forest and swamp and had few edible plants or game animals. The mixing of Sudanic and other traditions in this area produced unique new societies. To survive their challenging environment, the people lived mostly in small, self-sufficient villages with rich social networks. They practiced subsistence agriculture, with yams and bananas as the staple crops, often working the land communally. The Guinea peoples also traded with the Sudanic societies, over land or by boat up the rivers such as the Niger and Volta (VAHL-tuh), and thus became linked to wider networks of economic and cultural exchange. Many of the coastal societies came to practice some common customs, including Sudanese traditions such as theocratic political systems and pronounced social class divisions.

Guinea Coast

The Bantu-Speaking Peoples and Their Migrations

Over several thousand years, many iron-using speakers of Bantu languages had migrated from their original homeland in eastern Nigeria into Central and East Africa (see Chapter 3). During the Classical Era, Bantu peoples accelerated their expansion to the south and east. Some Bantu-speaking peoples moved into the southern Congo region now known as Katanga (kuh-TAHNG-guh), an area of savannah grasslands but prone to drought and disease. Much of the region south of the Congo Basin rain forest is relatively arid because of irregular rainfall. Fortunately, the Bantu successfully adapted sorghum and millet from the Sudanic region and Ethiopia to this dry southern climate. From Katanga many Bantu began moving to the west, south, and east. By 200 B.C.E. Bantu culture had reached the Zambezi (zam-BEE-zee) River Basin, and by the third century C.E. the first Bantu settlers entered what is now the nation of South Africa. Networks of trade and migration spanning vast distances eventually connected the southern third of Africa to the Sudan and the East African coast.

Settling Eastern and Southern Africa

Bantu-speaking migrants encountered local peoples and incorporated new influences. Because they worked iron, the Bantu possessed military and agricultural technologies more effective than those of many non-Bantu, some of whom were pushed into marginal economic areas suitable only for hunting and gathering. For example, the Mbuti Pygmies of the Congo region moved into thick rain forests, while many of the Khoisan (KOY-sahn) peoples in southern Africa, such as the Kung! hunters and gatherers discussed in Chapter 1, became desert dwellers. But many Bantu intermingled with, and probably culturally assimilated, those they met. Sudanese cultural forms carried by the Bantu, such as drums and percussive music, woodcarving, and ancestor-focused religions, became widespread. The contacts also influenced the Bantu cultures. For example, the Xhosa (KOH-sah) and Zulu peoples, who settled along the southeastern coast of today's South Africa, mixed their languages and cultures with the local Khoisan cattle herders, incorporating cattle herding into their economic life.

Cultural Mixing

The migrating Bantu also gradually absorbed various societies in East Africa, including pastoralists and farmers. Various ironworking pastoralists from the eastern Sudan, known as **Nilotes** (nie-LAHT-eez) because they speak Nilotic (nie-LAHT-ik) languages very different from the Bantu tongues, were also settling in East Africa. Their relationships with the Bantu were not always peaceful. Some Bantu adopted pastoralism (herding cattle and goats) while others mastered new crops, including Southeast Asian foods like bananas, coconuts, sugar cane, and Asian yams available on the East African coast. These foods, as well as domesticated chickens and possibly pigs, were brought to East Africa by Indonesian mariners and migrants early in the Common Era (see Chapter 5) and eventually spread throughout Africa. Some of the Indonesian mariners settled along the coast, establishing trading posts and marrying local people. Between 100 and 700 C.E. Indonesians settled the large and previously uninhabited island of Madagascar, implanting there a mixed Indonesian-Bantu culture and language that still survive.

Nilotes Ironworking pastoralists from the eastern Sudan who settled in East Africa and there had frequent interactions with the Bantu.

Maritime Trade and the East African Coast

The East African coast developed a cosmopolitan society based on maritime trade. The winds and currents in the Indian Ocean reverse direction every six months, allowing boats from

SECTION SUMMARY

- The Sudan region included trading hubs such as Jenne-Jenno, but the population in the Classical Era was not dense enough to require a powerful state; Ghana was the first state to arise, probably around 500 C.E.

- The Garamante peoples controlled the extensive caravan routes through the Sahara Desert to bring salt from the African Mediterranean coast to Sudan, which exported gold in return.

- The Bantu peoples, equipped with iron tools, continued to migrate south and east, mixing with and sometimes pushing out other peoples, as they made their way to South Africa by the third century C.E.

- Indonesian mariners settled on the East African coast and, to a greater extent, in Madagascar, where a mixed Indonesian-Bantu culture survives to this day.

- Winds that switched direction every six months made it easy to travel back and forth between East Africa and southwestern Asia, India, and Southeast Asia.

southwestern and southern Asia to sail to East Africa and back each year. The trading ports to which merchants from southern Arabia sailed were located along the coast from Somalia to present-day Tanzania. The main port city, Rhapta (RAHP-ta) in Tanzania, had a large Arab merchant community.

The east coast trade grew slowly during the Classical Era. A first-century C.E. Greek reported that ships left Egypt's Red Sea ports and then visited Adulis and various Somalian ports before sailing to East African ports such as Rhapta. They then headed to India rather than venturing farther down the coast, avoiding what they considered the mysterious ocean stretching southward. Growing numbers of traders came to the coastal towns. East Africa exported ivory, rhinoceros horn, and tortoise shell to Egypt, India, and western Asia and imported iron goods, pottery, and glass beads. Egyptian, Roman, and West Asian coins found in the region indicate trade with the Mediterranean area, and Persian pottery was distributed widely along the coast and inland. Eventually, the coast developed many port cities and a culture that mixed Bantu ideas with those of southwestern Asia. But it was many centuries before any ships established contact with the Western Hemisphere, to which we now turn.

CLASSICAL SOCIETIES AND NETWORKS IN THE AMERICAS

> How did the Mesoamerican, Andean, and North American societies compare with each other?

As in Eurasia and Africa, the first cities and states in the Americas developed during ancient times, including the Olmec in Mesoamerica and the Chavín in the Andes (see Chapter 4). Population increase helped to stimulate the growth of more American urban societies during the Classical Era. By around 1 C.E. there may have been around 15 million people in the Americas, over two-thirds of them concentrated in Mesoamerica and western South America, where several cities became the centers of prosperous states. Most of these American societies thrived from highly productive agriculture and developed diverse cultures, governments, and ways of life.

The Emergence of the Early Maya

Maya The most long-lasting and widespread of the classical Mesoamerican societies, who occupied the Yucatán Peninsula and northern Central America for almost 2,000 years.

To the east of the pioneering Olmec, in the lowland rain forests of Central America and the Yucatán (YOO-kuh-TAN) Peninsula in southeast Mexico, the **Maya** (MIE-uh) became the most long-lasting and widespread Mesoamerican society, forging a literate culture that excelled in some sciences and mathematics (see Map 9.2). Building on early regional traditions, Maya farming by shifting cultivation and ceramic making date back to at least 1100 B.C.E. The Maya introduced intensive cultivation of maize (corn) and other foods into the tropical forests. According to Maya legends, the gods had fashioned people out of corn. Maya farmers built artificial platforms and terraces on which they could grow enough crops to generate surpluses that supported a ruling elite, as well as large underground reservoirs to store groundwater where rainfall was scarce. As more productive agriculture led to more population, the Maya spread southward into the mountains and coastal zones of what is today Chiapas (chee-AHP-uhs) (Mexico), Guatemala (GWAHT-uh-MAHL-uh), Honduras, El Salvador, and Belize (buh-LEEZ).

Mayan Building Projects

As their power increased, the Maya elite organized ambitious building projects, constructing the first Maya pyramids and elaborate stone buildings by 600 B.C.E. Unlike Egyptian pyramids, which served as burial tombs for top leaders, Maya pyramids had temples on top to house the gods and were built for religious worship and ceremonies. According to Maya folklore:

There had been five generations of people since the origin of light, of life and of humankind. And they built houses for the gods, putting these in the center of the highest part of the citadel. After that their domains grew larger and more crowded.[8]

As notions of divine kingship became widespread, the Maya began making stone statues and carvings of their rulers and painting sophisticated murals illustrating Maya myths.

At the height of their culture, 150 B.C.E.–800 C.E., the Maya built many cities, each boasting masonry buildings, large temples, spacious plazas and pyramid complexes, and elaborate carvings (see Chronology: Classical Americas). Suburbs containing residences, markets, and workshops stretched for several miles out from the city centers. The major early city was El Mirador, where some of the earliest examples of Maya writing were inscribed on pot fragments and sculpture. Influenced by Olmec models, the Maya developed the most comprehensive writing system in the Americas, a hiero-glyphic script used for calendars, religious regulations, and many sacred books, as well as to record dynastic histories, genealogies, and military successes. A later Spanish observer admired "those who carried with them the black and red ink, the manuscripts and painted book, the wisdom, the annals, the books of song."[9]

Tikal (ti-KAHL), in what is today eastern Guatemala, was one of the major Maya cities between 200 and 900 C.E., with a population of 50,000 at its height. Tikal contained three hun-dred large ceremonial buildings dominated by temple pyra-mids 200 feet high that were decorated with carvings made of stucco plaster. The first ruler used the jaguar as the symbol of kingship, military bravery, and religious authority. His descendants, King Great Jaguar Paw and General Smoking Frog, led Tikal to a great victory over the rival city Uaxactun in 378 C.E., ensuring Tikal's regional supremacy for the next two hundred years.

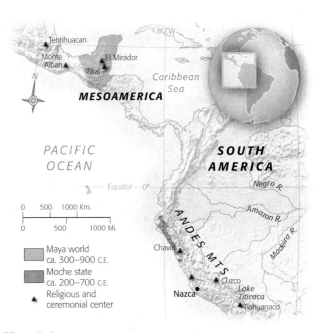

Map 9.2
Classical Societies in the Americas
The major American centers of complex agriculture, cities, and states emerged in Mesoamerica, where the Maya were the largest and longest-lasting society, and the Andes regions, where Chavín, Moche, and Tiwan-aku were important societies.

 **Interactive Map**

Maya Politics and Trade

Maya identity was more cultural than political. There was much cultural uniformity among the competing cities, probably because of the region's dense population and the close proximity of the trading cities with one another. Perhaps 10 million people lived in the Maya lowlands by 600 C.E. By around 500 C.E. the system shifted from one in which many small city-states competed to one in which a few cities, such as Tikal, dominated the others in their particular region. But no united Maya state or empire ever existed. Warfare between competing city-states over resources was frequent and brutal, and prisoners of war were usually enslaved or sacrificed. As in various Eastern Hemisphere and American societies, human sacrifice was common. Captured leaders from other cities faced especially agonizing deaths. Maya ruling families were interconnected, often marrying sons or daughters into ruling families of rival cities to cement alliances or dis-courage attack. Cities were ruled by kings and sometimes queens, who combined political, mili-tary, and religious leadership. The kings consolidated their position by linking themselves to gods and ancestors and erecting stone monuments containing inscriptions glorifying their deeds and ancestry. Because the scribes who wrote these inscriptions were a respected and influential group, when a city-state was defeated in battle the scribes of the losing king might also be killed.

Warfare and Leadership

Maya cities were linked in networks of interregional trade that were forged by hacking paths through the often dense rain forests. While rulers taxed and may have distributed goods, some recent findings suggest that many cities had marketplaces for traders. The Maya traded widely with non-Maya societies, some of them hundreds of miles away in central Mexico and deep into Cen-tral America. Dugout canoes carried Mayan and Central American goods to eastern Caribbean islands at least 1500 years ago. Merchants from the great non-Maya city of Teotihuacan (teh-o-tee-WAH-kahn), located near what is today Mexico City, lived in Maya cities, and Maya merchants and craftsmen settled in Teotihuacan. Mayan trading rafts probably sailed up and down the Central American coast and to some Caribbean islands. Unlike the societies of the Eastern Hemisphere,

Regional Networks

the Maya did not work bronze or iron, but they did use copper and imported gold from Panama. One of the most prized materials obtained through long-distance trade was jade, a very hard stone. Skilled Maya artists carved in jade, as well as in stone and wood, and their jade products were traded widely.

Maya Society, Religion, and Science

The Maya maintained a hierarchical social structure. The upper class included nobles, who staffed the bureaucracy, architects, priests, and scribes. Below them were many artisans, including sculptors, potters, painters, and stoneworkers. The laborers and farmers, who supplied manual work and food, occupied a lower rung still. Slaves, most of them criminals, war prisoners, orphans, or children sold by debtors, did the manual work of wealthy households. The strict legal code forced convicted robbers to restore stolen goods, pay for them, or work for the victim as a slave until the debt was paid.

The Maya had an extended, multigenerational family structure. Although descent was patrilineal, each person had two names, one from the father's family and one from the mother's. Parents arranged marriages for their children at an early age. Maya society accorded men more rights, prestige, and privileges than women. Boys and young men often lived apart from their families in special communal houses, learning the arts of war. Mothers kept their daughters close at hand, giving them a strict upbringing; girls, but not boys, were severely punished for compromising their chastity. Yet, some royal women wielded considerable power behind the kings, and a few served as rulers.

City people had some time for leisure activities. Regular festive local markets featured dancing to the drum and flute as well as ball games. Ball courts were built in all settlements. In the middle of each court was a stone ring, often 20 or 30 feet high, and players used a ball 6 inches in diameter, which they could only hit with their buttocks, fists, and elbows.

Maya Codex Only three Maya books (or codices) are known to have survived the Spanish conquest. This beautiful illustrated folding-screen book, the Dresden Codex, compiled around 1200 C.E., records astronomical calculations, tables of eclipses, and ritual detail. It is written on a long strip of bark paper coated with stucco.

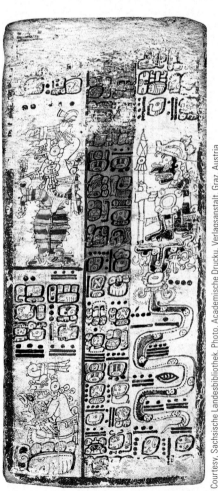

Courtesy, Sachsische Landesbibliothek. Photo, Academische Drucku. Verlagsanstalt, Graz, Austria

Since the main goal, directing the ball through the ring, was difficult, teams were probably also rewarded for keeping the ball in play as long as possible. The rapid action was exhausting. In an important match involving war captives, losers were sometimes sacrificed. The game, over 2,000 years old, is still played in some Mexico villages but without dire consequences for losing. Each city was fed by thousands of peasants growing maize and *cacao* (kuh-COW), from which chocolate is made. Cacao cultivation might go back to the Olmec. Although each farm family had its own plot, clearing and cultivating were done communally with neighbors. The Maya and other Americans had no draft animals to assist in farming, so they could not practice the intensive agriculture as people did in the Eastern Hemisphere. Instead the peasants had small plots, which they worked for perhaps fifty days a year. They were also subject to labor on public works or military duty.

Maya religion, science, and mathematics were linked together. The Maya worshiped a creator god and many other deities. The only surviving book of Maya religion, the *Popul Vuh* ("Book of Council"), claimed that the earth was sacred and that humankind was "given memory to count the days, [to be] bearers of respect for its divinity; to keep the rituals which connect humanity, nature and the heavens."[10] The Maya were obsessed with placating the gods through ritual practices, including human sacrifice. The gods needed victims, and so did the kings, to maintain their reputations for power. The Maya also emphasized purification of the body. There were many sweat baths, buildings fashioned to contain heat and steam generated by hot rocks. Sweat baths also may have been the scene of religious ceremonies.

The Maya's concern for using the correct times and seasons for religious celebrations motivated them to make calendars and to study astronomy. Cosmic phenomena determined which days were best for war, marriage, trade, rituals, and other activities. The Maya conceived of time as cyclical, and priests marked this time by observing the movement of planets and stars. The Maya secular calendar, based on a solar year at 365 days, was the world's most accurate before the sixteenth century. Their religious calendar, however, was based on 260 days. Every fifty-two years the two calendars coincided, at which time great festivals and religious observances were held.

Calendars
and Astronomy

The Maya were wise to study the sun, stars, and planets because cyclical variations in the sun's energy brought on debilitating droughts roughly every two hundred years. This climate change may have undermined the legitimacy of leaders linked to the gods and may also have provoked wars over scarce resources. Eventually increasing droughts probably contributed to the collapse of the Maya cities. The interest in time also contributed to a mathematics system simpler and much easier to use than the Roman numerals of Europe. Like the mathematicians of India, the Maya also introduced the concept of zero. Unfortunately, most of the Maya books (known as codices) were destroyed by the Spanish invaders in the 1500s C.E. Being zealous Christians, many Spanish considered the writing pagan, one arguing that the "books contained nothing [but] superstition and lies of the devil, [so] we burned them all which caused [the Maya] much affliction."[11] This terrible loss has made it much more difficult for historians to understand Maya history and culture.

Monte Alban and Teotihuacan

The Maya were not the only Mesoamerican peoples to develop cities and states in this era. By 400 B.C.E. small states were emerging among the Zapotec (ZAHP-uh-TEK) people in southern Mexico, especially around Monte Alban (MON-teh ahl-BAHN), a hilltop city and large ceremonial center with several huge pyramid platforms. Monte Alban was ruled by a hereditary elite of kings and priests. Many large carved stones may have been portraits of slain war captives, indicating military activity. Thanks to population growth and migration to the prosperous state, the capital city may have had a population of 25,000 to 30,000 people at its peak between 300 and 750 C.E. The Zapotec developed a complex alphabet and calendar that were similar to, and may have been derived from, those of the Olmec. Around 750 C.E. Monte Alban city began a long decline and was later mostly abandoned.

Mexican Cities

The large Valley of Mexico (the site of present-day Mexico City) also became an important site for urban societies. The valley had long been a center for mining *obsidian* (uhb-SID-ee-uhn), a glassy, volcanic rock prized for its razor-sharp edges. By 200 B.C.E. **Teotihuacan** ("the City of the Gods") became the largest city in the Americas and the capital of an empire in central Mexico, allowing the city to extend its influence over much of Mesoamerica. By 600 C.E. Teotihuacan was home to between 120,000 and 200,000 inhabitants, probably one of the half dozen largest cities in the world. It was laid out on a north-south axis that was bisected by wide avenues. The city boasted plazas, markets, apartment buildings, palaces, and hundreds of temples. Like the Harappan cities of ancient India, a complex drainage system aided removal of unwanted water. A huge Pyramid of the Sun rose over 200 feet high in the ceremonial center of the city, built from some 3 million tons of volcanic rock that was dug up and then transported to the city without benefit of iron tools or beasts of burden to pull wheeled vehicles. These American pyramids, smaller in size and built differently than the great Egyptian and Nubian pyramids, nonetheless demonstrate that the human mind can create the same symbols, however widely separated by geography and time. Teotihuacan also contained ball courts for games played with rubber balls.

Teotihuacan ("the City of the Gods") The largest city in the Americas and the capital of an empire in central Mexico during classical times.

Teotihuacan was a political, religious, and economic center. The kings seem to have been viewed as divine and left administration to bureaucrats and aristocrats. The people had writing and an ingenious numbering system, which no doubt assisted trade and administration. Priests and artisans, perhaps a quarter of the city's population, resided in houses built around small courtyards, where some fashioned obsidian tools or manufactured ceremonial pottery. Teotihuacan may also have functioned as the hub for the many trade networks spanning Mesoamerica and extending far to the north and south. Some neighborhoods were set aside for merchants and for sojourners or settlers, many of them traders and artisans, from the Maya cities and other regions, and Teotihuacan merchants also traveled widely. Maya-carved jade statues have been found in the city's ruins, and some archaeologists think there may have been close links between Teotihuacan and Maya royal families.

Teotihuacan
Government
and Economy

Eventually Teotihuacan society collapsed. The rulers seem to have become increasingly militaristic and human sacrifice became more common, earning Teotihuacan many enemies and

Georg Gerster/Photo Researchers, Inc.

Teotihuacan This overview shows the two largest pyramids at Teotihuacan, the Pyramid of the Moon (bottom center) and the Pyramid of the Sun. There were six hundred smaller pyramids in the city.

harming trade. In 750 C.E. invaders burned the city down, and the population scattered. The causes of the collapse may have been environmental (such as a prolonged drought) or the result of internal revolt or invasion by a rival state. But even in ruins the city's splendor lived on. A millennium later the Aztecs who had settled the area told the Spanish conquerors of their reverence for the sacred spirit of the pyramids: "And this they call Teotihuacan, because it is where they bury the lords."[12]

Andean Societies

The Maya and other Mesoamerican states were not the only societies that emerged and often flourished in the Americas during the Classical Era. The great Andes state of Chavín collapsed by 200 B.C.E., but some of the architectural and religious patterns it pioneered spread through the Andes and into adjacent lands, including **Moche** (MO-che), a prosperous and powerful state that formed around 200 B.C.E. in the desert region along the northern Peruvian coast. In this dry region farming required maintaining irrigation canals to channel the runoff from the Andes to grow corn, beans, peppers, squash, and cotton, which the Moche skillfully wove into textiles. They also exploited the abundant, protein-rich maritime resources just offshore, including fish and mollusks.

Moche A prosperous, powerful state that formed along the northern Peruvian coast from 200 B.C.E. to 700 C.E.

The Moche were part of a distinctive culture that emerged on the north coast of Peru in the second century B.C.E. These societies built monumental architecture, with platforms and courtyards, and fashioned beautiful jewelry, mirrors, and pottery. Coastal peoples traded some of their agricultural and maritime bounty to Andes societies for potatoes and other highland crops. Eventually trade networks linked distant societies over much of western South America. Some took up seagoing trade. Between 500 B.C.E. and the 1600s C.E., the Manteno people from the coast of Ecuador used balsa wood rafts equipped with sails and loaded with textiles, ceramics, precious metals, and prized shells to forge a coastal trade network stretching from Mexico to Chile. Because of such long-distance trade networks, coastal and interior peoples came to depend on each other, encouraging the formation of states in both places.

Coastal Societies

Moche Cities

The Moche capital city centered around two massive brick pyramids dedicated to the sun and the moon. The well-planned city was home to perhaps 10,000 people. Separate and perhaps hostile city-based Moche kingdoms were spread over hundreds of miles, all with similar customs, buildings, and pyramids. Burial chambers and a huge assortment of clay pottery painted with highly realistic scenes of social activity provide much knowledge of Moche society, such as the sometimes elegant, sometimes brutal life of the elite (see Profile: A Moche Lord). Enormous amounts of gold and silver artifacts were buried with Moche dignitaries.

The painted pots also reveal a colorful slice of everyday life. They show midwives attending birthing mothers and women carrying babies on their backs in shawls. Nearly everyone wears headgear in these scenes, from the feathered headdresses of the elite to the decorated cotton turbans of the common folk. Men often tattooed their faces. Like most Andes peoples, the Moche consumed maize beer. The paintings also show erotic scenes of lovemaking between men and women and between gods and humans, as well as scenes showing war leaders drinking the blood of their unfortunate captives. While many of their customs shock us and may not have made them popular neighbors, the Moche should be remembered for more than bloodshed. They were excellent gold workers and also made products from a copper and gold alloy as well as silver. They created one of the world's finest ceramic traditions and apparently also developed a mathematical system based on 10.

Eventually the Moche faced challenges they could not overcome, including a series of natural disasters, among them severe *El Ñinos* (el NEEN-yoz), the periodic warm water currents in the Pacific that bring higher temperatures and torrential rain to the region, as well as prolonged drought and massive earthquakes. Moche leaders may have responded to the resulting food shortages with increasing warfare to obtain resources and human sacrifice to appease the gods. The ecological and political crises that these disasters generated brought the Moche to an end by 650 or 700 C.E.

At about the same time that the Moche dominated the northern Peruvian coast, various states continued to rise and fall in the Andes and along the southern Peruvian coast. In the Lake Titicaca (tit-i-KAHK-uh) region (in modern Bolivia and southern Peru) of the Andes highlands between 600 and 100 B.C.E., the ancestors of the Aymara (AYE-muh-RAH) people built a state and constructed impressive stone sculpture. Even in ruins, their plazas, palaces, and brightly colored temples decorated with gold-covered reliefs could impress the Spanish 1,500 years later; one wrote: "There is a hill made by the hands of men, on great foundations of stone. What causes most astonishment are some great doorways of stone, some made out of a single stone."[13] The capital city, Tiwanaku (tee-wah-NA-coo), emerged by 100 C.E. and reached its height in 600 C.E., when it had a population of perhaps 40,000 and controlled much of the southern Andes. Tiwanaku was over 10,000 feet above sea level. A statue of the sun-god atop a platform greeted visitors, and in the city center was a huge, sacred platform, 650 feet long and 50 feet high. The rulers staged elaborate festivals with much drug and alcohol consumption to recruit labor for public works projects. Little is known of gender relations at Tiwanaku, but in the neighboring and rival state of Wari, just to the north, women of elite status operated a mountaintop brewery that made hundreds of gallons of corn beer every week.

Tiwanaku

Tiwanaku influenced a large region of western South America. The local art and the religion, which probably involved human sacrifice, seem to have spread into neighboring societies. The lands around the capital, rich in llama herds and a center of copper mining, flourished from a system of raised field agriculture—seeds planted on long artificial ridges separated by ditches—which improved drainage, replaced nutrients in the poor soil, and protected crops such as potatoes from frost. Tiwanaku agriculture was some 400 percent more productive than the farming in the region today. The Aymara, like other Andean peoples, were also skilled at using fibers. For example, they made boats to sail on the lake by weaving together reeds. But by 1100 C.E. the capital and surrounding fields were abandoned, perhaps because of climate change that generated a drought so severe that rivers dried up.

Another peoples, the Nazca (NAHZ-kuh), a decentralized agrarian society that flourished in the harsh desert in southern Peru from 200 B.C.E. to 600 C.E., became notable for the beautiful multicolored pottery and textiles it manufactured and the ceremonial centers it constructed. But the Nazca are most famous for creating geometric lines along their windswept plateau by clearing away surface stones to reveal the underlying rock and then laying the stones along the edges of the lines. Constructed on a huge scale, the lines depict either geometric shapes or animals such as monkeys and birds. These enigmatic markings have puzzled modern observers; scholars think they were created to mark the seasons, to communicate with gods believed to dwell in the nearby mountains, or to mark water sources. Or they may have just been artistic expressions of shapes and animals.

North American Societies

Sophisticated societies also emerged in North America before the Common Era. Several cultural traditions and permanent towns emerged among the desert farmers of the American Southwest, including the Hohokam (huh-HOH-kuhm), Anasazi (ah-nah-SAH-zee), and Mogollon

Southwestern Peoples

A MOCHE LORD

Outside of Mesoamerica, no American society left written records to help us understand individual lives. Nearly all we know of the Moche comes from recent archaeological investigations. As in Egypt, an arid climate preserved many objects and remains, allowing scholars to examine jewelry, weapons, clothing, ceramics, and skeletons. Many paintings on pots portray slices of Moche life. In addition, excavations at royal tombs in several cities have told us much about how the leaders of Moche society lived and died, even if we have no idea of their names, personalities, family ties, or precise governmental functions. These findings allow us to trace some of the experiences of one leader, probably a warrior-priest, who is known to archaeologists as one of the lords of Sipan, a Moche city. He was in his mid-thirties when he was buried around 390 C.E.

Archaeologists know what Moche men and women looked like. Moche men were stocky and averaged about 5 feet 3 inches in height, but this lord was 3 inches taller. He cut his hair in bangs over his forehead, wore it long in back, pierced his ears and nose, painted his face, and tattooed his arms and legs. The Moche women, such as those in the lord's family, stood about 4 feet 7 inches tall and wore their hair long, often braided with colorful woolen strands. At ceremonies women's dress consisted of a multicolored woven smock heavily laden with long strands of beads. Women lived much longer than men, but men had far richer costumes.

The lord of Sipan was buried in all the finery he probably wore in his official and ceremonial life. Like other warrior-priests, he dressed ostentatiously to demonstrate his wealth and power. He wore a long tunic completely covered with platelets of gilded copper, and he had copper sandals on his feet. On his wrists he sported large beaded bracelets of turquoise, gold, and shell. A beaded chest-plate and a spectacular necklace of gold and silver beads covered his chest and shoulders, and probably gleamed like the sun. Around his waist he wore a belt that supported crescent-shaped bells. A crescent-shaped gold nose ornament completely covered his mouth and lower face. Large ear ornaments were inlaid with gold and turquoise. On his head, the Sipan lord wore a large, crescent-shaped headdress ornament made of gold. In one hand he held a gold and silver scepter, an insignia of high rank. Moche art frequently depicted high-status men dressed like the Sipan lord.

The lord led a privileged life, but it was also one with many dangers. Moche society had a great concentration of wealth, and a few people, like the lord, lived in extreme opulence. Every valley may have had one or more royal courts that were connected to one another through marriage alliances and trade, like the kings of the Maya cities. Moche art frequently depicts warriors parading in front of royalty, perhaps preparing for war against rival courts. Like Maya royalty, the lord of Sipan may have gone into battle to personally fight rival lords.

Battle was a grueling and fateful experience for the combatants. Warriors used clubs to beat the heads of enemies, or they hurled stones and arrows with a sling. Like Roman gladiators, Moche warriors participated in hand-to-hand combat, with the ultimate goal of capturing the enemy for torture and sacrifice. A complex set of rules may have governed the conduct of warriors on and off the field. Battles ended when one warrior caught hold of another's hair and dragged him down. The loser, stripped of his clothes and weapon, was then paraded before the royalty of the winners. Painted bottles show the victorious lord presiding over a horrific sacrificial ceremony, drinking a goblet of blood drawn from the slit throats of captive enemy warriors. The lord of Sipan never suffered that fate. He was buried along with several young women, perhaps wives, concubines, or attendants; two burly men armed with shields and war clubs, possibly to protect him in the afterlife; and a dog, probably the lord's pet hound.

THINKING ABOUT THE PROFILE

1. How do burials and paintings on pots help us understand Moche life?

2. What do the lord's clothing and symbols of royalty tell us about Moche society?

3. What role did warfare play in the life of a Moche lord?

A Moche Lord   This Moche lord, memorialized for posterity in ceramic, wears the headgear and ear ornaments common to the Moche nobility. The potter skillfully captured the lord's facial features, giving the portrait a lifelike quality.

(MOH-guh-YOHN). By around 300 B.C.E. the Hohokam of what is now southern Arizona and northwest Mexico were trading extensively with other southwestern peoples and the southern California coast. Hohokam farmers used advanced irrigation, dams, terraces, and other strategies to grow maize, beans, squash, and cotton. The Hohokam survived for some 1,500 years, building large towns. The total Hohokam population in the vicinity of present-day Phoenix may have reached 40,000. The presence in Hohokam settlements of ball courts and rubber balls, as well as Mesoamerican-style platform mounds, indicates Mesoamerican influence over long-distance trade networks. But there is no evidence for human sacrifice or warfare. Eventually overpopulation, deforestation, and drier climates increased conflict and put more stress on the society, and by the fifteenth century the Hohokam settlements had been abandoned. Their modern descendants include the Pima and Papago Indians of Arizona.

The Anasazi and the closely related Mogollon culture were the direct ancestors of the Pueblo Indians in what is today Arizona and New Mexico. The Anasazi were once much more widespread and had towns in Arizona, Utah, and Colorado. The culture, which arose around the first century C.E., reached its high point between 750 and 900 C.E. The Mogollon peoples emerged around 200 B.C.E. and covered a territory stretching from central Arizona and New Mexico into northern Mexico. They flourished from a combination of corn growing and skillful gathering until the fifteenth century C.E.

Another great era of mound building characterized the eastern woodlands between around 500 B.C.E. and 400 C.E. Mound building had begun in North America around 2500 B.C.E. (see Chapter 4). But this new mound-building culture became even more widespread, encompassing the Mississippi, Ohio, Tennessee, and lower Missouri River Basins and their tributaries as well as the South Atlantic coast, a total area larger than India. The most prominent mound-builder tradition, known today as Hopewell, was centered in the Ohio River region. Hopewell artistic styles, maize cultivation, religious beliefs, ceremonial traditions, and burial customs spread throughout the eastern woodlands, but there is no evidence for any large state. The Hopewell peoples created extraordinary earthworks and other engineering projects. Elaborate geometric designs such as hexagons and circles mark their mounds. The Great Serpent Mound, built on a hilltop in Ohio around 2,000 years ago, was one of the most spectacular. Shaped like a snake, it ran 800 feet long from head to tail and was 4 feet tall and 20 feet wide. Some of the mounds were burial chambers for members of the elite. The Ortuna, a Hopewell culture in northern Florida, built a maze of 20-foot-wide canals that allowed them to reach both the Atlantic and Gulf coasts by dugout canoe, thus connecting them to a trading network stretching north to Ohio.

Eastern Moundbuilders

The Hopewell and other mound-building cultures were supported by two major economic changes. First, agriculture became more intensive, especially after the spread of maize. Second, long-distance trade expanded into a network spanning a large section of North America. Along the river trade routes moved obsidian from the Rocky Mountains, copper from the Great Lakes and later southern Appalachia, ceramic figurines and vessels from the lower Great Lakes, ore from Kansas, silver from Ontario, shells from the Gulf of Mexico and Florida, freshwater pearls from the Mississippi, and marine products from the Gulf coast such as sharks' teeth and turtle shells. Thanks to this trade network, sharks' teeth have been found in Illinois, over a thousand miles from the Caribbean.

The Hopewell culture began to decline around 300 C.E. and collapsed by 600 C.E. Overpopulation and the resulting competition for land might have put too much stress on the environment and economic system, and trade networks may have been disrupted. The maize crop diminished, possibly in part because of a cooling climate. In addition, around 300 C.E. someone invented or imported the bow and arrow into the region, altering the balance of power and stimulating warfare.

Changing States and the Spread of Cultures

While the traditions of the earliest urban societies, the Olmec and Chavín, remained influential in Mesoamerica and the Andes region, much change occurred over the centuries, although often on a different timeline from the Eastern Hemisphere. For example, around 200 or 300 C.E., various societies experienced a major transition. Small states such as Monte Alban, Teotihuacan, Tikal, and Tiwanaku grew into larger states, often regional empires. Long-distance trade increased, merchants became more influential, and ideas (such as writing and ball games in Mesoamerica) spread more widely. Many American peoples revered the land, seeing it as the source of both physical and spiritual life. The land also deserved reverence because of its close relationship to the supreme spirits or gods. As a result, people such as the Maya and some North American societies held maize as sacred, a gift from the gods.

SECTION SUMMARY

- The Maya society on the Yucatan Peninsula lived largely on corn, developed a comprehensive writing system and a numbering system that included zero, and built impressive buildings and large pyramids that served as religious centers.

- A few cities, such as Tikal, came to dominate Maya society, but there was no overarching Maya state.

- The Maya tried to please their gods through human sacrifice, which became more common with time, and self-purification, for which they used sweat baths; religion also motivated them to study astonomy and devise very accurate calendars.

- The Zapotecs built the city and state of Monte Alban.

- Teotihuacan, near present-day Mexico City, grew into one of the largest and best-designed cities in the world and had an extremely advanced infrastructure, including a complex drainage system.

- In the Andes, Chavín was succeeded by Moche, whose pottery depicts a violent culture of war and sacrifice but also of advanced metalwork and architecture.

- In the desert Southwest of North America, the Hohokam people developed extensive irrigation systems, and their cultural artifacts show some Mesoamerican influence.

- Supported by corn and expanded trade networks, mound-building cultures spread across eastern North America.

Except for the exceptionally enduring Maya and Tiwanaku, South American and Mesoamerican states exhibited a pattern of rise and fall after a few centuries, perhaps due in part to environmental and climate changes, which affected agriculture and fishing. Chronic warfare may also have played a role. Although the classical states established frameworks for later empires such as the Aztec and Inca, they did not survive in their original form, as the classical Chinese and Ethiopian states did.

The widespread presence of pyramids in Mesoamerica and South America has caused some observers to speculate about possible contacts across the Atlantic to North Africa and the Mediterranean long before the arrival of Norse Vikings around 1000 C.E. and, five centuries later, Spanish ships. But there is no firm archaeological evidence for any ties to the Eastern Hemisphere, and most specialists are skeptical that such contacts were ever made. Pyramids are based on practical principles of monument construction that were probably available to builders in any culture. Some American peoples were building mounds nearly as early as the first Egyptian pyramids.

Along the American west coast, from California to Peru, are scattered hints of trans-Pacific contacts in pottery design, artwork, and plants, leading to occasional speculation about possible Chinese, Japanese, or Polynesian voyages to the Americas. Some studies claim to find Japanese pottery in Ecuador, Olmec hieroglyphics that resemble Shang Chinese characters, Polynesian musical instruments and loan words in western South America, or Polynesian words and boat designs along the California coast. The world's most skilled mariners, Polynesians were capable of trips over several thousand miles of uncharted ocean, and they could have occasionally visited the American coast and then returned home. This might explain the presence of the South American sweet potato in Polynesia. However, no conclusive proof exists for any trans-Pacific contacts, and if any voyages did occur, they left no obvious long-lasting influence.

POPULATING THE PACIFIC: AUSTRALIAN AND ISLAND SOCIETIES

How were some of the notable features of Australian and Pacific societies shaped by their environments?

Although the original settlers of Australia and the Pacific islands migrated from or through Southeast Asia, the societies they developed remained largely isolated from the historical currents of Eurasia for many centuries. Australian Aborigines mastered a hostile environment and flourished from hunting and gathering. In extraordinary voyages, Austronesians migrated over thousands of miles of open ocean to inhabit most of the Pacific islands, adapting to new environments, creating diverse cultures, and developing long-distance trade networks.

Australian Geography and Aboriginal Societies

Geographical Foundations

Australia was settled at least 50,000 years ago. By 1000 B.C.E. Aboriginal tribes spoke some two hundred distinct languages. The environments that shaped the varied societies included the tropical, heavily forested coasts of the north and northeast, the temperate river basins and coasts of the southeast and southwest, and the deserts that dominate much of the interior. Aboriginal life was based largely on hunting and gathering, exploiting many food sources such as sea life along the coast and wild plants and insects in the harsh desert interior. Women gathered plants and small animals, prepared meals for the family, looked after the children, made the clothing, and built the huts. Men fished, hunted large animals, and manufactured implements. Aborigines developed an intimate understanding of weather patterns and their relationships to plants, animals, and land, knowledge still used by meteorologists today. In terms of nourishment, most Aborigines ate at least as well as peoples in Afro-Eurasia, and malnutrition and starvation were largely unknown. Agriculture never developed because most of the land was infertile, the rains erratic, and there were no native plants or animals capable of domestication. Even today large-scale irrigation is needed to sustain farming, and, as in ancient Mesopotamia, this irrigation has increased the salt content in groundwater, endangering fresh water supplies. Instead, Aboriginal societies developed land management and usage that enabled them to conserve their resources over thousands of years. They evolved a close relationship to the earth that remained at the center of their customs and beliefs over centuries. They also studied the night sky to survive the challenging landscape, using stories to explain the tides, eclipses, the rising and setting of the sun and moon, and the changing positions of the stars and planets throughout the year. The sky served as a calendar that indicated the change of seasons and when certain foods were available.

Many Aboriginal practices operated in tandem with the environment. For example, fire could be used to clear land to encourage regrowth of edible plants and rejuvenate the natural ecosystem. Whether deliberate or a result of natural processes, fires have always been a regular occurrence in Australia, but they have complicated modern life for the now urbanized regions. At least one Aboriginal society, the Gunditjmara in southern Australia, built an ingenious artificial lake where they operated eel farms beginning around 6000 B.C.E. The abundant eels raised there were traded around southern Australia. The Gunditjmara may also have lived in a permanent town with stone houses.

Aboriginal societies had many similar customs and beliefs. Since they had to move by foot with the seasons, most communities owned few possessions and prided themselves on not loading themselves down. Aboriginal men carried spear throwers and spears while women carried digging sticks and baskets to hold foodstuffs. Their seasonal moves, designed to maximize food availability, involved relocating to the same camps every year over regular trails. Aboriginal societies were divided into tribes organized either through the patrilineal or the matrilineal line, and nuclear families operated with considerable independence. Although few tribes had chiefs, older males exerted considerable influence in religious and social life. Women made critical decisions about the campsite and controlled their own ceremonial life. Relations between the genders were apparently flexible. Periodic disputes between neighboring tribes sometimes led to fighting, but they were usually settled by diplomacy involving the tribal elders.

Since most people had to spend only about three days a week in search of food, they had considerable time for rituals, ceremonial expression, and religious matters, including a widely shared belief in the mythology of the **dreamtime**, the distant past when the spiritual ancestors gave order and form to the universe at the world's creation. The dreamtime myths were remarkably consistent around the continent, passed down through countless generations by a rich oral literature. Aborigines also recognized an animistic world inhabited by many spirits and ghosts. Their art had a religious base and included body decoration, bark paintings, and especially rock carvings and paintings.

A complex trade system spanned the continent. Pearls and shells from the northern coast reached southern Australia, and quartz, flint, and other stones to make tools, as well as animal skins, wood products, and ornaments, were exchanged over wide areas. By classical times Indonesian trading ships probably visited the northwest coast to obtain pearls. Later, Chinese ships may have also engaged in such exchanges. But these outside contacts had little influence on most Australian societies. Today, after two centuries of change brought by European conquest and settlement, the life that sustained Australia's Aborigines for thousands of years has largely passed. Where once songs were sung about the history of the lands and the peoples, today, largely settled on rural land reserves or living in poor urban neighborhoods, the Aborigines lament the loss of their traditions. Their stories still recollect tribal pasts and beliefs, but the storytellers inhabit a very different reality from their ancestors.

Austronesian Expansion

Today some 1,200 different Austronesian languages are spoken from Madagascar eastward through Indonesia, Malaysia, the Philippines, and most of the Pacific islands. This book has elsewhere discussed the migrations of Indo-Europeans from southern Russia into Europe, western Asia, and India, as well as the long movement of Bantu-speaking peoples into the southern half of Africa. But no premodern peoples migrated over as wide an area in so short a time as did the Austronesians. Before the Classical Era some Austronesian-speaking peoples moved from Southeast Asia into the western Pacific islands just northeast of Australia (see Chapter 4). There they

Customs and Beliefs

dreamtime In Aboriginal Australian mythology, the distant past when the spiritual ancestors gave order and form to the universe at the world's creation.

Austronesian Migrations

encountered Melanesians (mel-uh-NEE-zhuhnz) who had earlier migrated from Southeast Asia. Over time the two traditions mixed, and Melanesians adopted Austronesian languages. Eventually some Austronesian-speaking peoples from the western Pacific sailed farther east and north to colonize other islands, in the process fostering new groups later known as Polynesians (PAHL-uh-NEE-zhunz) and Micronesians (MIE-kruh-NEE-zhunz).

Using only the stars, moon, sun, winds, and waves to guide them, the migrants endured the hardships of long open-sea voyages to discover new lands. Navigation and boat-building were a science; voyagers spent many days selecting the right tree for their canoes since worm-ridden wood might prove disastrous at sea. An ancient Tahitian prayer reveals the voyagers' fears: "O gods! Lead us safely to land. Leave us not in the ocean. Give us a breeze. Let the weather be fine and the sky clear."[14] These intentional migrations were spurred by overpopulation on islands with limited resources, fresh water, or fertile land. Some Pacific islands were mountainous and often covered by dense rain forests, while others were flat atolls only a few feet above sea level, which left the inhabitants vulnerable to high waves due to fierce storms. Islanders either learned to limit population growth or suffered the effects of deforestation and natural resource depletion, which generated conflict or migration. Excellent naval technology made the migrations possible: each double-hulled outrigger canoe, up to 100 feet long and consisting of two hulls with a platform lashed between them for living, cooking, work space, and storage, was capable of carrying up to eighty people, along with foods, plants, and animals.

Micronesians

The Micronesians, who settled many central and north Pacific islands, made ingenious navigation charts from cowrie shells tied together. The Austronesian-speaking ancestors of some Micronesians eventually colonized many small islands in the central Pacific, including the Carolines. The Marianas (MAR-ee-AN-uhz), including the islands of Guam and Saipan, may have been settled directly by Austronesians sailing east from the Philippines and possibly Taiwan between 1500 and 1000 B.C.E. (see Chronology: The Pacific Islands, 1500 B.C.E.–1000 C.E.). The Chamorro (cha-MOR-roe) people of the Marianas were the only Pacific society to grow Asian rice, suggesting they had continuing connections with the Philippines.

Polynesian Migrations and Societies

Polynesian Dispersal

Polynesian culture seems to have flowered first in the neighboring Fiji, Tonga, and Samoa (suh-MO-uh) island groups around 500 B.C.E. (see Map 9.3). Within a few centuries some were on the move again. By around 300 or 200 B.C.E. Polynesian mariners from Tonga may have reached the Marquesas (mar-KAY-suhs) Islands and soon thereafter Tahiti (tuh-HEE-tee), 1,500 miles east of Tonga. Polynesians sailed from Samoa 1,500 miles north to the Kiribati (kear-uh-BAH-tee) Islands, and then on to the Marshall Islands. Later, between 400 and 600 C.E., mariners from the

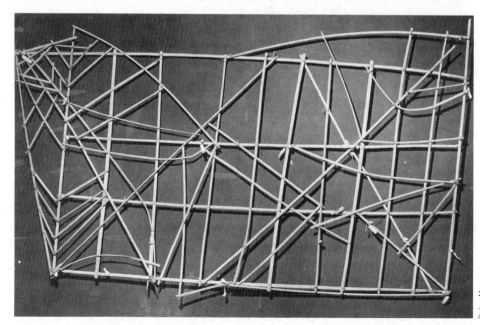

Polynesian Palm-Frond Navigational Map This nautical map, made in the Marshall Islands from palm fronds, shows distances between islands as measured by time traveled. The map may have originally had bits of shell or coral to mark islands. Polynesians and Micronesians often made such maps for their ocean voyages.

Bishop Museum

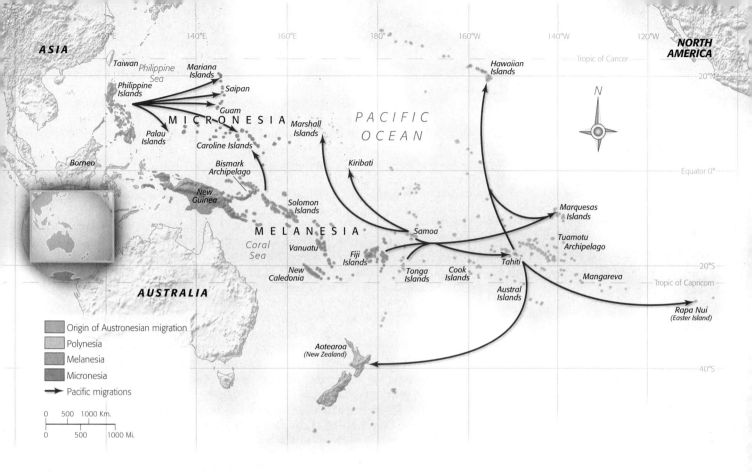

Map 9.3
Pacific Migrations in the Classical Era

During this era, Austronesian peoples scattered across the vast Pacific Basin, using ingenious canoes and navigation techniques to settle nearly all the inhabitable islands. From bases in Tonga and Samoa in the west, the Polynesians settled a large expanse of the basin ranging from Hawaii in the north to Easter Island in the east and New Zealand in the south.

Interactive Map

Marquesas settled Hawaii after crossing over 2,000 miles of ocean, followed around 1100 or 1200 C.E. by a migration from Tahiti 2,500 miles east to Easter Island. Finally, between 800 and 1000 C.E., some Tahitians moved west another 2,500 miles to Aotearoa (ow-TEH-a-ROW-uh) (which a Dutch explorer much later named New Zealand), the largest landmass settled by Polynesians. These settlers, the ancestors of the Maori (MAO-ree) people, faced a very different climate and topography from that of the tropical Pacific islands, as well as a new mix of plants and animals. Polynesian sailors may even have visited the Peruvian coast. Such contact might explain the presence of sweet potatoes, a South American crop, in eastern Polynesia and New Zealand for at least 1,000 years.

Polynesian agriculture was based on Southeast Asian crops such as yams, taro, bananas, coconuts, and breadfruit and animals such as pigs, chickens, and dogs. But survival required some modifications, including elaborate terracing, artificial ponds, and irrigation. Polynesians also exploited local food sources such as coconuts and the abundant marine life of the lagoons, coral reefs, and deep sea. Cloth made out of bark furnished clothing. But fragile island ecologies were easily unbalanced. Imported animals like pigs, dogs, and (unintentionally) rats consumed local birds. Overhunting eliminated some species, and deforestation was also a problem. As an extreme example, Easter Island, which was heavily forested when Polynesians arrived, was completely denuded over the centuries, and the people were reduced to poverty and chronic conflict over ever scarcer resources.

Early Polynesians lived in clans that were generally dominated by hereditary chiefs who controlled the lands. Conflict between rival clans over status and land led to tensions and sometimes war. Eventually the most elaborate social hierarchies emerged in Tonga, Tahiti, and Hawaii, where paramount chiefs ruled many thousands of followers and controlled much of the economy. While men held most political power, women often enjoyed a high status, and most Micronesian and some Polynesian societies were matrilineal. Polynesian women often ranked higher than their brothers in spiritual and ritual authority and, by marrying into other clans or ruling families, could help

Polynesian Agriculture and Cultures

SECTION SUMMARY

- Aboriginal Australians developed great understanding of natural phenomena and were very successful hunters and gatherers for thousands of years.

- Aborigines across Australia believed in the dreamtime of the mythic past and felt that spirits and ghosts inhabited much of the physical world.

- Austronesian peoples from Southeast Asia took to the sea and settled on various Pacific islands.

- Polynesian culture probably began in Fiji, Tonga, and Samoa, but it spread out over a remarkable expanse of the Pacific Ocean.

- An extensive trading network developed among the Pacific islands, and, despite their isolation from each other, the islands' cultures remained quite homogenous.

political relations. The far-flung Polynesian societies also shared many other cultural traits, including elaborate facial and body tattooing (the word *tattoo* is of Polynesian origin), myths, reverence for ancestors, and art forms such as woodcarving. Many of these customs were also common in Melanesia and Micronesia.

The huge triangle of Polynesia, anchored at the ends by Hawaii, New Zealand, and Easter Island, is one of the largest expanses of territory in the world. One of the first outsiders to explore the area, British captain James Cook, wrote in 1774: "It is extraordinary that the same [people] should have spread themselves over all the isles in this vast Ocean, almost a fourth part of the circumference of the Globe."[15] Migration over such vast distances did not necessarily mean isolation. Thanks to a large maritime network, obsidian mined on the island of New Britain, northeast of New Guinea, was traded as far west as Borneo and as far east as Fiji, some 4,000 miles apart. Nearby island groups traded with each other and maintained social links. For example, the Tongan and Fijian chiefly families frequently intermarried. But the sailing required remarkable observation and could be dangerous, as Captain Cook reported from Tonga in 1777: "In these Navigations the Sun is their guide by day and the Stars by night; when these are obscured they have recourse to the points from whence the Wind and waves come upon the vessel. If [these] shift, they are bewildered."[16] Even today Polynesian traditions honor great navigators of the past such as Moikeha and Pa'ao, who sailed back and forth between the Marquesas and Hawaii over a millennium ago.

CHAPTER SUMMARY

During the Classical Era some sub-Saharan Africans became more closely linked by trade with North Africa and Eurasia. Kush became a center for iron production, and Aksum, in the Ethiopian highlands, flourished as a trading hub. Cities and small states that emerged in the Sudanic region of West Africa participated in the growing trans-Saharan caravan trade network linking them with the Mediterranean world. Cities also appeared along the East African coast, tied by trade networks to the Mediterranean, western Asia, and India. Bantu-speaking peoples settled the southern half of Africa, carrying with them iron technology and many Sudanic influences.

Various urban societies dominated Mesoamerica and the Andes, including the Maya, Moche, Tiwanaku, Teotihuacan, and Monte Alban. The Maya forged a particularly enduring society based on competing city-states, developed a writing system, and understood much about astronomy and mathematics. The Moche on the Peruvian coast and Tiwanaku in the highlands formed empires. In Mesoamerica, Teotihuacan became the greatest city in the Americas and a major trading hub. In North America many peoples adopted farming, built permanent towns, and took up mound building. In the Pacific, Australian Aborigines adapted well to their harsh environment, flourishing for millennia from hunting and gathering. And various Austronesian peoples, particularly the Polynesians, made spectacular migrations into the vast Pacific Ocean by using remarkable seagoing technologies and adapting to diverse island environments.

KEY TERMS

Meroitic	Geez	griots	Teotihuacan
Coptic Church	Ghana	Nilotes	Moche
Aksum	Mande	Maya	dreamtime

EBOOK AND WEBSITE RESOURCES

e INTERACTIVE MAPS

Map 9.1 Classical Africa, 1500 B.C.E.–600 C.E.
Map 9.2 Classical Societies in the Americas
Map 9.3 Pacific Migrations in the Classical Era

LINKS

About Archaeology (http://archaeology.about.com/
library). About.com offers many essays and links
relevant to early Africa and the Americas.

Africa South of the Sahara: Selected Internet Sources
(http://www-sul.stanford.edu/depts/ssrg/africa/guide
.html). Useful collection of links from Stanford
University.

African Timelines (http://www.cocc.edu/cagatucci/
classes/hum211/timelines/htimeline.htm). Has many
links to specific periods and cultures as well as essays
on controversial topics.

Ancient Mesoamerican Civilizations (www.angelfire
.com/ca/humanorigins). Links and information about
the premodern societies.

History and Cultures of Africa (http://www.columbia
.edu/cu/lweb/indiv/africa/cuvl/cult.html). Extensive
links provided by Columbia University.

Internet African History Sourcebook (http://www
.fordham.edu/halsall/africa/africasbook.html). This
site, maintained at Fordham University, contains
much useful information and documentary material
on African societies.

Plus flashcards, practice quizzes, and more. Go to:
www.cengage.com/history/lockard/globalsocnet2e

SUGGESTED READING

Adams, Richard E. W. *Ancient Civilizations of the New World.*
Boulder: Westview, 1997. Brief survey of Mesoamerican and
South American societies before 1500 C.E.

Burstein, Stanley M. *Ancient African Civilizations: Kush and
Axum.* Princeton: Markus Wiener, 1998. Good brief introduction and collection of primary sources.

Coe, Michael. *The Maya,* 7th ed. London and New York: Thames
and Hudson, 2005. The standard overview of Maya history.

Connah, Graham. *African Civilization: An Archaeological Perspective,* 2nd ed. Cambridge: Cambridge University Press,
2001. An overview of early African societies, emphasizing
the rise of cities and states.

Ehret, Christopher. *An African Classical Age: Eastern and
Southern Africa in World History, 1000 B.C. to A.D. 400.* Charlottesville: University Press of Virginia, 1998. A pathbreaking
study rethinking the role of classical Africa in world history.

Fagan, Brian M. *Kingdoms of Gold, Kingdoms of Jade: The
Americas Before Columbus.* London and New York: Thames
and Hudson, 1991. A nicely illustrated and readable introduction to the premodern American societies.

Fischer, Steven Roger. *A History of the Pacific Islands.* New
York: Palgrave, 2002. A readable introduction to Pacific societies and history.

Kehoe, Alice Beck. *America Before the European Invasions.*
New York: Longman, 2002. A recent overview of the North
American peoples and history before 1600 C.E.

Kirch, Patrick. *On the Road of the Winds: An Archaeological
History of the Pacific Islands.* Berkeley: University of California Press, 2000. A comprehensive study of the Austronesians
in the Pacific.

Knight, Alan. *Mexico: From the Beginning to the Spanish Conquest.* New York: Cambridge University Press, 2002. An
introduction to Mesoamerican societies.

Mann, Charles C. *1491: New Revelations of the Americas Before
Columbus.* New York: Alfred A. Knopf, 2005. A readable summary of recent scholarship on the American societies.

Newman, James L. *The Peopling of Africa: A Geographic Interpretation.* New Haven, CT: Yale University Press, 1995. An
excellent summary of what we know about the early history
and migrations of Africa's people.

Nile, Richard, and Christian Clark. *Cultural Atlas of Australia,
New Zealand and the South Pacific.* New York: Facts on File,
1996. A well-written overview with much on early histories
and cultures.

Phillipson, David W. *African Archaeology,* 3rd ed. Cambridge:
Cambridge University Press, 2005. A general study of the
archaeology of premodern Africa, from prehistory into the
second millennium of the Common Era.

Phillipson, David W. *Ancient Ethiopia: Aksum, Its Antecedents
and Successors.* London: British Museum Press, 2005. A general study of the archaeology of premodern Africa, from prehistory into the second millennium of the Common Era.

Shillington, Kevin. *History of Africa,* revised 2nd ed. New York:
Palgrave Macmillan, 2005. A recent survey text.

Welsby, Derek A. *The Kingdom of Kush: The Napatan and
Meroitic Empires.* Princeton: Markus Wiener, 1996. A well-
illustrated and up-to-date survey of Kushite society.

Whitlock, Ralph. *Everyday Life of the Maya.* Reprint of 1976
edition. New York: Dorset Press, 1987. Although somewhat
dated, this remains an excellent introduction to Maya life.

The Afrocentric Challenge to Historians of Antiquity

For many years the writings by Western scholars about world history emphasized Europe, a biased perspective known as Eurocentrism. In the conventional story line, history began in Egypt, Mesopotamia, and Palestine before moving to Greece and Rome and then on to northwestern Europe and finally to North America. The rest of the world, except perhaps for India and China, constituted an exotic aside to the European mainstream. The academic fields of classics (the study of the Greco-Roman world) and Egyptology specialized in the ancient Mediterranean world, excluding the rest of Africa and Asia. Before the 1970s most Western historians either ignored Africa or argued that Africa was unimportant throughout world history.

THE PROBLEM

Today a historical perspective that incorporates Africa has become common, but for much of the twentieth century many scholars openly agreed with an eminent British historian, who wrote in 1928 that Africa had no history and that most Africans had stayed stagnant and sunk in barbarism for many centuries. In reacting to racial discrimination and lingering contempt for Africa's historical legacy, many historians have made a convincing case for the importance of Africa and its critical role in world history. But questions remain. Was Africa a central part of the larger ancient and classical world? Was Egypt essentially an African or a Mediterranean society? Finally, did Egypt strongly influence classical Greece?

THE DEBATE

In dramatic contrast to Eurocentrism, an alternative approach known as Afrocentrism emphasizes Africa's, rather than Europe's, centrality in history. The more radical Afrocentrists provide a mirror image to the old Eurocentric model, dismissing the older history as a lie designed to glorify European culture and perpetuate the power of white people. They assert that Africa was the fountainhead of Mediterranean culture and that a new way of understanding world history must be developed. Afrocentrists like the Senegalese Cheikh Anta Diop and the American Molefe Asante argue that black Africans, including Egyptians, originated and developed many of the arts, philosophies, and technologies of the ancient and classical Mediterranean societies.

Critics accuse the radical Afrocentrists, like the rigid Eurocentrists, of exaggeration and selectivity in their use of historical evidence, charging that they rely on largely outdated and discredited sources. Some Afrocentrists, for example, promote the dubious notions that Egyptian queen Cleopatra (a Hellenistic Greek) and Athenian philosopher Socrates were black, or that African mariners established the Olmec society of Mexico. Such unsubstantiated theories convince few scholars, regardless of their ethnic background. The British scholar Stephen Howe even asserts that Afrocentric writings replace outmoded Eurocentric scholarship with a misleading version that offers a fictional history.

One prong of the debate is whether ancient Egypt should be seen as essentially Mediterranean or as an African society rooted in African traditions. There is some truth to both propositions. Most scholars now acknowledge extensive Egyptian connections to Africa, western Asia, and southeastern Europe. African ties were certainly extensive. For example, the ancient Egyptian language was closely related to many African tongues. In addition, historians of Africa now believe that many ideas that Egyptians shared with African peoples diffused to Egypt from the south, including the notion and rituals of divine kingship that underpinned Egyptian royalty, various myths and gods, and much material culture. But Egypt's connections were diverse. Populated by migrants from all directions, Egypt produced people of many skin colors and physical features. As a trade crossroads, it maintained trade relations with Africans, Asians, and Europeans. People moved around and intermarried. Thus the Nile Valley was a zone of contact between many groups, where there was not only considerable mingling of people but also, with that, creative cultural borrowing and invention, making it difficult for historians to precisely identify the foreign influences on Egyptian culture.

Another controversy concerns whether Egypt spread African ideas and influences to the Greek culture emerging across the Mediterranean. In his three-volume study, *Black Athena*, the British-born, U.S.-based scholar Martin Bernal contends that, until the early nineteenth century, Western historians stressed the Afro-Asiatic origins of Greek culture, acknowledging Egypt and Phoenicia as core influences. Then, in a sharp turn from that position, he argues, because of increasing racism toward black people and rising European imperialism and nationalism, Western scholars began to stress the Greeks as being a creative source of culture rather than derivative—the pure and original source of European society. African and Middle East influences, such as those from Egypt and Phoenicia, were removed from the scenario.

To argue his point, Bernal uses the myths and historical writings of the Greeks themselves, including, for example, the claims by the Greek historian Herodotus that the Egyptians invented mathematics and that the names of Greek gods originated in Egypt. Herodotus spent time in Egypt around 450 B.C.E. and admired the Egyptian heritage. Influenced by his views, Bernal agrees with Diop that a significant proportion of Greek religion, political philosophy, architecture, science, and even language was imported from Phoenicia and Egypt. For example, Bernal suggests that Athena, the Greek goddess of wisdom and patron goddess of Athens, was a transplanted version of Neith, a goddess from the Nile Delta.

Bernal's work has provoked a storm of controversy. Critics accuse Bernal of misreading Greek myths and historical accounts. They suggest that the Greeks credited Egypt with these accomplishments because they wanted to legitimize their own position by connecting with the older and much respected Egyptian culture, a plausible argument. Furthermore, as most historians are aware, Herodotus often exaggerated or relied on unreliable hearsay, and so is not always a convincing source. Reliance on Herodotus, critics charge, led Bernal to unsubstan-

Alinari/Art Resource, NY

Athena, Greek Goddess of Wisdom Some scholars suspect that some Greek deities, such as Athena,
portrayed here in a Greek sculpture, were based on
Egyptian deities.

tiated links, such as one tracing the origins of Greek philosophy
to Egyptian literature on wisdom, despite many differences. In
one of the more articulate critiques of Bernal, Mary Lefkowitz links Bernal to radical Afrocentrism (an approach he criti-
cizes), deploring his scholarship for disputing that the Greeks
invented democracy, philosophy, and science.

In this debate, few classicists disagree that the Greeks
admired the Egyptians and traded with them extensively.
Some leading Greek thinkers, including Herodotus, Solon,
Plato, Thales, and Euclid, visited or studied in Egypt. But, like
Lefkowitz, many classicists believe Bernal greatly overstates
Afro-Asian influence and underestimates Greek genius. At the
same time, however, many other scholars defend Bernal, while
some, including the Africanist Basil Davidson and the classicist
Jacques Berlinblau, take a more balanced middle view. And
the controversy has also inspired more studies placing Egypt
and Africa in a larger regional or world context, such as those
by Schofield and Davies and by Gilbert and Reynolds.

EVALUATING THE DEBATE

Both sides of the debate have been accused of having a political agenda: to influence how the histories of Europe and Africa
are taught in North American and European schools. Hence,
the controversy illustrates the danger of what historians call

"present mindedness," the tendency to interpret the past
largely in light of present social and political concerns. While
we can never entirely escape this tendency, we can try to see
the people of the past as they saw themselves. This means not
using their experiences as ammunition in current social and
political debates, as both Eurocentric and Afrocentric historians have often done. While many particular points made by
Afrocentrists have found little favor among most historians, we
can credit Bernal and others for their useful critique of Eurocentric scholarship. In any case, the sources for Greek thinking may be less important than the creative uses they made
of them. Since the issues of how much Egypt contributed to
Greece and how much it reflected or stimulated sub-Saharan
African cultures are legitimate subjects for historical investigation, the debates will continue. But both Afrocentrism and
Eurocentrism are inadequate in providing a global framework
that looks at the contributions of all societies.

THINKING ABOUT THE CONTROVERSY

1. What is the argument labeled by critics as Eurocentrism?
2. What is the Afrocentric criticism of Eurocentrism?
3. What are the insights and problems of Bernal's *Black
   Athena*?

EXPLORING THE CONTROVERSY

Afrocentric history was pioneered by Cheikh Anta Diop in *Civilization or Barbarism: An Authentic Anthropology* (Brooklyn:
Lawrence Hill, 1991) and *The African Origin of Civilization:
Myth or Reality* (New York: Lawrence Hill, 1974). A more radical
approach can be found in Molefe Asante's *Afrocentricity* (Trenton: Africa World Press, 1988) and *The Afrocentric Idea* (Philadelphia: Temple University Press, 1987). The most significant
scholarly challenge to the views of mainstream classicists can
be found in Martin Bernal, *Black Athena: The Afroasiatic Roots
of Classical Civilization*, 3 vols. (New Brunswick, NJ: Rutgers
University Press, 1987, 1991, 2001). Bernal responds to his critics in *Black Athena Writes Back* (Durham, NC: Duke University
Press, 2001). The major rebuttals to Bernal and Afrocentrism
include Stephen Howe, *Afrocentrism: Mystical Pasts and Imagined Homes* (London: Verso, 1998); Mary Lefkowitz, *Not Out
of Africa: How Afrocentrism Became an Excuse to Teach Myth
as History* (New York: Basic Books, 1996); and Mary Lefkowitz
and Guy MacLean, eds., *Black Athena Revisited* (Chapel Hill:
University of North Carolina Press, 1996).

For thoughtful discussions of the Afrocentrist controversy,
see Basil Davidson, *The Search for Africa: History, Culture, Politics* (New York: Times Books, 1994); and Jacques Berlinblau,
*Heresy in the University: The "Black Athena" Controversy and
the Responsibility of American Intellectuals* (New Brunswick,
NJ: Rutgers University Press, 1999). Useful studies of Egypt and
Africa in world history include Louise Schofield and W. Vivian
Davies, eds., *Egypt, the Aegean and the Levant: Interconnec-
tions in the Second Millennium* (London: Trustees of the Brit-
ish Museum, 1995); and Erik Gilbert and Jonathan T. Reynolds,
Africa in World History: From Prehistory to the Present (Upper
Saddle River, NJ: Prentice-Hall, 2004).

Classical Blossomings in World History, 600 B.C.E.–600 C.E.

In the second century B.C.E. a Greek historian, Polybius, recognized the expanding horizons of his time and concluded that "the world's history has been a series of unrelated episodes, but from now on history becomes an organic whole. The affairs of Europe and Africa are connected with those of Asia and all events bear a relationship and contribute to a single end."[1] In his perception of increasing connections across cultures, Polybius identified a crucial transition. During the Classical Era a vast exchange of ideas, cultures, and products grew in the Afro-Eurasian zone. For example, the Chinese sent missions into western Asia, where they met Persians and Greeks. Alexander the Great, born on the northern fringes of Greece, conquered Egypt and later looked out on the Indus River in India, dreaming of moving on to the Ganges and even farther.

The commercial exchanges that were carried out along the trade routes represented the first glimmerings of a world economy centered on Asia. Greek merchants traveled as far as south India, and one, based in the Egyptian city of Alexandria, wrote a manual describing the ports and listing the products traded in East Africa and South Asia. Warehouses in the south Indian port of Pondicherry were filled with casks of Roman wine. Goods from Persia and Rome reached Funan in Southeast Asia, while the statue of an Indian goddess was carried to the Italian city of Pompeii. Romans craved Chinese silk, Arabian incense, and Indian spices. Merchants near Kabul, in today's Afghanistan, dealt in Greek glass, Egyptian pots, Chinese lacquer ware, and Hindu carvings.

Thanks in part to greater interregional communication over widening networks of exchange, the Classical Era was a period of blossomings of many kinds. Creative philosophies established new value systems or reinforced existing ones in the Mediterranean world and Asia. Between 350 B.C.E. and 200 C.E. the Afro-Eurasian world was also transformed by large regional empires. In the wake of these empires, universal religions such as Buddhism and Christianity crossed cultural boundaries, becoming permanent fixtures of world history. Classical peoples also refined their economic and social patterns. In this process, each society, while having its own dynamics, was also altered by contact with others.

The Axial Age of Philosophical Speculation

Between around 600 and 400 B.C.E., several societies of Eurasia faced a remarkably similar set of crises. People in China, India, Persia, Israel, and Greece were all beset by chronic warfare, population movement, political disruption, and the breakdown of traditional values. Improved ironworking technology produced better tools but also more effective weapons. Political instability was common, as rival states competed with each other for power in China, India, the Middle East, and Greece. These troubled conditions led to a climate of spiritual and intellectual restlessness, provoking a questioning of the old order. Because of the many influential and creative thinkers of this age, some scholars have called this an "axial period" or turning point, a crucial transition in history. This idea understates some crucial religious developments that occurred after 350 B.C.E., such as the reshaping of Hinduism, the division of Buddhism, and the rise of Christianity and Islam. The Axial Age also produced enduring philosophical, religious, and scientific ideas that became the intellectual underpinning of many cultural traditions and fostered new ways of thinking.

Axial Age Thinkers

Many of the greatest thinkers in history were near-contemporaries; that is, they lived at roughly the same time, between 600 and 350 B.C.E. Laozi (credited by tradition as the inspiration for Daoism) and Confucius in China lived and taught in the sixth century around the same time as Buddha and Mahavira (the founder of the Jain faith) in India and the Greek thinkers Thales and Heracleitus. Other major Axial Age thinkers included the Hebrew prophets Jeremiah, Ezekiel, and the second Isaiah, as well as Socrates, Plato, and Aristotle in Greece. Although he may have lived much earlier, the teachings of the Persian Zoroaster also became prominent in this era. Many people today are still influenced by these thinkers: Laozi's advice to live in accordance with nature, the Confucian dream of an ordered society based on proper ethical conduct, the Buddha's rules for ending human suffering, Mahavira's belief in absolute nonviolence, the prophetic Hebrew vision of universal justice and monotheism, the Greek emphasis on rational analysis, and the Zoroastrian notion of opposing forces of darkness and light still have meaning.

Some of these men were not only thinkers but also teachers. To pass along their ideas, leading intellectuals such as Confucius and Plato took on students. Confucius reflected the passion for education: "I am not someone who was born wise. I am someone who tries to learn [from the ancients]."[2] It was a time of exciting exchanges, as mystics and teachers traveled through India, dozens of philosophers spread their ideas in China, and students of Socrates competed with followers of the Stoics in the schools of Athens.

Causes and Characteristics of Axial Age Thought

In trying to identify the causes of the Axial Age, historians point to social and political instability, the effects of commercial exchanges along far-flung trade networks, economies productive enough to support a class of thinkers, and the first glimmerings of the belief that individuals have intrinsic worth apart from their role in society. Other possible causes include the increase in cultural exchanges among Afro-Asian peoples with the spread of writing, iron tools and vehicles, and

Confucius and Laozi in Conversation This picture engraved on a stone tablet in an old Confucian temple shows Confucius visiting Laozi in the city of Loyang and amiably discussing with him views on ritual and music.

improved boats. These inventions helped widen intellectual horizons and stimulated human intellect and imagination. Exactly where many of the great Axial Age ideas began, however, has led to controversy (see Historical Controversy: The Afrocentric Challenge to Historians of Antiquity).

Whatever the causes, several themes became common to Axial Age thinkers. First, especially in China and Greece, thinkers questioned the accepted myths and gods and promoted a humanistic view of life, one more concerned with the social and natural order than the supernatural order. Second, most thinkers stressed moral conduct and values, a vision that often rejected the violent, selfish pursuit of material power they saw around them. Some, like the Buddha, Mahavira, and Laozi, were pacifists who denounced all violence, the Jains going to the extreme of preventing harm even to insects. Third, Confucius, the Hebrew prophets, and several Greeks were also among the first people to think about history and its lessons for societies. Fourth, while few of these thinkers favored social equality, many argued that rulers should govern with a sense of obligation to the powerless and less fortunate. Finally, all the Axial Age thinkers believed that the world could be improved, either by the actions of ethical individuals or by the creation of an ideal social order, or both. For example, Plato devised a model government led not by kings but by a special class of wise men.

But the Axial Age thinkers disagreed as to whether truth was absolute. Socrates and Plato, for example, argued for universal concepts, Plato writing that "those who see the absolute and eternal have real knowledge and not mere opinions." Yet, some Greeks and Chinese also explored the notion that truth was relative and dependent on circumstances. As one Chinese thinker wrote: "Monkeys prefer trees: so what habitat can be said to be absolutely right? Fish flee at the sight of women whom men deem lovely. Whose is the right taste absolutely?"[3]

Philosophers still struggle with the question of universal or relative truth.

The Axial Age had not only philosophical and religious but also scientific and political consequences. Across Eurasia people raised fundamental questions about many phenomena and answered them by systematic investigation. Greek thinkers such as Aristotle, who pondered and classified everything from political systems to animals, influenced European and Middle Eastern science, and their ideas inspired new discoveries by Hellenistic, Roman and, later, Islamic scientists. At the other end of Eurasia, Chinese influenced by Confucianism and Daoism also created another rich scientific tradition. Indians became some of the classical world's greatest mathematicians and astronomers. Together, the classical Greeks, Chinese, Indians, and the ancient Mesopotamians and Egyptians built the foundations for modern science. Axial Age ideas also became the basis for new political ideologies. For example, in China, Confucianism mixed with Legalism provided the ideas for building stronger states, while Romans rose to power using modified Greek ideas of democracy. As a result of strengthening state institutions and leaders, in China, India, Persia, and Greece the Axial Age ended in mighty empires that reflected a new order of technological and organizational planning.

The Age of Regional Empires

The empires that arose in much of Eurasia during or at the end of the Axial Age were greater in size and impact than those that had flourished in ancient times. The Persian Empire set the stage, thriving for nearly three centuries. More regional empires appeared between 350 B.C.E. and 250 C.E., from China in the East to Rome in the West, that were much grander in scale than such earlier empires as the Assyrian and the Shang Chinese. In the Mediterranean Basin Rome built on the heritage of Alexander the Great. The Parthians and then the Sassanian Persians governed some of western and Central Asia, the Chinese Han Empire dominated much of East and Central Asia, and in India the Mauryan state controlled much of the subcontinent for over a century. Most of the empires built upon the ideas of classical sages and religious leaders, such as Confucius, Zoroaster, and Plato, in organizing society. In so doing they helped resolve the crises, such as political instability, that had sparked the rise of the Axial Age reformers. Empires also appeared in sub-Saharan Africa and the Americas, including Aksum, Teotihuacan, and Tiwanaku, but on a smaller scale than in Eurasia.

The Rise of Empires

The first great regional empires in the Eastern Hemisphere developed during the Axial Age. The Achaemenid Empire of Persia (550–334 B.C.E.) dwarfed its Middle Eastern predecessors and was the first large empire that ruled many diverse societies. At its height it reached from Egypt and northern Greece across western Asia to Central Asia and the Indus Basin. Persian kings had reason to brag, as did Xerxes, that they were kings of lands containing many people, of the great earth far and wide. Like many leaders, the Persian kings claimed to improve society. Darius I boasted that he had "changed many bad things that had been done to good things. . . . so that people did not kill each other any more."[4] The Hellenistic Empire created by Alexander and the Macedonian Greeks built directly on the experiences of Persian imperial rule. The dynasties that succeeded Alexander dominated much of western Asia, Egypt, and southeastern Europe for the next two centuries.

By the end of the Axial Age, in the third and fourth centuries, new empires arose in Eurasia in part as a result of increased warfare, such as fighting between warring states in India, China, and the western Mediterranean. In each region one state eventually subdued its rivals; the Mauryan, Han, and Roman Empires were the results of these conflicts. Changing social and economic conditions also helped spur the rise of these empires. Rapid economic growth due to expanding long-distance trade networks made merchants more important in all of these societies, and merchants then sought more political influence and social equality. The upper classes, such as the priestly brahman caste of India and the wealthy senatorial class in Rome, protected their own privileges while increasingly exploiting the peasants. The gap between rich and poor widened, causing increased tensions. Rulers surrounded themselves with the trappings of wealth and power, enjoying lavish ceremonies and giving themselves exalted titles. But the move toward empire alleviated some social conflicts by providing large, stable environments in which resources could be acquired and distributed. During this period, the growing states required extensive administrative machinery, larger armies, standardized laws, and governing philosophies. Administrators were needed to collect taxes, organize social services, and serve as judges. From China to Rome, provinces paid taxes and supplied sol-

diers to the large armies needed to sustain and expand the empires. For example, during the early Roman Empire the armed forces received 58 percent of all government revenue. At the same time the Han emperor stationed 300,000 troops along the Great Wall. Since everything was bigger and the stakes were higher, wars against competing states could be terribly destructive: after three wars with Carthage spanning more than a century, Rome razed that great city to the ground and laced salt into the soil to render it unfit for farming.

Philosophical and religious beliefs maintained community standards but were also used by rulers of these large states to sustain and legitimize their power. For example, Stoic philosophy encouraged Romans to accept their lot in life. In China Confucian ideas urged people to respect leaders, and Legalist thinkers told leaders to exercise power ruthlessly. Thus, the Confucian scholar Dong Zhongshu (ca. 179–104 B.C.E.) elevated the role of the Chinese emperor, arguing that "heaven, earth, and man are the source of all creatures. Heaven gives birth to them, earth nourishes them, and human beings complete them. Who else but a king could connect them all?"[5] In Mauryan India, Ashoka enhanced his position by using Buddhist moral injunctions emphasizing peace, tolerance, and welfare to win popular support. Ashoka recorded his goals on pillars: "All men are my children, and just as I desire for my children that they should obtain welfare and happiness, so do I desire [the same] for all men."[6]

Increasing Cultural Unity and Contact

These new regional empires imposed peace and uniformity within their boundaries. Bureaucratic structures standardized practices throughout an empire so that the weights, measures, currencies, calendars, tax codes, and official languages used throughout the far-flung provinces of an empire were the same. For example, Greek spread widely in the Hellenistic kingdoms of Asia. Latin became the common language in the Roman Empire, in the process fostering the western European "romance" languages, such as Spanish and French. Latin influences also found their way into Germanic languages such as English and German. But in Roman Asia few outside the political elite spoke or read Latin. Similarly, the northern Chinese dialect of Mandarin became China's official spoken language even though, outside of the educated class, few in the southern half of China spoke Mandarin.

By stimulating commerce and communication, the empires fostered the spread of ideas and technologies into neighboring societies and increased contact among distant peoples (see map). For example, Hellenistic Greeks and Mauryan Indians encountered each other in Afghanistan, a crossroads where Eurasian peoples both fought with each other and exchanged ideas. Spurred by imperial expansion, Roman culture and then Christianity permeated the Mediterranean Basin, Hellenistic Greek culture spread in western Asia and North Africa, and China influenced Japan, Korea, Vietnam, and Central Asia.

In Eurasia trade routes grew out of transportation systems constructed to channel resources to imperial capitals. China built canals unprecedented in scale, Achaemenid

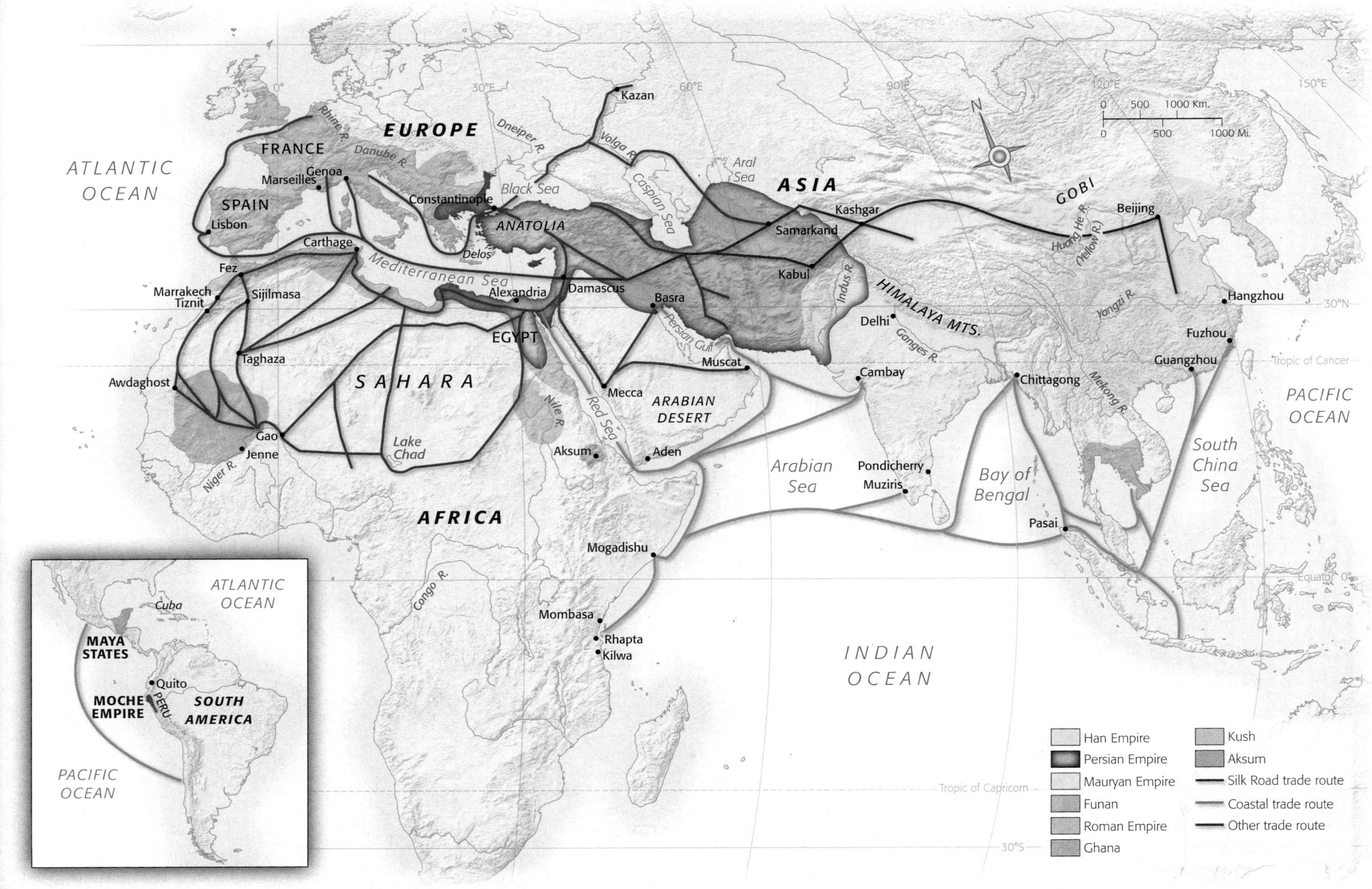

Great Empires and Trade Routes

During the Classical Era, great empires often dominated East Asia, India, western Asia, North Africa, and southern Europe. Extensive land and maritime trade routes linked East Asia with western Eurasia, West Africa with the Mediterranean, and East Africa with southern Asia.

e **Interactive Map**

Legend:

Kush
Aksum
Silk Road trade route
Coastal trade route
Other trade route

Han Empire
Persian Empire
Maunyan Empire
Funan
Roman Empire
Ghana

Persia and Mauryan India constructed east-west highways, and the Romans developed 150,000 miles of paved roads. These roads and canals, along with seaports, became linked to long-distance trade networks, which brought many societies, such as the Celts and Germans in northern Europe, the Sogdians in Central Asia, the Sudanic peoples of West Africa, the East African coastal dwellers, and the Japanese and Koreans, into closer contact with major empires.

Decline of Empires

Throughout history states rise and fall, and the classical empires did as well. While each of the great regional empires declined for different reasons, the Roman and Han Chinese Empires suffered from some of the same problems. Each empire expanded beyond its ability to support itself, weakening administrative structures and finances. Some conquered territories brought wealth to the empire, but others did not. The British Isles, for example, were a net drain on the imperial Roman treasury, and it was costly to maintain Chinese control in Central Asia. Both of these empires also suffered from civil wars and growing domestic unrest. Eventually both empires, unable to acquire new wealth through further expansion, made economic cutbacks and raised taxes to sustain the imperial structure, which caused widespread resentment. Contemporary observers recorded the decline. The third-century C.E. Roman writer Cyprian argued that "the World itself testifies to its own decline by giving manifold concrete evidence of the process of decay. This loss of strength and stature must end, at least, in annihilation."[7]

Both the Han and Roman Empires were also plagued by environmental problems. Because the empires formed as the global climate was warming, they could benefit from increased food supplies, and both flourished during the peak of warmth between 200 B.C.E. and 200 C.E. With the return of colder weather after 200 C.E., however, agricultural production declined and the great empires collapsed or weakened. Soil exhaustion in Italy was also a factor in Rome's declining food supply. In addition, diseases traveled along the land and sea routes, undermining Rome and China in the second century C.E. Some outbreaks, like the terrible plague identified with Justinian's Byzantium, killed millions and made life miserable over wide areas. Probably originating in Africa, the plague killed nearly half the population of Constantinople in the 540s. By the time the pandemic reached its end in the 590s, some 25 million West Asians, North Africans, and Europeans had perished.

When pastoral nomads began to put more pressure on the Roman and Chinese Empires, these states had been weakened so much by economic and environmental problems that they could no longer effectively resist. For instance, Chinese emperors could no longer afford to maintain the garrisons along the series of walls built across north China. The Germanic tribes proved a long-term threat to Rome, and various Central Asians, among them Huns, Scythians, and Turkish peoples, continuously intruded along the fringes of Persia, India, and China. By 200 C.E. population growth and climate change pushed some of them to more aggressively seek wealth in the declining Roman and Han Empires. In the end, the imperial orders were undermined in part by forces beyond their control.

Various peoples eventually conquered or displaced the great empires, although they also usually adopted Roman, Indian, Persian, or Chinese culture. But the imperial idea never died. It proved particularly strong in Persia, where the Achaeminid, Hellenistic Seleucid, Parthian, and finally Sassanian Empires succeeded each other over a millennium. Even in India, where fragmented states were the norm, the Gupta rulers claimed kinship with the Mauryas five centuries earlier. The belief in the need for large regional empires also endured for centuries in China and served as a model for later dynasties that conquered vast territories. Hence, the China of the eighteenth century C.E., which incorporated many non-Chinese societies, clearly descended in recognizable form from the Han of 150 B.C.E. Similarly, the Byzantine Empire controlled vast European and western Asian territories once part of the old Roman Empire. After the fall of the western Roman Empire, however, western Europeans never succeeded in reviving that empire, even though some Christian German kings centuries later claimed the title of "Holy Roman Emperor." In contrast to China, where the Sui dynasty revived much of the early Han system, western European societies were never able to restore the Roman heritage.

World Religions and Their Influences

During the later centuries of the Classical Era, universal religions became more prominent in Afro-Eurasia, marking another great transition that reshaped societies. Instead of the gods of the ancient world, which were local and identified with particular cities or cultures, these new religions were portable and appealed across cultural boundaries. They could be carried along trade routes, attracting believers far from their lands of birth. The Eurasian faiths with the most followers—Christianity, Buddhism, Hinduism, and Zoroastrianism—filled a vacuum created by political instability and cultural decline.

The Spread of Universal Religions

Religions spread along land and sea trade routes. Missionaries accompanied or were themselves traders, as a fourth-century C.E. Christian hymn in Syria acknowledged: "Travel like merchants, That we may gain the world. Fill creation with teaching."[8] About six centuries after its founding in India, Buddhism reached China via the Silk Road and Southeast Asia over the maritime trade routes. Christianity, with roots in the eastern Mediterranean, spread to Rome, where it became prominent by the fourth century C.E.; it permeated northern Europe beginning around 500 C.E. Christianity also established roots in western Asia, Egypt, Nubia, and Ethiopia. Other faiths also established a presence. Manicheanism, a mix of Christian and Zoroastrian influences, attracted believers from North Africa to China. Judaism also gained some converts in Arabia, the Caucasus, and Ethiopia. By 500 or 600 C.E. small Christian and Jewish communities had even been established in Central Asia, western India, and northern China. Networks of exchange helped shape religious traditions as well as spread them. For example, Zoroastrian ideas probably influenced Ionian Greek, Mahayana Buddhist, and Judeo-Christian beliefs and art forms.

The universal religions gave people hope in the face of the political and social crises that marked the decline of the great regional empires from the second through the fifth centuries C.E. Sometimes these new religions merged with or incorporated existing beliefs. In East Asia, for example, Buddhism gradually blended with or accommodated Confucianism, Daoism, and Shinto, and, in northern Europe, Christianity acquired a Germanic or Celtic flavor over the centuries. Not all the religious changes were accommodating, however. Religion could also divide families. In one case, a Roman writer told of conflict between a Christian wife and her husband, who practiced his traditional faith: "She is engaged in a fast; her husband has arranged a banquet. She celebrates the Easter Vigil throughout the entire night; her husband expects her in his bed."[9]

In sub-Saharan Africa and the Americas, some religious beliefs reached across many societies, becoming the counterparts to the organized Eurasian religions. The polytheistic beliefs of the Mande and other Sudanic peoples, for instance, gradually spread to the Guinea coast and Central Africa, and from there to eastern and southern Africa. In the Americas the Olmec introduced gods and views of the universe that contributed to the later religious beliefs of the Maya, and some Maya ideas may have spread to other Mesoamericans. Chavín religious traditions, including gods and shamanistic practices, probably influenced the views of other Andean peoples such as the Moche and Tiwanaku. Some of the American peoples practiced human sacrifice as part of their religious devotions, as offerings to the gods. Human sacrifice was also found in some Afro-Eurasian societies, among them the Celts, Minoan Crete, ancient Egypt, and Shang China.

Religion, Culture, and Society

The universal religions became a major force in shaping the societies and regions in which they became dominant, eventually creating, for example, a largely Hindu India, a Buddhist Sri Lanka, and a Christian Europe. To be sure, religion was only a part of life, and religions changed over time, dividing into varied sects such as the Mahayana and Theravada Buddhists. But after the regional empires collapsed into many rival states in the Mediterranean, India, and China, religious institutions transcended political divisions, fostering cultural unity across borders. Hindus, Buddhists, and Christians often saw themselves as part of larger communities. As a result, Chinese Buddhist pilgrims such as Faxian made the long and arduous journey to India to study with Indian Buddhists. And

King David   For centuries artists in the Christian Ethiopian kingdom, in the highlands of Northeast Africa, painted biblical figures on the pages of religious manuscripts. The artists often used Ethiopian motifs, and this painting of the Hebrew king David, adorned in rich robes and crown and playing a harp-type instrument, resembles that of an Ethiopian king.

Bibliotheque nationale de France

many Christians looked to the bishops in faraway cities such as Rome for guidance. Spirituality permeated the lives of people all over the world. Religion also offered the poor the hope that they might end their suffering and low status, if not in this life then through reincarnation or in some form of heaven.

All the universal religions, as well as the religions of urban American societies such as the Maya, had certain features, practices, and beliefs in common. They had sacred writings or scriptures, such as the Hindu Vedas and Christian Bible, strict moral codes, organized priesthoods, theologies laying out core beliefs, and some concept of existence after death. Most faiths also encouraged followers to treat others as they wanted to be treated themselves, although in practice many people ignored this advice. The devout shared a belief in the universal truth of their faith. All the religions were patriarchal to one degree or another, adding religious sanction to the growing suppression of women. Christian and Buddhist leaders also dispatched missionaries into neighboring societies, although Buddhism later lost most of its missionary zeal.

For all the spiritual comfort and insight they provided believers, these new religions, like their predecessors, were also important as forces of social control. For example, Hindu ideas of reincarnation and karma underpinned the Indian caste system, encouraging people to accept their status. Christians focused on attaining heaven and were warned that questioning religious authority and beliefs might prevent salvation. Some of the religious establishments grew intolerant of dissent. For this reason, Christian bishops established a consensus on doctrine, excluding ideas considered to be heresy. Those who disagreed with Christian or Zoroastrian orthodoxy might be banned or punished, and they were expected to face retribution after death in Hell, the abode of evil, an underworld for wicked people and disbelievers.

Monasticism and Its Diffusion

Some of the universal religions spawned a new social and spiritual movement, monasticism. It may have first developed as a movement within both Buddhism and Jainism. Buddha himself supposedly ordained the first monks as well as nuns, including his mother. In Theravada Buddhist societies most men spent some period as monks, bound by their rigid code of celibacy and poverty. But the concept then perhaps spread over the trade networks into western Asia. Whether or not inspired by Buddhist models, monasticism became a growing component of organized Christianity by the third century C.E.

Whether Christian or Buddhist, monasteries provided educational and charitable services while providing a focus for community religious life. In societies as far removed as England, Nubia, and China, a substantial number of men (and some women) joined monastic orders, abandoning the humdrum existence of everyday life for a focus on prayer and meditation. Most monks and nuns practiced austere religious practices to strengthen spiritual life. This could involve sexual abstinence, fasting, and solitary contemplation. In the Hindu tradition wandering holy men who abandoned the comforts of settled life and families provided a counterpart to organized monastic life.

Changing Economic and Social Patterns

Increased migration and communication fostered major social and economic changes. Population growth encouraged migration, which led to the intermixing of peoples and the exchange of ideas. Deadly disease epidemics moving along migration networks testified to this widespread contact between distant peoples. The long-distance trade routes also spread both diseases and new ideas. The result was that certain social attitudes became more common over a wide area, including attitudes toward women and slaves that lasted for centuries. The social and economic systems of the Classical Era, some alien and some familiar to modern people, suggest both how much and how little the world has changed since the Classical Era.

The Growth and Decline of World Population

Successful agricultural systems in the great empires allowed for substantial population growth from Europe to China. In 4000 B.C.E., at the dawn of the ancient world, the world population was well under 100 million. At the beginning of the Common Era there were probably between 200 and 250 million people, over 70 percent living in Asia and about 20 million each in Africa and the Americas. China was the largest society, with some 60 million people. In addition, more people now lived in cities. In 450 B.C.E. the world's largest city was probably Babylon, with 200,000 people. By 200 B.C.E. Patna in Mauryan India had 400,000, and by 100 C.E. Rome was the largest metropolis, with at least 500,000 people and perhaps a million.

But diseases began to limit population growth in the later Classical Era. Networks of communication were often networks of contagion, port cities being the major hubs of transmission. Epidemics of smallpox and plague resulted from travelers unknowingly spreading new diseases into areas where people had not yet built up immunities to them. Epidemic diseases may have killed as much as 25 percent of the population of China and the Roman Empire during the second and third centuries C.E. Indeed, plague outbreaks contributed considerably to the decline of the classical empires; for example, they undermined the Roman state and, by producing widespread misery and disillusionment, aided the spread of Christianity among demoralized or desperate Roman subjects. As a result of the various disease outbreaks, by 600 B.C.E. the world population remained between 200 and 240 million, similar to what it had been six centuries earlier.

Population growth led to increased movement, as people sought open lands and better opportunities. Responding to population pressures, Chinese migrants moved into central and southern China; Germanic and Turkish peoples spread into central Europe and western Asia, respectively; Bantu-speaking peoples occupied the southern half of Africa; and Austronesians settled remote Pacific islands. As groups migrated, they assimilated local peoples and cultures and adapted their lives to new surroundings.

Trade and Cultural Contact

The networks of trade, like those of imperial expansion and missionary activity, linked distant peoples while spreading the influence of cultures more widely. The Greeks picked up scientific and mathematical knowledge as well as some religious notions from the Egyptians and Phoenicians. Indian cultural influences, including Buddhism, spread over the trade routes into central, east, and southeast Asia, reaching as far as Korea, Japan, and Indonesia. Aksum was linked by commerce with the Mediterranean world and India, a link that brought Christianity to the Ethiopian highlands. Precious spices from southern Arabia, textiles from India, and gold from Malaya and West Africa found their way to the Mediterranean societies. The Roman writer Pliny was surprised at Roman demand for Indian pepper, which "has nothing in it that can plead as a recommendation [other than] a certain pungency; and yet it is for this that we import it all the way from India!"[10] Trade also connected Mesoamerica with neighboring regions and fostered networks of exchange in both eastern North America and western South America. For example, copper from the North American Great Lakes reached the Gulf Coast, and Mesoamerican ball games spread far and wide. Crops also traveled American trade routes; maize from Mexico became a major crop in both North and South America, and tomatoes from the Andes carried into Central America and Mexico.

Crossing the Pamir Mountains The Pamir Mountains, separating the deserts of what is now western China from the deserts and grasslands of Turkestan and Afghanistan, were one of the more formidable barriers faced by camel caravans traveling the Silk Road. To avoid the blistering summer heat of the desert, the caravans often traveled in winter and thus had to maneuver through mountain snows.

Michael Fairchild/Peter Arnold, Inc.

The Silk Road endured as a major overland long-distance network of exchange—in effect the first transcontinental highway—and allowed people, goods, and ideas to travel thousands of miles. As a Han dynasty historian put it: "Messengers come and go every season and month, foreign traders and merchants knock on the gates of the Great Wall every day."[11] In Eurasia the introduction of coinage encouraged trade by offering widely recognized tokens of value. Coins from Sassanian Persia and Byzantium as well as Chinese silk served as the network currency. Indeed, the huge amounts of gold and silver exported by Rome to pay for Chinese silk and Indian spices did some damage to the Roman economy. Overland trade expanded with the growing use of camels. After the invention of an efficient saddle allowed this pack animal to be used for longer journeys across the deserts and plains of Asia and Africa, camels became the trucks of the premodern Afro-Eurasian zone. And the merchants who used the camels carried not only bullion and products but also religions, especially Buddhism and Manicheanism, which spread along the Silk Road into Central Asia and China.

Cities grew up along the Silk Road across Central Asia to serve as suppliers and middlemen to the merchants. These cities, such as Kashgar in Xinjiang and Samarkand in Turkestan, became part of a contact zone linking many societies. Hubs at the eastern end of the Mediterranean, such as Petra, Palmyra, Alexandria, and Constantinople, served as transshipment points for goods traveling between China and Rome. This trade aided some societies. For example, Nabataean Arabs constructed a trade network linking Egypt, western Asia, and southern Europe, while the Sogdians dominated Central Asian trading cities and even had communities in western China. Chinese sources described the Sogdians as trained for trade: "At birth honey was put in their mouths and gum on their hands. They learned the trade from the age of five. On reaching twelve they were sent to do business in a neighboring state."[12]

Maritime trade also flourished during this period, enriching various ports. Hence, both trade goods and cultural influences were carried by sea between eastern and western Asia. Sailing networks connected the entire Mediterranean Basin. For several centuries one key network hub was the tiny Greek island of Delos (DEH-los) in the Aegean Sea, of which it was said, "Merchant, sail in and unload! Everything is as good as sold."[13] Merchants from all over, including Greeks from around the Mediterranean, Romans, Syrians, Jews, Phoenicians, Nabataean Arabs, and Yemenite Arabs, flocked to Delos to trade. Maritime counterparts to the overland trade diaspora of the Sogdians developed. For example, a Jewish trading community sunk roots in southwest India, Indian merchants settled in Funan (Cambodia), Indonesians and Arabs sailed to East Africa to trade or settle, and Greeks established communities all over the Mediterranean and Black Sea Basins.

Eventually a vast maritime route linked China, Vietnam, and Cambodia in the East through Malaya and the Indonesian archipelago to India and Sri Lanka, and then stretched westward to Persia, Arabia, and the East African coast. Europe and North Africa were connected to this system through the Arabs, Aksumites, and Persians. The Greek geographer Strabo wrote that since merchants from Roman-ruled Alexandria had sent trading fleets to India, "these regions have become better known to us today."[14] Some cities flourished as hubs for this maritime trade. For instance, between 100 and 500 C.E. the Egyptian port of Berenike on the Red Sea was regularly visited by ships from India. Products from as far away as Java and Cambodia reached the markets of Berenike, and eleven different written languages, including Greek and Sanskrit, were used there. Berenike was also linked through Alexandria to the Mediterranean societies.

Maritime commerce faced serious limitations, however. Because of formidable currents, only the strongest oars would allow a boat to pass through the Strait of Gibraltar separating Spain from North Africa. This problem inhibited trade between Mediterranean and Atlantic societies for many centuries. Similarly, the vast distances of the Pacific Ocean, crossed in that day only by outrigger canoes, limited the volume and type of goods carried along the trading networks there. Some people, using balsa rafts, traded along the Pacific Coast of South and Central America, while others used canoes to travel between Caribbean islands, but the volume and frequency of such maritime trade remain unclear.

Social Systems and Attitudes

The social systems and attitudes of the Classical Era set the patterns for centuries to come. In many places gender roles hardened. For example, in Greece and China, customs and laws allowed men far greater social freedom than women. Because the great empires were made through military conquest, they were very masculine in nature. In addition, patriarchal attitudes were encouraged by some of the new philosophies and religions. For example, Confucianism gave power to older men, and influential Christian leaders urged women to stay in the background. In addition, the faiths that replaced Greek and Roman religions removed goddesses as objects of worship in the Mediterranean world, although in southern Asia many Hindus continued to revere female deities.

Homosexuality existed in all classical societies and was generally tolerated in some, especially in Greece and Rome. Chinese historians reported that many emperors of the era, including the empire-builder Wu Di of the Han dynasty, had male lovers in addition to their wives and concubines. The Han era historian Sima Qian wrote numerous biographies of those men "who served the ruler and succeeded in delighting his ears and eyes, [winning] his favor and intimacy."[15] Chinese also tolerated lesbian relationships among women in polygamous households. But in many places official attitudes concerning gender roles and sexual behaviors became more rigid over time, pushing homosexuals to the margins of society.

Changing social and religious attitudes affected women. Although women had some legal protections in Greece and Rome, many also lived generally domestic and often secluded lives. For instance, when Roman women in 195 B.C.E. took to the streets to protest a law, passed during a costly war, that limited the amount of gold and finery a woman could wear, many men complained that women should stay home and out of politics. A Roman politician noted that "women cannot partake of [local office], priesthoods, [military] triumphs, badges of office, or spoils of war; elegance, finery and beautiful clothes are women's badges; in these they find joy and take pride."[16] Women faced increasing restrictions in China and northern India, where they were expected to be obedient to men. Patriarchy was also common in Africa, the Americas, and the Pacific islands. While there were notable exceptions, the leaders in Aksum and in the Maya city-states were mostly men.

But wherever they lived, women had varied experiences. Some were treated as property, assigned by their fathers to husbands, and many faced permanent dependency on fathers, husbands, and sons. But those who were well loved by male relatives could perhaps gain substantial personal advantages. Only a small minority of women anywhere were educated, Hypatia of Alexandria and Ban Zhao in China being notable examples. However, a few, such as Queen Zenobia in Palmyra, Cleopatra VII in Egypt, Queen Theodora in Byzantium, and several Kushite queens, attained great power. Some women asserted their own interests, a behavior reflected in some Greek plays. Thus, in *Antigone* (an-TIG-on-ee) by Sophocles, the main female character defies King Creon, who refuses to allow her to give her dead brother a proper burial.

Like patriarchy, slavery was practiced in many classical societies around the world. Most people saw slavery as a part of the natural order of things and essential to economic life. Slaves everywhere were bought and sold at the whim of the owner, and their lives and labor were controlled. Most slaves were poor, but not all lived in misery. Some Greek and Roman slaves held high positions in society or were attached to prosperous families. In societies such as Han China, Mauryan India, Aksum, and the Maya society, slaves were only one segment of the lower class, whereas in Greece and Rome slaves constituted a large part of the population and were used in every area of the economy, from mining and construction to prostitution and domestic work. For example, in Rome it was chiefly slaves who built the Colisseum, the Forum, and the great aqueducts that so impress modern tourists. Slavery mostly died out in China and India during the first millennium C.E. and became less important in Europe after the collapse of the Roman Empire, showing that societies do change, often dramatically, over time.

Suggested Reading

Books

Adas, Michael, ed. *Agricultural and Pastoral Societies in Ancient and Classical History*. Philadelphia: Temple University Press, 2001. A useful collection of essays on various topics.

Armstrong, Karen. *The Great Transformation: The Beginning of Our Religious Traditions.* New York: Knopf, 2006. Excellent introduction to the Axial Age and its thinkers.

Bentley, Jerry H. *Old World Encounters: Cross-Cultural Contacts and Exchanges in Pre-Modern Times.* New York: Oxford University Press, 1993. An up-to-date survey of trade routes and the spread of universal religions.

Bulliet, Richard W. *The Camel and the Wheel.* Cambridge: Harvard University Press, 1975. A classic study of the caravan trade in Asia and Africa.

Curtin, Philip D. *Cross-Cultural Trade in World History*. Cambridge: Cambridge University Press, 1984. Contains much material on long-distance trade in the Classical Era.

Fernandez-Armesto, Felipe. *Civilizations: Culture, Ambition, and the Transformation of Nature.* New York: Touchstone, 2001. A fascinating and wide-ranging survey across eras and regions that emphasizes adaptations to varied environments.

Foltz, Richard C. *Religions of the Silk Road: Overland Trade and Cultural Exchange from Antiquity to the Fifteenth Century.* New York: St. Martin's, 1999. Analyzes the spread of religions.

Headrick, Daniel. *Technology: A World History.* New York: Oxford University Press, 2009. Good summary of metallurgy and long distance trade in this era.

Lloyd, Geoffrey, and Nathan Sivin. *The Way and the Word: Science and Medicine in Early China and Greece.* New Haven, CT: Yale University Press, 2003. Compares these two great traditions of learning, arguing that modern science derives from both as well as from Indian, Islamic, and other cultures.

McClellan, James, and Harold Dorn. *Science and Technology in World History: An Introduction.* Baltimore: Johns Hopkins University Press, 1999. A survey of science and technology traditions.

Pearson, Michael. *The Indian Ocean.* New York: Routledge, 2003. A history of the maritime connections.

Prazniak, Roxann. *Dialogues Across Civilizations: Sketches in World History from the Chinese and European Experiences.* Boulder: Westview, 1996. Contains interesting comparative essays.

Smart, Ninian. *The Long Search.* Boston: Little, Brown and Co., 1977. A very readable introduction to the various universal religious traditions of Eurasia and their modern offshoots.

Super, John C., and Brian K. Turley. *Religion in World History.* New York: Routledge, 2006. A brief study of religious diffusion and change.

Wood, Frances. *The Silk Road.* Berkeley: University of California Press, 2002. Surveys 2,000 years of history.

WEBSITES

Ancient and Lost Civilizations (*http://www.crystalinks.com/ancient.html*). Contains essays and other materials on ancient and classical societies.

Exploring Ancient World Cultures (*http://eawc.evansville.edu/*). A very helpful collection of essays and other useful material.

Internet Ancient History Sourcebook (*http://www.fordham.edu/halsall/ancient/asbook.html*). An exceptionally rich collection of links and primary source readings.

Monks and Merchants (*http://www.asiasociety.org/arts/monksandmerchants/index.html***).** Interesting essays, timelines, maps, and images for an Asia Society exhibition on the Silk Road as a zone of communication.

Silk Road Narratives (*http://depts.washington.edu/uwch/silkroad/texts/texts.html***).** Explores cultural interaction in Eurasia through excerpts from Silk Road travelers.

EXPANDING HORIZONS: ENCOUNTERS AND TRANSFORMATIONS IN THE INTERMEDIATE ERA, CA. 600–1500

By 600 C.E. most of the great classical Eastern Hemisphere empires and states, such as Rome, Han China, Gupta India, and Kush, were only memories. The classical American societies, such as the Maya, were to flourish a few centuries longer, only to collapse. Yet vigorous new societies were emerging. Even while some classical patterns hung on or were modified to suit new needs, the Afro-Eurasian zone was in transition. During this era many societies developed a more cosmopolitan outlook. New trade networks emerged and old ones were revitalized. Though characterized by long periods of conflict, this era also saw worldwide innovations.

Historians disagree as to what this era should be called. Borrowing from European history, scholars often refer to the medieval period, a "middle ages" stretching from around 600 to 1500. The term *medieval* suggests societies with relatively weak governments, rigid social orders, and one dominating religion, a description that best fits Europe in this era and perhaps Japan and parts of India. However, the term has little relevance for China, the Islamic states, and most of Africa, Southeast Asia, and the Americas. *Intermediate Era* is a more neutral term to describe this creative transitional period, which linked the Classical Era, when contacts between distant societies were still limited, with the rise of global connections that marked the centuries after 1500.

The Intermediate Era experienced dramatic transformations of societies. The explosive rise of Islam from a local faith in Arabia in the early 600s to a hemisphere-wide religion by 1400 was one of the main transitions. The resurgence of China as a political, economic, and cultural force was another. Also during this time, Buddhism became a major influence in the eastern half of Eurasia, while Christianity became Europe's dominant faith. Mighty empires arose in Africa, Southeast Asia, and the Americas.

These nine centuries also differed from the preceding Classical Era by virtue of the increasing contacts between peoples. Contacts became more frequent and substantial beginning around 600. New interregional communications took place across Afro-Eurasia, including trade, cultural exchange, and religious links. As a result, a maritime trading network connected China and Southeast Asia through India and the Persian Gulf to East Africa

Courtesy, Museo Prehistorico et Etnografico, Rome

Sape Ivory Saltholder Africans had traded and carved ivory since ancient times. This magnificent ivory carving, made, probably in the fifteenth century, by an artist of the Sape people, who lived in what is today Sierra Leone in West Africa, was used to store salt. The carving reflected artistic influence brought to the region by the earliest Portuguese explorers and traders.

and the Mediterranean. A growing caravan trade across the Sahara Desert brought West Africa and the Mediterranean closer together. The spread of religions also reshaped societies. For example, Arab culture expanded with Islam. The cosmopolitan Islamic world, stretching from Morocco to Indonesia, enjoyed much cultural diversity but also shared many beliefs and practices. In the Western Hemisphere, Mesoamerican cultural and agricultural influences spread deep into North and Central America.

The era was also marked by conflicts that changed societies. Spurring the rise of interregional encounters was the expansion of several Central Asian peoples. Turkish migrations and conquests in western Asia occured throughout the period. In the thirteenth century the Mongols conquered the largest land empire in world history, stretching from Korea and China westward to Russia and eastern Europe, a momentous achievement with major consequences. For example, as a result, East Asian technology flowed along the trade routes to Europe. However, the Mongol period also witnessed the spread along these same trade routes of a catastrophic plague, known as the Black Death, that devastated societies all across Eurasia and North Africa, killing countless millions of Chinese, Persians, Arabs, and Europeans.

The Intermediate years also saw major innovations such as economic growth, technological change, the rise of new states, and maritime exploration. China became the world's most commercialized and industrialized society, often exercising influence far from its borders. In the early 1400s Chinese maritime expeditions reached East Africa and the Persian Gulf. Islamic states were also dynamic, and Muslim scholars and artisans made numerous contributions to the world. West African kingdoms, East African coastal cities, and Southeast Asian states were closely tied to world trade. In the Americas, the Aztec and Inca Empires had arisen on the foundations of earlier societies. Europeans made key intellectual and technological discoveries, and they also benefited when the expansion of Islam and the Mongols introduced to Europe Asian-derived ideas, plants, and tools. In the 1400s, making good use of naval technology and weaponry from all over Eurasia and energized by economic growth and religious fervor, Europeans began voyages of discovery that set the stage for connecting the entire world after 1500.

NORTH AND CENTRAL AMERICA
The Maya city-states flourished for centuries until the cities were abandoned. The Toltecs dominated central Mexico for two hundred years. In the 1400s the Aztecs conquered a large empire in Mexico and built a huge capital city. North of Mexico, societies such as the Anasazi lived in towns and farmed in the desert for centuries. To the east the Mississippian peoples built mounds and a grand city while trading over a vast area. Farming villages also dotted the east coast.

SOUTH AMERICA
For most of the era Tiwanaku, in the Andes, and the Chimu Empire, based on the Peruvian coast, were the dominant powers in western South America. In the 1400s the Incas conquered most of the region, creating the largest empire in the history of the Americas. Skilled farmers, the Incas used a powerful but paternalistic state to rule millions of people.

EUROPE

In western Europe a rigid society, dominated by a powerful Christian church, slowly emerged, reaching its zenith around 1000 C.E. Dozens of small rival states fought each other. Urban and commercial growth, technological innovation, and the Black Death eventually undermined feudalism and church power, and political, intellectual, artistic, and religious change began reshaping western Europe in the 1400s. At the same time, imported Chinese and Arab naval and military technology helped spur maritime explorations. Meanwhile, Byzantium struggled to hold its eastern Mediterranean empire but also spread its culture to the Russians.

WESTERN ASIA

The rise of Islam in Arabia in the 600s transformed the region. Arab Muslim armies conquered much of Western Asia, and most of the region's peoples eventually embraced Islam. Islam also spread west through North Africa and into Spain, as well as east to India, Central Asia, and Indonesia, linking Western Asians with a vast Islamic community. Islam divided into rival Sunni and Shi'a schools. Muslim scholars fostered science and literature, and major Islamic states, especially the Abbasid Empire, dominated the region. Eventually the Ottoman Turks formed the most powerful Western Asian state, conquering Byzantium.

EASTERN ASIA

China stood out for its influence and creativity. During the Tang and Song dynasties, China's economy grew rapidly and science flourished, attracting merchants and scholars from many countries. At the same time, Chinese cultural influences spread to neighboring Korea, Japan, and Vietnam. Under Mongol rule, China remained open to the world, but it later turned inward. Meanwhile, Japanese and Koreans combined Chinese influences, such as Buddhism, with their own traditions.

Map labels: ARCTIC OCEAN, RUSSIA, ENGLAND, EUROPE, FRANCE, Danube, BYZANTIUM, SPAIN, OTTOMAN EMPIRE, ABBASIDS (IRAQ), MOROCCO, EGYPT, Nile, ARABIA, MALI, AFRICA, Niger R., BENIN, KONGO, Congo R., SWAHILI, ATLANTIC OCEAN, ZIMBABWE, MONGOLS (MONGOLIA), ASIA, JAPAN, CHINA, HIMALAYAS, Ganges R., INDIA, PAGAN, Mekong R., VIETNAM, ANGKOR, INDIAN OCEAN, INDONESIA, AUSTRALIA

AFRICA

Islam swept across North Africa, becoming the dominant religion north of the Sahara. It also reshaped societies as it spread into West Africa and East Africa. Sub-Saharan African peoples formed large empires, such as Mali, and flourishing states, such as Benin, Kongo, and Zimbabwe. West African kingdoms and East African coastal cities were closely tied to world trade. In the 1400s the Portuguese explored the West African coast and disrupted African states.

SOUTHERN ASIA AND OCEANIA

Although politically fragmented into diverse rival states, India remained a major commercial and manufacturing center. Muslims from West and Central Asia conquered parts of north India, spreading Islam there. In response, Hinduism became reinvigorated. Southeast Asians flourished from farming and maritime trade, and major kingdoms, notably Angkor and Pagan, emerged. Southeast Asians imported ideas from India, China, and the Middle East, and many people adopted Theravada Buddhism or Islam. Maritime trade, especially the export of spices, and the spread of Islam and Buddhism linked Southeast Asia to the wider Afro-Eurasian world. Meanwhile, Polynesians settled the last uninhabited Pacific islands, including Hawaii and New Zealand.

THE RISE, POWER, AND CONNECTIONS OF THE ISLAMIC WORLD, 600–1500

Bibliothèque nationale de France

Pilgrimage Caravan
Every year caravans of Muslim pilgrims converged on Islam's holiest city, Mecca, in Arabia. This painting shows such a caravan led by a band. Pilgrims came from as far away as Morocco and Spain in the west and Indonesia and China in the east.

> *T*hen came Islam. All institutions underwent change. It distinguished [believers] from other nations and ennobled them. Islam became firmly established and securely rooted. Far-off nations accepted Islam.
>
> —IBN KHALDUN, FOURTEENTH-CENTURY ARAB HISTORIAN [1]

*I*n 1382 the author of these words on history, the fifty-year-old Arab scholar Abd al-Rahman Ibn Khaldun (AHB-d al-ruh-MAHN ib-uhn kal-DOON), left his longtime home in Tunis in North Africa and moved east to Egypt. He was already a well-traveled man and renowned as a thinker, and his work, like his life, reflected the expansive cosmopolitan nature of Islamic society, which crossed many geographical and cultural borders. He had recently completed his greatest work, a monumental history of the world known to educated Muslims. The book was the first attempt by a historian anywhere to discover and explain the changes in societies over time. Rational, analytical, and encyclopedic in coverage, it also offered a philosophy of history rooted in the scientific method.

Ibn Khaldun came from a family with roots in Arabia that had later settled in Spain and several generations later in Tunis. Ibn Khaldun visited and worked in various cities of North Africa and Spain, serving diverse rulers as a jurist, adviser, or diplomat. Now he was finally settling in Cairo, Egypt, a city he praised as the "metropolis of the world, garden of the universe, meeting-place of nations, ant hill of peoples, high place of Islam, seat of power."[2] Cairo remained his home as he served as a judge and a teacher, wrote voluminously, and traveled with high Egyptian officials to Palestine, Syria, and Arabia. Six centuries after his family left Arabia for the western Mediterranean, he could feel at home in their ancestral homeland. The Islamic world he chronicled enjoyed an extraordinary unity of time and space.

The rise of Islam that produced Ibn Khaldun was a major historical turning point that led to widespread social, cultural, and political changes over the centuries. The Islamic religion originated in seventh-century Arabia and eventually spread across several continents. Today Islam is, after Christianity, the largest religion in the world, embraced by about one-fifth of the world's population. A dynamic faith, Islam adapted to new cultures while remaining close to its founding ideals. It also had extensive dialogue with, and often tolerance toward, other traditions. For nearly a thousand years Islamic peoples greatly influenced or dominated much of the Eastern Hemisphere. Muslim thinkers salvaged or developed major portions of the science and mathematics that formed the basis for later industrial society, and Muslim sailors and merchants opened or extended networks that spread goods, technologies, and ideas throughout Afro-Eurasia.

FOCUS QUESTIONS

1. How did Islam arise and spread?
2. What were the major achievements of the Islamic states and empires?
3. What were the major concerns of Muslim thinkers and writers?
4. Why do historians speak of Islam as a hemispheric culture?

Visit the website and eBook for additional study materials and interactive tools: www.cengage.com/history/lockard/globalsocnet2e

EARLY ISLAM: THE ORIGINS AND SPREAD OF A CONTINUOUS TRADITION

How did Islam arise and spread?

The Islamic religion was founded in the Arabian peninsula, a parched land inhabited mainly by nomads who lived on the fringes of more powerful societies. A fervently monotheistic faith influenced by Jewish and Christian thought, Islam was inspired by the visions of a single influential man, Muhammad (moo-HAM-mad), considered by his followers to be the last of God's prophets. Islam quickly developed explosive energies that propelled it from a small Arab sect into the dominant faith of many millions of people from one end of the Eastern Hemisphere to the other. Within 130 years of Islam's birth, Arab armies and navies had conquered much of the territory from Spain to Persia and in the years to follow penetrated India, Central Asia, and China, in the process implanting Islam far from its homeland. These conquests and the accompanying spread of the new religion dramatically reshaped many societies across the Afro-Eurasian zone. Arab language and culture spread with Islam, providing a new identity for the once diverse Middle Eastern societies.

The Middle Eastern Sources of Islam

In Muhammad's day the Middle East, which includes western Asia and North Africa, was a region of great cultural diversity, a major factor in the rise of Islam. The Byzantine Empire had filled the vacuum left by the collapse of Roman control in western Asia and North Africa. Between 611 and 619 Sassanian Persia conquered Syria, Palestine, and Egypt. The Persians, Byzantines, and Ethiopians all interfered in Arabian politics. Many Middle Eastern people were Christians, including sects such as the Monophysites (among them the Copts of Egypt) and Nestorians, which were considered heretical by Roman Christians. These diverse traditions eventually influenced Islam.

Arab Society and Culture

Islam was also the product of a distinctive Arab society and culture. The Arabs, a Semitic people, occupied a desolate environment where life was sustained by scattered oases and a few areas of fertile highlands. Survival in a sparsely populated environment depended on cooperation within families, clans, and tribes. Each tribe was governed by a council of senior males, who selected a supreme elder respected for his generosity and bravery. Some Arabs, like the Nabataeans, became traders who ranged widely in the Middle East, and Arab trading cities and farmers flourished in Yemen in the south. But many Arab tribes were tent-dwelling nomadic pastoralists, known as **Bedouins** (BED-uh-wuhnz), who wandered in search of oases and grazing lands. Some resorted at times to raiding trade caravans. Poetry among the Arabs was so popular that, one month a year, raids and battles were halted so that poets could gather and compete. The Arab romantic poetry tradition may have been taken to Europe centuries later by Christian crusaders, probably influencing the chivalric love songs of medieval European performers known as troubadours.

Bedouins Tent-dwelling nomadic Arab pastoralists who wandered in search of oases, grazing lands, or trade caravans to raid.

Arabia was saturated with diverse religious traditions, including Judaism, Christianity, and Zoroastrianism. Like their Hebrew neighbors, the Arabs believed that they were descended from Abraham. While some Arabs had adopted Judaism or Christianity, most were polytheistic, believing in many gods, goddesses, and spirits. Some tribes believed that the chief god was housed in a huge sacred cube-shaped structure made out of stone, known as the **Ka'ba** (KAH-buh), in Mecca, a bustling trading city in central Arabia near the Red Sea to which people made annual pilgrimages. Meccan merchants obtained hides, leather goods, spices, and perfumes in Yemen and exchanged them in Syria for textiles, olive oil, and weapons.

Ka'ba A huge sacred cube-shaped stone in the city of Mecca to which people made annual pilgrimages.

The Prophet Muhammad and His Revelations

The founder of Islam was Muhammad Ibn Abdullah (ca. 570–632). Historians debate the origins of all the major religions, and Islam is no exception. Just as historians disagree about the accuracy of the historical accounts contained in the Hebrew Bible and the Christian gospels, and lack adequate sources to trace fully the lives of the Buddha and Confucius, there is controversy, especially among non-Muslim scholars, concerning Muhammad's life, how much Islamic thought arose out of older ideas, and the factors that shaped the expansion of the Arabs and Islam. The sources available for understanding early Judaism, Christianity, and Islam were com-

CHRONOLOGY

	Middle East	Europe	Central Asia
600	**622** Hijra of Muhammad to Medina **634–651** Arab conquests in Middle East **632–661** Rashidun Caliphate **661–750** Umayyad Caliphate		
700	**750–1258** Abbasid Caliphate	**711–1492** Muslim states in Spain	**705–715** Islamic conquests
1000		**1096–1272** Christian Crusades in Middle East	
1200			**1218–1360** Mongol conquests in Central and western Asia
1300		**1300–1923** Ottoman Empire	**1369–1405** Reign of Tamerlane

piled decades, sometimes centuries, after the events described and can be interpreted by historians in different ways.

According to the traditional accounts, Muhammad was a member of the Hashimite (HASH-uh-mite) clan of the prosperous mercantile Quraysh (KUR-aysh) tribe of Mecca (see Chronology: The Islamic World, 570–1220). Raised by an uncle after his parents died, he became a merchant, shipping goods for a wealthy twice-widowed older woman, Khadija (kah-DEE-juh), who had capitalized on the opportunities that city life sometimes gave ambitious women. They soon married. Although Muhammad's trade caravans flourished, he believed that Meccan merchants had become greedy and materialistic, contrary to Arab traditions of generosity.

In seeking answers to his concerns, Muhammad often meditated in the barren mountains around Mecca. In 610 he had a series of visions in which he believed God revealed the secrets of existence. He reported that he was visited by an angel, who brought God's command to "recite in the name of your lord who created the human."[3] Alarmed, he consulted one of his wife's cousins, a monotheist who encouraged him to accept the visions he received as revelations from God. Fearing that he was possessed by demons, Muhammad often agonized about the visions. The spiritual experiences continued over the next twenty-three years. However, Muhammad eventually came to accept the authenticity of the messages, largely because of the support given by his wife Khadija: "She believed in me when no one else did. She considered me to be truthful when the people called me a liar. She helped me with her fortune when the people had left me nothing."[4] Muhammad began preaching the new faith of *Islam* ("submission to God's will") to a few followers. The early believers, or *Muslims* (MUZ-limz) ("those who had submitted to God's will"), were mostly drawn from among his middle-class friends and relatives and a few other Meccans, some from lower-class backgrounds. Gradually some rich members of the Quraysh tribe also joined.

In the 650s, several decades after Muhammad's death, his followers compiled his revelations into an official version, the **Quran** (kuh-RAHN), meaning "Recitation." The Quran, beloved by Muslims for its beautiful poetic verses, became Islam's holy book, to believers the inspired word of God. A second book revered by many Muslims as a source of religious guidance and law, the **Hadith** (hah-DEETH), meaning "narrative," compiled by Muslim scholars into an official version during the ninth and tenth centuries, collected the remembered words and deeds of Muhammad himself.

Muhammad insisted that he was human, not divine, and his followers accepted him as a prophet whose visions were the last of several occasions in history during which God spoke to prophets. The earlier prophets were Adam, Abraham, Moses, and Jesus, and Muhammad was considered the final voice superseding the others (see Witness to the Past: The Holy Book, God, and the Prophet in the Quran). Muhammad's faith mixed older traditions with new understandings, and many of the principal ideas of Islam clearly resembled some beliefs of the Christians and Jews living in Mecca. Like these traditions, Muhammad's views were strictly monotheistic. All other gods were put aside, and believers were assured of an afterlife. In contrast to the dominant Arab social customs, Islam guaranteed women certain rights formerly denied them and promoted the equality

Primary Source: The Quran: Call for Jihad Discover what the Quran says about the duty of Muslims to defend themselves from their enemies, and how this duty is qualified.

Muhammad's Revelations

Quran ("Recitation") Islam's holiest book; contains the official version of Muhammad's revelations, and to believers is the inspired word of God.

Hadith ("Narrative") The remembered words and deeds of Muhammad, revered by many Muslims as a source of religious guidance and law.

CHRONOLOGY
The Islamic World, 570–1220

ca. 570   Birth of Muhammad in Mecca

622   Hijra of Muhammad and followers to Medina

632   Death of Muhammad; Abu Bakr becomes first caliph

634   Muslim conquests begin

632–661   Rashidun Caliphate

636–637   Arab military victories over Byzantine and Sassanian forces

642   Arab conquest of Egypt

651   Completion of Arab conquest of Persia

661   Murder of Ali and establishment of Umayyad dynasty in Damascus

705–715   Arab conquests of Afghanistan and Central Asia

711–720   Arab conquest of Spain

732   European defeat of Arabs at Battle of Tours

750   Abbasid defeat of Umayyads and new caliphate

756–1030   Umayyad dynasty in Spain

825–900   Arab conquest of Sicily

969–1171   Fatimid dynasty in Egypt and neighboring areas

1061–1091   Norman conquest of Sicily from Arabs

1071   Beginning of Seljuk Turk conquest of Anatolia

1085   Spanish Christian seizure of Umayyad capital

1095–1272   Christian Crusades in western Asia and North Africa

1171–1193   Reign of Saladin in Egypt

1218   Beginning of Mongol conquests in Muslim Central Asia

hijra The emigration of Muslims from Mecca to Medina in 622.

umma The community of Muslim believers united around God's message.

Allah To Muslims the one and only, all-powerful God.

---

of all believers. Muhammad also advocated principles of equality and justice, sharing all wealth, living simply, and creating a spirit of unity.

Emigration and Triumph

Muhammad soon faced challenges that led him to leave Mecca. His ideas divided his Quraysh tribe, and the Mecca leaders rejected Muhammad's views and following as a threat to their position. Some enemies harassed Muslims and even plotted Muhammad's murder. In 619 Khadija died, followed by the uncle who raised him, leaving Muhammad in despair. Meanwhile, the nearby city of Medina became engulfed in strife. To find a solution, the contending factions invited Muhammad, respected for his fairness and honesty, to come to Medina and arbitrate their disputes. In 622 Muhammad led seventy Muslims and their families from Mecca to Medina, an event known as the **hijra** (HIJ-ruh), or "emigration." Hence, to believers, 622, which begins the Muslim calendar, represents humanity's response to God's message. In Medina the Muslims formed a new community of believers, or **umma**. Many Medinans came to accept Muhammad as the Prophet, and he built his first mosque for worship and prayers. Muhammad was aided by his forceful personality and leadership. He also used a wise strategy of tolerating differences. For example, he accommodated Jews by respecting the stories of their past prophets.

Some historians argue that the boundaries between Muslims and Jews were not clearly defined at this time. Muhammad also said that the original Jewish and Christian teachings had been distorted by these religions' followers. In Medina Muhammad also took new wives. Because frequent warfare and raiding killed off many men, Arab men often had several wives so they could protect vulnerable women and procreate more children. Concerned for the welfare of women without husbands, Muhammad urged his men to marry widows. He also required that all wives be treated equally and fairly.

Muhammad's growing popularity earned him more enemies. Some Medina Jews mocked his beliefs. Muhammad urged his followers to respect sympathetic Christians and Jews, saying, "Dispute not with the People of the Book. We believe in what has been sent down to us, and what has been sent down to you; our God and your God is One."[5] But, believing he needed strong methods to preserve his umma, he expelled two Jewish tribes and had all the men of another killed because he suspected them of aiding his opponents. Muhammad's followers also fought and won various military skirmishes, usually against much larger armies. The Muslims, mostly city-dwellers, quickly learned desert warfare. In general Muhammad was a flexible, pragmatic leader, usually willing to negotiate and compromise rather than shed blood, but his brilliant military victories and shrewd diplomacy made him the most powerful man in Arabia. Muhammad pardoned most of his foes and assumed power in Mecca, sharing the taxes from trade with those who became Muslim. His triumph marked a shift of power and expanded the umma in central Arabia.

Muhammad's message of monotheism, community, equality, and justice proved a powerful attraction because it dissolved social barriers between tribes and encouraged a larger spiritual community. In his last sermon, Muhammad told his audience to deal justly with each other, treat women kindly, and consider all Muslims as brothers.[6] His message emphasized the one and only, all-powerful God, **Allah** (AH-luh): "He knows what is hidden and what is evident. He is the merciful lord of mercy. There is no God but him. He is the king, the holy, the peace, the faith keeper, the preserver, the strong, the all-disposing."[7]

Muhammad began delivering his message amidst social and economic changes in western Arabia. Meccan merchants had become more deeply involved in long-distance trade. Some Mec-

The Holy Book, God, and the Prophet in the Quran

The Quran is organized according to the length of individual chapters, so that early and later revelations are mixed together; it does not follow a rigid organization of thoughts. In addition, the beauty of the powerful, poetic writing style is not always apparent in English translation, where most of the nuances of the Arabic language are lost. In Arabic the Quran clearly comes across as both a scripture and an elegant literature that has inspired millions. The following brief excerpts present some basic ideas about the holy book itself, the unity and power of the monotheistic God, and the recognition of Muhammad as a human prophet or apostle to God.

In the name of the Merciful and Compassionate God. That is the Book! There is no doubt therein; a guide to the pious, who believe in the unseen, and are steadfast in prayer, and of what we have given them expend in alms; who believe in what is revealed to thee, and what was revealed before thee, and of the hereafter they are sure. These are in guidance from their Lord, and these are the prosperous. . . .

God, there is no god but He, the living, the self-subsistent. Slumber takes Him not, nor sleep. His is what is in the heavens and what is in the earth. Who is it that intercedes with Him save by His permission? He knows what is before them and what behind them, and they comprehend not aught of His knowledge but of what He pleases. His throne extends over the heavens and the earth, and it tires him not to guard them both, for He is high and grand. . . . On Him is the call of truth, and those who call on others than Him shall not be answered at all, save as one who stretches out his hand to the water that it may reach his mouth, but it reaches it not! The call of the misbelievers is always in error. . . . In the name of the Merciful and Compassionate God, Say "He is God alone!"

Muhammad is but an apostle; apostles have passed away before his time; what if he die or is killed, will ye retreat upon your heels? He who retreats upon his heels does no harm to God at all; but God will recompense the thankful. . . . Muhammad is not the father of any of your men, but the Apostle of God, and the Seal of the Prophets; for God all things doth know!

THINKING ABOUT THE READING

1. What is the purpose of the Quran?

2. What are the powers of God?

3. What is the relationship between Muhammad and God?

Source: Excerpts taken from Chapters 2, 3, 13, and 33 of the Quran, as reprinted in L. S. Stavrianos, ed., *The Epic of Man to 1500* (Englewood Cliffs, NJ: Prentice-Hall, 1970), 210–211.

cans had become richer and others poorer, fostering social instability. But Muhammad, like Jesus of Nazareth six hundred years earlier, emphasized social justice, thus winning support among the poor.

When Muhammad died at age sixty-two, the umma faced a challenge. Muhammad had left little guidance on future leadership, and the issue provoked disagreements. The four men closest to him formed a **caliphate** (KAL-uhf-uht), an imperial state headed by an Islamic ruler, or *caliph* (KAL-uhf), considered the successor of the Prophet in civil affairs. The umma was ruled from Medina by the Arab merchant aristocracy through Muhammad's four consecutive successors, known later as the Rashidun ("rightly guided") caliphs, between 632 and 661, but disagreements about succession continued.

caliphate An imperial state headed by an Islamic ruler, the caliph, considered the designated successor of the Prophet in civil affairs.

Islamic Beliefs and Society

Like Christians, Muslims considered their faith the last revealed religion, and they possessed a strong missionary impulse to share their faith with all people. The basic tenets of the religion provided a framework for a new world-view that changed history and for a sense of community in the wider brotherhood of believers. Believers have clear duties, known as the five pillars. These include, first, the profession of faith. Theologically the religion is blunt: "There is no God but Allah and Muhammad is his messenger."[7] Muhammad is not considered divine but a teacher chosen by God to spread the truth of a monotheistic God said to be eternal, all powerful, all knowing, and all merciful. Second is the formal worship, to be performed with words and action five times daily. The third pillar requires giving assistance to the poor and disadvantaged, for which Muslims are expected to donate a tenth of their wealth, which also benefits the giver. The fourth pillar, the annual fast or **Ramadan** (RAHM-uh-dahn), lasts one month, during which time Muslims have to abstain from eating, drinking, and having sex during daylight hours, to sacrifice for their faith and understand the hunger of the poor. They are supported

The Five Pillars of Faith

Ramadan The thirty days of annual fasting when Muslims abstain from eating, drinking, and sex during daylight hours, to demonstrate sacrifice for their faith and understand the hunger of the poor.

249

Muhammad Enters a City in Triumph

Although Islamic custom discourages painting images of the Prophet, Muslim artists, especially Persians and Turks, have done so over the centuries, emphasizing his spiritual qualities and destiny. This painting from an Islamic collection shows Muhammad leading his followers into Mecca for the first time after his exile while an angel on the gate cries, "Thou art the prophet of God."

haj The Muslim pilgrimage to the holy city of Mecca to worship with multitudes of other believers from around the world.

jihad Effort to live as God intended; a spiritual, moral, and intellectual struggle to enhance personal faith and follow the Quran.

Courtesy, Nasser D. Khalili Collection of Islamic Art

by lively gatherings of families and friends just before sunrise and then again following sunset. Finally, if possible, at least once in their lives Muslims make a pilgrimage, or **haj** (HAJ), to the holy city of Mecca, where they worship with other believers from around the world. Among other spiritual activities, pilgrims circle the great Ka'ba shrine, as Arabs had done before Islam.

Islam places other demands on believers. A puritanical moral code prohibits adultery, gambling, usury, or the use of intoxicating liquors. Heavy drinking was common among Arabs. Like Judaism, Islam also has strict dietary laws, including a ban on pork. An important concept is the necessity to pursue effort, or **jihad** (ji-HAHD), to live as God intended. Most perceive this as a spiritual, moral, and intellectual struggle to enhance personal faith and follow the Quran. However, a minority has interpreted jihad as involving military conflict or violent struggle with nonbelievers or enemies, somewhat like the Christian crusading tradition. Many Islamic beliefs are similar to Judeo-Christian beliefs. Muslims believe in angels, heavenly servants who serve as God's helpers, and a Devil who flouts God's command, and they also anticipate a last judgment, when each individual will be accountable for his or her own actions. The good will attain Heaven, a garden paradise, while the wicked will suffer an eternity in Hell.

Muslims applied the idea of unity to society, seeking to build a moral and divinely guided community by regulating how people lived together. People were asked to pursue justice, avoid excesses, and practice mercy. Islamic laws also protected the freedom of religious minorities to worship as they pleased, promoting toleration of Christians and Jews as "protected peoples." The Quran stated: "Lo! those who believe [in Islam], and those who are Jews and Christians, whoever believeth in Allah on the last day and doeth right—surely their reward is with their Lord, and no fear shall come upon them, neither shall they grieve."[8] Some Christian groups, angry with the corruption of the Byzantine Empire, aided the Muslim expansion and viewed the Arabs as liberators.

Islamic ideas influenced gender relations, improving the position of women in Arab culture. Before Islam, Arab women had few rights, and many were kept in seclusion. Men took as many wives as they could afford, and women were considered prized booty in raids. Under Islam, men could have up to four wives as long as they could support them and treated them equally, and men had more rights under the divorce and inheritance rules than women. However, women had some legal protection, could own property and engage in business, and were considered partners before God alongside men. Scholars debate how Muhummad viewed women's roles in society. Muhammad enjoyed the company of women, helped out with household chores, listened with interest when his wives asserted their own opinions, and emphasized that men should treat women kindly. He had taken more wives after Khadija's death, and his favorite wife, A'isha, played a prominent political role, especially after his death. Muhammad also encouraged female modesty in dress, suggesting that women draw their cloaks about them when they went out. Whether this meant full veiling of the face remains a matter of dispute. Veiling was common in many earlier Middle Eastern societies, going back to ancient Mesopotamia. Several generations after Muhammad, veiling became expected of devout women. While this enforced modesty has restricted women, many Muslim men and women have believed the custom protects women's dignity and virtue. This practice has also separated the sexes, preventing what most Muslims considered inappropriate romantic entanglements.

Islam and Women

Arab Conquests and the Making of an Islamic World

Arab Expansion

The Arabs rapidly expanded from their base in central Arabia. Between 634, shortly after the Prophet's death, and 651 Muslim armies conquered Iraq, Syria, Palestine, Egypt, and Persia.

A long siege; Muslims forced to withdraw

Under Muhammad, 622–632
632–656
656–750
750–900
★ Major battle

Map 10.1 Expansion of Islam, to 750 c.e.
The Arabs rapidly conquered much of western Asia, North Africa, and Spain, in the process expanding Islam into the conquered territories. By 750 their empire stretched from Morocco and Spain in the west to western India and Central Asia.

e Interactive Map

Arab ships sailed into the Mediterranean, taking Cyprus (649), Carthage (698), Tunis (TOO-nuhs) (700), and then Spain (711–720). In 732 Islamic expansion in Europe was finally stopped in southern France, at the Battle of Tours (toor), by a combined Christian force led by the Frankish general Charles Martel. Had Arab forces won that conflict, the history of Europe might have been different. Following the armies, Islam, within two centuries, had become the dominant religion in the Middle East and North Africa at the expense of Christianity and Zoroastrianism. In the centuries to follow, Islam spread across the Sahara to West Africa, down the East African coast, and north into Anatolia and then the Balkans. Arab expansion spread Arab identity and the Arabic language to many peoples in western Asia and North Africa. Adoption of the Arabic language and Islam united diverse peoples by transforming them into Arabs.

Arabs also expanded eastward, carrying Islam with them. After completing the conquest of Sassanian Persia, Arabs conquered Afghanistan, Sind (sind) in the lower Indus Basin, and Central Asia between 705 and 715 (see Map 10.1). By 751 Arab armies had reached the western fringes of the Chinese Empire, where they won a fierce engagement at the Talas River, blocking Chinese westward expansion and turning Central Asian Turks away from China and toward the Islamic world. Muslims now controlled most Silk Road cities, such as Samarkand and Bukhara. Muslim Arabs were already carrying out seaborne trade with China, and some Arab merchants settled in coastal cities there. In the eleventh century, Muslims began ruling large parts of India. Later, in the fifteenth and sixteenth centuries, Islam spread through the islands of Southeast Asia.

Historians have struggled to explain the energies involved in the rapid Arab expansion. Factors in Arabia, including long-term drought, poverty, and overpopulation, may have provided a spur to seek new lands. Arab leaders may have needed to capture lucrative trade routes and productive lands to obtain more resources to support their followers. In addition, the Byzantine and Sassanian Empires, exhausted from warfare and infighting, made an easy target for conquest. Furthermore, the Arab fighters were often motivated by religious faith. Yet most historians agree that Muslims made no systematic attempt to impose their religion on the conquered, and some suggest that Islam was still not clearly differentiated from Judaism and Christianity.

Factors in Expansion

SECTION SUMMARY

- Islam was born in Arabia, a harsh land where many people lived in cooperative tribes or clans.

- Islam's holiest book, the Quran, is believed to be a record of the divine revelations of the prophet Muhammad, who is considered the last prophet after Adam, Abraham, Moses, and Jesus.

- Facing some opposition in Mecca and drawn to resolve a dispute in Medina, Muhammad and his followers moved there and won many new converts.

- Muhammad's teachings were monotheistic (like Christianity and Judaism) and emphasized equality and mutual respect among peoples from different tribes.

- Islam is based on the five pillars: profession of faith; formal worship; charity; annual fasting, or Ramadan; and the pilgrimage, or haj, to Mecca.

- Islam spread extremely rapidly via Arab conquest of the Middle East, North Africa, Central Asia, and parts of India and Europe.

- Arab identity and language gradually spread to many of the conquered peoples.

- Explanations for the rapid Arab expansion include the need for resources, the weakness of other empires, and the need for a common cause to hold the Arabs together.

The dynamics within the fragile Islamic community itself provided a motive for expansion. Muhammad's death confronted his followers with a crisis, since they had lost their charismatic spiritual leader. By providing a common cause, conquest discouraged members from leaving the community. Warfare also capitalized on a long tradition of tribal fighting. Arab armies were cohesive, mobile, and well led. To prevent the rise of rival factions, Muhammad's first successor, his best friend Abu Bakr (ab-boo BAK-uhr), forbade people from leaving the umma and declared Muhammad God's final prophet. Abu Bakr allied with other tribes, among them often feuding nomadic Bedouins whose fighting spirit could be turned against non-Arab foes. Arab fighters divided up the spoils of conquest, spreading wealth within the community, maintaining unity, and keeping the allegiance of the many Muslims who believed strongly in a radical egalitarianism that challenged those with wealth and power.

By the eleventh century Islam had become the dominant religion over a wide area of Afro-Eurasia, joining older universal religions such as Buddhism and Christianity. Late-seventh-century Muslims thought of themselves as carriers of a global movement and new religion encompassing many peoples rather than an Arab cult. They ruled over self-governing religious communities of Greek Orthodox Christians, Nestorians, Copts, Zoroastrians, Manicheans, and Jews. Rather than remaining minority rulers over non-Muslim majorities, the Arab Muslims began encouraging conversion and cultural synthesis. Contrary to Western myth, conversion by force was the exception rather than the rule. Many found the religion and the increasingly cosmopolitan community of believers an attractive alternative to their old traditions.

EARLY ISLAMIC STATES AND EMPIRES

What were the major achievements of the Islamic states and empires?

Islamic expansion established a framework by which powerful states could rule millions of Muslims and non-Muslims, aided by unique concepts of government and law. For over half a millennium Arabic-speaking Muslims ruled a large segment of the Eastern Hemisphere. Great states and empires dominated the Middle East, and Islamic states on the fringe of Christian Europe served as conduits of knowledge. Peoples and ideas spread widely, fostering a dynamic society mixing Arab, Persian, Indian, and Greek cultures. But Islam also divided into rival sects, a split that created enduring tensions and that influenced Middle Eastern politics for many centuries.

Islamic Government and Law

sultan A Muslim ruler of only one country.

Shari'a The Islamic legal code for the regulation of social and economic as well as religious life.

Many Muslims viewed government and religion as the same, and Islamic states tended to punish those Muslims who violated religious prohibitions. Islamic political and religious power were often combined in a theocracy headed by a caliph or more commonly a **sultan**, a Muslim ruler of only one country. Although such far-reaching power could be easily abused, the moral authority of respected religious scholars could sometimes check abuses of political power. Muslim leaders established a legal code, or **Shari'a** (shah-REE-ah), for the regulation of social and economic as well as religious life. The Shari'a provided a comprehensive guide to life, covering areas such as divorce, inheritance, debts, and morality. Based chiefly on the Quran and the Hadith, it was also rooted in Arab cultural traditions and customs, supplemented by Persian and Byzantine concepts. But conflicts over the interpretation and application of the Quran led to the rise of several competing interpretive traditions that differed slightly in their emphasis on such tools as reasoning and scriptural authority.

Religious scholars such as judges, preachers, and prayer leaders played a major role in elaborating the Shari'a and in sustaining Islamic culture. Their legal decisions and writings provided cohesion and stability over the centuries, independent of the rise and fall of rulers. Muslims valued education based on studying with renowned religious and legal scholars, whose students then became teachers. By the tenth century religious boarding schools, known as **madrasas** (muh-DRAH-suhz), headed by a religious scholar, began appearing. Today thousands of these schools can be found all over the Muslim world.

madrasas Religious boarding schools found all over the Muslim world.

Early Imperial Caliphates: Unity and Strife

The imperial caliphates, beginning with the Rashidun, attempted to maintain unity but also faced challenges. After 661, the end of the Rashidun era, political power shifted outside of Arabia with two successive imperial dynasties, the Umayyad (oo-MY-ad) and the Abbasid (ah-BASS-id). Both dynasties were installed by members of Muhammad's Quraysh tribe. Arabia was the fountainhead, but power shifted elsewhere. While Mecca and Medina remained spiritual hubs, reinforced by annual pilgrimages, new cities emerged as more important political and economic centers for the Islamic world.

The sense of social and religious unity within a growing umma did not prevent political conflict. The early conquests greatly enriched Medina and Mecca merchant clans, and some Muslims grew critical of the new materialism. A full revolt against the Rashidun leadership erupted, and dissidents murdered the unpopular third caliph, Uthman (ooth-MAHN), installing Ali (ah-LEE) (ca. 600–661), Muhammad's son-in-law, as the fourth caliph. Although well qualified, pious, and generous, Ali proved weak. He moved the capital from Medina to Kufah (KOO-fa) in what is today Iraq, but others challenged Ali for leadership. Muhammad's widow, A'isha, helped rally the opposition to Ali, resulting in a civil war. Ali was finally killed by Uthman's relatives, who blamed him for their leader's murder. With Ali's death, the Rashidun era ended, but the divisions generated a permanent split in the Islamic world. Centuries later, many Muslims viewed the Rashidun period as a golden age with a simple government and a righteous cause, and some called for reinstating the caliphate to rule the Muslim world.

Sunni ("The Trodden Path") The main branch of Islam, comprising those who accept the practices of the Prophet and the historical succession of caliphs.

The caliphate moved to Damascus (duh-MAS-kuhs), in what is today Syria, under the leadership of the Umayyad dynasty (661–750). The Islamic empire was now led by men with no direct connection to, or descent from, the Prophet. With the move to Damascus, Arab politics came to be defined by large bureaucratic states with remote leaders who passed on their rule to their sons. Military expansion continued, and the Umayyad caliphs extended the Islamic empire deep into Byzantine territory. But the Umayyad system soon experienced unrest. Although the rulers encouraged Islam and called themselves deputies of God, they did not practice Islamic morality. Devout Muslims opposed to the Umayyads emphasized Muhammad's role as God's prophet, clearly setting Islam apart from rival monotheistic religions, and the Umayyads' legendary drinking, womanizing, and laxness in religious devotion generated civil war and division. Among the challengers was the Prophet's only remaining male heir, his grandson Husayn (hoo-SANE), who attracted support from those who believed the caliph must be a direct descendant of Muhammad. Husayn's rebellion in 680 failed, however, and he was killed in the Battle of Karbala (KAHR-buh-LAH), a city in Iraq. In death he and his father Ali, the murdered caliph, became martyrs against the Umayyads.

The Great Umayyad Mosque in Damascus This mosque, built between 709 and 715, is the oldest surviving monumental mosque.

Jane Taylor/Sonia Halliday Photographs

The Sunni-Shi'a Split

After the death of Ali, Islam began to split into two main branches due to disagreements over the nature of the umma and the full meaning of Muhammad's revelations. The main branch, **Sunni** (SOO-nee) ("The Trodden Path"), accepted the practices of the

Prophet and the historical succession of caliphs. Today about 85 percent of all Muslims, including most of those in North Africa, Turkey, the Balkans, South and Southeast Asia, and China, as well as the majority of Arabs, are Sunni. Sunni, which embraces a wide variety of opinions and practices and was probably not named until the ninth or tenth century, adheres to one of four main schools of Islamic law and a broad view of who qualifies for political power.

Shi'a ("Partisans" of Ali) The branch of Islam emphasizing the religious leaders descended from Muhammad through his son-in-law, Ali, who they believe was the rightful successor to the Prophet.

The other main branch began in a dispute over the leadership of the faithful. The **Shi'a (SHEE-uh)** ("Partisans" of Ali) emphasized only the religious leaders descended from Muhammad through his son-in-law, Ali, who they believed was the rightful successor to the Prophet. Karbala and nearby Najaf **(NAH-jaf)**, where respectively Husayn and Ali are buried, became holy Shi'ite pilgrimage centers. Over time Shi'ites provided an alternative religious vision to Sunni Islam. Shi'ism itself divided into three rival schools, based on which leader after Ali should be followed. The main concentrations of Shi'ites are found today in Iran, where most Persians adopted the school after 1500, and also in Iraq, Lebanon, and the Persian Gulf states. Smaller minorities are scattered across Central Asia, western India, and Pakistan.

Although they shared many commonalities, the differences between these two branches were deep. In general, Shi'ites followed strong religious leaders, a tradition not unknown to some Christians, ultra-Orthodox Jews, and Hindu sects. There was often much antagonism between the two groups, as there would later be, for example, between Catholics and Protestants in some Western countries. Sunni majorities sometimes persecuted Shi'ite minorities, producing a Shi'ite martyrdom complex and a tradition of dissent against Sunni rulers. Over the centuries Shi'ite movements established various states, often ruling uneasily over Sunni majorities.

Arabian Nights: The Abbasid Caliphate

The Abbasid Caliphate (750–1258), the next dynasty after the Umayyad, enjoyed great power and fostered a dynamic society for several centuries, surviving for half a millennium. The Abbasid caliphs embodied the unity of the Islamic umma and established a style for later Muslim rulers. The Abbasids, a Sunni branch of the Quraysh tribe descended from Muhammad's uncle, Abbas, had attracted support from both Sunnis and Shi'ites to defeat the Umayyad army. The lone Umayyad survivor fled to Spain, where he established a separate state that flourished for three centuries. The Abbasids expanded the empire to the east and maintained pressure against Byzantium in the west. By 800 the Abbasid Empire ruled some 30 million people (see Map 10.2).

The Abbasids moved their capital to Baghdad, located where the Tigris and Euphrates Rivers come closest together in today's Iraq. This move placed the capital strategically along major trade routes and in the middle of a farming district made fertile through irrigation. Baghdad became one of the world's greatest hubs, its bazaars filled with goods from as far away as China, Scandinavia, and East Africa, and the city boasted joint-stock companies and banks. In a public show of piety and generosity, the Abbasid government employed thousands of people in public works projects, building palaces, schools, hospitals, and mosques. Some Baghdad citizens, however, openly flouted Islamic prohibitions against hedonistic behavior, and in general Baghdad reflected the cosmopolitan flavor of Islamic society. In the 1160s a rabbi from Muslim-ruled Spain, Benjamin of Tudela, visited Baghdad and wrote of the ethnically diverse city and, in particular, its large Jewish community:

Abbasid Baghdad

> *This great Abbasid [caliph] is extremely friendly towards the Jews, many of his officers being of that nation. Baghdad contains about one thousand Jews, who enjoy peace, comfort, and much honor. Many of the Jews are good scholars and very rich. The city contains 28 Jewish synagogues.*[9]

Indeed, Islam became a far-reaching influence because of its ability to receive and absorb culture from all parts of the Eastern Hemisphere. For example, although the Abbasids were Arabs, Persian influence on their system was strong, and many Persians occupied high government positions. The Abbasids also acquired knowledge from faraway lands. Muslims first learned papermaking technology from Chinese captured in the Battle of Talas of 751, and by 800 Baghdad had its first paper mill. By the twelfth century paper was also manufactured in Morocco and Spain. Papermaking allowed for a wider distribution of the Quran, helping to spread Islam.

City Life

The height of Abbasid Baghdad conjures up the images of affluence and romance reported in *The Arabian Nights*, a cycle of stories that later also influenced European writers, artists, and composers. For example, the famous *Scheherazade* symphony by the nineteenth-century Russian composer Nikolai Rimsky-Korsakov **(RIM-skee KAWR-suh-kawf)** attempted to evoke the atmosphere

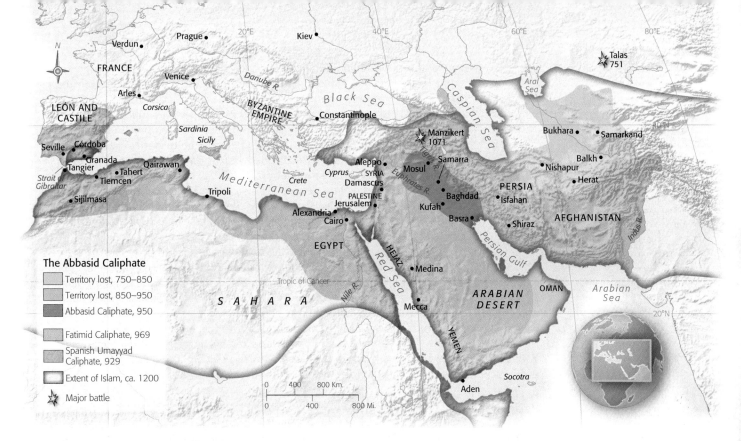

Map 10.2 The Abbasid Empire, ca. 800 C.E.

The Abbasids, a dynasty based in what is today Iraq, established the largest Muslim empire in the early Intermediate Era, ruling lands from Central Asia to Egypt before losing most of their territories. Among other major Islamic states, the Umayyads ruled Spain and Northwest Africa and the Fatimids ruled Egypt and neighboring lands.

Interactive Map

of Abbasid Baghdad. Some images of old Baghdad come from fanciful children's books and films based loosely on the great literary work, where we read of flying carpets and genies in magic lamps. Under the most famous Abbasid caliph, Harun al-Rashid (hah-ROON al-rah-SHEED) (786–809), there were no flying carpets, but many people enjoyed a comfortable life. Harun had a large harem of wives, concubines, and slave girls, perhaps 2,000 in all. The royal harems had an image, perhaps partly true, as a secluded world of luxury, idleness, and endless plotting for royal favor. Like some other Abbasid rulers, Harun also had a reputation for heavy drinking and pursuing the temptations of the flesh.

As they adopted the ways of the conquered, Arabs were gradually transformed from desert herders and traders into imperial rulers. The Abbasids often ruled through traditional leaders, such as the Coptic Church patriarchs of Egypt. In Iraq they resolved disputes among Nestorian Christians just as the Sassanian governors had done. Like the Sassanians, the caliphs patronized a state religion, now shifted from Zoroastrianism to Islam, and lavishly supported arts and crafts. They also appointed Muslim judges and built mosques.

The growth of cities followed Islamic conquests. New cities like Cairo began as Muslim garrisons. The caliphates needed administrative centers, however, and these drew in surrounding people seeking work. Hence Baghdad rapidly swelled to perhaps a million people by 900, becoming the world's largest city. The caliphs adopted the Sassanian system of dividing cities into wards marked by ethnic and occupational groups and of governing these groups through their own leaders.

Abbasid Decline and the End of the Arab Empire

Like all empires, the Abbasids eventually faced mounting problems and gradually lost their grip on power by the tenth century. Turkish soldiers, assigned to guard the caliphs, became more powerful in the government. Disaffected Shi'ites fomented bloody revolts as the caliphate became a mere figurehead, and parts of the empire broke away. Anti-Abbasid Shi'ites who claimed descent from Fatima, the daughter of Muhammad, established the Fatimid (FAT-uh-mid) Caliphate in Egypt and North Africa based in Cairo, which eventually became a rival to

255

Baghdad as an intellectual and economic center. The university founded in Cairo by the Fatimids in 970, Al-Azhar, became the most influential in the Islamic world and remains the unrivaled center of Islamic higher learning. Shi'ites also ruled various smaller states, where most of the population remained Sunni or non-Muslim yet generally enjoyed religious freedom. The Mongols, Central Asian nomads who built a great regional empire stretching from East Asia to eastern Europe in the thirteenth century (see Chapter 11 and the essay concluding Part III), were attracted by the wealth of the Abbasid realm. In 1258 Mongol armies sacked and destroyed Baghdad and executed the last Abbasid caliph (see Chronology: The Islamic World, 1095–1492), shattering the symbolic unity of the Muslim world. Throughout the Middle East, Arab dominance was challenged by Persians, Berbers, Kurds, and Turks as well as by Mongols.

Despite these setbacks, political weakness and loss of cultural dynamism did not become evident in the Islamic world until the sixteenth and seventeenth centuries, and even then there were important exceptions. Although few later Muslim rulers could match the power of the early Abbasids, Islamic society flourished and Islam accelerated its diffusion to new peoples. Between 1258 and 1550 the territorial size of the Islamic world doubled. Scholars, saints, and mystics assumed leadership throughout this world, establishing legal structures, dogmas, social forms, standards of piety, aesthetic sensibilities, styles of scholarship, and schools of philosophy that helped define the vital core of Islamic culture.

Cultural Mixing in Muslim Sicily and Spain

Islamic culture also flourished in Sicily and Spain, fostering a cosmopolitan mixed culture that brought prosperity and the sharing of scientific knowledge. Between 825 and 900 Muslim forces conquered Sicily, the largest Mediterranean island. Under Muslim rule, Sicily benefited from close ties to the Arab-dominated maritime trade system. Muslim rulers repaired long-decayed Roman irrigation works and vastly increased agricultural production. Many Arabs, Berbers, Africans, Greeks, Jews, Persians, and Slavs gravitated to the island, mixing with the local peoples and creating a cosmopolitan society. The Muslim capital, Palermo, was larger than any other city in Europe except Constantinople. But political divisions among Muslims left the island open to a gradual Christian reconquest. Between 1061 and 1091 the Normans, descendants of Vikings who had settled in France, replaced a Muslim government with their own. By 1200 Christian German rulers had established a Sicilian state and were persecuting Muslims and Jews, gradually bringing to an end an era when the islanders blended Islamic and Christian traditions into a dynamic fusion.

The Splendor of Cordoba

A more enduring Muslim society emerged in Spain, much of which was first conquered by Umayyad forces between 711 and 720. Their capital, Cordoba (KAWR-duh-buh), became Europe's largest city by 1000, home to half a million people. Under Umayyad rule, Spain was for several centuries a famed center of culture and learning, drawing scholars and thinkers from all over Europe and the Islamic world. Cordoba's library held 400,000 volumes, when libraries in Christian Europe owned only several hundred. The mood of tolerance generated a productive relationship between diverse peoples and traditions, with Christian, Muslim, and Jewish thinkers working together to share and advance knowledge. To one Arab poet, Cordoba was the garden of the fruits of ideas. Intellectuals discussed ancient Greek thought and the latest astronomical discoveries and translated books from and into Arabic. From this cosmopolitan intellectual milieu, much of the classical Greco-Roman heritage, Islamic and Indian science and mathematics, and some Chinese technology, such as papermaking, were passed on to Europe. Europe also benefited from Arab vocal and instrumental music, which were important in Islamic Arab culture for ceremonies, pleasure, and worship. Arab folk songs and musical instruments, such as the guitar and lute, diffused northward, influencing the courtly love songs of European troubadours and, later, Western popular music.

Decline and Conquest

By 1000 decline, marked by civil wars and factionalism, had begun to set in and the Umayyad government fragmented into smaller, often warring states. Intolerant Muslim invaders from Morocco took power in some regions and persecuted anyone not sharing their rigid interpretation of Islam. Many Spaniards had remained loyal to Catholicism, providing a base of support for efforts at reconquest, and much of northern Spain gradually came under Christian control. In 1085

Alhambra, Court of Lions The Alhambra, or Palace of Lions, built in Granada in southern Spain in the fourteenth century, is one of the finest architectural treasures from Muslim Spain. It features a courtyard with a fountain.

Everts/Visual Connection Archive

Christian knights conquered Cordoba, the center of Islamic power. Constant Christian military pressure gradually pushed Muslim rule into southern Spain, and by 1252 Christian princes controlled much of Spain and Portugal. Finally, in 1492, Christians took the last Muslim stronghold at Granada (gruh-NAHD-uh). The new Christian rulers, militant and intolerant, forced Muslims and Jews to either convert to Christianity or face expulsion. Many converted but thousands fled, usually to Muslim countries in North Africa or to Anatolia.

SECTION SUMMARY

- Muslim leaders imposed Shari'a, a legal code that regulated social, economic, and religious life.

- In the period of the early Rashidun Caliphate, dissidents murdered the third caliph and installed Muhammad's son-in-law Ali as the fourth caliph, and after Ali's murder Islam began to split into two branches: the Sunni majority branch and the Shi'a dissident branch who believed Ali was the only successor to the Prophet.

- Throughout history, Sunni persecution of Shi'ite minorities has created a Shi'ite martyrdom complex and a tradition of dissent against Sunni rulers.

- The Umayyad dynasty, which succeeded the Rashidun Caliphate, was led by men with no connection to Muhammad who extended the empire into Byzantine lands.

- Under the Abbasid Caliphate, during which *The Arabian Nights* was set, Baghdad became a cosmopolitan hub of trading and culture.

- As they expanded, Arabs adopted the imperial ruling structures of the peoples they conquered and were targeted by numerous invaders, including the Mongols.

- Spain and Sicily were ruled by Muslims for several centuries, though Christians gradually reclaimed them and failed to maintain the tolerance of the early Muslim rulers.

CULTURAL HALLMARKS OF ISLAM: THEOLOGY, SOCIETY, AND LEARNING

▌ What were the major concerns of Muslim thinkers and writers?

▌slamic expansion launched a thousand-year era, from the seventh to the seventeenth century, that brought many Afro-Eurasian peoples into closer contact with one another and allowed for a mixing of cultures within an Islamic framework. Muslims synthesized elements from varied traditions, including the Arab, Greek, Persian, and Indian, to produce a new hybrid culture, vital and durable, that was rooted in theology, social patterns, literature and art, science, and learning. Islamic theology continued to develop, fostering several distinct strands of thought and behavior, and Islamic societies fashioned a distinctive social system and a renowned cultural heritage. In addition, Islamic scholars contributed major scientific achievements and historical studies to the world.

Theology, Sufism, and Religious Practice

From the very beginning, Muslims' debates over theological questions led to divergent interpretations of the Quran. As in all religions, a variety of views about the great questions of life and death developed, reflecting the mixing of intellectual traditions. Some Muslim thinkers emphasized reason and free will, while others believed that Allah preordained everything. Throughout the Islamic world, influential thinkers mastered several fields of knowledge. Abu Yusuf al-Kindi (a-BOO YOU-suhf al-KIN-dee) (ca. 800–ca. 870), an Arab who lived in Iraq, praised the search for truth and popularized Greek ideas. Although he emphasized logic and mathematics, he also published work on science, music, medicine, and psychology. Abu Ali al-Husain Ibn Sina (a-BOO AH-lee al-who-SANE IB-unh SEE-nah) (980–1037), known in the West as Avicenna (av-uh-SEN-uh), was both a philosopher and a medical scholar. A native of Bukhara (boo-CAR-ruh), a Silk Road city in Central Asia, he spent most of his career in Persia. Ibn Sina believed everyone could exercise free will but that the highest goal was communion with God. Afghanistan-born Abu Hamid al-Ghazali (AH-boo HAM-id al-guh-ZAL-ee) (1058–1111), a teacher in Baghdad, used Aristotelian logic to justify Islamic beliefs. This rationalistic approach remained influential in Shi'a thinking but lost support in Sunni circles from the fourteenth century onward.

Theological Debates [margin note]

Among both Sunnis and Shi'ites a mystical approach and practice developed and gained many followers. **Sufism** (SOO-fiz-uhm) emphasized personal spiritual experience rather than nit-picking theology. Sufis stressed the superiority of the heart over the mind and sought communion with God. Such mysticism was suggested in the Quran: "Wherever ye turn there is the face of God."[10] A famous Sufi poet in Persia, Baba Kuhi, saw God in everything: "In the market, in the cloister—only God I saw; In the valley and on the mountain—only God I saw. Him I have seen beside me oft in tribulation; in favor and in fortune—only God I saw."[11] Many Sufis exchanged information with Christian, Hindu, and Jewish mystics, were willing to synthesize Islam with other ideas as long as the central spirit was maintained, and considered their practices useful even for non-Muslims. But Sufism constituted a supplement rather than a challenge to conventional Islam.

Sufism A mystical approach and practice within Islam that emphasized personal spiritual experience. [margin definition]

Sufis congregated in orders led by masters who taught prescribed techniques and attracted devoted followers. The whirling *dervishes* (DUHR-vish-iz) of Turkey are one of the most famous Sufi orders. Dervishes practiced special exercises and methods, including the trance dancing from which they get their name, to achieve a state of divine ecstasy. Several Sufi orders were renowned as peace-loving and tolerant of different views and customs. Followers credit some Sufi masters with magical powers and make their tombs pilgrimage destinations. However, Sufism remained a controversial movement. While the tendency to tolerate religious flexibility won Sufis converts, many non-Sufis condemned the way some Sufis suspended ordinary Islamic biases against wine, drugs, and music in worship. Sufis produced most Islamic poetry, and millions of Sufis revere the Persian Sufi poet Hafez (hah-FEZ) (1326–1389), who loved God and the grape with equal devotion: "Here we are with our wine and the ascetics with their piety. Let us see which one the beloved [God] will take."[12]

Diverse Practices [margin note]

As Islam spread into diverse cultures, it developed several distinct patterns of practice. The adaptationists showed a willingness to make adjustments to changing conditions. These Muslims have provided the base for reform and for secular and modernizing movements. Conservatives, on the other hand, strove to preserve established beliefs and customs, such as the rigid division of the sexes, and mistrusted innovation. The most dogmatic conservatives argued that the divine revelations channeled through Muhammad set a permanent standard to use in judging existing conditions, an unchangeable authority of universal validity. Finally, some stressed the personal aspects of the faith. These diverse patterns all have large followings among both Sunnis and Shi'ites, providing the basis for political and social conflict in Muslim societies.

Social Life and Gender Relations

As Islamic culture expanded and matured, the social structure became more complex and marked by clear ethnic, tribal, class, occupational, religious, and gender divisions, especially in the Middle East. Arabs generally had a higher social status than Turkish, Berber, African, and other converts. Those who can claim descent from the Prophet and members of the Hashimite clan to which he belonged have held an especially honored status in Islamic societies around the world. Many Arabs were also members of tribes, such as Muhammad's Quraysh tribe. In addition, because the first Muslims were merchants, the religion had a special appeal for people in the commercial sector, providing spiritual sanction of their quest for wealth, which could finance pilgrimages to Mecca and also help the poor through almsgiving. There was, however, discrimination against Christian and Jewish minorities, who did not always have the same rights as Muslims. They paid higher taxes and were prohibited from owning weapons, and so were exempt from military duty. However, they did enjoy some protection under the law. On the whole these communities were allowed to follow their own laws, customs, and beliefs and to maintain their own religious institutions.

Slavery was common. Slaves served as bureaucrats and soldiers, workers in businesses and factories, household servants and concubines, musicians, and plantation laborers. One Abbasid caliph kept 11,000 slaves in his palace. Islamic law encouraged owners to treat slaves with consideration, and many were eventually freed. Many slaves were war captives and children purchased from poor families or from Christian European states like Byzantium and Venice. In addition, for over a dozen centuries, but especially after 1200, perhaps 10 to 15 million African slaves were brought to the Middle East across the Sahara or up the East African coast by an Arab-dominated slave trade. African slave soldiers were common in Egypt, Persia, Iraq, Oman (oh-MAHN) in eastern Arabia, and Yemen.

Families were at the heart of the social system. Marriages were arranged, with the goal of cementing social or perhaps business ties between two families. Although Shari'a law allowed men to have up to four wives at a time, this privilege remained largely restricted to the rich and powerful. Many poor men never married at all because they could not afford the large bridal gifts expected. While divorce was theoretically easy for men, marriage contracts sometimes discouraged divorce by specifying that men pay a large gift to the wife upon divorce. Within the family, parents expected children to obey and respect them, even after they became adults. Family gatherings were usually segregated by gender and often involved poetry recitations, musical performances, or Quran readings. Although Islamic law harshly punished homosexuality, homosexual relationships were not uncommon, and same-sex love was often reflected in poetry and literature, most notably in Muslim Spain. European visitors were often shocked at the tolerant attitudes of Arabs, Persians, and Turks toward homosexual romantic relationships.

The status of women in Islamic society has been subject to debate by both Western and Islamic observers for centuries. For example, the philosopher Ibn Rushd (IB-uhn RUSHED) (1126–1198), known in the West as Averroes (uh-VER-uh-WEEZ), attacked restrictions on women as an economic burden, arguing that "the ability of women is not known, because they are merely used for procreation [and] child-rearing."[13] Although the Quran recognized certain rights of women, prohibited female infanticide, and limited the number of wives men could have, it also accorded women only half the inheritance of men and gave women less standing in courts

Persian Women at a Picnic This miniature from sixteenth-century Persia shows women preparing a picnic. The ability of women to venture away from home varied widely depending on social class and regional traditions.

of law. While some Muslims criticized the many restrictions on women as institutionalizing their social inferiority, other Muslim men and women have contended that these restrictions liberate women from insecurity and male harassment. Scholars have also disagreed over whether restrictions such as veiling and seclusion were based on Quranic mandates or on patriarchal pre-Islamic Arab, Middle Eastern, and Byzantine customs. Some Muslim communities in the Middle East, and many outside the region, never adopted these practices.

Gender Relations

Women played diverse roles. Some of the wives of Abbasid caliphs played political roles, albeit mostly behind the scenes. For instance, Khayzuran, noted for her compassion and generosity, rose from a simple Yemenite slave girl to become the great love and wife of the Caliph Mahdi, dominating his harem and investing in land reclamation and charitable works. On his death, she helped smooth the transition to the rulership of her son, Harun al-Rashid. During Abbasid times some elite women, while excluded from public life, enjoyed considerable power behind the scenes, and some exceptional women circumvented restrictions. For example, Umm Hani (also known as Mariam) in fifteenth-century Cairo studied law and religion with many famous teachers, wrote poetry, owned a large textile workshop, and became a renowned teacher and scholar of the Hadith. She also had seven children by two husbands and made thirteen pilgrimages to Mecca. While formal education for girls in the Middle East was generally limited, women monopolized certain occupations such as spinning and weaving, and they also worked in the fields or in some domestic industries beside men. And in some Muslim societies, particularly in sub-Saharan Africa and Southeast Asia, women often maintained their relative independence and were free to dress as they liked, socialize outside the home, and earn money. Turks and Mongols also seem to have been more liberal on gender issues than Arabs and Persians. In short, patterns of gender relations varied considerably.

Pen and Brush: Writing and the Visual Arts

Although Islamic societies became identified with literacy and literature, writing derived from pre-Islamic roots. The Arabic alphabet originated in southern Arabia long before Muhammad's time, and Islam enhanced the script further by emphasizing literacy. The Quran stated: "Read, and thy Lord is most generous, Who taught with the pen, Taught man what he knew not."[14] Muslims adopted the Arab poetic tradition but modified romantic ideas into praise not for a lover but for the Prophet and Allah.

Literature and Poetry

One of the greatest writers of Abbasid times, also an astronomer and mathematician, was the Persian Omar Khayyam (OH-MAHR key-YAHM). In his famous poem *Rubaiyat* (ROO-bee-AHT), he noted the fleeting nature of life: "One thing is certain, that Life flies; and the rest is Lies; the flower that once has blown forever dies." This fact led him to regret never knowing the purpose of existence:

Ah, make the most of what ye yet may spend, Before we too into the Dust descend; Dust unto Dust, and under Dust to lie, [without] Wine, Song, Singer, and End! Into this Universe, and Why not knowing, Nor Whence, like Water willy-nilly flowing; And out of it, as Wind along the Waste, I know not Whither, wily-nilly blowing.[15]

The most famous Sufi poet was the thirteenth-century Persian Jalal al-Din Rumi (ja-LAL al-DIN ROO-mee). Born in Afghanistan, as a youth he lived in Central Asia and Anatolia, a fact reflecting Islam's wide reach. Rumi blended liberal spirituality with humor in writings about love, desire, and the human condition, and he often danced while reciting his poems to disciples. He was optimistic, joyful, and ecumenical, stating: "I am neither Christian, nor Jew, nor Zoroastrian, nor Muslim."[16] At the beginning of the twenty-first century, over seven hundred years after his death, Rumi became the best-selling poet in the United States after his poems were translated into English.

History and Social Sciences

The modern study of history and of social sciences, especially geography, owes much to Muslim research and writing. With the expansion of Islam and Arab trading communities to the far corners of the Eastern Hemisphere, some Muslims traveled to distant lands. Educated Muslims enjoyed reading these travelers' accounts of other countries and peoples, and modern historians are indebted to travelers such as the Moroccan jurist Ibn Battuta (IB-uhn ba-TOO-tuh) for much of what we know today about sub-Saharan Africa and Southeast Asia from the ninth to the fifteenth centuries (see Profile: Ibn Battuta, a Muslim Traveler). Geographers and cartographers such as Al-Idrisi (al-AH-dree-see) from Muslim Spain also produced atlases, globes, and maps.

Ibn Khaldun (1332–1406), the well-traveled North African introduced at the beginning of the chapter, was the first known scholar anywhere to look for patterns and structure in history. His monumental work connected the rise of states among tribal communities with a growing feeling of solidarity between leaders and their followers. His recognition of the role in history of "group feeling" (what today we call ethnic identity) and of religion was pathbreaking. In studying other cultures, he advocated "critical examination":

> *Know the rules of statecraft, the nature of existing things, and the difference between nations, regions and tribes in regard to way of life, qualities of character, customs, sects, schools of thought, and so on. [The historian] must distinguish the similarities and differences between the present and the past.*[17]

Ibn Khaldun put the Arab expansion into the broader flow of regional history.

Some Muslims emphasized the visual arts. For example, since Arabic is written in a flowing style, the artful writing of words, or **calligraphy** (kuh-LIG-ruh-fee), became a much admired art form. An elegant script offered not just a message but also decoration. Islamic Persia, India, and Central Asia also fostered a tradition of painting, especially landscapes. In addition, Muslims produced world-class architecture that included lavishly decorated buildings such as the Taj Mahal in India. Some architecture, such as mosques with domes and towers, reflected Byzantine church influence. Then as now, Muslims were famed for weaving carpets and fabrics that were valued in many non-Muslim societies.

calligraphy The artful writing of words.

Science, Technology, and Learning

During the Islamic golden age many creative thinkers emerged. Muslims also borrowed, assimilated, and diffused Greek and Indian knowledge and were familiar with some Chinese technologies. Thanks to this knowledge, certain classical and Hellenistic Greek traditions of philosophy and science that had been nearly forgotten in Europe survived in the Middle East. Many advances in science and medicine were also made in the Islamic world as experts synthesized the learning of other societies with their own insights. Some of this knowledge was carried into the Middle East by Nestorian Christians, who taught Greek sciences under Abbasid sponsorship. The Abbasid caliphs opened the House of Wisdom in Baghdad, a research institute staffed by scholars charged with translating Greek, Syrian, Sanskrit, and Persian books on philosophy, medicine, astronomy, and mathematics into Arabic. Aristotle's writings were particularly influential. The institute also included schools, observatories, and a huge library. Other scientific centers arose, from Spain and Morocco to Samarkand in Central Asia. For example, in the tenth and eleventh centuries the Shi'ite Fatimids built the House of Knowledge in Cairo with a massive library holding 2 million books, many on scientific subjects.

Integrating Traditions

Arab and Persian scholars were not just translating but also actively assimilating the imported knowledge. As the influential eleventh-century Persian philosopher Al-Biruni (al-bih-ROO-nee) wrote: "The sciences were transmitted into the Arabic language from different parts of the world; by it [the sciences] were embellished and penetrated the hearts of men, while the beauties of [Arabic] flowed in their veins and arteries."[18] The dialogue resulting from a diversity of ideas produced an open-minded search for truth that is apparent in the work of Ibn Khaldun, Ibn Sina, al-Kindi, and Ibn Rushd. For instance, the philosopher al-Kindi wrote that Muslims should acknowledge truth from whatever source it came because nothing was more important than truth itself. Ibn Rushd (Averroes), who lived in Cordoba, influenced Christian thinkers with his assertion of the role of reason. In the eleventh century, Christian Europe became aware of the Muslim synthesis of Greek, Indian, and Persian knowledge from libraries in Spain.

Muslims also turned their attention to medicine. Although much influenced by Greek ideas, Muslim medical specialists did not accept ancient wisdom uncritically. Instead, they developed an empirical tradition. Baghdad hospitals were the world's most advanced. Muslim surgeons learned how to use opium for anesthesia, extract teeth and replace them with false teeth made from animal bones, remove kidney stones, and do a colostomy by creating an artificial anus. After many Islamic medical books were translated into Latin in the twelfth century, they became the major medical texts in Europe for the next five centuries. Two medical scientists, Abu Bakr al-Razi (a-boo BAH-car al-RAH-zee) (ca. 865–ca. 932) and Ibn Sina (Avicenna), compared Greek ideas with their own research. Al-Razi, a Persian, directed several hospitals and wrote more than fifty clinical studies as well as general medical works. The latter included the *Comprehensive Book,* the longest medical encyclopedia in Arabic (eighteen volumes), which was used in Europe into the 1400s. Al-Razi also studied what we would today call sociological and psychological aspects of medicine, and a century later Ibn Sina stressed psychosomatic medicine and treated depression. He also pioneered the study of vision and

Medicine and Chemistry

IBN BATTUTA, A MUSLIM TRAVELER

Among the Islamic travelers who journeyed to, and often sojourned in, distant lands, the most famous was Abdallah Muhammad Ibn Battuta, a gregarious and pious fourteenth-century Moroccan who spent thirty years touring the length and breadth of the Islamic world, as far east as Southeast Asia and, he claimed, the coastal ports of China. His travels demonstrated the reach of the Islamic community. He was a pilgrim, judge, scholar, Sufi, ambassador, and connoisseur of fine foods and elegant architecture. Ibn Battuta's writings about his remarkable journeys, the autobiographical *Rihla* (Book of Travels), provide detailed, often unique eyewitness accounts of many societies. A collaborator compiled the *Rihla* in a literary form near the end of the adventurer's life.

Born in Tangier, Morocco, in North Africa, to a Berber family of scholars and trained in Islamic law, Ibn Battuta left home in 1325 at the age of twenty-one to seek adventure and learning. His apparent wanderlust proved difficult to quench. Such extensive travel would have been impossible for any woman, Muslim or otherwise, in that era, since women were expected to stay close to home and family. Traveling by camel, horse, wagon, or ship, Ibn Battuta covered between 60,000 and 75,000 miles and visited dozens of countries. He never had a conventional family life and married several times for short periods, leaving children all over the hemisphere. The politically ambitious jurist often sojourned in a society for months or years; his largest career stint was seven years' service in the Delhi Sultanate of northern India. But wherever he went, Ibn Battuta made observations on a wide variety of subjects, from cuisine and botany to political practice and Sufi mystics. For example, he reported on the "continuous series of bazaars [along the Nile] from Alexandria to Cairo. Cities and villages succeed one another without interruption." And, coming from a more patriarchal North African society, he marveled at the "respect shown to women by the [Central Asian] Turks, for they hold a more dignified position than the men. Turkish women do not veil themselves."

Although a repeated visitor to Mecca and the Islamic heartland, his experiences in the frontier regions of Islam, such as India and the Maldive Islands, Southeast Asia, the East African coast, the western Sudan, Turkish Central Asia, Anatolia, and Mongol-ruled southern Russia, provide the most useful information for the historian. They reveal a vivid picture of an expanding, vigorous Islamic realm encountering diverse structures, peoples, and practices. For example, from him we learn about the sexual customs of the Maldive Islands, where he married the widow of a sultan, and the Arab religious scholars, Persian merchants, and Chinese painters who gathered at Delhi "like moths around a candle."

Whereas the Christian Marco Polo a century earlier was always a stranger in his travels in Asia, in most places Ibn Battuta went he encountered people who shared his world-view and social values. From Morocco to Central Asia and around the Indian Ocean Rim, people worshiped in mosques and recognized the Shari'a as a legal framework. Far and wide, Ibn Battuta enjoyed the company of merchants, scholars, Sufis, and princes, with most of whom he could converse in Arabic on many topics, including developments in faraway lands. His knowledge of Islamic law and Arabic allowed him to work as a judge and legal scholar from Morocco to India. But, while cosmopolitan and open-minded by the standards of the day, he was clearly uncomfortable in non-Islamic societies such as China and in those frontier Islamic cultures where Islamic orthodoxy was greatly modified by local custom, such as Mali in West Africa. The traveler finally returned home to Tangier, where he died around 1368.

THINKING ABOUT THE PROFILE

1. Why was Ibn Battuta one of the great travelers of the Intermediate Era?
2. What do his travels tell us about the values and reach of Islamic religion and culture?

Notes: Quotations from Ross Dunn, *The Adventures of Ibn Battuta: A Muslim Traveller of the 14th Century* (Berkeley: University of California Press, 1986), 45, 183; Nikki R. Keddie, "Women in the Middle East Since the Rise of Islam," in *Women's History in Global Perspective*, ed. Bonnie G. Smith, vol. 3 (Urbana: University of Illinois Press, 2005), 81.

Bibliotheque nationale de France

The Journey to Mali No known paintings of Ibn Battuta exist. However, this map of Africa and the Mediterranean world, made by a Jewish cartographer in Spain in 1375, features a drawing of a camel-riding Muslim traveler that some historians think represents the journey of the Moroccan to Mali.

eye disease and performed complicated operations on the eye. His medical encyclopedia provided about half of the medical curriculum in medieval European universities. Muslims also pioneered many of the apparatus, techniques, and language of chemistry later adopted in the West.

The scientific revolution that later occurred in Europe would have been impossible without Arab and Indian mathematics. In Baghdad the Persian Zoroastrian al-Khuwarizmi (al-KWAHR-uhz-mee) (ca. 780–ca. 850) developed the mathematical procedures he called algebra, building on Greek and Indian foundations. Omar Khayyam, the beloved Persian poet who worked at Baghdad's House of Wisdom, helped formulate trigonometry. From Indian math books Muslims adopted a revolutionary system of numbers. Today we know them as Arabic numerals because Europe acquired them from Muslim Spain. The most revolutionary innovation of Arabic numerals was not just their greater convenience but also the use of a dot to indicate an empty column. This dot eventually became the zero. All these innovations had practical uses. Thus, advances in mathematics and physics made possible improvements in water clocks, water wheels, and other irrigation apparatuses that spread well beyond the Islamic world.

Mathematics and Astronomy

Muslim astronomers combined Greek, Persian, and Indian knowledge of the stars and planets with their own observations to improve astronomical observations. Applying their knowledge of mathematics to optics, they constructed a primitive version of the telescope. One astronomer reportedly built an elaborate planetarium that reproduced the movement of the stars, and a remarkable observatory built at Samarkand in Central Asia in 1420 produced charts for hundreds of stars. Some astronomers noted the eccentric behavior of the planet Venus, which challenged the widespread notion of an earth-centered universe. Indeed, many Muslim astronomers accepted that the world was round.

Between the eighth and thirteenth centuries Islamic societies also made innovations in agriculture, demonstrating an expansion of production that amounted to what we today might call a "green revolution." As a result, improved diets and health spurred dramatic population growth. The agricultural improvement resulted partly from Islamic expansion. When the Arab conquests opened the door to India, Arabs could bring to the Middle East South Asian crops such as cotton, hard wheat, rice, and sugar cane; fruits such as the coconut palm, banana, sour orange, lemon, lime, mango, and watermelon; and vegetables such as spinach, artichokes, and eggplant. These imports from wetter lands encouraged better irrigation, including the use of enormous water wheels to supply water. Indeed, the spread of agricultural products was one of the Islamic peoples' major contributions to world history. Most of these crops filtered westward to Spain, where they thrived, and cotton became a major crop in West Africa. Many crops reached Christian Europe from Spain and Sicily, but they were adopted only slowly, since Europe at that time had a lower population density and limited irrigation technology.

SECTION SUMMARY

- Sufism, a mystical approach to Islam that emphasized flexibility and a personal connection with God, drew both Sunni and Shi'ite followers.
- Although the Quran and most Muslim societies restricted women, some Muslim societies did not, and both Muslims and non-Muslims have debated the origins and benefits of such practices as wearing a veil.
- Literature, especially poetry, was very important in Islamic culture, as was calligraphy, the artful writing of words.
- Islamic science and medicine were very advanced and pioneered such practices as anesthesia and the replacement of false teeth.
- The Scientific Revolution would not have occurred without the help of Islamic mathematicians who passed on to Europe Indian mathematics.
- Islamic peoples helped to spread a great variety of agricultural products across Eurasia.

GLOBALIZED ISLAM AND MIDDLE EASTERN POLITICAL CHANGE

Why do historians speak of Islam as a hemispheric culture?

The major theme of early Islam was the transformation of a parochial Arab culture into the first truly hemisphere-wide culture connected by many religious and commercial networks. Between the eighth and seventeenth centuries Islam expanded out of its Arabian heartland to become the dominant religion across a broad expanse of Africa and Eurasia, and Muslim minorities emerged in places as far afield as China and the Balkans. From this expansion was created **Dar al-Islam** (the "Abode of Islam"), the Islamic world stretching from Morocco to Indonesia and joined by both a common faith and trade. Networks fostered by Islam reached from the Atlantic eastward to the Pacific, spreading Arab words, names, social attitudes, cultural values, and the Arabic script to diverse peoples. Eventually several powerful military states

Dar al-Islam ("Abode of Islam") The Islamic world stretching from Morocco to Indonesia and joined by both a common faith and trade.

rose to power and ruled over large populations of Muslims and non-Muslims. The Islamic world also faced severe challenges—expanding Turks, Christian crusaders, Mongol conquerors, and horrific pandemics—that set the stage for the rise of new political forces in the fifteenth and sixteenth centuries. Yet, the Islamic tradition was resistant and overcame factionalism and political decay to remain creative well past the 1400s.

The Global Shape of Dar al-Islam

More than half of the world's 1.5 billion Muslims today live outside the Middle East, and Arabs are significantly outnumbered by non-Arab believers. The majority of all Muslims live in South and Southeast Asia. After the destruction of the Abbasid Caliphate, Arab political power diminished, but Islam grew rapidly in both Africa and South Asia (see Chapters 12–13). Dozens of prosperous Muslim trading cities, from Tangier in northwest Africa to Samarkand in Central Asia to Melaka in Malaya, offered goods from distant countries. Beginning in the thirteenth century, Muslims constructed a hemisphere-spanning system based not just on economic exchange but also on a shared understanding of the world and the cosmos, linked by informal networks of Islamic scholars and saints. The Quran and its message of a righteous social order provided a framework for Dar al-Islam.

The spread of Islam corresponded with the growth of Muslim-dominated long-distance trade, especially the maritime trade around the Indian Ocean Basin. Except for the Chinese, Arabs enjoyed the world's most advanced shipbuilding and navigation between 1000 and 1450. The lateen sails that Arabs devised, or perhaps adapted from Southeast Asians, later allowed European ships to undertake long-distance voyages in the 1400s. An increasingly integrated Muslim-dominated maritime trading system gradually emerged that linked the eastern Mediterranean, Middle East, East African coast, Persia, and India with the societies of East and Southeast Asia (see Map 10.3). One Arab merchant expressed his commercial ambitions: "I want to send Persian saffron to China, where I hear that it fetches a high price, and then ship Chinese porcelain to Greece, Greek brocade to India, Indian iron to Aleppo [a Syrian port], Aleppo glass to the Yemen and Yemeni material to Persia."[19]

Trade Networks

The Straits of Melaka in Southeast Asia and Hormuz (HAWR-muhz) at the Persian Gulf entrance stood at the heart of the key mercantile system of the Intermediate world. Over these sea routes the spices of Indonesia and East Africa, the gold and tin of Malaya, the textiles of India, the gold of southern Africa, and the silks, porcelain, and tea of China traveled to distant markets. The maritime network achieved its height in the fifteenth and sixteenth centuries, when Muslim economic and cultural power remained strong. Arab and Persian merchant communities could be found as far east as the ports of Korea and south China. By intermarrying with local women and practicing their faith, Muslim merchants in these trade diasporas converted others to Islam.

Turks and Crusaders

Between the eleventh and fifteenth centuries the Middle East faced a series of interventions by Turks and Crusaders that reshaped the region politically. The rise of the Turks is a major theme in this period of world history. The Turks were originally pastoral nomads from Central Asia who were divided by tribe and dialect. For centuries these skilled horsemen had intruded into Chinese, Indian, and western Asian societies, and some Turks adopted such religions as Nestorian Christianity, Judaism, and Buddhism. Gradually they drew closer to Middle Eastern cultural patterns, and most eventually embraced Islam. Some Turkish groups sent boys to the Abbasids, where they trained to serve the Abbasids as soldiers or administrators.

Rise of the Turks

Late in the tenth century a group of Muslim Turks, the Seljuks (SEL-jooks), achieved regional power. Expanding from Central Asia and recruiting other Turkish tribes into their confederation, they swept westward through Afghanistan and Iran into Iraq. Allied with the declining Abbasids, Seljuk forces conquered many Muslim and Christian societies in the Caucasus region, eventually creating a large empire stretching from Palestine to Samarkand. The weakening of the Byzantine state allowed the Seljuks in 1071 to seize much of Anatolia, which had for many centuries been populated largely by Greek-speaking Orthodox Christians. Even when the Seljuks' power soon diminished elsewhere and their empire crumbled, they continued to govern Anatolia.

The First Crusade

By the eleventh century some Islamic states faced increasing challenges from European Christians. Between 1095 and 1272 Christians from various European societies launched a long series of Crusades to win back what they saw as the Judeo-Christian Holy Land from Muslim occupation (see Chapter 14). The First Crusade capitalized on Muslim weakness, since the various feuding

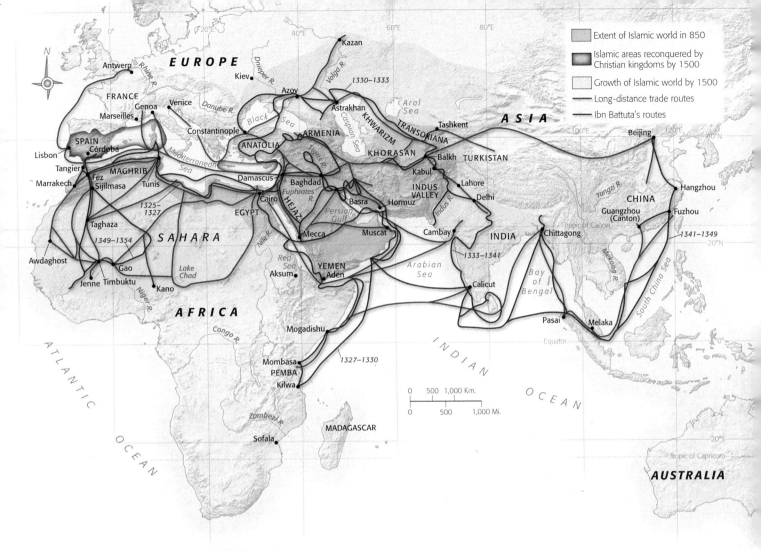

Map 10.3 Dar al-Islam and Trade Routes, ca. 1500 C.E.
By 1500 the Islamic world stretched into West Africa, East Africa, and Southeast Asia. Trade routes connected the Islamic lands and allowed Muslim traders to extend their networks to China, Russia, and Europe.

e Interactive Map

Muslim states could not cooperate. Some states, such as Fatimid Egypt, even maintained lucrative trade ties with Europe, and parts of the Middle East still had substantial Christian and Jewish populations as well as many dissident Muslims. In the end, however, the Crusades failed to achieve their goal.

The First Crusade (1095–1099) was triggered by the encroachment of Seljuk Turks on Byzantine territory and a division of the Christian church into rival branches in 1054. Roman popes, worried about Seljuk expansion and anxious to assert their primacy over the leaders of the breakaway Greek Orthodox Church based in Constantinople, promoted the idea of positive violence to defend the faith. Using untrue stories of Arab and Seljuk atrocities against Christians in Palestine, Pope Urban II called on Christians to reclaim the Holy Land and protect the churches and relics of Jerusalem. His plea attracted some 100,000 European volunteers, some pious, others just hungry for booty. The crusaders fought their way along the coast and reached Jerusalem in 1099, when they took the city and killed thousands of Muslims, Jews, and even local Christians. Some crusaders stayed on to guard the sites but also to colonize the surrounding territory, and four small crusader states were established in what is today Israel and Lebanon. As Muslim forces regrouped, another pope dispatched the Second Crusade (1147–1149), in which the crusaders mostly slaughtered Jews in Europe and pillaged the Byzantine Empire.

However, crusaders often fought each other, undermining their own power. In the mid-twelfth century Muslims effectively counterattacked, pushing back Christian forces and prompting the Third Crusade (1189–1192). The Muslim armies were led by General Salah al-Din, or Saladin (SAL-uh-din) (1138–1193), an Iraqi-born Kurd who once served the Fatimid rulers of Egypt, then deposed

Muslim-Christian Conflicts

them and became sultan, replacing Shi'ite with Sunni rule. Saladin's forces stopped a crusader invasion of Egypt and then, between 1187 and 1192, captured Jerusalem from the crusaders and extended his power into Syria. A tolerant leader, Saladin spared the Christians who surrendered in Jerusalem and employed the great Cordoba-born Jewish sage and legal authority Moses Maimonides (my-MAHN-uh-deez) (1135–1204) as his physician. His military exploits made Saladin a hero in Muslim eyes, and he is still revered today. The final six crusades failed to wrest control of North Africa, Jerusalem, and Anatolia from Muslim hands.

The Crusader's Legacy

Historians still debate the heritage of the Crusades. Many crusaders were undoubtedly inspired by a sincere religious zeal to preserve access to Christian holy sites, but many also looted captured cities and sacked the Orthodox Christian capital, Constantinople. Likewise, Muslim armies often showed little mercy on their enemies. Some believe that the militant Christian challenge to Islam represented by the Crusades ultimately made both religions less tolerant and more zealous, complicating relations between the two groups. For centuries afterward some Muslim rulers viewed their Christian subjects as untrustworthy, while Christians persecuted the remaining Muslim populations in southern Europe. Even today, hundreds of years later, Islamic militants still capitalize on lingering resentment against Western "crusaders."

Mongol Conquests and the Black Death

Another people from outside the region, the Mongols (MAHN-guhlz), also swept into western Asia, destroying various states, creating instability, and unwittingly laying the foundation for a hemisphere-wide disease that caused much devastation and death in the Middle East. The Mongols, Central Asian pastoral nomads, constituted a much greater short-term threat to Islam than the Christian crusaders. Led by Genghis Khan (GENG-iz KAHN) (ca. 1162–1227), the Mongols, prompted perhaps by environmental stress and overpopulation, began their expansion out of their Mongolian homeland in the late twelfth century. Between 1218 and 1221 they fought their way through the lands inhabited mostly by Turkish-speaking Muslims just north of Afghanistan, destroying several great Silk Road cities.

Mongol atrocities were legendary. For example, they killed 700,000 mostly unarmed residents in the Persian city of Merv. Their goal was to paralyze the Muslim societies with enough fear to prevent opposition. It usually worked. An Arab chronicler wrote of the Mongol invaders that "in the countries that have not yet been overrun by them, everyone spends the night afraid that they may appear there too."[20] After Genghis Khan's death in 1227, the Mongols turned to conquering China, Russia, and eastern Europe but also put pressure on the Caucasus and Anatolia. In 1243 they defeated the remnants of the Seljuk Turks.

Hulegu's Empire

In 1256 a grandson of Genghis Khan, Hulegu (hoo-LAY-goo) (1217–1275), led new attacks on the Middle East that had more lasting consequences for the region. Crossing the mountains into Iraq, Hulegu's army, faced with fierce resistance, responded with brutal force. In 1258 the Mongols pillaged Baghdad, burning schools, libraries, mosques, and palaces, killing perhaps a million people, and executing all the Abbasids. Some historians see Hulegu's destruction of Baghdad as a fateful turning point for Arab society that ended the prosperity and intellectual glory once represented by the now-gutted city. Hulegu's forces pushed on west, occupying Damascus and destroying the key eastern Mediterranean port of Aleppo (uh-LEP-oh). The pastoralist Mongols also badly disrupted agriculture, returning some farms to pasture and dispersing the peasants. In some places farming never recovered. But the Islamic tradition proved resilient. In 1260 Hulegu's armies tried to invade Egypt but were defeated by the Mamluks (MAM-looks), ex-slave soldiers of Turkish origin who had taken power in Egypt. Hulegu's Mongols stayed in Iraq and Persia, calling themselves the Il-Khanid (il-KHAN-id) dynasty, assimilating Persian culture, and eventually adopting Islam. Many descendants of Mongol invaders in Russia, known today as Tartars, also eventually became Muslim. The Il-Khanids practiced religious toleration and encouraged monumental architecture, learning, and a literary renaissance, during which scholars wrote pathbreaking histories of the world that tell us much about the Mongol empire.

The Great Pandemic

By building a large empire across Eurasia, the Mongols fostered overland trade and travel, but in so doing they also provided a path over which deadly diseases could spread. Like Europe and China, much of the Islamic world was deeply affected by the terrible fourteenth-century pandemic known in the West as the Black Death, a catastrophic disease, probably bubonic plague, that killed quickly and spread rapidly over the networks of exchange. Initially carried into the Black Sea region from eastern Asia by fleas infesting rats that stowed away on caravans along the Mongol-controlled Silk Road or on board trading ships, the pandemic hit the Middle East repeatedly over the course of a century, reducing the population of Egypt and Syria by two-thirds. Ibn Khaldun wrote that "cities and towns were laid waste, roads and way signs were obliterated, settlements and mansions became empty. The entire inhabited world changed."[21] Ibn Khaldun felt he might be living at the end of history, but by the 1400s the Middle East had stabilized and regained some of its lost economic and cultural dynamism.

The Rise of Muslim Military States

In the thirteenth and fourteenth centuries, several powerful Muslim military states arose, including those of the Mamluks in Egypt, the Timurids in Central Asia, and the Ottoman Turks in Anatolia. Gunpowder, a Chinese invention that filtered westward along the Silk Road during Mongol times, forever changed the nature of warfare and also had an impact on politics. After 1350 possession of firearms gave some states and groups an advantage over rivals and led to the rise of stronger, more bureaucratic states.

The Mamluks, who had thwarted Mongol expansion, ruled Egypt and Syria from 1250 to 1517, making Egypt the richest Middle Eastern state. After extending their power into Arabia and capturing Mecca and Medina, they were able to control and tax the flow of Muslim pilgrims. The Mamluks also enjoyed an active trade with the two major Italian trading cities, Genoa and Venice, that supplied valuable Asian goods to Europe. Merchants from Venice established trading posts around the Mamluk lands, where they exchanged timber, metals, and gold for spices, dyes, and Indian textiles. Eventually, however, Mamluk corruption and demands for increased taxes prompted seafaring European merchants to seek a maritime route to the East to avoid Mamluk territory. In 1516–1517 another Turkish group, the Ottomans, defeated the Mamluks and absorbed their lands into the growing Ottoman Empire (see Map 10.4).

Interactive Map

Map 10.4 The Ottoman Empire, 1566 Between 1300 and the mid-1500s the Ottoman Turks expanded out of western Anatolia to conquer a large empire in western Asia, Egypt and North Africa, and eastern Europe, making the Ottomans one of the world's largest states.

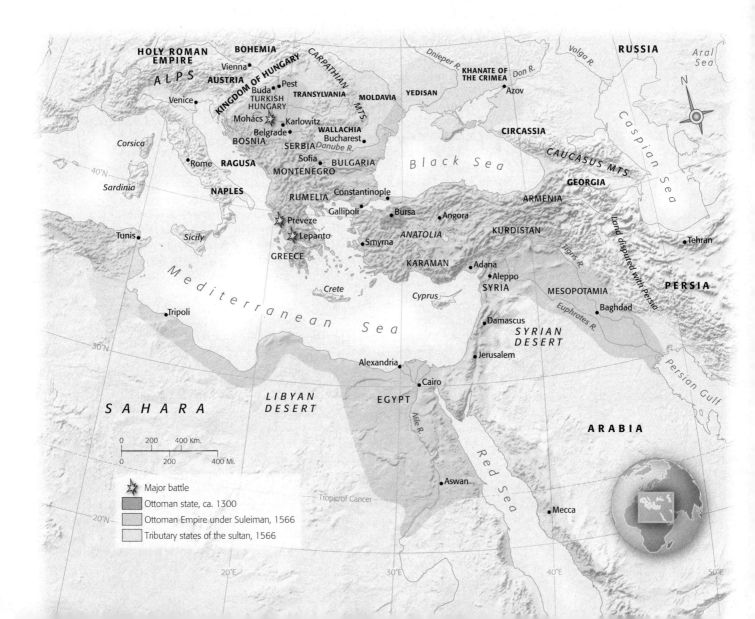

Venetian Ambassadors Visiting Mamluk Damascus Venetians and Genoese merchants, fierce rivals, regularly visited the Middle East to acquire silks, spices, and other valuable products. This painting from the 1400s shows Venetians being received by the Mamluk governor of Damascus, who wears a horned hat and sits on a low platform, in today's Syria.

Reunion des Musees Nationaux/Art Resource, NY

Tamerlane

In Central Asia, the Timurid state became the dominant regional power for over a century. The state's ruthless founder, Tamerlane (TAM-uhr-lane) (1336–1405), a Muslim prince of Turkish and Mongol ancestry, had been crippled by an arrow wound as a young man but hoped to emulate Genghis Khan. From his capital at Samarkand, Tamerlane's army rampaged through the Caucasus, southern Russia, Persia, Iraq, and Syria, killing thousands of people and destroying cities and farms. He then turned against India, wreaking havoc in the north (see Chapter 13). Only Tamerlane's death in 1405 halted his forces from invading China and Ottoman Turkey. Although Tamerlane protected merchants and Sufi mystics, his heritage was largely one of smoking ruins and pyramids of human heads. However, his successors built mosques and patronized scholars, and later his grandson established a great empire in India in the early 1500s.

The Ottomans

The most powerful and enduring military state was established by the Ottoman (AHT-uh-muhn) Turks. The Ottomans originated as a small Anatolian state led by a chief, Osman (ohs-MAHN) (*Ottoman* means "followers of Osman"), who came under the influence of Sufis dedicated to the destruction of Byzantium, which was reeling from temporary occupation of Constantinople by crusaders and weakening influence in Anatolia. The Ottomans capitalized on this vacuum and, by 1300, began raiding and then annexing the remaining Byzantine strongholds in Anatolia. Ultimately they used gunpowder weapons to conquer much of the Byzantine Empire, creating one of the most dynamic states in western Eurasia and a link between Middle Eastern Islam and European Christianity. The once great Byzantium was increasingly a shell of a state surrounding Constantinople.

Soon the Ottomans moved into the Balkans, where they defeated the strongest Christian power in southeastern Europe, Serbia. The Ottomans favored Muslims in taxes, and over the next several centuries many Albanian and Serb-speaking Christians adopted Islam, perhaps partly for economic reasons, creating a division in the Balkans between Catholic, Orthodox, and Muslim peoples that complicated politics for centuries to come. At the Battle of Nicopolis (nuh-KAHP-uh-luhs) in 1396, the Ottomans defeated a Hungarian-led force drawn from throughout Europe to oppose further Ottoman expansion. Then in 1453 Sultan Mehmed (MEH-met) the Conqueror (1432–1481) finally took Constantinople and converted the city into the Ottoman capital, eventually renamed Istanbul.

Ottoman Empire

The Ottoman Empire was now the major regional power, an empire of many peoples. Istanbul attracted a multiethnic and multireligious population and remained a major trade hub. Mehmed the Conqueror, who patronized the arts, even invited some of Italy's most famous artists and architects to work in his cosmopolitan capital, which by 1500 was Europe's largest city. Ottoman sultans used the administrative and military skills of the subject peoples and promoted men of merit regardless of their backgrounds. Through the **millet** ("nationality") system, the leaders of religious and ethnic minorities administered their own communities. For instance, the Greek patriarch had authority over all Orthodox Christians in Ottoman territory. Christians and Jews also practiced their religions freely for the most part. Thus the millet system allowed the Turks to divide and hence rule diverse peoples and faiths.

millet The nationality system through which the Ottomans allowed the leaders of religious and ethnic minorities to administer their own communities.

Under a dynamic and militarily powerful state, the Ottomans continued to expand. By 1500 they had solidified control over Greece and the Balkans (see Map 10.4). In the 1500s, the so-called Ottoman golden age, Ottoman rule was extended over much of western Asia as far east as Persia and also through North Africa from Egypt to Algeria. However, the Ottomans were defeated when they attempted to take Hungary in 1699. This event marked the end of Ottoman, and Islamic, expansion in western Eurasia and symbolized the decline of Islamic power, but the Ottoman Empire continued until 1923.

Islamic Contributions to World History

By linking peoples of varied cultures, ideas, religions, and languages, the Arab conquests fostered intellectual and artistic creativity. The Islamic faith and culture they spread profoundly influenced the development of Southern Asian, African, and European societies, and to the east the gradual Islamic conquest of India posed an alternative to Hinduism. As Islamic influence and Arab merchants traveled south across the Sahara and along the East African coast, various African societies also adopted the Islamic faith as well as some Muslim customs and technologies. From the ninth through the eleventh centuries, the Arabs in Sicily and Spain passed on some of the fruits of the advanced science, mathematics, and technology of the Middle East, India, and even China to Europe. In many respects the Muslims served as the critical link between the classical Greeks and Indians and the late medieval Europeans. Greco-Roman and Islamic learning was now studied in medieval universities. Western Europeans profited from this exchange of knowledge, and eventually it helped spark not only a scientific and technological revolution in Europe but also a questioning of the entrenched Christian church that ultimately led to more diverse ideas within Western societies. But the exchange was not one way, and Muslims also benefited from European knowledge of medicine, science, and art.

The mixing of Arab, Persian, Turkish, Byzantine, Christian, Jewish, African, and Indian influences created a hemispheric-wide Islamic world that connected culturally and politically diverse societies sharing a common faith and, often, values. While most people in what is today Iraq, Syria, Egypt, and North Africa adopted the Arabic language and called themselves Arabs, the Persians and Turks continued to speak their own languages, which they now wrote using the Arabic script. Indeed, for many centuries Persian remained a language of government and the elite, from the Seljuk Turkish empire in Anatolia to various Muslim states in India and Central Asia.

Cultural Mixing and Diversity

Non-Muslims played key roles in the Islamic world, especially in commerce. From the eighth through eleventh centuries Jews were the key trade middlemen between Christian Europe and the Muslim world. Hence, Jews from Narbonne in southern France traded in Spain, North Africa, and the eastern Mediterranean, becoming fluent in Arabic. After the eleventh century the Jews lost ground as intermediaries to the Italians in the west and the Armenian Christians in the east.

Muslim scholars were proud of the expanse of their horizons. For example, the Egyptian scholar Jalal al-Din al-Suyuti (juh-LALL al-din al-sue-YOU-tee) (1445–1505) boasted that he and his books had traveled as far as West Africa and India. Yet, after the defeat of the last Muslim kingdom in Spain in 1492, he also saw the Muslim world in need of intellectual and social renewal. Although the Ottoman Turks were on the rise, al-Suyuti could not know that after 1500 Muslim states would also have a resurgence in Persia and India, nor that various Europeans, benefiting from the encounter with Islam, would become serious rivals to Muslim power and a challenge to the interconnected Islamic world.

Several powerful Islamic states, including the Ottoman Empire, continued to exercise political and economic influence in the sixteenth and seventeenth centuries. But, with the occasional exception of Ottoman Turkey, technological innovation, scientific inquiry, and the questioning of accepted religious and cultural ideas fell off in the Middle East after 1500. The madrasas, while training Muslim clerics and providing spiritual guidance, tended to have narrow, theology-based curriculums that deemphasized

SECTION SUMMARY

- Trade routes spread Islam throughout the hemisphere, eventually creating Dar al-Islam, an Islamic world stretching from Indonesia to Morocco, in which Arabs constituted a minority of Muslims.

- The series of Christian Crusades to win back the Judeo-Christian Holy Land from Muslims led to long-lasting resentment on the part of Muslims.

- The Mongols, led by Genghis Khan and Hulegu, one of his grandsons, ruthlessly attacked Muslims in Central Asia and sacked Baghdad, but the Islamic tradition continued throughout Mongol rule.

- The arrival of gunpowder from China allowed Muslim military states, such as the Mamluks and the Timurids, to gain power.

- The Ottoman Turks established an extremely successful empire in the territory of the former Byzantine Empire by allowing subject minorities to administer their own affairs.

- By conducting and preserving a great deal of scientific and philosophical learning, the Muslims contributed much to European culture.

secular learning. Some historians believe this trend undermined the humanist, tolerant tradition of Islamic scholarship, such as the open-minded approach of Baghdad's House of Wisdom and the schools in Muslim Spain. Over the next three centuries, most of the Middle Eastern peoples who had boasted innovative and cosmopolitan traditions for a millennium gradually lost military and economic power while Europeans surged.

CHAPTER SUMMARY

The rise of Islam in Arabia during the seventh century changed world history. Islam forged a community of believers around a set of monotheistic ideas, and Muhammad's message proved so popular that, within a few decades, Muslim Arabs had conquered a large empire and spread Islam to many Arab and non-Arab peoples. Islam offered a distinctive set of religious, political, and social ideas, such as pilgrimage, annual fasting, a legal code, and an emphasis on social justice, but it also was influenced by Christian, Jewish, Persian, and other traditions. Islamic societies flourished under powerful theocratic governments, such as the Umayyad and Abbasid Caliphates, while Islamic writers and scientists assimilated and developed knowledge from many societies. Muslim thinkers preserved classical Greek learning while pioneering new ideas in astronomy, mathematics, the physical sciences, and agriculture. Arab links also contributed knowledge to medieval Europe, spurring the scientific and technological rise of the West.

The Islamic world became a cosmopolitan network of peoples, linked by trade and religious scholars. While the end of the Abbasids brought some political fragmentation, Islam still expanded, overcoming several challenges in the millennium after Muhammad. By 1500 the Ottoman Turks controlled a vast empire. Stretching from western Africa and southwestern Europe eastward to Southeast Asia and western China, Islam became a hemispheric culture, even extending its influences into non-Islamic regions. After 1500, however, the Islamic Middle East began to fade as a political power and a center for intellectual inquiry.

KEY TERMS

Bedouins	umma	jihad	Shi'a
Ka'ba	Allah	sultan	Sufism
Quran	caliphate	Shari'a	calligraphy
Hadith	Ramadan	madrasas	Dar al-Islam
hijra	haj	Sunni	millet

EBOOK AND WEBSITE RESOURCES

 PRIMARY SOURCE
The Quran: Call for Jihad

 INTERACTIVE MAPS
Map 10.1 Expansion of Islam, to 750 C.E.
Map 10.2 The Abbasid Empire, ca. 800 C.E.
Map 10.3 Dar al-Islam and Trade Routes, ca. 1500 C.E.
Map 10.4 The Ottoman Empire, 1566

LINKS

History of the Middle East Database (http://www
.nmhschool.org/tthornton/mehistorydatabase/
mideastindex.php). A fine set of essays and links on
the early and modern Middle East and Islam.
Ibn Battuta's Rihla (http://www.sfusd.k12.ca.us/schwww/
sch618/Ibn_Battuta/Ibn_Battuta_Rihla.html). A useful
site on Ibn Battuta and his wide travels.
Internet Islamic History Sourcebook (http://www
.fordham.edu/halsall/islam/islamsbook.html). A comprehensive examination of the Islamic tradition and
its long history, with many useful links and source
materials.

Islam and Islamic History in Arabia and the Middle East
(http://www.islamicity.com/education). A comprehensive site sponsored by a moderate Muslim organization.
Islamic Studies, Islam, Arabic, and Religion (http://www
.arches.uga.edu/~godlas). A comprehensive collection of links and resources maintained at the University of Georgia.
Virtual Religion Index (http://virtualreligion.net/vri/). Has
many links on all major religions, including Islam.

Plus flashcards, practice quizzes, and more. Go to:
www.cengage.com/history/lockard/globalsocnet2e

SUGGESTED READING

Armstrong, Karen. *Muhammad: A Biography of the Prophet.* San Francisco: Harper, 1992. A readable and sympathetic survey of Muhammad and his life.

Aslan, Reza. *No God but God: The Origins, Evolution, and Future of Islam.* New York: Random House, 2005. An account of Islamic religion and history by a liberal, Iranian-born, U.S.-based Muslim scholar.

Berkey, Jonathan P. *The Formation of Islam: Religion and Society in the Near East, 600–1800.* New York: Cambridge University Press, 2003. A fine scholarly study of the rise of Islam to 1500.

Bloom, Jonathan, and Sheila Blair. *Islam: A Thousand Years of Faith and Power.* New Haven, CT: Yale University Press, 2002. A well-written overview of Islamic history and society from 600 to 1700.

Dunn, Ross. *The Adventures of Ibn Battuta: A Muslim Traveller of the 14th Century.* Berkeley: University of California Press, 1986. A fascinating look at Dar al-Islam through the writings of the famed Arab traveler.

Eaton, Richard M. *Islamic History as Global History.* Washington, D.C.: American Historical Association, 1993. A valuable short pamphlet showing the significance of Islamic societies to world history.

Egger, Vernon O. *A History of the Muslim World to 1405: The Making of a Civilization.* Upper Saddle River, NJ: Prentice-Hall, 2004. A recent and comprehensive survey.

Esposito, John L. *Islam: The Straight Path*, revised 3rd ed. New York: Oxford University Press, 2005. Balanced and accessible introduction to Islamic faith and history.

Inalcik, Halil. *The Ottoman Empire: The Classical Age, 1300–1600.* London: Phoenix Press, 2000. A reprint of one of the best introductions to the early Ottoman Empire and society, first published in 1973.

Kennedy, Hugh. *The Great Arab Conquests: How the Spread of Islam Changed the World We Live In.* New York: Da Capo Press, 2007. Well-written overview of Islamic expansion.

Kennedy, Hugh. *When Baghdad Ruled the World: The Rise and Fall of Islam's Greatest Dynasty.* Cambridge, MA: Da Capo Press, 2005. A readable study of the Abbasid dynasty and era.

Lewis, David Levering. *God's Crucible: Islam and the Making of Europe, 570–1215.* New York: W.W. Norton, 2009. Recent study of Muslim-European exchanges.

Menocal, Maria Rosa. *The Ornament of the World: How Muslims, Jews, and Christians Created a Culture of Tolerance in Medieval Spain.* Boston: Little, Brown and Co., 2002. Uses profiles of historical figures to explore the cultural flowering of Muslim Spain.

Morgan, Michael H.. *Lost History: The Enduring Legacy of Muslim Scientists, Thinkers, and Artists.* Washington, D.C.: Smithsonian Institution, 2008. Profiles Islamic thinkers and their influence on Europe.

Nasr, Seyyed Hossein. *Islam: Religion, History, and Civilization.* San Francisco: HarperSanFrancisco, 2003. An insightful overview of the Islamic tradition by an Iranian-born scholar.

Risso, Patrica. *Merchants of Faith: Muslim Commerce and Culture in the Indian Ocean.* Boulder: Westview, 1995. A readable survey of Muslim trade networks.

Robinson, Francis, ed. *The Cambridge Illustrated History of the Islamic World.* Cambridge: Cambridge University Press, 1996. An authoritative, richly illustrated survey of Islamic society and history.

Walther, Wiebke. *Women in Islam from Medieval to Modern Times.* Princeton: Markus Wiener, 1999. One of the most valuable and readable studies of gender issues, by a German scholar.

EAST ASIAN TRADITIONS, TRANSFORMATIONS, AND EURASIAN ENCOUNTERS, 600–1500

Rafael Macia/Photo Researchers, Inc.

Giant Japanese Buddha at Kamakura
During this era, most Japanese adopted Buddhism, some expressing their faith in art. This gigantic statue, erected in the city of Kamakura in 1252, shows the Buddha in meditation.

China is a sea that salts all rivers that flow into it.

—ITALIAN TRAVELER MARCO POLO (1275 C.E.)[1]

Early in the twelfth century the Chinese artist Zhang Zeduan, noted for his realistic drawings, painted a massive scroll of people at work and leisure throughout the city of Kaifeng (KIE-FENG), then China's capital and home to perhaps 1 million people. Set during the annual spring festival, the scroll, the surviving portions of which are 17 feet long, portrays a bustling city, from its riverside suburbs to the high protective walls and the towering city gates to the downtown business district, during one of premodern China's most creative and prosperous eras. Kaifeng's streets are crowded with people (mostly men) going about their daily activities, including foreign merchants, streetside hawkers touting their goods, fortune tellers, scholars, and monks. The scroll also shows people working in warehouses, iron smelters, arsenals, and shipyards. Zhang's record of Kaifeng's commercial life is particularly vivid, showing building material suppliers, textile firms, and drug and chemical shops, as well as hotels, food stalls, teahouses, and restaurants. Cargo and pleasure barges cruise the river, while camels heavily laden with goods enter the city.

Much of the prosperous city life Zhang portrayed was familiar to Chinese of earlier and later generations, for Chinese society showed considerable continuity over time. The Han's eventual succession by the Sui and then by the Tang (tahng) and Song (soong) dynasties ensured that Chinese society continued along traditional lines, in contrast to the dramatic changes that took place in Japan, the Middle East, India, Southeast Asia, and Europe during the Intermediate Era. Once the Tang adopted a modified version of the Han system, the ensuing millennium proved to be a golden age, broken only occasionally by invasion or disorder. Some scholars call the Intermediate Era in world history the "Chinese Centuries." China became perhaps the world's richest and most populous society, enjoying a well-organized government and economy, a flourishing artistic and literary culture, and creativity in technology and science. Many commercial and cultural networks connected China to the rest of Eurasia. Furthermore, China's neighbors in Korea and Japan adopted many aspects of Chinese culture, though they also forged their own highly distinctive societies during this period. China did indeed, as Marco Polo recognized, influence or awe all those with whom it came into contact.

FOCUS QUESTIONS

1. **What role did Tang China play in the Eurasian world?**
2. **Why might historians consider the Song dynasty the high point of China's golden age?**
3. **How did China change during the Yuan and Ming dynasties?**
4. **How did the Koreans and Japanese develop their own distinctive societies?**

TANG CHINA: THE HUB OF THE EAST

What role did Tang China play in the Eurasian world?

The harsh Sui dynasty that united China after the disintegration of the Han ruled for only a short time (581–618 C.E.) before rebellions brought it to an end. The victor in the struggles between rival rebel forces established the Tang dynasty (618–907). The three centuries of Tang rule set a high watermark in many facets of Chinese life and provided a cultural and political model for neighboring Asian societies. The only comparable power in Eurasia at that time was the expanding Muslim Abbasid empire; India and Europe were divided into many small states and often threatened by invaders. Tang models shaped China until the early twentieth century.

The Tang Empire and Eurasian Exchange

In the seventh and eighth centuries Tang China—an empire of some 50 or 60 million people—was the largest and most populous society on earth, with immense influence in the eastern third of Eurasia (see Map 11.1). Like the Han before them, the Tang launched ambitious campaigns that brought Central Asia (as far west as the Caspian Sea), Tibet, Mongolia, Manchuria, and parts of Siberia under Chinese rule. Vietnam had long been a colony. The Koreans became a vassal state, and the Japanese established close ties. Chinese garrisons protected the Silk Road, fostering the flow of goods and people across Eurasia.

Silk Roads   The Tang were the most outward-looking of all Chinese dynasties, and during these years China became an open forum, a world market of ideas, people, and things arriving over the networks of exchange. The overland Silk Road across Central Asia remained a transcontinental high-

Map 11.1   The Tang Empire, ca. 750 C.E.

The Tang dynasty forged a large empire across Central Asia into Turkestan before their expansion was halted by Muslim armies at the Battle of Talas River in 751. Control of Central Asia allowed the Tang to protect the Silk Road trade route. The Tang also controlled Vietnam and dominated Korea.

e Interactive Map

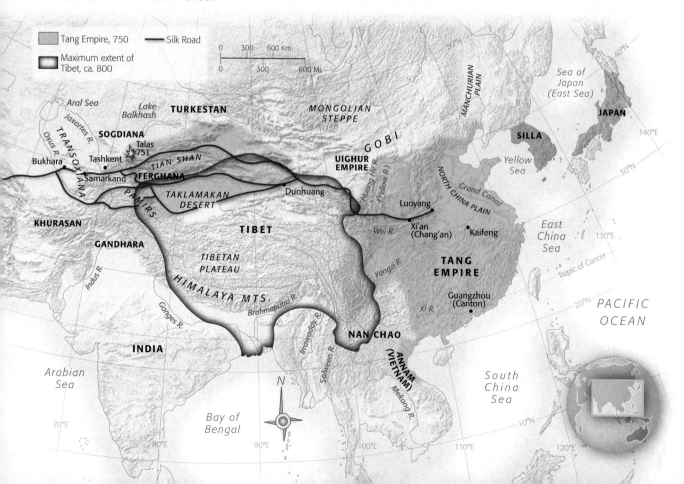

CHRONOLOGY

	China	Korea	Japan
600	**618–907** Tang dynasty	**676–918** Silla	**710–784** Nara period **794–1184** Heian period
900	**960–1279** Song dynasty	**935–1392** Koryo	
1100	**1279–1368** Yuan dynasty		**1180–1333** Kamakura Shogunate
1300	**1368–1644** Ming dynasty **1405–1433** Voyages of Admiral Zheng He	**1392–1910** Yi dynasty (Choson)	**1338–1568** Ashikaga Shogunate

way for traders, adventurers, diplomats, missionaries, and pilgrims traveling east or west, carrying goods and ideas. Nestorian Christian, Manichean, Buddhist, and Muslim missionaries arrived, and merchants from around Asia formed communities in several Chinese cities, many arriving by sea. Indeed, a lively sea trade, a kind of maritime Silk Road, linked China with Southeast Asia, India, and the Middle East. Perhaps two-thirds of the 200,000 inhabitants of the southern port of Guangzhou (gwahng-jo), also known as Canton, were immigrants, including Arabs, Persians, Indians, Cambodians, and Malays, and the city boasted both Sunni and Shi'ite mosques. Indian astronomers and mathematicians joined the Tang government as scientific officials. Meanwhile, several hundred Chinese scholars visited or sojourned in India, most of them seeking Buddhist literature.

Tang wealth and power stimulated commerce throughout Eurasia. By land or sea, many Chinese inventions reached into western Eurasia. In 753 C.E. a Chinese craftsman reported that, in Baghdad: "As for the weavers who make light silks, the goldsmiths who work gold and silver there, and the painters; the arts which they practice were started by Chinese technicians."[2] Chinese products such as silk and porcelain were much prized in Europe and the Middle East, and Chinese culture also spread to Korea and Japan. This multicultural exchange benefited China as well. Diverse societies in places such as Burma, Java, and Nepal regularly sent embassies to the Tang court bearing gifts, and renewed contacts with India and the Middle East fostered China's creativity. New products also appeared, most notably tea from Southeast Asia. After the Chinese began drinking tea, originally a medicinal substance, as a beverage, teahouses opened in every marketplace. Another new arrival was the chair from the Middle East, replacing seating pads; the Chinese became the only chair users in East Asia. However, some Chinese scholars criticized the cosmopolitan attitude and complained about too much foreign culture.

China and the World

The Eurasian exchange fostered dynamic and culturally rich cities. Tang China boasted many cities larger than any cities in Europe or India, and the capital, Chang'an (CHAHNG-ahn), present-day Xi'an (SHEE-AHN), had 2 million inhabitants. The world's largest city, Chang'an was a model of urban planning, with its streets carefully laid out in a grid pattern and the city divided into quadrants. The broad thoroughfares were crowded with visitors and sojourners from many lands, among them Arabs, Persians, Syrians, Jews, Turks, Koreans, Japanese, Vietnamese, Indians, and Tibetans. Many foreign artists, artisans, and merchants worked in the capital, as well as entertainers such as Indian jugglers and Afghan actors. The city contained four Zoroastrian temples, two Nestorian Christian churches, and several mosques. The only contemporary cities that could come close to matching Chang'an's size and amenities were Baghdad, the center of the powerful Abbasid Caliphate, and Byzantine-ruled Constantinople.

Chang'an

Imperial Government and Economic Growth

The centralized imperial government reached a high level of efficiency and maintained one of the world's most productive economies. Despite bloody rebellions, invasions, assassinations, palace coups, and dynastic upheavals, the hallmark of China's political system for many centuries was stability. Later dynasties followed the basic Tang model. According to Confucian theory, the family was the model for the state, so the emperor at the top of the system was the symbolic father of the people, governing by moral example, not physical force. The Chinese considered the emperor the Son of Heaven—not a divine figure but the intermediary between the terrestrial and supernatural realms—and the first scholar of the land. He held daily audiences during which diplomats from distant lands sometimes presented gifts as a symbol of their submission to his authority. In return the emperor bestowed on them a title, state robes, and gifts, a ceremony followed later by a banquet.

While women sometimes had power behind the throne, only one woman, the Empress Wu Zhao (woo chow) (625–705), ever officially led the government. She had become an imperial concubine at age thirteen and used her political skills and ruthless ambition to eventually displace the sickly emperor, maintaining her power for over fifty years. While Empress Wu generally ruled ably, Chinese scholars viewed her as an evil usurper and warned future generations that women should not rule the country.

In theory the emperor held absolute power, but his actual power was circumscribed in various ways. He had to consider the Censorate, an agency unique to China that monitored the workings of the government, rooted out corruption, proposed changes in state policies, and criticized the government for failings. Only the strongest emperors could punish the Censorate for criticism. Furthermore, the doctrine of the Mandate of Heaven, that people have a right to overthrow an evil, corrupt, or ineffective government, meant that emperors had to consider the consequences of their policies and behavior.

Because administering such a large and diverse empire required a competent bureaucracy, the Tang revived the competitive civil service exams from Han times. The Chinese believed that government officials, known as mandarins, should be the wisest and ablest men in the land. The merit-based exams were intended to seek out talented individuals, regardless of birth, for government service. To help train potential officials, the government also operated a national university and hundreds of local-level academies. During the Tang and the succeeding Song dynasties, perhaps 15 percent of the mandarins did not come from upper-class backgrounds, indicating that the examinations led to some social mobility.

The system consisted of a series of examinations at local, provincial, and national levels. Usually less than 5 percent of candidates passed and moved on to the next level. By passing the highest level a man received the equivalent of a PhD degree, a prerequisite to hold office. The exams largely tested knowledge of literary composition and the contents of the Confucian classics. This competitive merit exam system was the most important institution contributing to the long duration of the political system, giving the ruling elite a shared Confucian ideology emphasizing ethics and loyalty. The Tang bureaucracy numbered around fifteen thousand officials, an extraordinarily small number for a country as huge as China. Clearly they ruled with the cooperation of the local people. From now on whoever ruled China had to rule through the bureaucracy of scholars.

Tang officials pursued policies that maintained economic growth, especially agricultural production. The 80 percent of Chinese who tilled the soil were generally able—though often just barely—to produce a food surplus for the other 20 percent in towns and cities. The Chinese worked to achieve better yields and became one of the world's most efficient farming peoples. The Tang also attempted to circumvent the power of powerful landowning families by experimenting with land reform. In the "equal field system," officials assigned each peasant family a plot of around 19 acres, in the hope that this would provide enough for the family's needs. For a time the reforms brought the peasantry some prosperity. When the Tang declined after some 120 years, the equal field system also disintegrated. Still, throughout history some emperors and officials sought a more equitable land system.

Musicians on the Silk Road   This glazed pottery figurine, one of many similar pieces from the Tang era, shows musicians playing Persian musical instruments while riding a camel on their travels along the Silk Road to China, demonstrating China's ties to the Middle East.

© Cultural Relics Press

Religion, Science, and Technology

Buddhism in China

The early Intermediate Era was the golden age for Buddhism in Central, Southeast, and East Asia. Under the Tang, Buddhism grew to be a dominant faith, while Confucianism and Daoism remained influential. As Buddhist monks, pilgrims, and artists traveled between India and China, they drew the two societies into closer contact. However, competing Buddhist sects presented the government with some problems. Furthermore, the Buddhist monasteries came to control vast amounts of tax-exempt land and wealth, becoming an alternative power center. In the mid-ninth century the government cracked down on Buddhist institutions. Emperor Wuzong (woo-chong) (840–846), in desperate need of more revenues, seized 4,600 monasteries and defrocked all monks under the age of fifty. Although Wuzong's successors restored the monasteries, his actions reduced the political and economic power of the Buddhist orders enough to ensure that they never again exercised significant secular power.

Some new religions also moved east along the Silk Road. Nestorian Christianity, a sect considered heretical in Byzantium, gained a small following, and Islam became strong in northwest China and in pockets of southwest and southern China. Jewish merchants also settled in several northern China cities, founding Jewish communities that endured for centuries. Except for Wuzong, the Tang court generally took a tolerant, ecumenical view of religion. As one Tang emperor proclaimed: "The Way [truth] has more than one name. There is more than one sage. Doctrines vary in distant lands, their benefits reach all mankind."[3]

Tang scholars and craftsmen made significant scientific and technological achievements. Tang astronomers established the solar year at 365 days and studied sunspots, and some argued that the earth was round and revolved around the sun. They were also the first to analyze, record, and then predict solar eclipses. Chinese engineers built the first load-bearing segmental arch bridge. Another important development was the perfection of gunpowder, an elaboration of the firecracker. By using a mix of sulphur, saltpeter, and charcoal, Chinese military forces could now use primitive cannon and flaming rockets to protect their borders or resist rebels. Tang scholars made great strides by inventing woodblock printing. For centuries Chinese had carved texts into stone and then taken ink rubbings for mass distribution as demand for copies of religious and Confucian texts outpaced supply. Finally, some creative men began carving texts into wooden blocks, which could be used to reproduce text on paper with ink, satisfying the need to produce texts for the civil service exams and spread Buddhist writings. The first known book printed on paper with this method was a Buddhist text from 868 (see Chronology: China During the Intermediate Era). The Chinese had an insatiable desire to classify the wisdom of the past for use by future generations, and they could now compile encyclopedias to record their accumulated knowledge. Woodblock printing also gave rise to a written popular culture.

CHRONOLOGY
China During the Intermediate Era

581–618 Sui dynasty

618–907 Tang dynasty

751 Battle of Talas River

868 First books from woodblocks on paper

907–960 Five Dynasties

960–1279 Song dynasty

1167–1227 Life of Genghis Khan

1279–1368 Yuan dynasty (Mongols)

1368–1644 Ming dynasty

1405–1433 Voyages of Admiral Zheng He

The Arts and Literature

Some of China's greatest painters and sculptors lived in Tang times. Painting, an activity avidly pursued by scholars and government officials, was closely associated with calligraphy, the beautiful rendering of Chinese characters used to render a meaningful poem, quote, or passage in a refined, balanced form. Both calligraphers and painters used brush and ink on silk or paper. Chinese paintings were generally restrained, understated, and philosophical in presentation. Influenced by Daoism, many painters specialized in landscapes. An eleventh-century writer explained why: "Why does a virtuous man take delight in landscapes? That in a rustic retreat he may nourish his nature; amid the carefree play of streams and rocks, he may take delight. Haze, mist, and the haunting spirits of the mountains are what human nature seeks, and yet can rarely find."[4] But Confucian ideas were also expressed in the people who were usually a small part of the picture. Like Confucian philosophy, Chinese arts stressed order, morality, and tradition. But there were exceptions. Some artists were free spirits and experimented wildly; one eccentric flipped ink-soaked hair at silk, and another splashed while dancing. Artists also reflected their times. Wind-tossed bamboo and choppy water, for example, might indicate turbulent politics. The traveler to Tang China also experienced art when sipping tea from nearly transparent porcelain cups, the most sanitary utensils in the world at that time. China became famous for splendid lacquer ware, furniture made with mother of pearl, gold and silver inlay, and luxurious brocades.

Landscape Painting

Many of China's greatest poets lived in this era, and annual literary festivals were held in Chang'an to select prizewinners. Many poems depicted the hardships of life—poverty, war, the ups and downs of romantic love, the passing of time, the imminence of death—but many lyrical poems explored life and its wonders, as well as the parting of friends. Chinese poems usually blended emotion with restraint, reflecting their Daoist and Buddhist influences. For example, Wang Wei (wahng way) expressed a Daoist appreciation of nature: "Walking at leisure we watch laurel flowers fall. In the silence of this night the spring mountain is empty. The moon rises, the birds are startled, As they sing occasionally near the spring fountains." The poem describes a changing landscape of falling laurel leaves, a quiet spring mountain, a rising moon, and birds singing, all of which create Daoist feelings of peace, detachment, and purity.

Tang Poetry

The two giant figures of Tang poetry were Li Po (lee po) and Du Fu (too foo), close friends but very different in their personalities and styles. The eccentric Li (701–762) was romantic, disrespectful

The Nelson-Atkins Museum of Art, Kansas City, Missouri. Purchase: William Rockhill Nelson Trust, 47–71. Photograph by John Lamberton.

Song Landscape
This painting, completed around 1000 ᴇ shows a Buddhist temple dwarfed by towering mountain peaks.

of authority, and humorous but often melancholy: a true free spirit. Influenced by Daoism, Li said that a good person must be carefree, maintaining the heart and mind of a child. Li is believed to have drowned on a boat trip when he reached out in a drunken ecstasy for the reflection of the moon in the water. In "The Joys of Wine" he wrote: "Since Heaven and Earth love wine, I can love wine without shaming Heaven. With three cups I penetrate the Great Dao. Take a whole jugful and I and the world are one. Such things as I have dreamed in wine, Shall never be told to the sober."[5] Li also occasionally wrote about public issues. In a piece about the Tang military campaigns in Central Asia, he outlined the hardships of conscripted soldiers and wondered who would cultivate their fields.

The opposite of Li Po, Du Fu (712–770) was a Confucian humanist, the preeminent poet of social consciousness and deeply concerned with the human condition. Du's poems held up a mirror to his times. His antiwar poems remain powerful even a millennium later: "When will men be satisfied with building a wall against the barbarians? When will the soldiers return to their native land?" His sympathies were with the soldiers and their families rather than with imperial aims:

The war-chariots rattle, The war-horses whinny. Each man of you has a bow and quiver in his belt. Father, mother, son, wife, stare at you going. At the border where the blood of men spills like the sea. And still the heart of Emperor Wu is beating for war. Do you know that, east of China's mountains, in two hundred districts, And in thousands of villages, nothing grows but weeds? And though strong women have bent to the ploughing, East and west the furrows are all broken down.

Du was also capable of great tenderness and celebrated the pleasures of everyday life: "Clear waters wind, Around our village. With long summer days, Full of loveliness. My wife draws out, A chessboard on paper, While our little boys, Bend needles into fish hooks. What more could I wish for?"[6]

Changes in the Late Tang Dynasty

Significant changes took place in China between the eighth and tenth centuries. The overwhelming majority of Chinese now lived in central and south China, where the fertile Yangzi Basin was the most productive economic region. New crop strains were introduced from Southeast Asia that eventually made it possible to harvest two crops of rice a year. This increased productivity, combined with better transportation, led to more trade and substantial increases in the urban population. Crafts and merchant guilds and the world's first paper money appeared, and Chinese traders visited Southeast Asia to obtain luxury goods.

Like the Han, the Tang ultimately found its empire too expensive to maintain and too difficult to defend. After a bitter defeat by Arab forces at the Battle of Talas River (near Samarkand) in 751, the Tang declined as a military power in Central Asia. Muslim forces filled the vacuum, and Islam became the dominant religion in Turkestan and in the Xinjiang (shin-jee-yahng) region just west of China proper. Finally the Tang lost control of China itself. The country broke apart, and in 907 Chinese rebel bands, spurred by famine and drought, sacked Chang'an. The Tang demise allowed Vietnam to finally free itself from the long yoke of Chinese rule.

During the next five decades after the Tang collapse, China was divided into several competing states known as the Five Dynasties. But Chinese society was now too massive and deeply rooted to experience the centuries of anarchy that occurred between the Han and Sui, and from the Tang onward the interludes of disorder between great dynasties proved brief. Perhaps the Chinese might have remained more innovative if imperial unity had been replaced by smaller competing states, as

[5]Poem by Wang Wei "Bird-singing Stream" as seen in *The White Pony: An Anthology of Chinese Poetry* by Robert Payne (NY: Mentor, 1960). Poem by Li Po "Joys of Wine" as seen in *The White Pony: An Anthology of Chinese Poetry* by Robert Payne (NY: Mentor, 1960).

happened in western Europe. But the Chinese came to deplore disunity. A proverb stated: "Just as there cannot be two suns in the sky, there cannot be two rulers in China." The centralized imperial system remained in place for nearly a millennium after the Tang.

SECTION SUMMARY

- The Tang Empire was marked by ambitious expansion, inclusion of visitors from around the world, and the spread of Chinese goods across Eurasia.

- Under the Tang, stability was maintained by keeping the emperor's authority somewhat in check and by rewarding high achievers through the civil service exam system.

- Buddhism reached its peak influence during the Tang, but it was greatly weakened when Emperor Wuzong seized Buddhist monasteries.

- During the Tang, the first book was printed using woodblocks.

- Poetry and other arts were very popular during the Tang; while usually stressing Daoist harmony, they sometimes expressed criticism of the government.

SONG CHINA AND COMMERCIAL GROWTH

> **Why might historians consider the Song dynasty the high point of China's golden age?**

The next great dynasty, the Song (Sung) (960–1279), presided over a sophisticated period of achievement. Although lacking the Tang's empire building and world leadership, the Song was in many respects more refined in the arts of living and in technological development and material richness. Described by some historians as premodern China's most exciting period, the Song was characterized by unprecedented innovation, economic dynamism, urban sophistication, and cultural flowering. Late Song China contained perhaps 120 million people, between a quarter and a third of the world's total population, living in an area that stretched a thousand miles east to west and north to south.

Cities, Economies, and Technologies

Song China boasted the world's largest cities, at least five cities having populations over a million, and nearly fifty other cities each containing over 100,000 people. Meanwhile, once-great cities in western Eurasia had fallen in population: Rome to 35,000 and Baghdad to 125,000. Chinese urban residents enjoyed a high quality of life. A modern scholar described the vibrant activity in one of the cities:

> *The day started with the booming of temple bells. Peddlers began to make their way up and down the streets, calling out the foods they had for sale. Carts laden with meats and vegetables moved in toward the markets. Businesses of all kinds opened. Many of these, such as the tailors, hairdressers, dealers in paper and brushes, and caterers, served the city's taste for*

Scroll of Kaifeng
This segment from the scroll "Spring Festival on the River," discussed in the chapter opening, shows people thronging the Rainbow Bridge while boatmen lower their masts to pass under the cantilevered structure. Along the streets and bridge stalls sell their goods.

Werner Forman/Art Resource, NY

---

luxury. As night fell, lanterns lit up taverns and restaurants, the largest of which had staffs of hundreds. In the theater district dozens of houses offered varied bills, including the latest songs, puppet shows, acrobats, wrestlers, storytellers, and comedians.[7]

In the later Song era, when the government had been pushed south of the Yangzi River by nomadic invaders, the capital was Hangzhou (hahng-jo), a city of several million on the southern end of the Grand Canal (see Witness to the Past: Life in the Chinese Capital City). A later and well-traveled Italian visitor, Marco Polo, called it unquestionably the greatest city in the world. Hangzhou would be followed by Nanjing in the fifteenth century, and then Beijing from the sixteenth into the nineteenth centuries, as the world's largest cities.

Song Economy

The Song also marked the high point for Chinese commerce and foreign trade. The merchant class grew substantially, and tax revenues were three times higher than for the Tang. The Grand Canal, which linked the Yellow and Yangzi River Basins, provided an economic cornerstone, allowing the mass movement of goods between north and south. China also developed the world's first fully monetized economy, putting paper money and silver coins into wide use. In addition, Song China had the world's most advanced farming, with expanding productivity meeting the needs for agricultural products. Farmers doubled the rice crop and vastly increased the growing and marketing of sugar, once a minor crop. While foreign trade continued to flourish, now it was based more on maritime networks that connected China to the rest of Afro-Eurasia. Chinese merchants regularly visited Southeast Asia and traded around the Indian Ocean, and Chinese industrial and food products found markets as far away as Persia, East Africa, and Egypt. The cosmopolitan southern seaports of Guangzhou (Canton) and Quanzhou (Zayton) were home to thousands of foreigners, including many Arab, Indian, Persian, and even East African merchants. To accommodate these varied peoples, the cities contained numerous mosques and Hindu temples.

Primary Source: The Craft of Farming
Look inside a twelfth-century Chinese treatise on farming, with advice on when to plow, which crops to plant, and how to use compost as fertilizer.

Song China's industry was the world's most advanced. China's world leadership was reflected in its export of manufactured goods (silks, porcelain, books) and import of raw materials (spices, minerals, horses). Chinese porcelain was traded all over Asia, the Middle East, and parts of Africa, and the name *china* became synonymous with the very finest porcelain products. China's iron industry was the world's largest before the eighteenth century, producing the finest steel for tools, weapons, stoves, ploughshares, cooking equipment, nails, building materials, and bridges. Mass production and metal-casting techniques supplied standardized iron products to the world's largest internal market, and the Song mined coal for fuel and produced salt on an industrial scale. Spurred by domestic and foreign trade, Song China also developed a significant shipbuilding industry. Its huge compartmentalized ships had four decks and four to six masts and were capable of carrying five hundred sailors and extensive cargo. Thousands of cargo ships plied the rivers and canals. This maritime technology was the world's best at that time.

Technology and Science

The Song also maintained the Chinese technological and scientific tradition. Between the first and fifteenth centuries C.E., the Chinese produced a majority of the world's major inventions. For example, they built the world's longest bridge (2.5 kilometers) and expanded the use of water-powered clocks and mills. Major Chinese inventions of the era that later spread throughout Eurasia included the magnetic compass (for naval navigation), the sternpost rudder, and the spinning wheel. Song craftsmen also made movable type, first from fired clay and then from tin or copper, an invention that greatly facilitated the printing of books. In weaponry, Song technicians developed the fire lance, a bamboo tube filled with gunpowder that was the precursor of the metal-barrel gun. Song ships were fitted with missile launchers, flamethrowers, cannons, and bombs, all used to keep the coast free of pirates. Song engineers also invented a mechanized spinning process for the reeling of silk and later hemp thread. Developed over half a millennium before the Industrial Revolution began in western Europe, this was the world's first industrial machine. The Song also had notable achievements in astronomy and medicine. Today astronomers still use data the Song collected from observation of the skies, such as on the supernova that created the Crab Nebula. A Song calendar precisely measured the solar year (365.2425 days). In medicine, Chinese doctors inoculated against smallpox, a disease that ravaged much of Afro-Eurasia. Some Chinese medical ideas reached the Middle East and Europe by the thirteenth century.

Society and Religion

Men, Women, and Families

The Song also saw the development of an urbane elite culture. Printed books fostered the spread of education, exposing a wider audience to the values of the social and political elite, and the Song government established schools in every district. Although only a small percentage of these students ever became mandarins, a degree or some educated background became a certificate of status, even if it never led to a government post. The cultivated gentleman, whether or not in government service, was expected to be proficient in music (especially lute playing), chess,

Life in the Chinese Capital City

The following excerpts are from a description of Hangzhou, the capital city of China during the southern Song dynasty, written by a Chinese observer in 1235. It reveals the life of urban people in China during one of its most creative eras. The writer describes the city's many amenities, including shops, restaurants, and taverns, and also its cultural and social activities. The many specialized enterprises and diverse clubs indicate a highly complex society.

During the morning hours, markets extend from . . . the palace all the way to . . . the New Boulevard. Here we find pearl, jade, talismans, exotic plants and fruits, seasonal catches from the sea, wild game—all the rarities of the world. . . . In the evening . . . the markets are as busy as during the day. . . . In the wine shops and inns business also thrives. . . . In general the capital attracts the greatest variety of goods and has the best craftsmen. For instance, the flower company at Superior Lane does a truly excellent job of flower arrangement, and its caps, hairpins, and collars are unsurpassed in craftsmanship. Some . . . famous fabric stores sell exquisite brocade and fine silk which are unsurpassed anywhere in the country.

Among the various kinds of wine shops, the tea-and-food shops sell not only wine, but also various foods to go with it. However, to get seasonal delicacies . . . one should go to the inns, for they also have a menu from which one can make selections. The pastry-and-wine shops sell pastries with duckling and goose fillings. . . . In the large teahouses there are usually paintings and calligraphies by famous artists on display. . . . Most restaurants here are operated by people from the old capital [Kaifeng], like the lamb rice shops which also serve wine. . . . There are special food shops such as meat-pie shops and vegetable-noodle shops. . . . The vegetarian restaurants cater to [Buddhist] religious banquets and vegetarian dinners. . . . There are also shops specializing in snacks. Depending on the season, they sell a variety of delicacies. . . .

In the evening, food vendors of all sorts parade the streets and alleys . . . chanting their trade songs. . . .

The entertainment centers . . . are places where people gather. . . . In these centers there are schools for musicians offering thirteen different courses, among which the most significant is opera. . . . In each scene of an operatic performance there are four or five performers who first act out a short, well known piece. . . . Then they give a performance of the opera itself. . . . The opera is usually based on history and teaches a moral lesson, which may also be a political criticism in disguise. . . . There are always various acting troupes performing, and this usually attracts a large crowd.

For men of letters, there is a unique West Lake Poetry Society. Its members include both scholars residing in the capital and visiting poets from other parts of the country; over the years, many famous poets have been associated with this society. . . . Other groups include the Physical Fitness Club, Angler's Club, Occult Club, Young Girl's Chorus, Exotic Foods Club, Plants and Fruits Club, Antique Collector's Club, Horse-Lover's Club, and Refined Music Society. . . .

There are civil and military schools inside . . . the capital. Besides lineage schools, capital schools, and country schools, there are at least one or two village schools, family schools, private studios, or learning centers in every neighborhood.

THINKING ABOUT THE READING

1. What do the main goods sold in the markets say about economic prosperity?

2. What does the reading tell us about popular pleasures and entertainments in Hangzhou?

3. What do the main recreational and educational activities available suggest about leisure time and societal values?

Source: Reprinted with permission of The Free Press, a Division of Simon & Schuster Inc., from CHINESE CIVILIZATION AND SOCIETY, A Sourcebook, Second Revised & Expanded Edition by Patricia Buckley Ebrey. Copyright © 1993 by Patricia Buckley Ebrey. All rights reserved.

calligraphy, poetry, and painting. Although Song commercial growth allowed women to operate restaurants and sell fish and vegetables in markets, women experienced more restrictions than they had known earlier. Tang paintings and statues had shown aristocratic women in swept-up hair riding horses or standing dignified, wearing loose-fitting gowns. Now, however, women's status began to decline. Fearing that the new economic opportunities for women might undermine patriarchy, conservatives sought to limit women's roles. Men more often took concubines (official mistresses) in addition to their official wives, and families increasingly frowned upon remarriage for widows. Peasant wives had the most equitable position because they worked in the fields alongside men and were therefore crucial to family economic livelihood. Still, children belonged to the father's family, and the wife was ruled by her husband's mother. Divorce was possible but uncommon because it was a disgrace for the woman. In addition, old age was especially difficult for poor women, as a male Song writer sympathetically described:

For women who live a long life, old age is especially hard to bear, because most women must rely on others for their existence. Some wives with stupid husbands are able to manage the family's finances. But the most remarkable are the women who manage a household after their husbands have died leaving them with young children.[8]

Still another source of suffering for women was footbinding, which was introduced during the Song period among the elite and some of the common folk. Mothers tightly bound the feet of five- or six-year-old daughters to prevent normal growth, crippling a girl's feet and giving her a dainty walk, which enhanced what Chinese men viewed as her beauty and eroticism. But many peasants rejected the practice as too physically debilitating, since women's labor was necessary for family survival. Footbinding was not widespread until later dynasties.

neo-Confucianism A form of Confucianism arising in China during the Song period (960–1279) that incorporated many Buddhist and Daoist metaphysical ideas.

qi In Chinese thought, the energizing force pervading the universe.

The Song also saw the rise of **neo-Confucianism**, a form of Confucianism that incorporated many Buddhist and Daoist metaphysical ideas. Neo-Confucianism was associated particularly with Zhu Xi (JOO shee) (1130–1200), a child prodigy and one of the most influential thinkers in Chinese history, who resigned from government service in disgust at corruption. Zhu Xi believed that the original ideas of Confucius had become rigid and altered over the centuries, and he advocated rediscovering the essence of the sage's ideas. The influence of Daoism can be seen in Zhu Xi's rational and humane approach, which recognized a dualism between the material world and the energy thought by Chinese to pervade the universe, or **qi** (ch'i). Harnessing this qi for personal centering became the goal of *tai qi* (tai ch'i), exercises to build mind and body. In the spirit of Confucius, Zhu identified reason or principle as the unchanging law, and morality as the measure of all human affairs: "For every person the most important thing is the cultivation of himself as an ethical being."[9] However, because Zhu was indifferent to natural science, his ideas did not help sustain scientific inquiry. Over time neo-Confucianism became the dominant mindset of China's educated elite and a force for stability but not innovation.

The Song in World History

Barriers to Chinese Transformation

Although in many ways the Song could have been a turning point in Chinese and world history, they did not foster a major transition. The profound economic, technological, and urban developments remind some historians of eighteenth-century Europe at the dawn of rapid industrialization. But unlike that revolution's transforming impact in the West, the commercial and agricultural dynamism never revolutionized Chinese society. Instead, these developments were contained and absorbed. For example, the Chinese had the technology to sail the seas and colonize other lands, but they lacked the incentive because China was largely self-sufficient. Since the highly bureaucratic empire easily adjusted to economic change, it could keep the merchants from disrupting China's social order. With an agriculture productive enough to feed a huge population, convenient transportation by water through canals, and many natural resources, the Chinese had no great need to develop additional mechanized technologies. The Mongol conquest of the Song, as well as a cooler climate by the thirteenth century and the Black Death pandemic in the fourteenth, also undermined economic dynamism. Finally, population pressure became a growing burden as land available for farming filled up.

Confucian disdain of merchants also led to stagnation. In its domination of the merchants, the imperial government played a central role in containing economic growth. Song commercial growth resulted partly from the influence of unusually large number of mandarins from wealthy merchant families in this period. Yet, many essential commodities remained government monopolies, such as iron, grain, cloth, and salt, while public granaries to check famine were financed by taxes on the wealthy. This socialist policy reflected the low esteem accorded merchants in Confucian ideology. Monopolies over essential products enriched the state and protected the population from price and supply problems, but they restricted merchants to handling nonessential products.

The Song government, more interested in economic than political growth and empire, was generally disinterested in military expansion. Prosperity, trade, and urban living made peace more attractive than conquest. Although maintaining the world's largest army, the Song, unlike the Han and Tang, reduced the power of military leaders so they could not threaten civilian authority, a chronic problem in the Tang. As a result, the Song adopted a passive attitude toward controlling the pastoral nomads across the border, attempting not to conquer but to appease them with generous payments. Ultimately the policy failed. In the twelfth century a nomadic people, the Jin (Chin), conquered northern China, forcing the Song court to move south across the Yangzi, where it continued to rule central and southern China from Hangzhou until the invasion by the Mongols.

SECTION SUMMARY

- The Song dynasty was notable for its bustling urban life, its maritime trade, and its advanced economy.

- Song China made great advances in the manufacture of porcelain, ships, and bridges and in the prevention of disease.

- During the Song, the pursuit of education and cultivation became widespread among the elite.

- However, the status of women declined, and footbinding began to be practiced by the elite and some commoners.

- The Song's achievements did not lead to a major historical transition because China at this time felt self-sufficient, was not interested in conquest, and kept merchants out of important industries; it also tried to deal with neighboring pastoral nomads peacefully, a strategy that ultimately failed.

MONGOL CONQUEST, CHINESE RESURGENCE, AND EURASIAN CONNECTIONS

> **How did China change during the Yuan and Ming dynasties?**

From the thirteenth through the nineteenth centuries the Chinese way of life showed great stability. Three ruling houses held power between the downfall of the Song and the end of the imperial system in the twentieth century, an almost unprecedented record of political stability, perhaps matched only by that of the ancient Egyptian kingdoms. Two of the three dynasties were conquest dynasties imposed by non-Chinese nomadic peoples riding in on horseback. The two dynasties that held power between the thirteenth and seventeenth centuries were the Yuan (yu-wenn), established by invading Mongols, and the Ming, which marked a return to Chinese rule.

The Mongol Empire and the Conquest of China

For several millennia the Chinese had feared what they considered the "barbarian" scourge, fast-riding horsemen who came out of the Central Asian grasslands and deserts killing, looting, and taking captives. The strongest rulers could control these nomadic tribal peoples by conquest or effective divide-and-rule diplomacy. The ever-present Central Asian influence on China's political life was based on the close proximity of the arid grasslands north and west of China, which, compared to the lush farmlands of China, were suitable only for mobile herding. These contrasting environments had produced very different societies. In the grasslands a pastoral economy and few resources necessitated seasonal migration and chronic poverty for the tough, self-reliant herding people. When China was weak, the Great Wall proved no major barrier to peoples anxious to taste China's affluence. In the thirteenth century the Chinese realized their worst nightmare when a new confederation of warlike peoples, the Mongols, conquered all of China.

Central Asian Pastoralists

Before invading China the Mongols conquered much of Eurasia, including eastern Europe and western Asia. Traditionally divided into often feuding tribes, the Mongols became united under Temuchin (ca. 1167–1227), a ruthless but brilliant man of humble origins who defeated or co-opted his rivals and then changed his name to Genghis Khan (GENG-iz KAHN) ("Universal Emperor"). He had simple motives: "A man's greatest pleasure is to defeat his enemies, to drive them before him, to take from them that which they possessed, to see those whom they cherished in tears, to ride their horses, to hold their wives and daughters in his arms."[10] Skilled horse soldiers, more agile than their foes, the Mongols were formidable opponents. Their well-organized fighting units possessed powerful bows that could kill at 600 feet, disc-shaped stirrups that gave the rider maneuverability, and the world's most advanced siege weaponry, including catapults. Because of China's strength, it was one of the last countries to fall to Mongol control. Genghis Khan had conquered parts of northern China in 1215. The Mongol conquest of the rest of China, which came fifty years after the death of Genghis, was accomplished by his grandson, Khubilai Khan (koo-bluh KAHN) (r. 1260–1294), who created a new dynasty, the Yuan (1279–1368). China became, for the first and only time, part of a great world empire, one that stretched from eastern Europe to Korea and from the Black Sea to the Pacific Ocean (see Map 11.2 and the essay at the end of Part III).

Mongol Expansion

The Mongols imposed a distinctive government system and fostered new cultural forms in China. By Mongol standards Khubilai Khan was a rather enlightened ruler, far less cruel and more pragmatic than most of the Mongol leaders elsewhere in Eurasia. He patronized Buddhism, built granaries for food storage, operated an efficient postal system, and improved the transportation network. But Chinese historians have condemned Khubilai Khan for the sins committed by the Mongols generally, such as maintaining Mongol cultural identity and actively resisting assimilation into Chinese society. Later Chinese viewed the Yuan as China's darkest hour, an intolerable rule by aliens who would not be absorbed. Khubilai Khan moved the capital to Beijing ("Northern Capital"), before this a provincial city close to the Great Wall but situated alongside the major highways leading north and west. Except for brief periods since, Beijing has remained the capital of China, politically eclipsing more ancient cities like Chang'an and Hangzhou.

The Yuan Dynasty

The Mongols mistrusted and did not patronize intellectuals, but they were tolerant in religious matters. They invited missionaries from all over Eurasia to come to the court for religious debates, among them Christians of various sects (including Catholics); Khubilai Khan's mother was a Nestorian Christian. Khubilai Khan ruled over a religiously diverse society and wanted to avoid conflict. Indeed, China was far more accepting of religious diversity than Christian Europe. However, the Mongols had more rigid gender expectations and marriage practices than the Chinese, stressing

Map 11.2 China in the Mongol Empire

After the Mongols conquered much of Central Asia, western Asia, and eastern Europe, they added China and Korea to their huge empire, the largest contiguous land empire in world history. During the Mongol era many Asians and some Europeans, including the Italian Marco Polo, visited or worked in China.

e Interactive Map

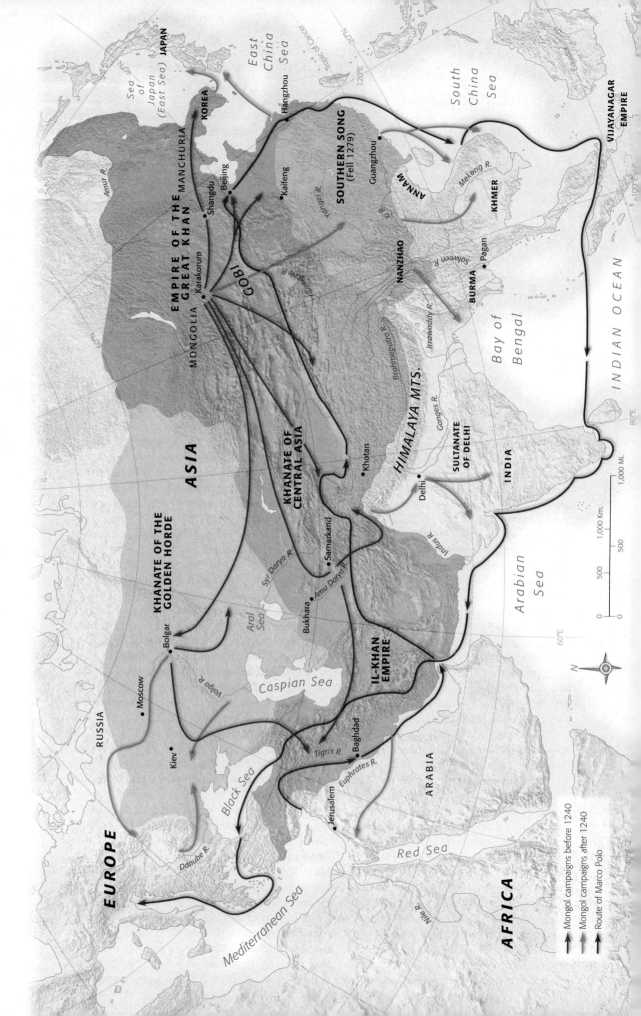

the need for widows to remain chaste and dutifully serve their aging parents-in-law. Chinese men now also expected women to remain at home and emphasize feminine behavior, including the growing fashion of tightly bound feet to set them apart from non-Chinese women.

Mongol China and Eurasian Networks

The Mongols paved the way for enhanced global communication, opening China's doors to the world. By protecting the Silk Road, the Mongols revived networks for the exchange of goods, ideas, and technologies between East and West. Chinese inventions like gunpowder, printing, the blast furnace for cast iron, silk-making machinery, paper money, and playing cards moved westward. Bubonic plague, which killed millions of Chinese during Mongol rule, also traveled the overland trade routes, fostering the Black Death that ravaged the Middle East and Europe in the fourteenth century (see Chapters 10 and 14). Many foreigners came to Mongol China by land and sea. Although Khubilai Khan attempted to win Chinese support by modeling his government along Chinese lines and dutifully performing Confucian rites, the Mongols failed to get the cooperation of most scholars and bureaucrats. To rule the vast country, they were forced to rely administratively on foreigners who came to China to serve in what was effectively an international civil service. These included many Muslims from Central Asia, western Asia, and North Africa, as well as a few Europeans who found their way to "fabled Cathay," as they called China.

One of the European visitors was the Italian merchant Marco Polo (ca. 1254–1324), who, with his father and uncle, initially went to China seeking trade goods but spent seventeen years there, mostly in government service. Eventually Polo returned to Italy and told of the wonders he had encountered (or heard about from other travelers). Europeans, few of whom knew much about the world east of Palestine, were unbelieving. Most dismissed Polo's book as full of lies, but the general accuracy of his account has been confirmed by historians. He was a keen observer and recorded the resentment of the Chinese people toward the Mongols, who once slaughtered a city's entire population for the killing of one drunk Mongol soldier. Polo wrote of China's great cities, such as Beijing and Hangzhou. Standing along the shores of beautiful West Lake, Hangzhou could not help but charm the Italian. Polo wrote in the thirteenth century that "the city is beyond dispute the finest and noblest in the world in point of grandeur and beauty as well as in its abundant delights. The natives of this city are of peaceful character, thoroughly honest and truthful and accustomed to dainty living."[11] The city boasted parks, a fire department, garbage collection, a pollution-control agency, and paved streets—all things nonexistent in Polo's much smaller Venice, then one of the major European cities. Indeed, China in this era was far more developed in many fields than the rest of Eurasia and probably had the world's highest standard of living. Polo noted, for example, that the Chinese had for a thousand years burned black stones (coal) for heat and that they took regular baths, astonishing information to medieval Europeans, who seldom if ever bathed.

While the Mongol conquests had enormous consequences for Central Asia, the Middle East, and Europe, Mongol rule in China lasted only a century and did not leave a deep imprint. Although the Mongols long dominated regions such as Russia and Turkestan, they failed to hold China. For one thing, they were always hated, and their leadership deteriorated after the death of Khubilai Khan. Furthermore, the Mongols in China lost their fighting toughness and came to desire luxury more than sacrifice. As Mongols in Central Asia and Persia adopted the cultures and religions of

Khubilai Khan and His Entourage Hunting This painting by a Chinese artist of the time shows Khubilai Khan, dressed in ermine, and Mongol colleagues, including a woman, hunting on horseback, a popular activity among Mongols.

Marco Polo in China

Mongol Decline

the conquered, Mongol unity fragmented and power struggles grew rampant. Then too, a terrible plague outbreak raged and the Yellow River flooded severely, bringing famine. Soon rebellions broke out all over China, and eventually a Chinese commoner established a new dynasty. Mongol military forces returned to Central Asia. Today Mongols venerate Genghis Khan as their greatest leader, building gawdy memorials and even a theme park to honor the conqueror.

Ming Government and Culture

The new Ming dynasty (1368–1644) fostered orderly government, social stability, and a rich culture. The founder, Zhu Yuanzhang (JOO yu-wen-JAHNG) (1328–1398), was a former Buddhist monk and the son of an itinerant farm worker who, like the founder of the Han, rose from abject poverty through sheer ability and ruthless behavior in a time of opportunity. Ming China's people lived for nearly three centuries in comparative peace and prosperity, with living standards among the highest and mortality rates among the lowest of anywhere in the world. During this time China more than doubled in population, from around 80 million to between 160 and 180 million.

The Ming installed a government similar to that of the Han and Tang but somewhat more despotic. Perhaps because of the bitter experience of Mongol rule, the Ming emperors exercised more power than earlier emperors and placed the bureaucracy under closer scrutiny, eliminating the office of prime minister, who had kept his hand on the pulse of the country. The Censorate also became more timid, reducing the checks on royal abuses. Hence, the Ming emperors became more isolated from the real world. As in previous dynasties, some Ming emperors had male lovers as well as many wives and concubines, a practice that reflected a tolerance of same-sex relationships among many Chinese court officials and commoners.

A sense of order infused the arts. Although culturally the Mongol period had proved relatively sterile, musical drama (Chinese opera) became a popular form of entertainment, appealing mostly to the Chinese common folk rather than the elite. In the Ming era, however, theater reached its highest level, with Chinese operas including extended arias and spoken dialogue. Each performance of a play aimed at harmonizing song, speech, costume, makeup, movement, and musical accompaniment. Much Chinese music was composed for operas or for ritual and ceremonial purposes. String, wind, and percussion instruments were popular, especially the flute, lute, and zither.

The Chinese began writing novels in Yuan times, an elaboration of age-old storytelling. The first novelists were intellectuals who refused to work for the Mongols but sought alternative sources of income by writing books for a popular audience. Although most Ming scholars considered fiction worthless, it had a large audience. Most novels had a Confucian moral emphasizing correct behavior, but some offered social criticisms or satires. Perhaps the greatest Ming novel, *The Water Margin* (also known as *All Men Are Brothers*), presented heroes who were also bandits, Robin Hoods driven into crime by corrupt officials. Ming authors also wrote some of the world's first detective stories. Rulers encouraged intellectual pursuits, expanding the *Hanlin* ("Forest of Culture") Academy established in the Tang. The brightest scholars were assigned there and paid to read and write whatever they liked. Ming scholars also compiled a 11,000-volume encyclopedia (with 20,000 chapters) and a 52-volume study of Chinese pharmacology.

A Ming Imperial Workshop Printers' shops, such as the one shown here, used movable type to publish encyclopedias with information on engineering, medicine, agriculture, and other practical topics.

Ming China and the Afro-Eurasian World

The early Ming rulers pursued territorial expansion, including a failed attempt to recolonize Vietnam. But China was now oriented more to the sea. Rather than send armies far into Central Asia, the emperor dispatched a series of grand maritime expeditions to southern Asia and beyond to reaffirm China's preeminence in the eastern half of Asia. Admiral Zheng He (jung huh) (Cheng Ho) (ca. 1371–1435), a huge man and a trusted court eunuch of Muslim faith, commanded seven voyages between 1405 and 1433. The world had never before seen such a large-scale feat of seamanship: the largest fleet comprised sixty-two vessels carrying 28,000 men, and the largest "treasure ships," as they were known, weighed 1,500 tons, were 450 feet long, boasted nine masts nearly 500 feet high, and carried a crew of five hundred. Observers must have been astounded as these ships approached their harbors. A few decades later Christopher Columbus sailed from Spain in three tiny vessels carrying a total of only about a hundred men.

Zheng He's extraordinary voyages carried the Chinese flag through Southeast Asia to India, the Persian Gulf, the Red Sea, and the East African coast (see Map 11.3). Had they continued, the Chinese ships could have sailed around Africa to Europe or the Americas, but they had no incentive to do so. During these voyages the Chinese undertook only a few military actions, but some thirty-six countries in southern and western Asia officially acknowledged Chinese preeminence. The ruler of the East African city of Malindi sent ambassadors bearing tribute, including a giraffe.

Exploring the Indian Ocean World

Historians still debate the reasons for Zheng He's great voyages. Some point to the desire to have so many foreign countries reaffirm the emperor's position as the Son of Heaven. Zheng He may also have sought to locate a deposed boy emperor who had disappeared, possibly fleeing into exile. Others suspect that the ambitious emperor wanted to demonstrate China's military capabilities. Some historians see commercial motives as primary, since these voyages occurred at a time of increased activity by Chinese merchants in Southeast Asia. During the early Ming many thousands of Chinese visited or had settled in the Philippines, Indonesia, Siam, and Vietnam, creating a closer commercial link to China, and Yuan and Ming porcelain was sold as far west as South-Central Africa.

Tribute System

Zheng He's voyages may also have revitalized the traditional tribute system, which during Han and Tang times shaped China's relations with its neighbors. China considered friendly East,

Map 11.3 The Voyages of Zheng He

After replacing the Mongols, the Ming reestablished a strong Chinese state, attempted to recolonize Vietnam, and rebuilt the Great Wall. Ming emperors also dispatched a series of grand maritime expeditions in the early 1400s that reached the Middle East and East Africa.

e Interactive Map

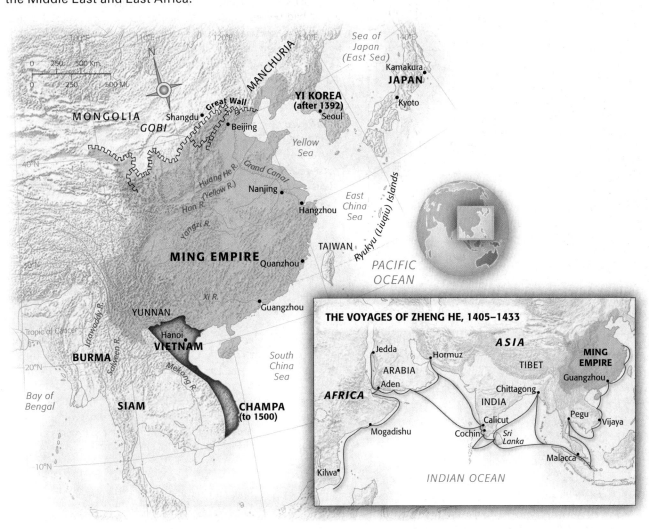

Southeast, and Central Asian states as vassals and granted them trade relations but rarely intervened to support their allies. In return the tributary states sent periodic envoys bearing gifts to the emperor, confirming his superiority in ritual form and playing along because they desired China's goodwill and trade goods. In Ming times tribute came regularly from states in Korea, Vietnam, Cambodia, Borneo, Indonesia, South Asia, and Central Asia.

Inevitably the Chinese saw themselves as the Middle Kingdom surrounded by barbarian societies. The Chinese never recognized any other society as an equal; they felt that they were superior not just materially but also culturally and that barbarians could not resist their appeal, a view reinforced when other East Asian societies borrowed from China. For the Chinese, to be civilized was to embrace Chinese culture, and a virtuous ruler, they believed, irresistibly attracted barbarians. When a tribute mission arrived in the capital, part of the rite was the **kotow**, the tribute-bearers' act of prostrating themselves before the emperor, a practice from which we get the modern English word *kowtow* ("to pander to authority"). This practice, above all others, left little doubt as to who was superior and who was inferior, reflecting a Confucian sense of hierarchy.

kotow The tribute-bearers' act of prostrating themselves before the Chinese emperor.

Ming China Turns Inward

Ending the Grand Voyages

In the early Ming, China remained perhaps the world's wealthiest and most developed country. Hindu India faced Muslim conquests, Middle Eastern societies struggled to overcome various setbacks, and western Europeans were just beginning to enjoy political and economic dynamism. Commercially vibrant and outward-thrusting, Ming China had the capability to open maritime communication between the continents and become the dominant world power. Instead China turned inward. The grand voyages and the commercial thrust to distant lands came to a sudden halt when the Ming emperor ordered them ended and outlawed Chinese emigration altogether. But some Chinese continued to illegally travel abroad for trade, and foreign merchant ships still came to China. The tribute system provided cover for extensive trade and smuggling.

The causes of the stunning reversal of official Chinese engagement with the world that, in the perspective of later history, seemed so counterproductive remain subject to debate. Perhaps Zheng He's voyages were too costly even for the wealthy Ming government. The voyages were not cost-effective, since the ships mostly returned with exotic goods rather than mineral resources and other valuable items. Unlike Christian and Muslim societies, the Chinese lacked any missionary zeal, having little interest in spreading Chinese religion and culture except to near neighbors such as Vietnam. Furthermore, despite their flourishing guilds and frequent wealth, the merchants held a low status in the Confucian social system. Ming leaders were convinced that profit was evil, and mercantile interests inevitably conflicted with political ones. Confucian officials often despised the merchants, and a later Ming scholar wrote that "one in a hundred [Chinese] is rich, while nine out of ten are impoverished. The poor cannot stand up to the rich. The lord of silver rules heaven and the god of copper cash reigns over the earth."[12] Hence many mandarins opposed foreign trade.

Military factors also influenced the turn inward. With the Mongols regrouping in Central Asia, the Ming court shifted its resources to defense of the northern borders and the pirate-infested Pacific coast, spending millions rebuilding and extending the Great Wall. What tourists see today of the Great Wall near Beijing is mostly work done by the Ming. In addition, military operations along the northern border and an ill-fated invasion of Vietnam generated a fiscal crisis that weakened the government.

Finally, after the bitterness of the Mongol era, the Chinese became more ethnocentric and antiforeign. China had always been land-based, self-centered, and self-sufficient. Later Ming Chinese believed that they needed nothing from outside. China remained powerful, productive, and mostly prosperous, enjoying generally high living standards, well into the eighteenth century, when profits from overseas colonies and the Industrial Revolution tipped the balance in favor of northwest Europe. By the later Ming, China had entered a period of relative isolation that was ended only by the forceful intrusion of a newly developed Europe in the early 1800s.

SECTION SUMMARY

- The ancient Chinese fear of Central Asian nomads was realized when the Mongols, under Genghis and Khubilai Khan, conquered China and established the Yuan dynasty.

- Khubilai Khan made a number of improvements in China's transportation system and moved the capital to Beijing.

- Because of lack of cooperation from Chinese scholars and bureaucrats, the Mongols established an international civil service, in which Marco Polo served.

- After the decline of the Mongols, the Chinese enjoyed three centuries of prosperity under the Ming dynasty, and their sense of well-being was displayed in Zheng He's grand sailing expeditions, which enhanced China's position among its neighbors.

- The Ming dynasty received tribute from many peoples throughout Asia.

- For reasons that are still debated, the Ming emperor suddenly ordered all overseas activity halted and China turned inward, beginning an isolation that ended only in the 1800s.

CULTURAL ADAPTATION IN KOREA AND JAPAN

> **How did the Koreans and Japanese develop their own distinctive societies?**

As the cultural heartland of East Asia, China strongly influenced its three large neighbors of Vietnam (see Chapter 13), Korea, and Japan. All derived considerable culture from China, including writing systems, philosophies, and political institutions. At the same time, they adapted these Chinese influences to their indigenous customs, retaining their cultural identity. During the second half of the Intermediate Era, the Japanese developed a very different way of life and outlook than they had enjoyed a few centuries earlier.

Korea and China

Several strong states emerged on the Korean peninsula. In the mid-seventh century the southern Korean state of Silla (SILL-ah) defeated its main rival, Koguryo, and eventually united most Koreans, but at the price of becoming a vassal of China. Political unity allowed Korean culture to become homogenized. Like earlier states, Silla also borrowed Chinese culture and institutions. Buddhism triumphed, and the Tang system became the model in government, with Confucianism used as a political ideology; many Korean monks also traveled to China. But Koreans were selective in their borrowing. The Korean social structure continued to place more emphasis than the Chinese did on inherited status instead of merit, and the gap between rich and poor was much wider than in China. Moreover, among Silla's rulers were three queens, suggesting less gender bias than in China. For example, Queen Sondok (r. 632–647) fostered science and promoted a tolerant mixing of Buddhism and shamanism. Silla women generally shared in the social status of their menfolk and enjoyed many legal rights.

Silla Society

During the period when Silla dominated much of the peninsula (676–935), Koreans adapted Chinese writing to their own very different spoken language, creating a distinctive literary tradition in history, religion, and poetry. To mass-produce these works, Silla craftsmen developed woodblock printing as early as China. The oldest still extant example of woodblock printing in the world, a Korean Buddhist writing, dates from 751. Koreans also studied astronomy. A great observatory built in this era is the oldest still standing in East Asia. Korea also formed connections with the rest of the world. Buddhist pilgrims came from as far away as India, and many Arabs traded or settled down there. One Arab wrote that "seldom has a stranger who has come there from Iraq or another country left it afterwards. So healthy is the air there, so pure the water, so fertile the soil and so plentiful of all good things."[13]

Gradually Silla declined, damaged by elite rivalries, corruption, and peasant uprisings, and it was replaced by a new state, Koryo (KAW-ree-oh), which lasted for over four centuries (935–1392). Chinese influence continued in politics and philosophy: Koreans set up an examination system, and neo-Confucianism became popular. But Koreans retained a distinctive political and social system. Korean kings, never as strong as Chinese emperors, were greatly influenced by the court, military, and aristocratic landowning families; unlike in China, Korean farming relied on large estates. The status of women also changed. In contrast to Silla, Koryo court women mainly exercised influence behind the scenes. For example, Lady Yu successfully urged her reluctant husband, Wang Kon, the founder of the Koryo dynasty, to seize power from a despotic ruler, arguing, "It is an ancient tradition to raise a banner of revolt against a tyrant. How can you, a great military leader, hesitate?"[14] While most Koryo women played a lesser role in public affairs, they took full responsibility for family affairs and farmed.

Koryo Society

Buddhism in Korea, which assimilated many elements from animism, gradually became a powerful economic and political force. But the involvement of monks in political life fostered religious corruption and a worldly orientation that alienated some believers. As a result, although for the past 1,500 years Korea has been a nominally Buddhist society, the religion gradually lost influence. A more secular interest fostered such developments as a publishing industry; by 1234 Koreans had invented the world's first metal movable-type printing.

After the Mongols conquered the peninsula, Koryo became a colony in their vast empire. When Koreans resisted, the Mongols devastated the land, carrying off hundreds of thousands of captives and imposing heavy taxes on peasants. Yet, thanks to closer links to trade networks, more Chinese and western Asian learning and technology reached Korea during the Mongol era. In 1392

Choson and the Yi Dynasty

Map 11.4   Korea and Japan, ca. 1300
Japanese society developed in an archipelago, the major early cities rising in central Honshu. In 1274 and 1281 the Japanese repulsed Mongol invasions by sea. Throwing off the Mongols, Korea was unified under the Yi dynasty in 1392.

 **Interactive Map**

a new Korean dynasty took over from the Mongols, the Yi **(yee)**, whose state was known as Choson **(cho-suhn)** (see Map 11.4). They lasted until 1910, an incredible longevity of 518 years.

Yi rulers maintained a tribute relationship with China, and Koreans learned to better use Chinese social and political models. Mastery of Confucian scholarship became the road to government careers, as Confucianism provided a philosophical justification for government by a benevolent bureaucracy under a virtuous ruler. Education expanded to prepare students for the civil service exams. Confucian influence also remade Korean social institutions such as the family. Believing that Korean women had too much freedom and hence behaved immorally, the Yi encouraged women's seclusion at home and imposed arranged marriages, veiling of the face when out in public, female chastity, and strict obedience to husbands and fathers. However, commoner women, who needed to work in the fields, usually had more freedom of movement. Today Confucianism is arguably a stronger force than Buddhism, especially in rural Korea.

Yi Korea continued to develop literature, technology, and science. King Sejong **(say-jong)** (r. 1418–1450) was a particularly strong supporter of scientific progress. Respected by his people for improving the Korean economy, helping poor peasants, and prohibiting cruel punishments, Sejong wrote books on agriculture and formed a scholarly think tank, the Hall of Worthies, where Yi scholars invented a phonetic system for indicating Korean pronunciation of Chinese characters and for writing the Korean language. But Chinese was still used for serious scholarship. These years also saw a renaissance of intellectual activity and technology. Koreans created the world's first rain gauges, which were installed throughout the country to keep accurate rainfall records. Choson remained among the more creative of the late Intermediate Afro-Eurasian societies.

Japan in the Nara Era

Although adopting many Chinese and Korean influences, Japan, like Korea, produced a highly distinctive society. In the mid-sixth century the Japanese embarked on three centuries of deliberate cultural borrowing from China, creating a robust, expansive, and sophisticated society. The changes began with the *Taika* **(TIE-kah)** ("Great Change") reform of 646 C.E., which the rulers hoped would transform Japan into a centralized empire on the Tang model, establishing a governmental system made to resemble, on the surface at least, the Chinese centralized bureaucracy. The Japanese now used the Chinese writing system. The adoption of Buddhism from China also brought with it a rich constellation of art and architecture.

The high point of conscious borrowing from China (710–784) takes its name from Nara **(NAH-rah)**, Japan's first capital city, which was built on the model of the Tang capital, Chang'an (see Chronology: Korea and Japan During the Intermediate Era). Nara had a population of some twenty thousand, while the total Japanese population was probably 5 or 6 million. During the Nara period land was nationalized in the name of the emperor and, using Tang models, reallocated on an equal basis to the peasants. In return, the peasants paid a land and labor tax. This system was abandoned as unworkable after a few decades, but it illustrated that in agrarian societies land control is the key to political power, a fact demonstrated vividly throughout Japanese history.

Although these changes were designed to strengthen imperial authority, the Japanese emperor never became an unchallenged and activist Chinese-style ruler. Powerful aristocrats maintained control of the bureaucracy and also retained large tax-exempt landholdings. In practice Japan became a **dyarchy**, a form of dual government whereby one powerful family filled the highest government posts and dominated the emperors, whose power was mostly symbolic.

Nara and the Tang

dyarchy A form of dual government that began in Japan during the Nara period (710–784), whereby one powerful family ruled the country while the emperor held mostly symbolic power.

King Sejong This modern painting portrays the Yi dynasty King Sejong, revered by Koreans for his political, economic, and scientific achievements, observing stars, supervising book printing, and contemplating a musical instrument he commissioned. Sejong patronized learning, supported agricultural innovations that increased crop yields, introduced humane laws, and fostered economic growth.

The emperors passed their lives in luxurious seclusion, guaranteeing an unbroken succession through having sons. This dyarchical system remained the pattern in Japan into the nineteenth century.

Nara leaders promoted aspects of Chinese culture but blended them with Japanese traditions. The rituals and ceremonies of the imperial court, largely based on Tang Chinese models, included stately dances and orchestral music using Japanese versions of Chinese musical instruments such as the flute, lute, and zither. They are still maintained at the Japanese court. More significantly, the Chinese written language gained great prestige, and Chinese ideographs were adapted to Japan's very different nontonal spoken language, in what must have been a difficult conversion process. Chinese literary forms, including poetry and calligraphy, became popular.

The Japanese also adopted and reshaped Chinese philosophical and religious doctrines that they found appealing. They modified Confucianism's ethical and political doctrines to suit their own social structure. They also borrowed Mahayana Buddhism, whose world-view that all things are impermanent greatly influenced their art and literature. Many artists and poets focused on the passage of time and the changing of the seasons. But the Japanese also retained their original animist religion known today as Shinto, a kind of nature worship. Shinto and Buddhism addressed different needs and easily blended into a synthesis. The deities of Shinto were not gods but beautiful natural phenomena such as Mt. Fuji **(FOO-jee)**, waterfalls, thunder, or stately trees. Shinto also stressed ritual purity, encouraging bathing and personal cleanliness. It offered no coherent theology or moral doctrine, no concept of death or an afterlife.

Religion and Culture

Economic unrest characterized the late Nara period. Peasants resented forced labor and military conscription, which often resulted in economic ruin. Many abandoned their fields, becoming wandering *ronin* **(ROH-neen)** ("wave people"), some of whom were hired by large landowners as workers. To stop people from becoming ronin, the government abolished compulsory service and gave the responsibility for police and defense to local officials. Eventually the ronin these officials hired as troops were transformed into the provincial warrior class, whose activities reshaped Japanese life.

Heian Cultural Renaissance

The imitation and direct cultural borrowing from China came to an end during the Heian **(HAY-en)** period (794–1184). After the capital moved from Nara to Heian, or Kyoto, 28 miles north, Japan gradually returned to relative isolation. The leaders discontinued foreign contacts in the ninth century and set about consciously absorbing and adapting the Chinese cultural patterns imported during the Nara era under the slogan "Chinese learning, Japanese spirit." Buddhism gradually harmonized with Shinto beliefs while generating new sects, art, and temple building. A rich and unique court society arose that fostered a distinctly Japanese writing system, literary styles, arts, and world-view. The

CHRONOLOGY

Korea and Japan During the Intermediate Era

646 Taika reforms in Japan

668 Destruction of Koguryo

676–935 Domination of Korea by Silla

710–784 Nara period in Japan

794–1184 Heian period in Japan

935–1392 Unification of Korea by Koryo

1180–1333 Kamakura Shogunate in Japan

1274, 1281 Mongol invasions of Japan

1338–1568 Ashikaga Shogunate in Japan

1392–1910 Yi dynasty in Korea

kana A Japanese phonetic script developed in the Heian period (794–1184) that consisted of some forty-seven syllabic signs derived from Chinese characters.

modification of Chinese influence was exemplified in the development of **kana** (KAH-nah), a phonetic script consisting of forty-seven syllabic signs derived from Chinese characters. Now Japanese could write their language phonetically, allowing more freedom of expression, especially when the kana letters were combined with Chinese characters. The Japanese written language of today combines the two systems.

Heian elite culture, a world enormously remote from us today in time, attitudes, and behavior, reached its high point around 1000 C.E. It flourished among a very small group of privileged families in Kyoto, which then had a population of around 100,000. Many elite residents derived their incomes from bureaucratic jobs and land ownership. The Kyoto aristocracy, extraordinarily withdrawn from the outside world, created a culture governed by standards of form and beauty in which the distinction between art and life was not clearly made. Passionately concerned with their social rank, they created some of Japan's greatest literature and art, admiring nothing so much as the ability to write in an artistic hand, compose a graceful poem, and create an elegant costume. The finest energies went into creating beauty, such as putting together harmonious syllables and lines of ink on the page or perfumes on the body. The Heian period was probably unique in world history for the careful attention spent in choosing an undergarment, or the time writing a love note, with perhaps a tastefully faded chrysanthemum to emphasize the melancholy nature of the contents. The superficial Heian aristocrats were not interested in pure intellect or social morality but were obsessed by mood, especially the sense of the transience of beauty.

Women's Roles

Women from affluent families had their highest position in Japanese history during the Heian era. Romantic affairs and sexual promiscuity were acceptable for both men and women. Aristocratic women spent their days playing games, writing diaries, listening to romantic stories, or practicing art. Some women, such as the novelist Lady Murasaki (MUR-uh-SAH-kee), gained a formal education and wrote because, without demanding jobs, they had abundant free time and could focus on their feelings (see Profile: Lady Murasaki, Heian Novelist). A poet might deftly turn a scene of nature into one of emotion: "The flowers withered, their color faded away, while meaninglessly, I spent my days in the world, and the long rains were falling."[15]

The Heian aristocracy saw love as an art to be cultivated. People wrote poems before meeting their lover and then the next morning following their meeting. Here are two morning-after poems from the diary of a prominent woman writer, Izumi Shikibu:

> Woman: "painful though it were, to see you leave before dawn [to avoid discovery], better by far than when the dawn's grey light, so cruelly tears you from my side." Prince: "to leave you while the leaves are moist with dew, is bitterer by far, than if I were to say farewell at night, without a single chance to show my love."[16]

Heian women wore their hair long to the ground, applied white skin powder and lipstick, plucked their eyebrows, and blackened their teeth with dye. In one novel, a lady refuses to do these things, and her attendants are disgusted: "Those eyebrows of hers, like hairy caterpillars, aren't they; and her teeth—like peeled caterpillars."[17] Men also used cosmetics and were equally concerned with their personal dress and appearance.

Heian Decline

Heian culture was perhaps too removed from real life to survive. Only a tiny fraction of Japan's population could afford to enjoy this hedonistic way of life. The common people outside Kyoto lived vastly different lives, usually working at bare subsistence levels as farmers and craftsmen. They were mostly illiterate and saddled by unremitting work, and most knew nothing of Heian court life or Chinese literature. Heian aristocrats called the provinces "uncivilized, barbarous, wretched" places.[18] The late Heian literature shows a growing pessimism as the Kyoto elite became aware that their world of aesthetic perfection might soon vanish. Such indeed was the case. Social and economic changes were clearing the path for a more decentralized system as powerful regional families gained considerable wealth and began building up their own warrior bands, based on kinship and vassal ties to their lord, to keep the peace. By the twelfth century the Heian era had ended and Japan had moved into a new phase of its history with a much different social system.

The Warrior Class and a New Japanese Society

The Heian aristocracy served as a transmitter of the now fully assimilated residue of Chinese culture to another vigorous group, the provincial warrior class, in whose hands the future of Japan was to lie. This warrior class gradually became the dominant force in Japanese politics

LADY MURASAKI, HEIAN NOVELIST

Women produced much of the best Heian literature. The greatest of the books was *The Tale of Genji*, the world's first psychological novel, written by a lady-in-waiting, Lady Murasaki (Murasaki Shibiku), beginning around 1008. Murasaki worked as the maid to Empress Akiko, who was a consort of the emperor and the daughter of a political leader. We know only a little of Murasaki's life, much of it from a diary she kept. She was born around 978 into a leading aristocratic family steeped in literature. Her grandfather was a famed poet and her father a provincial governor. Her father apparently lamented that she had not been a boy and allowed her to study. Murasaki's writing showed that she was familiar with Chinese history, literature, and poetry and had a considerable education. Indeed, she criticized young people who expected good jobs without undergoing the appropriate training.

Perhaps because she avidly pursued learning, she was married late, at age twenty, but her much older husband died only a few years later from illness. She had at least two children, including a daughter who later became a well-known writer. Murasaki is believed to have died sometime between 1025 and 1031, perhaps after several years as a Buddhist nun. Her self-description in her diary suggests an introverted woman:

Pretty yet shy, unsociable, fond of old tales, conceited, so wrapped up in poetry that other people hardly exist, spitefully looking down on the whole world—such is the unpleasant opinion that people have of me. Yet when they come to know me they say that I am strangely gentle, quite unlike what they had been led to believe.

Murasaki's novel, *The Tale of Genji*, is much more sophisticated in language and thoughtful in sensibility than the literature that came before in Japan. In *Genji* she made contemporary language rather than the formal Chinese writing style a medium for art. Even today words and phrases from *Genji* are common in Japanese language. She also had other goals, claiming that the novel should always have "a definite and serious purpose." In focusing on the emotional and psychological interplay of her characters, her writing betrays a strongly feminine perspective. *Genji* also constitutes a treasure trove on social history, revealing much about the times.

The engaging *Genji* story chronicles the life and amorous adventures of Prince Genji, the son of an emperor and a model for all the qualities of taste and refinement admired by the Kyoto aristocracy. Genji is an accomplished poet, painter, dancer, musician, and athlete. But his supreme gift is the art most prized: "pillowing" (lovemaking). Genji and his friends devote little time to their government jobs. They spend their days largely in the search for pleasure, attend countless ceremonial functions, recite poetry endlessly, and move from one romantic affair to another. The mood of the novel is subdued melancholy and nostalgia for the passing of lovely things. Both

Lady Murasaki This eighteenth-century painting of Lady Murasaki writing while observing the moon reflected the styles of the artist's times but also suggests the continuing significance of the beloved Heian era writer.

men and women freely express their emotions. Hence, Genji shows a keen sensitivity to nature: "I hope that I shall have a little time left for things which I really enjoy—flowers, autumn leaves, the sky, all those day-to-day changes and wonders that a single year brings forth; that is what I look forward to." The novel ends with Genji making plans to give up his posts and retire to a mountain village, perhaps to continue with his poetry, music, and painting while focusing more on religious knowledge.

THINKING ABOUT THE PROFILE

1. What sort of background did Murasaki come from?
2. Why is *Genji* such an important work of literature?

Notes: Quotations from Ivan Morris, *The World of the Shining Prince* (New York: Kodansha, 1994), 251; Ryusaku Tsunoda et al., eds., *Sources of Japanese Tradition*, vol. 2 (New York: Columbia University Press, 1958), 178–179; and Mikiso Hane, *Japan: A Historical Survey* (New York: Charles Scribner's, 1972), 56.

Rural Society

and society, helping to produce a very different Japanese government and culture. Rural society was changing. Powerful, land-hungry families and Buddhist communities were often able to seize land by force. By gaining tax exemptions, they increased the tax load on peasants, some of whom fled to the north or joined roving bands of unattached ronin. Other peasants signed over themselves and their lands to lords of manors, at the cost of becoming bound to the land and supplying food in exchange for protection. Thus the Heian era estates were replaced by a system in which a lord ruled over the villages on his parcel of land. By the end of the twelfth century, tax-paying land amounted to 10 percent or less of the total cultivated area, and local power had been taken over by the new rural aristocracy. Soldiers and ronin signed on as military retainers to aristocratic families headed by mounted warriors. Since conscription had ended earlier, imperial forces were weak, and political and military power dispersed to rural areas. Periodic fighting resulted in part from overpopulation: too many people competing for control of too little good land.

Warrior Society

This warrior class led Japan into a type of social and political organization more like that of Zhou China or medieval Europe than the centralized Tang state. Historians disagree as to when between the twelfth and fourteenth centuries the transition to a new Age of Warriors was completed, but it continued in some form to the nineteenth. During this time, military, political, and economic power all became defined in terms of rights to land and relations between lords and vassals. Despite many similarities between post-Heian Japan and medieval Europe, the Japanese rulers were at times stronger than most European kings.

samurai ("one who serves") A member of the Japanese warrior class, which gained power between the twelfth and fourteenth centuries and continued until the nineteenth.

Bushido ("Way of the Warrior") An idealized ethic for the Japanese samurai.

The warrior class, or **samurai** (SAH-moo-rie) ("one who serves"), who gradually assumed military supremacy over the emperor and the court, resulted from a relationship formed between the rural lords and their military retainers, based on an idealized feudal ethic later known as **Bushido** (boo-SHEE-doh) ("way of the warrior"), which was not completely developed until the seventeenth century. The samurai had two great ideals: loyalty to leaders, and absolute indifference to all physical hardship. They enjoyed special legal and ceremonial rights and in return were expected to give unquestioning service to their lords. Although only a few women of the samurai class engaged in combat, most received some martial arts training. Their main job was to run and defend the family estates.

Although the samurai occupied the highest level of the social system, they were a small percentage of the population. If a samurai failed to do his duty or achieve his purpose, suicide was a purposeful and honorable act that served as conclusive evidence that here was a man who could be respected by friend and enemy alike for his physical courage, determination, and sincerity. Homosexuality was also common among the samurai, as among several other warrior castes in history, such as the Spartans in classical Greece, perhaps because of male bonding and an ethic extolling male values. However, Japanese society generally tolerated same-sex relationships. Such unique cultural patterns as Zen Buddhism and the tea ceremony also rose to prominence among the samurai class.

The Shogunates and Economic Change

Kamakura Shogunate

By the twelfth century Japan was controlled by competing bands of feudal lords, and a civil war broke out between two powerful families and their respective allies. One lord, Minamoto-no-Yoritomo (MIN-a-MO-to-no-YOR-ee-TO-mo), emerged victorious and set up a military government in Kamakura (kah-mah-KOO-rah), near Tokyo (TOE-kee-oh), which lasted from 1180 to 1333. The emperor commissioned him **shogun** (SHOW-guhn) ("barbarian-subduing generalissimo"), in effect a military dictator controlling the country in the name of the emperor, who remained in seclusion in Kyoto. The shogun was responsible for internal and external defense of the realm, and he also had the right to nominate his own successor. No shogun seriously attempted to abolish the imperial house, which had become politically impotent but symbolized the people and the land. The Kamakura shoguns, nominally subordinate to the emperors, had real power, but before 1600 the system was not very centralized.

shogun ("barbarian-subduing generalissimo") A Japanese military dictator controlling the country in the name of the emperor.

During the Kamakura Shogunate the Mongols failed twice, in 1274 and 1281, to invade Japan. The 1281 Mongol attempt involved up to 150,000 men transported by over 4,000 conscripted Chinese ships, some armed with ceramic projectile bombs, the world's first known seagoing exploding projectiles. On both occasions, the Mongol armies landed, met fierce resistance, and were destroyed when great storms scattered and shipwrecked their fleets. These divine winds, or *kamikaze* (KAHM-i-KAHZ-ee), convinced the Japanese of special protection by the gods, and any inferiority complex toward China ended. Japan was not successfully invaded and defeated until 1945.

In 1333 the Kamakura Shogunate dissolved through intrigues and civil wars and was replaced by a government headed by the Kyoto-based Ashikaga (ah-shee-KAH-gah) family (1338–1568). But the Ashikaga shoguns never had much real power beyond the capital. Political power became increasingly decentralized as local lords struggled to obtain more land, leading to the rise of several hundred landowning territorial magnates called **daimyo** (DIE-MYO) ("great name"). Each daimyo monopolized local power, had his supporting samurai, and derived income from the peasants working on his land.

Between 1200 and 1500 Japan experienced rapid change in both economic and political spheres. Agriculture became more productive, and an increasingly active merchant class lived in the fast-growing towns. The Japanese developed a new interest in foreign trade, and Japanese sailors and merchants traveled to China and Southeast Asia. The rigid political and social system strained to accommodate these new energies. In the next century civil war and the arrival of European merchants and Christian missionaries aggravated these problems and resulted in a dramatic modification of the political system.

Japanese Society, Religion, and Culture

The new Japanese society and culture, shaped by the warrior class, reflected an even more rigid structure than before. Inequality started in the family, headed by a patriarchal male: children owed obedience to their parents, and the young honored the old. Women now commonly moved into their husband's household and were expected to be dutiful, obedient, and loyal to their menfolk. Marriages were arranged for the interest of the family, not from romantic love. While women lost some freedom, marriage became more durable and divorce more difficult, giving married women more security. Aristocratic women dominated the imperial court staff and ran the emperor's household. As in China, the interest of the group always took precedence over that of the individual.

Many Buddhist sects emerged, but three became the most significant. The largest, the *Pure Land,* emphasized prayer and faith for salvation, stressed the equality of all believers, and was very popular among the lower classes. It also rejected the notion of reincarnation, maintaining that believers went straight to nirvana. The *Nicheren* (NEE-chee-ren) sect has sometimes been compared to Christianity and Islam because of its militant proselytizing and concern for the afterlife. Whereas most Japanese Buddhist sects were peaceful and tolerant, Nicheren was angry, seeing rival views as heresy. The third major Buddhist sect, **Zen**, which originated in China under Daoist influence, emphasized meditation, individual practice and discipline, self-control, self-understanding, and intuition. Knowledge came from seeking deep into the mind, rather than from outside assistance. One Zen pioneer wrote, "Great is mind. Heaven's height is immeasurable but Mind goes beyond heaven; the earth's depth is unfathomable, but Mind reaches below the earth. Mind travels outside the macrocosm."[19] Zen practitioners expected enlightenment to come in a flash of understanding. The Zen culture was devised over the centuries to bring people in touch with their nonverbal, nonrational side. It stressed simplicity and restraint, contending that "great mastery is as if unskillful."[20]

Religious perspectives affected the arts. Zen values permeate Japanese rock gardens, landscape gardening, and flower arrangements. Gardens, ponds, and buildings, such as the beautiful Golden Pavilion of Kyoto, built in the thirteenth century, were all constructed in harmony with their natural surroundings. The tea ceremony emphasized patience, restraint, serenity, and the beauty of simple action involving the commonplace, that is, preparing and drinking tea. The highly formalized ceremony could last two hours, suggesting withdrawal from the real world. Japanese ceramics and pottery later became famous throughout the world for their subtlety and understated beauty. Potters made cups, bowls, and vases using rough textures and irregular lines to suggest weathering and the effects of time, a Japanese preoccupation. Japanese painting was also an old art and emphasized not creativity or self-expression but skill and technique through self-discipline. The **Noh** drama, plays that presented stylized gestures and spectacular masks, also appeared in this era.

Ashikaga Shogunate

daimyo ("great name") Large landowning territorial magnates who monopolized local power in Japan beginning during the Ashikaga period (1338–1568).

Japanese Buddhism

Zen A form of Japanese Buddhism called the meditation sect because it emphasizes individual practice and discipline, self-control, self-understanding, and intuition.

Japanese Arts

Noh Japanese plays that use stylized gestures and spectacular masks; began in the fourteenth century.

SECTION SUMMARY

- The Korean state of Silla was subordinate to China and borrowed a great deal from China's culture, adapting it to Korean traditions.

- The Koryo state was dominated by the aristocracy and saw the decline of Buddhist influence.

- The Yi, who ruled Korea after the Mongols, sought good relations with China and instituted the Chinese educational and civil service exam system.

- In the Nara period, Japan borrowed heavily from Chinese culture, but its government was a dyarchy in which one powerful family dominated the emperor, and imports such as Buddhism were melded with native cultural features such as Shinto.

- In the Heian period, borrowing from China ended, foreign contacts were stopped, and a small elite group, concerned almost exclusively with the pursuit of aesthetic beauty, created some of Japan's best art and literature.

- Affluent women in the Heian period had great sexual freedom and the time to learn to write.

- In Japan, the warrior class, or samurai, gradually attained supremacy over the emperor and the court, and an organization like that of medieval Europe, based on lords and vassals, became dominant.

- The Kamakura Shogunate began after the winner of a Japanese civil war was given the title of shogun, or military dictator, who ruled while the emperor retreated behind the scenes.

- The Ashikaga Shogunate, which followed the Kamakura, had little power over the provinces, which became ruled by landowning lords called daimyo.

- Three enduring Buddhist sects developed in Japan: Pure Land, which stressed equality; Nicheren, which was militant; and Zen, which stressed meditation, discipline, and simplicity, qualities that are shown in such Japanese arts as gardening, flower arranging, and the tea ceremony.

CHAPTER SUMMARY

The Intermediate Era was in many respects a golden age for much of East Asia. The Tang and Song dynasties represented perhaps the high point of Chinese history and culture. While the Tang enjoyed great external power, the Song featured dramatic commercial growth. The Chinese continued to develop distinctive forms of literature, visual arts, philosophy, and government, as well as new technologies and scientific understandings. The Mongol conquest and brief period of rule weakened China's dynamism but extended overland trade routes that linked China even more closely to the outside world and promoted the spread of Chinese science and technology to western Eurasia. During the Ming, China briefly reasserted its transregional power and maintained an advanced technology. But, in part because of the experience of Mongol rule, Ming China also increasingly turned inward, becoming less involved in world affairs.

The Koreans and Japanese synthesized Chinese learning, writing, Confucianism, and Buddhism with their own native traditions to produce highly distinctive societies. Significant change occurred in Japan as it moved from the aristocratic court culture of Heian to a warrior-dominated culture based on large landowning families and their military retainers, or samurai. By the end of the 1400s the East Asian societies remained strong but faced new challenges when Europeans began to expand their power in the world.

KEY TERMS

neo-Confucianism	dyarchy	Bushido	Zen
qi	kana	shogun	Noh
kotow	samurai	daimyo	

EBOOK AND WEBSITE RESOURCES

e PRIMARY SOURCE
The Craft of Farming

e INTERACTIVE MAPS
Map 11.1 The Tang Empire, ca. 700 ᴇ
Map 11.2 China in the Mongol Empire
Map 11.3 The Voyages of Zheng He
Map 11.4 Korea and Japan, ca. 1300

LINKS

Ancient Japan (http://www.wsu.edu/~dee/ANCJAPAN/ANCJAPAN-HTM). A useful site from Washington State University offering many essays and links on premodern Japan.

A Visual Sourcebook of Chinese Civilization (http://depts.washington.edu/chinaciv/). A wonderful collection of essays, illustrations, and other useful material on Chinese history.

East and Southeast Asia: An Annotated Directory of Internet Resources (http://newton.uor.edu/Departments&Programs/AsianStudiesDept/index.html). Varied collection of links, maintained at University of Redlands.

Internet East Asian History Sourcebook (http://www.fordham.edu/halsall/eastasia/eastasiasbook.html). An invaluable collection of sources and links on China, Japan, and Korea from ancient to modern times.

Internet Guide for China Studies (http://www.sino.uni-heidelberg.de/igcs/). A good collection of links on premodern and modern China, maintained at Germany's Heidelberg University.

Silk Road Narratives (http://depts.washington.edu/uwch/silkroad/texts/texts.html). Explores cultural interaction in Eurasia through excerpts from Silk Road travelers.

Plus flashcards, practice quizzes, and more. Go to: www.cengage.com/history/lockard/globalsocnet2e

SUGGESTED READING

Adshead, S. A. M. *China in World History*, 3rd ed. New York: St. Martin's, 2000. A study of China's relations with the world during this era.

Adshead, S. A. M. *T'ang China: The Rise of the East in World History.* New York: Palgrave Macmillan, 2004. A provocative examination of the rise and decline of China.

Benn, Charles. *China's Golden Age: Everyday Life in the Tang Dynasty.* New York: Oxford University Press, 2002. A comprehensive look at the society, economy, and culture of Tang China.

Cohen, Warren. *East Asia at the Center: Four Thousand Years of Engagement with the World.* New York: Columbia University Press, 2000. A good summary of China, Korea, and Japan in Eurasian history.

Ebrey, Patricia Buckley, Anne Walthall, and James B. Palais. *East Asia: A Cultural, Social, and Political History* 2nd ed. Boston: Houghton Mifflin, 2009. A readable, comprehensive survey, especially strong on the Intermediate Era.

Ebrey, Patricia Buckley. *The Inner Quarters: Marriage and the Lives of Chinese Women in the Sung Period.* Berkeley: University of California Press, 1993. A fascinating study of this neglected topic.

Gernet, Jacques. *Daily Life in China on the Eve of the Mongol Invasion 1250–1276.* Stanford: Stanford University Press, 1962. Dated but still a fascinating study of Song life.

Kuhn, Dieter. *The Age of Confucian Rule: The Song Transformation of China.* Cambridge: Harvard University Press, 2009. In-depth study of the Song era and society.

Lane, George. *Genghis Khan and Mongol Rule.* Indianapolis: Hackett, 2004. Good introduction with much on China.

Levathes, Louise. *When China Ruled the Seas: The Treasure Fleet of the Dragon Throne, 1405–33.* New York: Simon and Schuster, 1994. A recent study of the Ming voyages for the general reader.

Merson, John. *The Genius That Was China: East and West in the Making of the Modern World.* Woodstock, NY: Overlook Press, 1990. Lavishly illustrated with good coverage of Song and Ming China.

Morris, Ivan. *The World of the Shining Prince: Court Life in Ancient Japan.* New York: Kodansha International, 1994. A reprint of the classic 1964 study of Heian society and culture.

Rossabi, Morris. *Kublai Khan: His Life and Times.* Berkeley: University of California Press, 1987. A study of China under Mongol rule.

Seth, Michael J. *A Concise History of Korea from the Neolithic Times to the Nineteenth Century.* Lanham, MD: Rowman and Littlefield, 2006. Knowledgeable study of Korea and the larger East Asian context.

Shaughnessy, Edward, ed. *China: Empire and Civilization.* New York: Oxford University Press, 2005. Contains essays on many aspects of Chinese society in this era.

Souyri, Pierre F. *The World Turned Upside Down: Medieval Japanese Society,* translated by Kathe Roth. New York: Columbia University Press, 2001. A major scholarly study of later Intermediate Japan and warrior society.

Turnbull, Stephen. *Samurai: The World of the Warrior.* New York: Osprey, 2003. Well-written examination of samurai life.

Varley, Paul. *Japanese Culture,* 2nd ed. updated and expanded. Honolulu: University of Hawai'i Press, 2000. A good overview.

EXPANDING HORIZONS IN AFRICA AND THE AMERICAS, 600–1500

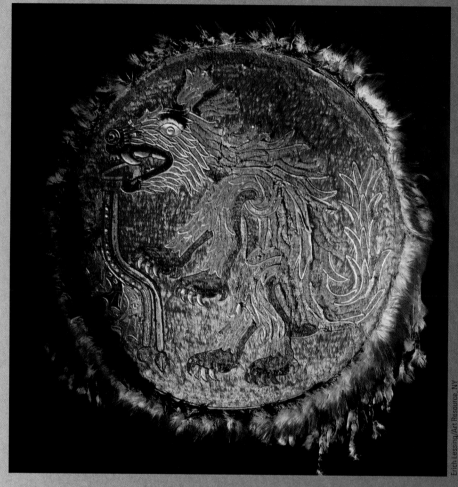

Erich Lessing/Art Resource, NY

Feathered Shield
This brightly colored feathered mosaic shield, used for ceremonial purposes by an Aztec warrior in the fifteenth century, has an image of the Aztec water god, a monster that resembled a coyote, outlined in gold.

Along time ago, when the Arabs arrived in Lamu [a port in today's Kenya, East Africa], they found local people there. The Arabs were received with friendliness and they wanted to stay on. The local people offered to trade land for cloths. Before the trading was finished, the Arabs had the land, and the [local people] had the cloth.

—A LAMU ORAL TRADITION[1]

FOCUS QUESTIONS

1. **How did contact with Islamic peoples help shape the societies of West and East Africa?**

2. **What were some distinctive patterns of government, society, thought, and economy in Intermediate Africa?**

3. **What factors explain the collapse of the early Intermediate Era American societies?**

4. **How were the Aztec and Inca Empires different, and how were they similar?**

Around 912 the Baghdad-born Arab geographer Abdul Hassan Ibn Ali al-Mas'udi sailed to East Africa with mariners from Oman, in eastern Arabia, on their regular trading expedition to what Arabs described as *Zanj* ("the land of black people"). The journey up and down the East African coast could be perilous, with reefs and strong winds that generated high waves. Al-Mas'udi spent three years visiting ports as far south as Sofala (so-FALL-a), a city in Mozambique (moe-zam-BEEK). After further travels to Persia, India, and China, al-Mas'udi finally settled in Cairo, where he wrote several scholarly books. The most influential, titled *Meadows of Gold and Mines of Gems*, described East African society in a key period of state formation while also recording the many links between these coastal towns, the Arabs, and other Eurasian societies. Al-Mas'udi praised the energetic traders and skilled workers of the coast, reported that the Sofala region produced abundant gold for export, and described how Arabs carried ivory from Zanj to Oman, from where they shipped it to India and China. He wrote that "in China the Kings and military and civil officers use ivory [to decorate furniture]. In India ivory is much sought after. It is used for the handles of daggers. But the chief use of ivory is making chessmen and backgammon pieces."[2]

During the Intermediate Era many societies in East Asia, Southeast Asia, South Asia, West Asia, North Africa, and Europe benefited from extensive links by which they exchanged technologies, products, religions, and ideas. As al-Mas'udi's description confirms, some sub-Saharan Africans also became connected to this vast network as trade expanded. African peoples like the gold producers near Sofala became integral parts of hemispheric commerce. But many sub-Saharan Africans had only indirect links, and the American societies across the Atlantic Ocean had no known links at all, to these busy Afro-Eurasian networks of exchange; thus they had to independently address the challenges they faced. Despite lack of contact with each other, Africans and Americans also shared some patterns of social and political development, some thriving in forbidding desert, forest, or highland environments. States rose and fell, among them a few regional empires. However, in contrast to the more densely populated areas of Eurasia, many Africans and Americans lived in self-governing villages rather than large, centralized governments. In the Western Hemisphere, trade routes existed over wide areas, but geography inhibited the growth of long-distance networks such as those linking East Africa to China. Only after 1492 did maritime exploration permanently connect African, American, and Eurasian peoples.

e Visit the website and eBook for additional study materials and interactive tools:
www.cengage.com/history/lockard/globalsocnet2e

Diverse African States and Peoples

How did contact with Islamic peoples help shape the societies of West and East Africa?

After 600, several important kingdoms arose in the Sudanic region and along the Guinea coast. As in Eurasia, empires sprouted, flourished, and decayed. Scholars studied and disputed in centers of learning, and what Chinese artists accomplished with ink and Europeans with paint, African artists achieved with bronze and wood. The rise of great Sudanic kingdoms coincided with the expansion of Islam and a global commerce that linked West Africa with North Africa, the Mediterranean Basin, and western Asia. Meanwhile, the expansion of Bantu-speakers continued as the Bantus settled the vast expanses of central, eastern, and southern Africa, some building great kingdoms. The East African coast became a flourishing mercantile region closely linked to Eurasia, allowing Islam to spread into the area. Like the Sudanic kingdoms and most Eurasian societies, some Bantu peoples built cities, kept records, engaged in extensive trade, and boasted diverse social classes.

Trade, State Building, and the Expansion of Islam in the Sudan

For hundreds of years camel caravans had plied the trackless Sahara sands, where dry conditions, towering sand dunes, and searing sun conspired against crops, grasses, and trees. The caravans transported gold, salt, ivory, slaves, and ceramics between West and North Africa. The people benefiting the most lived in the Sudan, the largely grasslands region just south of the Sahara. Because its generally flat geography and the long but sluggish Niger River allowed for easy communication, the Sudan became a meeting place of people and ideas.

Islam in the Sudan

Beginning in the 800s Islam filtered down the Saharan trade routes, carried peacefully by merchants, teachers, and mystics in much the same way it arrived in the islands of Southeast Asia (see Chapter 13). As Muslim merchants settled in Sudanic towns, they helped form stable governments to protect the trade. Many political and economic leaders, and eventually most Sudanic peoples, embraced Islam. Islamic influence produced changes in customs, names, dress, diet, architecture, and festivals, and Islamic schools spread literacy in the Arabic language. The Sudanic religious atmosphere promoted tolerance, by Muslims toward animists and vice versa. Still, Islamic practice was often superficial, and it took several centuries for the religion to permeate into the villages.

A few kingdoms already existed by the time that Islam reached the Sudan. The kings in these animist societies were considered divine, remaining aloof from the common people and ruled through bureaucracies. But many kings had to consult a council of elders, who frequently had to approve a decision to go to war, and some kings were elected by elders or chiefs. The women of the royal families also had great power, and, in a few societies, they could rule as queens. Some kingdoms became empires. States had no fixed territorial boundaries, only fluctuating spheres of influence, and they often included diverse ethnic groups, making them inherently unstable.

The earliest known Sudanic kingdom was Ghana, centered on the northwestern Niger River (see Map 12.1). Founded by Mande speakers of the Soninke (soh-NIN-kay) ethnic group, Ghana was probably established around 500 C.E. (see Chapter 9) but reached its golden age in the ninth and tenth centuries (see Chronology: Africa in the Intermediate Era), prospering from its control of the trans-Saharan gold trade. Of Ghana and its profitable commerce, the Spanish Muslim traveler Abu Hamid al-Andalusi wrote: "In the sands of that country is gold, treasure immeasurable. Merchants trade salt for it, taking the salt on camels from the salt mines. They travel on the desert as if it were a sea, having guides to pilot them by the stars or rocks."[3] Many of the 20,000 inhabitants of Ghana's capital, Koumbi, were immigrants, including Arab and Berber merchants. Ghana's rulers converted to Islam, increasing the wealth and splendor of the royal court. An Arab visitor wrote that the king's attendants had gold-plaited hair and carried gold-mounted swords, and that even the guard dogs wore collars of gold and silver. But a civil war erupted, and Berbers from North Africa attacked and destroyed the kingdom in 1203.

CHRONOLOGY

Africa in the Intermediate Era

ca. 500–1203 Kingdom of Ghana

1000–1200 Rise of Hausa city-states

ca. 1200–1450 Zimbabwe kingdom

1200–1500 Golden age of East African coastal cities

1220–1897 Kingdom of Benin

1234–1550 Mali Empire

ca. 1275 Rise of Yoruba kingdom of Oyo

1324–1325 Mansa Musa's pilgrimage to Mecca

ca. 1375 Rise of Kongo kingdom

1464–1591 Songhai Empire

1487 Bartolomeu Dias rounds Cape of Good Hope

CHRONOLOGY

	Africa	The Americas
700	**ca. 500–1203** Ghana	**700–1400** Anasazi
		800–1475 Chimu Empire
		900–1168 Toltec Empire
1000	**ca. 1000–1450** Zimbabwe	
1200	**1220–1897** Benin	
	1234–1550 Mali Empire	
1400	**1464–1591** Songhai Empire	**1428–1521** Aztec Empire
		1440–1532 Inca Empire

Mali and Songhai: Islam and Regional Power

The greatest Sudanic empire, Mali (MAHL-ee), was formed in 1234 by another Mande-speaking group, the Malinke (muh-LING-kay), led by the Keita (KAY-ee-tah) clan, whose leader, Sundiata (soon-JAH-tuh), became the **mansa** (MAHN-suh), or king, of Mali (see Profile: Sundiata, Imperial Founder). Farmers and traders, the Malinke conquered much of the western Sudan, including the territory once controlled by Ghana. The empire's total area stretched some 1,500 miles from east to west and incorporated dozens of ethnic groups. The Malinke mansa was both a secular and religious leader who surrounded himself with displays of wealth and ceremonial regalia and expected his subjects to approach him on their knees, instilling respect and obedience in his people. Sundiata apparently converted to Islam, perhaps to secure better relations with North Africa, but he never seriously practiced the religion and also made use of Malinke animism and magic.

Islamic influence gradually grew stronger, expanding communication and travel. Some later Mali emperors made glittering pilgrimages to Mecca. When Sundiata's descendant, Mansa Musa (MAN-sa MOO-sa) (r. 1312–1337), went to Mecca in 1324 riding a white Arab horse, he took fifty slaves bearing golden staffs, one thousand followers, and one hundred camels, each loaded with 300 pounds of gold. According to an Arab official writing of Mansa Musa's visit to Egypt en route to Arabia, he "spread upon Cairo the flood of his generosity; there was no person or holder of any office who did not receive a sum of gold from him. The people of Cairo earned incalculable sums from him, whether by selling or gifts."[4] An Arab observer credited Mansa Musa with building grand mosques in Mali and importing Islamic jurists. But the majority of Mali's people remained animist, and even the elite were lax in their Islamic practice.

Most Malians lived in small villages and cultivated rice, sorghum, or millet, supplemented by herding or fishing. Mali also supplied most of Europe's gold reserves and about two-thirds of the world's gold supply in this era. Local Africans mined the gold in open pits or in underground passages while women extracted the gold dust from the dirt dug out by the men. Gold traders then met salt merchants from the north and silently matched piles of gold and salt until a fair exchange was agreed upon. Imports came to Mali from as far away as China and India, and the Mali trading city of Timbuktu (tim-buk-TOO) emerged as the major southern terminus of the trans-Saharan caravan trade. The international links provided by Islam and the trans-Saharan commerce enticed many visitors and sojourners to Mali, including poets, architects, teachers, and traders from places such as Spain and Egypt, and at least one Italian merchant reached Timbuktu. The fourteenth-century Moroccan traveler Ibn Battuta spent months in Mali, whose many "admirable qualities" he admired, commenting that "they are seldom unjust, and have a greater abhorrence of injustice than any other people." He also found that "neither traveler nor inhabitant in it has anything to fear from robbers or men of violence."[5] But the pious Muslim frowned on what he considered the immodest dress and independent behavior of women and the custom of eating dogs.

Mali rapidly declined in the 1400s because of internal factionalism and raids by other peoples. Soon the fringes broke away, and by 1550 the Mali of former days was gone, replaced as the dominant Sudanic empire by Songhai (song-GAH-ee), a kingdom formed by several ethnic groups. By 1464 Songhai's empire was as large as the former Mali Empire. Some of the Songhai rulers were

Islam in Mali

mansa ("king") Mande term used by the Malinke people to refer to the ruler of the Mali Empire.

Malian Society

Rise of Songhai

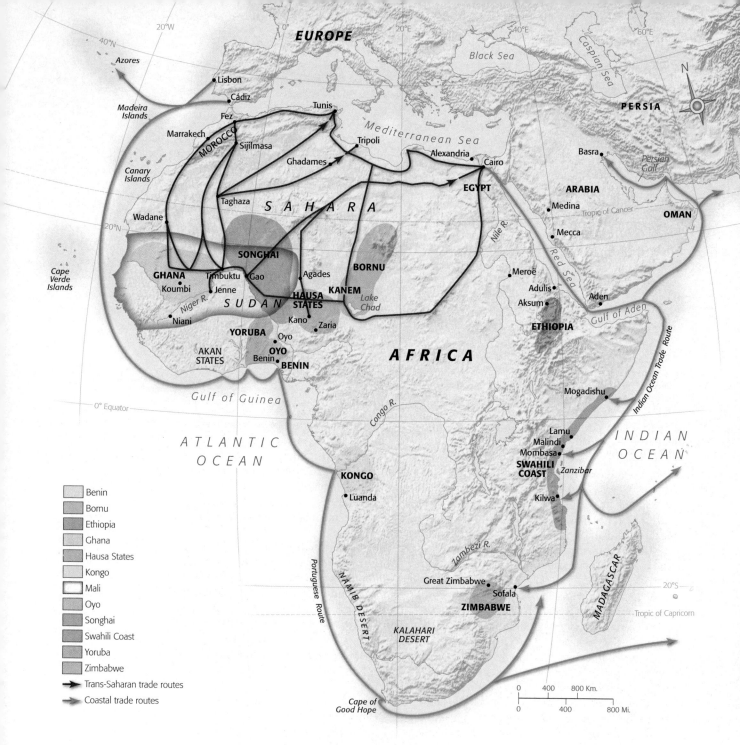

Map 12.1 Major Sub-Saharan African Kingdoms and States, 1200–1600 C.E.
Many large kingdoms and states emerged in Intermediate Africa. Large empires
dominated the Sudan in West Africa, while prosperous trading cities sharing a Swahili
culture dotted the east coast.

e **Interactive Map**

nominal Muslims, and others were devout. The most revered leader was Aksia (ACK-see-a) the
Great (1483–1528), a humane, pious, and tolerant man who was devoted to learning. The imperial
capital at Gao (ghow) on the Niger River was a substantial city containing perhaps 100,000 people.
As demand for gold and slaves increased in both North Africa and Europe, Songhai flourished from
the trans-Saharan caravan trade. Slaves were obtained from nearby peoples and sold in the Gao
slave market, and many were taken on the arduous journey across the Sahara to the Mediterranean
societies. In exchange for gold and slaves, Songhai received glass, copperware, cloth, perfumes,
and horses.

Under Songhai rule, Timbuktu flourished, becoming a major intellectual center with a famous
Islamic university that specialized in teaching astronomy, astrology, medicine, history, geography,

Arabic, and Quranic studies. The thousands of scholars and students in the city patronized bookstores and libraries containing thousands of books, many in African languages using Arabic script. In recent years over 30,000 lost books, hundreds of years old, on many subjects have been found underneath Timbuktu's mud houses and in nearby desert caves. One North African, on visiting Timbuktu, noted many shops and abundant food and described the people as "of a gentle and cheerful disposition, and spend a great part of the night in singing and dancing through all the streets of the city."[6] Songhai flourished until 1591, when Moroccans destroyed its military power.

The Central Sudan and Guinea Coast

After 1000 another dynamic Sudanic society developed farther east, in northern Nigeria, eastern Niger, and southern Chad, where the Hausa (HOUSE-uh) people erected fiercely competitive city-states, ruled by kings, that came to dominate some of the trans-Saharan trade. The prosperity of these city-states attracted many non-Hausa immigrants, including Arabs and Berbers, and Hausa society became increasingly Islamic. Hausa cities such as Kano (KAHN-oh) were centers for manufacturing cotton cloth and leatherwork, some of which was sold as far away as Europe. The Hausa were also farmers, famed craftspeople, and skilled traders, whose pursuit of wealth ranged all over West Africa. Today the Hausa language, which mixed Arab, Berber, and West African influences, remains the major trading language of the central Sudan and the most widely spoken sub-Saharan African language.

Hausa States

Like many Sudanic peoples, the Hausa possessed a strong class system, headed by royal families and the aristocracy. Islamic intellectuals, such as teachers, and wealthy merchants were influential. Hausa women enjoyed a high status compared with women in many African societies. In the fifteenth century a queen, Amina, ruled one of the major Hausa states, Zaria (zah-REE-uh). An oral poem praised her as "like the moon at its full, like the morning star. She is a lion as precious as gold among all women."[7]

Hausa Houses in Kano   Hausa towns and cities feature houses with large courtyards behind high walls. Structural beams made from local palm trees protrude from the walls.

Werner Forman/Art Resource, NY

SUNDIATA, IMPERIAL FOUNDER

According to tradition, the founder of the great Mali Empire was Sundiata Keita, the "Lion Prince" of the Malinke people. It is difficult to separate myth from fact about his life, but most historians believe there was a real Sundiata. Arab historians such as Ibn Khaldun mention him in their accounts. Nonetheless, any account must use oral epics, which tend to glorify his heroism and reflect a Malinke view of a glorious past.

At the time Sundiata was born in the early thirteenth century, Ghana was collapsing and various other groups were contending to fill the power vacuum. Sundiata was one of twelve sons of a Malinke king, Nare Fa Maghan, and Sogolon Conde, a hunchback. As a child Sundiata was sickly and had stiff legs that made walking difficult. Hence he was spared when a rival state, Kaniaga, under their brutal king, Sumaguru, conquered Sundiata's town, Niane, and executed all his brothers as potential threats. According to the oral epic:

> He had a slow and difficult childhood. At the age of three he still crawled along on all-fours. He had nothing of the great beauty of his father. He had a head so big that he seemed unable to support it. He was taciturn and used to spend the whole day just sitting in the middle of the house. Malicious tongues began to blab. All Niane talked of nothing but the stiff-legged son.

However, soothsayers predicted greatness for him, and eventually he overcame his physical problems so that "at the age of eighteen he had the stateliness of the lion and the strength of the buffalo."

As a young man he went into exile, and then he returned to rally his people against the tyrannical Sumaguru: "The sun will arise, the sun of Sundiata." Determined and diplomatic, he skillfully used traditional clan and kinship groups as well as a reputation for possessing knowledge of magic to build and solidify his power. Persuading other Malinke chiefs to surrender their titles to him, he became his peoples' sole king, enhancing his position in preparation for war. Sundiata put together a military force and triumphed over Sumaguru in the battle of Kirina about 1235, and then he conquered much of the old Ghana territories.

As king, Sundiata acquired the power to reshape Malinke government and society. According to the epics, "He left his mark on Mali for all time and his [rules] still guide men in their conduct [today]." As ruler for over two decades, Sundiata transformed his small state into the core of an imperial system based in his hometown of Niane, alongside the Niger River and near valuable gold fields. His rule brought peace, happiness, prosperity, and justice: "He protected the weak against the strong. The upright man was rewarded and the wicked one punished." The epic account is undoubtedly an idealized version of truth, but it also recorded that Sundiata punished his enemies. Malinke custom allowed high-status men to have many wives, and Sundiata, like his father, followed this practice, leaving many descendants.

Sundiata died about 1260, but his legend lived on. As the epics retold even today put it:

> Sundiata was unique. In his time no one equaled him and after him no one had the ambition to surpass him. Men of today, how small you are beside your ancestors. Sundiata rests but his spirit lives on and today the Keitas still come and bow before the stone under which lies the father of Mali.

THINKING ABOUT THE PROFILE

1. What does Sundiata's career tell us about the personal qualities admired by the Malinke people and helpful in forging a Sudanic empire?

2. How do the epic stories told over the centuries remember Sundiata and his deeds?

Note: Quotations from D. T. Niane, *Sundiata: An Epic of Old Mali* (London: Longman, 1965), 15, 40, 47, 81, 83–85.

From Ada Konare Ba, *Sunjiata: Le Fondateur L'Empire du Mali* (Dakar: Nouvelles Editions Africaines, 1983)

Sundiata This modern depiction of Sundiata Keita memorializes the legendary founder of the Mali Empire. Even today, nearly a millennium after his death, Sundiata remains a hero to Africans for his political and military skills.

Along the Guinea coast, a region of rain forest and grasslands just south of the Sudan, Sudanic influence and trade fostered the growth of states among societies like the Yoruba (YORE-uh-buh). By about 1000 the Yoruba in western Nigeria had developed several states, each based on a large city ruled by a king or prince. The kings were powerful and considered sacred, but they were influenced by elders and aristocrats. However, no united Yoruba kingdom existed: Yoruba identity was more cultural than political, based on a common language and culture, including complex animistic traditions that are still influential today. One Yoruba kingdom, Oyo (OY-oh), rose rapidly after 1275 to become the most powerful state in the area, flourishing until the late eighteenth century. Many towns dotted Yoruba country, serving as both commercial and political centers and ruled by elaborate bureaucracies. Merchants were respected and closely connected to the north-south trade networks. Since Yoruba women were not expected to work in the fields, many developed wealth and influence as traders. The Yoruba were also famed as artists. For example, the Yoruba at Ife (EE-fay) cast beautiful bronze portraits of their rulers. Since the Yoruba prized submissiveness to superiors and their culture discouraged conflict, crime was rare.

Benin King and Musicians This bronze plaque shows the king, preparing for war, wearing beads and flanked by royal musicians on both sides. Such plaques were hung on palace walls and pillars to glorify the ruler.

Another great Guinea kingdom, Benin (buh-NEEN), situated just east of Yoruba territory, was the state of the Bini (bean-ee) people, who shared some cultural traditions with the Yoruba. Benin emerged around 1220, and under King Ewuare (ee-WAHR-ee) the Great it established a sizable empire in the mid-1400s. Early kings like Ewuare were warriors, but later they became more spiritual leaders, leading secluded lives but subject to influence by powerful local chiefs. Benin artists cast beautiful bronzes and carved ivory to glorify the accomplishments of the king and state. Since Benin was located near the Atlantic coast, it was one of the first African kingdoms to be visited by Europeans in the 1400s, who wrote of the prosperous society they admired.

Benin city was protected by high walls and included an elaborate royal palace, neat houses with verandas (porches), and neighborhoods linked by broad avenues. An elite commercial class traded with the Hausa, Yoruba, and Songhai. Bini merchants dealt in woodcarvings, foodstuffs, ironwork, farm tools, weapons, and later cloth. Because they produced most of the cloth, Bini women also benefited from this trade. The upper classes dressed and dined well, consuming beef, mutton, chicken, and yams, while the poor ate yams, dried fish, beans, and bananas. However, the poor were protected from becoming beggars because an innovative welfare system supported those unable to work. Benin began to decline in 1550 but only collapsed in 1897.

The Bantu Diaspora

Bantu migrations persisted during the Intermediate Era. In eastern Africa the migrating Bantu came into contact with the Nilotic-speakers, who themselves had migrated from North-Central Africa. Bantu and Nilotes (NAI-lots) competed over good grazing land and salt, but they also traded, coexisted, and sometimes mixed together. For example, the Bantu Gikuyu (kee-KOO-yoo), who settled in Kenya, intermarried, traded, and sometimes fought with the Nilotic Masai (mah-SIE) people, who were mainly cattle herders.

Over time the Bantu peoples scattered over forest, savannah, and highlands in the southern half of Africa, developing diverse cultures, languages, political systems, and economic patterns but also maintaining many common traditions. Most Bantu-speakers remained farmers, practicing shifting cultivation where necessary but using more complex methods where possible. Bananas became the staple crop of East Africa. Some Bantu lived in towns, and centralized kingdoms on the Sudanic model appeared, especially in the Great Lakes region. But most kings had religious and ceremonial rather than real political power, and the village usually remained supreme.

East African Commerce and Swahili Culture

The expansion of both Islam and global commerce integrated the East African coastal peoples, including many Bantu, into Dar al-Islam and the wider world. The 1,200 miles of coast stretching from Somalia down to Mozambique was a cultural melting pot, where a growing trade network linking East Africa with the societies around the rim of the Indian Ocean brought in diverse

Indian Ocean Networks

cultures, languages, and religions, fostering a unique hybrid society. Because the prevailing monsoon wind patterns made it relatively easy to sail up and down the coast, the East African coastal peoples had long been in regular contact with seafaring folk from Arabia, Persia, India, and Southeast Asia. Indonesians visited East Africa for centuries, bringing with them bananas, coconuts, and yams, which spread throughout tropical Africa. Some Indonesians also settled on the island of Madagascar. Eventually seafaring Arabs from the Persian Gulf, Oman, and Yemen dominated the coastal trade, seeking ivory, tortoise shell, leopard skin, and later gold and copper.

As trade increased, many city-states developed along the coast, among them Mogadishu (mo-ga-DEE-shoo), Lamu (LAH-moo), Malindi (ma-LIN-dee), Mombasa (mahm-BAHS-uh), Zanzibar (ZAN-zuh-bahr), Kilwa (KILL-wa), and Sofala. Leaders of these states were chiefly interested in trade, not military expansion, and governed only a small hinterland. Settlers came from Arabia, Persia, and India. Each independent city-state was dominated by a royal court, often claiming Persian or Arab ancestry, and powerful trading families. Trade networks into the interior expanded with the discovery of gold in the highlands of Zimbabwe (zim-BOB-way). Because of its access to these gold fields, Sofala at the mouth of the Zambezi (zam-BEE-zee) River became a wealthy city.

City States

The golden age of the coast reached its peak from the twelfth through the fifteenth centuries as Islam became entrenched. Ships from Arabia, Persia, and India regularly visited. One passenger, the Moroccan jurist Ibn Battuta, traveled as far south as Kilwa, a prosperous city on an island off Tanzania, and described it as "one of the most beautiful and well-constructed towns in the world, elegantly built [with] good buildings of stone and mortar, entirely surrounded by a wall and towers."[8] Kilwa, which had perhaps 20,000 people, was a collection hub for goods coming in from north and south. The upper classes built three-story stone houses with indoor plumbing and lavished themselves with large quantities of gold and silver jewelry as well as Chinese silk and porcelain. Ibn Battuta described the Kilwa Muslims as devout, chaste, and virtuous and its rulers, a family claiming Yemenite descent, as humble and pious. Still, he disliked some local customs, such as their preference for a rich diet. He approved of the chicken, meat, fish, vegetables, and mangoes but not the rice cooked with butter and yogurt chutney, which probably had South Asian origins. His reports show that East Africans had become closely linked to the Islamic world by trade and religion but also maintained various local customs.

The East African city-states became an integral part of the greatest maritime trading network of the Intermediate world, a system of ports and trade routes that linked economies around the rim of the Indian Ocean stretching from Indonesia to East Africa. Foreign traders brought pottery, Chinese porcelain, glass beads, and Indian cotton to East Africa and traded them for iron, ivory, tortoise shell, leopard skins, gold, and slaves. The beautiful homes of the coastal cities, some with tropical gardens, fountains, and pools, attested to the wealth that was available to the upper and middle classes.

Swahili Name for a distinctive people, culture, and language, a mix of Bantu, Arab, and Islamic influences, that developed during the Intermediate Era on the East African coast.

Over time, intermarriage and the blending of Bantu, Arab, and Islamic influences in the coastal cities produced a distinctive new African culture and language, **Swahili** (Arab for "people of the coast"). The mixing of the Bantu and Arabic tongues created the new Swahili language, and Arabic script was used to produced poetry, historical legend, and religious speculation, in addition to commercial accounts. Eventually Swahili became the major trading language of the entire coastal region, its influence reaching as far inland as the eastern Congo River Basin. Today Swahili is second only to Hausa as a first or second language in sub-Saharan Africa.

The Swahili favored Arab architectural styles, ideas of inheritance, and dress, including long gowns for men and modest attire for women. Whereas the interior Bantu peoples practiced either patrilineal or matrilineal descent, the Swahili were, like Arabs, firmly patrilineal. However, it took many centuries for Islam to penetrate the hinterland. Islam spread in part because it was a flexible religion, willing to tolerate the incorporation of Bantu beliefs in spirits and ancestor worship. Today Muslims are numerous in all the East African countries, but five hundred years ago Islam was found mostly in the coastal towns.

Zimbabwe and the Kongo

Shona States

The East African trading cities were only a part of the wider Bantu diaspora, which also included various kingdoms in central and southern Africa. On the fertile plateau of south-central Africa one of the greatest kingdoms, Zimbabwe, which means "houses built of stone," emerged and flourished from trade with the coast. Today little remains of the kingdom's monumental buildings except for dozens of impressive stone ruins that dot the landscape for hundreds of miles. The Shona (SHO-nah) people constructed these buildings and a great state between the thirteenth

Visual Connection Archive

The Great Zimbabwe Complex Great stone enclosures, most probably used as royal residences or religious sanctuaries, were built around the Zimbabwe kingdom. This one, surrounded by high walls, was at the center of the kingdom's capital city.

and fifteenth centuries, eventually controlling much of the plateau. The granite buildings had various functions. Some were walls enclosing towns, and others seem to have been courts. In the heart of the capital city, which probably contained 10,000 to 20,000 people, the largest enclosure is an oval space surrounded by a wall 1,800 feet long, 32 feet high, and 17 feet thick that may have housed the royal family or perhaps served as a sanctuary in which the royal family worshiped their patron deity.

Mining was the key to Zimbabwe's prosperity. The Shona had migrated from the southern Congo River Basin, an area of many copper mines. Discovering gold, copper, and iron ore on the plateau, they extracted it from open-pit and occasionally underground mines and traded these minerals down the Zambezi River to the coast. By 1500 some 10,000 Arab and Swahili traders lived along the river, buying and then exporting the gold to the Middle East and India through Sofala and Kilwa. Shona exports corresponded to a rapid growth in the world demand for gold. In exchange Zimbabwe received Indian textiles and Chinese ceramics. Shona artists produced copper, bronze, and gold ornaments. In the 1400s the empire broke up into two rival states, and the capital city was largely abandoned by 1450. Perhaps Zimbabwe was a casualty of overpopulation, soil exhaustion, and overgrazing by cattle. As Zimbabwe declined, the trade routes and then the government may have shifted north to the upper Zambezi River Valley, but the Shona continued to export gold to the coast.

Zimbabwe's Mineral Wealth

Another great Bantu kingdom, Kongo, was established by the Bakongo (bah-KOHNG-goh) people in the 1300s near the Atlantic coast of northern Angola and western Congo. Eventually its population reached 2.5 million. The king's compound, nearly a mile around, was located in the capital city of Mbanga (um-BAHN-ga). Royal musicians bearing drums and ivory trumpets announced visitors and ceremonies. High-status people wore finely woven cloth fabrics, beautifully dyed, which European visitors compared to velvet, silk, and brocade. Although in theory absolute and divine, the king faced some restrictions: he was elected by elders and governors and had to seek advice from a council formed by the heads of the leading clans.

Kongolese Society

Kongo village chiefs settled disputes but referred serious quarrels or crimes to district judges. Villagers lived in houses with walls of palm matting and thatch roofs. Every day women ground millet into a white flour and stirred it in boiling water to make a stiff porridge, which was eaten with peas or beans and spicy sauces made of palm oil. Meat such as chicken, fish, or game, as well as bananas, yams, and pumpkins, provided some variety. Trade flourished, and people used a seashell-based currency to buy salt, colored cloth from India, palm cloth, palm belts, and animal skins.

SECTION SUMMARY

- The area south of the Sahara, known as the Sudan, benefited most from the Sahara caravan trade and gradually embraced Islam.

- In the kingdom of Ghana, which prospered from the trans-Saharan gold trade, councils of elders held the power of kings in check.

- The kingdom of Mali also grew fabulously wealthy because of the caravan trade, but like Ghana, it ultimately declined because of infighting and external threats.

- The Songhai, who split off from Mali, amassed great wealth from the demand for gold and slaves, and Timbuktu became a major center of Islamic learning.

- The Hausa city-states also participated in trade, and their women enjoyed high status.

- South of the Sudan, on the Guinea coast, the Yoruba developed a balance of power between kings and aristocrats and were generally peace-loving traders and artists, and the prosperous kingdom of Benin developed an innovative welfare system.

- The Bantu continued to expand across eastern and southern Africa and established numerous coastal city-states that were greatly influenced by trade with Arabs.

- The East African coast became largely Muslim, though it retained a great deal of its native African culture along with influences from such cultures as Arabia and South Asia.

- The fusion of Bantu, Arab, and Islamic culture yielded a new language, Swahili, and led to the adoption of many Arab practices by East Africans.

- Zimbabwe rose to prosperity as a result of mining and built large granite buildings whose precise use is still debated by historians.

AFRICAN SOCIETIES, THOUGHT, AND ECONOMIES

> What were some distinctive patterns of government, society, thought, and economy in Intermediate Africa?

Societies across Africa shared many common patterns of social organization, religion, culture, and economy. Nonetheless, African societies also varied considerably, depending partly on how closely they were connected to the Islamic world and on whether they had centralized or village-based governments. While intensive agriculture did not develop to the same extent as in Eurasia, trade with the wider world attracted European explorers to the region.

Political and Social Patterns

Stateless Societies

Although the powerful kingdoms such as Mali, Benin, and Zimbabwe governed many Africans, there were also many people who lived in stateless societies, decentralized, village-based political systems featuring self-governing villages where government involved family relationships. A council of elders normally assisted the chief and applied customary law to regulate conduct. Some of these stateless societies were small and some large, but each was unique. The Tiv (tihv) of eastern Nigeria developed an egalitarian society in which legal and economic rights were based on kinship. Their politics can be described as local democracy. Village elders and family heads allocated land, administered justice, and organized community activities, and custom influenced the authority of leaders and the behavior of citizens. Women controlled their own fields and did much of the farm work, but they were aided by men in harvesting and planting. The Gikuyu (kee-KOO-you), Bantu farmers in the temperate, green highlands around Mount Kenya in East Africa, had no local chiefs and mostly lived in individual family homesteads. Each extended family was headed by the senior male, who represented the family to the broader Gikuyu society. Younger Gikuyu men formed a special council that handled military affairs, and village councils elected representatives to district councils of elders. This democratic Gikuyu system relied heavily on group discussion and the power of public opinion.

Social Networks

Whether living in kingdoms or stateless societies, individuals were connected to others through varied social networks. The family formed an economic unit that cooperated in most matters and frequently included all the members of living generations and their spouses and children. Some societies practiced matrilineal kinship, tracing descent and inheritance through the female line. In kingdoms with kings, the queen sister or queen mother was usually a highly respected figure. For example, the Bini people still revere Idia, an early-sixteenth-century queen mother who raised an army and used her magical powers to aid her son in overcoming his enemies. Queen mothers often controlled access to rulers, managed treasuries, presided over court systems, and helped enthrone or depose rulers. Some queens ruled in their own right. However, women's status varied widely. Men dominated most families and often had multiple wives. Since the chief goal of marriage was children, a woman's status depended on her childbearing ability. To win the highest regard meant bearing many children, and women looked to their children rather than their husbands for support in old age.

A web of associations defined socially acceptable behavior. The family was part of a clan or lineage that traced descent to a particular ancestor. People related to other villagers through work or music groups, secret societies, religious cults, and age grades that promoted cooperation between people of the same generation. Most groups prized collective effort and responsibility instead of individual initiative. The *ethnic group,* often mistakenly called the "tribe" by modern observers, included people, not necessarily related by kinship ties, who spoke the same language, practiced similar customs, and lived in the same general territory. Some ethnic groups were quite large. Both the Yoruba and Hausa numbered in the millions and were divided into various states. Distinct cultures, languages, and religions marked off groups such as the Yoruba, Hausa, Shona, and Gikuyu.

Like many societies around the world, some sub-Saharan peoples condoned slavery and engaged in slave trading. Slaves were often war captives or debtors. Ibn Battuta wrote that, in many Sudanic cities, the wealthy "vie with one another in regard to the number of their slaves and serving-women. They never sell the educated female slaves, or but rarely and at a high price."[9] Slaves filled diverse social and economic roles. The Wolof (WOH-lohf) of Senegal assigned slaves to household work; Kongolese slaves were soldiers or plantation workers; the Akan (ah-KAHN) on the Guinea coast employed slave labor for gold mining; and some Hausa slaves were palace advisers and hence enjoyed a high social status. Some slaves were considered members of households, and many could marry and have their children freed. While slave life was often hard, among many African peoples slaves had more rights and could expect better treatment than slaves in most European, Islamic, Asian, and American societies.

African Slavery

Religious and Artistic Traditions

African religion was diverse, including not only Muslim and Christian believers but also many millions who practiced monotheism, a rich polytheism with many gods and spirits, animism (spirit worship), or a mix of the three. Africans often recognized a supernatural world of sorcery, magic, spirits, ancestors, and multiple gods that was mediated by shamans, male or female specialists who were skilled in curing disease and had knowledge about the spiritual realm. They were often successful as healers because they understood that many illnesses had spiritual and psychological as well as physical dimensions. Some male elders, considered sages, collected wisdom and challenged individuals to become better and more knowledgeable. Scholars compare these sages, who were constantly probing for truth, to classical Greek, Indian, and Chinese philosophers. Reverence toward cosmic forces blended into worship and spirituality, and many Africans believed in a life force that was part of all living and material entities. Deceased family members and ancestors, believed to be present in spirit, were also revered. Since most societies envisioned an unapproachable high god who held himself aloof from daily affairs, people prayed to ancestors and spirits.

Religious Diversity

The Dogon people, who live on an arid plateau in today's nation of Mali, may represent what African society and religion were like before the formation of states and the coming of outside religions. Their society is ruled by priest-chiefs. People work the fields collectively and center their lives on community religious festivals and arts. The Dogon order the cosmos and their society through myths that perceive the cosmos as dualistic, mixing male and female, order and change.

Africans also developed oral and written literatures. Most societies relied on **oral traditions**, verbal testimonies concerning the past passed down through the generations by professional rememberers, known as *griots* in West Africa, who served as local historians and recordkeepers and sometimes became councilors to kings and tutors to princes. Griots could recount past events while also updating the story with contemporary happenings, becoming walking libraries who transmitted knowledge to their successors. As a modern griot explained: "We are vessels of speech, the repositories which harbor secrets many centuries old. We are the memory of mankind."[10] Some griots concentrated on genealogy, remembering lists of kings or queen mothers. many top West African writers and popular musicians today come from griot families.

oral traditions Verbal testimonies concerning the past; the major form of oral literature in cultures without writing.

Some African peoples also had written languages and produced poetry and philosophical speculation. The most widespread written languages included Arabic, Hausa, Amharic, and Swahili. However, writing spread slowly because most Africans relied on well-defined customs to maintain order and so did not need written laws; because they had communal ownership, they also did not need to track land use and inheritance. Merchants in the Sudanic and East African cities recorded the buying and selling of large quantities of goods in Arabic or Swahili, but elsewhere writing was difficult, since paper deteriorates quickly in the tropical climate.

Art and Music

Africans produced a rich artistic heritage, including sculpture, dance, and music. Paleolithic Africans were among the first people anywhere to paint on rocks and cave walls. When farming developed, painting declined and sculpture in wood, clay, ivory, bronze, or gold became the major visual art form. Many Africans made wooden masks for religious festivals, as well as carvings of animal, human, and spiritual figures, and African sculpture has influenced modern artists around the world. Music and dance were both closely integrated into work, leisure, and religion and usually involved everyone's participation. Musical groups often accompanied people working in the fields, and at the end of the day the farmers and musicians returned to the village for an impromptu party. While African musicians emphasized percussion and used many types of drums, they also played various wind and string instruments. African musical traditions filtered into the Middle East along the trade routes, influencing Islamic music. Then, beginning in the 1500s, African slaves carried their musical traditions to the Americas, where they blended with European and Native American styles to foster many of the popular music styles of the twentieth century, such as blues, jazz, rock, calypso, salsa, and samba.

Agriculture and Trade

Sub-Saharan Africans successfully exploited the resources of their tropical environment to foster farming and trade. Whereas Eurasian societies had horses and oxen to pull plows and large wheeled carts, in much of tropical Africa these animals could not be bred or survive because of various tropical diseases or insect pests; they could only be used in the northeast highland regions and in the dry Sudan and Sahara. Because economic production and transportation therefore had to rely on human muscles, most Africans were small farmers who produced food primarily for their own use. With often poor soils, irregular rainfall, and no manure from draft animals for fertilizer, Africans could not match the highly productive agriculture found in China, India, and Europe. Instead many practiced shifting cultivation, a practical adaptation to local conditions. This system worked well as long as population densities remained small; by 1500 there were probably some 40 million people in sub-Saharan Africa, compared to over 100 million in China. More sophisticated techniques such as irrigation or terracing were used where possible.

Commercial Life

Trading networks interlaced tropical Africa. Great markets emerged at Sudanic cities such as Gao and Timbuktu, where traders bought and sold ivory, ebony, and honey from the Guinea coast and books, wheat, horses, dates, cloth, and salt from the north. Most market traders were women, and most traveling merchants were men. Some peoples were renowned as long-distance traders. Hausa merchants traveled to the Guinea coast to buy kola nuts, a rain forest tree crop that can be made into one of the few stimulants allowed Muslims. Various items, including gold, ivory, and kola nuts, were exported from tropical Africa to North Africa, Asia, and Europe. Both gold and cowry (KOW-ree) shells, collected on the Indian Ocean coast, were used as local currency.

However, local trade was often more essential than international commerce. People bought and sold things needed for everyday life, such as cloth, salt, ironware, and copper, and women made cloth from cotton and bark. Because sources of abundant salt were rare, it commanded a high price, and traders sometimes had to obtain it from hundreds of miles away. Iron ore was more common. Copper was valued from ancient times for making bangles and bracelets, but there were few good sources. The most extensive copper mining took place in the copper-belt region south of the Congo Basin and in South Africa.

Africans, Arab Slave Traders, and the Portuguese

Slave Trades

Africa was connected to Eurasia primarily by trade across the Sahara Desert or along the East African coast. As international trade expanded, Arab, Berber, and African traders shipped more African slaves north, where they were sold in North Africa, Iberia, Arabia, Persia, India, and Christian Europe. Between 650 and 1500 the trans-Saharan caravans transported perhaps 2 to 4 million slaves from West Africa to the Mediterranean societies, while up to 2 million were shipped from East Africa. These were significant numbers but considerably smaller in scale than the trans-

Atlantic slave trade carried out by Western nations between 1500 and 1850. African slaves in the Middle East became domestic servants, laborers, soldiers, and even administrators. Perhaps 250,000 descendants of African slaves, traders, and sailors live in India and Pakistan today.

The trans-Saharan slave trade inspired western Europeans to eventually seek slaves directly in West Africa. Portuguese exploration began a new era in African history. In search of Asian spices and African gold as well as slaves, the well-armed Portuguese began sailing south along the West African coastline in the early 1400s (see Chapter 14). They became involved in African affairs, colonizing the Cape Verde (VUHRD) Islands in the Atlantic and the nearby coastal region of Guinea-Bissau (GIN-ee bis-OW) and establishing various trading forts to obtain gold, ivory, and slaves. Some West Africans picked up artistic and religious ideas from the Portuguese merchants and Christian missionaries.

Portuguese Explorations

In 1487 a Portuguese expedition led by Bartolomeu Dias rounded the Cape of Good Hope at the tip of Africa and sailed into the Indian Ocean, thus opening up a whole new chapter in Western exploration and intensifying Portuguese interest both in Africa and the world to the east. Even after Christopher Columbus, sailing for Spain, announced his "discovery" of what he thought was India in 1492, the Portuguese concentrated on the sea route around Africa. In 1497 Portuguese ships commanded by Vasco da Gama sailed up the East African coast to the trading city of Malindi and, engaging an Indian or Arab pilot, sailed on to southern India. Da Gama had discovered the fastest oceanic path from Europe to the Indian Ocean maritime trading network.

In the 1480s the Portuguese began a long relationship with the Kongo kingdom, sending Catholic missionaries and skilled craftsmen. The resulting blend of Christian and Kongolese traditions reshaped the region. In 1491, after two court officials claimed that the Virgin Mary appeared to them in dreams, the Kongolese king, Nzinga a Nkuwu (en-ZING-a ah en-KOO-WOO), and some of the aristocracy adopted Christianity and sent their children to Portugal for study. The king wanted Portuguese teachers, craftsmen, and weapons to use against a rival kingdom. By the early 1500s, however, after the Portuguese realized the economic possibilities of the Americas, they became far more interested in obtaining slaves than in helping the Kongolese economy or treating the Kongolese as equals. In 1514 they began exporting Kongolese slaves to nearby islands, and eventually many Kongolese were shipped to the Americas. This began a new era for Africa and a direct relationship with the peoples of Europe and the Americas, the region to which we now turn.

SECTION SUMMARY

- Many Africans lived in "stateless societies" in which family relationships, rather than rulers or governments, organized people's lives.

- Africans were part of a variety of social networks, including the family, the village, and the ethnic group, often mistakenly called the "tribe."

- In addition to Muslims and Christians, many Africans were polytheistic, believers in multiple gods and spirits.

- In Africa the oral tradition was much stronger than the written one, and writing spread slowly because African custom did not depend on recordkeeping and important knowledge was passed down orally by griots.

- African agriculture faced a number of challenges, including the difficulty of obtaining and using draft animals, poor soil, and irregular rainfall.

- Several million African slaves were shipped to the Middle East, and the Portuguese laid the groundwork for the much larger European slave trade to the Americas.

AMERICAN SOCIETIES IN TRANSITION

What factors explain the collapse of the early Intermediate Era American societies?

Like Africans, most Americans creatively exploited their environments, whether they lived in urban societies or in smaller agricultural or nomadic communities. Whereas many Africans had direct or indirect contact with Eastern Hemisphere networks, Americans remained a world apart from that interconnecting zone and the influences that flowed through it. Furthermore, these American societies were often separated from each other by great distances and by more geographical barriers—high mountains, harsh deserts, and thick forests—than was true for their counterparts in Eurasia. Yet cultures, technologies, and trade goods spread over a wide area. Powerful states with dense populations in Mesoamerica and the Andes, such as the Maya, declined or collapsed, while less centralized governments formed elsewhere, including in North America.

The Collapse of the Classical States

Unlike their Afro-Eurasian counterparts such as Rome, Gupta India, and Han China, most of the major American states of the Classical Era survived into the early Intermediate Era. Great cities such as Teotihuacan, Tikal in the Maya lands, and Tiwanaku in the southern Andes had flourished for centuries. Their success was based on productive and innovative farming, trade, and metalworking, combined, in some cases, with warfare with their neighbors. Americans were creative plant breeders. Combining maize, a very nutritious crop, with beans, squash, and fish or game provided many people with a well-balanced, healthy diet. Americans also discovered many plant drugs still used today to cure disease or alleviate pain, including quinine and coca.

However, during the early Intermediate Era older centers of religious, economic, or political power were replaced by newer ones. In eighth-century Mesoamerica, Monte Alban, the capital of the Zapotec state, declined while Teotihuacan collapsed, removing a unifying commercial and political hub for central Mexico. Although the Maya had flourished for centuries, by 900 they had abandoned many of their cities. In South America, Moche collapsed around 700, but Tiwanaku only fell apart around 1000 (see Chronology: The Americas in the Intermediate Era). The reasons for these rapid changes of political and economic fortunes remain somewhat unclear, but climate change probably played a role. In Mesoamerica and the Pacific coast of South America, a warming climate baked the land as rains failed and brought drought. Grassy hillsides turned brown, streams dried up, and crops withered.

The Zenith and Decline of the Maya

The Maya of Yucatán and northern Central America declined rapidly and then suddenly collapsed, opening the way for new powers to rise. Maya society reached its peak between 600 and 800, with growing populations and massive monument building. Population densities reached a staggering 600 people per square mile, similar to China today, testifying to the Maya success in mastering a marginal environment for farming. Tikal may have contained 50,000 people. Complex irrigation systems supported a Mayan population of 3 to 5 million people between 600 and 900.

Warfare between states was frequent, but victories were short-lived and resulted in no large empires. The battles were mostly for royal glory and economic predominance, not conquest. The Maya were in close commercial contact with central Mexico; in Teotihuacan, for example, a whole neighborhood was reserved for Maya merchants. Maya also sometimes ventured by boat to Caribbean islands, trading jade, salt, feathers, and chocolate. They were excellent sculpturers, builders, astronomers, and mathematicians and had a well-developed writing system that could express any thought or concept. Thousands of folding-screen books called codices, made of bark paper, were produced, although only a handful survived after the Spanish arrival in the early 1500s. The early Maya evidently practiced forest conservation, considering certain groves of trees sacred, but as they built larger temples they increasingly cut down forests for timber.

Southern Mayan Collapse

Eventually this society faced the same transition as the other classical states. Between 800 and 900 most of the Maya cities in the southern lowlands were deserted, and the whole region lost perhaps two-thirds of its population. Climate change seems to have caused a drought lasting over a century, emptying the complex system of canals and reservoirs that collected rainwater for farming and drinking. Overpopulation may have prompted frantic attempts to increase agricultural productivity on marginally fertile land. The resulting soil degradation and deforestation may have fostered crop failures, reduced rainfall, famine, malnutrition, starvation, epidemics, and increased warfare. Governments may have become more unstable, prompting revolts. As people abandoned the southern Maya cities, some moved to fortified villages in remote areas. The political and religious hierarchy of kings, aristocrats, and priests may have disappeared, and merchants, scribes, and craftsmen ceased their work.

Northern Mayan Cities

However, these dramatic developments seem not to have affected the northern Maya cities such as Uxmal (oosh-MAHL), which flourished until around 1000. Only the northern Yucatán coast enjoyed continuity after 900. But more frequent warfare also engulfed this region, and human sacrifice increased. The city of Chichen Itza (chuh-chen uht-SAH), founded around 800, dominated the Yucatán Peninsula between 1000 and 1250, when it was succeeded by the state of Mayapan (MY-uh-PAHN), itself destroyed by a rebellion in 1441. By the 1500s the Yucatán Maya were fragmented into small states in chronic conflict with each other. The remnants of the Maya people still existed over a wide area of Mesoamerica, but their once-brilliant history was fading from memory.

The Toltecs and Chimu

Rise of the Toltecs

As the older Mesoamerican and Andean states declined or collapsed, other peoples established powerful states not unlike the kingdoms that flourished in West Africa. The Toltecs (TOLL-teks) moved into Mexico's central valley from the desert north and created an empire that lasted from 900 to 1168, systematically recording their history in writing. Their empire seems to have been a loose military alliance involving newcomers from the north mixing with the local people, whose roots lay in Teotihuacan. The Toltecs adopted the cult of **Quetzalcoatl** (kate-zahl-CO-ah-tal), the feathered serpent, which goes back deep in Mesoamerican history. In Toltec tradition, Quetzalcoatl was a human leader who was banished to sea by the war-gods, a story probably based on Topiltzin (to-PILLT-sen) (b. ca. 947), a cult high priest who succeeded his father as Toltec king but whose opposition to human sacrifice and promotion of peace angered more warlike leaders. Forced into exile, the man gradually blended into the god in myth. But the legend also said that the banished man-god, bearded and of fair complexion, would return to seek revenge, and this prophecy haunted later Mesoamericans.

Quetzalcoatl The feathered serpent, a symbol that goes back deep in Mesoamerican history.

The Toltecs achieved influence throughout the region, even over some of the northern Maya cities. Their capital city, Tula, was filled with ceremonial architecture and reached a population of 30,000 to 60,000. Tula was a center for obsidian mining, with Tula craftsmen producing obsidian and copper tools. The Toltecs may have even established some contact with societies in the Andes, and some Toltec trade goods have been found as far north as New Mexico and Arizona. But in the twelfth century the Toltec state, weakened by long-term drought, famine, and war, collapsed, disrupting the trade routes.

Along South America's Pacific coast, the Chimu (chee-MOO) Empire, whose ruling class may have descended from Moche nobles, rose to prominence around 800. By 1200 the Chimu controlled a sizable empire stretching some 600 miles north to south. Their capital, Chan Chan (CHAHN CHAHN), was a substantial city, filled with many adobe-walled compounds and a population of 25,000 to 50,000. The Chimu lords, who lived in seclusion in magnificent walled palaces up to three stories high, had elaborate funerals in which several hundred men and women were sacrificed to serve as attendants in the afterlife. Workers drafted into the army labored on vast construction and irrigation projects, including 25-foot-wide roads. To irrigate the fields of maize, beans, cotton, gourds, squash, peanuts, and fruits, they constructed hundreds of miles of terraces and large storage reservoirs that controlled the flow of water down the mountainsides. These activities allowed the Chimu to avoid all but the most severe droughts and to achieve two or three crops a year.

Rise of Chimu

Pyramid at Tula Each figure on this pyramid at the Toltec capital is made of fitted stone sections and represents a warrior carrying a throwing stick in one hand and a bag of incense in the other.

Map 12.2
Major North American Societies, 600–1500 C.E.

Farming societies were common in North America. The Pueblo peoples such as the Anasazi in the southwestern desert and the Mound Builders in the eastern half of the continent lived in towns. The city of Cahokia was the center of the widespread Mississippian culture and a vast trade network.

e **Interactive Map**

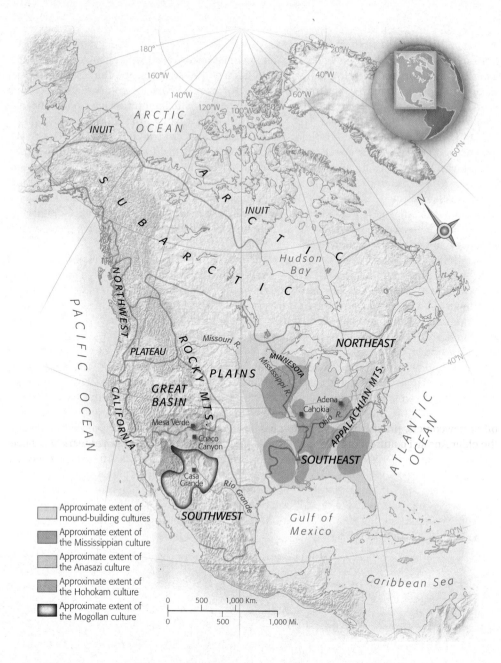

Approximate extent of mound-building cultures

Approximate extent of the Mississippian culture

Approximate extent of the Anasazi culture

Approximate extent of the Hohokam culture

Approximate extent of the Mogollan culture

Eventually, however, the Chimu faced challenges they could not overcome. Even with their productive farming, El Niño climate changes could disrupt irrigation. By the fourteenth century the Chimu were in decline, perhaps because of overpopulation and increased salinization of the soil. Around 1475 they were conquered by the Incas and incorporated into a vast Andean empire.

Pueblo Societies

While only a few American societies formed kingdoms or built large cities, many peoples creatively farmed in challenging environments and supported towns and long-distance trade. Some of the most successful societies developed in the southwestern desert of North America, whose modern descendants are known as the Pueblo Indians because of their permanent towns, called *pueblos* in Spanish. By learning to farm this dry region, the Pueblo peoples survived and sometimes flourished, becoming experts at selecting just the right soils for maize. Southwestern peoples also grew cotton and wove cotton cloth. Towns were often built around human-made dams, terraces, irrigation canals, and reservoirs. The Pueblo peoples also traded with central Mexico and the Pacific coast, mining and exchanging turquoise with Teotihuacan and the Toltecs for craft goods. Some Mesoamerican religious beliefs and customs, such as the tradition of the feathered serpent and ball courts and games, filtered north into some Pueblo communities.

Southwestern Peoples

By 700 the Hohokum and Mogollon societies dominated parts of southern Arizona, New Mexico, and northern Mexico (see Map 12.2). Among their large buildings, Casa Grande in northern Mexico, three stories high, was constructed around 1325 of thick adobe atop a platform mound. The surrounding town housed some 2,200 people. By 1000 the neighboring Mogollon people had developed masonry technology for house building. But climate change caused drought in the 1300s, and both the Hohokum and Mogollon settlements were eventually abandoned.

The Anasazi (ah-nah-SAH-zee), meaning "ancient ones" in the Navaho (NAH-vuh-ho) language, flourished between 700 and 1400, reaching their height of prosperity between 900 and 1250. Using huge sandstone blocks to build masonry houses, they constructed towns over large sections of Arizona, Colorado, New Mexico, and Utah, including major centers at Mesa Verde and Chaco (CHAHK-oh) Canyon. Mesa Verde, ingeniously built into steep cliff walls, probably housed 2,500 people, while another 30,000 lived in the surrounding area. In Chaco Canyon, eight adobe towns sat in or on the rim of the canyon, in which multistoried houses, some six stories high, were built around central plazas. The Anasazi constructed these pueblos with wood beams, stone, and clay carried from distant forests. Wide roads connected the Chaco pueblos with Anasazi towns a hundred miles away. The total Anasazi population probably numbered 100,000.

Anasazi Society

The Anasazi, like many Pueblo Indians, lived in egalitarian communities that practiced matrilineal kinship and matrilocal residence, with men moving into their wife's household. Women owned the houses, crops, and fields, but men dominated the council of elders who administered each town.

Environmental challenges eventually precipitated collapse. By 1200 Anasazi agriculture had declined from severe drought. Deforestation, soil erosion, disease epidemics, and invasions by outsiders may also have been factors. Hard times resulted in increased warfare between pueblos, and some pueblos, their social order undermined, may have resorted to human sacrifice or cannibalism. By 1300 many Anasazi had moved to the Rio Grande River Valley, where they mixed with other newcomers, producing the Pueblo peoples of central and northern New Mexico. By 1400 the older Anasazi culture had collapsed and the pueblos of Chaco and Mesa Verde had long been abandoned. Those Anasazi who survived were probably the ancestors of southwestern tribes like the Hopi (HOH-pee) and Zuni.

Anasazi Collapse

The Mississippian and Eastern Woodlands Societies

In the vast Mississippi and Ohio River Basins of eastern North America, where the land was more fertile than in the southwest, mound-building cultures flourished, based on trade and shifting cultivation of maize. The Mississippian culture, the most widespread between 700 and 1700, featured several cities, monumental architecture, social hierarchies, and religious art. The main Mississippian center, Cahokia (kuh-HOH-kee-uh), was strategically located near the juncture of the Mississippi and Missouri Rivers, a few miles from today's St. Louis. At their peak between 1050 and 1250, the city and suburbs probably had a population of 30,000 to 60,000. Cahokia was the North American counterpart to cities such as Teotihuacan and Tula, and Mesoamerican influences are clear in Mississippian communities, which had central plazas that included platform mounds topped by temples and elite houses, probably surrounded by markets. The largest Cahokia pyramid, 1,000 feet long, 700 feet wide, and 100 feet tall, was much larger than the Egyptian pyramids. Circles of standing timbers tracked the seasons by marking the sun's position. As in Mesoamerican cities, Cahokia's priest-rulers probably presided over lavish rituals atop the pyramids, and the chief religious cult worshiped the sun and had a religious symbolism of mythical creatures.

Cahokia

The matrilineal Cahokia society was divided into distinct classes. At the death of a ruler some commoners were sacrificed to accompany him on the voyage to the hereafter. According to oral traditions, a lord showed his status by riding in a flotilla of large canoes decorated with gold objects. Warfare over territory may have been common. Cahokia artisans made baskets, pottery, shell beads, leather clothes, copper ornaments, wooden utensils, and stone tools, and they carved artistic images into their buildings. Cahokia was the major hub of a vast trade network that stretched from the Great Lakes to the Rockies to the Gulf Coast along the Mississippi, Missouri, and Ohio Rivers. Cahokians imported Great Lakes copper to make jewelry, as well as marine shells and shark and barracuda jaws from the Gulf Coast. Cultural influences from Cahokia also spread through the eastern woodlands, including new strains of maize better adapted to cooler climates.

By 1550, the Mississippian culture had collapsed and the Mississippi River Basin population had dwindled, due probably to overpopulation, soil depletion, epidemics, and a cooling climate

SECTION SUMMARY

- American classical states survived longer than their counterparts in Eurasia, though they ultimately declined, perhaps because of climate change.

- The Maya supported an extremely dense population, but by 900 C.E. the southern Maya had collapsed, while the northern Maya continued on fitfully before collapsing by 1500.

- The Toltecs, a loose military empire based in central Mexico, adopted the cult of Quetzalcoatl, the feathered serpent.

- The Pueblo peoples of the American Southwest thrived on maize, grew and wove cotton, and were largely egalitarian and matrilineal.

- In the Mississippi and Ohio River Basins, mound-building cultures thrived on the fertile land and built some of the largest structures in the world.

that damaged agriculture. Growing tensions between the elites and the common folk also may have undermined the political system. By the early 1700s the surviving Mississippian peoples were devastated by diseases such as malaria and smallpox brought by European invaders. The last remnants of the Mound Builders, the sun-worshiping Natchez people in the lower Mississippi valley, were wiped out by French colonizers in a battle in 1731.

In the eastern woodlands of North America, few states had developed, and most farming communities resembled the African stateless societies such as the Tiv and Gikuyu. Although villages had chiefs, often elected by elders, they lacked much authority. Every family participated in decision making. Eastern woodland farming produced abundance. An English observer visiting Massachusetts in 1614 noted that the land was "so planted with gardens and corn fields, and so well inhabited with a goodly, strong people [that] I would rather live here than any where."[11] The men cleared the fields but were often gone for long periods, hunting or fighting. While warfare using bows and arrows was common, it generally led to few casualties. Since the women, working in groups, produced most of the food and many societies were matrilineal, their social and political status was high. Women elders often had the power to approve or prohibit warfare, and often a senior clan mother known for her wisdom nominated a new chief, who would then be elected or rejected by the rest of the tribe. The relative freedom of women resulted in a stronger emphasis on romantic courtship.

THE AMERICAN EMPIRES AND THEIR CHALLENGES

How were the Aztec and Inca Empires different, and how were they similar?

The collapse of the Maya and the decline of the Toltecs and Chimu resulted in the rapid rise of the Aztec (AZ-tek) and Inca (IN-kuh) societies, who built the largest empires and most sophisticated states ever seen in the Americas before 1500 (see Map 12.3). Thanks to strong armies and well-organized governments, both empires dominated large regions, but both also rapidly collapsed when confronted in the 1500s with the power of Spanish military forces and the epidemic diseases they brought from the Eastern Hemisphere.

The Aztec Empire, Religion, and Warfare

The Aztec society that developed out of the competition for power in Mesoamerica was created by the warlike Mexica, immigrants from the north known for their military skills who spoke Nahuatal (NAH-what-uhl). An early leader told them that "we shall conquer all peoples of the universe. I shall make you lords and kings of all that is in the world."[12] The Mexica took pride in their reputation as warriors and wrote much about their history, identifying themselves as the successor to the Toltecs and adopting many Toltec gods, rituals, and cultural forms. By 1325 they had established a strong state that soon controlled much of the Valley of Mexico, the lake-filled basin where Teotihuacan had once flourished and where they built their capital, Tenochtitlan (teh-noch-TIT-lan). In 1428 they expanded into neighboring regions. Their greatest ruler, Moctezuma (mock-teh-ZOO-ma) I (1440–1468), declared that war was the main Aztec preoccupation and its purpose was to gain new territories while acquiring prisoners for sacrifice to the gods. By 1519 the empire controlled much of central and southern Mexico, and it even collected tribute from people as far south as Guatemala and El Salvador. The tribute from the conquered became an important revenue source.

Foundations of Empire

Aztec Religion

Religion supported the warfare. The Aztecs believed the sun to be a warrior-god who daily battled his way across the skies to prevent the destruction of the universe by the forces of darkness. To help the sun-god remain fit for this struggle, the Aztecs had to feed the deity with blood from non-Aztec warriors captured in their frequent fighting, who were regularly sacrificed in gruesome

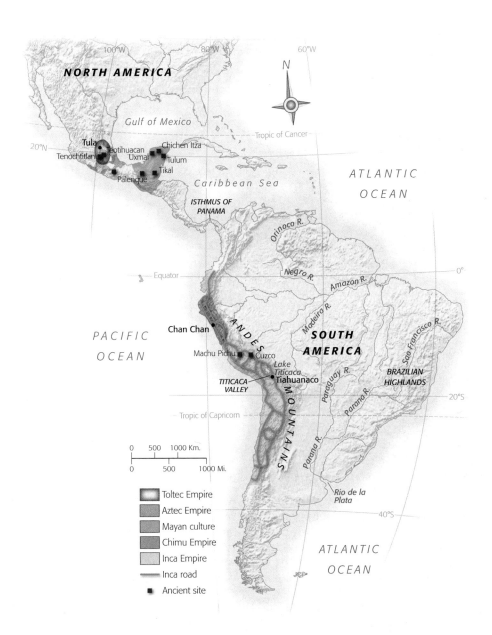

Map 12.3
South America
and Mesoamerica,
900–1500 C.E.
The Maya and Aztecs
in Mesoamerica and
the Incas in the Andes
forged the most
densely populated
societies, the most pro-
ductive farming, and
the best-organized gov-
ernments. The Incas
built one of the world's
largest empires. Other
urban societies also
flourished in Mexico
and South America.

Interactive Map

rituals. In Aztec myths, their god Huitzilopochtli (wheat-zeel-oh-POSHT-lee) ("The Humming-bird Wizard") commanded them to feed him with human hearts torn from the recently sacrificed. The Aztec practiced human sacrifice on a greater scale than any other major society ever did, sacrificing several thousand captured warriors a year throughout the empire. Other central Mexican people practiced blood sacrifice as well.

By 1500 the Aztecs faced growing economic, political, and military problems. The need for a regular supply of captives fostered a permanent state of war and terror, making for an unstable imperial system and fierce resistance. The conquered peoples paid tribute, but rebellions were frequent, providing an excuse to fight and obtain more captives. As a result of their brutal policies, the Aztecs had many enemies, some of whom were willing to cooperate with the newly arrived Spanish to invade Tenochtitlan. Even before this, Aztec leaders seem to have had a deepening sense of insecurity and to have been haunted by bad portents. These worries increased in 1518, when word reached Tenochtitlan of winged towers (Spanish ships) bearing white men with beards who were landing on Mexico's east coast. Because the Spanish arrival coincided with the prophesied return of Quetzalcoatl, historians debate whether Emperor Moctezuma II identified the Spanish with the god and thus lost the will to resist. However, the crucial fact was that Aztec tools and weapons were still based on sharp minerals, such as obsidian, which were no match for Spanish guns and steel swords. Although the Spanish encountered a vigorous Aztec society, Spanish conquest and occupation in 1521 ended the Aztec era.

Aztec Challenges

Aztec Warrior   These drawings, made by a sixteenth-century Aztec artist, show Aztec warriors, wearing costumes that reflect their status, who have defeated their opponents and forced them to kneel in submission. Many such captives would later be sacrificed.

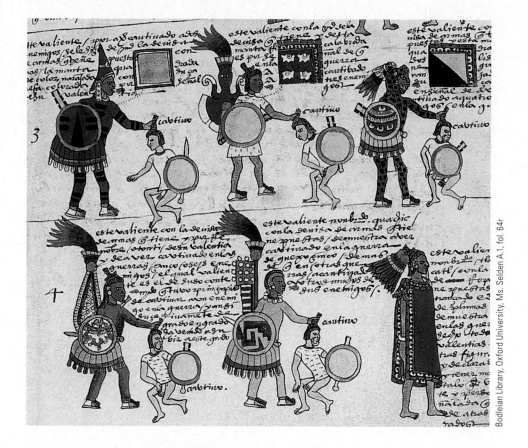

Bodleian Library, Oxford University, Ms. Selden A.1, fol. 64r

Aztec Economy and Society

The Aztecs developed a prosperous economy and a dynamic social system. Tenochtitlan (the site of today's Mexico City), on a swampy island in the middle of a large lake, was one of the world's great cities: large palaces, temples, forty pyramids, and diverse markets served some 150,000 to 300,000 residents. The Spanish marveled at the markets, where each kind of merchandise was sold in its respective street (see Witness to the Past: An Aztec Market). Thousands of canoes carrying passengers or produce traversed the six major canals daily. The first Spaniards to reach the city in 1519 were awed by the sight:

Trade and Agriculture

> *And when we saw all those towns and villages built in the water, and other great towns on dry land, and that straight and narrow causeway leading to Mexico [Tenochtitlan], we were astounded. These great towns and buildings rising from the water, all made of stone, seemed like an enchanted vision. Indeed, some of our soldiers asked whether it was not all a dream.*[13]

chinampas Artificial islands built along lakeshores of the central valley of Mexico for growing food.

Highly productive farming and trade underpinned the Aztec economy. The Aztecs grew their food on artificial islands, called **chinampas**, built on the lakes of the central valley, a technology that dated back hundreds of years. Tenochtitlan served as the core of a trade system that stretched into North America and Central America. Whole villages produced copper items or textiles. Merchants enjoyed a privileged position but were careful to maintain the state's goodwill, some probably serving as spies in outlying areas.

The Aztecs had a hierarchical social structure headed by emperors, true despots who were considered semigods and selected by a group of high officials, priests, and warriors. Then came the warrior-noble caste, whose men were divided into war lodges such as the eagle knights and jaguar knights. If captured by the enemy, they were expected to die with honor. According to an Aztec poem: "There is nothing like death in war. Far off I see it; my heart yearns for it!"[14] The priesthood, mostly celibate, played a key role in Aztec life, preparing the calendars and most of the books. An Aztec remembered the priests as "sages wise in words. They watch over, they read, they lay out the books. They lead us, they tell us the way."[15]

Social Classes

The elite classes held the commoners in contempt. Some commoners were entertainers and some were artisans, who created beautiful representations of the human figure for the elite. Indeed, Aztec sculpture, painted codex books, and murals were traded all over Mesoamerica. Many com-

An Aztec Market

The Spanish conquistadors who made their first visit to the Aztec capital of Tenochtitlan in 1519, two years before their conquest, were impressed with the wealth of foods and other trade goods available in the markets in and around the city. This account by Bernal Diaz del Castillo (DEE-as del kah-STEE-yoh), a Catholic priest who observed the Spanish conquest, describes the great market of Tlatelolco, near Tenochtitlan. Every day the market was thronged with as many as 25,000 people, and special market days might have attracted twice that number.

We were astounded at the number of people and the quantity of merchandise that [the market] contained, and at the good order and control that was maintained, for we had never seen such a thing before.... Each kind of merchandise was kept by itself and had its fixed place marked out. Let us begin with dealers of gold, silver, and precious stones, feathers, mantles, and embroidered goods. Then there were other wares consisting of Indian slaves, both men and women.... Next there were other traders who sold great pieces of cloth and cotton, and articles of twisted thread.... There were those who shod cloths of hennequen [a tough fiber] and ropes and the sandals with which they are shod....

Let us go and speak of those who sold beans and sage and other vegetables and herbs, ... and to those who sold fowls, cocks, ... rabbits, hares, deer, mallards, young dogs and other things of that sort in their part of the market, and let us also notice the fruiterers, and the women who sold cooked food, dough and tripe; ... then every sort of pottery made in a thousand different forms from great water jars to little jugs; ... then those who sold ... lumber, boards, cradles, beams, blocks and benches.... Paper ... and reeds scented with liquid [amber], and ... tobacco, and yellow ointments....

I am forgetting those who sell salt, and those who make the stone knives, ... and the fisherwomen and others who sell some small cakes ... [and] a bread having a flavor something like cheese. There are for sale axes of brass and copper and tin, and gourds and gaily painted jars made of wood. I could wish that I had finished telling of all the things which are sold there, but they are so numerous and of such different quality and the great market place with its surrounding arcades was so crowded with people, that one would not have been able to see and inquire about it all in two days.

THINKING ABOUT THE READING

1. What does the reading tell us about Aztec society and its material culture?
2. In what ways does the Aztec market remind you of a modern supermarket or department store?

Source: Bernard Diaz del Castillo, "The Discovery and Conquest of Mexico," trans. by A. P. Maudslay (NY: Farrar, Straus and Cudahy, 1956).

---

moners worked as tenant farmers on land owned by nobles. While the upper classes regularly ate sumptuous meals of meat, tortillas, and tamales, followed by a chocolate drink, commoners lived on ground maize meal, beans, and vegetables, cooked with chili, and rarely ate meat. At the bottom of society were many slaves, often debtors or criminals.

Men and women led very different lives. While their menfolk served the state, elite women enjoyed wealth but had two main roles: childbearer and weaver. Noble fathers advised their daughters "to learn very well the task of being a woman, which is to spin and weave. It is not proper for you to learn about herbs or to sell wood, peppers, [or] salt on the streets"[16] like the commoner women. Elite girls were kept at home until their arranged marriage, when they moved into their husband's family. In contrast, commoner women were freer to leave the house and pursue careers such as street vendors and midwives. While many young boys went to school to learn religion, history, rhetoric, and the arts of war, girls were taught domestic skills and religion as they prepared for marriage at around age sixteen.

Gender Relations

The Inca Imperial System

The Incas conquered an empire in the Andes much larger than the Aztec Empire. The Inca society, led by warrior chiefs, came together in central Peru around 1200. In the early 1400s a new leader, Viracocha (VEE-ruh-KOH-chuh) Inca, who claimed to be a living god, launched a new era of conquest with an army led by professional officers. By 1440 Viracocha's son, the pragmatic and visionary Pachacuti (PA-cha-koo-tee) ("World Remaker") (r. 1438–1471), became the major empire builder, eventually conquering the Lake Titicaca Basin and the Chimu Empire. By 1525, after uniting the highlands and the coastal zone for the first time, the Incas dominated nearly the whole region from southern Colombia to central Chile, ruling from their capital city, Cuzco (KOO-skoh), which contained between 60,000 and 100,000 people. Their empire stretched for nearly 3,000 miles, much of it above 8,000 feet in altitude, and became the most politically

Rise of the Incas

Machu Picchu This dramatic mountaintop settlement in the high Andes was probably built as a spiritual retreat for Inca royalty, who enjoyed its well-constructed drains, baths, fountains, and administrative buildings.

Alison Wright/Photo Researchers, Inc.

integrated in all of the Americas. The Incas also treated conquered peoples much more generously than did the Aztecs, incorporating them into their armies, rewarding their service, and tolerating their religions and cultures.

Empire building derived in part from the Inca religion and ideas of royalty, which considered kings to be divine, offspring of the sun and responsible for defending the order of the universe. The kings enjoyed great wealth and pomp. In describing a royal procession, a Spanish observer said that the king wore a collar of huge emeralds and was borne on a sedan throne made of massive gold, lined with the feathers of tropical birds and studded with gold and silver plates. On their death the kings' bodies were mummified and became the center of a cult. Since deceased kings were still considered the owners of their property and land, their successors had an incentive to seek new conquests so as to acquire their own property and land.

The Incas conquered or frightened into submission nearly all the farming societies, but their culture and power did not permeate far into the rain forests and deserts. The Incas deliberately resettled peoples to prevent rebellion or to develop new districts. In contrast to the brutal Aztecs, however, the Incas faced relatively few rebellions, in part because many non-Inca appreciated the peace imposed after several centuries of warfare. To win support, the Incas encouraged sons of non-Inca leaders to attend school with the sons of Inca nobles in Cuzco, where they studied history, geometry, military tactics, and oratory. Vast quantities of maize beer were consumed at festivals and celebrations to create goodwill and cooperation among the conquered. The Incas also practiced human sacrifice but on a smaller scale than the Aztecs, mostly on ceremonial occasions. For example, several children from noble families of conquered peoples might be killed on top of a mountain as honored gifts to the mountain gods, and their bodies were then mummified by the cold.

Like most empires, the Inca system was hierarchical and rigid. The royal family kept their bloodline undiluted by having siblings marry each other. Each ruler had a large harem of concubines but also a chief queen, his sister, who had her own magnificent palace and often considerable power behind the scenes. She headed a cult of the moon, led ceremonies for the major goddesses, and also gave birth to the male royal heirs. After some time rebellions became more frequent, and rivalry for the throne sometimes led to civil war. When the Spanish arrived in 1532, such a conflict had just ended, weakening the Inca resistance and allowing the Spanish to triumph militarily and replace the Inca political system with Spanish rule.

Inca Political Economy, Society, and Technology

The Inca Empire was supported by the most productive agriculture and creative technology in the Americas. Food collected by imperial storehouses was distributed as needed to others. In contrast to the Aztecs, the Inca state operated the imperial economy, taking the place of merchants in collecting and distributing goods. The state also required subjects to serve in the army, work state-owned farms, or serve on public works projects. Officials regularly visited villages to monitor work productivity or to check on sanitation.

Inca society was patriarchal, and most Inca commoners were part of large extended families. Both men and women made pottery and worked in the fields, the men plowing and the women sowing the seeds. Peasant women also spent considerable time each day weaving and collecting firewood or llama dung for cooking. The ancient Andean creator-god and chief Inca deity, Viracocha, had both male and female characteristics, and the Incas worshiped several female deities, including the Earth Mother.

Whereas the Aztecs mainly pursued sacrificial victims, the Incas wanted control of labor and land, building administrative centers throughout their territories. Some of these centers were retreats for the elite, such as Machu Picchu (MAH-choo PEE-choo), a spectacular collection of buildings built high atop a narrow mountain ridge above a remote river valley. Because communications were a priority in ruling conquered lands, the Incas linked this vast empire with 14,000 miles of roads radiating out from Cuzco. The roads were graded and paved and had gutters for drainage. Inca engineers even tunneled through rocks and built suspension bridges across gorges and pontoon bridges of reeds across rivers. The road system awed the Spanish, one of whom wrote, "I believe there is no account of a road as great as this, running through deep valleys, high mountains, banks of snow, torrents of water, living rock, and wild rivers."[17] Along these roads relay runners, averaging some 150 miles per day, conveyed administrative messages, and llama pack trains carried supplies.

Unlike the Mesoamericans, the Incas had no formal writing system, but they did have an efficient form of recordkeeping that involved differently colored knotted strings, called **quipus**, to record commercial dealings, property ownership, and census data. The Incas also created an oral literature with narrative power, including tales, prayers, and plaintive love songs, all passed down through the generations.

The Incas were particularly skilled in technology and science, and their vast agricultural engineering projects, such as terraces and irrigation canals, generated a widespread prosperity. An extensive irrigation system surpassed most of those in the Eastern Hemisphere, and Inca agriculture was far more productive than Peruvians can manage today. The main crops were potatoes, maize, peanuts, and cotton. Since the Incas practiced soil conservation, they rarely experienced famine. They also developed sophisticated medicine and surgical techniques, including simple anesthesia procedures. Using copper, bronze, and silver, they fashioned beautiful metal objects and were also among the world's greatest cloth makers, weaving luxurious woolen fabrics from the fleece of the alpaca and making bridges from cords and roofs from fibers. Engineers built fortresses and temples with great blocks of stone so perfectly joined that even a knife could not be inserted between them.

American Societies and Their Connections

The various American societies exchanged ideas and goods with each other over extended networks. As a result of trade and conquest, many people in western South America worshiped the same gods, shared mythologies, practiced human sacrifice, and made similar textiles, artworks, and metal products. Mesoamerican religious ideas, such as the cult of Quetzalcoatl, influenced the Anasazi and even reached into the Mississippi Valley. Mesoamericans traded with the Pueblo peoples for turquoise and with Central Americans for jade. But the Andean and Mesoamerican societies were separated by thousands of miles of forests and mountains, which limited direct contact. The only known direct communication between the two regions was undertaken by traders known as the Manteno, from coastal Ecuador, who for centuries had sailed large balsa rafts carrying cargo up and down the Pacific coast from Chile to Mexico.

However, geographical barriers did not prevent the Andean and Mesoamerican societies from developing some common social and political features. Gender relations, for instance, were very similar in the two regions. Unlike North America, where matrilineal patterns were common, these were patriarchal societies in which men dominated central governments and village life, and older males led the extended family households. Women took care of food, wove cloth, and ran households. Unlike the kings and nobles, who might have several wives, most commoners practiced monogamy. In both regions, warfare was common but ritualized, and conflict involved much protocol, including declarations of war. Armies in close formation fought hand to hand, with the goal of capturing rather than killing opponents. Since most battles occurred far from cities, civilians and settlements were largely left alone.

The Americas had far fewer people than the Eastern Hemisphere. Historians debate the size of the Western Hemisphere population in the late 1400s, but recent studies estimate 60 to 75 million. Mesoamerica had the most people, perhaps 20 to 30 million, while the Andes region was home to 12 to 15 million. Perhaps 7 million lived in North America, two-thirds of them in the eastern woodlands and southwestern regions. Compared to the Eastern Hemisphere, Americans faced fewer deadly diseases, and some peoples were quite healthy. Yet, farmers and urbanites, especially Mayans,

- The Aztecs lived in a state of constant war and conquest, sacrificing thousands of enemy warriors a year, but their enemies helped the Spanish to conquer them.

- The Aztecs were productive farmers and active traders, and they had a hierarchical social structure in which priests played a central role.

- The Incas conquered a wide area in the Andes and had a hierarchical social structure, but they were far more inclusive and tolerant than the Aztecs.

- Trade in the Inca Empire was tightly controlled by the state, and an extensive irrigation system and soil conservation program yielded a consistent and abundant food supply.

- Despite extremely limited contact between Andean societies and Mesoamerican ones, they were similar in terms of gender relations and warfare protocols.

experienced more health risks than hunters and gatherers and general health seems to have been deteriorating for some centuries prior to the Columbian voyages. Famine caused by sporadic climate change was a bigger problem.

Eventually, however, the American societies faced a challenge coming from the Eastern Hemisphere. The only known European visits to the Americas before 1492 took place in eastern Canada. Around 1000 C.E. a small group of Greenland-based Norse (Norwegian) Vikings led by Leif Ericson visited the area and established a base camp in Newfoundland (see Chapter 14). The Vikings alienated the local people and abandoned their settlement after a few years, but occasional Norse trading visits to the area may have continued for decades, even centuries. The isolated Norse did not publicize their discoveries to Europe, although Portuguese fishermen who visited Iceland may have picked up some information.

Five centuries later a more enduring connection between the hemispheres was forged. In search of Asia, a Spanish expedition led by an Italian mariner, Christopher Columbus, ventured out in three small ships, eventually reaching the Bahamas. In later voyages Columbus visited more parts of the Caribbean and the coast of South America. Even before 1492 some Americans had premonitions of a coming disaster. A chronicle compiled a few years earlier by the Tarascan (tuh-RAH-skuhn) people of western Mexico, rivals of the Aztecs, forecast a time when

there will be no more temples or fireplaces, everything shall become a desert because other men are coming to the earth. They will spare no end of the earth, and everywhere all the way to the edge of the sea and beyond.[18]

Despite creating technologies and ways of life that met their needs, thousands of years of isolation had left the Americans vulnerable to the devastating diseases and more effective steel weapons brought from more densely populated Afro-Eurasia. The new oceanic link altered American history forever, as epidemics wiped out millions of people, great empires fell, and Europeans colonized the hemisphere.

CHAPTER SUMMARY

African and American societies were separated by a vast ocean but shared certain patterns. They both formed some great centralized kingdoms and empires as well as many village-based stateless societies, and their contacts with Eurasian states and networks ranged from modest to none. Most Africans were settled ironworking farmers. The Sudanic kingdoms of Ghana, Mali, and Songhai had a complex political, cultural, and intellectual life, as well as trade connections to the Mediterranean. The increase in long-distance trade and the widespread acceptance of Islam helped integrate West Africa into hemispheric networks. Similar trends reshaped the East African coast, where city-states emerged and became linked to the Middle East and the great Indian Ocean maritime trade networks. Some coastal Bantu blended Islam and Arab culture with their own traditions, creating a Swahili culture. Other Bantu formed great kingdoms such as Zimbabwe, which flourished from gold exports. Throughout Africa, however, many people lived in small stateless societies. African religion included both polytheistic and monotheistic traditions, and many people believed in diverse spirits.

Across the Atlantic in the Americas, the classical states, including the long-enduring Maya and its cities, eventually collapsed from climate change and chronic warfare. These societies were replaced by vigorous new peoples, such as the Toltecs and Chimu. The Aztecs and Incas built the largest empires that ever existed in the Americas. The Americans also showed a pattern of continuity with the past. Both the Aztecs and Incas made use of long-established religious traditions and highly efficient agricultural techniques. The Aztecs practiced human sacrifice and commerce on a much greater scale than the Incas, while the Incas were outstanding engineers and road builders. Both empires had productive agriculture and well-organized states, but neither was prepared for the diseases and iron weapons that were brought by the Spanish.

KEY TERMS

mansa	oral traditions	chinampas
Swahili	Quetzalcoatl	quipus

EBOOK AND WEBSITE RESOURCES

 PRIMARY SOURCE
The Chronicles of Cieza

INTERACTIVE MAPS
Map 12.1 Major Sub-Saharan African Kingdoms and States, 1200–1600 C.E.
Map 12.2 Major North American Societies, 600–1500 C.E.
Map 12.3 South America and Mesoamerica, 900–1500 C.E.

LINKS

Africa South of the Sahara (http://www-sul.stanford.edu/depts/ssrg/africa/guide.html). Useful collection of links from Stanford University.

Ancient Mexico.com (http://www.ancientweb.org/mexico/). Contains useful features on art, culture, and history.

Ancient Mesoamerican Civilizations (http://www.angelfire.com/ca/humanorigins/). Links and information about the premodern American societies.

Civilizations in Africa (http://www.wsu.edu/~dee/CIVAFRCA/CIVAFRCA.HTM). Contains useful essays on premodern Africa.

History and Cultures of Africa (http://www.columbia.edu/cu/lweb/indiv/africa/index.html). Provides valuable links to relevant websites on African history.

Internet African History Sourcebook (http://www.fordham.edu/halsall/africa/africasbook.html). This site contains much useful information and documentary material on ancient Africa.

The Aztecs/Mexicas (http://www.indians.org/welker/aztec.htm). Essays and information on the Aztecs.

Plus flashcards, practice quizzes, and more. Go to: www.cengage.com/history/lockard/globalsocnet2e

SUGGESTED READING

Connah, Graham. *African Civilization: An Archaeological Perspective*, 2nd ed. Cambridge: Cambridge University Press, 2001. An overview of early African societies, emphasizing the rise of cities and states.

D'altroy, Terence N. *The Incas*. Malden, MA: Blackwell, 2003. An excellent, up-to-date introduction to the Andes societies in this era.

Davidson, Basil. *The Lost Cities of Africa*, rev. ed. Boston: Atlantic-Little, Brown, 1987. A revision of a classic and a very readable study of early African societies from the Sudan to Zimbabwe.

Ehret, Christopher. *The Civilizations of Africa: A History to 1800*. Charlottesville: University of Virginia Press, 2002. A survey text with detailed coverage.

Fagan, Brian M. *Kingdoms of Gold, Kingdoms of Jade: The Americas Before Columbus*. London and New York: Thames and Hudson, 1991. A nicely illustrated, readable introduction to the American societies.

July, Robert W. *A History of the African People*, 5th ed. Prospect Heights, IL: Waveland Press, 1998. A very readable survey of African history.

Kehoe, Alice Beck. *America Before the European Invasions*. New York: Longman, 2002. A recent overview of the North American peoples and history before 1600 C.E.

Knight, Alan. *Mexico: From the Beginning to the Spanish Conquest*. New York: Cambridge University Press, 2002. An introduction to Mesoamerican societies through the Aztecs.

Longhena, Maria and Walter Alva. *The Incas and Other Ancient Andean Civilizations*. New York: Barnes and Noble, 2007. Lavishly illustrated study of pre-Inca and Inca cultures.

Mann, Charles C. *1491: New Revelations of the Americas Before Columbus*. New York: Alfred A. Knopf, 2005. A readable summary of recent scholarship on the American societies.

Nurse, Derek, and Thomas Spear. *The Swahili: Reconstructing the History and Language of an African Society, 800–1500*. Philadelphia: University of Pennsylvania Press, 1985. An excellent summary of what we know about the Swahili and their early history.

Pearson, Michael. *The Indian Ocean*. New York: Routledge, 2003. Integrates East Africa into the hemispheric trading system.

Shaffer, Lynda Norene. *Native Americans Before 1492: The Mound-building Centers of the Eastern Woodlands*. Armonk, NY: M. E. Sharpe, 1992. A brief overview, for the general reader, of some early North American societies.

Smith, Michael E. *The Aztecs*, 2nd ed. Malden, MA: Blackwell, 2003. A recent scholarly study.

Thobhani, Akbarali. *Mansa Musa: The Golden King of Ancient Mali*. Dubuque, IA: Kendall-Hunt, 1998. A readable introduction to Mali and its rulers.

Townsend, Richard F. *The Aztecs*, rev. ed. New York: Thames and Hudson, 2000. A readable, well-illustrated survey of Aztec history and society.

SOUTH ASIA, CENTRAL ASIA, SOUTHEAST ASIA, AND AFRO-EURASIAN CONNECTIONS, 600–1500

Fujita Art Museum

Xuan Zang Arriving in China
A seventh-century Buddhist Chinese pilgrim, Xuan Zang, spent many years travel-ing in India, collecting Buddhist wisdom and observing Indian life. This Chinese painting shows him and his caravan returning to China with pack loads of Buddhist manuscripts.

I ndia's shape is like the half-moon. The administration of the government is founded on benign principles. The taxes on the people are light. Each one keeps his own worldly goods in peace. The merchants come and go in carrying out their transactions. Those whose duty it is sow and reap, plough and [weed], and plant; and after their labor they rest awhile.

—Xuan Zang, seventh-century Chinese visitor to India[1]

I n 630 C.E. a determined Chinese Buddhist monk, Xuan Zang (swan tsang) (ca. 600–664), traveled the Silk Road to India on an extended pilgrimage to collect holy books and ended up spending fifteen years visiting every corner of the subcontinent. He was very observant and politically astute, but he also chafed at the perception of many Indian Buddhists that China was too remote to truly claim Buddhism. In a debate at the great Nalanda (nuh-LAN-duh) Monastery, Xuan Zang told the monks that

Buddha established his doctrine so that it might be diffused to all lands. Who would wish to enjoy it alone? Besides, in my country the emperor is virtuous and the subjects loyal, parents are loving and sons obedient, humanity and justice are highly esteemed.[2]

FOCUS QUESTIONS

1. How did Hinduism and Buddhism change in this era?
2. How did Islam alter the ancient Indian pattern of diversity in unity?
3. What political and religious forms shaped Southeast Asian societies in the Early Intermediate Era?
4. What was the influence of Theravada Buddhism, Confucianism, and Islam on Southeast Asia?

Xuan Zang found much to admire in India, including the Indian tolerance for diverse viewpoints. Even though Hinduism was dominant, Buddhism enjoyed protection and royal patronage. Xuan Zang's writings described an Indian society that had a rigid social structure but was also creative and open to foreign influences, including regular contact with China, Europe, the Middle East, and Indonesia. Xuan Zang was also much impressed with India's high standard of living, efficient governments, and generally peaceful conditions. But some customs troubled him. Despite the bias in Indian religions against eating animals, many Indians consumed fish, venison, and mutton. He also criticized the caste restrictions, such as confining untouchables to their own shabby neighborhoods. After covering some 40,000 total miles in his many years of travel, Xuan Zang returned to China in 643, taking with him hundreds of Buddhist books to be translated into Chinese. He also became a confidant of the Tang emperor and fostered closer relations between India and China.

India's cultural diversity and openness to foreign influence were due in part to the repeated invasions of Central Asian peoples, who brought with them varied beliefs and customs. Hindu religion and society absorbed these newcomers and their ideas. Groups with differing customs generally lived peacefully side by side, and Indian ideals spread to neighboring peoples. But Hindu political domination and the assimilation of newcomers faced a particularly severe challenge with the arrival of Muslims, who gained control over large parts of the subcontinent. Having their own strong religious ideas, Muslims were not easily absorbed into the complex world of Hindu culture. The coming of Islam constituted a great turning point in the region's development, a transition comparable to that initiated by the Aryan migrations into India several millennia earlier.

e Visit the website and eBook for additional study materials and interactive tools: www.cengage.com/history/lockard/globalsocnet2e

Southeast Asians also adopted new political systems and religions. Powerful kingdoms emerged, some of them strongly influenced by Indian culture. By the fifteenth century new faiths from outside, Theravada Buddhism and Islam, had reshaped the political map and created diverse cultures that remained a hallmark of Southeast Asian societies.

HINDUISM, BUDDHISM, AND SOUTH ASIAN SOCIETY

How did Hinduism and Buddhism change in this era?

No Hindu leaders recreated an empire like the Maurya or Gupta Empire. Instead India encompassed many states, cultures, and languages. Despite a broad Hindu tradition and the common heritage it created, India became a collage of microcultures in which many images coexisted on the same canvas, shaping each other while retaining their own distinctive character, thus demonstrating one of the great themes in Indian history: diversity in unity. Although dividing into competing schools of thought and practice, Hinduism experienced a Renaissance and grew in popularity. While Hinduism increasingly shaped Indian life, Buddhism faded in India but found new influence in neighboring societies. Hindu culture flourished in India for half a millennium before facing the concerted challenge from Islamic peoples.

Unity and Disunity in Hindu India

The political disunity following the fall of the Gupta state in the fifth century proved to be a long-term pattern. King Harsha Vardhana (600–647) briefly united parts of north India (see Chronology: South Asia, 600–1500). A man of enormous energy, he amassed a formidable army of 100,000 cavalry and 60,000 elephants and skillfully held together his small empire while cultivating close relations with Tang China. Harsha had a fondness for philosophy and was renowned as a poet. While enjoying the pomp of kingship, he also listened patiently to the complaints of his humbler subjects. A strong Buddhist like Ashoka, he tolerated all faiths but also prevented his beloved sister, a Hindu, from committing sati at her husband's cremation. Harsha ruled for forty-one years, but his empire collapsed on his death.

Harsha

Despite Harsha's brilliant reign, dozens of states proliferated in the subcontinent. Many Hindu states were absolute monarchies in which rulers owned many economic resources, such as forests, mines, and weaving operations, and tried to control outlying regions through appointed governors. Holding a precarious position of power, they buttressed their rule by claiming a divine mission and employed Brahmans (Hindu priests) as court advisers to give them legitimacy.

Rajputs ("King's Sons")
A Hindu Indian warrior caste formed by earlier Central Asian invaders.

North and south India developed somewhat different political patterns. **Rajputs** ("King's Sons"), members of a Hindu warrior caste formed by earlier Central Asian invaders, controlled some north Indian states. Rajputs were raised in traditions of chivalry, honor, and courage not unlike those of Japanese samurai or medieval European knights, their code emphasizing mercy toward enemies and precise rules of conduct in warfare. However, the Rajput-led kingdoms often fought wars against each other for regional power. In contrast, many south Indian states were oriented to the sea and hence specialized in piracy and foreign trade. South Indian merchants had more political influence than north Indian merchants and continued their lucrative maritime trade with Southeast Asia, China, and the Middle East. Indeed, many visited or settled in Southeast Asia, bringing with them lasting south Indian ideas on art, politics, and religion.

Village Life

Whatever the fragmentation of politics and regions, the continuity of Indian culture was reflected in the countless villages that remained the basic unit of Indian life. Even today, about 80 percent of Indians still live in villages. Farmers had to feed an Indian population that reached around 100 million by 1500. Land was regarded as the property of the ruler, who was entitled to either a tax or a share of the produce. The land tax remained the main source of state revenue and the main burden on the villagers. As long as they regularly met their tax obligations, peasants had the hereditary right to use the land they farmed. Village governments included a council elected annually from among village elders and caste leaders that dispensed local justice and collected taxes.

The typical village remained largely self-sufficient and organized through the caste system, which promoted stability. Members of different castes lived separately in their own neighborhoods, but all contributed to the livelihood of the larger community. Each village had a potter, carpenter,

CHRONOLOGY

	South Asia	Southeast Asia
600	**600–647** Empire of Harsha	**600–1290** Srivijaya Empire
800	**846–1216** Chola dynasty	**802–1432** Angkor Empire
1000	**1192–1526** Delhi Sultanate	**1044–1287** Pagan kingdom
1200	**1336–1565** Vijayanagara state	**1238–1419** Sukhotai state
1400		**1403–1511** Melaka state

blacksmith, clerk, herdsman, teacher, astrologer, and priest as well as many farmers who served each other on a barter basis in what was essentially a symbiotic community. Some modern writers romanticize traditional village life, portraying people living peacefully together, and village life did offer psychological and economic security. Each villager had a recognized status, rights, and duties, a supportive caste community, and many personal relationships. When the rulers maintained peace, repressed banditry, and kept the tax burden reasonable, most people were probably contented.

Many Indians also lived in towns and cities. Merchants helped administer the towns, but, as in China, they were heavily taxed and not allowed to become too independent of government. During the eighth century, to escape the Islamic conquest of Persia, some Zoroastrians fled to western India, where they formed the distinctive *Parsee* (Persian) community and became known as businessmen and manufacturers. Indeed, India was one of the world's leading manufacturing centers. Urban workshops produced cloth, textiles, pottery, leather goods, and jewelry for local use or export to markets as distant as China, Africa, and eastern Europe. India and China provided most of the world's industrial goods until the eighteenth century, and the average per capita incomes for Indians remained high by world standards.

CHRONOLOGY
South Asia, 600–1500

600–647 Empire of Harsha in north India

620–649 First Tibetan kingdom and introduction of Buddhism

711 First Muslim invasion of northwest India

846–1216 Chola kingdom in south India

1192–1526 Delhi Sultanate

1336–1565 Kingdom of Vijayanagara in south India

1398–1399 Devastation of Delhi by Tamerlane

The Hindu Social System and Scientific Traditions

The Hindu social system demonstrated great continuity over the centuries and, as in China, subordinated the individual to the group. Indians owed their most basic obligations to their extended family, a relationship described in an old saying as "joint in food, worship, and property." The family, which included people of several generations, lived together in the same household, enforced caste regulations among their members, and also collectively owned their economic assets, such as farmland. Because families shared their wealth, they constituted an effective source of social security. Most families, especially in north India, were patriarchal, headed by a senior male, although older women enjoyed considerable influence. Children lived in close contact with cousins, aunts, uncles, and grandparents. Child rearing became a group obligation.

Family System

Marriage customs reflected regional differences. In north India, parents arranged marriages. Girls were married off young, sometimes by the age of seven or eight, usually to a boy in a neighboring village. Because the bride's family paid for the wedding and was expected to give lavish presents, families preferred sons. In South India girls were more likely to marry boys whom they already knew, often a cousin. In Kerala (CARE-a-la) in southwestern India, one large group practiced **polyandry**, marriage of a woman to several husbands. Most Indian families viewed divorce as a humiliation.

polyandry Marriage of a woman to several husbands.

The Indian social system favored men, who enjoyed many privileges, and male leaders became obsessed with preserving social stability and controlling female sexuality. From puberty females of all castes were taught to keep a distance from all men except their closest relatives. High-caste women were expected to spend their time at home, only occasionally visiting friends or family. Low-caste and untouchable women enjoyed more mobility because they had to earn the incomes needed for family survival. Most women led lives marked by obedience, sacrifice, and service, submitting to parents, husband, and children. The young bride, usually much younger than her

Gender Relations

Benoy K. Behl

Sculpture of Two Lovers from Konarak Temple This sculpture of two embracing lovers comes from the Konarak temple in the north Indian state of Orissa. The Hindu temple, dedicated to the sun-god, was built in the thirteenth century and featured many erotic sculptures.

husband, moved into her husband's household and obeyed her new mother-in-law. Yet, husbands often treated their brides indulgently. Indians also revered motherhood. After she bore children (especially sons), the wife's status improved considerably, and she enjoyed more freedom and respect. As a woman grew older and became a mother-in-law herself, she gained even more influence.

Of course, not all wives were silent and subservient. Women also enjoyed some legal rights, and ill-treatment of women was condemned, although it was undoubtedly common. But widowhood could prove catastrophic if a woman had no son. Since Hindu custom frowned on remarriage, to be a young and childless widow was to face a difficult situation. To avoid surviving their deceased husband, some women, especially in north India, chose or were forced to die on their husband's funeral pyre. An ancient Indian expression captures the challenge for women: "As a girl she is under the tutelage of her parents; as an adult her husband; as a widow her sons."

Indians held diverse views about sex. Many books commended celibacy and advised married men to exercise their sexual prerogatives sparingly if they wanted health and virtue. Yet, the worldly views of many are reflected in many Indian texts such as the *Kama Sutra*, a manual of lovemaking and related matters. Even the Hindu gods and goddesses were portrayed in art and writings as highly sexual beings, a view very unlike that of the virginal Madonna and celibate Jesus of Christian tradition, the image of a spiritually and morally pure Buddha, and the puritanical restrictions of Islam. During this era Indians made many contributions in mathematics and science. One of the greatest Indian mathematicians and astronomers, Bhaskara (bas-CAR-a), living in the twelfth century, proved that zero was infinity. He also designed a perpetual motion machine by filling a wheel rim with quicksilver. Bhaskara's book on the subject, translated into Arabic, later reached Europe and inspired drawings of quicksilver wheels that influenced modern scientific thought. The first weight-driven clocks, built in Europe after 1300, may have been based in part on Bhaskara's ideas.

Some Indian astronomers and mathematicians found employment in Tang China, fostering a fruitful exchange of knowledge between the two societies. However, while Indians developed a rational system of mathematics and the basis for scientific reasoning, the indifference of the higher castes to applied or practical inquiry hindered the development of science. As the brahmans became more powerful, those with technical expertise lost status. Some visitors reported a growing disdain among Hindu thinkers for foreign ideas. An astute Muslim observer wrote that "the Hindus believe that there is no country, king, religion, [or] science like theirs."[3]

Hindu Diversity and Renaissance

Diverse Beliefs

Hinduism provided the spiritual framework for the great majority of South Asians until the coming of Islam. Its strength lay in its diversity, which could accommodate all classes, personalities, and intellects. It gave the scholars and mystics abstract and speculative thought and the more worldly individuals a wealth of ritual, art, and gods for every occasion. The values of Hinduism permeated the diverse Indian society. Recognizing that individuals varied in their spiritual and intellectual capacities, Hindus tolerated many different practices and beliefs and relied on no fixed and exclusive theology. As the earliest Hindu holy book, the *Rig Veda*, put it: "Reality is one; sages speak of it in different ways."[4] Concepts of spiritual power ranged from an indescribable but all-pervading, omnipotent God, to personal gods with human attributes, to demons and spirits. Hinduism remained undogmatic, a philosophy and way of life with no central institution or church to monitor the faith or to codify beliefs. Muslims introduced the collective term *Hindu*, from the Persian term for "Indians," to describe the varied Indian sects, and in the nineteenth century Europeans began referring to the diverse collection of Indian beliefs as "Hinduism."

The tradition of tolerance suggested that all approaches to God were valid, although mystics and intellectuals tended to consider their approaches more worthy. For example, mother-goddess worship was common among the lower castes, especially in south India, but was less popular among the higher castes. People worshiped the many gods and goddesses in various ways. Many men and women believed that the wives and consorts (companions) of the main male gods were more responsive to their needs than the male gods. Thus many cults worshiped Shiva's wife, Shakti (SHAHK-tee), who was kind and beautiful but also cruel and fearsome. Most Hindus perceived the universe as a collection of temporary living quarters inhabited by individual souls going through a succession of lives. The most devout had the ultimate goal of being liberated from human consciousness and freed from the endless cycle of birth and rebirth, but only a small minority seriously sought to escape from the earthly world with all its pain and pleasures. While wandering holy men were respected for their withdrawal from worldly activities, most Hindus met their social obligations to family, caste, and village while practicing moderation and temperance.

Hindu Tolerance

Hinduism helped establish a common culture throughout India. Brahmans served as advisers to kings, standardizing political ideas and rituals. But while they monopolized reading the Sanskrit scriptures, the Hindu classics were available to all through storytellers. The collections of ancient prayers and hymns, the Vedas, were also translated from Sanskrit into regional languages.

Many thinkers who embellished or revitalized Hindu traditions lived during these centuries, creating the Hindu Renaissance. Through his itinerant preaching, debates with rivals, and written commentaries on the *Upanishads*, Shankara (shan-kar-uh) (788–820), a south Indian brahman, revitalized the mystical *Vedanta* tradition, with its belief in the underlying unity of all reality. To Shankara, all the Hindu gods were manifestations of the impersonal, timeless, changeless, and unitary Absolute Reality, *Brahman*, and the individual soul only a tiny part of the whole unity of the universe. While accepting the Hindu scriptures as divine revelation, he wanted to prove them through logical reasoning and debate, yet he also argued that all knowledge was relative because humankind's grasp of reality is warped by ignorance. The truth of existence could only be understood through ascetic meditation. Shankara's views remain very popular among modern Indian intellectuals.

The Hindu Renaissance

Other philosophers offered different visions of Hinduism. Ramanuja (RAH-muh-NOO-ja) emphasized **bhakti**, devotional worship of a personal god, arguing that the gods should be accessible without priestly help. A few centuries later some Christian reformers in Europe would develop a similar notion of establishing a personal relationship with God without priestly aid. The bhakti tradition emphasized pilgrimage to holy places such as the city of Benares (buh-NAHR-uhs) (Varanasi), alongside the Ganges; Hindus who died in Benares had their sins washed away. Many early bhakti thinkers, most of them non-brahmans, also opposed or downplayed the caste system. The bhakti tradition appealed particularly to women. An early female poet, Antal, urged women devotees to revere Lord Krishna (an incarnation of Vishnu).

bhakti Devotional worship of a personal Hindu god.

The Hindu Renaissance included the building of flamboyant temples, whose sculptural art illustrated the intricate mythology of the faith. One of the best examples was a temple constructed in Khajuraho (kah-ju-RA-ho) that was dedicated to Vishnu. Sculptures carved into the temple walls suggested the delights enjoyed by the gods, including lovemaking. The erotic, sexually explicit paintings or carvings in many Hindu temples reflected a rather open view about portraying sexuality.

Transitions in Indian and Tibetan Buddhism

While Hinduism was enjoying its resurgence, the influence of Indian Buddhism gradually declined except in northeast India, where governments patronized the religion and its institutions, such as the college at the Nalanda Monastery, which attracted religious students from around Asia. Pilgrims from distant lands, such as Xuan Zang, showed how much Buddhism was becoming a major influence in the eastern half of Eurasia as the faith spread in Central Asia, Tibet, China, Korea, Japan, and Southeast Asia, adapting to different cultures. The intellectual environment of northeast India also promoted a dialogue between Hinduism and Mahayana Buddhism, fostering new schools of Buddhist and Hindu thought. One new Buddhist school, the **Vajrayana** ("Thunderbolt"), featured female saviors and magical powers. It spread during the eighth century into Nepal and Tibet.

Vajrayana ("Thunderbolt") A form of Buddhism that featured female saviors and the human attainment of magical powers.

In Bengal the contact between Mahayana Buddhists and Hindu followers of Shiva who revered his consort, the goddess Shakti, led to **Tantrism** (TAN-triz-uhm), which worshiped the female essence of the universe. Both the Tantric and Vajrayana schools exalted female power as earth mother and divine strength. Tantric sects developed within both Hinduism and Buddhism, and some were mystical sects that presented male-female sexual union as a symbolic unity between

Tantrism An approach within both Buddhism and Hinduism that worshiped the female essence of the universe.

the earthly and cosmic worlds. Other sects promised release from life's pain in a single lifetime to those who cultivated hedonism, pleasure, and ecstasy. Tantric Hindus were often hostile to the caste system. Most Hindus and Buddhists denounced Tantrism as an excuse for debauchery and sexual desire, and Tantrism gradually became a minor strand in the two religions.

While Buddhism declined in India, the remote high plateau of Tibet became a refuge for the religion. The first known pre-Buddhist Tibetan state emerged when Songsten-gampo (SONG-sten-GOM-po) (r. 620–649 C.E.) unified several tribes. Interested in connecting to an Asian world where Buddhism was expanding, he established close relations with Tang China and married a Chinese princess. Although not a Buddhist, he allowed the religion to spread in his kingdom. Tibetans also made the Sanskrit script from India their written language. By the eighth century Buddhism had become the dominant Tibetan faith, and its monasteries enjoyed many legal protections and financial support from the government. But many Tibetans also continued to follow the ancient folk religion, *bon*. The two faiths competed for popular support and political influence, and violent religious conflicts destroyed the unified state.

However, both Tibetan Buddhism and state building were later reinvigorated in the thirteenth century when many Buddhist monks fled to Tibet to escape Islamic persecution in India. Political relations with the predominantly Buddhist Mongols, who had conquered China and established some control in Tibet, also boosted Tibetan Buddhism. A unified Tibetan government was reestablished in 1247 under the leadership of one Buddhist sect and then by aristocratic families, which persisted into the seventeenth century.

Tibetans developed a distinctive religious tradition in their harsh highlands environment. Their Buddhism is often termed **Lamaism** (LAH-muh-iz-uhm) because of the centrality of monks, or *lamas* (LAH-muhz), and huge monasteries. Perhaps a quarter to a third of male Tibetans became career monks, and Buddhism came to permeate every aspect of Tibetan life. Believers practiced magic, made pilgrimages to shrines, and provided generous support to monasteries and Buddhist teachers. Tibetans also blended Buddhism with strong beliefs in the supernatural, including evil spirits. For example, people spun hand-held or roadside prayer wheels and carved prayers into stones, seeking the help of the Buddha.

Rise of Tibetan Buddhism

Lamaism The Tibetan form of Buddhism, characterized by the centrality of monks (*lamas*) and huge monasteries.

SECTION SUMMARY

- In the Intermediate Era, India was fragmented into many small states; the north was influenced by earlier Central Asian invaders and the south by maritime trade with Southeast Asia.

- The village, which was based on cooperation and caste, remained the basic unit of Indian life and provided people with a sense of security.

- Indian merchants in the cities were heavily taxed, but India and China produced most of the world's manufactured goods in this era.

- In the Hindu social system, the individual was subordinate to the group and people tended to live in extended families that supported their members.

- Indian men had much more power than women, who were forced to marry early and earned respect through bearing children, particularly boys.

- The mathematician Bhaskara discovered perpetual motion, which influenced science in the West.

- Hinduism adapted itself to the needs of a wide variety of people, from the worldly to the scholarly, and helped to establish a common culture throughout India.

- Shankara, a major thinker of the Hindu Renaissance, emphasized the importance of reason and of ascetic meditation, while Ramanuja emphasized the worship of a personal god.

- Indian Buddhism declined generally, but it remained important in the northeast, where Vajrayana and Tantrism grew out of the interplay between it and Hinduism.

- Buddhism became the dominant religion in Tibet, where it became Lamaism, and many Indian Buddhist monks took refuge there to escape Islamic persecution.

THE COMING OF ISLAM TO INDIA AND CENTRAL ASIA

How did Islam alter the ancient Indian pattern of diversity in unity?

The spread of Islamic religion and government in India was a major transition in Indian history, as important as the coming of the Aryans several millennia earlier. Since Muslims and Hindus were almost exact opposites in their beliefs, Islam created a great divide in South Asian society. As Al-Biruni, an eleventh-century Muslim scholar, put it: "Hindus entirely differ from us in every respect. In all manners and usages they differ from us to such a degree as to frighten their children with us."[5] For centuries Hinduism had absorbed invaders and their faiths, but Islam, a self-confident, missionary religion, could not be assimilated. The tension between the two faiths sometimes resulted in conflict. However, Islam enriched Indian culture, establishing new connections with western Asia while also promoting the spread of Indian ideas, especially in mathematics and science, to the Middle East and Europe. Many Indians embraced the new faith, and Muslims also gained political dominance over large parts of India.

Early Islamic Encounters

Islamic forces reached Central Asia and India within a few decades of the religion's founding. Western Asians had long been linked to Central Asia through Silk Road trade, and they were well aware of India's riches. Arab sailors had been active in South Asia for centuries before the rise of Islam, linking India by trade to western Asia and East Africa. Islamic rulers hoped to dominate these valuable regions, and military conflict increased.

The Kutb Minar Tower in Delhi The 240-foot-high Kutb Minar temple in Delhi was built between the twelfth and fourteenth centuries to celebrate Muslim victory in north India.

Robert Harding World Imagery

During the seventh century Arab forces expanded into Afghanistan. By 673 Arab armies were moving into Silk Road cities such as Bukhara and Samarkand, dominated by the Sogdian (SOG-dee-uhn) merchants, mostly Buddhists and Zoroastrians. The rival Central Asian city-states could not come together against the dynamic Arabs, and although many Sogdians resisted, by the early eighth century Arabs had conquered most of the cities. The Arab defeat of Chinese forces at the Battle of Talas River in 751 marked the end of serious resistance to Muslim dominance in Central Asia, and eventually most Central Asians adopted Islam. In India, conflict between Hindus and Muslims began slowly. In 711 Indian pirates plundered an Arab ship near the mouth of the Indus River, and Arab armies responded by briefly conquering the western Indus Basin. But not all encounters were violent. Arab traders from Yemen settled in the ports of southwestern India, bringing Islam to some of the people there.

The expansion of Islam through western and Central Asia presented a challenge to India. By the eleventh century various Turkish peoples had formed Islamic sultanates in Afghanistan, of which Ghazni (GAHZ-nee) was the most powerful. Sultan Mahmud (MACH-mood) of Ghazni (r. 997–1030) led his soldiers on campaigns into India, as much for plunder as for conquest. Seeing the multitude of Hindu idols as an abomination to Islamic monotheism, the invaders destroyed Hindu temples while they looted cities. The vast wealth they took from northwestern India to Ghazni helped that city become a great center of Islamic learning and arts that attracted famed scholars such as the Persian Al-Biruni.

Afghan Sultanates

The Rajputs led the major Indian opposition to Muslim invaders, maintaining a spirited Hindu resistance for many decades. But Rajput military tactics were outdated, and the military forces were divided in their political loyalties. In addition, Indian wars had been fought largely between rulers and their respective warrior castes rather than by conscripted civilians. The caste system allowed only warriors such as the Rajputs to be trained in arms, so they could not effectively mobilize other Indians to help in the fight. Eventually the Rajput armies were defeated by the more mobile, horse-riding Muslims.

Muslim Conquests

The pillaging and destruction by the early Muslim invaders fostered long-term Hindu antipathy toward Muslims. Many Hindus were killed, enslaved, or robbed. For example, even Al-Biruni concluded that Mahmud "utterly ruined [India's] prosperity. To Mahmud the Hindus were infidels, to be dispatched to hell as soon as they refused to be plundered."[6] The Muslim newcomers zealously persecuted Buddhists as well, destroying their monasteries and schools, including the

**Map 13.1
India and the
Delhi Sultanate,
ca. 1300 c.e.**

At its height, the Delhi Sultanate controlled much of northern India. South India was divided into many major states, with the Cholas and Pandyas the largest. Indian ports were connected by a vigorous maritime trade to the Middle East, East Africa, and Southeast Asia.

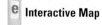 **Interactive Map**

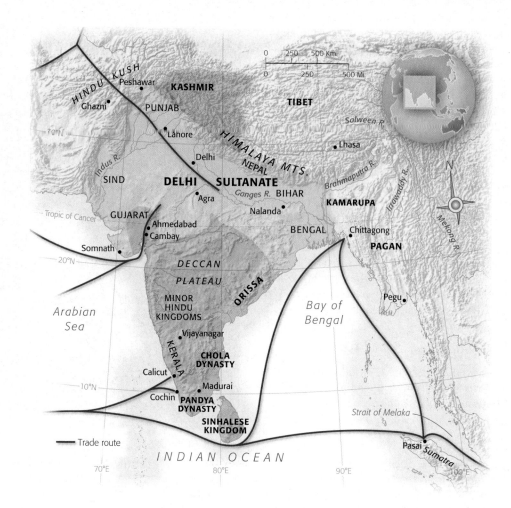

complex at Nalanda. Thousands of monks either were killed or fled to sanctuary in the Himalayas or Tibet. This repression helped eradicate Buddhism from the land of its birth.

The Rise and Fall of the Delhi Sultanate

A new chapter in Muslim expansion began in 1191 when a Turkish prince, driven by religious fervor and lust for the region's riches, conquered most of northern India and founded the Delhi Sultanate (see Map 13.1). The sultanate (1192–1526) reached its height in the 1200s and 1300s and brought political unity to north India for the first time in centuries. Under the Delhi regime Islamic authority and religion spread throughout north India. But the Delhi system was unstable and experienced frequent bloodshed and treachery as leaders competed for power.

Delhi Sultans

The Delhi sultans had diverse ruling styles. Some were patrons of the arts, supporters of science, experts in Greek philosophy, and builders of architecturally splendid structures. Many others, however, were tyrannical and cruel, routinely killing rivals and their families. Some ruined the country with reckless spending. All the sultans employed Persian-style royal pomp, but they also styled themselves after Hindu monarchs, demanding prostration and toe-kissing from subordinates. This blending of ruling styles suggests that Muslim and Hindu cultures were mixing among the elite. Some sultans expanded Delhi's power into central India and, briefly, south India, creating an empire larger than the Gupta realm.

Two of the most able Delhi sultans were Iltutmish (il-TOOT-mish) (1211–1236), who made the Delhi Sultanate the most powerful state in north India, and his remarkable daughter, Raziya (r. 1236–1240). Iltutmish kept out the Mongol armies of Genghis Khan by skillful diplomacy, gradually followed more tolerant policies toward Hindus, and welcomed Muslim refugees, among them scholars and artists, fleeing the Mongols. Their large numbers helped to abort any possibility of Hinduism gradually absorbing Islam. Iltutmish's chosen successor, Raziya, became the only female Muslim ruler in Indian history, praised by scholars of her time for fostering trade, building roads, planting trees, supporting poets and artists, and opening schools. A male Muslim observer described her as "a great monarch, wise, just and generous. She was endowed with all the qualities befitting a king, but she was not born of the right sex, and so in the estimation of men all these virtues were worthless."[7] Raziya was resented as a female leader in a patriarchal society. She further offended Muslim conservatives by abandoning the veil, dressing in male garb, and having a close, perhaps romantic, relationship with a male personal attendant. She died defending her position from male rivals.

By the mid-fourteenth century north India was humbled by severe drought and famine caused in part by climate change. The Delhi Sultanate went into a rapid decline, devastated by rebellion and civil war. Meanwhile, a new Muslim threat appeared in the northwest, the Mongol and Turkish forces of Tamerlane (1336–1405). The ruthless warrior had already conquered Central Asia and Persia, creating the Timurid Empire based at Samarkand (see Chapter 10). In 1398 Tamerlane's forces invaded India, looting Delhi and killing perhaps 100,000 inhabitants in the city, mostly Hindus. Thousands more were dragged away as slaves. Tamerlane defended his actions, arguing that "although I was desirous of sparing them it was the will of God that this calamity should befall the city."[8] Tamerlane and his army returned to Central Asia, leaving Delhi's few surviving inhabitants to perish by plague or starvation. His invasion had a great impact on India, destroying the grand city of Delhi and with it political unity in north India. The Delhi Sultanate survived for several centuries, but in a shrunken form. By the fifteenth century India was fragmented into dozens of Muslim and Hindu states.

Hindu Politics and Culture

While the Delhi Sultanate governed part of India, various Hindu monarchies survived elsewhere, especially in south and east India. Like post-Heian Japan and medieval Europe, these states featured economic self-sufficiency and political decentralization, with warriors receiving land from the monarch in exchange for military service. Commerce flourished, especially in south India. Merchants on the southwest coast, including Jews and Arabs, maintained close ties to western Asia and North Africa and enjoyed wealth. Ports such as Cochin (KOH-chin) and Calicut (KAL-ih-cut) in Kerala and Cambay (kam-BAY) in Gujarat (GOO-jur-ot) played major roles in Indian Ocean trade.

The Tamil (TAA-mill) people of southeast India, controlled by a Hindu dynasty known as the Cholas (CHO-luhs) (846–1216), profited from both piracy and foreign trade. The powerful Chola navy controlled the eastern Indian Ocean and conquered both Kerala and Sri Lanka (Ceylon). Chola merchant castes organized a dynamic maritime trade that brought great wealth to the society and revenue to the kings, and sometimes Chola seafaring led to plunder and conquest as far away as Southeast Asia. Some Chola rulers also established close diplomatic and trade ties to Burma, Cambodia, and China.

The Tamils developed an outstanding artistic tradition, including many fabulous Hindu temples featuring magnificent bronzes. Perhaps the greatest creation was made by some unknown tenth-century genius, a bronze figure of Shiva portrayed as "Lord of the Dance," ready to commence the cosmic dance of life and restore vitality to the world. For centuries artists and historians praised this work, one writing that

> *rarely has an artist achieved such perfect balance and harmony in any medium as in this metal statue, whose symbolism embraces all of Hindu civilization in its mythic power. . . . The workmanship of the artists was flawless in its beauty, magically transmuting metal to flesh-like texture, imparting the breath of life to their subjects.*[9]

The Cholas declined, and the power vacuum was eventually filled by another Hindu kingdom, Vijayanagara (vij-uh-yuh-NUHG-uhr-uh) ("City of Victory"), established in 1336. This militarily powerful state, which eventually dominated much of south and central India, built a magnificent temple-filled capital city but was destroyed by rivals in 1565. The persistence of Hindu rule in southern India preserved Hindu customs and institutions, disappearing in some northern areas.

Vijayanagara

Shiva as Lord of the Dance This famous bronze statue of Shiva as Lord of the Dance was made by Chola artists in southeast India. Displaying himself as a god of many qualities, Shiva grasps the flame of destruction in one hand and the drum of creation in another. The small figure under his foot represents the illusions that Shiva undermines.

The Nelson-Atkins Museum of Art, Kansas City, Missouri. Purchase: William Rockhill Nelson Trust, 34-7. Photography by Jamison Miller

Muslim Rule and the Reshaping of Indian Life

Hindu-Muslim Conflict

The growing number of Muslims and Islamic political power changed Indian history. Muslims and Hindus experienced chronic conflict, the natural result of tensions created by their very different values. To Muslims, Hinduism, with its many deities, elaborate rituals, powerful priests, fondness for images, and preference for eating pork but not beef, constituted the opposite of all Islam held sacred. At the same time, Hindus despised the intolerance of some Muslim rulers and desperately resisted Muslim control. Since Muslim governments could not afford to permanently alienate their Hindu subjects, who constituted a huge majority of the population, some compromises between rulers and ruled were made. Although Muslim rulers often confiscated the wealth of rich Hindu nobles, life in the villages went on largely undisturbed. Eventually many Muslim scholars and leaders came to respect Hindus and the small Zoroastrian community as peoples of the book, counterparts to Christians and Jews in western Asia. But non-Muslims still faced second-class status and special tax payments.

Growth of Islam

Over the centuries many Indians converted from Hinduism to Islam, especially in the Indus River Valley in the northwest and in Bengal in the northeast. A much smaller proportion of southerners embraced Islam. Converts included rich Hindus who wanted to safeguard their positions and secure government offices in Muslim-ruled states, as well as many poor Hindus who converted to escape low or untouchable status and to avoid the heavier taxes on non-Muslims. Over 90 percent of today's Muslims in South Asia are descendants of converts from Hinduism or Buddhism rather than Muslim immigrants. Today Muslims constitute one-fourth of the South Asian population. Sufi mystics, who sought personal union with god, were the key to many Hindus' conversion. Bengali folk tradition celebrates a Sufi who moved to a village and built a mosque: "For the whole day [he] sat under a fig tree. His fame soon spread far and wide. Everybody talked of the occult [healing and psychic] powers he possessed."[10] People respected the intensity of the Sufis' spiritual discipline and the depth of their religious understanding. Perhaps the Sufi message also became popular because it closely resembled bhakti Hinduism, which also emphasized emotional commitment. Today many South Asian Muslims and some Hindus still venerate Sufi mystics of earlier centuries as saints.

purdah The Indian Muslim custom of secluding women.

Religious and cultural mixing occurred. Some Hindu and Muslim mystics came together to form a group emphasizing a love of god. Some poets, honored later as saints, promoted a mixture of Sufi and bhakti ideals, among them Kabir **(kah-BEER)** (1440–1518), a member of a low-status caste of weavers from Benares (see Witness to the Past: The Songs of Kabir). Although blind and illiterate, Kabir wrote poetry that is still revered today by both Hindus and Muslims. The cultural mixing also fostered a new language, Urdu **(ER-doo)**, a combination of Persian, Turkish, Arabic, and Indian words superimposed on a Hindi grammar and written with the Arabic script, that was used by many Muslims in north and northwest India. Muslim influences, including Persian words and Persian food, were also incorporated into Hindu social life. Many Hindu males adopted Muslim clothing styles, and in north India some Hindus began practicing the local Muslim custom of **purdah**, seclusion of women. Some intermarriage also occurred, and, at the village level, Muslims fit themselves into the caste system to some extent. Thus the Muslim society that developed in India, like the Hindu society, was not egalitarian but rather was led by an upper class who descended from immigrants.

However, despite some mixing, from the thirteenth century onward, the life of India became two distinct currents flowing side by side. Under the challenge of the missionary Islam, Hinduism became more conservative, emphasizing tradition and priestly leadership, while most Muslims refused to be assimilated into the social and religious fold of Hinduism and remained disdainful of Hindus and of the caste system. But, unlike Buddhism, which was centered in vulnerable monasteries, Hinduism's decentralized structure proved stable. Thus Hindus and Muslims mingled to some extent along the lines of contact but never formed a single stream. This persistent division greatly affected twentieth-century India, when the British colony of India (most of the subconti-

SECTION SUMMARY

- Hindu warriors fended off Muslim invaders for a time, but they were outmatched and eventually defeated by their aggressive opponents.

- The destruction inflicted by Muslim invaders caused long-term Hindu resentment and also contributed to the decline of Buddhism in India.

- The Islamic Delhi Sultanate brought unity to north India for the first time in centuries, but its rulers ranged from the enlightened to the tyrannical.

- Various Hindu monarchies, including the Cholas, maintained power in southern and eastern India, while Hindu traditions died out in the north.

- The Delhi Sultanate declined because of climate change and civil war, and north Indian unity was shattered by the invasion of Tamerlane.

- Muslim and Hindu beliefs were radically opposed, but over time Muslim rulers came to tolerate Hindu subjects, many of whom eventually converted to Islam.

- While there was some cultural interchange between Hindus and Muslims in India, for the most part, the traditions remained separate.

The Songs of Kabir

Coming from a Hindu family that had recently converted to Islam, Kabir was well acquainted with both religious traditions. His mystical poems of passionate love for a monotheistic god rejected religious prejudice, rigid dogmatism, and the caste system. Modern Indian intellectuals seeking to bridge the gap between the two faiths particularly admired his attempt to see beyond the limitations of the two religions and his absolute opposition to violence. The following poem argues that individuals must experience God for themselves.

O servant, where dost thou seek Me? Lo! I am beside thee.

I am neither in temple nor in mosque; I am neither in Kaaba [Muslim shrine] nor in Kailash [abode of Shiva].

Neither am I in rites and ceremonies, nor in Yoga and renunciation.

If thou art a true seeker, thou shalt at once see Me: . . .

It is needless to ask of a saint the caste to which he belongs; For the priest, the warrior, the tradesman, and all the thirty-six castes, alike are seeking for God.

It is but folly to ask what the caste of a saint may be; The barber has sought God, the washerwoman, and the carpenter . . .

Hindus and Muslims alike have achieved the End, where remains no mark of distinction. . . .

O brother! when I was forgetful, my true Guru [Hindu teacher] showed me the Way.

Then I left off all rites and ceremonies, I bathed no more in the holy water: . . .

From that time forth I knew no more how to roll in the dust in obeisance:

I do not ring the temple bell; I do not set the idol on its throne; I do not worship the image with flowers.

It is not the austerities that mortify the flesh which are pleasing to the Lord,

When you leave off your clothes and kill your senses, you do not please the Lord,

The man who is kind and who practices righteousness, who remains passive amidst the affairs of the world, who considers all creatures on earth as his own self,

He attains the Immortal Being, the true God is ever with him.

Kabir says: "He attains the true Name whose words are pure, and who is free from pride and conceit."

If God be within the mosque, then to whom does this world belong?

If Ram [God] be within the image which you find upon your pilgrimage, then who is there to know what happens without?

Hari [Lord Vishnu] is in the East; Allah is in the West. Look within your heart, . . .

All the men and women of the world are His Living Forms. Kabir is the child of Allah and of Ram [God]: He is my *Guru*, He is my *Pir* [Sufi saint].

THINKING ABOUT THE READING

1. Why would someone of mixed religious background be open to questioning rigid doctrines?
2. What does Kabir think about the traditions of organized religions?
3. Where does Kabir believe that God is to be found?

Source: William Theodore De Bary, ed., *Sources of Indian Tradition*, Vol. 1 Copyright © 1958 Columbia University Press. Reprinted with permission of the publisher.

---

nent) was eventually divided into separate nations, the Hindu-dominated India and the Muslim-dominated Pakistan. A third religion also maintained a South Asian base, since the island of Sri Lanka remained a bastion of Theravada Buddhism.

CULTURAL ADAPTATION AND KINGDOMS IN SOUTHEAST ASIA

> What political and religious forms shaped Southeast Asian societies in the Early Intermediate Era?

Owing partly to the stimulus from India and, to a lesser extent, China, several great Southeast Asian kingdoms developed near the end of the first millennium C.E., establishing their main centers in what is today Cambodia, Burma, the Indonesian islands of Java and Sumatra, and Vietnam (see Map 13.2). These Southeast Asian states mixed outside influences with their own traditions to foster new societies (see Chronology: Southeast Asia, 600–1500).

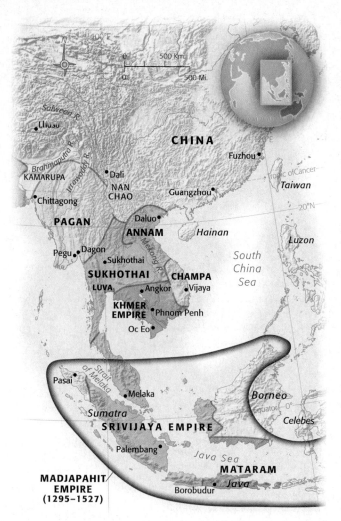

**Map 13.2
Major Southeast
Asian Kingdoms,
ca. 1200 C.E.**

By 1200 the Khmer
Empire (Angkor), which
once covered much of
mainland Southeast
Asia, had declined.
Sukhothai, Pagan,
Srivijaya, Champa, and
Vietnam were other
major states.

e **Interactive Map**

Indianized Kingdoms and Societies

From early in the Common Era until around the fourteenth century, many Southeast Asian societies made selective use of Indian models in shaping their political patterns, a process known as Indianization. For example, the rulers declared themselves god-kings, not just China-style intermediaries between the human realm and the cosmos but rather a reincarnated Buddha or Shiva worthy of cult worship. By maintaining order in the world, they ensured cosmic harmony. Kings enjoyed enormous prestige but also faced continuous threats from rivals, who often succeeded in acquiring the throne, and neighboring states.

The economic foundations of the Indianized kingdoms differed. Some were based largely on agriculture, while others, including the states alongside the Straits of Melaka, depended heavily on maritime trade. These contrasting patterns represented skillful adaptations to the environment. In the agriculture-based economies, rice-growing technology became productive enough to sustain large centralized states, but in places with large areas of swampland people compensated for their lack of good farmland by maximizing their access to the open frontier of the sea.

The migration and mixing of peoples and their cultures were significant themes in Southeast Asia, as they had been in India, Europe, and Africa. Peoples such as the Burmans (BUHR-muhnz) in the ninth century and the Tai (tie) peoples in the seventh to thirteenth centuries moved from Tibet and China into mainland Southeast Asia. The Burmans established the dynamic state of Pagan (puh-GONE) in central Burma (1044–1287).

Religion played a central role in the new states. Though the peasantry remained chiefly animist, Southeast Asian elites adopted Mahayana Buddhism and Hinduism. At its height in the twelfth century, the city of Pagan was one of the architectural wonders of the world, filled with magnificent temples and shrines for the glory of Buddhism and Hinduism. At Pagan and elsewhere religion infused government and the arts, and Hindu priests became advisers on court rituals. Hindu Indian epics such as the *Ramayana* and *Mahabharata* became deeply imbedded in the cultures, and the Hindu kings, gods, and demons animated the arts.

Southeast Asian societies shared many common features. Extensive trade networks, both land and maritime, had linked the region from earliest times, and many people specialized in local or foreign commerce. Most of the larger states were multiethnic in their population, including many foreign merchants, a diversity that fostered a cosmopolitan attitude. Still, most Southeast Asians were farmers and fishermen and lived in villages characterized by a spirit of cooperation for mutual survival. Unlike in India, however, Southeast Asian family patterns ranged from flexible structures to a few patriarchies and matriarchies. In contrast to India and China, women held a relatively high status in most Southeast Asian societies, and some, like the Burmese queen Pwa Saw (pwah saw), exercised political influence behind the scenes (see Profile: Pwa Saw, a Burmese Queen). An enduring gap in world-views separated the social and cultural traditions of the courts, including the royal families, administrations, and capital cities, from the villages. For example, Indian scripts became the basis for many Southeast Asian written languages, such as Khmer, Burman, and Thai, and fostered poetry, religious speculations, and historical chronicles, important components of Southeast Asia's elite culture.

The Angkor Empire and Society

The Khmer people created the greatest Indianized state, the kingdom of Angkor (ANG-kor) in Cambodia. A visionary king, Jayavarman (JAI-a-VAR-man) I (r. 802–834), who identified himself with the Hindu god Shiva, established the state in 802, and his successors extended the kingdom, which persisted until 1432. The magnificent temples still standing today testify to the prosperity and organization of Angkor society. By the twelfth century the bustling capital city, Angkor Thom

(ANG-kor tom), contained perhaps a million people, making it much larger than medieval European cities and comparable to all but the largest Chinese and Arab cities. Trade with China and other countries flourished, and many Chinese merchants lived in the kingdom.

At its height in the twelfth and thirteenth centuries, Angkor had an empire controlling much of what is now Cambodia, Laos, Thailand, and southern Vietnam. The Khmers acquired and maintained their empire by warfare, diplomacy, and pragmatism, usually giving regional governors considerable autonomy. Many kings were art patrons and builders of roads and temples. Zhou Daguan (joe ta-kwan), a Chinese ambassador in Angkor in 1296, left vivid descriptions of Angkor, including the system of justice presided over by the king: "Disputes of the people, however insignificant, always go to the king. Each day the king holds two audiences for affairs of state. Those of the functionaries or the people who wish to see the king, sit on the ground to wait for him."[11] The well-financed state held much power over the population and supported substantial public services, including hospitals, schools, and libraries. Conscripted workers constructed an extensive canal and reservoir network for efficient water distribution and storage, exhibiting some of the most advanced civil engineering in the premodern world. The Khmers also may have had the most productive agriculture in world history, producing three to four crops of rice a year.

Religion played an important political and cultural role. The Angkor government resembled a theocracy: it presided over a cult for the popular worship of the god-kings, and priestly families held a privileged position. The numerous temples and Hindu priests controlled massive wealth. Hindu values were also reflected in theater, art, dance, and the many magnificent stone temples, some of them as huge as small mountains. Designed to represent the Hindu conception of the cosmos centered on the abode of the gods, the temples provided vivid symbols of a monarch's earthly power, since the construction involved amazing engineering skills and massive conscripted labor. The largest religious complex in the premodern world, Angkor Wat (ANG-kor waht), was built by some 70,000 workers in the twelfth century. The reliefs carved into stone at Angkor Wat and other temples provide glimpses of daily life, showing fishing boats, midwives attending a childbirth, merchant stalls, festival jugglers and dancers, peasants bringing goods to market, the crowd at a cockfight, and men playing chess.

In exchange for material security, Khmer commoners tolerated a highly inequitable distribution of wealth and power as well as substantial labor demands. Angkor had numerous slaves and people in temporary servitude. Although no India-style caste system existed despite the strong Hindu influence, the social structure was rigid. Each class had its appointed role: below the king were the priests, and below them were the trade guilds. The vast majority of the population were of the farmer-builder-soldier class. Khmer women played a much more important role in society and politics than women did in most other places in the world. According to Zhou Daguan, women operated most of the retail stalls: "In this country it is the women who are concerned with commerce."[12] Some royal women were noted for intellectual or service activities. Jayarajadevi (JAI-ya-RAJ-adeh-vee), the first wife of King Jayavarman VII, took in hundreds of abandoned girls and trained and settled them. After her death the king married Indradevi (IN-dra-deh-vee), a renowned scholar who lectured at a Buddhist monastery. Women dominated the palace staff, and some were even gladiators and warriors. Chinese visitors were shocked at the liberated behavior of Khmer women, who went out in public as they liked. Women were also active in the arts, especially as poets.

Indianized Urban Societies in Java and Sumatra

Several Indianized states developed in the Indonesian archipelago on the large islands of Java and Sumatra. The encounters between Indian influence and local traditions produced in Java a distinctive

CHRONOLOGY
Southeast Asia, 600–1500

192–1471 Kingdom of Champa

600–1290 Srivijaya Empire

802–1432 Angkor Empire

939 End of Chinese colonization in Vietnam

1044–1287 Pagan kingdom in Burma

1292–1527 Madjapahit kingdom on Java

1238–1419 Sukhotai kingdom in Siam

1350–1767 Ayutthaya kingdom in Siam

1403–1511 Melaka kingdom and Sultanate

1428–1788 Le dynasty in Vietnam (founded by Le Loi)

Angkor Wat Temple Complex This photograph shows the inner buildings of the Angkor Wat temple complex in northern Cambodia. The towers represented the Hindu view of the cosmos. Mount Meru, the home of the gods, rises 726 feet in the middle.

Robert Harding World Imagery

PWA SAW, A BURMESE QUEEN

Women in royal families played important political roles in many Southeast Asian states, mostly behind the scenes, but few had the influence of thirteenth-century Queen Pwa Saw of Pagan. Much of what we know about her life comes from a chronicle of the country's history compiled by Burmese scholars in the nineteenth century, and modern historians are divided on whether it represents more myth than fact. Whatever the accuracy, in their traditions the Burman people remember Queen Pwa Saw as witty, wise, and beautiful and as exercising political influence for forty years during one of their most difficult periods.

The girl who would become queen was born to a prosperous peasant family in a remote village around 1237. According to the legends, a deadly king cobra approached her when she was asleep but failed to attack, considered a favorable omen for a bright future, and a jasmine bush she tended astonished her neighbors by blooming in three colors. This unusual event drew the attention of the young King Uzana (r. 1249–1256), a playboy fond of hunting and drinking who was visiting the district with a large entourage of attendants. The unexpected visit of a king and his party riding on elephants spurred the villagers into frenzied preparations for a proper reception to demonstrate their respect. Infatuated with the bright, pretty, graceful, and talkative sixteen-year-old girl, Uzana took her back to Pagan as one of his many wives and appointed her a deputy queen. A short time later, Uzana died in an accident while hunting wild elephants.

With her husband's death, Pwa Saw was thrown into the schemes and rivalries of the royal court as various factions maneuvered for power. Placed in a precarious position as a young bride resented by rival queens, she quickly forged an alliance with the able and wily Chief Minister Yazathingyan (YAH-za-THING-yan), who feared the accession of the king's oldest son, the unpopular Prince Thitathu (thee-TAH-thoo), with whom he had long quarreled. Together they convinced officials to support another son, Narathihapade (NAR-a-THITH-a-PAH-dee) (r. 1256–1287), as king and make Pwa Saw chief queen. But the young king proved arrogant, quick-tempered, and ruthless, alienating many at court and earning the nickname "King Dog's Dung." While the economy declined, the king boasted that he was "the commander of 36 million soldiers, the swallower of 300 dishes of curry daily," and had 3,000 concubines. His zeal to build an expensive Buddhist pagoda fostered the proverb that "the pagoda is finished and the great country ruined." Pwa Saw remained loyal but lost respect for the king.

After her ally Yazathingyan died leading royal forces to suppress a rebellion in the south, Pwa Saw skillfully survived the king's paranoid suspicions and the constant intrigues of the court nobles, attendants, and other queens. Because the king trusted the widely revered queen, she could often overrule his destructive tendencies and talk him into making wiser state decisions. She also convinced the erratic king to appoint capable officials. But she had to maintain her wits. Increasingly paranoid, Narathihapade executed any perceived enemies and burned another queen to death. In the 1270s, anxious to prove himself a great leader, he rejected Pwa Saw's advice to meet Mongol demands for tribute and avoid conflict and instead escalated tensions, thus bringing on war, disaster, and the temporary Mongol occupation of Pagan.

Even as the Pagan state declined, Pwa Saw asserted a benevolent influence. For instance, in 1271 she donated some of her lands and properties to a Buddhist temple, expressing hope that in future existences she would "have long life, be free from illness, have a good appearance, melodic of voice, be loved and respected by all men and gods, [and] be fully equipped with faith, wisdom, nobility." In 1287 the mad king was murdered by one of his sons. In 1289 Queen Saw and surviving ministers selected a new king, Kyawswar (kee-YAH-swar) (1287–1298). With that last effort to help her country, she retired in style to her home village.

THINKING ABOUT THE PROFILE

1. What skills did Pwa Saw use to influence the court?

2. What does this profile tell us about the relations between queens and kings at Pagan?

Notes: Quotations from D. G. E. Hall, *A History of South-East Asia,* 4th ed. (New York: St. Martin's Press, 1981), 169; and Michael Aung-Thwin, *Pagan: The Origins of Modern Burma* (Honolulu: University of Hawaii Press, 1985), 41.

Court Life of Pwa Saw No known paintings of Pwa Saw exist. This fresco, from the Ananda Buddhist temple at Pagan, shows rich court ladies, much like Pwa Saw herself, relaxing in an upstairs room of a magnificent Buddhist temple while, downstairs, stallholders hawk their wares to visitors.

Robert Harding World Imagery

religious and political blend known as Hindu-Javanese, which was based on an agricultural economy. According to Hindu-Javanese thinking, because the earthly order mirrored and embodied the cosmic order, people must avoid disharmony and change to preserve the cosmic order. The god-king's duty was to prevent social deterioration and maintain order in a turbulent human world. The greatest Javanese kingdom, Madjapahit (MAH-ja-PA-hit) (1292–1527), reached its peak in the fourteenth century under the fabled Prime Minister Gajah Mada, when it loosely controlled a large empire embracing much of present-day Indonesia. As in Angkor, the capitals and palaces of Javanese kingdoms like Madjapahit were built to imitate the cosmic order. Hindu-Buddhist ideas can be seen vividly in temple complexes such as the temple mountain of Borobodur (BOR-uh-buh-door) in central Java, as well as in the shadow puppet plays, or **wayang kulit** (WHY-ang KOO-leet), which were based on the Hindu epics like the *Ramayana* but had much local content as well.

Social inequality permeated Hindu-Javanese society, and a complex etiquette regulated the relations between those of varied status. The aristocracy, who administered the realm, expected deference from commoners, most of whom lived in villages whose cultures differed substantially from those of the royal capitals. Much village work was planned and carried out on a communal basis, following a tradition of mutual aid. Peasants identified more with their village community than with distant kings in their palaces.

Coastal states on Sumatra were shaped more heavily by international trade than were the agricultural kingdoms of Java and Cambodia. The Straits of Melaka separating Sumatra from the Malay Peninsula was a major passageway through which a complex maritime trading system gradually emerged that linked the eastern Mediterranean, Middle East, East African coast, Persia, and India with East and Southeast Asia. Between 600 and 1290 many of the small trading states in the Straits region came under the loose control of Srivijaya (SREE-vih-JAI-ya), an empire based in southeastern Sumatra that exercised considerable power over the region's international commerce and maintained a close trade relationship with powerful China. Srivijaya's naval force both fought and engaged in piracy. Srivijaya was also a major international center of Buddhist study, attracting thousands of Buddhist monks and students from many countries.

International Influences and the Decline of the Indianized States

The great Indianized states of Southeast Asia came to an end between the thirteenth and fifteenth centuries, but the changes were mostly gradual. Some causes of decline were internal. Angkor experienced a combination of military expansion that overstretched resources; increased temple building that resulted in higher tax levies and forced labor that antagonized much of the population; and growing breakdown of the irrigation system, which took more and more labor to maintain. Increasingly unpredictable rains due to climate change overstretched the hydraulic system. But international influences also played a role in the disintegration of Angkor and neighboring states.

Over several centuries various groups from mountainous southwestern China speaking Tai languages migrated into Southeast Asia, some of them setting up their own states in the Mekong Basin and northern Thailand. These were the ancestors of the closely related Siamese (SYE-uh-meez), today known as the Thai, and the Lao (laow) peoples. As they moved south, the Tai conquered or absorbed the local peoples while also adopting some of their cultural traditions. Eventually they came into conflict with Angkor, repeatedly sacking the capital and seizing much of the empire's territory. The Khmer Empire soon disintegrated, and the Angkor capital was abandoned. As the monuments to their glorious past were overtaken by jungle, the Khmers became pawns perched uneasily between the expanding Vietnamese and Siamese states.

Meanwhile, the Mongols encountered Angkor's neighbors. After conquering China, in 1288 they attacked Pagan because the Burmans refused to recognize Mongol overlordship. When the Mongols soon withdrew, they left instability in Burma as rival groups competed for power. Elsewhere in Southeast Asia the Mongols found mostly frustration. Although a land-and-sea invasion of Vietnam and Champa inflicted terrible damage, it was ultimately repelled by a temporary Vietnamese-Cham military alliance. A Mongol naval expedition to Java also proved a costly failure. Southeast Asians were among the few peoples to successfully resist Mongol conquest and power.

A third force for change was religion. By early in the second millennium of the Common Era, Theravada Buddhism and Islam began filtering peacefully into the region from outside. Theravada Buddhism had been a strong influence in Burma, but a revitalized form came from Sri Lanka and provided a challenge to the Indianized regimes. The Buddhist message of egalitarianism, pacifism, and individual worth proved attractive to peasants weary of war, public labor projects, and tyrannical kings. Theravada Buddhism was a tolerant religion able to exist alongside the rich animism of the peasants, who could honor the Buddha while worshiping local spirits. By the fourteenth

Hindu-Javanese Society

wayang kulit Javanese shadow puppet play based on Hindu epics like the *Ramayana* and local Javanese content.

Trading States

Migrations and Invasions

Theravada Buddhism and Islam

century most of the Burman, Khmer, Siamese, and Lao peasants had adopted Theravada Buddhism, while the elite mixed the faith with the older Hindu–Mahayana Buddhist traditions.

From the thirteenth through sixteenth centuries, Sunni Islam filtered in from the Middle East via India and spread widely. Like Buddhism, Islam offered an egalitarian message and a complex theology that appealed to peasants and merchants in the Malay Peninsula, Sumatra, Java, and some of the other islands. Some adopted Sunni Islam in a largely orthodox form, while others mixed it with animism or Hinduism Buddhism. Sufism also blended well with the existing mysticism. Only a few scattered peoples maintained Indianized societies. Among the Balinese (BAH-luh-NEEZ) on the Indonesian island of Bali, Hinduism and other classical patterns remained vigorous, emphasizing arts like dancing, music, shadow plays, and woodcarving. Thus the many visitors to Bali today can glimpse patterns that were once widespread in the region.

SECTION SUMMARY

- Southeast Asian kingdoms were heavily influenced by India, and, as in India, their rulers considered themselves god-kings, although their power was limited in the provinces.

- Most Southeast Asian states were multiethnic and were influenced by immigrants and the migration of Mahayana Buddhism and Hinduism from India.

- The Indianized kingdom of Angkor controlled a large swath of Southeast Asia and completed advanced civil engineering projects, such as an extensive canal system and the huge temple complex of Angkor Wat.

- Hindu priests played a very important role in Angkor, and the social structure was extremely rigid, though an Indian-style caste system did not take hold and women were more important in society and politics than in most places in the world.

- On Java, a highly stratified Indianized society that championed harmony developed, while on Sumatra, Srivajaya became a powerful commercial empire.

- Southeast Asians fended off the Mongols, but new peoples such as the Tai invaded and destroyed Angkor, and the gradual introduction of Theravada Buddhism and Sunni Islam challenged the hierarchical order and displaced Indian influence in many states.

BUDDHIST, CONFUCIAN, AND ISLAMIC SOUTHEAST ASIAN SOCIETIES

> What was the influence of Theravada Buddhism, Confucianism, and Islam on Southeast Asia?

By the fifteenth century Southeast Asia had experienced a major transition. The Indianized kingdoms had gradually been replaced by less despotic states, and networks of trade and religion linked the region even more closely to Afro-Eurasia. The major Southeast Asian societies diverged from the earlier Indian and Chinese-influenced patterns, and Theravada Buddhism, Confucianism, and Islam permeated further into the countryside. By the fifteenth century three broad but very distinctive social and cultural patterns had developed: the Theravada Buddhist, the Confucian-Buddhist Vietnamese, and the Malayo-Muslim or Indonesian.

Theravada Buddhist Society in Siam

Rise of Siamese States

The Siamese established several states in northern and central Thailand. Sukhotai (SOO-ko-TAI) (1238–1419), founded by former Angkor vassals, controlled much of the central plains of Thailand. According to Siamese tradition, Sukhotai's glory was established by Rama Kamkheng (RA-ma KHAM-keng) ("Rama the Brave"), a shrewd diplomat who established a close tributary relationship with China. Sukhothai adopted the Khmer script and incorporated Khmer influences in literature, art, and government. Siamese chronicles portray Rama as a wise and popular ruler. A temple inscription tells us that

> the Lord of the country levies no tolls on his subjects. If he sees someone else's wealth he does not interfere. If he captures some enemy soldiers he neither kills them nor beats them. In the [palace] doorway a bell is suspended; if an inhabitant of the kingdom has any complaint or any matter irritates his stomach and torments his mind, and he desires to expose it to the king ring the bell.[13]

This may have exaggerated his merits, but Rama did make Theravada Buddhism the state religion and adopted humane laws. By 1350, however, Sukhotai was eclipsed by another Siamese state with its capital at Ayutthaya (ah-YUT-uh-yuh), which developed a regional empire whose influence extended into Cambodia and the small Lao states along the Mekong River. Its rivalry with the Burmans and Vietnamese for regional dominance occasionally led to war.

Class System and Gender Relations

In most Theravada Buddhist states, people viewed kings as semidivine reincarnated Buddhas. Kings lived in splendor, advised by Brahman priests in ceremonial and magical practices. They had many wives and therefore many sons, all of whom could be rivals for the throne, and unclear political succession rules meant chronic instability. Despite a bureaucratic government, royal power lessened as distance to the capital increased.

The Siamese society had many similarities to those of the Theravada Buddhist Khmer, Burmans, and especially the Lao. The Siamese social order was divided into a small aristocracy, many commoners, and some slaves (many of them prisoners of war). Deference to higher authority and recognition of status differences were expected. In contrast to the extended families of China or India, small nuclear families were the norm. While Theravada peoples encouraged cooperation within the family and village, they also valued individualism. Although women did not enjoy absolute equality and were expected to show their respect for men, free women enjoyed many rights. They inherited equally with men, could initiate marriage or divorce, and operated most of the stalls in village or town markets. Visitors from China, India, Europe, and the Middle East were shocked at the relative freedom of Siamese women. A Muslim Persian diplomat in Ayutthaya wrote that "it is common for women to engage in buying and selling in the markets and even to undertake physical labor, and they do not cover themselves with modesty. Thus you can see the women paddling to the surrounding villages where they successfully earn their daily bread with no assistance from the men."[14]

Siamese society reflected Theravada Buddhist values, such as gentleness, meditation, and reincarnation, as well as the concept of *karma*, the idea that one's actions in this life or past lives determined one's destiny. To escape from the endless round of life, death, and rebirth, believers were expected to attain merit by performing generous deeds, with the ultimate goal of reaching *nirvana*, or release from suffering. Many men became Buddhist monks who played key roles in local affairs and operated many village schools, with the result that Theravada societies had some of the highest literacy rates (especially for males) in the premodern world. Women could not gain merit as monks, although some became nuns. Most Siamese were tolerant of those who were less devout, believing that an individual's spiritual state was his or her own responsibility. Peasants moved easily between supporting their local Buddhist temple and placating the animist spirits of the fields.

Theravada Buddhist Values

Confucianism, Buddhism, and Vietnamese Society

Vietnam, another important Southeast Asian state, had been a Chinese colony for over a thousand years, but a Vietnamese rebellion finally succeeded in pushing the Chinese out in 939 and establishing independence. Vietnam continued to borrow ideas from China and even became a vassal state, sending tribute missions to the Chinese emperor. By the fourteenth century it offered a striking contrast to Theravada Buddhist societies.

Despite Vietnam's formal subservience, Chinese forces occasionally attempted a reconquest, inspiring the Vietnamese to become masters at resisting foreign invasions. In 1407 the new Ming dynasty invaded and conquered Vietnam. In response to the harsh Chinese repression, Le Loi (lay lo-ee) (1385–1433) organized a Vietnamese resistance movement that struggled tenaciously for the next two decades. After finally expelling the Chinese in 1428, Le Loi founded a new Vietnamese dynasty, the Le (1428–1788). His social and economic reforms and victory over Chinese domination made him one of the heroes of Vietnam's long struggle for independence. As Le Loi told his people: "Over the centuries, we have been sometimes strong, sometimes weak; but never yet have we been lacking in heroes. In that let our history be the proof."[15] Thus over the centuries, a sense of common identity and national feeling greatly aided Vietnamese survival on the fringes of powerful China. When the country was at peace, literature, poetry, and theater flourished.

Vietnam and China

Vietnam's imperial system was modeled on China's, headed by an emperor considered a "son of heaven," an intermediary between the terrestrial and supernatural realms ruling through the Mandate of Heaven. As in China, emperors governed through a bureaucracy staffed by scholar-administrators (*mandarins*) chosen by civil service examinations designed to recruit men of talent. The official ideology of Confucianism stressed ethical conduct, social harmony, and hierarchy. Vietnam also sought to influence or control the peoples of the highlands as well as the neighboring Cham, Khmer, and Lao states.

Le Dynasty Ruler This Vietnamese drawing shows the Le emperor being carried in state, accompanied by his mandarins, parasol- and fan-bearers, and a royal elephant. The drawing was printed in an eighteenth-century British book, with an English description of the procession.

Peasant society differed considerably from the imperial court and political elite. In the villages religious life mixed Mahayana Buddhism, Confucianism, and Daoism, all adopted from China, with spirit and ancestor worship. Villages were self-governing, their autonomy summarized in the expression that "the authority of the emperor ends at the village gate." Communal land in the village was set aside to be farmed by landless peasants. Although the Vietnamese social system was patriarchal, women dominated the town and village markets, doing most of the buying and selling of food and crafts, and they saw their influence increase with age.

Vietnamese Expansion

Beginning in the tenth century, some Vietnamese left the overcrowded Red River Valley and Tonkin Gulf to migrate southward. These Vietnamese settlers, supported by imperial forces, overran the Cham people in central Vietnam and by 1471 the kingdom of Champa had ended. By the sixteenth century the Vietnamese were pushing toward the Khmer-dominated Mekong River Basin in southern Vietnam. As a result of this migration, the Vietnamese became more involved with Southeast Asia, and the central and southern dialects and cultures gradually came to differ from those in the northern part of Vietnam.

Islam, Maritime Networks, and the Malay World

Maritime Trade

Southeast Asians had long excelled as seafaring traders, traveling as far away as East Africa. During the Intermediate Era Southeast Asian port cities became essential intermediaries in the trade between China, India, and the Middle East. This trade brought Southeast Asians into contact with the Muslim Islamic merchants from Arabia, Persia, and India, who spread Islam along the Indian Ocean trading routes. Commercial people were attracted to a religion that sanctioned the accumulation of wealth and preached cooperation among believers, and some Hindu-Buddhist rulers of coastal states in the Malay Peninsula and Indonesian islands grew eager to attract Muslim traders. Impressed by the cosmopolitan universality of Islam, they adopted the new faith, converting themselves into sultans. The increased trade spurred the growth of cities and new maritime trading states and gave merchants more influence in local politics. This transformation in the international maritime economy created an unprecedented commercial prosperity and cosmopolitan culture in Southeast Asia. At the same time, more intensive agricultural growth, including new crops and varieties of rice, spurred population increase, migration, and more bureaucratic states.

Rise of Melaka

The spread of Islam in the region coincided with, and was spurred by, the rise of the great port of Melaka **(muh-LACK-uh)** on the southwest coast of Malaya facing the Straits of Melaka. In 1403 the Hindu ruler of the city, Parameswara, adopted Islam and transformed himself into a sultan. The Melakans blended Islamic faith and culture with the older Hindu-Buddhist and animist beliefs, creating an eclectic cultural pattern. Because Islam in the region was closely identified with the Malay people of Melaka, historians often refer to the Muslim Southeast Asian societies as Malayo-Muslim. Malay identity spread to many societies in Malaya, Sumatra, and Borneo who practiced Islam and spoke the Malay language.

Melaka replaced Srivijaya as the region's economic power and became the crossroads of Asian maritime commerce. Its rulers sent tributary missions to China and made their port a waystation for the series of grand Chinese voyages to the western Indian Ocean led by Admiral Zheng He (see Chapter 11). In exchange for Melaka's service, the Ming supported the young state in regional disputes. Soon merchants from around Asia began coming to the new emporium, rapidly transforming the port into the archipelago's major trading hub, as well as the southeastern terminus for the Indian Ocean maritime trading network. One of the major commercial centers in the world, Melaka rivaled other great trading ports such as Calicut, Cambay, Guangzhou (Canton), Hormuz, Alexandria, Genoa, and Venice. In 1468 Melaka's sultan Mansur wrote to the king of the Ryukyu Islands, "We have learned that to master the blue oceans people must engage in commerce. All the lands within the seas are united in one body. Life has never been so affluent in preceding generations as it is today."[16] Gradually, Melaka became the center of a highly decentralized empire that dominated much of coastal Malaya and eastern Sumatra.

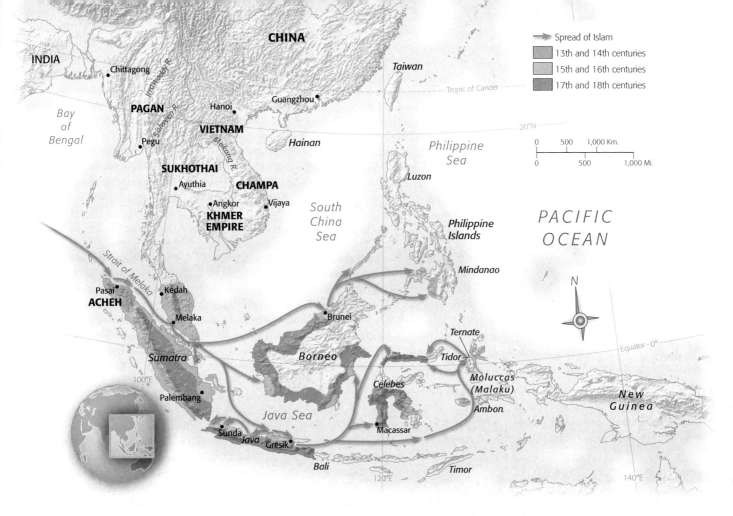

**Map 13.3
The Spread of Islam in Island Southeast Asia**

Carried by merchants and missionaries, Islam spread from Arabia and India to island Southeast Asia, eventually becoming the major faith on many islands and in the Malay Peninsula.

Interactive Map

Melaka flourished until 1511 as a vital link in world trade. An early-sixteenth-century Portuguese visitor wrote that it had "no equal in the world" and extolled the importance of Melaka to peoples and trade patterns as far away as western Europe: "Melaka is a city that was made for merchandise, fitter than any other in the world. Commerce between different nations for a thousand leagues on every hand must come to Melaka."[17] Melaka had a special connection to the Indian port of Cambay, nearly 3,000 miles away. Every year trading ships from around the Middle East and South Asia gathered at Cambay and Calicut to make the long voyage to Melaka, carrying with them grain, woolens, arms, copperware, textiles, and opium. Goods from as far north as Korea also reached Melaka.

The flourishing trading port attracted merchants from many lands. By the late 1400s Melaka's 100,000 to 200,000 people included 15,000 foreign merchants, whose diversity reflected Melaka's global importance. The foreigners included Arabs, Egyptians, Persians, Armenians, Jews, Ethiopians, Swahilis, Burmese, and Indians from the west, and Vietnamese, Javanese, Filipinos, Japanese, and Chinese from the east and north. Some eighty-four languages were spoken on the city's streets. Visitors claimed that more ships crowded the Melaka harbor than in any other port in the world, attracted by a stable government and a free trade policy. City shops offered textiles from India, books from the Middle East, cloves and nutmeg from Maluku, batiks and carpets from Java, silk and porcelain from China, and sugar from the Philippines. Gold brought from various places was so plentiful that children played with it.

Melaka also became the main center for the spread of Islam in the Malay Peninsula and western Indonesian archipelago (see Map 13.3), spurring political change and economic growth as rulers embraced the new faith for religious, political, and commercial reasons. Some Islamic states, such as Acheh (AH-chay) in northern Sumatra, became regional powers. The sultanates of Ternate (tuhr-NAH-tay) and Tidor (TEE-door) in the Maluku (muh-LUKE-uh) (Moluccan) Islands of northeastern Indonesia prospered from the spices they produced (especially cloves and nutmeg) that were prized in Europe and the Middle East. Gradually many people followed the example of their rulers and adopted Islam, joining Southeast Asia to the wider Islamic world. But there also remained many village-based societies, some of them still practicing animism, in more isolated or fringe areas such as the Philippine Islands, with no political authority higher than local chiefs.

Spread of Islam

Islamic Diversity

Various patterns of Islamic belief and practice, more diverse than elsewhere in the Islamic world, emerged in the scattered island societies. In most cases Islam did not completely displace older customs. For example, on Java Indianized kings and courts combined Islamic beliefs with older Hindu-Buddhist ceremonies and mystical traditions. Yet, many peasants maintained their mystical animist beliefs and practices under an Islamic veneer, tolerating diverse religious views, while others (especially merchants) adopted a more orthodox Islamic faith, following prescribed Islamic practices and looking toward the Middle East for models. The complex Javanese religion mirrored a hierarchical social system. The sultans in their palaces remained aloof from the people, while the aristocracy remained obsessed with practicing refined behavior rooted in mystical Hinduism. Javanese of all classes placed a great value on avoiding interpersonal conflict.

Southeast Asia and the Wider World

Southeast Asia had long been a cosmopolitan region where peoples, ideas, and products met, and visitors and sojourners from many lands continued to reach the region. For example, the intrepid Italian traveler Marco Polo passed through in 1292 on his way home from a long sojourn in China. His writings praised the wealth and sophistication of Champa, Java, and Sumatra, arousing European interest in seeking direct trade connections with these seemingly fabulous lands. Polo wrote that "Java is of unsurpassing wealth, producing all kinds of spices, frequented by a vast amount of shipping. Indeed, the treasure of this island is so great as to be past telling."[18]

Indeed, the Southeast Asia Marco Polo and other travelers such as the Moroccan Ibn Battuta encountered was one of the world's more prosperous and urbanized regions. Major cities like Ayutthaya, Melaka, and Hanoi (Vietnam) were as large as the major European urban centers like Naples and Paris. By the 1400s, though having perhaps 15 to 20 million people, Southeast Asia was still dwarfed by the dense populations of nearby China and India. Still, blessed with fertile land and extensive trade, Southeast Asians often enjoyed better health, more varied diets, and adequate material resources than most peoples.

Southeast Asia's connections to the wider world, as well as its famed wealth, eventually attracted arrivals who were not welcome. By the beginning of the sixteenth century a few Portuguese explorers and adventurers, with deadly weapons, state-of-the-art ships, Christian missionary zeal, and desire for wealth, reached first India and then Southeast Asia seeking "Christians and spices." The Portuguese standard of living was probably inferior to that of Siam, Vietnam, Melaka, or Java, but the Portuguese were the forerunners of what became a powerful, destabilizing European presence that gradually altered the region after 1500.

SECTION SUMMARY

- Siamese states such as Sukhotai and Ayutthaya were Theravada Buddhist monarchies that valued individualism and peacefulness, offered women a fair amount of freedom, and were permeated by Buddhist values.

- Despite gaining freedom from Chinese rule, Vietnam retained a great deal of Chinese cultural influence.

- Inhabitants of the Malay and Indonesian archipelagoes embraced Islam, which arrived via increasing maritime trade, and grafted it onto Hinduism and Buddhism to create many different patterns of Islamic belief, while native animist traditions survived to some extent in the villages.

- Melaka displaced Srivajaya as the center of Southeast Asian trading power and became an international crossroads.

- Southeast Asia would eventually attract less friendly visitors, such as the Portuguese.

CHAPTER SUMMARY

Although many earlier patterns of life and thought persisted in India and Southeast Asia during the Intermediate Era, these regions also experienced tremendous changes. A constant stream of West Asian and Central Asian peoples into India brought more diversity to Indian social patterns and beliefs. Although India remained politically fragmented, Hinduism enjoyed a kind of renaissance. Most people owed allegiance to their family, caste, and village. Hinduism spawned diverse ideas and cults and gradually brought some cultural unity, while Buddhism gradually lost influence in much of India. Hindu society faced its greatest challenge from Muslim conquerors, who became politically dominant in north India. Muslims would not be assimilated, although there was some mixing of Hindu and Muslim traditions. Islam added a major new strand to India's heritage, influencing the political, religious, and cultural realms but increasing diversity at the expense of unity.

Hindu and Buddhist ideas along with various other Indian traditions diffused to Southeast Asia, where they helped foster the rise of great kingdoms. The Angkor Empire dominated much of mainland Southeast Asia by mixing Indian and local patterns. New religions and new peoples, especially the Tais, eventually reshaped Southeast Asia. Theravada Buddhism became a major influence in several societies, including Siam, while Islam became strong in peninsula and island societies such as Melaka and Java. International trade fostered economic dynamism, and Melaka served as a major international port in which many cultural traditions flourished.

KEY TERMS

Rajputs	bhakti	Tantrism	purdah
polyandry	Vajrayana	Lamaism	wayang kulit

EBOOK AND WEBSITE RESOURCES

e INTERACTIVE MAPS

Map 13.1 India and the Delhi Sultanate, ca. 1300 C.E.

Map 13.2 Major Southeast Asian Kingdoms, ca. 1200 C.E.

Map 13.3 The Spread of Islam in Island Southeast Asia

LINKS

Internet Indian History Sourcebook (http://www .fordham.edu/halsall/india/indiasbook.html). An invaluable collection of sources and links on India.

WWW Southeast Asia Guide (http://www.library.wisc .edu/guides/SEAsia/). An impressive, easy-to-use site from the University of Wisconsin-Madison.

WWW Virtual Library: South Asia (http://www.columbia .edu/cu/web/indiv/southasia/cuvl/). This Columbia University site offers many useful resources.

WWW Virtual Library: Southeast Asia (http://www .library.leiden.edu/collections/special/intro_se_asia .jsp). A Dutch site offering portals to all the countries of the region.

Plus flashcards, practice quizzes, and more. Go to: www.cengage.com/history/lockard/globalsocnet2e

SUGGESTED READING

Andaya, Barbara Watson, and Leonard Andaya. *A History of Malaysia*, 2nd ed. Honolulu: University of Hawaii Press, 2000. Contains an overview of Melaka and the spread of Islam in Southeast Asia.

Asher, Catherine B. and Cynthia Talbot. *India Before Europe*. New York: Cambridge University Press, 2006. Contains a good summary of this era.

Aung-Thwin, Michael. *Pagan: The Origins of Modern Burma*. Honolulu: University of Hawaii Press, 1985. The most comprehensive study of the Pagan society in Burma.

Avari, Burjar. *India: The Ancient Past: A History of the Indian Sub-Continent from c.7000 BC to AD 1200*. London: Routledge, 2007. Useful survey by an Indian scholar.

Basham, A. L. *The Wonder That Was India*, 3rd rev. ed. New Delhi: Rupa and Company, 1967 (reprinted 1999). Although dated, this is still a valuable general study of pre-Islamic India.

Chaudhuri, K. N. *Trade and Civilization in the Indian Ocean: An Economic History from the Rise of Islam to 1750*. Cambridge: Cambridge University Press, 1985. A scholarly study of trade and Islam, with much on India and Southeast Asia.

Hall, Kenneth R. *Maritime Trade and State Development in Early Southeast Asia*. Honolulu: University of Hawaii Press, 1985. One of the few studies of trade and politics in Southeast Asia before 1500 C.E.

Higham, Charles. *The Civilization of Angkor*. Berkeley: University of California Press, 2001. A scholarly but readable summary of Cambodia's early history.

Kulke, Hermann, and Dietmar Rothermund. *History of India*, 4th ed. London and New York: Routledge, 2004. A concise but stimulating general history, incorporating recent scholarship on India in this era.

Mabbett, Ian, and David Chandler. *The Khmers*. London: Blackwell, 1995. An authoritative study of Cambodian history, with much on Angkor.

Risso, Patricia. *Merchants and Faith: Muslim Commerce and Culture in the Indian Ocean*. Boulder: Westview, 1995. Connects Islam and Indian Ocean commerce, with much of southern Asia.

Rizvi, S. A. A. *The Wonder That Was India*, Part 2. New Delhi: Rupa and Company, 1987 (reprinted 2000). A comprehensive discussion of India under the impact of Islam from 1200 to 1700.

Taylor, Jean G. *Indonesia: People and Histories*. New Haven: Yale University Press, 2003. Well-written examination with much on this era.

Thapar, Romila. *Early India: From the Origins to A.D. 1300*. Berkeley: University of California Press, 2003. A recent revision of the standard work by an Indian historian.

CHRISTIAN SOCIETIES IN MEDIEVAL EUROPE, BYZANTIUM, AND RUSSIA, 600–1500

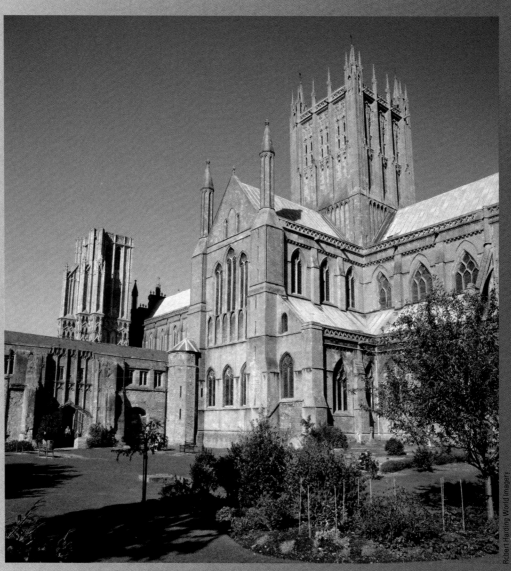

Robert Harding World Imagery

Wells Cathedral The importance of Christianity in European life was symbolized by magnificent cathedrals. This cathedral, built in the town of Wells in England in the thirteenth century C.E., was designed to reflect the glory of God.

> The most Christian man beloved by God, the glorious king of the Franks, while he was building this [Christian] monastery, wished that [its] consecration and the battles which he [waged] should not be consigned completely to oblivion.
>
> Monastery dedication attributed to Charlemagne, ninth-century Frankish Emperor[1]

It was Christmas, 800 C.E., and the city of Rome, filled with magnificent buildings and monuments, still possessed majesty and was the center of western Christendom. Along one of the many roads that connected the fabled metropolis to a wider Europe had come the most powerful ruler in Europe, Charlemagne (SHAHR-leh-mane), the king of the Germanic people called the Franks, arriving from his capital of Aachen (AH-kuhn), some 700 miles away in northwest Germany, to celebrate Christmas mass with Pope Leo III, the head of Christendom. A towering man, 6 feet 4 inches tall, and wearing a Roman toga and Greek cloak, Charlemagne entered the spectacular St. Peter's cathedral. When the Christmas service ended, the pope placed upon Charlemagne's head a golden crown encrusted with sparkling jewels while the crowd chanted, "Crowned by god, great and peace-loving Emperor of the Romans, life and victory."[2] For the first time the pope had crowned an emperor of a new, church-blessed Roman Empire. For the next few centuries popes tried to influence secular affairs and shape monarchies, while kings worked to control the church and, like Charlemagne, used religion—even the building of monasteries—for their own purposes. The complex relations between the Roman church and diverse European states helped shape the tapestry of European life in this era.

In the 1400s Italian historians first coined the term *medieval* to describe the centuries, in their view a superstitious and ignorant "Dark Age," between the classical Romans and their own time. But the reality of what later scholars often called the "Middle Ages" in Europe was more complex. Linked by faith and culture, western Europeans combined Christianity with practices inherited from both the Romans and Germanic groups like the Franks. Although the mixing of religion and politics went back to ancient times, in both western Europe and Byzantium to the east, the strong influence of the Christian churches in all aspects of society, including politics, was an innovation, and medieval people tended to think of themselves as part of Christendom rather than Europe. Christian culture spread into northeastern Europe and Russia; at the same time, however, Europeans borrowed much from other cultures, especially from Muslims. Finally, the many tensions of European life, including conflicts between Christian leaders and kings for power, struggles between kings and nobles, debates over how to reconcile faith and reason, and the differing priorities of the rural-based aristocracy and urban merchants, fostered a competitive spirit that helped spur overseas exploration in the fifteenth century.

FOCUS QUESTIONS

1. How did Europeans create new societies between 500 and 1000?
2. What institutions and ideas shaped medieval European life?
3. How did Byzantine society differ from that of western Europe?
4. What developments between 1300 and 1500 gave Europeans the incentive and means to begin reshaping the world after 1500?

medieval A term first used in the 1400s by Italian historians to describe the centuries between the classical Romans and their own time.

Visit the website and eBook for additional study materials and interactive tools:
www.cengage.com/history/lockard/globalsocnet2e

FORMING CHRISTIAN SOCIETIES IN WESTERN EUROPE

▌ How did Europeans create new societies between 500 and 1000?

The disintegration of the western Roman Empire in the fifth century led to political and social instability, clearing the ground for the rise of new societies between 500 and 1000. These were centuries of creativity, spurred by the mixing of Roman and Germanic traditions as well as by relations with non-European peoples. While western European societies varied, they also developed many common features, including a dominant Christian church and similar social, political, and economic systems. Economic change and technological development also set a foundation for a new Europe.

Environment and Expanding Christianity

Climate and Geography

Climate change and disease shaped post-Roman Europe. A cooling climate brought shorter growing seasons between 500 and 900, after which warmer trends returned. The terrible plague that devastated Europe during Justinian's time reappeared occasionally. Given these challenges, it was not surprising that people turned to religion for support. Between 200 and 800 western Europe also suffered repeated incursions by migrating peoples. Various Germanic groups occupied much of the region, destroying forever the western Roman Empire and culture and preventing any imperial restoration like that in China, where classical society reemerged during the Tang dynasty. Today few people study the Latin that was once the dominant language of the Mediterranean world.

Yet, Europe's favorable geography enabled similar religious, social, economic, and political patterns to spread. Much of western and central Europe was blessed by fertile, well-watered plains rich in minerals, while a long coastline offered many fine harbors along the Mediterranean and Baltic Seas and the Atlantic Ocean. Long navigable rivers such as the Danube (DAN-yoob) and Rhine and accessible mountain passes through the Alps made communication within the region much easier than for Asia, Africa, and South America. Hence, land and sea networks linked diverse societies, fostering the movement of ideas, products, peoples, technologies, and diseases.

Rise of the Roman church

As Roman power melted away, the church became the major source of authority, and local bishops and monasteries were often the only government in rural areas. Over time the bishops of Rome gained authority, eventually claiming the title of pope (Holy Father) and heading the vast church apparatus. Increasingly the papacy meant an independent church that was not controlled by any one government and that could assert its influence over kings. The popes continued their efforts to spread the faith to those Germanic peoples who still followed their ancient gods. Around 600 Pope Gregory I sanctioned turning pagan worship sites into churches rather than destroying them. As a result of missionary efforts, the Anglo-Saxon kingdom of Kent in England converted, and from its capital, Canterbury, missionaries were sent to German lands. The most famous, Boniface (BON-uh-face) (ca. 675–754), a member of the Benedictine order, won many converts in Germany.

Christians helped spread the faith by blending German values and practices into their religion. For instance, the pagan use of special amulets or charms to ward off evil was changed to the Christian practice of wearing medals around the neck honoring Jesus or his mother. Once they had acquired key positions in governments, Christians often persecuted non-Christians by destroying their houses of worship or denying them government positions. Since many church bishops came from upper-class German families, Christian leaders began valuing warriors and fighting, which was not a prominent feature of early Christianity. Even local church leaders often were more concerned with protecting their territory and family than they were with promoting Christian values.

Religious Orders

The church also included religious orders. From Christianity's earliest centuries, some men and women had tried to escape what they felt were the corruptions of cities by moving to isolated places to pray and prepare for Heaven. Many monks joined monasteries, communities for men who had taken holy orders. Monasteries grew their own food, and monks cleared forests for crops. Some of the large monasteries provided social services such as shelter for travelers, emergency food, and clothing for the poor. Some women also joined convents for lives of service or prayer. While monks and nuns tried to escape the concerns of society, they actually helped create a new culture. With the slogan "to work is to pray," monks filled their lives with activity to avoid idleness; one form of

CHRONOLOGY

	Early Medieval Western Europe	Later Medieval Western Europe	Byzantium and Russia
600	**750–1200** Viking attacks in Europe **768–814** Reign of Charlemagne		
800	**843** Treaty of Verdun		**988** Russian conversion to Christianity
1000		**1066** Norman conquest of England **1095–1272** Crusades	**1054** Schism between Roman and Byzantine churches
1200		**1337–1453** Hundred Years War **1348–1350** Peak of Black Death	**1237–1241** Mongol invasions
1400		**1420** Beginning of Portuguese exploration of Africa	**1453** Fall of Constantinople to Turks

work, copying manuscripts, eventually created the bound book. The willingness of monks to serve God and their neighbors with their hands as well as their hearts gave manual labor a respect that it never had in the classical Mediterranean world.

The Frankish and Holy Roman Empires

Between 500 and 1000 the political map of Europe changed. Muslim armies conquered North Africa, the eastern shore of the Mediterranean, and most of Spain during the seventh and eighth centuries (see Chapter 10), and Muslim bands raided Italy and France. The victory of the Frankish ruler Charles Martel at the Battle of Tours in 732 finally stopped these raids (see Chronology: The Early Middle Ages, 500–1000). Following this victory, the Franks created a large state in western Europe. In 753 Pope Stephen sought the aid of the Franks against the Germanic Lombard kingdom in northern Italy, which was threatening papal control of central Italy. He then anointed the Frankish king Pepin **(PEP-in)** the Short as the special protector of Italy, indicating the sacred nature of kingship in Christian thought and the pope's belief that he had the right to designate political rulers. In return for the pope's blessing, Pepin defeated the Lombards and donated land in central Italy to the pope, the basis of a collection of small Papal States surrounding Rome that remained under papal control for over 1,000 years. From this time on the attention of western Europe's chief religious leaders became divided between their spiritual and earthly concerns.

Rise of the Franks

The special relationship between the popes and the Franks grew during a new dynasty known as the Carolingians **(kah-roe-LIN-gee-uhnz)** after their greatest ruler, Charlemagne (r. 768–814), who, as dramatized in the chapter opener, was crowned by the pope in Rome. Charlemagne spread Frankish power from France and northern Italy deep into the lands of another Germanic people, the Saxons, in north and central Germany, temporarily uniting the heart of western Europe (see Map 14.1). Charlemagne took great interest in the religious lives of his people. He promoted both education and Christianity, using the church to strengthen his empire as he appointed bishops and priests, influenced ceremonies and doctrines, ordered execution for those who violated religious obligations, and controlled the monasteries. To enhance his power, he also sent diplomatic missions to Byzantium and various Islamic states. Charlemagne told Pope Leo III that he would defend the church from its enemies and that the pope's job was only "to assist the success of our arms with your hands raised in prayer to God."[3] In return for this protection and promotion of Christianity, the Carolingians expected church leaders, from priests and bishops to abbots of monasteries, to be loyal to the king.

The Carolingians

When the pope crowned Charlemagne "Emperor of the Romans," he revived the Roman Empire in the west symbolically. However, papal relations with the Carolingian rulers also set the stage for later church-state conflict. Popes argued that lay control over church matters should only be exercised with papal approval, while later German rulers wanted some political control in Italy.

**Map 14.1
Europe During the
Carolingian Empire**

At the height of their
power under Charle-
magne, the Carolingian
rulers of the Franks
controlled much of
northwestern Europe,
including what is
today France, the Low
Countries, western and
southern Germany, and
northern Italy.

e | Interactive Map

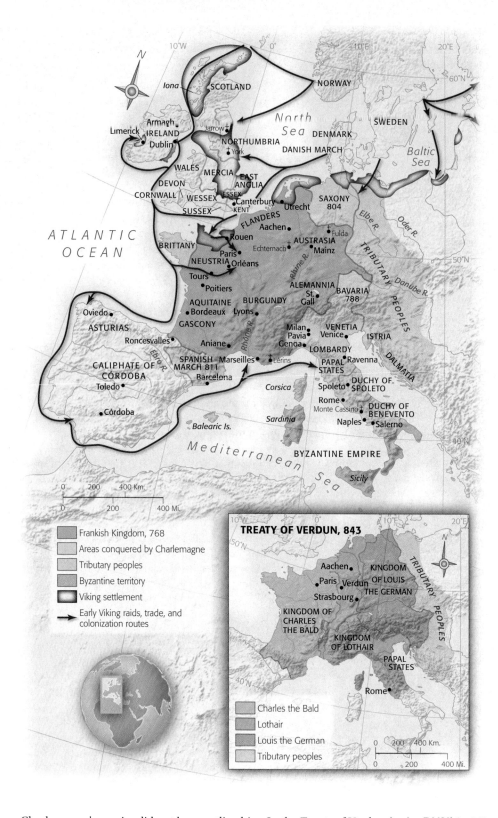

Rise of Holy
Roman Empire

Charlemagne's empire did not long outlive him. In the Treaty of Verdun (vuhr-DUN) in 843, it was divided among his three grandsons, and eventually other Germanic peoples challenged the Franks for influence. The Saxon ruler Otto I, known as Otto the Great (r. 936–973), built a new Ger-man empire by establishing his control over rebellious princes in Germany and leading an army into northern Italy, and in 962 the pope declared Otto "Roman Emperor." From this point until 1806, rulers in Germany retained this title, eventually proclaiming their lands to be the "Holy Roman Empire." But this empire had little in common with the classical Roman Empire. Much of its territory had never been under Roman control, and most Germans, Italians, Slavs, Czechs, and Hungarians within its domains had little sense of common citizenship or even much awareness of the political connections beyond the local level. Like the Carolingians, Otto and his successors continued to both defend and dominate the church, even appointing bishops in their lands.

Vikings and Other Invaders

The European heartland continued to attract other peoples seeking wealth. The biggest threat came from the Vikings, or Northmen, who faced population pressures that led them to launch raids out of Scandinavia, a region with limited productive farmland. Viking warriors burned and looted towns and monasteries in England, France, Holland, and Ireland. While rumors may have exaggerated Viking atrocities, it was a scary time, and people prayed: "From the violence of the men from the north, O Lord, deliver us."[4] The Vikings were also skilled craftsmen who built ingenious shallow-draft boats capable of both oceanic and riverine voyages.

Between 750 and 1200 various Vikings raided, traded, and settled around Europe. After some time the Scandinavians adopted Christianity and established the kingdoms of Denmark, Norway, and Sweden. Some Swedish Vikings moved east into the heartland of Russia, establishing several states and also sailing downriver to the Black Sea to trade with Byzantium and the Middle East. Danish and Norse Vikings established permanent settlements in coastal England, Ireland, and the islands north of Scotland. Other Vikings settled down in western France, in Normandy (named after Normans or Northmen). Normans who descended from these Vikings conquered England in 1066.

Eventually the Vikings gave up raiding for trade and farming. Those who settled outside Scandinavia adopted the cultures of the local Celtic, Latin, Germanic, or Slavic peoples. But their heritage remains in the many place names and words in the local languages. The Vikings left other legacies as well. Among the world's greatest maritime explorers, Norse Vikings began settling Iceland in 874 and founded several settlements on Greenland around 986. Then around 1000 a small group of Greenland Vikings established an outpost along the coast of eastern Canada, and Vikings made occasional trading visits to the area for the next several centuries. These Viking explorers also fostered a democratic ideal. Icelanders created an elected assembly in 930 to make and administer laws.

Two other warlike peoples, the Bulgars (BUL-gahrz) and Magyars (MAG-yahrz), migrated from Russia into central Europe. The Slavic Bulgars created a large state but were contained by

Bulgars and Magyars

CHRONOLOGY
The Early Middle Ages, 500–1000

529 First Benedictine monastery

732 Battle of Tours

750–1200 Viking attacks in Europe

756–1492 Muslim states in Spain

768–814 Reign of Charlemagne over Franks

800 Papal crowning of Charlemagne

843 Division of Carolingian Empire in Treaty of Verdun

874 Viking settlement of Iceland

955 Defeat of Magyars

962 Revival of Holy Roman Empire by Otto the Great

986 First Norse settlements in Greenland

© University Museum of Cultural Heritage, University of Oslo, Norway

Viking Longship
This longship from the ninth century, excavated from a burial mound in Norway in 1904, boasted intricate decorations and carvings. Probably used for ceremonial purposes, it became the burial chamber of a royal Viking woman.

"Tilling the Fields"   Most medieval Europeans were peasants growing food. This French painting from the 1400s shows peasants working land on a manor.

The Bridgeman Art Library International

Byzantine armies, and eventually they converted to Eastern Orthodox Christianity and settled in the eastern Balkan region known as Bulgaria. The Magyars, excellent horsemen who spoke a Ural-Altaic language related to Turkish, moved into the Hungarian plain and threatened Germany and Italy. However, German forces under Otto the Great crushed a large Magyar army in 955, and the Magyars then settled permanently in Hungary and adopted Roman Christianity.

Early Medieval Trade, Muslim Spain, and Technology

Merchants

Trade also shaped the new Europe. While most Europeans were peasants, growing food or raising livestock, some were merchants who traded wool hides, salt, fish, wine, and grain over long distances, often by sea or riverboat. Trade continued briskly in the eastern Mediterranean, where it was tightly controlled by the Byzantine rulers. As time passed, the east-west trade grew dynamic. The Italian city of Venice was an active trading center throughout the Middle Ages, and Venice and Genoa competed to dominate trade with the Middle East and Byzantium. Other Italian cities remained connected to the Byzantine economy. Even the most remote northern towns received occasional visits from merchants, and aristocrats purchased luxury goods such as silk produced in the East. By 800, multiple networks of exchange were reconnecting western Europeans to each other and to eastern Europe and the increasingly Islamic Middle East.

Islamic Influences

Europeans benefited from the growing connections with, and borrowings from, the Muslim world. Islamic expansion stimulated a wider movement of people, goods, and information, such as Asian science and classical Greek thought, that gradually influenced many Afro-Eurasian societies. The exchange of products and ideas between Christian Europe and cosmopolitan Islamic Spain and Sicily, where various cultures met, proved especially fruitful for European intellectual life. Scholars and merchants from all over the Mediterranean world and the Frankish kingdom gravitated to Spanish cities such as Cordoba (see Chapter 10). The meeting of Christian, Jewish, and Muslim traditions in Muslim-ruled Spain and Sicily allowed the philosophical, scientific, and technological writings of many Classical Greek and Indian as well as Persian and Arab thinkers to spread among educated Europeans. In the 1140s, an Italian translator of Arabic texts wrote that "it befits us to imitate the Arabs especially, for they are our teachers and the pioneers."[5]

Technological Innovation

Various technological improvements, some originating in Asia, came into common use in western Europe during these early centuries, laying the basis for European expansion after 1000. Some of the major technological innovations improved agriculture, spurring the higher grain yields that sparked population growth in Europe. The rugged *moldboard plow* included a blade that dug the earth and an attached moldboard that turned over the furrow, enabling farmers to turn and drain the heavy, wet soil of northern Europe, where difficult farming conditions had kept the populations sparse. The horseshoe, which Europeans adopted from Central Asians in the ninth century, allowed farmers to make greater use of horses to plow fields, especially when they were combined with the horse collar. Invented in China, the horse collar distributed the weight of the burden across the animal's shoulders so that the horse could pull more weight and work longer hours. The most crucial agricultural improvement was the three-field system, which replaced the Roman two-field system. Europeans divided their fields into three parts and let only one-third lie fallow each year, increasing their yield by planting winter and summer wheat in the other two fields. Increased grain consumption produced a better-balanced diet.

Other innovations fostered the growth of industry. First invented in Roman times, watermills were built along rivers and streams to generate power, freeing up human and animal labor for other tasks. By 1056 over 5,600 watermills in England provided power for such activities as sawing logs and grinding wheat into flour. Waterpower thus allowed some industries to be mechanized. By the 1100s Europeans also used windmills, invented in Persia around 650, to generate power for such industries as grinding grain. By then the wheelbarrow had also reached Europe from China.

SECTION SUMMARY

- With the decline of the Roman Empire, the Christian church became a power in its own right with influence over kings, and monasteries created a new culture that respected manual labor.

- Under Germanic influence, Christians more aggressively spread their faith, assimilating pagan practices and transforming them into Christian ones and sometimes persecuting non-Christians, as well as beginning to value warfare and fighting.

- During this time the Papal States were created, Charlemagne's Carolingian empire temporarily united much of Europe, and Otto the Great began the tradition of calling Germany the "Holy Roman Empire."

- The Vikings of Scandinavia, who raided European lands for over four centuries, were also good traders and eventually settled in Iceland, Greenland, and various European territories; they also made forays to eastern Canada and experimented with democracy.

- As merchants engaged in growing networks of exchange, trade with the expanding Muslim world and contact with Muslim Spain introduced Europeans to Classical Greek, Indian, Arab, and Persian ideas.

- Technological advances such as the moldboard plow, the horseshoe, and the horse collar improved agriculture, as did the three-field system, and the watermill helped to improve European industry.

MEDIEVAL SOCIETIES, THOUGHT, AND POLITICS

What institutions and ideas shaped medieval European life?

Medieval Europe was dominated by three institutions between 800 and 1300. The papacy was significant in religion and church state relations, feudalism in the realm of politics and social structure, and manorialism in the economic realm. Both feudalism and manorialism developed from roots in the late Roman Empire and varied greatly across western Europe. The pluralism of religious, social, political, and economic institutions forged in early medieval Europe, combined with an unusually warm climate, spurred changes in many areas of life between 1000 and 1300, centuries historians term the "High Middle Ages." The power of the Roman church and its popes grew, fostering conflict with rulers and intellectuals. European societies were beset by tensions not only between religious and lay rulers but also between Roman and Byzantine Christian leaders and between Christians and Muslims. These varied conflicts, along with the growing divergence between cities, with their merchant classes, and the traditional feudal aristocrats ruling in the countryside, helped reshape European society.

The Emergence of Feudalism

Although some historians consider the concept to be misleading and overgeneralized, most have characterized the complex and decentralized social, political, and economic system of these centuries as **feudalism**, a political arrangement characterized by a weak central monarchy ruling over smaller states and aristocratic families that were largely autonomous but owed military and labor service obligations as vassals to the monarch. In turn, these nobles ruled as lords over the warriors and farmers on their estates, who, as subordinates, owed them service as **vassals**. Church leaders supported this arrangement, arguing that "it is the will of the Creator

feudalism A political arrangement characterized by a weak central monarchy ruling over smaller states or influential families that were largely autonomous but owed service obligations to the monarch.

vassals In medieval Europe, a subordinate person owing service to a lord.

that the higher shall always rule over the lower. Each individual and each class should stay in its place [and] perform its tasks."[6] This feudalistic political and social formation was strongest in France, England, and parts of Italy. Although many monarchs had little power beyond the region around their capital, some small states were part of a larger unit, such as the Holy Roman Empire, their princes owing allegiance to the king but also exercising power in the states they ruled.

Despite the Christian church's role in creating a common culture and the accomplishments of strong rulers such as Charlemagne and Otto the Great, certain forces worked toward the decentralization that characterized feudalism. The old Roman roads had fallen into disrepair, disrupting transportation and trade, and Europe remained sparsely populated with few cities. By 1000 the most densely populated region, France, boasted a population of only 8 or 9 million people, England had only a million and a half, and Europe as a whole only around 40 million, less than half of Song China's 100 million. Since both money and talent were scarce and land was the source of wealth, Charlemagne rewarded his best soldiers and officials by giving them control over land. Vassals who held such grants of land from a lord, called **benefices**, took an oath of personal loyalty to the king and promised him military service. In return they had a free hand to govern their territory, collect taxes from the inhabitants, and administer justice.

benefices In medieval Europe, grants of land from lord to vassal.

Feudalism also refers to legal relations between lords and vassals, including the *fief*, the thing granted in a feudal contract, usually land but sometimes something such as the right to collect tolls on a bridge. If a fief of land were large enough, the vassal could subdivide it and have vassals of his own. Thus feudalism allowed a king to rule a large country without personally administering it. This rule through subordinates was most common in England, especially after William, Duke of Normandy, conquered that island in 1066 and set up a feudal monarchy (see Chronology: The High Middle Ages, 1000–1300).

fief In medieval Europe, the thing granted in a feudal contract, usually land.

Feudal society included **knights**, armored military retainers who swore allegiance to their lord and who fought mostly on horseback. Since warhorses and elaborate armor were expensive, lords imposed this expense on their vassals. Knights had a rigid code of behavior, including a sense of duty and honor known as **chivalry**. A thirteenth-century French writer explained the chivalric ideal: "A knight must be hardy, courteous, generous, loyal and of fair speech; ferocious to his foe, frank and debonair to his friend. [He] has proved himself in arms and thereby won the praise of men."[7] Despite romantic images of knights wielding lances in jousts or defending maidens from fire-breathing dragons, the reality was usually more mundane. Knights wore 60 pounds of chain-mail armor and were often felled by heat exhaustion. The steel suits of armor seen in museums did not come into general use until the 1400s. Since states and rival lords fought each other regularly, knights were kept busy. But despite the dangers, the rewards could be great, including acquiring wealth and marrying into an aristocratic family. The mounted cavalry was the chief fighting force, made possible by the stirrup, brought by Central Asians who probably adopted it from the Chinese. The stirrup enabled the knight to stand when delivering a blow, making him much more powerful than if he delivered a blow while seated.

knights In medieval Europe, armored military retainers on horseback who swore allegiance to their lord.

chivalry The rigid code of behavior, including a sense of duty and honor, of medieval European knights.

Manors, Cities, and Trade

manorialism The medieval European system of autonomous, nearly self-sufficient agricultural estates.

The rural economy was based on **manorialism**, a system of autonomous, nearly self-sufficient agricultural estates. As the Roman cities became expensive places to live, wealthy Romans retreated to their large country estates and hired low-wage agricultural workers. Eventually these Roman estates and villages became the manors. With money and trade goods in short supply, each manor supplied its own needs, from mills to grind the grain to blacksmiths to shoe the horses. The manors, often organized around a castle, were owned by nobles who had the right to the produce grown by the large class of hereditary **serfs**, peasants who were legally bound to their lord and tied to the land through the generations. Serfs tilled the lord's fields as well as their own and were given the use of the manor's resources, such as farming tools or crafts, and protection in the manor house or castle in case the settlement was attacked. Serfs were not allowed to change their status or leave without permission, but they could not be dispossessed unless they failed to live up to their obligations. Warned to work hard to receive their eventual reward in Heaven, they paid for their security with a lifetime of drudgery. Occasional peasant revolts indicated some dissatisfaction.

serfs In medieval Europe, peasants legally bound to their lord and tied to the land through generations.

Although serfdom became far more pervasive, slavery did not disappear altogether in Europe. Mostly farmers or domestic servants, slaves constituted perhaps 10 percent of the English population until the eleventh century, were common in Italy and Spain, and also worked papal estates and the farms of French monasteries. Leading Christian thinkers like St. Thomas Aquinas argued that slavery was morally justified and an economic necessity. An active Mediterranean slave trade based in Byzantium acquired slaves, mostly Slavs, Greeks, and Turks, from the Black Sea region and shipped them to southern Europe and North Africa. The Carolingians and Venetians also sold European slaves to the Arabs, and Vikings sold English and French slaves to Byzantium and Islamic Spain. By the 1400s Arabs and Portuguese were selling enslaved West Africans in southern Europe.

During the High Middle Ages, populations, towns, and cities grew. Compared to Byzantium, China, and the Islamic world, early medieval western Europe was economically underdeveloped and its cities small: by 1000 Rome had only 35,000 people, Paris 20,000, and London 10,000. By contrast, Constantinople had 300,000, Kaifeng in China had 400,000, Cordoba in Muslim Spain nearly 500,000, and the world's largest city, Baghdad, a million people. However, between 1000 and 1300 the increased food resulting from the new methods of growing crops spurred a doubling of Europe's population to about 75 million. Western European cities increased in population and became centers of trade and industry. Milan and Paris grew to almost 100,000 during these three centuries. London had 30,000 people and a problem with air pollution due to the burning of coal.

Urban Growth

As in our own day, some medieval people thought cities were degenerate places. An eleventh-century English monk detested London:

> I do not like that city. All sorts of men crowd together there from every country. Each race brings its own vices. No one lives in it without falling into some sort of crime. Actors, jesters, smooth-skinned lads, flatterers, effeminates, pederasts, singing and dancing girls, quacks, belly-dancers, sorceresses, extortioners, magicians, mimes, beggars, buffoons: all this tribe fill all the houses. Therefore, if you do not want to dwell with evildoers, do not live in London.[8]

Indeed, urban life and the money to be made attracted many people to cities. A German expression, "city air makes one free," referred to the fact that a serf who left the manor and was able to spend "a year and a day" in a city without being caught was considered legally free. Thus cities increasingly operated outside the feudal social and political structure. City craftsmen and merchants organized themselves into **guilds**, fraternal organizations designed to protect the economic interests of members and to win exemptions from feudal obligations. Eventually city charters, secured from the local lord or the king, allowed the cities to have their own courts and other privileges of self-government. Rulers granted such privileges because of the wealth that city commerce and payments brought them.

guilds In medieval Europe, collective fraternal organizations of craftsmen and merchants designed to protect the economic interests of their members.

The expansion of cities and commerce opened new possibilities for merchants, but they had to overcome social prejudices. In feudal society, people belonged to one of three categories, in order of importance: "those who prayed" (churchmen, priests, and monks), "those who fought" (aristocratic warriors, knights), and "those who worked" (peasants). Merchants and bankers had no place in this hierarchy unless they could marry the daughter of an impoverished aristocrat and hence acquire land. But most merchants also shared society's values and Christian faith. The English merchant Godric of Pinchale (ca. 1069–1170) left home as a teenager to peddle goods in nearby villages, then traded goods by sea between England, Scotland, Denmark, and Holland. Eventually he owned a small fleet of vessels and became quite wealthy, even making pilgrimages to Jerusalem. He never married and later in life gave away all his wealth to the poor and became a hermit, writing religious poetry and gaining fame for his piety.

Rise of Merchants and Bankers

People resented merchants because they sold goods for more than they paid for them and consorted with foreigners. Greed was considered a serious sin, and the practice of loaning money at interest was regarded as **usury**, a sin because the lender was making a profit without doing any labor. But moneylending was necessary to commerce, and even popes borrowed money at interest. While Italians became renowned as bankers, moneylending was often left largely to Jews, thus allowing Christians to benefit from borrowing money without committing usury. Gradually using and lending money became more acceptable

usury The practice of loaning money at interest; considered a sin in medieval Europe, although necessary to commerce.

Long-distance trade reached its peak between 1100 and 1350 as western Europeans shipped woolen textiles, flax, hemp, wines, olive oil, fruit, and timber to the East in return for luxury goods from Byzantium and Asia such as spices, silk, perfumes, and precious gems. Trade and commerce around Europe also grew and prejudice against merchants declined. Cities such as Constantinople, Venice, Genoa, Bruges (broozh) and Amsterdam in the Low Countries, and Strassburg in the Rhineland became major commercial hubs. Italian merchants acquired goods from the Middle East and Byzantium and shipped them over the Alps to Belgium and Holland in exchange for woolen

Long Distance Trade

A Medieval Town
This painting shows a variety of town enterprises, including a tailor's shop, barbershop, and an apothecary.

Bibliotheque nationale de France

textiles. One feudal French ruler, the Count of Champagne (shahm-PAHN-yuh), established the "fairs of Champagne" where goods were displayed at town fairs lasting seven weeks, with the count providing various services for the merchants. The wealth created by such activities fostered a commercial revolution and made merchants and bankers more influential.

Eventually commerce became more central to the European economy than agriculture, although the broad repercussions of the commercial revolution—the rise of capitalism; the incorporation of merchants as a vital social class; stronger monarchies; and the weakening of both feudalism and the Christian church—became clear only centuries later. In the short term, both the popes and the political leaders of Europe seemed stronger than ever, but the merchant class gradually gained political and economic power to challenge feudal nobles and eventually the monarchies.

Social Life and Groups

Families and Gender Relations

Medieval society was patriarchal, though family life and gender relations varied with social status and local customs. Generally, men supported the family and women ran the household and raised children. Sons were considered more important than daughters because they passed on the family line, property, and name. Parents arranged most marriages. Men were allowed to have sex outside marriage, while women were valued for their virginity and faithfulness. From the church's perspective, marriage was a necessary evil, and it legitimized sex only for procreation, not pleasure. A leading theologian, St. Thomas Aquinas, contended that "woman was created to help man, but only in the act of procreation, because in all other tasks he can find far better support elsewhere." One priest even warned married people to avoid sex on the Sabbath because "monsters, cripples, and all sickly children [are] conceived on Saturday nights."[9] However, rulers often flouted custom. Charlemagne enforced rigid Christian morality on his people while also marrying four times, having five mistresses, and siring eighteen children.

Today's Western middle-class model of a husband, wife, and their unmarried children living in one independent household, separate from the larger family, was the exception rather than the rule. Many medieval women tended to marry late, and large numbers of both men and women remained unmarried. Children often left their birth families at an early age to become apprentices in a trade, servants, or novices in religious orders. Laws favoring men spurred many young women to join Christian convents, all-female religious communities where they could find physical and social protection and possibilities for leadership.

Medieval society had an almost contradictory view of women. On the one hand, gender stereotypes in the Bible led people to believe that women had to be subordinate to men and were depraved, leading men into sin, as Eve did Adam. Women were also considered intellectually inferior to men. On the other hand, Mary, the Virgin Mother of Jesus, became one of the most popular objects of devotion. Many cathedrals were named after Notre Dame (NO-truh DAHM) ("Our Lady"). Furthermore, women could inherit property, and they worked in many occupations, including farming, ale making, small-scale trade, glassmaking, and the textile industry.

By the 1100s **courtly love**, a new concept of passionate but pure relationships between knights and ladies and celebrated in song by wandering troubadours, brought romance to male-female relations and, combined with the cult of the Virgin Mary, elevated the status of aristocratic women. Courtly love probably originated in Muslim Spain, where women poets flourished. But whether courtly or not, romantic love existed mostly outside of marriage. In medieval tales, knights often sought the favors of fair maidens (usually the wife of another, perhaps their lord) who were unattainable. Since adultery was considered a high crime, the knight's love was usually unrequited.

courtly love A standard of polite relationships between knights and ladies that arose in the 1100s in medieval Europe. Courtly love was celebrated in song by wandering troubadours.

The early Christian tolerance of homosexuality survived through the Early Middle Ages. Although various church leaders and rulers condemned what they called "sodomites," after the immoral inhabitants of the biblical city of Sodom, public attitudes toward same-sex relationships were often more accepting. Indeed, considerable homosexual fiction and poetry was published in the eleventh and twelfth centuries, and several prominent bishops and English kings were thought to be homosexuals. Beginning in the thirteenth century, however, public attitudes shifted. As states became stronger, they promoted uniformity in social relations and religious views and fostered suspicion of those perceived as outside the social and religious mainstream. The church launched a violent campaign against heresy and unconventional behavior that often targeted people suspected of homosexuality. Whereas in 1250 homosexual behavior was legal in most of Europe, by 1300 it had become a capital offense in many societies.

Outsiders

Medieval society was tightly ordered but also rife with tensions. Daily life was precarious for rich and poor alike, and violent crime remained common. Many tensions arose because of a major distinction between Christians and "outsiders"—nonbelievers, Muslims, Jews, and heretics. Christians used the term *pagan* to describe Muslims, who reciprocated by calling Christians *infidels* (unbelievers). The drive to destroy all beliefs outside of the Christian mainstream eventually led to a long series of crusades against Islam and persecution of Jews.

Many European towns had Jewish communities. Jews worked in many occupations but were best known as merchants and bankers because Christians were forbidden to loan money at interest. Resentment of their commercial success and moneylending made them scapegoats for misfortunes, such as epidemics, that were hard to explain. Although Christians mostly tolerated the Jews before 1150, anti-Semitism (AN-tee-SEM-uh-tiz-uhm) increased dramatically as more Christians took up banking and as Christians became more militant in asserting their faith. In 1182 the Jews were ordered to leave France, and this expulsion was imitated in other countries during the next three centuries. Governments also placed restrictions on Jewish businesses and residences. Our modern term *ghetto* originally described the part of medieval cities where the Jews were compelled to live. Many expelled Jews migrated to Poland and Byzantium, which developed large Jewish populations.

Christians and Jews

Disdain was also directed at people considered to be heretics. Christians struggled to differentiate correct belief from heresy. Some devout Christians criticized church corruption, including ill-educated priests and arrogant bishops, but church leaders viewed reformers challenging their power as heretics. As a result, they organized military attacks on the Albigensians (AL-buh-JEN-shunz), a group in southern France who criticized the church's material wealth, urged clerical poverty, and wanted the Bible to be translated from Latin into the vernacular languages such as French and German so that ordinary people could read it for themselves. The church destroyed the Albigensians by killing their followers and confiscating their property.

The Church as a Social and Political Force

Europeans experienced both exuberance and turmoil during the High Middle Ages. Massive cathedrals with lofty spires inspired deep emotions, and the church claimed to help its members reach Heaven and avoid Hell. But the church of the High Middle Ages was also a powerful social and political force. The basis of clerical power was the sacrament, a rite believed to be a spiritual milestone. Medieval Christians measured the stages of their lives by sacraments such as baptism and matrimony, which had to be administered by a priest. In the village church, people did not just receive spiritual nourishment but also registered births and marriages and paid taxes. Because they had the power to deny someone the sacraments, which were considered

Church Sacraments

excommunicate To expel a person from the Roman Catholic Church and its sacraments.

necessary for salvation, medieval priests had enormous power. They could also **excommunicate**, or expel a person from the church and its sacraments, an act that was psychologically devastating.

Not all priests and bishops lived up to their responsibilities or growing expectations for celibacy. Many priests had so little education that they could barely recite the Latin liturgy, and some were corrupt and took bribes. Many priests and monks were also married, a practice that reformist church leaders attempted to end because they felt priests should not be distracted by families and did not want priests to pass on their parishes to their children. Nonetheless, even after the final ban many priests were married, kept mistresses, or were either homosexual or assumed to be so. Many people had ambivalent attitudes toward the clergy, fearing priests because of their power and ridiculing them because of their shortcomings.

Reformers

In the eleventh century, reformers attempted to change the church and end abuses by priests, monks, and high officials. New religious orders tried to restore monastic life to its original purity, insisting that all monks remain celibate, and several German rulers revived the papacy by appointing reform-minded popes who tried to end **simony** (SIGH-muh-nee), a common practice whereby wealthy families paid to have their sons appointed bishops. Such an appointment was desirable because bishops collected significant revenues in their territories. In an attempt to keep European rulers from interfering in papal elections, the church also established the College of Cardinals in 1059 to elect the pope. Churchmen made Roman law the basis of church law because it referred all matters to the person at the top, in this case the pope.

simony In medieval Europe, a practice whereby wealthy families paid to have their sons appointed bishops.

The Papacy

The papacy's growing political power was made clear when a major church-state conflict erupted over the appointment of bishops. For centuries rulers had appointed their leading nobles to key church offices. But in 1075 Pope Gregory VII (ca. 1020–1085) excommunicated the German emperor for appointing the archbishop of Milan (mi-LAHN). Gregory had a low opinion of kings, who, he said, "derive their origin from men ignorant of God who raised themselves above their fellows by pride, plunder, treachery, murder, at the instigation of the Devil."[10] In 1122 both men compromised and agreed that both emperor and pope would invest the new bishops. This dispute strengthened papal authority and weakened the German emperors. As German rulers began intervening in Italian politics to regain control over the church, they lost influence over their own princes at home, leading eventually to decentralized government and political warfare in the German-speaking lands. Another pope, Innocent III (r. 1198–1216), dramatically extended papal authority over secular rulers, using his control over the sacraments to force King John of England to accept the pope's candidate for archbishop of Canterbury and requiring the king of France to take back a wife he had divorced. In 1215 he required Jews to wear distinctive clothing and also aggressively punished "heretical depravity."

Holy Inquisition A church court created in 1231 in medieval Europe to investigate and eliminate heresy; inquisitions continued into the 1600s.

The papal drive to investigate and eliminate heresy led to the **Holy Inquisition**, a church court created in 1231. Churchmen tried thousands of people with views outside the mainstream, and popes sanctioned torture and starvation to induce confessions. Those found guilty faced punishments, including penances, banishment, prison, mutilation, and death. Over the next two centuries several thousand people were executed. The most notorious inquisition began, under state rather than church control, in Spain in 1478 and perpetrated brutal persecution of Jews and Muslims, burning at least 2,000 people at the stake. The inquisitions continued into the 1600s and also included bans on books viewed as dangerous to the faith.

Beliefs on History and Nature

Christians had adopted from the ancient Jewish tradition ideas about nature and history still apparent in the West today, including the concept of progress. Early Christian thinkers supported the notion of human society improving with time, an idea then foreign to most of the world. This linear rather than cyclical concept viewed history as leading from one point to another in a line of progressive movement. The basis for the view was found in the seven-day creation story in Genesis. To many Christian thinkers, God planned the world, including the natural environment, for human benefit, which necessitated exploiting nature. Hence, no item had any purpose but to serve humans, and it was God's will that people improved land by clearing forests and wetlands, which some monasteries did with great enthusiasm. The crass medieval attitude toward nature gave ideological justification for the great technological and economic development to later emerge in the West but also caused environmental problems.

Some Christian and Jewish thinkers dissented from these views and affirmed that nature was also God's creation and required care and stewardship. One was St. Francis of Assisi (1182–1226), who renounced wealth to found a new religious order, the Franciscans (fran-SIS-kuhnz), dedicated to lives of poverty, humility, and serving the urban poor. St. Francis saw all creatures as part of God's plan. And the twelfth-century Jewish philosopher Moses Maimonides wrote that "it should not be believed that all beings exist for the sake of the existence of man."[11] In addition, kings and lords often protected the forests where they enjoyed hunting.

New European States

Threatened by the increase in papal power, and with less need for feudal vassals as economies grew, rulers sought to gain more control over their lands (see Map 14.2). The English kings were most successful at this centralization of power. After leading the Norman conquest of England in 1066, William of Normandy (1027–1087) had divided the land among his chief vassals. But by the 1100s, William's successors were taking authority away from the local nobility, appointing justices and tax collectors. King Henry II (r. 1154–1189) expanded the power of the royal courts over feudal and church courts. He also invaded Ireland in 1171 and established English control of the island's eastern region.

However, some of Henry II's successors unintentionally laid the foundations for a later representative government in England. John (the Prince John of the Robin Hood legend) weakened royal power in 1215 by signing the **Magna Carta** (MAG-nuh KAHR-tuh) or "Great Charter," an agreement that limited the feudal and taxation rights of the king and his officials while protecting the rights of the church, lords, and merchants. The Magna Carta was later used to support the notion that rulers had to have the consent of their subjects, one of the foundations of modern English constitutional monarchy. Henry III (r. 1216–1272) also contributed to representative government. His incessant demand for taxes to fight foreign wars made him unpopular, and, in 1265, rebellious barons called together a parliament (literally, a "speaking place") that included middle-class townspeople and knights to air their grievances and demand that the king consider their views. This parliament became the model for later meetings called by kings to secure approval of their policies.

The Capetians (kuh-PEE-shuhnz), who succeeded the Carolingians as kings in France (987–1328), also tried to increase their power and expand their territory. King Philip II (r. 1180–1223) gained control over Normandy, replacing noblemen with paid officials who would be more loyal to the crown. Louis IX, or St. Louis (r. 1226–1270), a pious man, curbed the power of the nobility while persecuting heretics and Jews. Philip the Fair (r. 1285–1314) may have had the most impact on France and Europe. To raise money for his wars, he arrested all the Jews and seized their property before expelling them from the kingdom in 1306. He also had the leaders of a militant religious order, the Knights Templar (TEM-plahr), burned at the stake as heretics so that he could default on a loan they had given him. When Pope Boniface VIII (r. 1294–1303) challenged Philip's growing power, Philip accused the pope of sexual perversion and murder and sent a force to Italy to arrest him. Townspeople rescued the pope by driving French troops away. For the next seventy years (1305–1377), the College of Cardinals, bowing to French pressure, elected popes, most of them French, who chose to live in the papal territory of Avignon (ah-vee-NYON) in southern France. Philip's ruthless action showed that the days of papal control over European rulers were ending and that France was emerging as the strongest kingdom in western Europe.

German rulers of the Hohenstaufen (HO-uhn-SHTOU-fuhn) dynasty (1152 and 1254) had the least success in centralizing their lands, largely because they spent too much time trying to control Italy while the feudal nobility in Germany remained powerful. Frederick I (r. 1154–1190) reasserted his authority as Holy Roman Emperor over the wealthy cities in northern Italy, but this involved war with the pope, who organized an Italian coalition that defeated Frederick's forces. Frederick I's successors gradually lost power to German princes. It would be seven hundred years before Italy, divided up into small papal-ruled and nonpapal states, and Germany finally achieved the territorial unity enjoyed by France and England.

The Crusades and Intellectual Life

The religious and political tensions helped foster the Crusades, a series of military expeditions or holy wars between 1095 and 1272 to reclaim the "Holy Land," Palestine, from Muslim control (see Chapter 10). European Christians had long made pilgrimages to Jerusalem and considered the city part of their world. The crusading began after the Byzantine emperor sought help to dislodge the Muslim Seljuk Turks, who now dominated much of western Asia. Medieval Christians had a militant zeal to spread their faith and destroy Islam, through the use of force if necessary, and early Christian thinkers like Augustine of Hippo had sanctioned war to defend the faith. Except for Islam, no other world religion maintained such a strong missionary impulse to convert the world to what its believers considered the only true faith. Although many crusaders were motivated by religious beliefs and idealism, these often became mixed with lust for wealth and land. Political rivalries between European leaders also played a role.

In 1095 Pope Urban II urged Christian rulers to unite to protect the Christian holy sites, prompting the first of nine crusades by land and sea. Fabricating or exaggerating stories of Muslim

---

English Monarchs

Magna Carta ("Great Charter") An agreement signed by King John of England in 1215 that limited the feudal rights of the English king and his officials while protecting the rights of the church, lords, and merchants.

French and German Monarchs

Primary Source: Magna Carta: The Great Charter of Liberties Learn what rights and liberties the English nobility, on behalf of all free Englishmen, forced King John to grant them in 1215.

Christian-Muslim Conflict

Map 14.2 Medieval Europe, 900–1300
During the High Middle Ages, the Holy Roman Empire, comprising dozens of smaller states, covered much of what is today Germany, Austria, eastern France, and northern Italy. France, England, Hungary, and Poland were also major states.

e Interactive Map

atrocities against Christians, he proclaimed that the Turks "have completely destroyed some of God's churches. They ruin the altars with filth and defilement. They are pleased to kill others. And what shall I say about the shocking rape of the women."[12] Various kings, nobles, and bishops joined the cause. Some crusaders temporarily occupied parts of the Holy Land, such as Jerusalem, even establishing crusader-led states, but eventually they were forced out. Other crusaders were diverted to ransacking Constantinople or Egypt.

Looting and pillaging cities, the crusaders often slaughtered thousands of Muslims, Jews, and Byzantine Christians, burning mosques and synagogues with people inside. The Muslim defenders often responded by killing local Christians. The streets of Jerusalem, it was said, ran ankle-deep in blood. Crusaders even slaughtered 12,000 Jews in Germany in 1096. Non-Christians viewed crusaders as terrorists. In the thirteenth century, however, the crusading energies dissipated. The long conflicts left a bitter heritage between Christians and Muslims that still complicates political and cross-cultural relations in the modern world.

Rise of Universities

Some medieval tensions also derived from robust intellectual debates, often in universities, involving theologians and philosophers. By the twelfth century, guilds of scholars formed centers of higher learning. While universities had existed earlier in India and the Islamic world, they mostly specialized in religious studies. European universities taught not only religion but also secular knowledge, such as the ideas of Aristotle, raising eyebrows among church leaders (see Profile: Heloise, a French Scholar and Nun). The most famous European universities were at Paris, Oxford

HELOISE, A FRENCH SCHOLAR AND NUN

A scandalous love affair between two brilliant people, Abelard and Heloise, reveals much about the life and values of medieval times, including church politics and attitudes toward sexuality. Over the centuries the romance and its sad repercussions inspired countless works of poetry and prose. Often portrayed as a forbidden affair between a smitten schoolgirl and her unprincipled teacher, a famed but controversial theologian, the relationship between the two figures was in reality far more complex.

Heloise (1101–1164) was the niece of a high church official in Paris. Coming from a wealthy, influential family, she had more educational opportunities than most women of her time and was educated at a well-financed convent, where she showed a keen intelligence. In 1117 her uncle Fulbert, a high-ranking cleric, arranged for the seventeen-year-old to study with Peter Abelard (1079–1142), the most famous teacher and a nonclergyman, at the school of the Notre Dame Cathedral. Born into an aristocratic family in Brittany, Abelard had studied with renowned teachers and had taught at several schools. He was notorious for both his arrogance and his intellect and made enemies in the church by championing reason, logic, and progressive thinking on religious doctrine.

Despite a twenty-year age difference, Abelard and Heloise fell passionately in love. Abelard wrote of how they went from reading books to kissing. They composed love songs and letters to each other, but their affair also reflected a friendship and intellectual respect, and her letters reveal a good knowledge of Roman and Christian writers. The two lovers tried to keep their affair quiet and were secretly married after she became pregnant. Their romance came at a time when the church was not just encouraging but mandating that clergy as well as secular teachers, such as Abelard, and students in church schools remain celibate. Abelard realized that his marriage would end his current position and his future church career. Heloise gave birth to a son, who was raised by Abelard's sister and eventually became a church official. However, when Heloise's family learned of the affair, they sought revenge, and Fulbert hired two men to beat and then castrate Abelard. Now disgraced, Abelard joined a Benedictine monastery, and, at his encouragement, Heloise entered a convent. Eventually she became the community's director.

Although separated, Heloise and Abelard continued to write letters to each other. Expressing her affection, Heloise wrote him that "I seek to please thee rather than [God]. Thy command brought me, not the love of God, to the [nunnery]." Strongly influenced by the thought of Aristotle, Abelard restored his scholarly reputation by writing books and essays about the possibilities of mixing philosophy and religion, for which he was for a time condemned as a heretic. Later, as an abbot (head) of a large monastery, he helped Heloise and her nuns establish a new convent, although he maintained a personal distance from her. Her ability to gain support and funding helped her convent to flourish. She remained ambivalent about her career, however, writing Abelard that "I am judged religious at a time when there is little in religion that is not hypocrisy." Heloise became known for her learning, and one top male cleric praised her knowledge of the liberal arts, saying, "You have surpassed all women and have gone further than almost every man." However, Heloise resented Abelard's desire to remain aloof from her, and she wrote, "Of all the wretched women I am the most wretched, for the higher the ascent, the heavier the fall."

Although they died twenty years apart, the pair were buried alongside each other at the convent, a fitting conclusion to a relationship and an era. Heloise was one of the last educated churchwomen to maintain close contact with male scholars and church officials. Obsessed with celibacy, the church increasingly separated the men and women engaged in religious life.

THINKING ABOUT THE PROFILE

1. What does the love affair and its consequences tell us about life at this time?

2. How did the different ways in which Abelard and Heloise rebuilt their lives reflect the values of medieval people?

Notes: Quotations from Barbara A. Hanawalt, *The Middle Ages: An Illustrated History* (New York: Oxford University Press, 1998), 88; Jane Slaughter and Melissa K. Bokovoy, *Sharing the Stage: Biography and Gender in Western Civilization*, vol. 1 (Boston: Houghton Mifflin, 2003), 255, 261–262; and James Burge, *Heloise and Abelard: A New Biography* (San Francisco: HarperSanFrancisco, 2003), 271.

Bridgeman-Giraudon/Art Resource, NY

Heloise and Abelard   This painting, from a fourteenth-century French manuscript, shows Heloise (in nun's habit) and Abelard in conversation, years after their torrid love affair had shocked church authorities.

in England, and Salerno and Bologna (boe-LOAN-yuh) in Italy. Students learned the "seven liberal arts"—astronomy, geometry, arithmetic, music, grammar, rhetoric, and logic—and then specialized in medicine, law, or philosophy. As today, students did not spend all of their time studying. When one student wrote home for money because "the city is expensive and makes many demands," his father replied: "I have recently learned that you live dissolutely, preferring play to work, and strumming your guitar while others are at their studies."[13]

Debating Faith and Reason

Heated debates over the relative importance of faith and reason, often against church opposition, contributed much to later Western thought. Thomas Aquinas (uh-KWINE-uhs) (1225–1274), an Italian monk of the Dominican order and professor at the University of Paris, argued that much could be determined by reason, even the existence of God, but that at some point a believer had to accept on faith many mysteries. He also believed that human domination over nature was part of a divine plan and that women were passive and incapable of moral perfection. Some thinkers influenced by Aristotle argued that real knowledge came only from direct observation, a position that supported scientific inquiry.

Literature

Literature was diverse and contradictory. The *Song of Roland*, from twelfth-century France, described the great deeds of a loyal knight who died fighting in Charlemagne's army. But the warlike tone of this epic contrasted with many French lyric poems and stories that exalted personal happiness and romantic love as an ideal in a society that generally arranged marriages. Writers all over Europe took up the Celtic legend of the British King Arthur and his court. In some versions Arthur's wife, Guinevere (GWIN-uh-veer), and his best friend, Lancelot, followed their hearts and became doomed lovers. In a lighter vein, we have this parody of the Christian Apostles' Creed written by a student more delighted by spirits than by the Spirit: "I believe in the tavern of my host, More than in the Holy Ghost. The tavern will my sweetheart be, and the Holy Church is not for me."[14]

SECTION SUMMARY

- Feudalism was a medieval political arrangement in which a king gave nobles the right to rule over sections of his territory in exchange for their allegiance.

- The owners of rural manors had a right to the crops of their serfs, peasants who were bound to the land, and they were protected by their knights, armored warriors on horseback.

- Agricultural advances helped to fuel growing populations in European cities, though they remained smaller than cities in the Muslim world and China.

- As trade in luxury goods flourished, European merchants gradually gained influence, but they suffered from people's image of them as greedy and usurious.

- Medieval society was patriarchal and considered women to be inferior to men; children usually left home early; and most marriages were arranged by parents.

- In the Early Middle Ages homosexuality was widely tolerated, but by the Late Middle Ages it had become unacceptable.

- Many of the tensions in medieval society were caused by the intolerance for "outsiders": non-Christians and heretics, Muslims, and Jews, all of whom were disdained and treated harshly, killed (as in the Crusades), or expelled.

- The church and its priests had a great deal of power over people's lives, but many priests were unqualified or incompetent.

- In some instances, popes became more powerful than kings, and they also orchestrated the Holy Inquisition, which killed thousands of "nonbelievers."

- Christians adopted the Jewish belief in progress over time and the belief that everything in the world was for the use of humans, a view that laid the ground for later industrialization in the West.

- While English rulers eventually consolidated their power and Philip the Fair of France ruthlessly seized power and property and even attacked the pope, German rulers had trouble centralizing their lands because they were too interested in struggling with the pope in Italy.

- Spurred on by a mix of religious idealism and greed, Christians mounted a series of Crusades to wrest the "Holy Land" from Muslim control, thereby creating a resentment among Muslims that has lasted to today.

EASTERN EUROPE: BYZANTINES, SLAVS, AND MONGOLS

How did Byzantine society differ from that of western Europe?

Byzantium, and the eastern European societies it influenced, remained very distinct from western Europe. Despite Christianity and long-standing trade connections, deep political, economic, and religious differences separated them and still do. Demonstrating a remarkable longevity, the Byzantine Empire fought for its life but, from the eleventh century, experienced steady political decline until its final defeat by the Ottoman Turks in 1453 (see Chronology: Byzantium, Russia, and Eastern Europe, 600–1500). In the process, it served as a buffer zone protecting central and western Europe against Muslim, Slavic, and Mongol invaders. Most of the Slavic societies in eastern Europe adopted Eastern Orthodox Christianity, and one of these, the Russians, eventually created a powerful state.

Byzantium and Its Rivals

Byzantium faced nearly continuous pressure from neighboring peoples. In the sixth and seventh centuries the Sassanian Persians and Byzantines fought wars that weakened both empires and made Arab conquest of their lands easier. The Arabs attacked Constantinople in 673 and 717, but the Byzantines survived. For the next three and a half centuries, they were challenged by various Slavic peoples who had begun moving into eastern Europe in late Roman times, becoming the dominant population in a vast region of mountains, forests, and grasslands stretching north from Greece to the eastern Baltic and eastward through Russia. The major Slavic threats came from the Bulgars and Serbs. The Byzantine ruler known as "Basil the Bulgar-Slayer" defeated a Bulgar army in 1014 and blinded 15,000 Bulgarian prisoners of war before releasing them to return home. The defeat of the Bulgars opened the door to the Serbs, who set up several small states in the Balkans, bringing them into conflict with Byzantium. After a series of wars, the Ottoman Turks conquered the Serbs in 1459.

Byzantine political fortunes declined. In 1071, Byzantine forces were driven from southern Italy by Norman knights, and in 1091, at the Battle of Manzikert (MANZ-ih-kuhrt), they were defeated by Seljuk Turks in eastern Anatolia. The shrunken Byzantine territories now faced regular attacks from both east and west. Turks soon completed the conquest of Anatolia and left Constantinople a beleaguered fortress. The desperate Byzantines requested the help of western knights to defend them against the Turks, but instead crusader armies occupied Palestine and Syria between 1096 and 1200. The Byzantines also did not expect the crusaders in 1204, bribed by the Venetians, Byzantine trading rivals, to use a disputed imperial succession in the empire as an excuse to conquer Constantinople itself and govern it until forced out in 1261. Capitalizing on these disasters, the expanding Ottoman Turks finally conquered Constantinople and the surrounding territory in 1453, ending the Byzantine state and transforming the capital city, which the Turks eventually renamed Istanbul.

Byzantine-Turk Conflicts

Despite its many misfortunes, the Byzantine Empire survived as long as it did because of its economic and religious strengths. Because Constantinople lay astride the principal trade routes between Europe and Asia, the merchant class remained vital. Slave traders shipped eastern European slaves, many of them Slavs from the Black Sea region, to be sold in the Mediterranean. Our English word for "slave" comes from the word *Slav*. Taxes from these goods and people as well as silk production enriched the treasury, and Byzantine coins were used around Eurasia.

Byzantine church and state were intertwined, with Christianity and its rituals influencing all aspects of society and filling it with lengthy religious ceremonies and an intense prayer life. Unlike in western Europe, however, governments dominated the church, and rulers regularly interfered in church affairs. Byzantines also engaged in hair-splitting theological disputes. For example, they bitterly disagreed on the use of icons, painted images of holy figures, and over whether the Holy Spirit proceeded from God or from both God and Jesus. Byzantine Christians refused to recognize the supreme position of the bishop of Rome over other bishops. These conflicts over theology and authority spurred the final split between the Roman Catholic and Greek Orthodox Churches, which came when the pope and the patriarch of Constantinople angrily excommunicated each other in 1054.

Church and State

Although the Byzantine church supported male power, a few women achieved political or intellectual influence. Empress Irene, an orphan who married an emperor, ruled Byzantium for two decades (780–802). Although her detractors considered her cruel and ruthless, Irene fostered prosperity, made peace with Muslim states, and temporarily resolved the dispute over icons. Byzantium's best-known historian, the princess Anna Comnena (1083–1148), studied literature, astronomy, medicine, and Greek philosophy.

CHRONOLOGY

Byzantium, Russia, and Eastern Europe, 600–1500

632 First Arab expansion into the Byzantine Empire

825 First Swedish Viking bases in Russia

863 Cyrillic alphabet created

988 Conversion of Vladimir of Kiev to Christianity

1054 Schism between Roman and Byzantine churches

1091 Battle of Manzikert

1237–1241 Mongol invasions of Russia and eastern Europe

1453 Ottoman Turk conquest of Constantinople

1459 Ottoman Turk defeat of Serbs

Byzantium, Russians, and Mongols

Spread of Byzantine Culture

The Byzantines held off foes long enough so that Byzantine culture spread north and east, allowing Byzantine religion and culture to survive the defeat of the empire. The differences between eastern and western versions of Christianity gave some of the eastern European peoples a choice of which to adopt. In the ninth century, two Byzantine brothers, known later as Saints Cyril and Methodius (mi-THO-dee-uhs), converted many Slavs to eastern Christianity. The brothers devised an alphabet, known as Cyrillic (suh-RILL-ik), for the Slavs, and Cyril began translating the Bible and other church writings from Greek. The Bulgars, Serbs, Russians, and many Ukrainians eventually adopted Byzantine culture, including Orthodox Christianity. The Russians and other societies they influenced, including the Georgians in the Caucasus, learned their Christian culture and their politics from a society with an autocratic emperor and close connections between church and state, in contrast to western Europe, where church-state conflicts remained common. Other Slavs, among them Croats (KRO-ATS), Czechs (checks), Lithuanians (lith-oo-ANE-ee-uhnz), Poles, Slovaks (SLO-vaks), Slovenes (SLO-veenz), and many Ukrainians, adopted Roman Catholicism. Eastern and western European cultures remain distinct even today, partly because of the differences between the Greek and Roman churches of 1,000 years ago.

Rise of Russia

Russian identity descended from the Rus (roos), whose capital was at Kiev (KEE-yev), in today's Ukraine (you-CRANE). Swedish Vikings, who founded trading cities in the Slavic regions, had become the Rus ruling class, both trading with and raiding the Byzantines. Viking trade networks crisscrossed the Russian and Ukrainian plains, and the Vikings were eventually assimilated by the Slavs. From the tenth to the twelfth centuries, the Russians expanded, forming settlements as far north as Novgorod (NOHV-goh-rod), from which timber was shipped south to the Black Sea. The Rus ruler Vladimir (VLAD-ih-mir) I (ca. 956–1015) in Kiev opened the doors to Byzantine influence. Vladimir had several wives and eight hundred concubines but, hoping for political advantage, sought marriage to a Byzantine princess. After she refused to marry a pagan polygamist, he agreed to accept Orthodox Christianity in 988 and make her his only wife. When Vladimir ordered his soldiers to be baptized, he guaranteed that a large part of eastern Europe would become Eastern Orthodox.

By the time western Europeans heard rumors about the brutal Mongols, the Russians had already encountered them. Mongol armies conquered Central Asia and parts of China and the Middle East (see Chapters 10 and 11 and the essay at the end of Part III) and repeatedly sacked Russian cities beginning in 1237. A papal envoy who visited Kiev after an attack reported, "We found lying in the fields countless heads and bones. [The city] has been reduced to nothing: barely 200 houses [still] stand there."[15] Until the fifteenth century most Russians remained subject to the Golden Horde, a Mongol state on the lower Volga River. Muscovy (MUSS-koe-vee), a Russian state centered on Moscow, benefited, since the Golden Horde treated its ruler as the senior Russian leader.

Western Europe was fortunate to escape Mongol conquest. In 1241, Mongol armies moved far into Europe, crushing Polish and Hungarian forces sent against them. Soon they stood at the Danube contemplating an invasion into German lands. But the Germans and Europeans farther west were spared because Mongol generals returned to Mongolia when they heard of the death of the Mongol leader, Ogodei. Had the Mongol conquests continued westward, European history might have been very different. But Europe was much less tempting than the far richer societies of China and Islamic western Asia.

Eventually Muscovy became the dominant Russian state as Mongol political power declined and the head of the Russian Orthodox Church, appointed by the patriarch of Constantinople, moved from Kiev to Moscow. During the reign of Ivan III (1440–1505), Muscovy escaped Mongol control and established domination over other Russian states. Ivan began to call himself *czar* (meaning "caesar") to indicate his superiority over lesser rulers, and he married the niece of the last Byz-

An Orthodox Church in Novgorod, Russia   The distinctive architecture of this church represents the fusion of Slavic, Byzantine, and Viking influences.

Novosti

antine emperor. The Russian Orthodox Church broke with the patriarch of Constantinople, and Russian clergy began referring to Moscow as the Third Rome, successor to Constantinople. The Russians also expanded into the territories of the Catholic Lithuanians, adding religious antagonisms to the political tensions between Orthodox and Catholic peoples in eastern Europe.

SECTION SUMMARY

- The Byzantines were under almost constant attack by Sassanian Persians, Bulgars, Slavs, and western European Christians, but Byzantium survived until it was conquered by the Turks in 1453.

- Byzantium's culture and Orthodox Christianity survived because they were spread to many eastern European

peoples, including the Russians, the Bulgars, the Serbs, and many Ukrainians.

- The Russians, who had adopted Orthodox Christianity, were attacked by the Mongols but emerged as one of the strongest societies in eastern Europe.

LATE MEDIEVAL EUROPE AND THE ROOTS OF EXPANSION

> What developments between 1300 and 1500 gave Europeans the incentive and means to begin reshaping the world after 1500?

The Late Middle Ages (1300–1500) were a period of transition. For a century the population shrunk dramatically as a result of famine, plague, and warfare, contributing to the gradual end of feudalism. Royal power increased many places at the expense of the feudal nobility, while the Roman church also lost influence as questioning of church practices and beliefs increased. Yet, the ferment fostered intellectual and cultural creativity, trade increased, and brave mariners began exploring the world beyond Europe, fostering the resurgence of the West.

The Black Death and Social Change

Late medieval Europe was an unhappy place, ravaged by famine, disease, and war. Europe's climate turned colder about 1300, fostering "the Little Ice Age." As a result, the Norse farming settlements in Greenland collapsed from deforestation, expanding glaciers, and conflict with the local Inuit. The same cooler temperatures shortened the European growing season, causing serious food shortages.

Europe also repeatedly suffered from the Black Death, a terrible *pandemic,* or massive epidemic that crossed many regions, named for the black bruises that appeared under the skin. In 1347 a trading ship coming from the Black Sea limped into a Sicilian harbor with all of the crew either dead or dying from a deadly infection spread by fleas that lived on rats who had scampered aboard ship—probably bubonic plague, perhaps mixed with pneumonic (noo-MON-ik) plague. The pandemic caused unprecedented death and suffering as it spread along and disrupted the networks of exchange all over Eurasia and North Africa (see Chronology: The Late Middle Ages, 1300–1500). During its peak years from 1348 to 1350, the pandemic killed a third of all Europeans. Over 65 percent of the population in some congested cities died, greatly reducing commerce, and Europe's population in the fourteenth century dropped from around 70 or 75 million to some 45 or 50 million people, most killed by either a fast-acting respiratory infection or by swelling and internal bleeding. Pope Clement VI wrote that "the living were barely sufficient to bury the dead, or so horrified as to avoid the task. So great a terror seized nearly everyone."[16] The horrors endured in nursery rhymes: "Ring around the rosies, a pocketful of posies, ashes, ashes, we all fall down." Those who survived developed some immunities: although the Black Death reoccurred for decades, it killed fewer people each time.

The troubles reshaped European social patterns, especially for the upper classes. With far fewer peasants alive to till the fields, those remaining asked for more privileges and money, and peasant revolts demanding an end to serfdom increased, most notably in France in 1358 and in England in 1381. Meanwhile, some people challenged social norms. In addition to writing works of history, ethics, and poetry, the French author Christine of Pasan (1364–ca. 1430) proclaimed that women were equals of men, systematically disproved all the negative stereotypes men held of women's character, and shrewdly critiqued the patriarchal social structure. She wrote that "those who blame women out of jealousy are those wicked men who have seen many women of greater intelligence

Hemispheric Pandemic

Impacts on Society

and nobler conduct than they themselves possess."[17] Some literature, such as the fiction of the fourteenth-century English writer Geoffrey Chaucer (CHAW-suhr) (see Witness to the Past: A Literary View of Late Medieval People), reflected the changing social customs and relations.

The death and despair influenced emotional and social life. Many people assumed the pandemic was divine punishment. Feelings of utter hopelessness overwhelmed people who vainly tried to dig graves for their family members before they too succumbed to death, which usually came in a matter of days. While famine and disease raged, aristocrats regaled themselves with magnificent banquets and pageants and wore ostentatious clothing. The poor sought escape through prayer, meditation, and self-flagellation, imitating the torture of Jesus by beating themselves with whips until their blood flowed. Some places people, looking for scapegoats, blamed outsiders, especially Jews, for the troubles. In the mid-1300s thousands of Jews were burned alive or driven out of cities, especially in the German states.

The pandemic's impact on western and eastern Europe proved quite different. Because eastern Europe had fewer cities and more villages, fewer peasants died. Since the eastern monarchs were also weaker, the aristocracy imposed serfdom on many of their peasants, creating large agricultural estates. The nobility were strengthened socially, while their western European counterparts were weakened by labor shortages and higher costs. Hence, eastern Europe remained primarily an agricultural area, while western European rulers continued to strengthen their central governments.

Warfare and Political Centralization

The Hundred Years War

Warfare in late medieval western Europe, which was common, strengthened kings and states (see Map 14.3). For example, the intermittent fighting between English and French troops known as the Hundred Years War (1337–1453) enhanced royal power in France and also, eventually, in England. This war, caused by the English kings' desire to hold on to their feudal lands in France, eventually resulted in a French victory. At first the English gained victories by using trained commoners

The Metropolitan Museum of Art, the Cloisters Collection, 1954 [54.1.1]. Photograph © 1987 The Metropolitan Museum of Art

and a new weapon, the longbow, that launched powerful arrows and thus diminished the knights as an effective fighting force. However, aided by Jeanne d'Arc (zhahn DAHRK) (ca. 1412–1431), a sixteen-year-old peasant who believed that voices from saints told her to lead troops into battle, the French broke the English siege of the city of Orleans (or-lay-AHN) and slowly recovered most of the English-held territory in France. Jeanne, meanwhile, was captured and burned at the stake, becoming the most famous martyr to French nationhood.

During the conflict's final stages, the French monarchs introduced new direct taxes that lessened their dependence on the feudal nobility. Kings also reorganized the royal armies to depend more on mercenary troops hired with tax revenues. In England, military defeat fostered a long conflict between two rival royal houses, the War of the Roses (1455–1485), that ended with Henry VII founding a new Tudor dynasty. Henry VII sent in armies to reclaim Ireland, which were followed by English settlers who repressed the Celtic Irish. The Tudors established England as a world power during the 1500s.

Royal power also increased during the late 1400s in Spain. In 1085 Christians began the long reconquest of the peninsula

Praying for Relief This image of survivors carrying away plague victims in Rome was commissioned by a French duke for an illuminated book in the early 1400s. It illustrates the despair and devastating loss of life caused by the Black Death, especially in cities.

A Literary View of Late Medieval People

The English writer Geoffrey Chaucer (ca. 1340–1400) wrote one of the best-known books of the Late Middle Ages, *The Canterbury Tales*, set in the time of the Black Death. Born in London, Chaucer was a cosmopolitan poet, soldier, and diplomat who served in the English Parliament and was familiar with French and Italian intellectual and cultural trends. His writings reflected these trends while also strongly influencing spoken and written English. *The Canterbury Tales* also offered a witty and sophisticated picture of English society. This excerpt presents stereotypical and satirical views of various pilgrims on their way to visit Canterbury, the seat of church power in England.

The knight there was, and he was a worthy man, Who, from the moment that he first began To ride about the world, loved chivalry, Truth, honor, freedom, and all courtesy. . . . Of mortal battles he had fought fifteen . . . And always won he sovereign fame for prize . . . He never yet had any vileness said [about him] in all his life . . . He was a truly perfect, gentle knight. . . .

There was also a nun, a prioress, Who, in her smiling, modest was and coy . . . At table she had been well taught withal, And never from her lips let morels fall, Nor dipped her fingers deep in sauce, but ate With so much care the food upon her plate That never driblet fell upon her breast. In courtesy she had delight and zest. . . .

A monk there was, one made for mastery [and loved hunting] . . . A manly man, to be an abbot able. Full many a blooded horse had he in stable: And when he rode men might his bridle hear A-jingling in the whistling wind as clear, Aye, and as loud as does the chapel bell Where this brave monk was of the cell. . . . This said monk let such lowly old things [strict old monastic rules] slowly pace And followed new world manners in their place. What? Should he study as a madman would Upon a book in cloister cell? Or yet, go labor with his hands and . . . sweat [as St. Augustine commanded]? . . .

There was a merchant with forked beard, and girt . . . Upon his head a Flemish beaver hat; His boots were fastened rather elegantly. He spoke [his opinions] pompously, Stressing the times when he had won, not lost [his profits] . . . At money changing he could make a crown. This worthy man kept all his wits well set; There was no one could say he was in debt, So well he governed all his trade affairs. . . .

There was a good man of religion, too, A country parson, poor . . . but rich he was in holy thought and work. He was also a learned man also [a scholar] . . . who Christ's own Gospel truly sought to preach. Devoutly his parisoner's would he teach . . . Benign he was and wondrous diligent, Patient in adverse times and well content . . . But rather would he give . . . unto those poor parishioners about, Part of his income, even of his goods . . . That first he wrought and after words he taught [first he practiced, then he preached]. . . .

THINKING ABOUT THE READING

1. What are the various clerical stereotypes presented?

2. How is the merchant portrayed?

Source: General Prologue to Geoffrey Chaucer's *Canterbury Tales*, electronic edition prepared by Edwin Duncan (*http:www.towson.edu/~duncan/chaucer/titlepage.htm*)

from Muslims. By 1249 they had reclaimed Portugal, and by the 1300s Spanish Christians had displaced all of the Muslim states except for Granada (gruh-NAH-duh) in the far south. In 1469 the two largest kingdoms were united when King Ferdinand of Aragon (AR-uh-gon) married his cousin, Isabella of Castile (kas-TEEL). These monarchs finally crushed Granada in 1492 and then, obsessed with religious uniformity, demanded that the Spanish Jews and Muslims either convert or be expelled. Hoping to increase royal wealth, they also sponsored the first trans-Atlantic voyage by the Italian mariner, Christopher Columbus, in 1492.

The nobility remained strong in the Holy Roman Empire, which included many of the German-speaking lands and parts of Italy. The Habsburg (HABZ-berg) family, who took power in 1273, were unable to create a strong centralized state. In 1356 they reduced the pope's influence over the election of Holy Roman Emperors but also confirmed the power of the princes. During the coming centuries imperial Habsburg rulers concentrated on increasing the personal territorial holdings of their family. In the later 1400s, by royal marriage alliances, they gained control of the Netherlands and much of southern Italy.

Holy Roman Empire

Hemispheric Connections, New Intellectual Horizons, and Technology

Long Distance Trade

The Late Middle Ages fostered new intellectual horizons and technologies, some of them derived from contacts with Asia and Africa. The Mongols did not conquer western Europe but reenergized

Map 14.3
Europe, 1400–1500
During this period France became western Europe's strongest kingdom, but Spanish kings gradually reunified much of the Iberian peninsula. The Holy Roman empire remained decentralized. Meanwhile, Lithuania, Hungary, and Poland controlled much of eastern Europe.

e Interactive Map

Spread of Roman Christendom

- In 1000 C.E.
- Added 1000–1200
- Lost 1000–1200 (Regained 1200–1500)
- Added 1200–1500
- Lost 1200–1500
- English holdings, 1360
- Boundary of the Holy Roman Empire

N

ATLANTIC OCEAN

North Sea

IRELAND
Dublin

SCOTLAND

WALES
ENGLAND
London

Baltic Sea

NORWAY
Oslo

SWEDEN
Stockholm

DENMARK
Copenhagen
Hamburg

ESTONIA
NOVGOROD

PRUSSIA
Riga

GRAND PRINCIPALITY OF MOSCOW
Moscow

KHANATE OF THE KAZAN

Volga R.

KHANATE OF THE GOLDEN HORDE

KHANATE OF THE ASTRAKHAN

Don R.

KHANATE OF THE CRIMEA

Dnieper R.

Kiev

GRAND PRINCIPALITY OF LITHUANIA

PRUSSIA
Königsberg
Danzig
Warsaw

POLAND

BOHEMIA

Elbe R.

Rhine R.

Frankfurt

HOLY ROMAN EMPIRE

AUSTRIA
Vienna

STYRIA
TYROL

SWITZERLAND

A L P S

MILAN
Po R.

GENOA

MILAN
Venice

VENETIAN REPUBLIC

Adriatic Sea

FLORENCE

PAPAL STATES

Rome

BUDAPEST
Budapest

HUNGARY

MOLDAVIA

WALLACHIA

Danube R.

SERBIA

BOSNIA

MONTENEGRO

ALBANIA

Black Sea

Constantinople

OTTOMAN EMPIRE

Athens

Crete

Rhodes

Cyprus

FLANDERS

LUXEMBOURG

CHAMPAGNE

BURGUNDY

FRANCHE-COMTÉ

Paris
Orléans

BRITTANY

FRANCE

Lyons

SAVOY

Rhône R.

Avignon

Marseilles

AQUITAINE

NAVARRE

Ebro R.

Barcelona

KINGDOM OF ARAGON

Toledo

KINGDOM OF CASTILE AND LEÓN

PORTUGAL
Lisbon

Granada
GRANADA

MOROCCO

ALGIERS

TUNIS

Mediterranean Sea

Corsica

Sardinia

KINGDOM OF NAPLES

Naples

Sicily

Malta

Rome

Tigris R.

Euphrates R.

0   150   300 Mi.
0   150   300 Km

Eurasian trade, allowing inventions and ideas to flow to Europe from China and western Asia. Some of these inventions, such as printing, gunpowder, and the compass, eventually revolutionized European technology. Europeans, especially Italians, imported spices, carpets, silks, porcelain, glassware, and even painting supplies from Muslim Spain, Ottoman Turkey, Mamluk Egypt, and Persia. The cosmopolitan Ottoman ruler Mehmed the Conqueror (1430–1481) read and published Greek and Latin books on history and philosophy and invited Italian merchants, craftsmen, artists, and architects to work in Istanbul (formerly Constantinople). Some Italians, especially Venetians, were influenced by the magnificent palaces and mosques they saw in Islamic cities. By the later 1400s the Portuguese brought back artworks and fabrics from West Africa and the Kongo that also influenced European artists.

At the same time, moral and political corruption contributed to the decline of papal political power and the Roman church. Some historians argue that all power tends to corrupt. In the case of the church, dissidents complained about the buying of church offices, favoritism to relatives, and the absenteeism of bishops who served more than one diocese; to collect the extra revenue, such bishops were necessarily absent from one or other of their jobs. His detractors claimed that Cardinal Wolsey, archbishop of both Canterbury and York in England, entered the cathedral at York only once, for his funeral. Skeptics also viewed practices such as venerating holy relics and making pilgrimages as superstition that encouraged fraud, while defenders argued that relics and pilgrimages gave people something tangible to cling to when seeking God's help.

Papal Decline

Papal prestige declined after the popes moved to Avignon in southern France (1309–1377). The Avignon popes required that candidates for bishop pay a large sum to the papal treasury, a form of extortion that reserved high church offices for the wealthy. When the papacy finally returned to Rome, two men claimed to be the rightful pope, and Europeans picked sides in this "Great Schism" (1378–1417). Although the split ended, much damage had been done to the papacy's prestige. After a council of bishops unsuccessfully tried to replace papal monarchy with a church government by such councils, popes refused to call any further councils on church reform.

Imported ideas and products along with dissent in the church contributed to the dramatic flowering of arts and learning later known as the **Renaissance**, or "rebirth," that began in the Italian city-states around 1350 and intensified through the 1400s and 1500s, spreading to other societies. In Florence, artists and thinkers rediscovered the ideas of the Classical Greeks and Romans. Renaissance philosophy, called **humanism**, emphasized humanity, worldly concerns, and reason rather than religious ideals. The books of Dante Alighieri (DAHN-tay ah-lee-GYEH-ree) (1265–1321), especially *The Divine Comedy*, attacked the pope and promoted vernacular language, in this case Italian, rather than Latin, while painters in Italy, such as Sandro Botticelli (SAHN-dro BOT-i-CHEL-ee) (1445–1510), and in the Netherlands depicted space and the human figure realistically. Scholars debate whether the Renaissance undermined medieval world-views by fostering individualism, secularism, and scientific inquiry or was mainly a cultural movement among a small privileged elite that had little impact on the larger society. Nonetheless, Renaissance artists and writers emphasized tolerance of diverse views and new ideals of beauty, weakening church influence. The Renaissance eventually spread into northern Europe in the 1500s.

The Renaissance

Renaissance ("Rebirth") A dramatic flowering in arts and learning that began in the Italian city-states around 1350 and spread through Europe through the 1500s.

humanism The name for the European Renaissance philosophy, which emphasized humanity, worldly concerns, and reason rather than religious ideals.

Extraordinary technological development, greatly aided by imports from other regions, also characterized late medieval Europe. European scholars translated Arab and Greek scientific writings in Muslim Spain, while Asian and Muslim technologies reached Europe, including the Chinese spinning wheel and loom, which spurred improved textile manufacturing. During the fourteenth and fifteenth centuries western Europeans developed better ships, in part by improving Chinese inventions such as the compass and sternpost rudder and by adapting the Arab lateen sails. By the 1490s, thanks to these advances in navigation, sailing, and weaponry, Europeans were masters of the oceans. They also devised time-measuring devices, including mechanical clocks, that allowed people to control and standardize units of time.

New Technologies

Perhaps the most crucial invention was printing by movable type, allowing information to be produced and spread in unlimited quantities. The Chinese invented woodblock printing and movable type made of clay and metal centuries earlier (see Chapter 11), and knowledge of Chinese techniques may have traveled the trade routes to Europe. By the 1400s Europeans used block printing for books and playing cards, and in 1455 the German goldsmith Johann Gutenberg (yoh-HAHN GOO-ten-burg) (1400–1468) introduced the first known metal movable type outside of East Asia, using it to print a Bible. From then on the printed word became an essential medium of mass communication and no longer the monopoly of the few who could afford the expensive hand-copied volumes. This development undermined both feudalism and the church.

Imported technology, especially gunpowder from China, made for more lethal warfare. By the 1200s, the Chinese had developed primitive guns capable of ejecting flame and projectiles 40 yards, a major reason it took the Mongols so long to conquer China. This and other weapons reached

Europe during the Mongol era and were then improved, making warfare far deadlier than it had been before. But gunpowder weapons, while killing many knights and nobles in wars, also gave Europeans a huge military advantage over societies that did not have them, among them those in sub-Saharan Africa and the Americas.

Population and Economic Growth

Technological advance was matched by population and economic growth. Increased agricultural development spurred a European population increase of 40 to 50 percent between the tenth and fourteenth centuries, the highest rate in the world. After the Black Death, Europe's population again increased rapidly, grain production doubled, and many peasants moved into eastern Europe to open lands.

Expanding Commerce

Commerce also expanded. When feudalism and manorialism were dominant, merchants mostly dealt in luxury goods for the aristocracy. Indeed, the feudal ethic was somewhat hostile to the accumulation of wealth, and it devalued merchants. By the 1300s, however, this feudal ethic began to break down. As foreign trade became more economically important, commerce became a part of everyday life. Valuable spices from India and Southeast Asia were distributed by Venetian merchants who had trading posts all over the Middle East and around the Black Sea, as well as from Genoa. Observers were awed by the vast quantity of merchandise, much of it from the East, in fifteenth-century Venice:

> It seems as if the whole world flocks here. Who could count the many shops so well furnished that they seem almost warehouses, with so many cloths of every make—tapestry, brocades, carpets of every sort, silks of every kind; and so many warehouses full of spices, groceries and rugs. These things stupefy the beholder.[18]

Gold from West Africa, used in coins, treasuries, and jewelry, also stimulated the European economy. European merchants borrowed and used Arab trading practices and mathematics. In the early 1200s Fibonacci (fee-bo-NACH-ee), a merchant from Pisa in Italy, wrote of the Arab and Indian numerals and calculations he had studied in Algeria, Egypt, and Syria. Soon the mathematical and commercial innovations he learned were adopted in Venice, Genoa, and Florence.

Unique Cities

Western European cities were unique in their growing political power and autonomy. Unlike in centralized China or the Ottoman Empire, these cities existed in a politically fragmented region and thus could bargain with kings for advantages and autonomy. In 1241 various north German cities expanded a trade alliance, the Hanseatic (han-see-AT-ik) League, that eventually had over 165 member cities, including some in Holland and Poland, and its own army and navy, making it almost an independent political power. These developments gave European merchants a status and power unique in the world. In China, for instance, merchants, while often prosperous, had a low ranking in the Confucian social system, were heavily taxed, and faced many restrictions. In western Europe merchants steadily gained influence, becoming city political leaders. Governments now supported merchants and their interests, fostering a social and institutional structure that encouraged profits. Not everyone approved, however. The Dutch philosopher Erasmus complained about greed, asking, "When did avarice reign more largely and less punished?"[19] Nonetheless, late medieval Europeans laid the foundation for an economic revolution that began to fundamentally alter western European life in the 1500s and later spread its influences around the world.

The Portuguese and Maritime Exploration

In the 1400s a few Europeans, pushed by the growth of commerce, and taking advantage of the new maritime and military technologies, began to explore the world beyond Europe by sea. The Portuguese, who had recently been unified in a kingdom and whose standard of living was probably lower than that of many Africans and Asians, began sailing south in search of slaves, gold,

Portuguese Motives

and other trade goods. Although shocked at the wealth of some of the societies they encountered, they enjoyed the advantage of guns, better ships, and a maritime tradition, and they were motivated by a missionary desire to outflank Islam and spread Christianity, as well as a compelling appetite for plunder and conquest. The Portuguese also had a larger strategic purpose: to find a way around Africa and sail directly to the fabled lands of Southeast Asia, the source of the spices so valued in Europe. They also sought the sources of African gold. Finally, European legends spoke of a great Christian emperor in Africa, "Prester John," perhaps derived from the king of Ethiopia, who they believed could be a possible ally against Muslims.

Hence, in search of, in their words, "Christians and spices," the Portuguese began systematically exploring the West African coast in 1420 under the sponsorship of Prince Henry the Navigator (1394–1460), an innovator in shipbuilding design and cartography. Soon Henry's caravels, small ships that could sail both on the ocean and into shallow coastal waters and rivers, discovered Madeira (muh-DEER-uh) Island and the Azores (A-zorz) and Canary Islands in the Atlantic off North Africa. By the 1480s the Portuguese had visited much of the African coast as far south as Angola (see Chapter 12). In 1487 Portuguese ships led by Bartolomeu Dias (DEE-uhsh) reached the Indian Ocean, intensifying Portuguese interest both in Africa and the world to the east. One of the sailors who had manned Portuguese ships was a Genoese immigrant to Portugal, Christopher Columbus, who later developed an alternative strategy for reaching the East. In 1492 Columbus, under Spanish sponsorship, sailed west across the Atlantic to the Americas, changing world history forever.

Portuguese Discoveries

SECTION SUMMARY

- The Black Death killed a third of Europe's people and reduced the power of western European nobles while increasing the power of eastern European nobles.

- French rulers increased their power in the Hundred Years War, England's Tudor dynasty later made England a world power, and Spanish Christians gradually drove out the Muslims, while in Germany and Italy the nobility remained strong.

- The church entered a decline in power and prestige as it came to be seen as corrupt, and the papacy was weakened by the Great Schism.

- During the Renaissance, artists and writers rediscovered classical influences and championed worldly concerns, individualism, and realism rather than spirituality.

- Major technological developments, influenced in part by ideas imported from China and the Muslim world, included the printing press, which further undermined the church, and guns, which killed many in European wars and were especially deadly against Africans and Americans.

- Despite the Black Death, Europe's population soared and its merchants grew increasingly successful and powerful.

- The Portuguese were the first to begin exploring the West Coast of Africa for slaves, gold, and other trade goods, and their adventures eventually led to Columbus's voyage to the Americas.

CHAPTER SUMMARY

European societies changed dramatically between 600 and 1500. By mixing Greco-Roman, Christian, and Germanic legacies between 500 and 1000, western Europeans constructed new societies based on new values and practices. These societies also acquired knowledge from and traded with the Islamic world, especially Muslim Spain. Feudalism, manorialism, and the papacy became the major medieval institutions, but they generated conflict between popes and kings, kings and nobles, nobles and merchants, cities and countryside, and Christians and outsiders. The church played a crucial social and political role in European societies. Priests dominated village life, while popes fought heresy and spurred crusades against Muslims.

The social, political, economic, and religious systems of Byzantium were different from those in western Europe. The Byzantine emperors were more powerful and had more control over the church. Eventually the Byzantine church broke completely with the Roman church, becoming the Greek Orthodox Church. Byzantium also passed on many traditions to various eastern European societies such as the Russians. Russia later became a strong state with a rival Orthodox Church.

Western Europeans were linked by trade networks to other societies of Eurasia and North Africa. These networks, including those formed by the Mongol expansion, allowed the movement from east to west not only of valuable goods, technologies, and ideas but also of diseases such as the Black Death. Between 1300 and 1500 western European states grew larger and, in some cases, more centralized, the church faced decline as a political force, and warfare became more deadly. Sparked in part by Afro-Asian influences, the Renaissance fostered new humanistic ideas and artistic currents, while economic growth and social change enhanced the influence of merchants. In the fifteenth century, aided by Asian and Islamic seafaring technologies, western Europeans began exploring the world.

KEY TERMS

medieval	knights	usury	Magna Carta
feudalism	chivalry	courtly love	Renaissance
vassals	manorialism	excommunicate	humanism
benefices	serfs	simony	
fief	guilds	Holy Inquisition	

EBOOK AND WEBSITE RESOURCES

ⓔ PRIMARY SOURCE

Magna Carta: The Great Charter of Liberties

ⓔ INTERACTIVE MAPS

Map 14.1 Europe During the Carolingian Empire
Map 14.2 Medieval Europe, 900–1300
Map 14.3 Europe, 1400–1500

LINKS

Byzantium: Byzantine Studies on the Internet (http://www.fordham.edu/halsall/byzantium). Contains useful texts, images, essays, and bibliography.

The Internet Medieval Sourcebook (http://www.fordham.edu/halsall/sbook.html). This is one of the best, most extensive sources for texts and essays.

Lectures in Medieval History (http://www.ku/kansas/medieval/108/lectures/index.html). Many useful essays for the general reader by a leading expert.

Medieval and Renaissance Europe: Primary Historical Documents (http://eudocs.lib.byu.edu/index.php/Main_Page). Many links to primary sources.

The WWW Virtual Library: Medieval Europe (https://www.msu.edu/~georgem1/history/medieval.htm). Contains many links to many topical sites.

The World of the Vikings (http://www.worldofthevikings.com). Contains many links to texts, images, and essays.

Plus flashcards, practice quizzes, and more. Go to: www.cengage.com/history/lockard/globalsocnet2e.

SUGGESTED READING

Bridenthal, Renate, et al., eds. *Becoming Visible: Women in European History,* 3rd ed. Boston: Houghton Mifflin, 1998. Valuable essays.

Brotton, Jerry. *The Renaissance Bazaar: From the Silk Road to Michelangelo.* Oxford: Oxford University Press, 2002. An important revisionist interpretation by a British scholar that places European developments in a hemispheric context.

Cruz, Jo Ann, H. Moran, and Richard Gerberding. *Medieval Worlds: An Introduction to European History, 300–1492.* Boston: Houghton Mifflin, 2004. A readable and comprehensive recent text.

Cunliffe, Barry. *Facing the Ocean: The Atlantic and Its Peoples, 8000 BC–AD 1500.* New York: Oxford University Press, 2001. Examines the societies on Eurasia's western rim.

Davies, Norman. *Europe: A History.* New York: Harper Perennial, 1998. A fascinating examination with much on this era.

Gies, Frances, and Joseph Gies. *Marriage and the Family in the Middle Ages.* New York: Harper and Row, 1987. A thorough account of marriage and family life, written for the general reader.

Hanawalt, Barbara A. *The Middle Ages: An Illustrated History.* New York: Oxford University Press, 1998. A well-written overview aimed at the general reader.

Kelly, John. *The Great Mortality: An Intimate History of the Black Death, the Most Devastating Plague of All Time.* New York: HarperCollins, 2005. A readable account of the calamity and its effects on people.

Logan, F. Donald. *The Vikings in History,* 3rd ed. London: Routledge, 2005. A wide-ranging survey that stresses the importance of the Vikings in European history.

Lowney, Chris. *A Vanished World: Medieval Spain's Golden Age of Enlightenment.* New York: Free Press, 2005. Examines Islamic Spain's connections to Europe.

Madden, Thomas F. *A New History of the Crusades.* Lanham, MD: Rowman and Littlefield, 2005. A recent and well-written overview.

McCormick, Michael. *Origins of the European Economy: Communication and Commerce, A.D. 300–900.* New York: Cambridge University Press, 2001. Pathbreaking work.

Ostrowski, Donald. *Muscovy and the Mongols: Cross-Cultural Influences on the Steppe Frontier, 1304–1589.* Cambridge: Cambridge University Press, 1990. A scholarly study of Byzantine and Mongol influences on the Russians.

Treadgold, Warren. *A Concise History of Byzantium.* New York: Palgrave, 2001. A comprehensive recent survey.

Wells, Colin. *Sailing from Byzantium: How a Lost Empire Shaped the World.* New York: Delta, 2006. Readable study of Byzantium and its legacy.

Eastern Predominance in the Intermediate World

For over a century now the prosperous and powerful nations of North America and western Europe—often known today as the West—have dominated the world economically and politically. But before 1500 the world looked very different, and various societies in Asia and North Africa were much stronger and more influential than they are today. Some Eastern societies enjoyed power and status far beyond their borders, helping to shape much of the Eastern Hemisphere in these centuries. However, historians debate to what degree we can consider this to have been an era of Eastern predominance in Afro-Eurasia.

THE PROBLEM

Some historians believe that the rise to influence and prosperity of the East, especially China, India, and various Islamic societies, was a major theme of the Intermediate Era. In their view, for most of these centuries, these Eastern peoples developed and sustained more dynamic governments, productive economies, and creative technologies than any other societies. Others disagree, contending that after 1000 the advantage shifted to western Europeans, who laid the foundations for rapid growth and eventual world dominance. These arguments are part of a vigorous scholarly debate.

THE DEBATE

Many historians identify Eastern predominance in this era, but they disagree on which society made the greatest contributions to the world. The largest number point to China as the Eurasian leader in the Intermediate Era, and they offer a variety of factors to explain China's status. S. A. M. Adshead, for example, sees Tang China as taking center-stage in the world economy and becoming the world's best-ordered state between 600 and 900. William McNeill refers to an era of Chinese predominance especially from 1000 to 1500, with China as the engine of the Eurasian economy. Various historians of Asia, among them Rhoads Murphey, describe an especially dynamic and creative Song China that had many of the conditions that would, in the later eighteenth century, foster industrialization in northwest Europe: urbanization, commercialization, widening local and overseas markets, rising demand, and mechanical invention. A few scholars such as Mary Matossian label the entire Intermediate Era the "Chinese Millennium," when China was more populous, productive, and wealthy than any other society, enjoying an orderly society and advanced technology.

There is a growing consensus among world historians that Chinese innovations and commercial expansion energized Eurasian trade and that Chinese inventions contributed much to the Intermediate world. The British scholar Robert Temple goes even further, crediting the Chinese with inventing modern agriculture, shipping, astronomical observatories, oil industries, paper money, decimal mathematics, wheelbarrows, fishing reels, multistage rockets, guns, umbrellas, hot-air balloons, chess, whiskey, and even the essential design of the steam engine. Without Chinese naval technology, he and others argue, Columbus would never have sailed to America. China and India

were the two great centers of world manufacturing before 1500, and their exports fueled Afro-Eurasian trade.

But China was not the only Asian powerhouse and great source of knowledge. Indians fostered two universal religions, Buddhism and Hinduism, while inventing and exporting scientific, technological, and agricultural techniques to China, the Islamic world, and later Europe in a process the historian Lynda Shaffer terms "southernization." Such innovations as Indian granulated sugar crystals, the decimal system, "Arabic" numerals, and cotton plants had revolutionary implications for Eurasia. Then there are historians of the Middle East, such as Marshall Hodgson and Richard Eaton, who argue for the centrality of the Islamic societies. They contend that, before 1600, the Islamic culture and economy were the world's most expansive, influential, and integrating force. Islam provided a widespread, sophisticated culture as many peoples joined the Muslim-dominated hemispheric economy. Islam was cosmopolitan, egalitarian, and flexible, allowing Muslims to rebound from the Mongol conquests and Black Death and reestablish powerful states such as Ottoman Turkey.

Still other historians think China, India, and Islam all played key roles as powerhouses in an Eastern-dominated Intermediate world. For instance, Robert Marks argues that the Eastern Hemisphere in the 1300s and 1400s had three centers, with dynamic but linked regional systems based on China, India, and Islam. In the 1400s, from Ottoman Turkey eastward to Japan, agricultural efficiency, consumer goods, social welfare, and civilian and military technology were generally the equal of, and often superior to, European counterparts. British scholar John Hobson makes a strong case that the rise of the East made possible the later rise of the West. He argues that the globalization of the era allowed the advanced Eastern inventions, the products of more dynamic societies, to flow westward, where they were gradually assimilated by Europe. Many historians contend that Europe in this era was economically weak, with small, insignificant states, and did not show renewed vigor until 1400. Nor did Europe have, as some historians suggest, any unique cultural advantages. Jack Goody concludes that there were few decisive cultural differences between East and West in rationality, economic tools, family patterns, and political pluralism.

Other scholars doubt that any Eastern societies had a great advantage in this era, and they contend that medieval Europe was not backward compared to China, India, or Islam. David Landes, for example, while conceding that Europe was well behind China and Islam in many areas of life in 1000, suggests that things had changed considerably 500 years later. With what he considers many cultural and geographical advantages, Europeans, argues Landes, caught up to the East with the growth of manufacturing and trade. Landes and others describe an inventive Europe with impressive technological progress using increased nonhuman power, especially in agriculture. Toby Huff has favorably contrasted European science with its Chinese counterpart, especially after 1200. Restless human energy, influential merchants, and competing states made late medieval Europe dynamic. Rodney Stark credits the medieval Catholic Church's emphasis on reason and belief in progress for fostering economic growth, asserting that these ideas were lacking in other religions, a view many scholars have challenged. Landes and Huff also challenge the notion of Eastern leadership. They see China by 1450 as overpopulated, intellectually dormant, indifferent to technology, negating commercial success, and resistant to change. Some historians of China, such as Adshead, concur that the balance of power was shifting toward Europe in the later Intermediate Era.

If several Eastern societies, and especially China, did have some advantages and great power during much of the Intermediate Era, they lost their predominance between 1450 and 1800, raising the question of when and how the East declined. As for when, some historians believe the decline of the East preceded and made possible the rise of the West. Janet Abu-Lughod describes a well-integrated hemispheric system linking Afro-Eurasia by trade for several centuries, with no single country dominant. This network declined after 1350, reducing Europe's commercial competition. Other historians blame Eastern decline on the Mongols and their heirs, who devastated western Asia and North India and ended the creative Song dynasty.

Others credit what the historian L. S. Stavrianos termed the "Law of the Retarding Lead"—that nothing fails like success—for undermining China and helping underdeveloped Europe. This concept holds that the best-adapted, most successful societies have the most difficulty in changing and retaining their lead in a period of transition. They lose their dynamic thrust. Conversely, the less successful societies are more likely to eventually adapt and forge ahead. In the 1400s China still had an edge over other societies, with an advanced technology, efficient government, great regional power, and the world's largest commercial economy. As a result, the Chinese had a stake in preserving rather than dramatically altering their system, which seemed to work so well. Indeed, some argue that the leading Eastern societies, especially China, remained successful until overtaken by a rising West between 1600 and 1800.

EVALUATING THE DEBATE

A plausible case can be made for Eastern predominance, and most global historians now agree that, while other societies played key roles, China and the Islamic world were the two major poles of global trade and technological innovation for much of this era, at least before the 1400s. But the Eastern advantage was eventually lost. We are left with tantalizing questions. What if the Mongols or Ottomans had conquered some of western Europe, or Ming admiral Zheng He had continued his voyages and headed all the way to West Africa, Europe, or the Americas? Had they occurred, these Mongol, Ottoman, or Chinese achievements might have created a world unrecognizable to us today. Perhaps China, with many prerequisites already in place and enriched by greater trade with West Africa and Europe, might have sparked an industrial revolution. It did not happen, however. Humanity stood at a crossroads in the middle of the millennium, posed between several very different futures. During the next several centuries Europe gradually forged ahead—what some historians call "the rise of the West"—partly by assimilating Eastern technologies and science, while

Chinese Foundries By the second century B.C.E. Chinese iron masters had developed highly sophisticated techniques for producing iron and steel, including a basic blast furnace similar to those invented in Europe in the nineteenth century.

the Islamic societies, India, and finally China struggled, making the world after 1500 very different from the world before it.

THINKING ABOUT THE CONTROVERSY

1. Why do some historians emphasize China as the predominant power in this era?
2. What role did India and the Islamic societies play in the Intermediate world?
3. What points support the argument that Europe began its rise to world power in this era?

EXPLORING THE CONTROVERSY

Among books making the case for Eastern predominance and leadership are John M. Hobson, *The Eastern Origins of Western Civilisation* (New York: Cambridge University Press, 2004); Robert B. Marks, *The Origins of the Modern World: A Global and Ecological Narrative* (Lanham, MD: Rowman and Littlefield, 2002); and Jack Goody, *The East in the West* (Cambridge: Cambridge University Press, 1996). On China as the major power, see S. A. M. Adshead, *Tang China: The Rise of the East in World History* (New York: Palgrave, 2004); William H. McNeill, *The Pursuit of Power: Technology, Armed Force, and Society Since* A.D. *1000* (Chicago: University of Chicago Press, 1982); Rhoads Murphey, *East Asia: A New History*, 3rd ed. (New York: Longman, 2004); Mary Kilbourne Matossian, *Shaping World History: Breakthroughs in Ecology, Technology, Science, and Politics* (Armonk, NY: M.E. Sharpe, 1997); and Robert Temple, *The Genius of China: 3,000 Years of Science, Discovery and Invention* (London: Prion Books, 1986). For Indian and Islamic influence, see Lynda Shaffer, "Southernization," *Journal of World History* 5, no.1 (Spring 1994): 1–22; Marshall Hodgson, *Rethinking World History* (Cambridge: Cambridge University Press, 1993); and Richard Eaton, *Islamic History as Global History* (Washington, DC: American Historical Association, 1993). Among books that argue for European superiority are Toby E. Huff, *The Rise of Early Modern Science: Islam, China, and the West* (Cambridge: Cambridge University Press, 1993); David S. Landes, *The Wealth and Power of Nations: Why Some Are So Rich and Some Are So Poor* (New York: Norton, 1998); and Rodney Stark, *The Victory of Reason: How Christianity Led to Freedom, Capitalism, and Western Success* (New York: Random House, 2005). For a broader study of the rise and demise of the East, see Janet L. Abu-Lughod, *Before European Hegemony: The World System* A.D. *1250–1350* (New York: Oxford University Press, 1989).

Expanding Horizons in the Intermediate Era, 600 B.C.E.–600 C.E.

Societies change largely in interaction with one another rather than in isolation, and world historians emphasize these interactions. In world history, the formation of broad connections among peoples is more crucial than the rise and fall of individual states and even great empires. World history differs from regional history primarily because the world historian stresses contacts, collisions, and networks of exchange, as well as the spread from one society to another of products, technologies, ideas, and people. From earliest times parts of Eurasia and North Africa formed an interconnecting zone, and the links continually expanded to incorporate more of Eurasia and Africa and then, after 1500, the Americas and Oceania.

These patterns can be clearly seen in the Intermediate Era, or Middle Ages between 600 and 1500 C.E., when the world changed profoundly. During this time, the Chinese, Indian, and Islamic societies stood out for their power and creativity, but by the 1400s western Europe was also emerging as a dynamic center. In the Eastern Hemisphere vigorous societies also flourished in Northeast Asia, Southeast Asia, Central Asia, and sub-Saharan Africa. Many far-flung cultures became linked as people, armies, goods, and religions moved more easily and frequently, expanding horizons. These movements and exchanges connected peoples from one end of Afro-Eurasia to the other and generated several transitions, such as the reshaping of many societies by the spread of universal religions. Connections were also growing within the Americas. Large empires such as those of the Aztecs, Incas, and their predecessors enjoyed widespread influence, and trade networks bound societies over great distances. Thanks to European voyages of discovery, by 1500 the long divided Eastern and Western Hemispheres came into regular communication, furthering global contacts.

Today the term *globalization* refers to the increasing interconnectedness of nations and peoples around the world through international trade, investment, ideas, popular culture, and travel. Globalization is sometimes viewed as a twentieth-century phenomenon. But extensive exchanges between widespread peoples and travel over vast distances came many centuries earlier, especially in Afro-Eurasia. An English observer, William Fitzsteven, described the results of such connections in the 1170s when he noted how the markets of London carried products that reflected the cosmopolitan tastes of the city's people:

> Gold from Arabia, from Sabaea [Yemen] spice
> And incense; from the Scythians [Central Asians] arms
>   of steel
> Well-tempered; oil from the rich groves of palm
> That spring from the fat lands of Babylon;
> Fine gems from Nile, from China crimson silks;
> French wines; and sable . . .
> From the far lands where Rus and Northmen [Vikings]
>   dwell.[1]

This essay examines some of these early forms of globalization during the Intermediate Era, such as long-distance

trade, the spread of world religions and the social changes they fostered, the connections sparked by the Mongol expansion, and the acceleration of maritime exploration in the Late Intermediate Era.

Increasing Economic Exchange

Interregional trade was a major theme in world history, especially because it fostered other forms of exchange, including the spread of religions, cultures, and technologies over trade routes. Merchants carried with them their own traditions and learned of other traditions in their travels. During the Intermediate Era, several trade zones developed in the Americas, while in the Eastern Hemisphere overland trade routes reached across Eurasia and Africa. Maritime trade also flourished around the rim of the Indian Ocean. Though it was dominated by Islamic merchants, who spread their faith far and wide, many peoples of various faiths engaged in long-distance commerce by land and sea, serving as links between diverse societies.

Trade and Interregional Contact

The roots of the growing commerce between societies go far back in history. Long-distance trade routes had long existed to move cargo and people by boat, camel, or horseback. The contacts between societies that occurred through trade and military expansion spread various cultural and religious ideas (see map). For instance, Indian influences, including Buddhism, were carried over the trading routes into Central Asia, Tibet, China, Japan, and Southeast Asia between 200 B.C.E. and 1500 C.E. Similarly, between 700 and 1500, Islam expanded by land and sea into West and East Africa, southern Europe, India, and Southeast Asia. Muslim-dominated trade routes ultimately reached from the Sahara to the South China Sea. Once established, these trade routes became a stimulus for travel. Indeed, the annual pilgrimage of devout Muslims proved a boon for merchants as pilgrims from all over brought their local products to Mecca, transforming it into one of the world's great fairs. In 1184 one observer marveled that "no merchandise in the world is absent from this meeting."[2]

Beginning around 200 B.C.E., the Silk Road, a 4,000-mile-long route linking China through Central Asia to India, western Asia, and the Mediterranean, provided the most outstanding example of overland trade and a symbol of east-west contacts. Cities such as Samarkand and Bukhara grew up along the overland Silk Road routes across Central Asia to service trade and merchants. The people in these cities prospered as middlemen between merchants and suppliers of caravans. Chinese silk, porcelain, and bamboo were carried west to Baghdad and the eastern Mediterranean ports, from which they were shipped by sea to Constantinople and Rome. Silk clothes were coveted by European bishops and aristocrats as well as by Mahayana Buddhist monks. The lively caravan trade that developed along

Bildarchiv Preussischer Kulturbesitz/Art Resource, NY

Silk Road Travelers
The Silk Road remained a key trade route during this era. This painting, from a fourteenth-century atlas made in Spain, shows one of the horse and camel caravans that traveled between China and Central Asia.

the Silk Road had other consequences too. Over the centuries many Chinese inventions, such as gunpowder, wheelbarrows, and the compass, were transported westward over the Silk Road and profoundly changed Western society. The trade even influenced food preferences. Chinese noodles, for example, spread widely in Asia, and Arabs may have brought Chinese-derived pasta to Italy. But the exchange was not entirely one way. Arabs marveled at a Chinese scholar who sojourned in Baghdad around 900, learned Arabic, and made copies of important medical texts to take back to China.

The Silk Road was not the only major land trade network. Other major overland trade routes linked West Africa and the Mediterranean across the Sahara Desert, allowing the movement of commodities such as salt and gold. Land and riverine routes also tied northern and eastern Europe into the broader Eurasian trade system. For example, between 800 and 1000 Swedish Vikings established a major trading network stretching from Scandinavia through Russia to Byzantium. Persia, Mali in West Africa, Byzantium, the northern Italian city-states, and Muslim Spain also prospered from their strategic locations along major trade routes. An Arab source reported that, thanks to their extensive travels, Jewish merchants who came to Cordoba in Spain "speak Arabic, Persian, [Italian], and the language of the Franks and Slavs."[3] At about the same time that these routes were expanding in Eurasia and Africa, in the Americas overland trade also carried Mesoamerican influences deep into North America while spreading Andean technologies, crops, and religious cults widely around South America. Although oceanic exchange in the Americas was limited, people in North and South America moved products by canoe along rivers, a lively canoe and raft trade linked the Caribbean islands, and some traders sailed along the Pacific coast on rafts.

The Rise of Maritime Trade

By 1000 an increasingly lucrative maritime trade, perhaps spurred by improving naval technology, grew in the Eastern Hemisphere, despite the dangers from pirates and storms. At one end of the Afro-Eurasian zone, much trade crisscrossed the Mediterranean, around which Venice, Genoa, Constantinople, Aleppo in Syria, Alexandria, and Algiers served as the major ports. Sailing networks along Europe's Atlantic coast later linked the Baltic and North Seas to Mediterranean ports and helped foster the Hanseatic League of Baltic ports.

Farther east, the Indian Ocean routes became the heart of the most extensive maritime trade network in the Intermediate world. The Abbasid caliph al-Mansur, writing from Baghdad, boasted that "there is no obstacle to us and China; everything on the sea can come to us on it."[4] The Indian Ocean system linked China, Japan, Vietnam, and Cambodia in the east through Malaya and the Indonesian archipelago to India and Sri Lanka, and then westward to Persia, Arabia, Russia, the eastern and central Mediterranean, and the East African coast as far south as Mozambique. Over these routes the spices of Indonesia, the gold and tin of Malaya, the textiles, sugar, and cotton of India, the cinnamon of Sri Lanka, the gold and ivory of East Africa, the coffee of Arabia, the carpets of Persia, and the silks, porcelain, and tea of China moved to distant markets. Many of these products reached Europe, sparking interest there in reaching the sources of the riches of the East.

The spices, aromatic and pungent derivatives of vegetables grown in tropical lands, were among the main products moving from east to west. Black pepper was cultivated chiefly in India, Siam, and Indonesia, while cloves, nutmeg, and mace came from the Maluku (Moluccan) Islands of eastern Indonesia. Cinnamon was grown in Indonesia and Sri Lanka. All of them found a market in the Middle East and Europe. Asia was not the only source for spices, since red or cayenne pepper from West Africa was traded to the Middle East and reached Europe in the 1300s. While they became ingredients in cosmetics and perfumes, spices were more commonly used as medicine or as condiments to flavor food. Intermediate Era people treated a range of illnesses and aided digestion with spices, and many

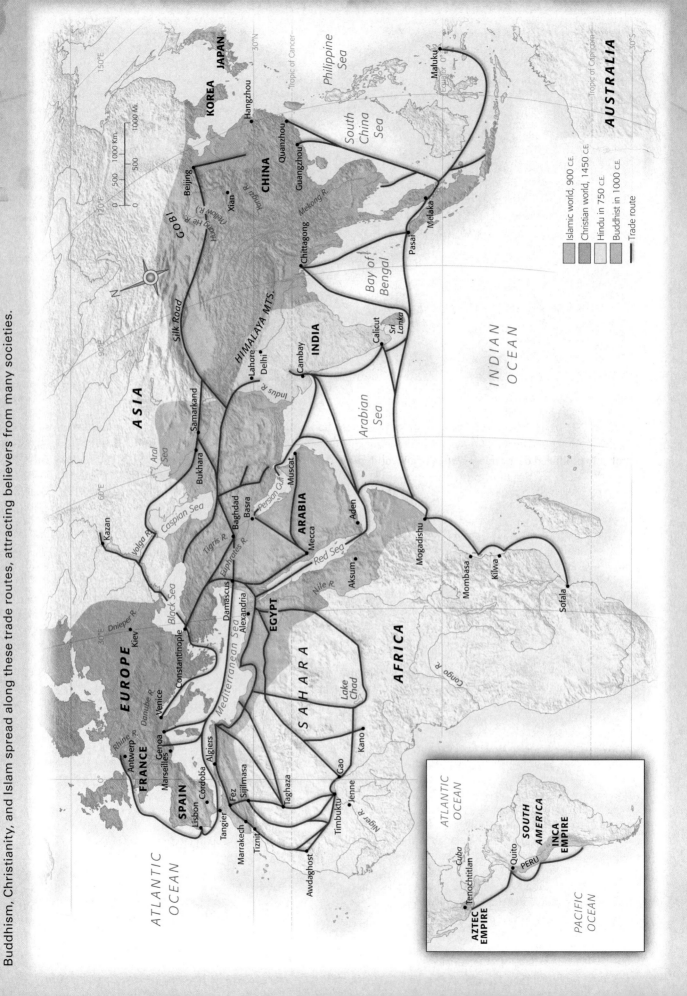

World Religions and Trade Routes, 600–1500

Much of the Eastern Hemisphere was linked by land and maritime trade routes. Along with goods and travelers, Buddhism, Christianity, and Islam spread along these trade routes, attracting believers from many societies.

e Interactive Map

Legend:
- Islamic world, 900 C.E.
- Christian world, 1450 C.E.
- Hindu in 750 C.E.
- Buddhist in 1000 C.E.
- Trade route

cultures used copious quantities of spices in cooking. Asian spices such as almonds, ginger, saffron, cinnamon, sugar, nutmeg, and cloves improved late medieval European diets. An English book from the early 1400s reported the popularity of pepper, which helped disguise the bad taste of heavily salted preserved meat during the long European winter: "Pepper is black and has a good smack, And every man doth it buy."[5]

Various states around the Persian Gulf, Indian Ocean, and South China Sea were closely linked to maritime trade. However, no particular political power dominated the Indian Ocean trading routes. The trade dynamism depended on cosmopolitan port cities, especially hubs such as Hormuz in Persia, Kilwa in Tanzania, Cambay in northwest India, Calicut on India's southwest coast, Melaka in Malaya, and Quanzhou (chwan-cho) in southern China. These trading ports became vibrant centers of international commerce and culture, drawing populations from various societies. The thirteenth-century traveler Marco Polo was fascinated by the coming and going of ships at Quanzhou: "Here is a harbor whither all ships of India come, with much costly merchandise. It is also the port whither go the [Chinese] merchants [heading overseas]. There is such traffic of merchandise that it is a truly wonderful sight."[6]

A hemispheric trade system developed in which some people came to produce for a world market. This system was fueled by China and India, the great centers of world manufacturing in this era (see Historical Controversy: Eastern Predominance in the Intermediate World). Together China and India probably produced over three-quarters of all world industrial products before 1500. China exported iron, steel, silk, refined sugar, and ceramics, while India was the great producer of textiles. Their industrial products might be transported thousands of miles. Hence, the work of a cotton weaver in India might be sold in China or East Africa, and Chinese ceramics might reach Zimbabwe and Mali. The Muslim soldiers who resisted the Christian crusaders used steel swords smelted in India from East African iron. Merchants from all over Afro-Eurasia—Arabs, Armenians, Chinese, Indians, Indonesians, Jews, Venetians, Genoese—traveled great distances in search of profits, often forming permanent trade diasporas. For instance, it was said of the Genoese, whose merchant networks stretched from Portugal to the Middle East and Russia, that they were so spread "throughout the world that wherever one goes and stays he makes another Genoa there."[7] One Cairo-based Jewish family firm had branches in India, Iran, and Tunisia. Most of the goods traded over vast distances were luxury items meant for the upper classes, but some goods, such as pepper and sugar, also reached consumers of more modest means.

Universal Religions and Social Change

The power and reach of universal, or world, religions such as Buddhism, Christianity, and Islam increased during the Intermediate Era. Religion and its mandates dominated the lives of millions around the world. These religions were early agents of globalization, propagating ideas and fostering trade across regional boundaries. By 1500 the religious map of the Eastern Hemisphere looked very different than it had in 600. Millions of people had embraced ideas, beliefs, and ways of life vastly different from those of their ancestors. The religions promoted moral and ethical values that helped preserve harmony in societies that were increasingly cosmopolitan. The Christian injunction to "love thy neighbor as thyself," the Buddhist emphasis on good thoughts and actions, and the Muslim ideals of social justice and the equality of believers fostered goodwill and cooperation. Religious beliefs also spurred the emergence of new values and social forms.

The Triumph of Universal Religions

During the Intermediate Era, most people in Eurasia and many in Africa eventually embraced one or another universal religion. Islam became the most widespread, rapidly expanding through the Middle East and eventually claiming Central Asia and parts of Europe while gaining a large following in West Africa, the East African coast, South Asia, China, and Southeast Asia. Islam fostered religious, social, and economic networks that linked peoples from Morocco and Spain to Indonesia and the Philippines with a common faith, values, and trade connections. Some Muslim scholars and jurists, such as the Moroccan Ibn Battuta, traveled, sojourned, and even settled thousands of miles from their homelands.

Older faiths also spread in this era, changing societies in varied ways. Theravada Buddhism was established in Sri Lanka and then expanded into mainland Southeast Asia, where it gradually displaced earlier faiths and reshaped cultures by teaching moderation, pacifism, unselfish acts, and individualism. To the north, Mahayana Buddhism first reached Central Asia and then China early in the Common Era, and during the Intermediate Era it became entrenched in Japan, Korea, Vietnam, Mongolia, and Tibet. In most places Buddhism existed alongside rather than replacing earlier religious traditions, such as animism in Siam and Tibet, Shinto in Japan, and Confucianism in China. By 1000 a Buddhist world incorporating diverse societies and several sects stretched from India eastward to Vietnam and Japan, but the temples, pagodas, and statues constructed to honor the Buddha reflected local styles and taste. Whereas many kinds of people, including merchants and jurists, moved along Islamic networks, Buddhist networks tended to facilitate the movement of pilgrims, such as the seventh-century Chinese monk Xuan Zang (swan tsang), who sojourned in India.

Christianity expanded to encompass nearly all of Europe in its fold by 1200, filtering north into the Germanic and Celtic lands and east among the Slavs. But the original Christian church divided. The Roman church dominated the west while the Orthodox church claimed Russia and much of eastern Europe. Although Christianity was pushed back by Islam in western Asia and North Africa, sizable Christian communities grew and sometimes flourished in these regions, aided by the tolerance Muslims usually accorded Christian practice. Nonetheless, chronic tensions arose between Christian Europe and the Islamic world, derived from political and economic conflicts as well as a clash between the strong missionary impulses of both religions. Christians and Muslims often viewed each other as barbarians. A tenth-century Arab geographer argued after visiting Europe that the manners of Christian Europeans "are harsh, their understanding dull and their tongues heavy. Those of them who are furthest to the north are the most subject to stupidity, grossness and brutishness."[8] Tensions between the two rival faiths generated the European Crusades to regain the Holy Land, which left a legacy of bitterness on both sides.

All universal religions nurtured a respect for learning. An admiring Arab described a great library, the House of Knowledge, opened by the Shi'ite Fatimid caliph in Egypt in 1005: "People could visit it, and whoever wanted to copy something that interested him could do so. Lectures were held there by the Quran readers, astronomers, grammarians, philologists, and physicians."[9] The House of Wisdom in Abbasid-ruled Baghdad attracted scholars from all over the Islamic world and beyond, and scholars from Arabia and Spain even made the long journey across the Sahara to West Africa to teach or study in the university at Timbuktu. Some Buddhist centers of higher education, such as the university at Nalanda in India and the monasteries in Srivijaya, in Sumatra, attracted students from all over Asia. In Europe, various Christian orders and thinkers encouraged the preservation of knowledge, laying the foundation for universities, such as Paris and Oxford, and spurring philosophical speculation. Eventually the European universities broadened their studies, mixing theology with secular subjects such as science and logic. Confucians also revered knowledge, and Chinese rulers patronized centers of scholarship such as the Hanlin Academy. Jewish communities honored theologians and produced philosophers such as Spanish-born Moses Maimonides (971–1030), an expert on Aristotle who became a court physician in Egypt.

Gender Roles and Family Patterns

The expansion of universal religions during the Intermediate Era, combined with increasing trade, also influenced many aspects of social life, thought, and attitudes. All of the religions had patriarchal institutional structures that were led by men who promoted notions of female inferiority. For instance, even humanist Christian thinkers believed that women belonged in the home. A fifteenth-century Italian warned that "it would hardly win us [men] respect if our wife busied herself among the men in the marketplace. It also seems somewhat demeaning to me to remain shut up in the house among women when I have manly things to do among men."[10] Islam incorporated many Arab and Persian customs that constrained women, including those that prescribed female seclusion and modesty, but seclusion and veiling of women became the main pattern primarily in Muslim societies that already had a strong patriarchal tradition, such as Arabia, Egypt, north India, and the former Byzantine territories. Where pre-Islamic cultures had less rigid gender roles, as in Spain, Southeast Asia, and West Africa, Islamic patriarchy was considerably modified. The pious Arab traveler Ibn Battuta, for example, was astonished that, in his view, the Mali women wore much too revealing clothing and seemed to have a higher status than the men.

The status of women varied around the world. As Confucianism dug deeper roots in East Asia, patriarchy became a stronger force there than it had been in classical times. By Ming times it was more common to seclude upper-class Chinese women, and even bind their feet. Japanese society also became more patriarchal, as the warrior culture replaced the Heian culture in which elite women had flourished. But some Mahayana Buddhists favored gender equity, at least in principle. The Japanese Zen master Dogen (DOE-joan) argued that

there was nothing special about masculinity: "The elements that make up the human body are the same for a man as for a woman. You should not waste your time in futile discussion of the superiority of one sex over another."[11] In mainland Southeast Asia, Theravada Buddhism proved a generally moderating force in gender relations, although men had more opportunity than women to acquire the merit needed to reach nirvana because only men could become monks. In societies as different as Byzantium, Carolingian France, West Africa, Southeast Asia, and the Inca Empire, individual women, such as the Burmese queen Pwa Saw, could still gain power as queens or as powers behind the throne. But in most societies religious hierarchies and military organizations remained mostly male, with priesthoods and warfare giving men more access to prestige and resources. In addition, in most places education was largely restricted to boys.

Religious values influenced family patterns and sexual attitudes. Islam allowed men to have four wives, but polygamy for some men meant that women were unavailable to others, who then could not marry. Christian teachings favored monogamy and marriage, but many men and women joined clerical orders or for other reasons never married. And European kings often flouted church teachings by having concubines and mistresses. Only a minority of western Europeans, mostly in the middle class, lived in nuclear families like those common today in the West. In many societies around the world, men of elite status, and especially in royal families, had multiple wives and concubines. Only a few societies allowed women to have more than one husband.

Attitudes toward homosexuality and gender identity varied widely. Followers of Christianity, Judaism, Islam, and Confucianism all shared an aversion to homosexual relations, in part because they did not produce children. But this sexual behavior had long been practiced and even tolerated in all these traditions. Christian tolerance turned to fierce repression only in the thirteenth century, and such repression was not a global pattern. Perhaps because there were many unmarried Muslim men, and also owing to the rigid segregation of the sexes, some Islamic societies ignored homosexual activity. Homosexual literature was common in western Asian cities under the Abbasid Caliphate. The Japanese, Chinese, and some Southeast Asian and Native American societies also tended to accept homosexuality as part of life. Gender categories could be flexible. Some Asian and American tribal peoples identified more than two genders, including homosexual or heterosexual men who lived as women and served the village as shamans.

Slavery and Feudalism

Most societies were hierarchical, and many people lived in slavery or faced severe restrictions on their freedom. Sanctioned by various religions or simply by custom or economic necessity, slavery had long been common throughout the world and remained so in the Intermediate Era, except for East Asia, where it largely died out by 1000. Islam permitted slavery but encouraged owners to treat slaves well. In Arab, Persian, and Turkish societies, the availability of slaves to do the physical work made the seclusion of elite women possible. Many Muslim African societies, and some that were non-Muslim, had slaves, including the West African kingdoms and East African city-states, although their status varied widely. Africans had been shipped north for centuries to work in the Islamic world, and some African slaves in the Persian Gulf region revolted. Slaves were also common in Southeast Asian societies such as Angkor and Siam. A Persian observer wrote that, in Indonesia, the people "reckon high rank and wealth by the quantity of slaves a person owns."[12] Various American peoples, among them the Mayas and Aztecs, enslaved prisoners of war, debtors, and criminals.

In Europe, slavery's decline after the end of the Roman Empire, and gradual replacement by serfdom, a less restrictive form of bondage, did not end the slave market there. Some slaves still labored in parts of western Europe, sometimes even on lands of Christian monasteries. An active Mediterranean slave trade shipped Slavs, Greeks, and Turks from the Black Sea region to southern Europe and North Africa. Some northwestern Europeans were also sold as slaves to Mediterranean societies. By the fifteenth century Africans appeared in southern European slave markets.

Although some scholars question the usefulness and scope of the concept of feudalism, others identify it as a major new social and political pattern in the world in the Intermediate Era. In feudal societies, relations between people of different status, especially between lords and vassals, were prescribed by agreements or law, and governments were weak or decentralized. The feudal model, which included lords and knights, independent manors, serfdom, small states, and chronic warfare, was best represented by some medieval European societies between 800 and 1300. Some historians also apply feudalism to post-Heian Japan under the warrior class and shogunates, and others to parts of India and Southeast Asia, where many small states competed for power. Feudal societies such as Norman England, the Carolingian realm, and perhaps Ashikaga Japan differed in many ways from the large centralized states such as Song China, Abbasid Iraq, Mali, or the Inca Empire, where emperors or kings exercised great power through bureaucracies.

In most hierarchical societies, whether feudal or centralized, political, military, and religious elites lived off wealth from the primary producers, such as peasants, herders, and artisans. Workers were more or less controlled by, and owed obligations to, those in power, such as Inca kings and Chinese emperors, who ruled despotically. For example, in medieval Europe the dominant Christian church encouraged people who wanted to reap rewards in Heaven to accept the social order, and some governments standardized work requirements. Hence, in 800 the Frankish king Charlemagne proclaimed that the peasant living on church and royal estates "must plow his lord's land a whole day [but not also be asked] to do handiwork service during the same week. The dependent shall not withdraw from these services and the lords shall not ask more from them."[13] In both western Europe and Japan, feudalism established a basis for future change by building up intense pressures that eventually erupted.

The Mongol Empire and Hemispheric Connections

The Mongol expansion, which united a large chunk of the Eurasian population and indirectly affected millions of other people, was one of the most crucial developments in world history. Between 1250 and 1350 the Mongols established the largest land empire in world history, stretching from lands on the western shores of the Black Sea east to the Pacific coast of China and Korea. The building of the Mongol Empire was a ruthless but amazing feat. Within the span of a century the Mongol armies, supported by a Mongol population of less than 2 million, swept out of their arid Central Asian grasslands to put over 200 million people under their control. By reopening Central Asian trade routes closed by political turmoil and by connecting with many different peoples and countries, the Mongols fostered communication networks and the transfer of technology between once remote parts of the Eastern Hemisphere. In doing so, they were major catalysts of change, laying a foundation for the gradual transition from the Intermediate to the Early Modern Era.

The Mongol Empire

The forces prompting the Mongols to build their empire are not altogether clear. Warfare was common among the Mongols, who were tough steppe herders of horses and camels. Historically, various other Central Asian pastoralists, including Turks, Huns, and Tibetans, had forged large but short-lived empires

Catapults The Mongols used advanced military technology, including catapults, to conquer cities. This battle scene, painted by a Persian artist, shows the Mongols attacking a city around 1300.

Edinburgh University Library, Orms. 20, fol. 124v

or confederations. Various factors in Central Asia, including ecological instability, climate change, and population growth, may have prompted the Mongol expansion by fostering competition for limited resources. Another factor was the religions, such as Mahayana Buddhism and Nestorian Christianity, that reached remote Mongolia, which heightened awareness of the riches to be found in the world beyond the steppes. These forces led to the emergence of Genghis Khan (ca. 1162–1227), a visionary leader who effectively united the Mongol tribes. His warriors, mounted and well armed, and aided by siege weaponry and innovative military strategies of rapid attack, made a formidable fighting force.

Within a few decades Mongol armies conquered Central Asia, Tibet, Korea, Russia, part of eastern Europe, Afghanistan, and a large part of western Asia, including Persia and Anatolia. The Mongols were at the Danube, preparing to sweep through Hungary into western Europe, when Genghis Khan's successor, his son Ogodei (1185–1241), died, aborting that thrust. Thus western Europe did not suffer the ravages experienced by other peoples. In the mid-1200s the Mongols expanded their domination in western Asia, overpowering the Arab Abbasid Caliphate. The widespread destruction they caused in the Middle East and Central Asia ended the Islamic golden age and reshaped politics and agriculture in these regions. Later, China, the most formidable foe and tempting prize, and Korea were also eventually added to the Mongol-ruled realm.

Coming from a harsh environment with few resources, the Mongols, with an army of perhaps 130,000 men, sometimes used brutal methods, as had conquerors of earlier eras such as the Assyrians and Alexander the Great. Contemporary accounts credit the Mongols with massacring hundreds of thousands, perhaps millions, of people and burning many cities. A Persian historian concluded that "it is unlikely that mankind will [ever again] see the like of this calamity."[14] The death toll, however, was probably exaggerated by both Mongols and their foes. Some historians doubt that many civilians were killed en masse, since they were needed for production and transportation.

However, the Mongol Empire proved short-lived. One reason was that the Mongols never connected with maritime commerce. They were also victims of their success. Before he died, Genghis Khan worried that his successors would forsake the rigorous life for the comforts of wealthy conquered peoples such as Arabs and Chinese, predicting that "after us, [our] people will wear garments of gold; they will eat sweet, greasy food, ride splendid coursers, and hold in their arms the loveliest women, and they will forget that they owe these things to us."[15] This warning proved prophetic. The Mongols succumbed to wealth and power, their harsh and increasingly corrupt rule provoking rebellions that would end their domination.

The Heritage of the Mongols and Their Networks

In 2000 some world historians named Genghis Khan the most crucial figure of the second millennium C.E. because, despite his brutality, the Mongol conquests he led established an early form of globalized communication characterized by technology and product transfer moving chiefly from east to west along the Silk Road. During the Mongol era, for example, Chinese inventions such as the spinning wheel, medical discoveries, and domesticated fruits and plants such as the orange and

lemon reached Europe and the Middle East. People moved by way of these routes, too. A Chinese Nestorian Christian monk of Turkish ancestry, Rabban Sauma, even visited Rome, France, and England in 1287 as a diplomat for the Mongol ruler of Persia, the first known visitor to western Europe from East Asia and an early example of politics on a hemispheric scale.

Because of the Mongols, travel from one end of Eurasia to the other became easier than ever before. During Mongol times many men of talent moved from west to east. In China the Mongols relied administratively on a large number of foreigners who came to serve in the civil service. These included many Muslims from West and Central Asia and a few Europeans such as Marco Polo who found their way to the fabled land the Europeans called Cathay. Polo's reports on his travels increased European interest in Asia and inspired later explorers, such as Christopher Columbus, to seek a sea route to East Asia.

Some historians consider the Mongols the great equalizers of history by having made possible technology transfer from East Asia to western Europe and the Middle East. The Mongols unwittingly set in motion changes that allowed Europeans to acquire and improve Chinese technologies such as printing, gunpowder, and the magnetic compass while developing new inventions of their own. These Chinese inventions had a major impact in Europe. In the seventeenth century the English philosopher Francis Bacon noted that Chinese printing, gunpowder, and the magnet "changed the whole face and state of things" in European literature, warfare, and navigation.[16] Europeans improved Chinese weapons such as flamethrowers and primitive guns, making late medieval warfare far deadlier. Gunpowder and Chinese military technology, coming by way of routes opened by the Mongols, also helped reshape Middle Eastern politics and fostered the rise of the Ottoman Empire.

Disaster and Dynamism in the Late Intermediate Era

A combination of natural disasters, including a terrible pandemic and abrupt climate change, also helped reshape Eurasian societies. Increased trade by land and sea and the migration of peoples such as the Turks, Germans, and Mongols fostered the spread of diseases across the Eastern Hemisphere. Many regions also experienced much cooler climates beginning around 1300, which caused agricultural failures and with them, widespread famine. But these disasters also sparked dynamic new energies that revived trade, which in turn spurred maritime exploration.

The Spread of Diseases

Diseases have long played a major role in human life. Sometimes they have come in terrible pandemics, deadly disease outbreaks affecting millions of people in many societies. Among the most dangerous diseases was bubonic plague, carried by fleas that infested rats. The fleas jumped from rats to humans, causing enlarged lymphatic glands in the victim's groin, armpit, or neck and a high fever, usually followed by death. The disease was sporadic, often not returning for many years. Pandemics had political consequences. A major plague epidemic from the sixth through eighth centuries, for example, weakened both Byzantium and Sassanian Persia, making it more difficult for these empires to repulse Islamic forces.

The worst pandemic in world history, known in the West as the Black Death, may have resulted from the Mongol conquests, in particular the greater contact they brought between Eurasian societies. Climate change may also have been a factor. Eurasia was unusually wet during the 1300s, perhaps increasing the number of fleas and rats. The Black Death, which most scholars think was chiefly caused by bubonic plague, apparently originated in China or Central Asia, where it killed millions. By the mid-1300s it had been carried by merchants and soldiers along the Silk Road to southern Russia. Ships leaving the Genoese trading colony at Calfa, on the Crimean peninsula at the north end of the Black Sea, carried it unwittingly to the Middle East and Europe, where it raged through cities and towns. In the affected societies, from China to Egypt to England and even to fishing villages in remote Greenland, perhaps a third of the total population died in the first outbreak, the higher mortality being in congested cities. Surveying the damage, the Italian writer Petrarch wrote that future generations would be "incredulous, unable to imagine the empty houses, abandoned towns, the squalid countryside, the fields littered with dead, the dreadful silent solitude which seemed to hang over the whole world. Physicians were useless, philosophers could only shrug their shoulders and look wise."[17] Millions more died as the pandemic reappeared in intervals in western Eurasia over the next century.

Ultimately the Black Death disrupted the complex system of interregional trade and communication that had flourished around Eurasia in the thirteenth and fourteenth centuries. Agricultural and industrial production declined and financial crises and labor shortages wrecked economies from China to France. The pandemic also helped undermine Mongol rule in East Asia and the Middle East. Some of the problems resulted from the huge population losses. When the Black Death came to an end, a spurt of growth saw population levels soar from East Asia to Europe. By 1500 the world population had reached between 400 million and 600 million people, about twice the population of 1000. China accounted for a fourth of the total, and India for at least a fifth. Europe, including Russia, grew rapidly to 70–95 million. The Black Death did not affect sub-Saharan Africa or the Americas, each of which probably had 60 to 80 million people by 1500.

Climate Change and Societies

Climate change has helped shape, and sometimes destroyed, societies since the dawn of humankind. It spurred the transition to farming in western Asia 10,000 years ago, undermined the Mesopotamian and Indus societies 4,000 years ago, and hastened the decline of the Chinese Han and Roman Empires around 200 C.E. Eurasian weather became more erratic during the 1200s, and the fluctuations may have helped prompt the Mongol expansion. In the Americas climate change during the Intermediate Era probably contributed to the collapse of various societies, including Tiwanaku, Moche, Teotihuacan, the southern Maya, and the Anasazi.

Around 1300 an unusually warm period gave way to much cooler weather that lasted until 1850, sparking what scientists call the "Little Ice Age," with serious results for societies. Whatever the causes, which are still debated, longer and more frigid winters periodically affected Europe, North America, Central Asia, and China. Bitter cold drove the Norse Vikings out of Greenland, and Icelandic farming floundered. Severe storms and flooding in Europe were followed by drought and crop failures, causing widespread famine. Rivers and canals froze, inhibiting boat traffic. Between 1315 and 1317 perhaps 15 percent of Europe's population starved to death. Hunger apparently made northern Europeans and Chinese less resistant to the Black Death. In addition, rainfall declined in India and Africa, drying up many lakes.

In North America great droughts in the late 1200s may have contributed to Cahokia's decline and caused the dispersal of the Anasazi. Pueblo peoples responded to hard times by migrating, as they said in their songs and poems: "Survival, I know this way. It rains. Mountains and canyons and plants grow. We traveled this way."[18] The Hohokum and Mogollon societies collapsed from drought, and their people moved elsewhere in the southwest. The North Atlantic climate became even colder from the mid-1600s to mid-1700s, and such discomfort may have inspired some adventurous Europeans to seek greener pastures abroad, in the Americas.

The Roots of Oceanic Exploration

The Mongol conquests had connected distant peoples and fostered trade. With the Mongol Empire's demise, however, and the security of Silk Road travel reduced, maritime trade became more crucial and naval technology improved considerably. As a result, late in the Intermediate Era there was a trend toward oceanic exploration over vast distances. The fame of Melaka, Calicut, Hormuz, and other Asian ports as commercial hubs for valuable goods had reached Europe, and by the late fourteenth century some European merchants were beginning to dream of a sea route to the East that would enable them to trade directly with China and the Indies.

By the early 1400s the Chinese had the most advanced ships and navigational techniques and the most outward-looking attitude. The Chinese took the initiative of exploration, dispatching unprecedented voyages of discovery led by Zheng He that sailed as far as the Middle East and East Africa. Zheng's ships followed long-established maritime networks, reflecting the crucial role played in world history by Afro-Eurasian maritime commerce. This Chinese thrust did not have lasting effects on the world, however. Although they had the naval capability, the Chinese, unlike the Europeans, lacked the economic incentive and religious zeal, and hence never sailed around Africa in search of Europe. However, some historians think a few Arabs and Indians may have. A navigation manual written by the Arab navigator Shihab al-Din Ahmad Ibn Majid (SHE-hob al-DIN AH-mad ibn MA-jeed) in the later 1400s, and probably based on earlier voyages, gives quite detailed, and mostly accurate, instructions for sailing down the East African coast, around the Cape of Good Hope, up the West African coast, and then into the Mediterranean.

The Portuguese and then the Spanish, both peoples with long maritime traditions and coastal locations, used Chinese, Arab, and European naval technology to construct ships and equip crews for successful long-distance voyages. In search of gold, spices, slaves, and other resources, Portuguese ships sailed to West and Central Africa, where they established outposts and eventually colonies. By the end of the fifteenth century the Portuguese had rounded the Cape of Good Hope to reach the Indian Ocean, the East African trading ports, and finally India. The Portuguese were not the only Europeans dazzled by Asian wealth. A historian in the early 1500s reported on another mariner and his ambitions:

> *Christopher Columbus, a Genoese, proposed to the Catholic King and Queen [of Spain] to discover the islands which touch the Indies. He asked for ships, promising not only to propagate the Christian religion, but also certainly to bring back pearls, spices and gold beyond anything imagined.*[19]

The Spanish expedition led by Columbus landed in the Americas in the 1490s. With these new networks of communication between distant societies, the history of the world was profoundly altered. An even more connected world and the Early Modern Era were at hand.

Suggested Reading

Books

Bentley, Jerry H. *Old World Encounters: Cross-Cultural Contacts and Exchanges in Pre-Modern Times*. New York: Oxford University Press, 1993. An up-to-date survey of trade routes and the spread of universal religions.

Curtin, Philip D. *Cross-Cultural Trade in World History*. Cambridge: Cambridge University Press, 1984. A sweeping examination of world trade and cross-cultural exchange.

Fernandez-Armesto, Felipe. *Millennium: A History of the Last Thousand Years*. New York: Scribner, 1995. An idiosyncratic but interesting overview of the world over the past millennium, for the general reader.

Gilbert, Erik, and Jonathan Reynolds. *Trading Tastes: Commodity and Cultural Exchange to 1750*. Upper Saddle River, NJ: Prentice Hall, 2006. A readable survey of the salt, silk, spice, and sugar trades and their impacts.

Gordon, Stewart. *When Asia Was the World: Traveling Merchants, Scholars, Warriors, and Monks who Created the "Riches of the East."* Philadelphia: Da Capo, 2008. Profiles eight great travelers and their experiences in Eurasia.

Headrick, Daniel R. *Technology: A World History*. New York: Oxford University Press, 2009. Good survey of maritime, military, and productive technologies.

Hobson, John M. *The Eastern Origins of Western Civilisation*. New York: Cambridge University Press, 2004. A fascinating, well-researched study offering an Asia-centric history of the era.

Keay, John. *The Spice Route: A History*. Berkeley: University of California Press, 2006. Readable description of Afro-Eurasian trade.

Lane, George. *Daily Life in the Mongol Empire*. Indianapolis: Hackett, 2006. Readable account of societies and cultures.

Larner, John. *Marco Polo and the Discovery of the World*. New Haven, CT: Yale University Press, 1999. A readable study of the impact of Marco Polo's writings on European exploration.

McNeill, William H. *Plagues and Peoples*, rev. ed. Garden City, NJ: Anchor, 1998. One of the best studies of the history and role of diseases, including the Black Death.

Morgan, David. *The Mongols*. New York: Basil Blackwell, 1986. A fine study of the Mongols and their empire.

Pacey, Arnold. *Technology in World Civilization*. Cambridge: MIT Press, 1990. Discussion of Asian and European technologies in this era.

Pearson, Michael. *The Indian Ocean*. New York: Routledge, 2000. A comprehensive look at the role this ocean played in world history.

Ringrose, David R. *Expansion and Global Interaction, 1200–1700*. New York: Longman, 2001. Explores the relationship between expansion and global interaction that began with the Mongols.

Risso, Patricia. *Merchants and Faith: Muslim Commerce and Culture in the Indian Ocean*. Boulder: Westview, 1995. A readable survey of Islam-centered commerce from the beginning through the nineteenth century.

Stearns, Peter. *Gender in World History*. New York: Routledge, 2000. A brief but general study with good material on this era.

Super, John C., and Briane K. Turley. *Religion in World History*. New York: Routledge, 2006. A brief overview of religious traditions and change.

Weatherford, Jack. *Genghis Khan and the Making of the Modern World*. New York: Crown, 2004. A readable and provocative examination of the Mongol role in world history.

Whitfield, Susan. *Life Along the Silk Road*. Berkeley: University of California Press, 1999. A readable portrait of Silk Road life through the experiences of travelers and residents.

WEBSITES

Internet Global History Sourcebook (*http://www.fordham.edu/halsall/global/globalsbook.html*). An excellent set of links on world history from ancient to modern times.

Silk Road Narratives (*http://depts.washington.edu/uwch/silkroad/texts/texts.html*). Explores cultural interaction in Eurasia through excerpts from Silk Road travelers.

Virtual Religion Index (*http://virtualreligion.net/vri/*). An outstanding site with many links on all major religions from ancient times until today.

Notes

Chapter 1 The Origins of Human Societies, to ca. 2000 B.C.E.

1. Brian Swimme and Thomas Berry, *The Universe Story* (San Francisco: Harper, 1992), 2.
2. From the *Rig Veda*, quoted in Carolyn Brown Heinz, *Asian Cultural Traditions* (Prospect Heights, IL: Waveland, 1999), 132.
3. Genesis 3:17–19, *The Holy Bible*, New King James Version (Chicago: Thomas Nelson, 1983), 3.
4. From Plato's *Critias*, quoted in L. S. Stavrianos, *Lifelines from Our Past: A New World History*, rev. ed. (Armonk, NY: M.E. Sharpe, 1997), 65.
5. Genesis 1:28, *Holy Bible*, 2.

Chapter 2 Ancient Societies in Mesopotamia, India, and Central Asia, 5000–600 B.C.E.

1. The quote is from the Oriental Institute, the University of Chicago.
2. The quote is from the Oriental Institute, the University of Chicago.
3. Quoted in Frederick Gentels and Melvin Steinfield, *Hangups from Way Back: Historical Myths and Canons*, vol. 1, 2nd ed. (San Francisco: Canfield, 1974), 64.
4. The quotes are from William H. Stiebing, Jr., *Ancient Near Eastern History and Culture* (New York: Longman, 2003), 48.
5. The quotes are from Brian Fagan, *The Long Summer: How Climate Changed Civilization* (New York: Basic Books, 2004), 138.
6. Quoted in Michael Wood, *Legacy: The Search for Ancient Cultures* (New York: Sterling, 1994), 34.
7. Quoted in G. R. Driver and John C. Miles, eds., *The Babylonian Laws*, vol. II (Oxford: Clarendon Press, 1952), 7.
8. Quoted in N. B. Jankowska, "Asshur, Mitanni, and Arrapkhe," in *Early Antiquity*, ed. I. M. Diakonoff (Chicago: University of Chicago Press, 1991), 256.
9. Samuel Noah Kramer, *The Cradle of Civilization* (New York: Time-Life Books, 1967), 75.
10. Quoted in Wood, *Legacy*, 32.
11. *The Epic of Gilgamesh*, trans. by N. K. Sandars (New York: Penguin Books, 1960), 108.
12. Quoted in John Keay, *India: A History* (New York: Atlantic Monthly Press, 2000), 35.
13. Quoted in Hermann Kulke and Dietmar Rothermund, *History of India*, 3rd ed. (New York: Routledge, 1998), 35.
14. William McNaughton, ed., *Light from the East* (New York: Laurel, 1978), 398.
15. Quoted in Burton Stein, *A History of India* (Malden, MA: Blackwell, 1998), 53.
16. Quoted in A. L. Basham, *The Wonder That Was India* (New York: Grove Press, 1959), 241.
17. Quoted in Romila Thapar, *Early India from the Origins to AD 1300* (Berkeley: University of California Press, 2002), 116.

Chapter 3 Ancient Societies in Africa and the Mediterranean, 5000–600 B.C.E.

1. Quoted in Lionel Casson, *Ancient Egypt* (New York: Time Incorporated, 1965), 120.
2. Quoted in David Phillipson, *African Archaeology*, 2nd ed. (Cambridge: Cambridge University Press, 1993), 152.
3. Quoted in *Egypt: Land of the Pharaohs* (Alexandria, Va.: Time-Life Books, 1992), p. 142.
4. Quoted in Casson, *Ancient Egypt*, p. 95.
5. Quoted in Carl Roebuck, *The World of Ancient Times* (New York: Charles Scribner's Sons, 1966), p. 72.
6. Quoted in Egypt: Land of Pharaohs, p. 89.
7. Quoted in Felipe Fernandez-Armesto, *Civilizations: Culture, Ambition, and the Transformation of Nature* (New York: Simon and Schuster, 2001), p. 195.

8. Quoted in Brian M. Fagan, *People of the Earth: An Introduction to World Prehistory*, 9th ed. (New York: Longmans, 1998), p. 407.
9. Quoted in Ezra Pound and Noel Stock, *Love Poems of Ancient Egypt* (Norfolk, Conn.: New Directions, 1962).
10. Quoted in Barbara Mertz, *Red Land, Black Land: Daily Life in Ancient Egypt*, rev. ed. (New York: Dodd, Mead and Company, 1978), p. 56.
11. Quoted in *Africa's Glorious Legacy* (Alexandria, Va.: Time-Life Books, 1996), p. 18.
12. Nahum 3:7, 19, *The Holy Bible*, New King James Version (Chicago: Thomas Nelson, 1983), p. 908.
13.. Psalm 137:1, *Holy Bible*, p. 639.
14. Isaiah 45:21–22, *Holy Bible*, p. 721.
15. Isaiah 42:6–7, *Holy Bible*, p. 717.
16. Ezekiel 27:3–4, 9, *Holy Bible*, p. 835.

Chapter 4 Around the Pacific Rim: Eastern Eurasia and the Americas, 5000–600 B.C.E.

1. From the ancient Chinese *Book of Songs*, quoted in Herlee Glessner Creel, *The Birth of China: A Survey of the Formative Period of Chinese Civilization* (New York: Frederick Unger, 1937), 64.
2. Quoted in Michael Wood, *Legacy: The Search for Ancient Cultures* (New York: Sterling, 1994), p. 96.
3. *The Book of Songs*, translated by Arthur Waley (London: George Unwin, 1954), p. 162.
4. Quoted in Felipe Fernandez-Armesto, *Civilizations: Culture, Ambition, and the Transformation of Nature* (New York: Simon and Schuster, 2001), p. 214.
5. The quotes are in John Minford and Joseph S. M. Lau, eds., *Classical Chinese Literature: An Anthology of Translations*, vol. 1 (New York: Columbia University Press, 2000), pp. 16–17, 20.
6. Quoted in Creel, *Birth of China*, pp. 228–229.
7. Quoted in Benjamin I. Schwartz, *The World of Thought in Ancient China* (Cambridge: Harvard University Press, 1985), p. 39.
8. In Minford and Lau, *Classical Chinese Literature*, p. 150.
9. The two songs come from Waley, *Book of Songs*, pp. 68, 203.
10. Waley, *Book of Songs*, p. 205.
11. Quoted in Nguyen Ngoc Bich, "The Power and Relevance of Vietnamese Myths," in David P. Elliott et al., eds., *Vietnam: Essays on History, Culture and Society* (New York: Asia Society, 1985), p. 62.
12. Quoted in Brian M. Fagan, *Kingdoms of Gold, Kingdoms of Jade: The Americas Before Columbus* (New York: Thames and Hudson, 1991), p. 55.

Societies, Networks, Transitions: Ancient Foundations of World History, 4000–600 B.C.E.

1. From Homer's *The Odyssey*, quoted in Rodney Castledon, *Minoans: Life in Bronze Age Crete* (New York: Routledge, 1993), 111.
2. Quoted in Lewis Mumford, *The City in History: Its Origins, Its Transformations, and Its Prospects* (New York: Harcourt, Brace and World, 1961), 68.
3. Quoted in Lionel Casson, *The Ancient Mariners: Seafarers and Sea Fighters of the Mediterranean in Ancient Times*, 2nd ed. (Princeton: Princeton University Press, 1991), 9.
4. From the *Brahmanas*, quoted in F. R. Allchin, *The Archaeology of Historic South Asia: The Emergence of Cities and States* (New York: Cambridge University Press, 1995), 86–87.
5. Quoted in John Keegan, *A History of Warfare* (New York: Alfred A. Knopf, 1993), 143.
6. Quoted in Barbara Mertz, *Red Land, Black Land: Daily Life in Ancient Egypt*, rev. ed. (New York: Dodd Mead, and Company, 1978), 135–136.
7. *The Book of Songs*, translated by Arthur Waley (London: George Allen and Unwin, 1954), 121.
8. Nahum 3:2–3, *Holy Bible*, 907.

9. Isaiah 2:4, *Holy Bible*, 683.

10. Quoted in Merry E.Wiesner-Hanks, *Gender in History* (Malden, MA: Blackwell, 2001), 61.

11. From Homer's *The Odyssey*, quoted in Castledon, *Minoans*, 9.

12. Quoted in Stephen L. Sass, *The Substance of Civilization: Material and Human History from the Stone Age to the Age of Silicon* (New York: Arcade, 1998), 13.

13. Quoted in Herlee Glessner Creel, *The Birth of China: A Survey of the Formative Period of Chinese Civilization* (New York: Frederick Unger, 1961), 256.

Chapter 5 Classical Societies in Southern and Central Asia, 600 B.C.E.–600 C.E.

1. Quoted in Jeannine Auboyer, *Daily Life in Ancient India: From 200 BC to 700 AD* (London: Phoenix, 2002), 62.

2. Quoted in Lionel Casson, *The Ancient Mariners: Seafarers and Sea Fighters of the Mediterranean in Ancient Times*, 2nd ed. (Princeton: Princeton University Press, 1991), 202.

3. Quoted in Stanley Wolpert, *A New History of India*, 5th ed. (New York: Oxford University Press, 1997), 48.

4. From Swami Prabhavananda and Frederick Manchester, eds., *The Upanishads: Breath of the Eternal* (New York: Mentor, 1957), 62.

5. C. E. Gover, *The Folk-Songs of Southern India* (London: Trubner and Co., 1872), 165.

6. Quoted in Wolpert, *New History*, 54.

7. Quoted in Roy C. Amore and Julia Ching, "The Buddhist Tradition," in *World Religions: Eastern Traditions*, ed. Willard G. Oxtoby (New York: Oxford University Press, 1996), 230.

8. Quoted in Rhoads Murphy, *A History of Asia*, 4th ed. (New York: HarperCollins, 2003), 74.

9. Quoted in Lucille Schulberg, *Historic India* (New York: Time-Life Books, 1968), 80.

10. From William McNaughton, ed., *Light from the East* (New York: Laurel, 1978), 377.

Chapter 6 Eurasian Connections and New Traditions in East Asia, 600 B.C.E.–600 C.E.

1. *Records of the Historian: Chapters from the Shih Chi of Ssu-ma Ch'ien*, translated by Burton Watson (New York: Columbia University Press, 1969), 274.

2. Quoted in Arthur Cotterell and David Morgan, *China's Civilization: A Survey of Its History, Arts, and Technology* (New York: Praeger, 1975), 58.

3. Quoted in H. G. Creel, *Chinese Thought from Confucius to Mao Tse-Tung* (New York: Mentor, 1953), 32.

4. Quoted in Ch'u Chai and Winberg Chai, *Confucianism* (Woodbury, NY: Barron's, 1973), 45.

5. Quoted in Dun J. Li, ed., *The Essence of Chinese Civilization* (Princeton: D. Van Nostrand, 1967), 6.

6. The quotes are from Patricia Buckley Ebrey, ed., *Chinese Civilization: A Sourcebook*, 2nd ed., revised and expanded (New York: Free Press, 1993), 43–44.

7. The quotes are from Lionel Giles, *The Sayings of Lao Tzu* (New York: E.P. Dutton, 1908), 19, 22, 25.

8. Quoted in Creel, *Chinese Thought*, 85.

9. Quoted in Arthur Waley, *The Way and Its Power: A Study of the Tao Te Ching and Its Place in Chinese Thought* (New York: Grove Press, 1958), 210.

10. Quoted in William McNaughton, ed., *Light from the East: An Anthology of Asian Literature* (New York: Laurel, 1978), 132.

11. Sima Qian, quoted in Arthur Cotterell, *The First Emperor of China* (New York: Penguin, 1988), 106.

12. Quoted in Frances Wood, *The Silk Road: Two Thousand Years in the Heart of Asia* (Berkeley: University of California Press, 2002), 55.

13. From John Minford and Joseph S. M. Lau, eds., *Classical Chinese Literature: An Anthology of Translations*, vol. 1 (New York: Columbia University Press, 2000), 387.

14. Ebrey, *Chinese Civilization*, 61–62.

15. Quoted in ibid., 73.

16. Quoted in Robin R. Wang, ed., *Images of Women in Chinese Thought and Culture: Writings from the Pre-Qin Period Through the Song Dynasty* (Indianapolis: Hackett, 2003), 254.

17. Ibid.

18. Quoted in David John Lu, ed., *Sources of Japanese History*, vol. 1 (New York: McGraw-Hill, 1974), 21–22.

Chapter 7 Western Asia, the Eastern Mediterranean, and Regional Systems, 600–200 B.C.E.

1. Quoted in Norman Davies, *Europe: A History* (New York: Harper, 1996), 117.

2. Quoted in Lindsay Allen, *The Persian Empire* (Chicago: University of Chicago Press, 2005), 27.

3. Quoted in A. T. Olmstead, *History of the Persian Empire* (Chicago: University of Chicago Press, 1959), 125.

4. Quoted in William H. Stiebing, *Ancient Near Eastern History and Culture* (New York: Longman, 2003), 303.

5. From George Rawlinson, trans., *The Histories of Herodotus*, vol. 1 (London: Dent, 1910), 131–140.

6. From Loren J. Samons III, ed., *Athenian Democracy and Imperialism* (Boston: Houghton Mifflin, 1998), 216–217.

7. Quoted in Robert Flaceliere, *Daily Life in Greece at the Time of Pericles* (London: Phoenix, 2002), 56.

8. Quoted in Rex Warner, *The Greek Philosophers* (New York: New American Library, 1958), 24.

9. The quote is from Martyn Oliver, *History of Philosophy: Great Thinkers from 600 B.C. to the Present Day* (New York: MetroBooks, 1997), 16–17.

10. Quoted in Mortimer Chambers et al., *The Western Experience*, vol. 1, 5th ed. (New York: McGraw-Hill, 1987), 96.

11. Quoted in C. Warren Hollister, *Roots of the Western Tradition: A Short History of the Ancient World*, 5th ed. (McGraw-Hill, 1991), 109.

12. From Barbara Hughes Fowler, *Archaic Greek Poetry: An Anthology* (Madison: University of Wisconsin Press, 1992), 131.

13. Quoted in Robert Flaceliere, "Women, Marriage, and the Family," in *Everyman in Europe: Essays in Social History*, ed. Allan Mitchell and Istvan Deak, vol. 1 (Englewood Cliffs, NJ: Prentice-Hall, 1974), 53.

14. From *Medea*, quoted in Frank J. Frost, *Greek Society*, 2nd ed. (Lexington, MA: D.C. Heath, 1980), 94.

15. From Aristophanes, *Lysistrata and Other Plays*, trans. Alan H. Sommerstein (New York: Penguin, 1973), 200–208.

16. Reported by Thucydides, quoted in L. S. Stavrianos, ed., *The Epic of Man to 1500* (Englewood Cliffs, NJ: Prentice-Hall, 1970), 120–122.

17. Quoted in Michael Chauveau, *Egypt in the Age of Cleopatra: History and Society Under the Ptolemies* (Ithaca: Cornell University Press, 2000), 188.

18. Quoted in Francis Chanoux, *Hellenistic Civilization* (Malden, MA: Blackwell, 2003), 319.

19. "Diogenes," in *Biographical Encyclopedia of Philosophy* (Garden City, NY: Doubleday, 1965), 76.

Chapter 8 Empires, Networks, and the Remaking of Europe, North Africa, and Western Asia, 500 B.C.E.–600 C.E.

1. Quoted in Tim Cornell and John Matthews, *The Roman World* (Alexandria, VA: Stonehenge, 1991), 51.

2. Livy, quoted in Frederick Gentles and Melvin Steinfield, eds., *Hangups from Way Back: Historical Myths and Canons*, vol. 1, 2nd ed. (San Francisco: Canfield, 1974), 173.

3. Diodorus, quoted in Barry Cunliffe, *The Extraordinary Voyage of Pytheas the Greek* (New York: Penguin, 2002), 52.

4. Gentles and Steinfield, *Hangups from Way Back*, 167.

5. From Plutarch, *Life of Antony*, in *Readings in Ancient History*, ed. William S. Davis, vol. 2 (Boston: Allyn and Bacon, 1913), 163–164.

6. Quoted in Jerome Carcopino, *Daily Life in Ancient Rome*, 2nd ed. (New Haven, CT: Yale University Press, 1968), 202.

7. Quoted in Norman Davies, *Europe: A History* (New York: Harper, 1998), 193.

8. Diodorus Siculus, in Jo Ann Shelton, *As the Romans Did: A Sourcebook in Roman Social History* (New York: Oxford University Press, 1988), 175.

9. The quotes are from Henry C. Boren, *Roman Society: A Social, Economic and Cultural History,* 2nd ed. (Lexington, MA: D.C. Heath, 1992), 279, 219.

10. Quoted in Susan Whitfield, *Life Along the Silk Road* (Berkeley: University of California Press, 1999), 21.

11. Tacitus, *Agricola,* quoted in Moses Hadas, ed., *A History of Rome from Its Origins to 529 A.D. as Told by the Roman Historians* (Garden City, NY: Doubleday Anchor, 1956), 126–127.

12. Matthew 22: 37-39, in *The Holy Bible,* New King James Version (Chicago: Thomas Nelson, 1982), 957.

13. Quoted in Michael McCormick, *Origins of the European Economy: Communication and Commerce, A.D. 300–900* (New York: Cambridge University Press, 2001), 27.

14. From A. Atwater, trans., *Procopius: The Secret History* (Ann Arbor: University of Michigan Press, 1963), 8.

15. Quoted in Daniel Del Castillo, "A Long-Ignored Plague Gets Its Due," *Chronicle of Higher Education,* February 15, 2002, A22.

16. Quoted in Philip Sharrard, *Byzantium* (New York: Time-Life, 1966), 36.

17. Quoted in Patricia Crone, "The Rise of Islam in the World," in *The Cambridge Illustrated History of the Islamic World,* ed. Francis Robinson (New York: Cambridge University Press, 1966), 4–5.

Chapter 9   Classical Societies and Regional Networks in Africa, the Americas, and Oceania, 600 B.C.E.–600 C.E.

1. From *The Horizon History of Africa* (New York: American Heritage, 1971), 207.

2. Ibn Battuta, quoted in Robert W. July, *Precolonial Africa: An Economic and Social History* (New York: Charles Scribner's, 1975), p. 183.

3. Quoted in Stanley Burstein, ed., *Ancient African Civilizations: Kush and Axum* (Princeton, N.J.: Markus Wiener, 1998), p. 41.

4. Quoted in Derek A. Welsby, *The Kingdom of Kush: The Napatan and Meroitic Empires* (Princeton: Markus Wiener, 1996), p. 40.

5. From *Horizon History,* p. 78.

6. Quoted in Basil Davidson, *African Kingdoms* (New York: Time-Life, 1966), p. 42.

7. Quoted in Graham Connah, *African Civilization. Precolonial Cities and States in Tropical Africa: An Archaeological Perspective* (Cambridge: Cambridge University Press, 1987), p. 78.

8. Quoted in Robert W. July, *A History of the African People,* 5th ed. (Prospect Heights, Ill.: Waveland, 1998), p. 45.

9. Rufinus, quoted in Burstein, *Ancient African Civilizations,* p. 95.

10. Quoted in Christopher Ehret, *An African Classical Age: Eastern and Southern Africa in World History, 1000 B.C. to A.D. 400* (Charlottesville: University of Virginia Press, 1998), p. 275.

11. From the Popul Vuh, quoted in Brian M. Fagan, *Kingdoms of Gold, Kingdoms of Jade: The Americas Before Columbus* (London and New York: Thames and Hudson, 1991), p. 94.

12. Father Bernardino de Sahagun, quoted in Richard E. W. Adams, *Prehistoric Mesoamerica* (Boston: Little, Brown, 1977), p. 110.

13. Frey Diego de Landa, quoted in T. Patrick Culbert, *Maya Civilization* (Washington, D.C.: Smithsonian, 1993), p. 23.

14. Quoted in Michael Wood, *Legacy: The Search for Ancient Cultures* (New York: Sterling, 1994), p. 166.

15. Frey Diego de Landa, quoted in Culbert, *Maya Civilization,* p. 22.

16. Fra Bernardino de Sahagun, quoted in Juan Schobinger, *The First Americans* (Grand Rapids, Mich.: William B. Eerdmans, 1994), p. 97.

17. Cieza de Leon, quoted in Fagan, *Kingdoms of Gold,* p. 192.

18. Quoted in Brian Fagan, *The Long Summer: How Climate Changed Civilization* (New York: Basic Books, 2004), p. 213.

19. Quoted in Judy Thompson and Allan Taylor, *Polynesian Canoes and Navigation* (Laie, Hawaii: Institute of Polynesian Studies, 1980), p. 32.

20. Quoted in Peter Bellwood, *The Polynesians: Prehistory of an Island People,* revised ed. (London: Thames and Hudson, 1997), p. 7.

21. Quoted in Peter Bellwood, *Man's Conquest of the Pacific: The Prehistory of Southeast Asia and Oceania* (New York: Oxford University Press, 1979), p. 300.

Societies, Networks, Transitions: Classical Blossomings in World History, 600 B.C.E.–600 C.E.

1. Quoted in Michael Wood, *Legacy: The Search for Ancient Cultures* (New York: Sterling, 1994), 192.

2. Quoted in Patricia Buckley Ebrey, *The Cambridge Illustrated History of China* (New York: Cambridge University Press, 1996), 46.

3. The quotes are from Felipe Fernandez-Armesto, *Ideas That Changed the World* (New York: DK, 2003), 117, 119.

4. Quoted in Lindsay Allen, *The Persian Empire* (Chicago: University of Chicago Press, 2005), 43.

5. From Patricia Buckley Ebrey, ed., *Chinese Civilization: A Sourcebook,* 2nd ed., revised and expanded (New York: Free Press, 1993), 57–58.

6. Quoted in Romila Thapar, *Asoka and the Decline of the Mauryas* (Delhi: Oxford University Press, 1997), 147.

7. Quoted in Robert P. Clark, *The Global Imperative: An Interpretive History of the Spread of Humankind* (Boulder: Westview, 1997), 3.

8. Quoted in Richard C. Foltz, *Religions of the Silk Road: Overland Trade and Cultural Exchange from Antiquity to the Fifteenth Century* (New York: St. Martin's, 1999), 62.

9. Tertullian, quoted in Erik Gilbert and Jonathan T. Reynolds, *Africa in World History: From Prehistory to the Present* (Upper Saddle River, NJ: Prentice-Hall, 2004), 74.

10. Quoted in Kenneth R. Hall, *Maritime Trade and State Development in Early Southeast Asia* (Honolulu: University of Hawaii Press, 1985), 29.

11. Hou Han Shu, quoted in *Monks and Merchants: Silk Road Treasures from Northwest China* (http://www.asiasociety.org/arts/monksandmerchants/index.html).

12. Quoted in Frances Wood, *The Silk Road: Two Thousand Years in the Heart of Asia* (Berkeley: University of California Press, 2001), 66.

13. Quoted in Lionel Casson, *The Ancient Mariners: Seafarers and Sea Fighters of the Mediterranean in Ancient Times,* 2nd ed. (Princeton: Princeton University Press, 1991), 166.

14. From Basil Davidson, *African Civilization Revisited: From Antiquity to Modern Times* (Trenton, NJ: Africa World Press, 1991), 64.

15. Quoted in Louis Crompton, *Homosexuality and Civilization* (Cambridge: Harvard University Press, 2003), 218.

16. Quoted in Peter N. Stearns, *Gender in World History* (New York: Routledge, 2000), 28.

Chapter 10   The Rise, Power, and Connections of the Islamic World, 600–1500

1. From *The Muqaddimah: An Introduction to History,* translated by Franz Rosenthal and edited by N. J. Dawood (Princeton: Princeton University Press, 1967), 25–27.

2. Quoted in Albert Hourani, *A History of the Arab Peoples* (Cambridge: Belknap Press, 1991), 3.

3. Quoted in Jonathan Bloom and Sheila Blair, *Islam: A Thousand Years of Faith and Power* (New Haven, CT: Yale University Press, 2002), 29.

4. Quoted in Wiebke Walther, *Women in Islam* (Princeton: Markus Wiener, 1993), 104.

5. Quoted in Karen Armstrong, *Muhammad: A Biography of the Prophet* (San Francisco: HarperSan Francisco, 1992), 160.

6. Quoted in Arthur Goldschmidt, Jr., *A Concise History of the Middle East,* 4th ed. revised (Boulder: Westview, 1991), p. 37.

7. Quoted in Francis Robinson, *The Cultural Atlas of the Islamic World Since 1500* (Oxford: Stonehenge, 1992), p. 180.

8. Quoted in Henry Bucher, *Middle East* (Guilford, Conn.: Dushkin, 1984), p. 19.

9. Quoted in Manuel Komroff, ed., *Contemporaries of Marco Polo* (New York: Horace Liveright, 1928), pp. 286–292.

10. Quoted in Alfred Guillaume, "Islamic Mysticism and the Sufi Sect," in Swisher, ed., *Spread,* p. 153.

11. "Baba Kuhi of Shiraz," translated by Reynold A. Nicholson. Quoted in Mary Ann Frese Witt et al., *The Humanities: Cultural Roots and Continuities*, vol. 1, 7th ed. (Boston: Houghton Mifflin, 2005), p. 270.

12. Quoted in Adam Goodheart, "Pilgrims from the Great Satan," *New York Times*, March 10, 2002, p. A12.

13. Quoted in Walther, *Women in Islam*, p. 40.

14. Quoted in Mervyn Hiskett, "Islamic Literature and Art," in Swisher, ed., *Spread*, p. 120.

15. Excerpted in John Yohannan, ed., *A Treasury of Asian Literature* (New York: New American Library, 1965), pp. 261–262.

16. Quoted in Jonathan P. Berkey, *The Formation of Islam: Religion and Society in the Near East, 600–1800* (New York: Cambridge University Press, 2003), p. 233.

17. Quoted in Hourani, *History of Arab Peoples*, p. 201.

18. Quoted in Bernard Lewis, *The Arabs in History* (New York: Harper and Row, 1960), p. 131.

19. Hariri, quoted in Fernand Braudel, *A History of Civilizations* (New York: Penguin, 1995), p. 71.

20. Ibn Al Athir, quoted in Mike Edwards, "Genghis Khan," *National Geographic* (December, 1996): p. 9.

21. Quoted in Francis Robinson, *The Cambridge Illustrated History of the Islamic World* (Cambridge: Cambridge University Press, 1996), p. 198.

Chapter 11 East Asian Traditions, Transformations, and Eurasian Encounters, 600–1500

1. Quoted in John Merson, *The Genius That Was China: East and West in the Making of the Modern World* (Woodstock, NY: Overlook Press, 1990), 14.

2. Quoted in John A. Harrison, *The Chinese Empire* (New York: Harcourt Brace Jovanovich, 1972), 239.

3. Quoted in C. P. Fitzgerald, *China: A Short Cultural History* (New York: Praeger, 1961), 336.

4. Quoted in Derk Bodde, *China's Cultural Tradition: What and Whither?* (New York: Holt, Rinehart and Winston, 1957), 31.

5. The Wang and Li poems are from Robert Payne, ed., *The White Pony: An Anthology of Chinese Poetry* (New York: Mentor, 1960), 154, 174.

6. Du's poems are from Cyril Birch, ed., *Anthology of Chinese Literature from Early Times to the Fourteenth Century* (New York: Grove Press, 1965), 240–241; and *Tu Fu: Selected Poems* (Peking: Foreign Languages Press, 1962), 100.

7. John Meskill, "History of China," in *An Introduction to Chinese Civilization*, ed. John Meskill (Lexington, MA: D.C. Heath, 1973), 127–128.

8. Yuan Tsai, from Patricia Buckley Ebrey, ed., *Chinese Civilization and Society: A Sourcebook* (New York: The Free Press, 1981), p. 96.

9. The quotes are from Dun J. Li, ed., *The Essence of Chinese Civilization* (Princeton, NJ: Van Nostrand, 1967), p. 88; and James Zee-Min Lee, *Chinese Potpourri* (Hong Kong: Oriental Publishers, 1950), p. 319.

10. Quoted in H. D. Martin, *The Rise of Chingis Khan and His Conquest of North China* (Baltimore: Johns Hopkins University Press, 1950), 5.

11. R. E. Latham, trans., *The Travels of Marco Polo* (Baltimore: Penguin Books, 1958), 184–187.

12. Zhang Tao, quoted in Timothy Brook, *The Confusions of Pleasure: Commerce and Culture in the Ming* (Berkeley: University of California Press, 1998), vii.

13. Quoted in Bruce Cumings, *Korea's Place in the Sun: A Modern History* (New York: W.W. Norton, 1997), 37.

14. Quoted in Yung Chung Kim, ed. and trans., *Women of Korea: A History from Ancient Times to 1945* (Seoul: Ewha Women's University Press, 1977), 32.

15. Quoted in Donald Keene, "Literature," in *An Introduction to Japanese Civilization*, ed. Arthur E. Tiedemann (Lexington, MA: D.C. Heath, 1974), 395.

16. Quoted in Ivan Morris, *The World of the Shining Prince: Court Life in Ancient Japan* (New York: Kodansha, 1994), 229.

17. Quoted in ibid., 204.

18. Quoted in Mikiso Hane, *Japan: A Historical Survey* (New York: Charles Scribner's, 1972), 56.

19. From Ryusaku Tsunoda et al., eds., *Sources of Japanese Tradition*, vol. 2 (New York: Columbia University Press, 1958), 236.

20. Quoted in Noel F. Busch, *The Horizon Concise History of Japan* (New York: American Heritage, 1972), 58.

Chapter 12 Expanding Horizons in Africa and the Americas, 600–1500

1. Quoted in Patricia W. Romero, *Lamu: History, Society, and Family in an East African Port City* (Princeton: Markus Wiener, 1997), 14.

2. Quoted in Esmond Bradley Martin and Chryssee Perry Martin, *Cargoes of the East: The Ports, Trade and Culture of the Arabian Seas and Western Indian Ocean* (London: Elm Tree Books, 1978), 9.

3. Quoted in *Africa's Glorious Legacy* (Arlington, VA: Time-Life Books, 1994), 90.

4. Quoted in E. Jefferson Murphy, *History of African Civilization* (New York: Dell, 1972), 120.

5. The quotes are from E. W. Bovill, *The Golden Trade of the Moors*, 2nd ed. (London: Oxford University Press, 1970), 95.

6. Leo Africanus, quoted in Kevin Shillington, *History of Africa*, rev. ed. (New York: St. Martin's, 1995), 105.

7. Quoted in Constance B. Hilliard, ed., *Intellectual Traditions of Pre-Colonial Africa* (New York: McGraw-Hill, 1998), 311–312.

8. Quoted in John Middleton, *The World of the Swahili* (New Haven, CT: Yale University Press, 1992), 40.

9. Quoted in Bovill, *Golden Trade*, 96.

10. Djeli Mamoudou Kouyate, quoted in D. T. Niane, *Sundiata: An Epic of Old Mali* (London: Longman, 1965), 1.

11. John Smith, quoted in Charles Mann, "The Pristine Myth," *The Atlantic Online*, March 7, 2002 (http://www.theatlantic.com/unbound/interviews/int2002-03-07.htm)

12. Quoted in Richard F. Townsend, *The Aztecs*, rev. ed. (New York: Thames and Hudson, 2000), 59.

13. Quoted in Brian M. Fagan, *Kingdoms of Gold, Kingdoms of Jade: The Americas Before Columbus* (London: Thames and Hudson, 1991), 7.

14. Quoted in ibid., 224.

15. Quoted in Robert M. Carnack et al., *The Legacy of Mesoamerica: History and Culture of a Native American Civilization* (Upper Saddle River, NJ: Prentice-Hall, 1996), 415.

16. Quoted in Marysa Navarro, "Women in Pre-Columbian and Colonial Latin America," in *Restoring Women to History* (Bloomington, IN: Organization of American Historians, 1988), 6.

17. Pedro Cieza de Leon, quoted in Terence N. D'Altroy, *The Incas* (Malden, MA: Blackwell, 2002), 3.

18. The Chronicles of Michoacan, quoted in Melvin Lunenfeld, ed., *Discovery, Invasion, Encounter: Sources and Interpretations* (Lexington, MA: D.C. Heath, 1991), p. 262.

Chapter 13 South Asia, Central Asia, Southeast Asia, and Afro-Eurasian Connections, 600–1500

1. From L. S. Stavrianos, *The Epic of Man to 1500* (Englewood Cliffs, NJ: Prentice-Hall, 1970), 160, 162–163.

2. Quoted in Tansen Sen, *Buddhism, Diplomacy, and Trade: The Realignment of Sino-Indian Relations, 600–1400* (Honolulu: University of Hawaii Press, 2003), 11.

3. Al-Biruni, quoted in Romila Thapar, *Early India: From the Origins to AD 1300* (Berkeley: University of California Press, 2002), 437.

4. Quoted in Paul Thomas Welty, *The Asians: Their Evolving Heritage*, 6th ed. (New York: Harper and Row, 1984), 68.

5. Quoted in Lucille Schulberg, *Historic India* (New York: Time-Life Books, 1968), 11–12.

6. Quoted in Debiprasad Chattophyana, *History of Science and Technology in Ancient India*, vol. 3 (Calcutta: Firma KLM Private Ltd., 1996), 60.

7. Minhaju-s Siraj, quoted in John Keay, *A History of India* (New York: Atlantic Monthly Press, 2000), 245.

8. Quoted in Keay, *History of India*, 274.

9. Stanley Wolpert, *A New History of India*, 5th ed. (New York: Oxford University Press, 1997), 113.

10. Quoted in Richard Eaton, "Islamic History as Global History," in *Islamic and European Expansion: The Forging of a Global Order*, ed. Michael Adas (Philadelphia: Temple University Press, 1993), 21.

11. Quoted in Christopher Pym, *The Ancient Civilization of Angkor* (New York: New American Library, 1968), 118.
12. Quoted in David Chandler, *A History of Cambodia*, 2nd ed. updated (Boulder, CO: Westview Press, 1996), 74.
13. From ibid., 41.
14. Ibn Muhammad Ibrahim, from Michael Smithies, *Descriptions of Old Siam* (Kuala Lumpur: Oxford University Press, 1995), 91.
15. Quoted in Ralph Smith, *Viet-Nam and the West* (Ithaca, NY: Cornell University Press, 1971), 9.
16. Quoted in Anthony Reid, *Southeast Asia in the Age of Commerce, 1450–1680*, vol. 2 (New Haven: Yale University Press, 1993), 10.
17. Tome' Pires, quoted in Paul Wheatley, *The Golden Khersonese* (Kuala Lumpur: University of Malaya Press, 1961), 313.
18. Quoted in Kenneth R. Hall, *Maritime Trade and State Development in Early Southeast Asia* (Honolulu: University of Hawaii Press, 1985), 210.

Chapter 14 Christian Societies in Medieval Europe, Byzantium, and Russia, 600–1500

1. From a fourteenth-century legend, quoted in Amy G. Remensnyder, "Topographies of Memory: Center and Periphery in High Medieval France," in Gerd Althoff et al., eds., *Medieval Concepts of the Past: Ritual, Memory, Historiography* (New York: Cambridge University Press, 2002), p. 214.
2. Quoted in *What Life Was Like in the Age of Chivalry: Medieval Europe, AD 800–1500* (Alexandria, Va.: Time-Life Books, 1997), p. 17.
3. Quoted in James C. Russell, *The Germanization of Early Medieval Christianity* (Oxford: Oxford University Press, 1994), p. 186.
4. "Charlemagne's letter to Pope Leo III, 796," from C. Warren Hollister et al., *Medieval Europe: A Short Sourcebook*, 2nd ed. (New York: McGraw-Hill, 1992), p. 78.
5. Quoted in F. Donald Logan, *The Vikings in History*, 2nd ed. (New York: Routledge, 1991), p. 15.
6. Hugo of Santalla, quoted in Jerry Brotton, *The Renaissance Bazaar: From the Silk Road to Michelangelo* (Oxford: Oxford University Press, 2002), p. 195.
7. Quoted in John M. Hobson, *The Eastern Origins of Western Civilization* (New York: Cambridge University Press, 2004), p. 113.
8. Quoted in Jo Ann H. Moran Cruz and Richard Gerberding, *Medieval Worlds: An Introduction to European History, 300–1492* (Boston: Houghton Mifflin, 2004), p. 388.
9. Quoted in *Eileen Power, Medieval People*, new rev. ed. (New York: Barnes and Noble, 1963), p. 18.
10. Richard of Devizes, quoted in Jacques Le Goff, ed., *The Medieval World* (London: Postgate Books, 1997), p. 139.
11. The quotes are from Frederic Delouche, et al., *Illustrated History of Europe: A Unique Portrait of Europe's Common History* (New York: Barnes and Noble, 2001), p. 170; and Georges Duby, "Marriage in Early Medieval Society," in *Love and Marriage: The Middle Ages*, translated by Jane Dunnett (Chicago: University of Chicago Press, 1994), p. 11.
12. Quoted in Carolly Erickson, *The Medieval Vision: Essays in History and Perception* (New York: Oxford University Press, 1976), p. 73.
13. Quoted in Cruz and Gerberding, *Medieval Worlds*, p. 277.
14. Quoted in Clive Ponting, *A Green History of the World: The Environment and the Collapse of Great Civilizations* (New York: Penguin, 1991), p. 144.
15. Quoted in Thomas F. Madden, *A Concise History of the Crusades* (Lanham, Md.: Rowman and Littlefield, 1999), pp. 8–9.
16. Quoted in C. Warren Hollister, *Medieval Europe: A Short History*, 8th ed. (Boston: McGraw-Hill, 1998), p. 296.
17. Quoted in ibid., p. 273.
18. Quoted in Nicholas V. Riasanovsky, *A History of Russia*, 5th ed. (New York: Oxford University Press, 1993), p. 72.
19. Eustache Deschamps, quoted in J. Huizinga, *The Waning of the Middle Ages* (Garden City, N.Y.: Doubleday Anchor, 1954), p. 33.
20. Quoted in Delouche, *Illustrated History*, p. 168.
21. Quoted in Brotton, *Renaissance Bazaar*, p. 75.
22. Canon Pietro Casola, quoted in ibid., p. 38.
23. Quoted in Edith Simon, *The Reformation* (New York: Time-Life Books, 1966), p. 71.
24. Cadamosto, quoted in Peter Russell, *Prince Henry "the Navigator": A Life* (New Haven, Conn.: Yale University Press, 2000), p. 225.

Societies, Networks, Transitions: Expanding Horizons in the Intermediate Era, 600 B.C.E.–600 C.E.

1. Quoted in Jack Turner, *Spice: The History of a Temptation* (New York: Vintage, 2004), 103.
2. Quoted in Fernand Braudel, *The Wheels of Commerce* (New York: Harper and Row, 1979), 127.
3. Abdul Kassim ibn Khordadbeh, quoted in Elmer Bendiner, *The Rise and Fall of Paradise* (New York: Dorset Press, 1983), 101.
4. Quoted in John M. Hobson, *The Eastern Origins of Western Civilisation* (New York: Cambridge University Press, 2004), 40.
5. Quoted in M. N. Pearson, "Introduction," in *Spices in the Indian Ocean World*, ed. M. N. Pearson (Aldershot, UK: Valiorum, 1996), xv.
6. Quoted in Philip D. Curtin, *Cross-Cultural Trade in World History* (New York: Cambridge University Press, 1984), 125.
7. Quoted in John Kelley, *The Great Mortality* (New York: HarperCollins, 2005), 2.
8. Quoted in Peter N. Stearns, *Western Civilization in World History* (New York: Routledge, 2003), 52.
9. Al-Musabbihi, quoted in Heinz Halm, *The Fatimids and Their Traditions of Learning* (New York: I.B. Taurus, 1997), 73.
10. Leon Battista Alberti, quoted in Jeremy Brotton, *The Renaissance Bazaar: From the Silk Road to Michelangelo* (London: Oxford University Press, 2002), 73–74.
11. Quoted in Peter N. Stearns, *Gender in World History* (New York: Routledge, 2000), 52.
12. Quoted in Anthony Reid, *Southeast Asia in the Age of Commerce, 1450–1680*, vol. 1 (New Haven: Yale University Press, 1988), 1.
13. Quoted in Adriaan Verhulst, *The Carolingian Economy* (New York: Cambridge University Press, 2002), 48.
14. Ibn al-Athir, quoted in David R. Ringrose, *Expansion and Global Interaction, 1200–1700* (New York: Longman, 2001), 22.
15. Quoted in Rene Grousset, *The Empire of the Steppes: A History of Central Asia* (New Brunswick: Rutgers University Press, 1970), 249.
16. Quoted in L. S. Stavrianos, *Lifelines from Our Past: A New World History*, rev. ed. (Armonk, NY: M.E. Sharpe, 1997), 58.
17. Quoted in Frederick F. Cartwright, *Disease and History: The Influence of Disease in Shaping the Great Events of History* (New York: Thomas Y. Crowell, 1972), 37.
18. Quoted in Brian Fagan, *The Long Summer: How Climate Changed Civilization* (New York: Basic Books, 2004), 224.
19. Peter Martyr, quoted in Turner, *Spice*, xi.

INDEX

Abacus, 147

Abbasid caliphate, 243, 254–256 *and map*; cities in, 254–255; decline of, 256; homosexuality in, 380; maritime trade of, 377; Mongols and, 266, 382; Turks in, 264

Abbas (uncle of Muhammad), 254

Abelard and Heloise, 361 *and illus.*

Aborigines of Australia, 14–15, 98, 222–223

Abortion, 13, 188

Abraham, 65; Islam and, 246

Abu Bakr (Muhammad's first successor), 252

Abu Hureyra, 5, 15, 17*(illus.)*

Abu-Lughod, Janet, 374

Abu Simbel, statues at, 50*(illus.)*

Academies: *See also* Schools and scholars; in Athens, 165; in China, 276, 286, 380

Achaemenids (Persia), 156–161, 200, 232. *See also* Persian Empire; decline of, 159–160

Acheh, Sumatra, 343

Achilles, 70

Acropolis, in Athens, 168 *and illus.*

Actium, Battle of (31 B.C.E.), 185

Acupuncture, in China, 147

Administration. *See also* Bureaucracy; Civil service; Government; Sumerian, 33; Assyrian Empire, 35, 36; Harappan, 40; Egyptian, 54, 98; Chinese, 79, 276; cities as centers of, 98; Teotihuacan, 217; Inca, 321; Ottoman, 268

Adshead, S. A. M., 373, 374

Adulis (Masawa), 210, 211, 214

Aeneid (Virgil), 189

Aeschylus (Greek playwright), 165, 170

Afghanistan (Afghans), 131, 171, 232; China and, 140; Persia and, 156, 170; Greco-Bactrian kingdom, 114, 117, 172, 173*(map)*; Kushan empire and, 117, 200; Sassanian, 200; Islam in, 251; Arab armies in, 331

Africa (Africans). *See also* Bantus; East Africa; North Africa; Sub-Saharan Africa; Sudanic Africa; West Africa; *and specific countries and peoples;* human origins in, 7, 8, 9; agricultural origins in, 3, 17, 18, 19*(map)*; chronology (800 B.C.E.–500 C.E.), 207; long distance trade and, 205; ironworking in, 3, 60–61, 62, 98; Islam in, 207, 269, 300; American societies compared, 311, 322; chronology (500–1487), 300; social

patterns in, 308–309; stateless societies in, 308; Portuguese expeditions in, 311; religious and artistic traditions of, 309–310

African Origins theory, 9

African slaves (slavery), 309, 380–381

African slave trade, 212, 259, 302; trans-Saharan, 310–311

Afro-Asiatic languages, 52. *See also* Bantu; Semitic languages

Afrocentrism, 228–229

Afro-Eurasia: human evolution in, 9; peoples of, 29; Bronze Age in, 96; India and, 118; pastoral nomad threat in, 101; regional empires in, 105–106, 145; Roman Empire in, 183–184; exchange in, 230; Ming China and, 286–288

Afterlife, belief in: mummification and, 58, 89; in China, 75; in Egypt, 58, 103; in Buddhism, 146; in Zoroastrianism, 159; in Christianity, 195; in Islam, 250; in Japan, 295; in Chimu, 313

Agade (Mesopotamia), 29, 34

Agamemnon (Aeschylus), 165

Agamemnon (Greece), 69–70

Agriculture: *See also* Farmers and farming; Irrigation; Landowners (landownership); Peasants; Plows; Rural society (rural areas); *and specific crops;* origins of, 5, 19*(map)*; population growth and, 15, 17, 22, 101; shifting cultivation, 17, 60; technology and, 21, 22; transformation in, 15, 17–21; chronology (9500–500 B.C.E.), 18; globalization and diversity of, 18, 19*(map)*; environment and, 17, 20–21; in India, 47; in Africa, 60–61, 212; in China, 74–75, 79, 142, 276, 280; in Korea, 84; Native American, 88–89; in Southeast Asia, 82, 83; as historical transition, 96; in Korea, 148; Roman, 180; in Ethiopia, 209; Maya, 214, 216; Andean peoples, 219, 321; shifting cultivation, 212, 214; terracing in, 89, 209, 221, 313, 321; Mongol conquests and, 266; spread of Islam and, 263; in Japan, 295; in sub-Saharan Africa, 310; in Southeast Asia, 336; medieval Europe, 352–353 *and illus.*; manorialism, 354; in Eastern Europe, 366, 370

Ahura Mazda (god), 159, 160

Ainu culture (Japan), 84–85, 86, 149

Air pollution, coal burning and, 355

A'isha (wife of Muhammad), 250, 253

Ajanta, cave temples at, 121*(illus.)*

Akan people (Guinea), 309

Akhenaten (Amenophis), 55

Akkad (Akkadian Empire), 34–35, 101

Akkadian language, 98, 100*(illus.)*

Aksia the Great (Songhai), 302

Aksum Empire (Ethiopia), 207, 208*(map)*; Christianity in, 107; legacy, 210; social patterns and culture, 209–210; stele monoliths of, 61*(illus.)*, 204*(illus.)*, 210; trade in, 209, 211, 233*(map)*, 237

Al-Andalusi, Abu Hamid (Muslim traveler), 300

Alaska, 12; land bridge to, 11*(map)*, 12, 86

Al-Azhar University, 256

Albigensian heresy, 357

Al-Biruni (Muslim scholar), 261, 331

Alchemy, 147

Alcoholic beverages. *See also* Beermaking; Wine; Islamic prohibition on, 250

Aleppo, Mongol destruction of, 266

Aleutian Islands (Aleuts), 84, 86

Alexander the Great, 107, 173 *and map.* *See also* Hellenistic Age; Diogenes and, 174; in India, 113–114, 115*(map)*, 171, 230; Persia and, 160, 171, 172 *and illus.*

Alexandria, 172, 173, 184; Christianity in, 196, 197 *and illus.*; cosmopolitanism in, 173, 175; library of, 174

Algebra, 147. *See also* Mathematics

Algeria, 58; rock art in, 4*(illus.)*

Al-Ghazali, Abu Hamid (Islamic mystic), 258

Alhambra, Court of Lions, 257*(illus.)*

Ali (Muhammad's son-in-law), 253, 254

Al-Iridisi (Muslim mapmaker), 260

Al-Kindi, Abu Yusuf, 258, 261

Allah (god), 248, 249, 250, 258, 260

Alpacas and llamas, 19*(map)*, 20, 89, 219, 321

Alphabets: phonetic, 147; Phoenician, 68, 69, 70, 170; Greek, 70, 180; Aksumite, 209; Meroitic, 206; Zapotec, 217; Arabic, 260; Cyrillic, 364

Al-Rashid, Harun, Caliph, 255

Al-Razi, Abu Bakr, 261

Al-Suyuti, Jalal al-Din (Egyptian scholar), 269

Altamira, Spain, cave paintings in, 14*(illus.)*

Amanitere (Meroë), 209*(illus.)*

Amaterasu (sun goddess), 149

Amazon Basin, agriculture in, 15, 18, 89

Amenophis (Akhenaten), 55